Bobby
and
J. Edgar

Bobby
and
J. Edgar

THE HISTORIC FACE-OFF BETWEEN THE KENNEDYS AND J. EDGAR HOOVER THAT TRANSFORMED AMERICA

Burton Hersh

CARROLL & GRAF PUBLISHERS
NEW YORK

For Ellen,
Early and late

BOBBY AND J. EDGAR
The Historic Face-off Between the Kennedys and J. Edgar Hoover
That Transformed America

Carroll & Graf Publishers
An Imprint of Avalon Publishing Group, Inc.
245 West 17th Street
11th Floor
New York, NY 10011

AVALON
publishing group incorporated

Copyright © 2007 by Burton Hersh

First Carroll & Graf edition 2007

Library of Congress Cataloging-in-Publication Data is available.

ISBN-10: 0-7867-1982-6
ISBN-13: 978-0-78671-982-2

9 8 7 6 5 4 3 2 1

Interior Design by Meryl Sussman Levavi

Printed in the United States of America
Distributed by Publishers Group West

Contents

Foreword

It's been the best part of a century since Joseph P. Kennedy first poked his head above the turbulent shallows of Massachusetts politics and informed the lurking press: "For the Kennedys from now on it's going to be either the White House or the shithouse." His breakthroughs and setbacks have impacted an amazing amount of our collective history, forced us to reexamine our purposes, and subjected a lot of us, more than once, to an abiding anguish. What began as the dogged financier's campaign of self-realization turned into a national saga. We share those moments of glory as well as no small residue of collective guilt.

For twentieth-century America the Kennedys amounted to the House of Atreus, that clan of Attic kings whose agonies impel classic theater. As they were driven, so we are driven. Having authored two books about the family already, principally centered on Edward Kennedy, I thought I might be exempted from reconnoitering this wide a historical orbit, a treatment that, if honestly done, was likely to scorch out sources and friends whom I have cherished since the middle sixties. When I decided several years ago to think about the largely unpublicized vendetta involving Attorney General Robert Kennedy and J. Edgar Hoover, the obsessively territorial Director of the FBI, it was my intention to limit the scope of my story to the face-off between two colorful, authoritarian bureaucrats.

That didn't work out. I wasn't very deep into the research before I could see that the thrust of Robert Kennedy's attorney-generalship was plainly to root out organized crime in America. My next revelation—I'd had an inkling that this was true for years, but now the evidence was overwhelming—involved the career-long participation of Joseph P. Kennedy in the criminal underworld. It doesn't require Carl Jung to conclude that there are archetypes roaming the foliage here, or Freud to identify the Oedipal implications. But even that oversimplifies the forces at work. What looked for a while like a three-part disharmony—Joe, Edgar, and Bobby—now began to spread out onto a national stage and turned into a full-blown operetta.

Large personalities at the margins began to introduce themselves. Cardinal Spellman and Johnny Rosselli, Joe McCarthy and Gloria Swanson and Roy Cohn. Martin Luther King and Jimmy Hoffa and Carlos Marcello and John Kennedy himself and Marilyn Monroe and Jack Ruby and Carroll Rosenbloom and Lyndon Johnson and Hoover's handpicked instruments, the pious, intrigue-loving Cartha "Deke" DeLoach, offset by the Director's grubby little axman, Billy Sullivan. Against all these contesting lives, mid-century America ground forward. History tends to spit into the wind, so let the reader be forewarned.

It's fruitless to explain in advance too much of what a writer intends to say. That's what the book is for. I like to imagine that this work will present the principals with a unique and unsentimentalized clarity, at no point damning or canonizing. Bobby was no saint, nor Hoover a complete monster. Each of them adored power and used it to push the country in a direction he intended it to go. Paradoxically, when dealing with the largest endeavors—curbing the Cosa Nostra before it dominated the society, reversing Jim Crow—these two natural antagonists found themselves trapped in an uneasy collaboration. Out of this collaboration came today's America.

Since the early fifties, when Joe Kennedy got serious about moving Jack toward the White House, successive waves of biographers have engaged the public with fundamentally opposed readings of who the Kennedys were and what they intended to do. The first books, influenced heavily by the Hearst and Time, Inc. profiles the Ambassador himself promoted, adhered to *The Amazing Kennedys* or *A Hero for Our Time* model and roped in serious academics as well as hacks delighted to be supplied with background material and flattering if temporary acquaintance with the celebrity powerful. Once Kennedy became president, wordsmiths from the Right moved in, and the negative clipping files compiled by the likes of Victor Lasky and Ralph de Toledano descended, well calculated to dull the gloss.

Very little in either category revealed a great deal about the Kennedys. One of the first books to genuinely open up the subject was Joan and Clay Blair Jr.'s 1972 volume *The Search for JFK*. Along with the carefully culled oral histories the Kennedy Library overseers of the period were willing to release, the Blairs hunted down and interviewed a wide variety of Kennedy social friends and paid help over several generations and produced a long, rather fragmentary study of John Kennedy's life throughout his years in Congress. The Blairs winkled out testimony as to Kennedy's emotionally starved boyhood, his controversial performance as a PT-boat skipper in the Solomons, his wretched health, culminating in the diagnosis of full-blown Addison's disease, and his compulsive Don Juanism. "Jack grew up," the Blairs concluded, "in the shadow of a domineering, unscrupulous absentee father, a devoutly religious absentee mother, and a bullying sibling, Joe Jr."

Many of the Blairs' judgments were foreshadowed in *The Founding Father*, Richard Whalen's landmark 1964 treatment of the career of Joseph P. Kennedy. Joe Kennedy was a handful; he evidenced few scruples about grabbing what he wanted; yet, once I began to work my way through the memoirs and letters and documents along with the reminiscences of contemporaries, I found myself revising my assumptions about who, exactly, Joe Kennedy was. My many conversations with Ted Kennedy over the years, supplemented by several days of frank exchanges with Bob Kennedy shortly before he died, had long ago convinced me that Joe's children genuinely loved him, and he them, with an unconditional intensity. Whatever they were, whatever they did, he would be there to look after their interests and guarantee their success. This put a strain on every one of them and stunted their development in many ways, but in other ways it imparted the drive and conviction of their own special destiny that distinguished them even as children.

It is a cliché in Kennedy literature that Joe Kennedy made Jack Kennedy president to fulfill his own unrealized ambition. It is equally likely that Joe Kennedy moved Jack Kennedy toward the presidency because he intended to present this fey, disease-ridden son the realization of his invalid dreams. By the middle fifties, their doting if pragmatic father was worried that his surviving boys had learned their lessons too well, that recklessness and insensitivy to competing interests might bring down reversals and tragedies even he couldn't prevent.

Joe remained insistently aware that his sons were really not ready for all that power, and expected that he—along with Lyndon Johnson—would remain in place to negotiate crises. For many years, long before Jack Kennedy assumed the presidency, his father had interposed himself between his idealistic youngsters and darker, more implacable elements in American society—the important political bosses, the strategists of the Mob, J. Edgar Hoover. The December morning in 1961 a massive stroke incapacitated Joseph P. Kennedy, his children were on their own.

Many of these stresses collected in the tightly knit Bobby. Pugnacious, brooding, insecure, Robert Kennedy succumbed to the demands of his father after the election in 1960 and took on the responsibilities of attorney general. He was clearly intended to function as his father's surrogate. He would protect Jack and subjugate Joe Kennedy's unpredictable crony over the years, the slippery, lethal Director of the FBI. Yet, even before Joe Kennedy collapsed, the vendetta between Bobby and the unhappy Edgar had started and, as it played out, turned into perhaps the last of the great untold donnybrooks of contemporary American history.

BOOK ONE

THE PRELUDE TO POWER

◆

John F. Kennedy "told his good friend John Sharon that if he had his life to live over again, he would have a different father, a different wife, and a different religion."

—RALPH MARTIN, *Seeds of Destruction*, p. 443

Hiding Joe

July in Greater Los Angeles can provide a month in the frying pan, what with the wind off the arid, remorseless desert pulling through the five oceanside counties. All through the Democratic convention week in 1960 exceptionally fine weather held. For the Kennedy family, obsessed as they were that year with nailing down the nomination for Jack, this run of reliable cloudless days was enough to inflate confidence. They were all superstitious, although none so profoundly as the temperamental patriarch. Enough bad weather, especially when the wind was up and keening off the water, could find him locked in his room or flying out of town in a headlong panic. He refused to stomach any reminders that death was imminent.

While most of the political business at the Democratic convention was conducted on the middle floors of the Biltmore Hotel in the far-flung commercial district, Joe Kennedy and Rose and several of their adult children were lying low in Marion Davies's sprawling, Spanish-style *residencia* in Beverly Hills. The mansion was secluded enough at the end of a quarter-mile drive, protected by interwoven stands of eucalyptus and bougainvillea. A battery of telephones next to Joe Kennedy's chair beside the pool, hooked up by direct line to the frenzied four-room Kennedy headquarters in Suite 8315 at the Biltmore, permitted minute-to-minute consultation.

One visitor nobody spotted around the residence was its owner, Marion Davies, under treatment that summer for a stubborn malignancy.

A warmhearted, somewhat zany Ziegfeld hoofer and pioneering film come-dienne better known as the mistress of press baron William Randolph Hearst and the hostess of San Simeon, Davies helped provide an unwritten footnote to Joe Kennedy's complicated emotional history. Hearst himself had passed on in 1951; on hearing the news, Kennedy propped up Marion's photograph on his night table in Hyannis Port. "She was a woman who understood men," he confided to his chauffeur. "She understood men who wanted great things. She understood me." It was the only photograph in his bedroom.

Joseph P. Kennedy's association with Hearst and his dipsomaniacal chatelaine went back to the 1920s, when the single-minded fledgling moviemaker and would-be financier had started to commute for months at a stretch to the ramshackle Hollywood film studios among the orange groves. The day he arrived, Joe knew very little more about the industry than that he intended to take his piece of the action away from all those Jewish "pants pressers" manifestly getting too rich too fast. Marion Davies had wel-comed him.

Now, close to four decades later, Joe Kennedy was back in town to relish the culminating moment of his life. His son was about to be nominated by his party to run for president of the United States. In 1945, tipped off to James Michael Curley's looming bankruptcy problems by J. Edgar Hoover, Joe Kennedy had moved in behind the scenes to lock up Jack Curley's seat in the U.S. House of Representatives. From then on, behind virtually every move his sickly, pleasure-loving son attempted, there lay the hand—and power—of the omnipresent father. They were very close to triumph that July, and the unrelenting Ambassador intended to make sure that nothing went wrong.

Joe Kennedy had been in and out of California by then for several months, tenderizing influential politicians around the state in behalf of Jack's candi-dacy. His base of operations all spring and summer was the Cal-Neva Lodge. Well up in the Sierras overlooking Lake Tahoe and strategically positioned to straddle the California–Nevada line, along with invigorating mountain air the Cal-Neva offered a wide range of gaming tables supplemented by call girls—and boys—to exhaust every appetite. On paper, the owner of the resort was the lippy, social-climbing crooner Frank Sinatra, although with the help of one of his many proxies Joe Kennedy himself had recently grabbed off a percentage of the place. Another partner was Sam ("Momo") Giancana, just then an intimate of Frank's and the Mafia don who dominated the Chicago

Outfit. J. Edgar Hoover and the FBI were maintaining a running log on every arrival and departure.

The governor of California during the months leading up to the convention was Edmund—Pat—Brown. A gregarious if somewhat naïve politician preoccupied with secondary issues like abolishing the death penalty, Brown was being romanced hard that spring by Lyndon Johnson's operatives. As an attractive Catholic, Brown could be assured of finding himself at the top of the vice-presidential list if he would only commit to Lyndon. The problem with going along with that was, remembers Brown's key aide, Fred Dutton, "Pat really took to Kennedy, I thought a little too much." Just then the wily Dutton was serving as Brown's assistant attorney general in charge of law enforcement, and throughout the decade coming up would distinguish himself as a trouble-shooting assistant in the Kennedy White House and Robert Kennedy's confidant and traveling companion. That spring before the convention in 1960, Dutton remembers, Joe Kennedy would not stop calling, determined to set up a meeting with the governor in Sacramento.

"He finally came down and had dinner at the governor's house," Dutton recalled. But the Californians were well-informed and wary. "We were trying to avoid anything to do with the Cal-Neva. There was a guy sent by the Daley organization in Chicago to stay with Joe Kennedy. He was there the whole time before the Democratic convention. We knew there were unsavory types, which was one of the reasons we were trying to keep our distance. I would occasionally call Bob Kennedy just to keep him up to date. So we could minimize the dealings with the father."

By 1960, power relationships among the Kennedys were shifting. Contemporaries preferred to talk with Bobby. That was not to say that Bob at thirty-four was a lot easier to deal with than his vehement old man, who at least had a certain amount of give to him once he calmed down. Conservative activists like John Roche had been heard to remark that Robert Kennedy was little better than "a clone of the Ambassador," a political mechanic who "couldn't distinguish a principle from a fireplug." The thing was, Bob was realistic—demanding, but realistic. Whatever he arranged for tended to happen. A jingle then making the rounds tipped off the insider consensus: "Jack and Bob will run the show/While Ted's in charge of hiding Joe."

As Jack's campaign manager, Bobby had been carrying the weight for close to a year; with all the delegates converging in Los Angeles, he expected to get—and got—almost no sleep the week of the convention. JFK had arranged to rent Jack Haley's hideaway apartment for himself at North Rossmore Avenue, where he could daydream to his Ella Fitzgerald records and entertain Judith Campbell along with an unstinting supply of party girls ushered through by Peter Lawford. Jackie was in Hyannis Port, waiting out her pregnancy. The second night, Kennedy went over the back fence to dine at Puccini's, the restaurant Lawford and Frank Sinatra co-owned. Marilyn Monroe was along, and the playful actress pronounced the candidate's behavior afterward as "very democratic" and "very penetrating." "They were good together," Lawford had to admit.

Bobby caught what rest he could slumped in a chair in his tumbledown hideaway office off Suite 8315. His spare, knobby frame and pasty-faced scowl reminded anybody who looked in of a stoned-out adolescent.

It was a constant effort for Bob to maintain civility. "That young man never says please," Adlai Stevenson lamented. He referred to Kennedy privately as "the Black Prince." Stevenson was in anguish as hour by hour the Democratic Party prepared to anoint another champion: "He never says thank you, he never asks for things, he demands them." Bobby was too tired by then to mask his presumption. The party's grand duchess, Eleanor Roosevelt, sailed like a creaking galleon in and out of the mingled delegations, disparaging the frontrunner as that season's corporate type, empty, "someone who understands what courage is and admires it, but has not quite the independence to have it." The whole scene set Bobby's maloccluded teeth on edge.

Politicians respond to expansiveness, but in Robert Kennedy they had to deal with a surrogate for the father who was not only terse but downright unsettling, an incoherent roughneck who felt so much, had so much to say, that he frequently gave you nothing. Bobby reddened easily. His slump-shouldered gait, those hooded eyes normally directed at the floor—people sensed more resignation than assurance.

All week he held himself in, rarely letting too much impatience or contempt creep into his abbreviated exchanges. He could be whimsical, even engaging sometimes, if rarely around this collection of hacks. The forty-plus Kennedy volunteers keeping tabs on the delegates nursing their cigars throughout the corridors or grazing at the noisy lobby buffet tables were liable to return to the back room in the Kennedy suite to find Bobby climbed up onto a chair, methodically counting heads, clicking off the whereabouts of his coordinators. A scrawny, tousled bird, his rubbery lips writhing with impatience around the assertive front teeth, those pale assessing eyes beneath their sweeping folds aglitter beside his harsh chopped beak of a nose. Sleeves rolled up, by midmorning the shirttail would be blousing out and the knot of his necktie worked halfway down his front. Perspiration stood in dark blotches. All business every minute, running down the delegate count.

"If you think it's more important to go to Disneyland than nominate the next president of the United States," he seethed at one belated volunteer, "you ought to quit right now." Arthur Schlesinger Jr. would memorialize in his journal those last hours before the vote on Wednesday, Bob carping until he got "the name, address and telephone number of every half-vote. 'I don't want generalities or guesses,' he would say. 'There's no point in fooling ourselves. . . . If we don't win tonight, we're dead.'"

There remained all along the danger of a sentimental breakout to Adlai Stevenson, but the ogre who threw the shadow across Jack's prospects was Lyndon Johnson. In 1959, sounding out the prospects for Jack, Bob had stopped off for a quick visit to the LBJ ranch in Texas. He hadn't enjoyed it. Lyndon promised to stay out, but Johnson's lugubrious, overhearty swings of emotion annoyed the shy but acutely judgmental middle brother. To the imperious Johnson, Robert Kennedy was little better than a clerk with the bad judgment to have disgraced himself as "one of McCarthy's toadies."

Bob watched while throughout the spring and summer the big, shambling Majority Leader let Hubert Humphrey provide a stalking horse, meanwhile locking up the Southern delegations almost to the man while confident that his own enormous and inescapable presence, once he arrived at the convention, would bully and persuade enough delegates to abandon the presumptuous Kennedys. He anticipated a brokered convention.

Since the middle fifties, there had been another influential heavyweight in this compounding melodrama, still largely off-stage but implicated in every move. As early as 1955 Joe Kennedy had reportedly approached Thomas Corcoran, Washington's most renowned arranger of political marriages. If Corcoran could contrive to bring about a Johnson–Kennedy ticket in 1956, "I'll make you rich, Tommy," the Ambassador had assured Corcoran, and spoke of oil leases and undiscovered Western lands. That same year the impatient financier had written Johnson directly: "As I told you in our telephone call awhile back, both Jack and I are ready to support you in 1956, if you decide. . . . Jack feels he owes a debt to you, but especially to the country. . . ." Only Lyndon wasn't interested. He had been shaken too recently by his heart attack.

By 1960 the majority leader had recovered. Paddling in and out among the delegation chairmen, he referred to JFK as a "little scrawny fellow with rickets," a cipher in the Senate with ankles no bigger around than the circle

Lyndon could describe by touching his enormous thumb to the tip of his forefinger. Johnson stand-ins spread the word that Jack was dying of Addison's disease. Eleanor Roosevelt was right when she called Jack Kennedy a creature of his father's ambition. The brothers were fags. If Jack ever did wind up in the White House, the nation would fall under the control of an appeaser, and worse: "I was never any Chamberlain umbrella policy man," Johnson blared in debate with Jack before the Texas delegation. "I never thought Hitler was right."

Johnson had a powerful undisclosed ally. His neighbor on Thirtieth Place N.W., J. Edgar Hoover, was known to incline toward a Nixon presidency; but if a period of Democratic administration was unavoidable, the FBI Director preferred Lyndon.

J. Edgar Hoover and Joseph Kennedy had been in touch for many years. Along with his fellow ex-bootlegger Lewis Rosenstiel, Kennedy became an early co-underwriter of the J. Edgar Hoover Foundation. At one point during the fifties, the Ambassador, as he preferred to be addressed, had written Hoover a very fervent fan letter in which he offered to back the Director if *he* might decide to run for president. Joe was a "special service contact" for the Bureau, and he and the Director habitually traded tips and favors. Kennedy offered Hoover—never oblivious to money—a salary of $100,000 annually should he ever see fit to come to work for Joseph P. Kennedy, Inc. This was roughly three times the amount that Hoover was earning with the government at the time, but Hoover, who secretly and perhaps correctly conceived of himself as the most powerful individual in America, never took the offer seriously. A special agent of the FBI was posted in Hyannis Port largely to look after the Kennedys at play. The two autocrats continued to com-pare opinions from time to time, and occasionally Hoover and his gloomy shadow Clyde Tolson would arrive for an extended weekend at the Kennedy winter quarters on North Ocean Boulevard in Palm Beach. Hoover was a world-class freeloader.

This long and mutually beneficial association in no way inhibited Hoover (one of the nation's finest at dealing off the bottom of the deck) from intervening covertly to bust the Kennedy presidential momentum. Jack was a lightweight. Worse, a lightweight with unmistakable liberal tendencies and compiling obligations to the left-leaning Reuther wing of organized labor. The Director had already suffered through a couple of run-ins with Bobby while he was tearing the country up ramrodding the Senate Rackets Committee. Edgar invariably preferred to head off trouble.

The rumors about Joe Kennedy's Nazi-lining days and Jack Kennedy's precarious health, which Johnson and his Citizens-for-Johnson sidekick India Edwards were promulgating among the delegates, undoubtedly originated with Hoover. The Director had documentation a great deal more compromising in his closely guarded Secret and Confidential archives. He would yet determine how much he needed to release to maintain control.

Hoover never minded waiting. Increasingly reclusive, the Director had arrived at his final and absolute state. More beefy than corpulent, Edgar's big old head was sunken entirely into jowls, his ripples of receding hair now processed straight back to avoid that detested biracial look. He boasted a perfectly flat profile, excepting only the squashed-looking nose. His eyes were very dark, garnished by a disturbing profusion of lashes. Impeccably dressed at all times, the Director never relinquished his iconic stature. Sixty-five, Hoover still spat out language a mile a minute, G-man style. Among politicians who understood what was going on he emitted exceedingly dangerous radiations.

If Hoover was making himself felt that July in 1960, the Kennedys didn't pick up on it until after Jack got nominated. There tended to be a lag at times inside the Kennedy operation even among the principals, episodes of the murderous one-upmanship so prevalent around the Hyannis Port dinner table. For example, Jack had found out from Eugene Keogh in Pennsylvania that party boss Bill Green had finally given in to the Ambassador and agreed to swing his state's support behind Jack. The candidate told his father but neglected to tip off Bobby, who was out sweating delegates in the Pennsylvania hustings with Kenny O'Donnell. "Why didn't you tell me?" the exasperated Bobby demanded of his brother when he finally found out.

"Because you and Kenny talk too much," Jack told him. Stay in line.

One newspaperman closer to the action than most that July was John Seigenthaler. A reporter for the *Nashville Tennessean* who supplied Bob leads on union violence around the border states during the Rackets Committee investigations, in 1959 the courtly young Seigenthaler had taken a leave of absence to join Bob in the deserted summer manse at Hickory Hill and help grind out Bobby's memoir about labor corruption, *The Enemy Within*. The *Tennessean* was backing Lyndon, and in 1960 sent

Seigenthaler out to Los Angeles to forage for inside dope around the Kennedy camp. Two days before the roll call for the nomination, Seigenthaler spotted Bobby emerging from a telephone alcove in the Biltmore Hotel with Missouri Senator Stuart Symington, the photogenic, well-liked ex-Secretary of the Air Force under Harry Truman. Treat this as originating with a confidential source, Bobby cautioned Seigenthaler, but he and his brother had decided that Symington would definitely be the vice-presidential choice. Seigenthaler wrote his story, which was picked up around the country. Privately, Bob Kennedy was known to favor Scoop Jackson.

Soon after that, Bobby was able to lean on his father to let Seigenthaler through the gates of the Davies property for a personal interview. "The old man had run the *Los Angeles Times*' guy off the premises a day earlier, so this was a big deal," Seigenthaler laughs now.

Less than a year earlier, Seigenthaler had joined Bobby for a couple of dinners with the crusty Ambassador at Pavillon, the sumptuous Manhattan eatery in which the father reportedly owned a percentage. Joe Kennedy was fidgeting on the inside seat of a banquette, upset, as he told them immediately, "because he thought Ted Sorensen had taken too much credit for writing *Profiles in Courage*," the book of sketches for which the Ambassador had finagled the Pulitzer Prize for Jack.

"He began to lecture me about loyalty," Seigenthaler remembers, "and ego, and ambition. I was a little slow; I didn't know whether he was talking to his son or to me." Ed Sullivan, the television impresario, was at the next table, "and the next thing I know, he's got Sullivan entering into the lecture. When I finally got it I said, 'Look, this is your son's book, I've agreed to help edit . . . we signed a contract, and I'm perfectly satisfied.'" The financier calmed down little by little, flaring up again at the end of the meal at the maitre d' because he had been charged $10 for two saucers of ice cream.

When they next met, again at Pavillon, *The Enemy Within* was out and doing quite well. Robert Kennedy inscribed Seigenthaler's first edition on the way in from the airport. It was a celebratory evening, with champagne toasts and the Ambassador holding forth about how "you fellas knew exactly what you were doing, you never took your eye off the ball, everybody I've talked to thinks it's a great book. . . .

"And Bob says, 'John, show Dad how I signed your book.'" Seigenthaler handed it over. Bob had written: "To John Seigenthaler. Who wrote my book for me."

Glowering, the founding father looked up. "Bobby," he erupted, "you're a goddamn fool. That'll be in the *New York Post* in two weeks!"

"He was sending his father a little needling message," Seigenthaler says, "and he laughed, and I laughed, and finally the old man laughed too."

Daggers out, *en famille*. When, early that convention week, Seigenthaler was finally able to elbow his way into Joe Kennedy's presence, he found the Ambassador a little bit shopworn-looking, initially quite defensive. He was not enthusiastic about being interviewed. "My sense of it," Seigenthaler says, "was that he was sort of a lonely old man sittin' out there, hidden away, nowhere near the action, when he could have been pretty much any place he wanted to be."

Kennedy had opened the door for Seigenthaler himself, and if there were servants on the premises Seigenthaler never noticed any. Joe ushered Seigenthaler into a chair by the pool, across from his own, and adjusted the beach umbrella so that the hot California sun baked the reporter as he attempted to write. "I think he wanted to sweat me," Seigenthaler saw, "but I wasn't going to let him get away with that." Attired in matching faded top and trunks, the father submitted, haltingly at first, to questions. At seventy-two, his silver hair was now thinned back above his temples almost to the crown of his long, freckled, Irish head. Maintaining himself bolt upright largely by force of character but exposing the usual contingent of skin tags and exploded veins along his skinny limbs, Joe Kennedy now settled into his chair and regarded this collaborator with one of his children through those famously analytical eyes, magnified by his trademark eyeglasses. He had a straw hat, which he put on whenever the house telephone rang and he had to make his way across the intervening forty or fifty yards of the vast court-yard to answer it.

"I thought his attitude was just as advertised," Seigenthaler concluded. "Tough as nails, sort of a biting, self-deprecating wit. . . ." A few hours earlier, the Texas delegation had put out word that it wanted Jack Kennedy to drop by and debate Lyndon. In Joe Kennedy's opinion, that would be "a damn-fool thing to do, a distraction," especially within view of the television cameras, since Jack had the nomination sewed up by then. Children were perverse. "But, Daddy," Kennedy's pregnant daughter Jean, down for a swim, argued on her way by. "It's a challenge."

"See what I mean?" Joe queried Seigenthaler. A story had broken in the national press a few days before about the lobotomizing of the Kennedy daughter Rosemary, and unless Jack Kennedy did awfully well against Johnson the feeling in many circles was bound to be heightened that the

Kennedys had no compunctions when it came to buying whatever the hell they wanted. Appearances were all-important. All afternoon, the father was obviously waiting for Jack to call and solicit his advice about debating Johnson, but the candidate never did. Instead, Jack went ahead and debated. When word came in by radio that JFK would appear before the Texas delegation, Joe's response was automatic: "He will absolutely take this fellow apart." But the old man dreaded a misstep.

The flurry of press about Rosemary obviously summoned up complicated feelings in the brooding Ambassador. "Who knows why God makes one child as dull as a dollar and another as bright as sunlight," the patriarch mused. He got up to answer the telephone again—more wasted time, a wrong number—and once he got back to the side of the pool he readjusted the beach umbrella so as to throw a relieving shadow on Seigenthaler. Seigenthaler left a few minutes later, wondering how a dollar could be so dull to somebody like Joe Kennedy.

While the Ambassador waited for results, antagonism between the Johnson and Kennedy supporters was intensifying by the hour. When Robert Kennedy found out that the ever-wavering Stevenson had decided at the last minute to announce his own candidacy and that Hubert Humphrey was supporting him, Kennedy cornered AFL-CIO chief Walter Reuther and chewed him out. Seigenthaler overheard Bob, "quite testy" by then, demand of Reuther: "Can't you explain to Humphrey that Adlai's decision is really a ploy by Lyndon to deflect support from us?" From poolside, the Ambassador was haranguing Stevenson directly. Through Mob interface Jake Arvey, Joe had contributed to Adlai's earlier campaigns and preferred to think of the whimsical Democrat as another of his discoveries.

Minnesota Senator Eugene McCarthy—never much of a Kennedy admirer—went on to nominate Stevenson with the most inspiring speech registered at the convention. Nerves were very tight. When Bobby Baker, Johnson's manikin-of-all-work as Secretary to the Senate Majority, invited Bob Kennedy to join him and his wife for breakfast in the Biltmore's coffee shop, Baker remarked that Teddy Kennedy had been "a little rough" in alluding to Lyndon's heart attack while canvassing Texas for delegates.

For years, by then, Baker had been available for all manner of personal favors around the Senate for Jack. But at that moment, only the nomination existed. "You've got your nerve," Bobby Kennedy unexpectedly lashed out. "Lyndon Johnson has compared my father to the Nazis and John Connally and India Edwards lied in saying my brother is dying of Addison's disease. You Johnson people are running a stinking damned campaign, and you're gonna get yours when the time comes." Fists clenched, Bob Kennedy had leaned provocatively into Baker's face.

By that late hour, Johnson and his supporters were badly deluded, and Jack Kennedy was nominated on Wednesday night on the first ballot. Never much of a sport, Johnson took it extremely hard. He refused to appear at an impromptu reception that Baker, Senator Clements of Kentucky, and the governor of Tennessee sponsored to thank important campaign contributors and delegates who stayed with the Majority Leader. Celebrated for his geniality, Baker got thoroughly disheartened waiting for his hero to make an appearance and wound up stinking drunk.

At 6:30 the following morning, Johnson aide Bill Moyers was banging on Baker's door at the Biltmore. "The Leader wants to see you," Moyers kept shouting.

"Tell him to go to hell. He's rude, and all the people that supported him were disappointed in him," Baker told Moyers.

Five minutes later, Moyers was back. "Bobby, this is a crisis, you gotta come."

"So I take a cold shower—I had a terrible hangover," Baker recollects, "and I go down the corridor to Johnson's rooms. Johnson is there, and Lady Bird, and he says 'Your buddy Senator Kennedy called and *demanded* that he come here to my suite to see me. What do you think?'"

Resorting to that solicitous, roundabout testing for sentiment in which people from the deep South delight, Baker explained to his Leader that he himself was a Baptist married to a Catholic, so he knew something about them, that "Kennedy thinks you're the ablest guy he's ever known, that he knows a Catholic has never been elected in the history of this country, and that he wants you to be his running mate."

"What shall I do?" Johnson cut him short.

Baker launched into another stemwinder, based on the advice he had given Adlai Stevenson when he himself was executive director of the Democratic Platform Committee in 1956. He quoted Speaker of the House Sam Rayburn as having opined that "in these thermonuclear times you must select a man, one, that is the best for your country, two, that you trust so much that he would be the trustee for your wife and children when you die. When you tell us who that man is, he'll be your running mate."

By now Johnson's emotions were aroused. Still, in Baker's recollection, "Johnson bein' the coward that he was, when Kennedy comes around and offers it to him, he says, 'Well, I gotta consult with the Speaker.' Bobby was the campaign manager, and I guess Jack thought he didn't have to consult with him."

Johnson's mentor, Rayburn, didn't care for the offer at first. Senate Finance Committee Chairman Robert Kerr, a tough ex-wildcatter, was so outraged by the whole idea that he clocked Baker for not talking Lyndon out of it. But by the middle of the day Lyndon Johnson's mighty vanity was involved, and he was doing everything he could to establish enough leverage on Jack.

Baker's picture of Lyndon Johnson as the flabbergasted virgin, scooped up as the party's choice to accompany their prince to the ball—that undoubtedly needs updating. Memories differ, but there is a lot of consensus behind the version of events that insists, as Baker maintains, that "Joe Alsop and Phillip Graham and ol' man Joe Kennedy prevailed on Jack to get Johnson on the ticket." Graham, the publisher of the *Washington Post* and a long-standing backer of the Majority Leader, had his staffers writing all week that "Kennedy would probably offer the Vice-Presidency to Johnson." Privately, the financier conceded that the liberals might recoil, but Johnson "will look good a couple of weeks from now." Give the oil interests something.

According to Michael Janeway, whose influential father Eliot labored for the Luce publications throughout the convention and was a highly regarded spear-carrier inside the post-Rooseveltian entourage, "Joe Kennedy worked Johnson over on the back channel." Away from the "campaign rhetoric," the founding father presented the upset Lyndon "his own version of the future, whereby 'these boys' are not ready to run the country, which means that 'you and I, Lyndon' are going to have to run it for them." Joe allegedly offered Johnson $1 million to settle his campaign debts, which the Leader accepted. Johnson was calming down. Meanwhile, the Ambassador himself was urging on anybody he spoke with his own belief that this election would be closer than people expected. Johnson was in the best position to carry the South. By early Thursday morning, Lyndon Johnson was back in the hunt and John Kennedy had evidently been softened up.

"Around noon, when Kennedy said 'I want Johnson as my running mate,' that ended it," Baker says. Robert Kennedy had been assuring progressives like Joe Rauh for days that Lyndon was not under consideration. "That was the worst hurt Bobby ever suffered. In view of all the work he had done, he had been mistreated," Baker concluded. Worse, "Walter Reuther and all of them, they were gonna bolt the convention." Reuther, Arthur Goldberg, virtually the entire heavy artillery of the legitimate American labor movement descended on John Kennedy. "I was so furious that I could hardly talk," O'Donnell said afterward. "I felt we had been double-crossed."

Dangerously pale with anger and uncertainty, John Kennedy talked fast, rationalized that "I won't be able to live with Lyndon as the leader of a small minority in the Senate," that "I don't see any reason in the world why he would want it." To his brother's consternation, the pounding he was taking had paralyzed the candidate. "He was an extremely hesitant person," his economic adviser Paul Samuelson saw, "who checked the ice in front of him all the time." His father nourished deeper doubts. "You can trample all over him," the Ambassador told Tip O'Neill, "and the next day he's there for you with loving arms." As he watched Jack continually shift his ground, Bobby got more and more upset. He told Charles Bartlett later that it was the worst day of his life.

In time, it would become evident that outside forces were being brought to bear. Jack Kennedy's personal secretary, Evelyn Lincoln, was stationed outside the bedroom of the suite inside which the brothers were attempting to cope. John Kennedy was pacing, and Robert Kennedy had collapsed on a bed. Mrs. Lincoln kept bringing in messages from outside. "It was the information J. Edgar Hoover passed to Johnson," she revealed years afterward. "About womanizing, and things in Joe Kennedy's background, and anything he could dig up. He was using that as clout. Kennedy was angry, because they had boxed him into a corner."

By 1960 Hoover's files on the Kennedys were already voluminous. Along with the 1942 wiretap transcriptions bearing on the love affair of Jack and Inga Arvad, the Danish beauty queen alleged to have been close at one point to Goering and Hitler, there were the reported 343 closely held case files on the business activities of Joseph P. Kennedy, starting with the bootlegging years and including coverage of several illegal—treasonous, even—transactions brought off while Kennedy was Ambassador to the Court of Saint James; the decades of wary collaboration with senior personalities throughout organized crime; the parties brother-in-law Peter Lawford arranged for the boys at the Hotel Carlyle, replete with "mulatto prostitutes"; memos about the supposed ill-advised Palm Beach marriage of Jack Kennedy, which the Ambassador was said to have stepped in to annul; the various paternity claims. It was a very extended series.

That Thursday in July, the Kennedy brothers were privileged to review little more than a sampling. But it was enough. Whether the founding father himself connived secretly with the FBI Director to move his boys in the direction he intended them to go would be hard to establish. What they were expected to take in were the consequences of dropping Johnson, unless he actually decided to renege on his own. Hoover was well known for his propensity to leak his timeliest discoveries to the press.

That Thursday, Bobby dropped in on Johnson three times: once to try to gauge his mood, and the second time to suggest with as much delicacy as was in him that Johnson consider withdrawing his acceptance—there was a lot of opposition, certainly among the labor people, why split the party? What would he think of Chairman of the National Committee . . . ? During Bob's last visit, Johnson had assumed that well-practiced hangdog look of his, the long, meaty folds of his face swelling with unhappiness, and then he "burst into tears," Bob would subsequently tell Arthur Schlesinger Jr., and shook, and said, "I want to be Vice President, and, if the President will have me, I'll join him in making a fight for it."

Prowling the convention floor, U.S. House Majority Leader John McCormack was keeping the fidgety Ambassador apprised minute to minute. "How many votes did you figure in that total?" another reporter who made it through the security overheard the old man demanding on the telephone, tilted back in his chair beside the pool. "There should be some Southern votes in there too . . . well. . . ."

Once JFK started wavering, Joe Kennedy himself quickly heard about it and immediately got Johnson on the line to salve his abraded feelings and urge him emphatically to take the vice-presidential offer. "Hell, Scoop," LBJ told Henry Jackson when it was all over. "They didn't want me. They wanted you. It was the old man who wanted me."

Johnson sympathizers would claim that Bobby was still pushing on Johnson the logic of renouncing his own candidacy when Phil Graham, looking in on "the turmoil in Johnson's private headquarters," called the hectored nominee. Jack informed Graham that his brother was "out of touch." The deal was down; Lyndon was on the ticket. Robert Kennedy was apparently the last to know. "And that's why Bobby hated Lyndon so," Bobby Baker concludes.

That night the boys took dinner at the Marion Davies estate. Watching over the younger generation splashing around the fountain in front, the

Ambassador greeted his victorious sons waiting "grandly in the doorway," Arthur Schlesinger reports, in a velvet smoking jacket. "Don't worry," Joe assured the nominee. "Within two weeks, they'll be saying it's the smartest thing you ever did."

The next day, his purposes at the convention served, the cunning old speculator flew back early to New York to pull strings to get Jack elected. On November 9, once he had finally conceded, the penetrating if embittered Dick Nixon telegraphed congratulations to Joseph P. Kennedy. "You have not lost a son," Nixon assured his one-time backer. "You have gained a country."

2

The Legacy

That week of backstage strategizing which left John Kennedy nominated and Lyndon Johnson in place as his running mate tested the aging financier. He'd brought it off. It hadn't been the first time Joe had found a way to utilize the baleful, disruptive presence of J. Edgar Hoover. Johnson would be helpful, whether Jack or Bobby sounded enthusiastic or not. It was rarely necessary to concede too much to either of the boys.

"My father lived four lives," Jack Kennedy mused after the old man was incapacitated. Joe was an American original, a lone-wolf capitalist who decided on the rules as he went along. In both his family life and his business the patriarch was hit-and-run, intensely focused and productive until he got what he wanted, then inclined to grab his profit and disappear. What left the deepest impression on his children were his absences, punctuated by his heartfelt, bromide-rich letters. In person, he evoked something close to adoration in all of them, laced with considerable fear.

Joe Kennedy is routinely termed his family's "founding father," but in truth the first fortune began with *his* father, Patrick Joseph Kennedy, "Pat the Barkeep." Patrick was the only son of a widowed hairdresser. A stocky community mainstay with luxuriant handlebar moustaches, P. J. started out as a stevedore and, fortified by the savings of his immigrant mother, scraped together enough cash at twenty-six to buy into a saloon in East Boston's Haymarket Square. He parlayed *its* profits into several additional bars, a whiskey dealership—he distributed Haig and Haig—and land and commercial holdings which included shares in the Suffolk Coal Company and the fledgling Columbia Trust, where even reputable Irishmen were permitted occasionally to borrow. Well regarded throughout the neighborhood, open-handed with the poor, P. J. was elected by heavy majorities to the Massachusetts House of Representatives and ultimately the state Senate. In the end, he decided to exert himself politically on the city's Board of Strategy, where power brokers from the districts met to parcel out jobs and marshal the Irish vote. Another Board of Strategy regular was John Francis ("Honey Fitz") Fitzgerald, a short, corner-cutting, self-advertising politico the sober-sided P. J. remained at pains to tolerate.

P. J. married up. His selection, Mary Augusta Hickey, a hefty woman with three prominent brothers, was approaching thirty when she got a ring on Pat. For all her social airs, the marriage proved workable from the start; Pat referred to his generously proportioned bride as Mame. The arrival within a year of Joseph Patrick Kennedy delighted the ambitious mother, who conspicuously favored her enterprising single son over her subsequent two daughters. In later years Joe Kennedy was fond of telling reporters that he grew up "on the mud flats of East Boston," but in fact he spent his boyhood in a well-staffed four-story townhouse on Webster Street, a prime site overlooking the booming harbor.

His mother coddled Joe, reminding him often that his uncle John, an M.D., had matriculated at Harvard; she curtailed his aptitude for deviltry with "the Hickey look," a protracted, unsettling glance of disapproval. By the time the tall, scrappy redhead graduated from Boston Latin he exhibited the bearing that was to cow so many: the long feral face, marked by full, demanding, rather brutal lips reminiscent of his son Jack's and an appraising stare that modulated as the situation required to reflect sardonic disapproval or mock astonishment or abrupt, terrifying displays of anger. Mame's baby was already in the habit of dealing with the world with a scion's disdain.

At the exacting Boston Latin School his academics were indifferent, but his cocksure, wisecracking personality ultimately commanded a following. He was a quick study. He found that he needed a great deal of pocket money and scrambled around the neighborhoods peddling newspapers, raising pigeons, even lighting the gas lamps and stoves of the orthodox Jews on Saturday. He was a gung-ho baseball player, twice captain of his team, an accomplishment made easier by the additional year it took the slapdash scholar to graduate.

Joe's hauteur was already starting to raise hackles. "The trouble with you, Joe," the baseball coach at Boston Latin told him, "is that your father holds political office. Everybody's been toadying to you for years and you think you're better than the other boys." There was a reprimand here, but also—coming from these Protestants—the suggestion of an ethnic slight. When finally Joe did graduate, Kennedy's yearbook inscription predicted that he would arrive at fortune "in a very roundabout way." Allowing for Kennedy's background, deviousness was to be anticipated.

A similar quirky performance played through at Harvard. He started out expecting to specialize in history and economics. Naturally quick with numbers, Joe found accounting too demanding, and in the end would drop enough courses to wind up majoring in music, which became a secret, life-long outlet for the pent-up financier. Eager to advance socially, Kennedy made it his business to room in the Yard with two of the obvious class leaders, the All-American Bob Fisher and the Philadelphia Social Register blue-blood Robert Potter. Kennedy wangled his way into the Hasty Pudding and the less prestigious Dickey and Delta Upsilon but got nowhere aspiring to the better, socially restricted final clubs. A classmate would remember the loudmouthed youngster as "an unctuous, totally unabashed social climber." He was already pursuing Rose, the mayor's sprightly daughter, behind her disapproving father's back.

Most unnerving of all, he failed to snag a berth on the varsity baseball team. A passable fielder, Joe ran, by one report, "like an ice wagon." Then, just before the all-important Yale game, the star who had beaten Kennedy out for first base, Chick McLaughlin, approached the coach and prevailed on him to put Kennedy in for long enough to earn his Harvard H. It would develop that McLaughlin intended to apply for a license to run a movie theater once he graduated; several associates of P. J. had taken Chick aside and made it clear that, if McLaughlin hoped to get his license, Joe would have to letter.

There was a lesson here the graduating senior never forgot. Things didn't just happen; intermediaries made them happen, normally behind the scenes. Having taken this in, Joe Kennedy was primed. "Joe was the kind of guy," one of his teammates divulged to biographer Richard Whalen, "who, if he wanted something bad enough, would get it, and he didn't care how he got it. He'd run right over anybody."

A bona fide Harvard graduate, Kennedy snagged an appointment as a state bank examiner after a word from his father's friends and devoted himself to courting Rose. Long-jawed and compact, convent-bred, brimming over with herself, Honey Fitz's favorite daughter amounted to royalty in Irish-Catholic Boston; her father wouldn't let this gum-chewing offspring of Pat the Barkeep into the house. But when Joe Kennedy rigged a coup that prevented a takeover of the Columbia Trust and emerged in 1913, at twenty-five, the youngest and best-publicized bank president in America, Fitzgerald gave it up and the two were married at a small, private nuptial mass by Cardinal O'Connell. Weeks later they settled into the unprepossessing house on Beales Street in Brookline that would wind up a national monument.

Capitalizing on "a contagious laugh, a vitality that magnetized a room," Kennedy lobbied his way into a trustee's chair on the moribund Massachusetts Electric Company. The meetings were slow, he conceded to a friend, but how else "to meet people like the Saltonstalls?" Riding the mayor's coattails, he joined his father-in-law in hiking up city license fees and splitting the surcharges while prodding the effervescent Honey Fitz for introductions to luminaries like Bernard Baruch. Bystanders found the self-important banker confusing to read. As quick to foreclose a shaky mortgage and grab a quick and heartless turnover as the most hardened Presbyterian, Kennedy betrayed from time to time an unbankerly susceptibility to a hard-luck story, a welling-up of human sympathy he did his damnedest to suppress. Kennedy's entire career would be peppered with acts of cold-blooded self-interest interspersed with outbursts of generosity.

When World War I threatened to interrupt his fortune-building, Kennedy recruited Guy Currier, a high-rolling Harvard classmate already piling it up as a lobbyist for Bethlehem Steel, to scout out a defense-related situation guaranteed to protect his deferment status. Through Charles M. Schwab, Currier arranged for Kennedy to step in as an assistant to Joseph Powell, the general manager of Bethlehem Ship at Fore River, Massachusetts. Kennedy promptly underwrote a profitable private commissary. In times to come, the eager executive liked to expand on his version of a contretemps with Assistant Secretary of the Navy Franklin D. Roosevelt. Roosevelt demanded that Bethlehem turn over a couple of battleships the yard had built for the Argentine Navy. After Kennedy proved balky about delivery until the government's check cleared, Roosevelt ordered in tugboats and towed both battleships out. "When I left his office," Kennedy would assure his listeners, "I was so disappointed and angry that I broke down and cried." But Kennedy was rarely inclined to joke about another setback, FDR's intervention to prevent Kennedy from firing five thousand irreplaceable shipyard workers rather than honor a scheduled pay raise. When word of that fiasco reached the home office, Kennedy was reportedly demoted.

Other executives supplied more detail. "Joe was just accommodated to skip the draft during World War I because of a lot of pressure from his father-in-law, Honey Fitz," one Bethlehem colleague recalled. "He was given some kind of office job. . . ." Another biographer maintains that, as exemption requirements tightened, Kennedy secretly rummaged through the office paperwork until he stumbled across incriminating evidence of war profiteering: "The threat of its exposure convinced Joseph Powell . . . to contact the Boston draft board to help keep Joe out of the military."

After 1918, the market for boatbuilders dried up and Kennedy moved on. He himself would circulate the story that all it took was to slip into a commuter seat next to Galen Stone, talk fast, and promote himself a job as manager of the investment division at Hayden, Stone in Boston and New York. As always with Kennedy, footnotes got left out. As part of her dowry from Honey Fitz, Rose Kennedy had come into five thousand shares of the Atlantic, Gulf and West Indies Shipping Line, AGWI, where Stone himself sat in as chairman. At the time, five thousand shares represented an important position. AGWI stock was under assault, and with Joe Kennedy on the payroll Stone could count on Rose's proxies.

These were unsettling years for the self-aggrandizing Harvard graduate, what with the children starting to come along and the skeptical, outspoken Honey Fitz hovering over the household. Between Rose and her loquacious father, Joe needed to watch his step. By now Kennedy was commuting regularly to Manhattan, where his sharp eye for chorus girls produced a liaison with the honey-blonde film sensation Betty Compson. Rose, pregnant with her fourth, moved back in with her father, who found her fretful and bossy underfoot and pushed her back, still bitter but permanently resigned, on Joe.

It was the era of unlimited margin. Kennedy borrowed heavily and too often lost heavily, most embarrassingly after Mexican bandits vandalized AGWI's oil holdings, a setback compounded by a bear raid on the company which gutted Rose's position. Sharpshooters around the State Street financial district misled the cocky newcomer. "If you have enough inside information and unlimited credit," he said later, "you are sure to go broke." "When you deal with a businessman," Joe would tell his children, "you screw him first or he'll screw you. . . ."

Never temperamentally a plunger, Kennedy made a killing or two with the help of insiders like Galen Stone, who tipped him in time to the takeover of the Pond Coal Company by Henry Ford. By then Joe's ulcers were kicking up, and the stolid P. J. was "afraid he's bitten off more than he can chew." What increasingly tempted Kennedy was a sure thing. Reliable setups took work, specialized information, undisclosed money changing hands. But with diligence, they paid off.

By 1920, bootlegging was a sure thing. With the enactment of the 1919 Volstead Act, the anguish of prohibition had descended on a parched America. Here was an opening Kennedy had the bloodlines to exploit. Not only was P. J. connected in the trade; two of Honey Fitz's younger brothers were energetically running booze. Kennedy started out trafficking in legal "medicinal permits." Early evidence that the stockbroker was branching out appeared during the Harvard Tenth Reunion of the Class of '12. "Joe was our chief bootlegger," one classmate laughed afterward. "Of course, he didn't touch a drop himself, but he arranged with his agents to have the stuff sent in right on the beach at Plymouth. It came ashore the way the Pilgrims did." Days before he died, the sleek, faux-genteel paymaster for the New York Families, Frank Costello, told Peter Maas that his decades of partnership with Kennedy began when the financier sought him out to make sure Scotch got to the Cape Cod reunion.

By early 1923 Kennedy had detached himself from Hayden, Stone and set up offices as an independent banker. A team of working-class Irishmen he had recruited in Fore River, Charley Sullivan, E. B. Derr, and Ted O'Leary, as well as Kennedy's discreet personal factotum, the one-time secretary to Honey Fitz, Edward Moore—the boss's reliable "Four Horseman"—moved in as backup. James Seymour signed on, once Kennedy started in California, with John J. Ford and Pat Scollard backing up the raiders in Kennedy's Wall Street offices. Innocents they would deal with throughout the next few decades characterized Kennedy's flunkies as "gangsters in appearance," but they were scrupulously trained by their employer to function at critical junction points of his interflowing enterprises. O'Leary, a heavy-set, florid Dartmouth graduate with the agility of a bouncer, took day-to-day responsibility for the boss's clandestine liquor business. Once the Kennedy family relocated to Riverdale, Ted was to be contacted through the New York Athletic Club.

Kennedy kept "the liquor business" at arm's length. A 1926 Canadian government Royal Commission on Customs and Excise investigation revealed that Kennedy had all along been purchasing whiskey from the Hiram Walker distillery in shipload lots. Kennedy was also a major customer for the Seagram product from the Bronfmans. While Joe Kennedy personally was very rarely in evidence, the "rum fleets" he underwrote offloaded the contraband Scotch and gin onto secluded inlets up and down the lower Massachusetts coast, where, along with Kennedy's employees, Costello's minions would see after distribution throughout the major Eastern markets. Kennedy personally looked in on the important retail outlets. Most of the important mobsters in the bootlegging industry emerged from prohibition well stocked with Joe Kennedy anecdotes. Like other underworld dignitaries, the murderous little English thug Owen Madden, who monopolized the nightclub trade throughout the New York boroughs, raved later about the youthful Bostonian's maturity of outlook and "business judgment."

Occasionally there were ugly setbacks. Reminiscing to his biographers in Israel during an interlude of forced retirement, Meyer Lansky lamented an incident in 1927 when a contingent from the "Lansky–Luciano organization" ambushed one of Joe Kennedy's boatloads as it came onto the beach from Ireland. When they attempted to resist, eleven of Kennedy's punks were shot to death and the whiskey grabbed. This wasn't Lansky's style; when he began to dress down his most promising honcho, the trigger-happy Bugsy Siegel, Siegel protested: "It really wasn't our fault. Those Irish idiots hire amateurs as guards." Kennedy lost a great deal of money.

Throughout the twenties, boats chartered by the enterprising banker came across the water whenever people were thirsty. California took on booze via Catalina Island. Kennedy serviced the Caribbean from the Bahamas to Palm Beach County, unloading the high-grade stuff from international waters, just beyond the reach of the U.S. Treasury Department and its hard-bitten Alcohol, Tobacco and Firearms operatives. A lot came in over the Great Lakes. Several sources credit talk of a lively spaghetti supper hosted by Al Capone during which the Chicago kingpin and Joe worked out a schedule for the exchange of Irish whiskey for the equivalent in cases from Big Al's Canadian distillery, the swap to be effected on Mackinac Island.

The advisability of dealing with Joe remained a matter of controversy inside the Chicago Outfit. Of all Capone's top heirs, the Outfit's consigliere Murray Llewellyn ("The Camel") Humphreys, a Welchman who dealt with tax planning and kept after legal matters for his impulsive Sicilian associates, remained the most skeptical when it came to this brash Boston Irishman who negotiated so easily and was so hard to hold to his promises. During the ensuing decades The Camel—who was a lot more presentable than Jake ("Greasy Thumb") Guzik or the beetle-browed Momo Giancana— actually maintained a kind of sporadic acquaintanceship with Kennedy, and visited him at several of his homes. Also known as Curly or The Hump, the farsighted Welshman wrote Kennedy off privately as a "four-flusher and a double-crosser" for having "highjacked his own load that had already been paid for and took it and sold it somewhere else all over again."

Stories made the rounds in Chicago to the effect that a panicked Kennedy had been forced to appeal to the Windy City's Diamond Jim Esposito to lift a contract on his life taken out by the deadly Jews of Detroit's Purple Gang, who intended to retaliate against the banker for smuggling rum across Michigan without their say-so. Esposito stepped in; Joe invested in alcohol and sugar from Diamond Jim to liven up his more proletarian brands.

Out West, Kennedy reaped a certain cachet as the bootlegger for the film community. One grateful customer was the comedienne Marion Davies, already living in quasiroyal splendor as the official mistress of William Randolph Hearst. Joe and Marion probably met when Marion was a leggy bombshell with the Ziegfeld Follies during the early twenties. Ever openhearted, Davies had taken spontaneously to this hard-pitching Bostonian always willing to supply a bottle she could work on behind W. R.'s back. Her W. R., for all his plump, wastrel looks and the killer forelock, didn't really approve of drinking.

It was the heyday of newspapering, and the many Hearst publications controlled public opinion. Joe Kennedy was beginning to factor in the uses of publicity. He'd gotten a lot of attention when he was America's youngest bank president; his composed, unlined visage, looking mildly up from his desk at the bank, made editions across the country. He rarely ducked interviews.

Even before he finally captured Rose, Kennedy seemed to luxuriate naturally in the company of showgirls, with all their resilience and informality. Kennedy and the offhand Davies understood each other. "Joe Kennedy was a good friend of W. R.'s, and I always liked him," Marion would subsequently write. "He was a good Irishman." Joe, and later his sons, could always depend on hospitality at the Hearst properties. "DEAREST JOE:" runs a 1922 telegram, "SO SORRY I DID NOT SEE YOU BEFORE YOU LEFT BUT IT WAS WONDERFUL SEEING YOU EVEN FOR SUCH A SHORT TIME. I DO HOPE IT WILL NOT BE LONG BEFORE WE MEET AGAIN. LOTS OF LOVE—MARION."

After starchy, withheld Boston, California was a tonic to the senses, an orchard of expectations where dreams were forever ripening. While still at Hayden, Stone, Kennedy led a group that acquired thirty-one small movie theaters in New England. He dabbled in production. In 1925, after rounding up backing from several of the WASPiest moguls around Boston led by the plutocratic Guy Currier, Kennedy boosted himself into control of the Film Booking Office of America, FBO, a British producer and distributor of movies.

Still written off as the mayor's self-promoting son-in-law around judgmental Back Bay and blackballed when he came up for membership at the Cohasset Country Club, Kennedy decided to reignite his career. He decided to relocate his expanding family to Greater New York, where nobody was likely to ask too many questions about the quantum appreciation of his assets or find him pretentious for hiring a chauffeur. Early in 1926, he moved the Kennedys to a much more appropriate residence in Riverdale and regrouped to become a player in the emerging motion picture industry. "Look at that bunch of pants-pressers in Hollywood making themselves millionaires," he advised one friend. "I could take the whole business away from them."

Like the old money around Boston, the hard-bellied little cloak-and-suiters who built the industry showed limited interest in offering up their domain to Joseph P. Kennedy. While he would later claim that he modeled his family life on the dedicated parenting he encountered in Hollywood, the fact is these shrewd, tough-minded, pinochle-playing Jews could more than handle any threat this self-anointed boy banker posed. Furthermore, like Kennedy, they had no scruples about playing rough. Virtually from the beginning, most of them depended on Mob ties—the indelicate ex-fence Harry Cohn at Columbia was completely subservient for financing to underworld money. Mob-dominated unions collaborated to set everything from production costs to projectionist wages. Kennedy's later, vaunted anti-Semitism undoubtedly owed a great deal to a superstitious dread that, if he ever looked away, these Hebrews would clean out everything he had.

One source has it that Kennedy himself was regarded by the Capone organization as a stalking horse for Chicago's interests on the Coast. Kennedy had arrived in Hollywood to find the directors at FBO grinding out low-budget shoot-'em-ups and horse operas, one every couple of weeks. The ambitious banker rented himself a base of operations on Rodeo Drive and, deploying Moore, Sullivan, et al., "tight-lipped men with loud ties," attempted to take things over. One early gesture involved persuading the dean of the Harvard Business School to invite the reigning studio heads to deliver a series of lectures on the history of the industry. It was like a convention of Rodney Dangerfield clones, with subliterate ex-furriers and ragpickers from the bowels of the Lower East Side holding forth in Yiddified English while peeping about warily—a number were suing one another—to identify likely process servers.

Kennedy wanted something big, major. His first instinct was to isolate a star, Gloria Swanson, and enshrine her publicly as his trophy mistress. Gloria was a tiny woman with sharp, perfectly cut features and pouty bee-sting lips, a lynx-eyed twenty-eight-year-old film celebrity quite worried just then about finding enough money to support her extravagant lifestyle along with her high-minded third husband, The Marquis Le Bailly de la Falaise de la Coudraye. Swanson had just finished the production of *Sadie Thompson,* a dramatization of Somerset Maugham's story *Rain.* The first time Swanson spotted the name Joe Kennedy was as a signatory, among others, to a telegram to her studio head protesting the release of such "salacious books and plays." Kennedy had started out in California by cultivating Will Hays, Hollywood's top crusader for propriety.

As it happened, *Sadie Thompson* was a critical and popular success. But while she waited for the film to premiere, Swanson was running out of money, and a go-between put her in touch with Kennedy, reputed to exert influence with several New York banking houses. At their initial lunch, Swanson found the banker alarmingly heavy-duty: "His suit was too bulky, and the knot of his tie was not pushed up tight." Approaching forty, "With his spectacles and prominent chin, he looked like any average working-class person's uncle." She was put off by his need to throw in the facts that his father-in-law had been the mayor of Boston and that he had studied at "Hah-vad" every few minutes, not to mention his tendency to talk with his hands and thwack his thigh each time he was amused.

Yet something about this big Irishman's urgency and the intensity of his desire to involve himself in her life touched Gloria Swanson, and before very long she had turned her business affairs over to him. Her current and future assets were funneled into the Gloria Production Company, the stock of which was issued in the name of one of Kennedy's key executives in Manhattan, Patrick Scollard. Scollard had his reservations: "IF I DON'T GO TO JAIL OVER THIS DEAL, I NEVER WILL," he wired his California counterpart, Ed Derr.

Not long after that, while the faithful Eddie Moore had taken her husband the Marquis out deep-sea fishing off Palm Beach, Gloria Swanson would one day write, Kennedy mounted her "like a roped horse," followed by a premature ejaculation. The romance was on.

It was a bad idea. Rose was fairly hardened by then and entertained Gloria in Hyannis Port and joined her and her husband and others on a boat trip to Europe. Swanson found herself being dressed down by Cardinal O'Connell, a nondescript old man all dressed in red who smelled of incense and moved "with a rustle of taffeta or silk." O'Connell informed her that she had become "an occasion of sin" for Joe. Meanwhile, the "important" film they intended to create together, ultimately entitled *Queen Kelly*, was turning into a financial and artistic Moloch.

Directed by the central European émigré Erich von Stroheim, by reputation "an underwear fetishist with a streak of sadism," the story line followed the ordeal of "a convent-bred girl who inherits a string of African bordellos. . . . A strong suggestion of necrophilia was the kicker." Originally titled *The Swamp*, this primal affront to the Hays Office would never be released and was reported to cost Joe Kennedy $800,000. In truth, most of the capital required to produce *Queen Kelly* had come from shaky little Columbia Trust in Boston, borrowed in Swanson's name and released piecemeal by Eddie Moore as the film's expenses were covered by Gloria's earnings.

Kennedy had been wary all along. On May 18, 1929, Joe's father P. J. died of liver cancer. Accosted by an angry cousin—"You son of a bitch. . . . You were too busy on the West Coast chasing Gloria Swanson around"—for neglecting to make it back for his father's funeral, Joe pleaded his priorities: "I couldn't leave. If I left for two days, the Jews would rob me blind." Here was a profound apprehension, too deep to argue with.

Not that he hadn't reinsured. One of the Horsemen, Kennedy's designated accountant E. B. Derr, was in place to buffer Joe off by personally assuming power of attorney for Gloria. As the misery settled, Gloria was gradually made aware that most of the splashier favors the high-spirited banker had been bestowing on her over the past few years—furs, her luxurious bungalow on the lot, a Cadillac Joe impulsively presented to an innovative scriptwriter—came entirely from her side of the ledger. Worse, future earnings her Gloria Productions racked up would go to Kennedy. Gloria came out of it effectively broke, and her enthusiastic partner had moved on.

Like every other producer, Kennedy depended on gangster elements around Southern California to head off labor unrest. The International Alliance of Theatrical Stage Employees and Motion Picture Operators—the Stagehands Union—worked essentially for the studios, a company device to keep costs down. Organized crime in California was just emerging from the Black-Hand-Unione-Siciliano phase as the first generation, the Mustache Petes, died off and more contemporary hoodlums like Anthony ("Tony the Hat")

Cornero and Jack Dragna introduced a measure of rationality to rumrunning and gambling. One punk who worked for them both was Johnny Rosselli, a gaunt and observant youngster who had already risen to the dignity of midlevel gunsel under Al Capone. Roselli's tubercular lungs couldn't take the raw winds off Lake Michigan, and he relocated in 1924 to Los Angeles.

Paperwork on Rosselli is spotty, but it is quite plain that this immigrant who arrived at five with his family from the Hill Country of Campania and resettled in Boston's North End in 1911 took to the streets early. Fillipo Sacco had already renamed himself Johnny Rosselli by 1925, after a forgotten fifteenth-century Florentine painter, and the disgruntled young hood who appears in a mug shot from the period (grand larceny and carrying a concealed weapon) looks well turned out, bound for serious endeavor. FBI records tick off a rap sheet which includes charges for illegal possession of a firearm, dealing in narcotics, and importing "old members of the Al Capone gang" to intimidate the Stagehands Union. Before the twenties ended, Rosselli was well enough entrenched with Dragna to look after labor conciliation work—strikebreaking—for both the film producers and the Hays office, as well as lay off major bets with the national syndicate. The man he ran hooch for before Capone, Abner ("Longie") Zwillman, the Philadelphia gangland potentate, deputized Rosselli to keep an eye on his protégé on the coast, the white-blonde film phenomenon Jean Harlow. When Harry Cohn required $500,000 in a hurry to buy out his disconcertingly scrupulous brother, Rosselli got financing overnight from Zwillman. In time, Zwillman and Rosselli would combine to produce several profitable Grade B suspense thrillers.

Sources close to the likeable gangster insist that, before he coordinated shipments for Zwillman, the adolescent Rosselli broke into the trade carting crates ashore for Joseph P. Kennedy. By the end of the twenties, the versatile young thug and Kennedy had settled into a productive acquaintanceship, frequently sharing a card game or a round of golf; Dade County police files document their get-togethers in Florida. The emaciated, coughing contract killer from Chicago was transforming himself into a kind of bicoastal sophisticate, a skilled intermediary whose warm gray eyes and mild-mannered approach to the challenges of the world, with expensive suits set off by matching gaudy tie and handkerchief, reassured starlet and tycoon equally. Whatever you were after, this handsomely pompadoured problem solver for the syndicate could come up with something. Here was an individual it would be foolhardy *not* to know.

* * *

One of the calamities that helped sabotage *Queen Kelly* was the fact that, just as production ended, *The Jazz Singer* with Al Jolson hit the marketplace as the first blockbuster talking movie. This meant that *Queen Kelly*, too, would have to be reshot and dubbed at enormous expense. Apart from the money required, the perversity of many of the brothel scenes heightened by the human voice took viewers over the top.

Back in New York, a lot less driven by his glands to undergo those three-day transcontinental train rides, Kennedy was in a position to capitalize on the recurrent buzz that he knew something about the cockamamie picture business. He brought a fresh eye: Kennedy discovered the young Walt Disney designing animated commercials in Kansas City and signed him for FBO, where Disney developed Mickey Mouse. Overnight there were several sound systems out there, and leaders like David Sarnoff of RCA wanted theirs to become the industry standard. Sarnoff bought into FBO to make sure RCA equipment went into its theater chain. Then Kennedy found financial backing to acquire control of the Keith-Albee-Orpheum vaudeville and film chain, which owned most of Pathé-De Mille Productions. Kennedy assigned his energetic lieutenant, John J. Ford, to oversee his unwieldy movie acquisitions, and, when the pompous Edward F. Albee strolled into his office one day with a suggestion, Kennedy closed the old man down with a reminder quoted widely along Wall Street: "Didn't you know, Ed? You're washed up. You're through."

Kennedy was piecing together the media conglomerate that would emerge as RKO. He would need all the outlets he could get. One chain he had his eye on was the Pantages system, sixty movie houses out West, perfect for balancing his holding. But the elderly immigrant Greek Alex Pantages wouldn't sell. Kennedy started by denying the chain major first-run films; when that didn't move Pantages, in August 1929 a scene was apparently choreographed which featured a fetching seventeen-year-old Los Angeles girl, Eunice Pringle, erupting from a janitor's closet with her dress torn and a hysterical tale about old Pantages having assaulted her, proceeding from "kissing me madly" to biting one of her breasts. As trials and appeals worked their way up the court system, Pantages stock dropped. RKO soon acquired most of the Pantages holdings at less than half the price originally offered. "On her deathbed," Eunice Pringle "confessed that it had been Kennedy who masterminded the frameup."

As RKO came together, Kennedy was working every angle, paying himself high multiple salaries for guiding each of the constituents, establishing several classes of stock, and quietly switching his own holdings to the detriment of ordinary shareholders while creating huge option allotments for company officers guaranteed to deplete the treasury. His longtime backer, Guy Currier, whom Kennedy had persuaded to buy into Western Electric to pipeline insider data to Joe, discovered that in his absence Kennedy had "pillaged his files for inside information. . . ." Shortly before the Crash, behind Currier's back, Kennedy arranged to sell out almost all of their combined position in RKO to David Sarnoff.

Three intense years in the motion-picture business had left Kennedy thirty pounds lighter and a reported five million dollars richer. Joe sold his huge block of RCA securities at 50; the stock reached 114, then began its long, bumpy descent. Together with the off-the-books proceeds from his mysterious "liquor business," cashing out gave the hard-driving banker meaningful capital of his own. Throughout the twenties, Kennedy let it be bruited about that he was the gunslinger you wanted when your company was endangered. Typical was his intervention in 1924 when Yellow Cab underwent a bear raid, and Kennedy sweated together a boiler-room operation to shore the stock price up. He emerged, briefly, as a partner in the company by forging a merger with Fifth Avenue Coach, the New York bus company. Subsequently, when Yellow Cab collapsed again, its rough-hewn founder, John D. Hertz, became convinced that Kennedy had jumped on inside information to short the stock himself before bailing out, as it was becoming apparent that Hertz had been paying off New York's Mayor John F. Hylan.

By October 1929, when the economic collapse began in earnest, Kennedy masterminded a complex series of flanking attacks on the weakened market, organized around pools of like-minded raiders. While maintaining a regular trading desk at Hall and Steiglitz, he shorted the troubled Blue Chips mercilessly through straws at Oliphant as well as Bache. He formed a backroom alliance with the notorious bear Ben ("Sell 'em Ben") Smith, who tipped Kennedy off whenever the top grizzlies had their claws in a company. As throughout his arm's-length trafficking with the Mafia, Kennedy provided these omnivorous bears a legitimate spokesman while Wall Street underwent its gruesome rending.

As conditions deteriorated, Kennedy sensed a profound answering rumble working its way closer throughout the substructure of politics. He identified New York Governor Franklin D. Roosevelt as the approaching force. Louis

Howe, Roosevelt's irritable Svengali, never had much use for the glad-handing Wall Streeter, but the campaign needed money badly, and Kennedy was eager to prove his sincerity with a $25,000 outright gift and a $50,000 loan to the Democratic Party. Bought in by Henry Morgenthau Jr. and welcomed by the campaign's gusty top kick, James Farley, Kennedy raised a lot of money anonymously—which he was careful to contribute to the candidate under his own name. Franklin Roosevelt's intimate secretary Missy LeHand teamed up with Kennedy to work on then-Bishop Francis Spellman to help extract the Massachusetts delegates from the Al Smith campaign and deliver them to FDR.

A Hollywood Kennedy contact, Twentieth Century Fox founder Joe Schenck, was reputed to have pipelined "half a million to Roosevelt's campaign for the syndicate through Postmaster General Farley." Despite Jimmy Roosevelt's efforts at intervention, Schenck would do time when an IRS investigation proved he had neglected to declare a $400,000 handout from the Mob. At the 1932 Democratic convention in Chicago, Frank Costello, Lucky Luciano, and Meyer Lansky showed up to look after their respective interests, sharing suites at the Francis Drake with their Tammany Hall counterparts.

Most useful just then, Kennedy offered *himself* as an emissary to William Randolph Hearst. Through Kennedy, Hearst worked on Roosevelt to declare openly that he would not join the League of Nations. As the convention dragged through its third ballot without a nomination for Roosevelt, Kennedy telephoned the autocrat of San Simeon and warned him that delegates were starting to line up behind Newton Baker, a defender of the League. "If you don't want Baker, you'd better take Roosevelt," Kennedy warned the press czar, who reluctantly released his California delegates. Kennedy telephoned Gloria Swanson to inform her that he had "the next president of the United States" on the line for her. Miffed with her slippery paramour, Gloria refused to take the call.

By October, Hearst had sent through a sizable check to the Democratic campaign, and Kennedy was minueting in place to reassure him: "I realize that this check coming to the Committee through me helps a great deal in having consideration paid to any suggestion that I might want to make," Kennedy admitted. "You may rest assured, and this I want to say to go on record, that whenever your interests in this administration are not served well, my interest has ceased."

The terror of East Boston was learning.

* * *

For the rest of the decade, Kennedy either had a prestigious post in Washington or he was bucking for one. During much of the fall, Kennedy was permitted to join the presidential party racketing across the country on the campaign train and snagged a berth on FDR's vacation yacht. The banker quickly found himself watching FDR's oldest son Jimmy, the lanky, balding aide-de-camp to his father whose greed and relative slowness on the uptake would make him useful to any number of unscrupulous associates. A general agFent in Boston for Travelers Insurance, Jimmy Roosevelt was grateful when Kennedy shooed business in his direction—along, reportedly, with girls—and functioned as Kennedy's voice in his father's ear.

In September 1933, with prohibition about to end, Kennedy and Rose, with Jimmy and Betsy Roosevelt, took a tour of England and Scotland. Showing off the president's son, Kennedy lined up American distributorships for Haig and Haig and John Dewar Scotch and Gordon's Gin. Flush with cash just then from a pool he was running to cannibalize Libby-Owens-Ford stock, throughout the final months of prohibition Kennedy arranged for the importation of thousands of cases of liquor covered by "medicinal licenses" to the warehouses of his newly formed Somerset Importing Company. He reportedly named the company after a Boston club he was confident would never let him in. Kennedy's specialist in moving liquor around, Ted O'Leary, ran Somerset day by day. When Jimmy Roosevelt hinted that *he* might like a little of this action, Joe fobbed him off with a knowing laugh and the avuncular aside that "you can't do that, it would embarrass your father." Jimmy reportedly settled for $25,000.

Kennedy expected appointment to secretary of the treasury. When that wasn't forthcoming, he made do with a seat on the newly formed Securities and Exchange Commission, alternately sulking and strong-arming himself into place as the initial Chairman. Experienced speculator that he was, Kennedy had few problems devising a pattern of regulation very effective in frustrating the fly-by-night securities promoters, bucket-shop operators, and panic-loving bears accustomed to victimizing their momentary clients. Kennedy rented a suburban showplace, Marwood, within commuting distance in the Maryland estate country, and settled in with Eddie Moore. Exploiting Marwood as a base, Kennedy entertained lavishly. Presenting himself as one servant of the people to whom wealth remained incidental, the extroverted millionaire drew heavily on several of the members of his commission, especially Harvard law professor James Landis and the Yale expert on corporate finance, William O. Douglas. Both remained productive family friends long after their SEC days.

In 1933, Kennedy had acquired a five-bedroom Addison Mizner mansion on North Ocean Boulevard in Palm Beach. Kennedy loved to shuffle friends and promising acquaintances in and out of both properties. Franklin Roosevelt grew fond of bantering with the slangy, outspoken banker over the perfect mint juleps that Joe—himself an unapologetic teetotaler—delighted in presenting the president while FDR relaxed in his wheelchair in the basement screening room at Marwood. James Farley came out. Brought into the picture by Bernie Baruch, the *New York Times*'s man in Washington, Arthur Krock, a fast-rising young snob determined to conceal his small-town Jewish origins, had started to haunt the place. Krock never forgot the day he walked in on Joe winding up a telephone call to FDR. "Listen, boy," Kennedy was roaring at the president, "if we do that we'll land in the outhouse where we belong." Even Eleanor applauded the forthright Kennedy during those exultant break-in months. FDR's personal secretary and substitute wife, Missy LeHand, slipped in and out both at Marwood and around the Palm Beach establishment.

As the thirties deepened, dignitaries throughout the press and political worlds showed up to bake in the hot sun at La Guerida, the gracious Kennedy Florida property. With certain of his female guests—Clare Boothe Luce, the wife of the Time, Inc. founder; by several reports the discreet Missy LeHand—Kennedy conducted diplomatic relations in the European tradition, below the belt. Cardinal Spellman came down. In time, accompanied by his lean and constant companion, Clyde Tolson, the brisk and increasingly celebrated Director of the FBI, J. Edgar Hoover, had started to put in an occasional appearance.

It was during FDR's tenure that Hoover managed to emerge from bureaucratic anonymity and take up his calling as a national archetype. As it happened, the role largely came to him. If the Kennedys were entrepreneurial, the Hoovers were primarily about entrenching position. Like *his* father, Hoover's father Dickerson worked for the U.S. Coast and Geodetic Survey, a worried-looking print manager with soulful eyes and a soup-strainer mustache. Psychologically, Dickerson remained delicate, and he was in and out of sanitariums while the baby of the family, sickly, fearful little Edgar, began groping for his own purchase on the world.

Enough family letters survive to establish the anxiety level. Attempting to recuperate in St. Louis, Dickerson writes his son: "This is a big city and it is full of people, some parts are very pretty but I don't think you or mama would like it—Everybody is in a rush, but as yet I have not seen any bad people and the police is as scarce as they can be.—The Mississippi River is very high and the water is like clay. The drinking water here has to be filtered when it comes out of the spigot it is very dark." Another letter refers to "a terrible lightening storm [sic], it lasted one & one half hours and it was some storm, it broke over us all of a sudden, flash after flash it was something awful." Feebly, the distant father attempts to build his nine-year-old up: "It is cold here, and if you was here that big overcoat would be just right to keep you warm, I sleep in your little bed and I wish that you were here so that I could fight you in the morning. Mama might think you ain't strong but just let her try to fight you and she will find out."

Essentially, raising Edgar would fall to the mother, née Annie Marie Scheitlin. A short, round-faced, rather dumpy woman with the eyes of an *Infanta,* the overbearing Annie represented coherence to Edgar while his father was increasingly disabled with what was then called melancholia, a variety of clinical depression. Of impeccable Swiss stock, Annie took a lot of pride from the fact that her grand-uncle had been the Swiss Republic's first honorary consul general to the United States. Another relative, William Hitz, was a D.C. judge.

Enough money came through to permit Annie to operate their modest, two-story stucco row house with the widow's walk across the front, everything wrapped and slip-covered. Even as a child, Edgar had about himself that welcome Swiss mania for orderliness. He started a newspaper at eleven, *The Weekly Review,* which memorialized everybody else's comings and goings. He nudged the family to transfer its allegiance from the local Lutheran congregation to the socially prestigious Old First Presbyterian at the foot of Capitol Hill. Little Edgar's voice changed late, and for several years he was able to sing soprano parts in the choir.

At fourteen Hoover arranged to transfer to distant Central High, just then the most highly regarded of the D.C. schools. He was still short for his age, slight, but keyed-up, assertive, and sure of himself. Relatives would remember a fidgety, rather driven adolescent, a top student, a compact busybody who rose quickly to become the captain of his high school ROTC marching unit. Asked whether Hoover dated, one classmate ventured that "He was in love with Company A." To quell an annoying stutter, Edgar made himself develop into an outstanding debater, purportedly nicknamed

"Speed" for his ability to crank out language so fast and hot and heavy that he could drown out any exchange. He taught a Sunday School class.

Whatever the neighbors thought, he was his mother's darling. During their infrequent separations, her letters are replete with good advice and domestic suggestions. "My dear old man," one note from Boston opens and closes "with hugs and kisses to your own dear self." Another recommends that "if the same girl waits on the table and does the bedroom work you had better give her a dollar the same as you give Aunt Harriet." Another remarks that "Papa is home with me this week" while "They have commenced to dig up the street in front. . . ." "Was so glad to hear you were perfect in your spelling and Arithmetic. Study hard both your lessons and your music, and try and be a very good boy, for Mama wants you to have the trip to Baltimore."

As Dickerson became marginalized, Edgar—the only child still around and unmarried—accepted his responsibility for keeping the household afloat. He decided that his older siblings shirked responsibility for the parents and ultimately cut them off. Dickerson would collect no pension and incarnated the horrors of forced retirement. Edgar took a job at the Library of Congress. Inside that unending labyrinth of corridors and files Hoover discovered his lifelong metier, the sifting and control of information, and advanced unerringly from messenger to cataloger to clerk while signing up for night law at George Washington University. He pledged a fraternity, Kappa Alpha. Annie became its "unofficial housemother." After law school, Hoover appears to have persuaded Judge Hitz to find him something in the Justice Department. It was 1917, the country was at war, and a government job guaranteed a deferment.

The Hoover of 1917 was already taking on the proportions of the icon to come. His first name, John, had been reduced to a J, to give his signature a fillip of distinction. He was a very busy fellow, sculptured and grave-looking at his desk, gazing out with cold impatience at the photographer from those wide-set, slightly protuberant eyes beneath his high thinker's forehead. Visitors were trying.

Looked after at home, he would remain a minimalist when it came to personal life. Hoover seemed to require one friend, somebody he could eat and travel with while chewing over the business of the day. First in this line was Hoover's Kappa Alpha brother Thomas Franklin—Frank—Baughman. Also a law student, Frank Baughman sat quietly during Hoover's diatribes against booze and gambling and tolerated his incessant practical jokes.

Decked out in fresh white linen suits, the two would float around what nightlife there was in the District and drop into the neighborhood vaudeville acts. Baughman brought his mother over to the Hoovers' for bridge with Edgar and his mom. Dickerson, a creature of the shadows by now, stayed out of sight. When Baughman signed up as a captain of artillery, Hoover and Annie saw him off at Union Station.

Hoover remained Over Here. Once Baughman got back in 1919, he discovered Hoover orchestrating the Justice Department's roundup of aliens from his desk in the Radical Division of the Bureau of Investigation. Hoover brought Frank in to help him deal with the paperwork. For the next ten years Baughman functioned as Hoover's alter ego. Then Frank Baughman decided he wanted to get married and that ended that.

Woodrow Wilson's attorney general was A. Mitchell Palmer. Palmer was a fluttery Quaker lawyer with aspirations to the presidency. On June 2, 1919, an anarchist with a bomb blew off the front of his house, spreading body parts across the lawn. Insisting he had inside information of an "attempt to rise up and destroy the government at one fell swoop," Palmer secured a special Congressional appropriation and pushed for a mass deportation of alien radicals. He put young Hoover, twenty-four, in charge of this momentous— and unconstitutional—assault on the American Left.

Wartime experience had accustomed Hoover to incarcerating or deporting enemy nationals without concerning himself about due process. A rash of strikes as well as random terrorist acts was riling the bourgeois establishment. Hoover settled into a crash course on Marxism-Leninism which left him convinced absolutely that here was the Antichrist, that all measures curricular and extracurricular were justified to extirpate radicalism in America. There was little distinction between the egalitarianism of a Eugene Debs and the machinations of the OGPU (Soviet secret police).

What strikes the historian is the thoroughness and efficiency with which this high-strung young fanatic brought down the "Palmer raids" on thousands of suspect foreigners. Within months, according to Senate investigators, Hoover had built up inside his General Intelligence Division a card-index file covering four hundred and fifty thousand individuals. By the end of 1919 and into 1920 ten thousand people were rounded up in nationwide dragnets, almost always without warrants, and manhandled into cells that "within a few days became stinking cesspools." Hoover himself drew up the briefs on which the arrest warrants were based and personally coordinated the raids. Foreigners caught the brunt of it—Spanish and Italian anarchists, along with the Union of Russian Workers—even though no evidence ever surfaced to tie the targets of this roundup to terrorism.

Congressional testimony Hoover prepared for Palmer was replete with the white-hot assault rhetoric typical of the intense young bureaucrat: These agitators were "avowed revolutionaries" and "Out of the sly and crafty eyes of many of them leap cupidity, cruelty, insanity, and crime; from their lopsided faces, sloping brows, and misshappen features may be recognized the unmistakable criminal type."

Hoover put a face to this purge by arranging personally to deport Emma Goldman and Alexander Berkman. Showcase anarchists, Berkman had confirmed his bona fides years before by shooting Henry Frick. The stout, bespectacled Emma was a legendary stump-speaker, feminist, and bugbear of governments everywhere. By tagging Emma as Queen of the Reds and America's foremost advocate of free love, Hoover positioned himself solidly as a spokesman for America's fearful propertied classes.

But rationality was overtaking this flank attack on individual rights. Louis Post, acting secretary of labor, canceled over 70 percent of Hoover's deportation orders. A Congressional committee moved in to investigate the onslaught, spurred on by union spokesmen and a private study underwritten by the National Popular Government League and the American Civil Liberties Union (ACLU) and signed by leaders of the American bar from Zechariah Chafee to Roscoe Pound and Felix Frankfurter. Hoover's campaign amounted to a "continued violation of the Constitution . . . under the guise of . . . the suppression of radical activities."

Hoover joined the posse. Years afterward, Hoover would confess to a reporter: "I deplored the manner in which the raids were executed then, and my position has remained unchanged." In 1920 the election of Warren Harding inaugurated twelve years of conservative Republican signal-calling. As head of the Bureau of Investigation, Harding appointed William J. Burns, founder of the famous detective agency. Within the disorganized government, the Bureau of Investigation promptly degenerated into a dumping ground for hacks, most notoriously Gaston B. Means, who wholesaled out of his office everything money could buy from liquor licenses to administrative pardons.

By now number two within the Bureau, Hoover bided his time. In 1924, Harding died of a heart attack and Calvin Coolidge became president; he appointed as attorney general Harlan Stone, the principled ex-dean of Columbia Law School. The Ohio Gang was finished.

Stone fired Burns, but he inquired widely before he promoted Hoover. Hoover was still very young—twenty-nine—and his staccato, hair-trigger personality could make him an embarrassment. His prejudices weren't easy to mistake. By 1919, for example, Hoover had his eye on Marcus Garvey, putting together the Black Star Steamship Line as the basis for a black-owned economic empire. Since, "unfortunately," there were no infractions of federal statue through which to railroad Garvey, Hoover tagged him with mail fraud and got Garvey deported in 1925. Pretensions among the coloreds disturbed the ambitious bureaucrat. Society required protection.

Little escaped those wide-set, gleaming eyes. He lived at home still, fussed over by his mother. He became a Mason and joined a country club. Dickerson finally passed away in 1922. With one colored servant, Annie babied her late-born treasure; she cooked and cleaned and made sure the parquet floor in the dining room "was kept waxed," cousins would remember, "to within an inch of your life." After a long night locked up in his room with Bureau paperwork, Edgar would tiptoe down to breakfast and examine the poached egg and take perhaps a bite or two before lowering the plate gently to the overpolished floor to be dealt with by the Airedale, Spee De Bozo. Speedy Number Two, Hoover's animal counterpart. Until the day he died, he kept the Airedale's picture on his desk, the only family portrait.

Then he would walk the dog and saunter off early for work.

Harlan Stone had little choice. On May 10, 1924, according to Hoover, the attorney general summoned the prodigy. Stone was a great bulky fellow, with a scholar's frown. He offered Hoover the post of Acting Director of the Bureau of Investigation.

"I'll take the job," Hoover supposedly shot back, "on certain conditions. . . . The Bureau must be divorced from politics and not be a catchall for political hacks. Second, promotions will be made on proven ability and the Bureau will be responsible only to the Attorney General."

"I wouldn't give it to you under any other conditions," Stone responded and scowled one final time. "That's all. Good day."

Hoover kept a photograph of Stone on his office wall for the next fifty years.

Young Hoover turned intently to the reformulation of the Bureau of Investigation. Tonally, life in the FBI fluctuated between a rolling YMCA staff meeting and twenty years at Parris Island. The Director's private fetishes controlled the rulebook. Ultimately it was not permitted to question even the most outlandish order, drink coffee at work, marry a woman not "Bureau material," go bald, or take a left turn with the Director in the car. The atmosphere was top-down authoritarian, Mussolini without the chuckles.

To rid the Bureau of hackers and potential appointees, Hoover mandated that all applicants be graduate lawyers or accountants. In time, this standard was quietly waived. Not enough were signing up. The applicant pool tended heavily toward men whose background made it easy to comply: originally small-town Protestants, after 1940 Irish Catholics of modest background, Mormons. Obedience was paramount. Little or no priority went to individuals prepared to do what the Bureau supposedly existed to do—investigate. Hoover himself was innocent of standard police procedures, and every once in a while a renegade ex-special agent or a disgruntled Congressman would point that out, to the Director's fury. To pump his image up, Hoover would then arrange to have himself photographed during the arrest of that week's Public Enemy. Behind his back, Hoover's own men were known to shrug off these bravura performances—"You can come out now, Mister Director— we've got the son of a bitch in handcuffs."

Still touchy about the Palmer raids, Hoover disavowed the entire episode and proclaimed that there was "no federal statue against entertaining radical ideas, and we are wasting no time collecting information that we cannot use." ACLU founder Roger Baldwin would write of the "unfortunate performance of the Bureau in a previous administration in which Hoover doubtless played an unwilling part."

Meanwhile, Hoover continued to raise his standards and shrink his organization; the Bureau's agent count dropped from 579 in 1920 to 339 as the decade closed; by 1932, the number of field offices was down from 53 to 22.

From the D.C. headquarters in the Justice Department—the SOG, Seat of Government, in Bureau parlance—the instructions went out to the special agents around the country. Each SAC—Special Agent in Charge— was expected to maintain his field office in a close-to-inhuman state of readiness. One disillusioned special agent, Joe Schott, wrote of the dreaded inspections. Hoover "knew there were weaklings and malingerers out there flouting his rules and goofing off." Periodically he "sent forth raiding parties to attack field offices and tear them apart in search of heresy and disloyalty. He called these depredations office inspections. They resembled the corn-field scene in *Planet of the Apes*—when the apes came galloping through on their horses, lassoing all the humans in sight. In The Bureau, the apes were called inspectors—or, in Bureau vernacular, 'goons.'"

Each raid was inexorably followed by a blizzard of letters of censure or letters of commendation. These documents would wind up in personnel files and determine whether each man would get promoted, fired, or sent along the Trail of Bureau Tears (the "Bureau Bicycle") on a long, demoralizing series of reassignments from Butte, Montana, to Anchorage, Alaska, until he buckled ultimately and resigned. The pay was high—twice that of counterparts across the federal bureaucracy. Pension opportunities were unparalleled. The dropout rate remained staggering.

In 1928 Hoover replaced his best friend. Hoover's interest in Frank Baughman had started to wane, especially after Baughman got engaged, and little by little he was demoted from oversight of the headquarters staff to gunnery instructor at the training facility. Clyde Anderson Tolson came aboard and within two years had risen to assistant director.

Tolson was a go-getter. A presentable lawyer from rural Iowa with the uneasy sideways glance of a farm boy in the city, Tolson played first base on the headquarters team. His reputation as a manager had preceded him from the War Department, where he kept track of administrative details for almost a decade. He could be snappish, withering, in situations in which Hoover might be inclined to soften. Hoover kept him busy struggling with the problems of organization and personnel throughout the headquarters divisions. The two ate lunch together at the Mayflower Hotel almost every day, took trips together, and inspection tours and vacations; and before long Hoover let it be known that any social invitations would have to include Clyde, whom he called "Junior." Tolson called Hoover "Boss" sometimes, sometimes "Eddie," and, when his blood was up, "Speed." Their bond became increasingly obvious, but anybody who suggested that anything more was involved Hoover lambasted as an "obvious degenerate" and a "despicable foul-minded malicious rat." That tended to back people off.

Even around the office, Tolson would take special pains to maintain his status as a colorless background functionary, ancillary to the Boss. An anteater for details like Tolson was indispensable, once Hoover started building out his card-catalog system of raw files until its entries numbered into the millions. The Bureau was already tapping telephone lines, experimenting with microphones. In 1924 Hoover arranged for a Congressional appropriation to consolidate the nation's fingerprint collections, everything from urban municipalities to post office employees and members of the military, into the Bureau's master system. Local cops could come to him to run a set of prints. In 1930 the Bureau began to publish its Uniform Crime Reports, a compilation of the country's lawbreaking statistics.

Hoover intended to *know* whatever was going on, but he had also resolved to obligate the Bureau as little as possible. Police chiefs could send what talent they had to the Bureau's National Academy for their three-month introduction to the high-tech gadgetry in Hoover's Crime Lab. Each recruit went home with an idealized picture of the Director, signed, and a confidential telephone number he could call if he were ever moved to turn in one of his superiors. For the watching Director, until the day he died, the game was mostly about capitalizing on information. Information was like bullets in this perilous, compounding government. Each of these tough, handpicked young men would protect the Republic. Its bodyguard. *His* bodyguard. The threats were out there, constantly.

What he did not want was too much responsibility. To make sure those clean-cut professionals of his got nowhere near corrupting elements of society, where the money was huge, Hoover arranged with Congress to leave the more pernicious social evils—drugs, gambling, prohibition enforcement, labor racketeering, extortion, loan-sharking, tax evasion—to local law enforcement or elements outside the Justice Department, like Internal Revenue or the Narcotics Bureau. Since drugs, gambling, and the rest provided the lifeblood of organized crime, Hoover wanted nothing to do with any of them. In one of those gestures of selective aphasia that came to characterize the Boss, Hoover would flatfootedly deny that there was anything like organized crime out there, let alone the Mafia. This did not mean that the Director was about to ignore his opportunity to keep track of tens of thousands of hooligans and miscreants. But that was largely for the files. Day-to-day, the FBI would remain accountable for car theft, kidnapping, and the headline-grabbing exploits of small-time bank robbers.

Successful year after year in ratcheting up his Congressional appropriation, Hoover had discovered almost immediately that he needed to sell the Bureau with statistics: how many man-hours, how much paperwork, what percentage of convictions? To improve the efficiency of the Bureau, he expected each agent to contribute as much as 3-1/2 unpaid hours a day. Filling in the reports produced a lot of sotto-voce carping, much falsification of records, and many stolen afternoons in bowling alleys, topless bars, and out on golf courses. As the system proliferated into fifty-eight field offices and hundreds of smaller resident agencies, verifying everybody's time card was out of the question.

To stay on top of things Hoover required a human computer, and Tolson was a close as Washington could provide. Good-looking in the bloodless, firm-jawed way that caught Hoover's eye, Tolson was a clean-desk man, the sort who could peruse a ten-page document in seconds and pick out the one mistake likely to mess them up. Apparently unflappable, the dour Tolson couldn't seem to get enough of his superior's yarns or miss his cue when it came to suggesting that the boss would "go down in history as the greatest man of the century." Tolson took a lot of pressure off Hoover by internalizing the stresses of the day, a problem Hoover advised him to deal with by putting up a punching bag in his office or simply calling somebody in when he got nervous and dismissing the unlucky slob "with prejudice."

Even this heaven-sent relationship suffered its break-in problems. During the early years, Tolson betrayed an awareness of women. The monastic Hoover found these symptoms disquieting, presaging less-than-adequate commitment. From time to time Hoover permitted himself to be glimpsed taking Ginger Rogers's mother to dinner, or dropping in on Dorothy Lamour when he happened to swing through Los Angeles. The Director handled such social contacts the way he did his expanding collection of antique figurines—with chivalric restraint, gallantly dusting them off every once in a while if only to reassure himself that they were still in his life.

Overloaded with responsibility, Tolson inveigled his roommate at the Westchester Apartments, Guy Hottel, into signing on to back him up. Hottel was a wisecracking powerhouse, a bull of a man who had played tackle on his college team and remained, according to one agent of the period, a go-getter who, "when he figured you'd been in the telephone booth long enough, would drag you out." Already preoccupied with his own safety, Hoover requisitioned Hottel as his personal troubleshooter and bodyguard. Hoover and Hottel were photographed in tandem at racetracks and watering holes on both coasts, Hoover with an arm lapped over Hottel's powerful shoulder, beneath which a bulging holster was visible. Unlike the decorous Tolson, Hottel was generally amused by Hoover's self-important free-loading ways. The three went everywhere together, a worried-looking Tolson bringing up the rear.

Tolson watched with building concern. A high-spirited roustabout, Hottel had no compunction about showing up at the office with a black eye after an all-night poker game. Worse, he had a taste for the ladies, and in the end married four times. The inevitable crisis arrived one Christmas in Miami in the middle thirties. Ex-FBI man William Turner details the end of the affair: "After settling in, Tolson and Hottel announced to Hoover that they had female dates that evening. With that Hoover flew into a tantrum, locking himself in the bathroom and banging on the wall. The burly Hottel had to knock in the door and slap around the FBI Director to bring him to his senses."

Here was a weakness, this hysterical revulsion at the very thought of uncountenanced sexual activity, and once he returned to himself Hoover took the overdue steps. He moved Hottel out of his immediate circle and into a slot as Special Agent in Charge of the Washington Field Office. In time, when Hottel's scattergood administration threatened scandals, Hoover quietly cashiered Hottel but found him a sinecure on the racing commission. Years later, an insider would maintain that Hottel survived despite his reputation as a wife-beater because "he has openly stated that Hoover and Tolson, whom he knows intimately, and some of their friends, are homosexuals." Such rumors were cropping up all the time, and it was Bureau policy to dispatch an intimidating team of agents to squelch these demeaning allegations. But, when Hoover suspected his attackers had the goods, he tended to back down silently and let the suspicions blow over.

Their flutter with Hottel now laid to rest, the Director and Tolson settled into a long-term association that would often be compared with a bourgeois marriage. Archived photographs would catch the pair in gleaming paper hats at play on New Year's in the Stork Club, or snapping each other's pictures on the patio beside a beach. There were reportedly spats once in a while, with fierce exchanges and broken dishes. But normally they ate lunch together at the Mayflower and dinner at their customary table at Harvey's. They continued to live apart, and, before it got too late most evenings, Hoover could be depended on to make his dutiful way home to Annie.

3

Two Confidence Men

As the Roosevelt administration entrenched itself, Hoover the media celebrity came into ever sharper focus against the daily backdrop of breadlines and veterans' marches. Films of the era featured fast-talking, indomitable crimebusters like Jimmy Cagney and Edward G. Robinson, lambasting evil and reasserting national values at a time when very little was going well. With his rat-a-tat delivery and air of absolute ethical certainty, Hoover seemed to millions their champion in real life. He and his G-men would conduct the helpless, luckless men and women of America through this Slough of Despond. This bucked people up.

Hoover understood that politics at the street level must be presented as a morality play, supplied with villains and heroes. The Left wasn't available for the time being. To replace Emma Goldman, Hoover contrived to concentrate newspaper attention on a succession of kidnappers and bank robbers and, once war broke out, spies. They tended to be noisy and colorful, if distinctly minor-league, good copy and outstanding publicity for the ascending Bureau.

How deliberately Hoover anticipated this role was evident by the spring of 1932, when the Director gatecrashed the investigation by the New Jersey State Police of the kidnapping of the Lindbergh baby. Repeatedly denied authority, Hoover bombarded the media with press releases until the general public became convinced that Hoover was in charge and Congress caved in and passed the Lindbergh Law, which accorded Hoover's Bureau of Investigation sole jurisdiction in kidnapping cases. The trial two years later of Bruno Richard Hauptmann produced a mélange of conflicting evidence and the statement by the eternally clueless Lindbergh crediting Elmer Irey of the Treasury Department. But the Bureau's Crime Records Division made sure its Boss remained identified with this historic triumph.

As it happened, Hoover himself had been very lucky to hang onto his disputed directorship as the administration changed hands. The attorney general-designate, the crusading ex-Senator Thomas Walch, had been a bitterly critical member on the Senate subcommittee that investigated the Palmer raids and was well aware of the extent of Hoover's implication. He had already announced that the Justice Department could expect "almost completely new personnel" when the recently married Walch's postwedding exertions in a sleeper crossing North Carolina evidently brought on a fatal heart attack. Near panic, Hoover himself met Walch's train as it steamed into Union Station and brought with him experts prepared to testify that "a thoroughly documented medical examination was made." Edgar was totally in the clear. Homer Cummings, Walch's far more political replacement, kept the eager-beaver Hoover on.

Early in the Roosevelt years a rash of bank robberies was alarming the citizenry. A 1934 shootout in Kansas City led to the passage of nine crime bills—prodded hard by Hoover—which extended the reach of what would from now on be labeled the *Federal* Bureau of Investigation. Its mandate expanded from auto theft and bankruptcy and white slavery cases to include the robbery of any bank in the Federal Reserve System. Further obligations would include "the transportation of stolen property, the transmission of threats, racketeering in interstate commerce, and the flight of a witness across state lines to avoid prosecution or giving testimony." Hoover chose to ignore the thrust of several of these additional provisions, which would have given the FBI more justification than it wanted to go after organized crime.

What rang the bell were bank robberies, brought off in most cases by gun-crazy backwoods dimwits. Hoover fed the newspapers details that encouraged the dumbfounded reading public to personalize the self-dramatizing thugs he intended to hunt down. In time he would eliminate them all—"Baby Face" Nelson and "Creepy" Karpis, "Machine Gun" Kelly and "Pretty Boy" Floyd, Bonnie and Clyde, Ma Barker. The prize Hoover lusted after longer than he cared to was "Handsome Johnny Dillinger."

Full of country aplomb, Dillinger had been caught once after robbing a couple of crossroads banks, then broken out of an "escape-proof" Indiana jail, stolen the sheriff's car, and made it into Illinois. Hoover's diminutive special agent in charge in Chicago, Melvin Purvis, had tracked Dillinger and his men to an empty Wisconsin summer resort and botched the siege. A lawman and at least one civilian died, and Dillinger got away again. As newspaper readers began to root for the rangy desperado, Hoover started feeling the heat. He got his own back when Purvis convinced a brothel madam named Anna Sage—the Lady in Red—to sell Dillinger out; the gallant bank robber went down in a fusillade outside Chicago's Biograph Theater, shot dead by a couple of Western gunslingers Hoover had been provident enough to put on the payroll, gonzos with very little education but a lot of experience with firearms.

Purvis reportedly tore the buttons off his coat groping for his revolver. "The shooting and killing of John Dillinger by the Agents of your office," Hoover wrote Purvis the next day, "under your admirable direction and planning are but another indication of your ability and capacity as a leader and executive." But the national acclaim Purvis reaped sat poorly with the Director. Shunned, Purvis left the Bureau to establish the Melvin Purvis Law-and-Order Patrol under the sponsorship of Post Toasties. Hoover's ghostwritten first book, *Persons in Hiding,* reduced Purvis's involvement to the vanishing point, and Hoover changed the status of Purvis's resignation to "termination with prejudice"—fired. There would be room for only one FBI personality in the national spotlight.

With Dillinger effectively disposed of, Hoover hit the law-and-order lecture circuit and treated his colleagues to the paranoid vernacular he was cultivating: "I'm going to tell the truth about these rats," he stormed to one critic. "I'm going to tell the truth about their dirty, filthy, diseased women. I'm going to tell the truth about the miserable politicians who protect them and the slimy, silly or sob-sister convict lovers who let them out on sentimental or ill-advised paroles. If the people don't like it, they can get me fired. But I'm going to say it."

This outburst hints strongly at Hoover's increasingly schizoid existence. Unflinchingly judgmental around the Washington Headquarters, on regular visits to Manhattan the FBI Director was something of a nightclub toff. He liked best the converted speakeasies that were emerging as watering holes for the rich and unscrupulous, especially Toots Shor's and Sherman Billingsley's Stork Club. Both Shor and Billingsley were recently retired bootleggers, Joe Kennedy's reliable customers. When Hoover bustled in, normally trailed by Tolson, he got a hearty greeting and the chance to pose for photographers with a big plastic toy machine gun. For somebody who never had occasion to fire a weapon in his life, adulation like this provided a confirmatory thrill.

Hoover's appearance on The Great White Way was as calculated as everything else he was doing. A letter of appreciation to Hearst's star gossip columnist Walter Winchell in 1934 induced the fawning Winchell to introduce the Director and Clyde around the Stork Club, the habitués of which were impressed by this rising crimebuster. Winchell went on the FBI's special correspondents list, entitling him to receive all FBI releases. "I am looking forward to many evenings in the future when we can get together and have some real fun and settle the momentous questions of the nation," Hoover wrote his gabby new friend.

Their friendship was tested when Hoover found himself under pressure the summer of 1939 to bring in Louis "Lepke" Buchalter. Lepke—"Lepkeleh" to his mother, Little Louis—ran Murder, Incorporated and specialized in labor racketeering and extortion. Understated in manner but a stone killer on the street, Lepke's notoriety was such that New York District Attorney Tom Dewey had a put a $25,000 bounty on his head, matched by the U.S. attorney general. To protect his inflated reputation, Hoover was forced to hurl the Bureau into this manhunt; one account maintains that "Hoover had threatened Mob heads Joey Adonis and Frank Costello that unless Lepke surrendered, the FBI would arrest every suspected Italian gangster in the country."

Hank Messick, no doubt the most encompassing historian of the Mob so far, maintains that details from suppressed FBI files indicate that "The head of a giant liquor company, whose roots went back to Prohibition and whose friends included Johnnie Torrio and Meyer Lansky, made contact with a high-ranking subordinate of Hoover and arrangements were made to surrender Lepke. The aide was told that Lepke would be promised no state prosecution; Hoover was not informed of the promise. The aide was later given a good job by the liquor man."

The liquor company president was unmistakably Lewis Rosenstiel, who years afterward would personally fund the J. Edgar Hoover Foundation and hire as a vice-president of Schenley's distillery Louis Nichols, "Nick the Greek," the bombastic publicity coordinator who became head of Hoover's Crime Records Division in 1937 and almost single-handedly masterminded the Boss's legend. Everybody involved was excited at the prospect of taking Lepke. Winchell put the word out on his radio program. There now ensued weeks of false starts and phony rendezvous arrangements, which took their toll on the high-strung Hoover. "I am fed up with you and your friends," Hoover shrieked at Winchell in front of his claque of tipplers at the Stork.

"They can make a fool out of you, but they can't make a fool out of me and my men."

"These aren't my friends, John," Winchell protested.

"They are your friends, they are your friends. And don't call me John!"

But a day later the jumpy Louis Buchalter turned himself in. Escorted by Winchell himself not long after 10 P.M. at Twenty-eighth Street and Fifth Avenue, Lepke slid in alongside the apprehensive Director to discover that there was no deal. The country's most barefaced killer would attempt to save his skin by threatening to implicate Franklin Roosevelt's senior labor statesman, Sidney Hillman of the Amalgamated Clothing Workers, who kept Lepke on a weekly retainer ($50 of which got shunted off to Lucky Luciano) to terrorize both laborers and manufacturers into obedience. By then it didn't matter. Lepke got the chair in 1944, and Hoover battened on the story for the rest of his life.

What comes up through the floorboards is the extent to which Hoover was not merely aware of but habitually traded favors and threats with personalities in organized crime. After Dewey put Lucky Luciano away in 1936, the leadership shifted itself to Frank Costello. Born Francesco Castiglia in Italy, Costello spent his entire life endeavoring to improve himself. A porcine, self-examining criminal strategist rarely to be seen outside a $350 suit, Costello abhorred violence unless nothing else worked. Costello's specialty was greasing the establishment, from police officials to aldermen. Every morning he strolled into the barbershop in the Waldorf and settled into the chair for his daily trim and a manicure.

By the later thirties, an admirer was comping Hoover to a suite at the Waldorf Towers whenever he deemed to visit Manhattan. An acquaintanceship developed, supplemented from time to time by the exchange of confidences on a bench in Central Park. Columnist Earl Wilson insisted that when Hoover invited Costello to join him at the Waldorf coffee shop, the mobster warned him: "I got to be careful of my associates. They'll accuse me of consortin' with questionable characters." Sometimes they simply ran across each other. "I heard Hoover in the Stork Club one night," one insider would later divulge, "tell one of the toughest guys in the country . . . a Mafia boy who always went to the barber shop at the Waldorf that as long as he stayed out of Edgar's bailiwick, he [Hoover] would stay out of his." Costello was a resource.

It went beyond that. Hoover had discovered vacations, initially in the Miami area, where the ponies ran. Reluctant his whole life to part with his own limited money, the Director was unabashed about jumping on the offer of Meyer Schine, the one-time candy butcher putting together a string of hotels. Schine put up Hoover and Tolson in his Gulfstream Hotel on Miami Beach, headquarters for the Mob's betting-parlor impresario Frank Erickson. The boys had taken to doping a nag occasionally, and mostly through Walter Winchell the word got passed to Edgar. "The *horse* races," Costello croaked to Bill Hundley when Hoover's passion for the track came up. "You'll never know how many races I had to fix for those lousy ten-dollar bets of Hoover's." Meyer Lansky's bookmakers reportedly handled Hoover's major bets, which would be processed only if the Director won. Even Costello may well have been taken in: "Hoover would let himself be photographed at the two-dollar windows," crime historian Stephen Fox has written, "while FBI agents placed other bets for him at the hundred-dollar windows." On days in Florida when no word reached him from the top of the Mob, Hoover was not above summoning some minor wiseguy hanging around the paddock and demanding an inside tip. In time he himself recognized that he had better not be photographed with any of these thugs and authorized a Miami Hoodlum Squad to point out to him the established gangsters.

The increasingly hardened Director attached great importance to aboveboard relations with the Mafiosi. After Lepke was apprehended, U.S. Attorney General Frank Murphy summoned Hoover and suggested strongly that the FBI chief turn the killer over to the eager Tom Dewey—after all, "you know the man is guilty of eighty murders." Hoover immediately launched into one of those fits of pique already dreaded throughout official Washington. "Mister Attorney General," he rapped out, "the man doesn't live who can break my word to the underworld." Lepke was ultimately sandbagged, but Hoover was on record.

Despite denials from Nichols and, later, DeLoach, the evidence that Lewis Rosenstiel played a role in expediting Costello's decision to cough up Lepke suggests that the heavy-handed master at Schenley's was intriguing with the FBI boss all along. Designated—self-designated—throughout his empire of booze the "Supreme Commander," the highfalutin distiller maintained on his payroll an assortment of live wires, from ex-Boston bootlegger Joe Linsey to the uncrowned king of the California Assembly, lobbyist Arthur Samish. Pensive, hyperalert Meyer Lansky frequented his salon.

One recent Hoover biographer maintains that Hoover first met Rosenstiel through Joe Kennedy, very much a member in good standing of the retired bootleggers' association throughout the Roosevelt years. It was an interval when Kennedy and Hoover were both highly regarded by the happy hotdogs closest to the president's ear. The extent of the reforms being rammed into place by the New Dealers, Kennedy included, was stirring dark thoughts inside the surviving corporate interests. A representative approached Major General Smedley Darlington Butler, a recent commandant of the Marine Corps, in hope of persuading him to lead a coup d'etat against "the Communist menace," by which they meant the government. The American Liberty League was formed, a kind of nativist Croix de Feu movement which catered to right-wing aspirations to a fascist takeover. Reactionaries, from Fritz Kuhn's German-American Bund to the demagogic radio priest Father Coughlin, openly threatened the survival of constitutional government.

Butler approached Hoover. On August 24, 1936, FDR summoned Hoover to the White House, along with Secretary of State Cordell Hull. Himself much more concerned about Harry Bridges and the Communist West Coast Longshoremen's Union, Hoover agreed, with a certain reluctance, to fire up his boys and assist the president in "obtaining a broad picture" of the extremist movements. But only if the matter was formally referred to the Bureau by the Department of State. "Go ahead and investigate the hell out of those cocksuckers," Cordell Hull broke in. Here was the go-ahead Hoover had been pining for since the Palmer raids aborted, and it wouldn't take long before Hoover had reconstituted his General Intelligence Division, shut down in the aftermath of the Palmer raids, and with it "extensive indices of individuals, groups, and organizations engaged in subversive activities. . . ."

Big Brother was back. This time he would be a lot better advised as to tactics and publicity. "One hears in Washington that Hoover has secret dossiers on all left-wingers," Jack Alexander wrote in *The New Yorker* in 1937, "and is just awaiting a chance to clap them into concentration camps." But Hoover himself soft-pedaled that, since "it is now anyone's privilege to advocate overthrow of the government so long as no overt act is committed."

Joe Kennedy might not have gone that far. Civil liberties were never much discussed around his dinner table. Both emerging powers, Edgar Hoover and Joe Kennedy were already swapping cordialities; before long the FBI Director and Tolson were weekending at the Kennedy hacienda on North Ocean Boulevard in Palm Beach. An FBI resident agent kept watch over the Kennedy estate in Hyannis Port. The gregarious financier made sure that a case each of Jack Daniels Black Label and Haig and Haig from Somerset

Importers showed up before Christmas at FBI headquarters, earmarked for Hoover and Tolson respectively.

For Hoover's purposes, Kennedy functioned as a spotter for one of his primary targets, the Detroit rabble-rouser Father Charles Coughlin. With his following of millions, the hearty, backslapping priest was fond of trading racy stories with the effusive speculator. Coughlin favored open invective—"Kill the Jews!" he would blare out during his broadcasts, which was a heart-stopper even then. As a heavily promoted layman in the American Catholic community, Kennedy was prominent enough to help conduct the future Pope Pius XII, Eugenio Cardinal Pacelli, through a meeting with Roosevelt at Hyde Park and broker a deal with Pacelli to help tone Father Coughlin down.

The issue was already moot as to the extent of Kennedy's own anti-Semitism. While vociferous at times once he identified Jewish interests at work—"They have surrounded you with Jews and Communists," he erupted at Roosevelt—many of Kennedy's breakthroughs required help from those devilishly subtle Jews he cultivated. With an assist from Bernie Baruch, Kennedy enlisted the magisterial Herbert Bayard Swope, editor of the *New York World* and on occasion a fellow corporate raider and trading partner, along with Arthur Krock of the *New York Times,* to procure for him the chairmanship of the SEC. Swope's associates had included Arnold Rothstein, the bootlegging impresario and obsessive gambler who fixed the 1919 World Series.

Again and again, from drafting Joe's self-serving book *I'm for Roosevelt* in 1936 to stacking the jury which awarded Jack his unlikely Pulitzer Prize for *Profiles in Courage* in 1957, Krock was alternately cozened and enticed to exploit his position with the *Times* to Joe Kennedy's benefit. "He was terribly generous to his friends," Krock ultimately told an interviewer. "I've often reflected since those days that he probably never liked me at all, but found me useful and thought he might be able to make use of me." When Joe called to inform Krock that if he would "look out the window Christmas morning . . . you'll see an automobile," Krock responded "'I will see nothing of the kind. I'll have it towed away if it's there.' And that was the end of that. That was a pretty coarse kind of bribe. He didn't need it. That was the way his mind worked."

The Jews Kennedy dealt with were often as hard-nosed and self-interested as he himself. In 1936, mired in an outdated corporate structure, David Sarnoff brought in as a well-paid consultant the man from whom he had recently bought many of the components of RCA. For top dollar, Kennedy straightened things out. He moved on the same year to tackle Paramount

Pictures, Gloria Swanson's home studio and the creation largely of the immigrant Hungarian Adolf Zukor, whom Kennedy had romanced a few years earlier. Kennedy now pronounced the studio "incompetent, unbusinesslike and wasteful. . . ."

One industry chronicle has Kennedy explaining to the Paramount board that a lot of the problem was the public's annoyance at the fact that Jews controlled the film business. "To reduce the pressure," Kennedy advised the directors, President Roosevelt was convinced the owners should sell the company. To Kennedy.

It happened that one of the board members was Edwin Weisl Sr., a top New York investment banker with Tammany connections and, like Kennedy, an adviser to Hearst. Weisl knew Harry Hopkins, FDR's closest adviser. Weisl telephoned Hopkins to investigate this unexpected development.

"Hey, chief," Hopkins called across the office to Roosevelt.

"What, Harry?"

"What's this about Joe Kennedy and Paramount?"

"What's Paramount?"

"There's your answer," Hopkins informed Weisl. The board selected Weisl to go fire Kennedy. Weisl would recall that "In his warmhearted Irish way," Joe Kennedy told a mutual friend: "'I'll get that dirty Jew son of a bitch if it's the last thing I do.'" All this would reverberate years later, when Weisl had become an intimate adviser to Lyndon Johnson.

Whatever you asked Joe to do, he had his own agenda, which usually trumped yours. When his vintage admirer William Randolph Hearst determined that his newspaper empire had started to crumble, W. R. retained Kennedy. Kennedy quickly offered to relieve Hearst of his magazines for $8 million, far below the breakup price. Hearst found other backing.

Another media mogul Kennedy hosted regularly was *Time*'s Henry Luce, whose beautiful and opportunistic wife Clare rarely saw any reason not to console Joe in bed. When *Fortune* decided to print a profile of Joe in 1937 which referenced Gloria Swanson, Kennedy scanned the galleys and then took Luce to lunch. "You publish that story and you're going to lose your *Time* magazine," Kennedy advised the publisher, plainly threatening a buyout. Luce edited back the piece, and while he continued to help pump up the mystique of the Kennedy family—though not too shy to accept a heavy subvention from Joe under the table for a cover story about Jack—bitterness ultimately set in. "He'd call everybody a son of a bitch except the man he happened to be having dinner with at the moment," Luce would reflect. Rose confirmed this judgment. When it came to Joe's vast acquaintanceship,

"We never grew very intimate with any of them. Joe had his own friends . . . and he'd keep them on his own personal payroll."

A lot of Kennedy was bluff, the threat of banging you over the head with a fortune which was a lot smaller than people imagined. An analysis by *The New Republic* showed that "Mr. Kennedy caught the small and weak companies by the heels, and stuffed them through his office wringer. It also shows, however, that the big, strong companies either fought him to a standstill, or else obtained what they wanted." Privately dreading the possibility that he could lose what he had, Kennedy continued to feather his nest whether he found himself in public office or on the street. Even during the thirties, damaging details leaked out and soiled his reputation.

When Franklin Roosevelt invited Kennedy to become head of the Maritime Commission in 1937, the speculator's response was wholly in character: "If it's all the same to you, let some other patriot take it on the chin. There's a lot of money to be made in the market. I'd like to skim off my share of the profits." Between Harry Bridges's rioting longshoremen and the stolid, oversubsidized shipowners, the industry was hopeless, and Kennedy moved on within the year.

Since Roosevelt was unbudgeable about granting him Treasury, Kennedy had inaugurated a backstairs campaign spearheaded by Jimmy Roosevelt to snag the Court of Saint James, Ambassador to Great Britain. FDR confided to White House insiders that he was sending the restless and potentially divisive Kennedy to England to get him out of the way, where he could be watched. Kennedy would insist that the president was prompted by more compassionate motives. "Joe, you've been working hard for a long time," Kennedy quoted FDR to one early reporter; "go over to London and take it easy for a while. You know, they have weekends over there that last from Thursday until Tuesday. . . ."

Joseph Kennedy's tenure in the British Isles began with a heavy surge of tabloid publicity concentrated on Rose's still-trim figure and the nine handsome children. It ended a few years later with the demoralized Ambassador on a kind of permanent, unacknowledged leave of absence, alternately hiding out in Palm Beach and granting to Louis Lyons of the *Boston Globe* a disastrous interview in which he stated that England was finished and democracy was probably finished, "bunk," overseas and here. After the initial flurry in 1938, it hadn't been long before the British press began to pick up on the outspoken ambassador's underlying defeatism, his awe of the Nazis, and dedication to peace at any price. A State Department summary cites a report to Hitler quoting Kennedy as saying to the German ambassador in Washington that "it was not so much the fact that we wanted to get rid of the Jews that was harmful to us, but rather the loud clamor with which we accompanied this purpose."

British antipathy rose after a second look. "He was not only the first Irish Catholic to defile the London Embassy," one writer sniffed, "but he was rambunctious and ill tempered, worse than careless with his language, vulgar in the eyes of the nicer people, anything but bashful, and filthy with American dollars. He chewed gum. He put his feet on the desk and he called the Queen 'a cute trick.'" Kennedy found his natural supporters among the appeasers of the Cliveden Set. "Who would have thought the English could take into camp a red-headed Irishman?" FDR marveled.

A lot of Kennedy's opinions arose out of his cold, professional realism. The Nazis were genuinely intent on getting rid of the Jews. Soon after he arrived in London he promulgated an initiative—after consultation with Helmut Wohlthat, the architect of Goering's five-year economic plan for Germany—that would help distribute Germany's Jews around the British Empire and the United States; Hitler's imposition of a billion-mark ransom on the Jewish community in Germany to compensate for the shooting of the third secretary at the Paris Embassy by a disturbed seventeen-year-old Polish Jew, Herschel Grynszpan, spiked Kennedy's proposals and instead brought down *Kristallnacht.* Simultaneously, the Ambassador worked on Count Ciano to ease back on anti-Semitic measures coming into force in Italy.

But, enraged by the attacks in the American media on the Hitler regime, Kennedy became obsessed with the notion that American Jews in influential places were precipitating a world war, and he was rarely hesitant to make his opinions felt. A report from J. Edgar Hoover to presidential secretary Steve Early passed on Kennedy's remarks to members of the British government. The Ambassador had suggested to his defeatist English contacts that they ignore Roosevelt's statements, since, "(1) 'It will be my friends that are in the White House in 1940' and, (2) 'Roosevelt is run by the Jews and all the anti-fascist sentiment in the United States is largely created by the Jews who run the press.'" With a friend like Edgar, most of Kennedy's enemies were insignificant.

Observers on the scene judged Kennedy as "permanently 'on the make,'" or preoccupied with "movies and liquor" while "operating the stock market seven ways 'til Wednesday." Roosevelt heard from Harry Hopkins that, as Czechoslovakia slid into crisis, Kennedy shorted Czech securities and picked up $500,000. A public relations man Kennedy took to England from the Maritime Commission, Harvey Klemmer, was ordered to capitalize on the prestige of the embassy to keep Somerset Importers at the front of the line when shipping became available, procuring space for Kennedy for two hyndred thousand cases of whiskey when nobody else moved much of anything.

With the coming of the Blitz, perhaps the worst of the rumors about the garrulous American ambassador started to make the rounds. "For a man with a weak stomach," his father wrote Jack in September 1940, "these last three days have proven very conclusively that you can worry about much more important things than whether you are going to have an ulcer or not." Since he remained unsatisfied with air-raid provisions at the embassy, Joe quickly leased country residences out beyond the target area, purportedly to protect vital embassy records and codes.

For years by then Arthur Krock had been performing his editorial soft-shoe in the columns of the *New York Times* to explain away Kennedy's shortcomings in London. Privately, he knew how indefensible it was. "Harry Hopkins had come back from London and told Roosevelt that the reason that Joe Kennedy had taken a house in Ascot where he slept was because he was afraid," Krock admitted many years later. "Whereas Kennedy's reason was that he didn't think it was a very good idea for the American Ambassador to be killed because he was trying to keep us out of the war. And so Hopkins told Roosevelt and Roosevelt told many that Kennedy was yellow."

This was a judgment Kennedy did not care to live with, and, even less, his sons. Franklin Roosevelt himself was increasingly weary of Kennedy's antics. The seemingly blasé president was particularly concerned about the extent to which Kennedy had been manipulating his vulnerable son Jimmy. Openly on the take, Jimmy Roosevelt had proposed to William O. Douglas, Kennedy's successor at the SEC, that he participate in a fee-splitting arrangement according to which the big public utilities would pay off a middleman to avoid regulatory sanctions. "What chance do we have when the Republicans take over?" Jimmy demanded of Douglas. When the incensed Douglas took this scheme to FDR, the upset president wept openly.

For some years, Roosevelt appears to have imagined that Joe Kennedy might help restrain his high-stepping and dangerously venal oldest son. In letters between Joe and Jimmy the speculator refers to himself as young Roosevelt's "foster-father." Joe reportedly shared the harem of chorus girls provided by Morton Downey with the ever-available Roosevelt. Not long after their 1933 tour of the important British distillers, Joe wangled Jimmy a sinecure as the president of the National Grain Yeast Corporation of Belleville, New Jersey, producer of the important ingredient in the production of whiskey, under investigation at the time for bootlegging.

But Roosevelt was quickly let go for negligence. He was then enlisted as his father's secretary and aide-de-camp in the White House. Up or down, young Roosevelt remained on tap to promote Joe Kennedy's interests, and, when Kennedy's appointment as ambassador to London wasn't coming through as fast as Joe would have liked, obsequiously wrote his mentor to hang on, since "It is almost done. I haven't failed you yet."

A December 10, 1939 entry in Kennedy's diary goes into a discussion with Missy LeHand concerning the president's worries about Jimmy's impending divorce from Betty Cushing. "She said President was worried and hoped to get it settled up. Was much surprised at how little money Jim had." After six years throughout which his son had abased himself pulling chestnuts out of the fire for Joe, the Hudson Valley squire no doubt expected that Jimmy would emerge with a presentable bank account.

In 1942, after Roosevelt had soft-soaped Joe into keeping his mouth shut throughout the run-up to the 1940 election, FDR eventually blew up during a confrontation in Hyde Park. "I never want to see that son of a bitch again as long as I live," the president choked out to Eleanor. "Take his resignation and get him out of here." Kennedy had reportedly been agitating for last-minute concessions to Hitler, and to hell with London.

For once, Kennedy's stubbornly suppressed wife broke ranks. "We had everything," Rose ultimately confessed to one younger cousin. "Everything. But Joe didn't have an ounce of humility, and in London he refused to learn anything. After a while I tried to tell him what I felt. He didn't listen, though—Joe never listened—but maybe I should have said even more."

Ever responsive to shifting political winds, J. Edgar Hoover now supplied the failing president with raw files to reinforce his suspicions: "In April, 1942 a source of unknown reliability advised that James Roosevelt traveled to England just prior to the repeal of prohibition and secured extensive U.S. liquor rights," one memo read. "Due to pressure from U.S. liquor interests, James Roosevelt allegedly transferred these contracts to Kennedy who was reportedly appointed Ambassador to England so he could handle the contract." This was a little far afield, but not something FDR was pleased to discover circulating about his son.

The same year, Hoover sent over a letter via presidential assistant "Pa" Watson to let the president know that another source of unknown reliability had indicated that Joe Kennedy and James Roosevelt had arranged for pay-offs to Jim Farley while he was still Postmaster General in the expectation of lower tariffs and taxes on liquor imports, a boon to Somerset Importers. The beleaguered president was already on edge after perusing intelligence reports from the previous year alleging that Kennedy's fellow market raider, "Sell-'em-Ben" Smith, was negotiating through Vichy to bribe Hitler with gold bullion to stave off war. Hoover now informed Roosevelt that Smith and Kennedy met Hermann Goering and "donated a considerable amount of money to the German cause." It would appear that Kennedy himself never felt that he could afford to worry about the source of all these damaging reports. "Joe Kennedy thought that Hoover was quite a guy," Hoover's own brain bank and attack dog, William Sullivan, concluded, "and never caught on that he was quite a con man too."

A lot of Hoover's dredgings from his raw files were little more than hearsay, but to a president whose health was deteriorating every day, these aspersions on his son were galling. Jimmy's influence-peddling might very well have landed him in jail. Kennedy was non grata, forever. Later on, himself manipulated by old Joe in West Virginia to assure the primary for Jack, Franklin D. Roosevelt Jr. would sum up his family's assessment of the financier. He was "one of the most evil, disgusting men I have ever known," FDR Jr. announced.

The fact that Hoover continued to lay these torpedoes into Kennedy's standing around the White House didn't mean that he'd cooled on the Ambassador personally. For Hoover the Roosevelt years were providing a consolidation phase, the chance to relegitimize the techniques of control he hadn't quite dared reassert. After months of interdepartmental skirmishing, he was able to back off Attorney General Robert Jackson and formally reacquire the right to bug and tap, subject to the perplexing proviso enunciated by the Supreme Court which determined that while the divulging of tapped exchanges was prohibited, the use of evidence they produced was not.

Typically, Hoover made a point of bristling self-righteously when FDR demanded that he tap Postmaster General Farley—whom the president feared as a possible opponent in 1940: "I cannot do that." If the existence of such a tap ever leaked, "the damage to you would be irrevocable. I cannot do it. I will not do it."

After such a noble stand, Hoover could unleash his "Sound School" graduates on anybody of less than Cabinet stature and trot out his liveliest discoveries, like Lindbergh's German mistress, before the gossip-loving president. The Director's aim was rarely to indict, but rather to alert his victims and control events. Individuals were fallible, and it was Hoover's job to readjust their reality. "I have no intention of becoming the chief of the department of blackmail," he had announced with characteristic grandiosity. Good Edgar actually meant that, although Bad Edgar very rarely resisted the compulsion to poke around in other people's lives.

The imminence of war appeared to justify everything. In January 1940, the FBI grabbed seventeen members of Father Coughlin's Christian Front for stockpiling ammunition and explosives, a "vast plot," as Hoover saw it. The next month he rounded up a dozen members of the Abraham Lincoln Brigade, supporters of the anti-Franco left in Spain, and had them led away, chained, before photographers. Put off by the prodigious sexual requirements of the British-run spy Dusko ("Tricycle") Popov—"As I recall," one FBI special agent said later, "Popov was partial to twins, but, lacking a matched pair, often made do with a couple of other accommodating ladies"—Hoover left out of his summary for the president of Popov's face-to-face warnings of an aerial assault on the U.S. fleet, delivered two months before the Japanese attacked Hawaii. This "irrational, ranting man," Popov said later on, "was the person responsible for the disaster of Pearl Harbor."

What mattered was shaping events, at least for public consumption. Perhaps most telling was the bonanza of publicity the Bureau reaped in June 1942 for capturing four German saboteurs landed by submarine on a remote Long Island inlet, along with another four put ashore near Jacksonville, Florida. Two weeks later the Bureau had rounded up the lot, no damage done. Even Roosevelt was led to believe that brilliant detective work by the Director and his men alone accomplished this prodigious feat. What the FBI press releases left out was the fact that the two leaders of the Long Island team, George John Dasch and Ernst Peter Burger, both of whom had lived in the United States for many years, had no intention of blowing up anything. After getting nowhere with FBI agents in the field, Dasch took a train to Washington and appeared at FBI headquarters.

Even there, Dasch got treated as a crackpot. Only when he sprang the clasps on the suitcase he had brought along and dumped the $84,000 in cash the Abwehr had provided him for living expenses did he get his audience with Hoover. Dasch, then Burger, gave the feds everything—targets, cover names, contacts—and the eight were quickly rounded up.

Now it became important to present a scenario which glorified the FBI and covered up the fact that the Bureau had been handed this triumph. Bureau releases specified that Dasch had been "apprehended" in New York

City several days after he actually surrendered to Hoover personally in D.C. The records were sealed. All eight Germans were immediately found guilty, and six were electrocuted within the month. Dasch bumped into Hoover at his trial. "Mr. Hoover, aren't you really ashamed of yourself?" he cried out.

A nearby special agent smashed Dasch in the face, sending him sprawling. He watched Hoover waddle out of sight, "seemingly surrounded," he later wrote, "by an impregnable wall of justice and strength."

Enough of the truth reached the powers-that-be in time to commute the sentences of Burger, who got hard labor for life, and Dasch, who got thirty years. Lou Nichols pitched hard but failed to procure for Edgar the Congressional Medal of Honor. The entire travesty produced the best-coordinated cover-up the Bureau would attempt until John Kennedy was assassinated.

The Director's aptitude for intervening, like some divinity from Olympus toying with everyday men, was exemplified nicely in his involvement with the star-crossed love affair between the young ensign Jack Kennedy and his increasingly perplexed Danish conquest, Inga Arvad. Between the technical attentions of the FBI and Joe Kennedy's unremitting vigilance, the whole affair played out like a rehearsal on a sound stage.

By January 1942 Joseph Kennedy was finished politically. His insistence on appeasement reinforced by the persistent rumors that he was prepared to underwrite some isolationist candidate, quite possibly himself, to unhorse Roosevelt in 1940 left Joe cast out of circles of significant power in Washington. He had a reputation, according to *New York Times* columnist Scotty Reston, as a wanna-be who "never met a man—or a woman, for that matter—he didn't think he could conquer, but he couldn't keep his mouth shut or his pants on." The one offer he did get, to run a shipyard, he dismissed as insulting. Through much of the early war, the only top official interested in taking his calls was J. Edgar Hoover. There would be other administrations, Hoover knew, and besides, Kennedy could be openhanded. In 1943 the Director arranged for Kennedy to serve as a Special Service Contact of the Boston office of the FBI. There was the thought that Joe might be willing to inform on the shipping industry or those movieland free thinkers out in California.

There was an understanding between Joe and Edgar that the Bureau would keep an eye on Kennedy's adult children. In mid-January 1942 this precaution paid off. Joe Kennedy got a wake-up call from Hoover alerting him, according to Jack's amanuensis William Sutton, that "Jack was in big trouble and he should get him out of Washington immediately."

Behind everything was Jack's front-burner affair with Inga Arvad, a quick-witted Danish beauty with eyes to drown in and full, pert, insinuating lips. At twenty-eight, she was four years and a world of sophistication beyond the pallid ensign whose father had manipulated him a direct commission in the Navy in October 1941 along with a safe desk in D.C. editing the *Daily Digest* for the chief of naval operations. Inga, quite expert at merchandising what she had in four languages, had landed a personality column in the Washington *Times-Herald,* where Kathleen ("Kick") Kennedy worked. Kick talked Jack up to Inga, who found him charming indeed, "exuding animal magnetism." She did a profile of Jack for her paper, and after that the two tumbled without qualm into their historic embroilment.

In what developed overnight into the most intense romantic involvement of Jack Kennedy's life there appear to have been four fascinated participants: Jack, Inga, the FBI, and Joe. It was Inga's assumption that the investigation started when an FBI plant in the purchasing department of the *Times-Herald* came across a photograph of her standing beside Adolf Hitler during the 1936 Olympic Games in Berlin. The isolationist *Times-Herald* editor had recently published highly classified U.S. military plans, and the paper's ownership had abruptly found its patriotism called into question by the December bombing of Pearl Harbor.

The Bureau's informant at the *Times-Herald* tipped off the young reporter who was sharing an apartment with Inga, Page Huidekoper, not many months earlier an aide to Joe Kennedy in London, who supposedly had her eye on Jack. Page hurried to the office to rat Inga out to Cissy Patterson, the paper's impulsive owner. Mrs. Patterson told Page and Inga and the newspaper's editor-in-chief to drop everything and march across town and explain the embarrassing photo cut to Mr. Hoover.

They got as far as Clyde Tolson—Hoover preferred to lurk in the background—but the more details the effusive Inga provided, the more titillated the leadership around the Bureau got. Raised as a kind of all-purpose prodigy by her ambitious, widowed mother, Inga had been trained as a dancer at the Royal Theater in Copenhagen, studied the piano under Max Rytter, and been crowned the Beauty Queen of Denmark at sixteen. Turning down the Folies-Bergere, she married and divorced an Egyptian diplomat before the age of twenty.

At twenty-one she married Dr. Paul Fejos—a one-time Hungarian cavalry officer who took up film before moving on to archaeology—so Inga reinvented herself as the Berlin correspondent for a Copenhagen newspaper and alternatively smoothed and elbowed her way into the affections of most of the leading Nazi potentates. She attended Goering's wedding to Emmy Sonnemann as a guest, and in her dispatches described the Führer as "exceedingly human, very kind, very charming, and as if he had nothing more important in this world than to convince me that in National Socialism lay the salvation of the world."

Even more intriguing to Hoover's watchdogs was the continuing connection between Dr. Fejos and Axel Wenner-Gren, the "Swedish Sphinx." Underwritten by Wenner-Gren, Fejos's Wintergreen expeditions to locate the lost cities of the Incas were quite possibly propaganda forays to soften up South America, a well-established Nazi target. The founder of Electrolux, Wenner-Gren had a bank in the Bahamas and dealt with finances for the exiled Nazi-lining Duke of Windsor. Wenner-Gren's gigantic yacht, the *Southern Cross,* was believed by the Office of Naval Intelligence to be refueling Nazi U-boats.

In fact, months before she showed up outside his office, Hoover had himself called for a full-court press on Kennedy's Inga Binga. A column by Inga that dealt flippantly with Clyde Tolson as well as Hoover's personal secretary Helen Gandy had long since raised those famous hairs on the back of the Director's neck, reputed to stand straight up "just like an Airedale's when it gets mad." Inga's FBI interviewer found her "a rather haughty person" who emphasized her "pull with prominent persons." She demanded that Hoover present her with a letter of exoneration. She dropped Bernard Baruch's name and insisted that she had the "utmost contempt for the German people."

So FBI counterintelligence had known Arvad for a long time before Jack Kennedy showed up. The woman was unabashed about trading what she had for what she wanted. One surveillance in June 1941 tracked her through a long evening with Wenner-Gren, which included an hour alone with him at the Shoreham Hotel. Three days later, the two are on record as having spent an afternoon in Wenner-Gren's room. Wenner-Gren was supplying Inga cash in $5,000 increments. "I think we ought to run these leads down . . . ," Hoover noted in the margin. "There has been much rumor about the Arvad woman."

Interestingly, the Washington Field Office of the FBI, which had a watch on Inga's apartment, encountered great problems establishing the identity of her regular visitor, an ensign with "a gray overcoat with raglan sleeves and gray tweed trousers. He does not wear a hat and has blonde curly hair which is always tousled . . . known only as Jack."

Meanwhile, Inga's upset husband, Dr. Paul Fejos, hired a detective of his own and quickly identified the mysterious naval officer. Fejos promptly contacted Joseph P. Kennedy in New York; Hoover himself now put the situation together, called Joe, and planted an item in Walter Winchell's January 12, 1942 column: "One of Ex-Ambassador Kennedy's eligible sons is the target of a Washington gal columnist's affections. So much so she has consulted her barrister about divorcing her exploring groom. Pa Kennedy no like." Joe Kennedy had a working relationship with James Forrestal, the Undersecretary of the Navy, and within twenty-four hours Jack Kennedy had received orders transferring him to Charleston, South Carolina.

Key figures around Washington had started to notice the vivacious Dane. On January 24, Wild Bill Donovan of the OSS sent Hoover a heads-up about the connection between Inga and Wenner-Gren, who "has been placed on the American black-list." By May Wenner-Gren was banned from the country, and FDR sent Hoover an advisory suggesting that it might be "just as well" to have Inga "watched specially."

Not happy decrypting routine messages in Charleston, Jack Kennedy sweet-talked Inga into a series of weekend visits. The FBI was already tapping their telephone calls. Microphone surveillance devices—bugs—were quickly installed in the room Inga usually took at the Ft. Sumpter Hotel. Transcriptions from an even fatter file on the couple were soon flowing across the Director's mahogany desk.

What arises from all this paperwork could provide the libretto for an operetta. The Savannah Special Agent in Charge sent up Arvad's vital statistics—"28 yrs., 5'7-8, 135 lbs., Blonde, Blue, Fair"—and as for Appearance concludes: "Heavy legs; smart dresser: fast walker—described by Hitler as 'a perfect Nordic beauty.'"

Throughout the many telephone calls, Inga—who is very feline, very adept at kissing and then scratching and then drawing back, hurt, and then risking everything with an impudent remark or two—plays with her appealing if suggestible young ensign. She keeps him worried. Kathleen has tipped Jack off that Inga felt he wasn't much of a dresser, that a mutual friend had a better tailor. "That's no reflection on your clothes," she twits him. "Darling, you look best without anything."

A few days later, after Inga has made a quick trip to Manhattan, Jack calls again. "I heard you had a big orgy up in New York," he drops on her, half in jest.

"I'll tell you about it," Inga comes back. "I'll tell you about it for a whole weekend if you like to hear about it. My husband has his little spies all over the place."

"Really."

"No, he doesn't. But he told me all sorts of things about you, none of which were flattering. He knew every word you had said to your father about me. It made me look like—it amused me very much. . . . He said, 'Jack Kennedy shrugged his shoulders and said "I wouldn't dream of marrying her; in fact, I don't care two bits about her. She's just something I picked up on the road."' It's very amusing, darling. Tell me, when are you going away?"

The shadow of the patriarch descended across Jack's urge to investigate his deeper feelings. The editor of the *Times-Herald,* Frank Waldrop, would recount later how "Joseph Patrick Kennedy came boiling down here again, and I sat in on one of the head-butting sessions with his children." Before long, "the word in the city room was that when Joe Kennedy burst out 'Dammit, Jack, she's already married,' the boy said he didn't care."

Except that he cared. Like any experienced courtesan, Inga attempted in the European manner to exploit sex to infuse some real maturity into this buoyant yet profoundly unripe discovery of hers and found herself wrestling for his soul. In one letter she went so far as to describe Jack to himself: "He is so big and strong, and when you talk to him or see him you always have the impression that his big white teeth are ready to bite off a chunk of life. There is determination in his green Irish eyes. He has two backbones: His own and his father's." She would recall old Joe as a charmer when they were all together but hard underneath, "a good handshaker with a flashy smile but cold eyes" who, "if she left the room, he'd come down on Jack about her and if Jack left the room, he'd try to hop in the sack with her. . . ."

"She thought the Kennedy family was weird," Inga's son, Ronald McCoy, would ultimately remark to interviewer Clay Blair Jr. "The family was just an extension of the old man's hard-line schizophrenic condition. . . . The way she thought of it, the old man would push Joe, Joe would push Jack, Jack would push Bobby, Bobby would push Teddy, and Teddy would fall on his ass. Jack was going through a hell of a crisis about that."

It was as if the financier's unfulfilled ambitions somehow kept the boys in a panic, prevented them from establishing their own rhythms. Afterward, embittered, Inga complained to Arthur Krock that Jack really wasn't much of a lover, a "boy, not a man, who was intent upon ejaculation and not a woman's pleasure." She would not be the last woman to complain. Sex for Jack Kennedy would remain a brush-and-run affair, a series of quick, unfulfilled conquests, a technique to dodge a migraine.

Half-joking yet profoundly serious, he blamed the FBI. "But you know, goddamn it, Henry, I found out that son-of-a-bitch Hoover had put a micro-phone under the mattress!" Jack erupted to one friend. Along with Naval security, FBI agents were openly stalking the pair—in their hotel room, in restaurants, even window-shopping in Charleston—and keeping the Director on top of things. Nothing ever hinted of espionage. Kennedy "spent each night with subject in her hotel room . . . engaging in sexual intercourse on numerous occasions," one FBI synopsis goes. Another has Inga accusing Jack of "taking every pleasure of youth but not the responsibility." Referring to a recent trip to the pistol range, Jack asked "if she can do it, and she said she can kill any one with looks so not to worry about the pistol."

Meanwhile, Joe Kennedy kept after his son. One of Hoover's lieutenants contacted the financier directly to inform him that he too was implicated in the spreading Arvad investigation; this meant that Jack's romance was endangering the family. By now, the continuing strain was causing Jack's back to act up. On March 6, Inga, crushed, effectively ended it. The Kennedys were too much. Now hounded quite openly by the FBI, Inga left for Reno to get her divorce from Fejos.

Jack himself was reassigned to a combat unit. "He wasn't at all interested in going to fight the war," Ronald McCoy subsequently told the Blairs. "He came back later and said his father had called up an old Wall Street friend, Undersecretary of the Navy James V. Forrestal, and asked him to transfer Jack to sea duty, to the Pacific. Apparently he was really pissed off at the old man. He asked Inga to wait for him." Flouting his father's wishes, while changing duty stations Jack stopped over in Washington to spend a few hours with the one woman who opened his heart. The FBI intercepted a call she made soon after. Her impulse to mother him survived the pain. "Only, you know, his back," Inga lamented to a friend. "He looks like a limping monkey from behind. He can't walk at all. That's ridiculous, sending him off to sea duty."

Among his uneasy siblings, there was an awareness that Jack had been thwarted from exploring what could have turned into a breakthrough romance. The father was largely instrumental, but none of them could deal with that. This left the FBI. Bobby, already nursing the grudges for the rest of them, was becoming aware of J. Edgar Hoover.

Gangster Values

Hoover's adroitness at every stage of the Arvad episode impressed Joe Kennedy. Nursing doubts in any case about the Wenner-Gren/Fejos/Arvad group, the FBI director proceeded to ascending levels of surveillance. From routine background checks to inserting an informant at the *Times-Herald* to the authorization of full-bore tapping and bugging, the investigation processed beautifully. Joe Kennedy was informed at the right moment, and a squib went into Walter Winchell's column to function as a warning, a flare of exposure to make the principals scramble. There were no arrests, which the Director preferred where people of consequence were involved. Inga went her way, and before too long she married the film cowboy Tim McCoy. Public order survived. Hoover remained its unseen guardian.

A past master himself at rigging desirable outcomes, Kennedy appreciated good technique when he ran across it. One aphorism Joe favored, Rose would recall, was "Things don't just happen, they are made to happen." Success meant controlling events, facing down or obliterating whatever stood in the way. Preoccupied with his children now, Kennedy would devote the rest of his life to opening and closing doors and locking in results.

Underneath such an approach, of course, lay a profound distrust of society. Underneath the distrust was fear. Overmatched since boyhood by his censorious mother, Joe lived with the assumption that those condescending

WASPS and Jews out there *were* smarter, stronger, waiting complacently to devour him. For all his bravado ultimately a very guarded man, subject at every age to phobias; any setback or failure tended to paralyze Joe, to make him sick. This meant that even to survive it was critical to win, to dominate, and these apprehensions he would pass along to his surviving sons. Anxiety gnawed constantly; even starting out, he was incapacitated by nephritis and ulcers. Survival meant demonstrating every day that he could still perform. The much-trumpeted business triumphs, the procession of women—everything was emblematic. Failure stank of catastrophe.

As his fortune accumulated, Kennedy engineered for himself a kind of well-buffered multiple existence, forever in and out of not only the Bronxville mansion and the Palm Beach and Hyannis Port properties but also of a suite he kept in the Waldorf Towers and, as opportunity afforded, residential units in one of his Park Avenue apartment buildings or off Central Park or high in the Marina Twin Towers in Chicago or at a sumptuous rented villa on the Cote d'Azur. He was frequently spotted, almost always without Rose, recuperating at one of the vast Hearst estates, or gambling and wenching vigorously above Lake Tahoe. His decision to commit a little time to vacations with his children turned into an event; they competed ferociously to impress and propitiate him. He did a great deal of parenting by letter.

An intuitive administrator, Kennedy kept a constant eye out for underlings he could use, normally good solid hero-worshipping blue-collar Irish Catholics, and did not scruple to hang on them legal responsibility should anything turn rotten. Where business was concerned, he permitted himself few prejudices and employed serviceable Jews; associates like Phil Reisman at RKO would remain, as Ted Kennedy wrote, "a trusted ally whose company Dad enjoyed as much as any man's." While he was stationed in England, Kennedy repeatedly attempted to hire Carmel Offie, William Bullitt's fawning, sinister, ultra-efficient right hand, indifferent to the fact that Offie was a flamboyant homosexual. He offered a position to the fast-moving young Thomas Corcoran. Conniving employees sometimes provided an extra layer of protection. Around the offices, Kennedy was all business.

The wayward children of East European Jewish peddlers and Siciliano bolita runners who invented big-league crime in America shared more than territory with their celebrated Irish colleague. They assumed, like Joe, that the Protestant Ascendancy had no intention of turning over very much to them. Whatever they got, they took, operating inside the laws when that was conducive to their purposes and flouting them, very often violently, under normal circumstances. Success entailed "arrangements," most often a bribe or payoff, after which results were gratifying. Subservience to the Calvinist guidelines produced squat. Women had a part to play, either as diversions, entertainment, or, inside the subculture, as well-decorated spouses tucked away for breeding purposes. A display of wealth was de rigueur.

It would be surprising if no gangster values seeped into the Kennedy ethos, and a great many did. What made Kennedy different was his itch for respectability, his conviction that even the "nice people," in Rose's phrase, would esteem them if he could only get rich enough and deploy his fortune where society's leaders noticed. Even as a fresh-faced banker, Joe made it a point to be seen weekly at the Boston Symphony with Rose; in London—not without fanfare—Kennedy arranged to spring Toscanini from Mussolini's Italy. Sometimes these gestures tended to become ludicrous, as when he tried to browbeat the renowned Socialist thinker Harold Laski into endorsing his sons' geopolitical sputterings. Where Kennedy was truly inspired was in manipulating his own publicity. Once he became ambassador, he pumped up the public perception of his family as glamorous, irresistible, until before too long much of the newspaper-reading public bought in. "It's not what you are, it's what people think you are," Kennedy hammered at offspring. Here was a formula for disaster down the road, but things went so well for so long that nobody was looking ahead.

One avenue that opened up early was Kennedy's emergence as a Leading Catholic Layman. He and his family would be received regularly in private audiences with the Holy Father; he became a Knight of Malta; Rose became a Papal Countess; Joe went onto the board of Notre Dame for a time and cultivated its indulgent president, Father John Cavanaugh. He solicited for Catholic charities, often depositing whatever gifts he collected in his own bank account and writing a tax-deductible covering check to the Holy See for whatever he decided. Most significant, lured in by the plump little sexually ambiguous Francis Cardinal Spellman, Kennedy's became a well-attended voice in Catholic geopolitics. This involvement would invite very severe global consequences.

Periodically the pressure became insupportable and Kennedy dropped out. Red Chandor, a New York socialite who was acquainted with the Kennedys, remembered being filled in by a member of the Adams family who put in time in a sanitarium with Joe during the middle Twenties: "Joe Kennedy was there having a nervous breakdown from, I guess, having too much money or something. . . . Joe would get all the most important—you know, CEO's and people like that were there—and Joe would talk to them about their business and he would help them make out their income tax forms. . . . And he said to my friend, who he roomed with . . . This guy—That guy is so dumb, I'm going to take his company away from him one day. . . ." Sick as he got sometimes, the drive never wavered. "I'm gonna make one of my sons the first Catholic president," Joe told Adams. "If one of my sons doesn't get it, another one will."

That made it excruciating when anything went sour. After all those months in California, Gloria Swanson would recount, determined as he was to "challenge all the swells to remember that this was the saloonkeeper's son" taking over the industry, Joe Kennedy degenerated into a chain-smoker and lost thirty-two pounds. The day he realized his make-or-break movie *Queen Kelly* had collapsed, Joe stalled out completely. "Stopping abruptly," Gloria later wrote, "he slumped into a deep chair. He turned away from me, struggling to control himself. He held his head in his hands, and little, high-pitched sounds escaped from his body, like those of a wounded animal whimpering in a trap. He finally found his voice. It was quiet, controlled. 'I've never had a failure in my life,' were his first words. Then he rose, ashen, and went into another searing rage at the people who had let this happen. But he was too hurt and stunned to get properly angry. He yanked me into his arms, and soon my face was wet with tears."

Emerging from the early recession with a personal fortune of perhaps ten million dollars, Kennedy began to organize much of his estate into trust funds for his children. He was doing this, he assured cronies, to make his children independent of him. They must be free enough to tell him to "go to hell." Jack would laugh this off: "He was speculating," JFK remarked. "It was a very risky business. He was speculating pretty hard and his health was not good at the time, and that was the reason he did it. There was no other reason for it."

Another panic set in once the Battle of Britain threatened to engulf his ambassadorship. A pariah across most of the British establishment by then, Kennedy found himself eating dinner alone much of the time, mostly the scrambled eggs and soft food his inflamed digestion could tolerate. He lost fifteen pounds and his hair went gray. Fighting hysteria, he regaled visitors with his conviction that the British Empire was lost, that the world economic system was on the edge of devastation, that he and his family would shortly be ruined. One afternoon the unnerved Ambassador telephoned the embassy to alert his staff that the Nazi invasion of England would begin at three. When Kennedy finally escaped to the United States for long enough to undergo his regular physical at the Lahey Clinic, he was diagnosed, alarmingly, with very severe gastritis and acute colitis. There was a suspicion of cancer.

Except for Rosemary, who had been tucked away in an English retreat, Kennedy's family was out of harm's way at home. Rose couldn't have helped in any case. One commentator has written of Rose that she possessed "a mind with the simple, functional strength of a crowbar" and remained "half Irish charm and all business." Another noted that Kennedy's priest-ridden wife "loved him so much she denied him sex except for procreation so he could concentrate on his work" and "did not comprehend how he could seek women who thought so little of his business needs that they gave him their bodies with what presumably was uncontrolled abandon."

In April 1940, increasingly alone and trapped, Kennedy slipped across the Channel for a rendezvous in the Paris Ritz with Clare Boothe Luce. Clare was as businesslike as Rose, although, throughout her decades of celebrity as a cocktail-party wit and Broadway playwright and Congresswoman, she livened up her marriage to the crusty, halting publisher of *Time* magazine by including among her professional qualifications a no-nonsense availability between the sheets. Her reactionary opinions and snide anti-Semitism accorded perfectly with Kennedy's—especially under so much pressure—and helped him justify the outrageous views he was to express too openly throughout the Blitz. That season Clare was after Joe to dump FDR. Before long, Kennedy had effectively sealed his own political doom.

Along with the parade of popsies and "secretaries" and "actresses" Joe kept his friends and family scrounging to come up with, the defunct Ambassador was beginning to feel the need for something more sustaining. A substitute wife. His decade with Daye Eliot evidently began while he was still in London and she was dancing with Fifi Ferry's Les Girls troupe out of Le Touquet in France. Still recovering from a busted marriage to a minor hoodlum, the twenty-one-year-old Daye was in need of what was then referred to as a "woman's operation."

Daye brought out a side of Joe he hated to expose. He was a soft touch for people in trouble, especially if he got to Dutch-uncle their lives. Joe bought her operation, then introduced her to Cardinal Spellman, who arranged for her conversion to Catholicism. The columnist Doris Lilly, an intimate of Eliot's, observed shrewdly that the Ambassador "paid for this surgery before he was even involved sexually with her and it wasn't a question in those days as money was not discussed between people . . . he took for granted that by doing this, she would be his girl at a later point. She realized it too, but it wasn't anything they really talked about, and, in fact, he probably savored that whole aspect of the relationship when he was helping her more than the physical part that followed."

Maybe. Kennedy needed to start again. In time, he called in his markers with the voluptuous brunette and installed her in a ground-floor Manhattan apartment on Beekman Place. He came and went inconspicuously by the garden door. Over the years he presented her with a set of square-cut emeralds mounted in platinum, introduced her to Gloria Swanson, and at one point shepherded her to Hyannis Port to make the acquaintance of Rose. He did not appear alarmed if she dated other men.

This was a lonely man, hungering for human contact. Kennedy literature is peppered with anecdotes about old Joe lingering embarrassingly in the rooms of his sons' dates, trolling for "just one kiss." Respectable women he had barely met found his face plastered all over theirs, wet and unwelcome. "Be sure to lock the bedroom door," Jack warned female sleepovers, more amused than appalled. "The Ambassador has a tendency to prowl late at night." Friends of his daughters from boarding school would confess many years later that Joe had slipped into their beds during the wee hours and clapped a hand over their mouths and muttered: "This is going to be something you'll always remember." No doubt they did.

One judgment the literature won't touch is how such license impacted on his children. It is a truism that the boys chased because the father chased, but that was superficial. Even a glimpse in passing of their seminal demigod (on whom they all depended utterly) fondling some glassy-eyed "secretary" in the basement projection room, or "getting at . . . this young girl . . . under the table" at the Caravelle—how could it ever be less than traumatizing? What began as a deep, desperate need in the father would turn into obsessive, joyless, hit-and-run behavior with the boys.

Sex would become a rivalry, a matter of performance, especially between Joe and Jack. "Why don't you get a live one?" the Ambassador demanded of one of Jack's dates as the young people left for the movies. He confided to George Smathers and others that Jack was a "poor lover" and to Henry Luce that he didn't believe his second son was going to get very far, he "wasn't very bright." "Women?" the financier came back at one acquaintance who congratulated him on Jack's reputation with the ladies. "Older women, maybe."

Jack would tell friends that his father was "stern," "brusque," "rather curt" a lot of the time, and "pretty caustic when we lost." "There isn't a motive in him which I respect except love of family," JFK admitted privately during the 1960 campaign, "and sometimes I think that's just pride." What Jack did respect was the old man's judgment, his hard, seasoned, in-the-world appraisal of whatever was important. Eclectic himself, Jack

appreciated the old battler's perspective: "Even if my dad had even ten percent of his brain working, I'd still feel he had more sense than anybody else
I know."

Joe Kennedy spoiled his children; he micromanaged their lives along
with their careers, pestering their friends and staffers on the telephone by the
hour, automatically disposing of their bills through his Park Avenue bookkeeping operation and shipping in lawyers or accountants or detectives
when something threatened to get out of hand. He maintained a chokehold
on the press. Between dependency and love there is a fine bleeding edge.
Along with a lot of funds, they needed his emotional support. "My father
would be for me if I were running as head of the Communist Party," Jack
himself remarked. JFK was "quite in awe of his father," George Smathers saw.
"You have to understand that Jack was totally devoted to his father," Chuck
Spalding told one interviewer. "He loved Old Joe more than he ever loved
any other human being."

What haunted their relationship was the fact that Jack wasn't Joe Jr. Jack
had been sickly all along, never really a contender—at two, his son had been
so ill with scarlet fever that Joe had pledged to contribute half his estate to
the Church if the boy recovered. When Jack finally made it, Joe wrote the
check, although only after signing over assets to Rose. Even then he intended
to outsmart God.

Joe Jr. had been the self-assured heir apparent with the bearing of a born
naval officer as well as perfect ideological pitch, resonating to his father's
opinions. In 1933, touring Nazi Germany, Joe's eldest had written home that
Jews dominated the professions during the years of the Weimar Republic,
"but their methods had been quite unscrupulous." A purge was coming, for
"in every revolution you have to expect some bloodshed."

Well accustomed to eclipsing his raffish, unkempt, semi-invalid of a
younger brother, Joe Jr. had been startled and disapproving when Jack got
shipped out to the Solomons as a lieutenant j.g. in command of PT-109, and
thunderstruck when he came back a year later to national acclaim, the recipient of the Navy Cross. His father made sure that John Hersey's treatment in
The New Yorker of Jack's amazing performance while saving his crew got
reprints in the mass-market *Reader's Digest*. At home on leave to celebrate
the Ambassador's birthday, young Joe's smile froze and his face reddened
when a guest raised a glass to "our own hero, Lt. John F. Kennedy of the
United States Navy." He sobbed himself to sleep that night, and on returning
to England volunteered for "Zootsuit Black," a high-risk mission in August
1944 to dump a dynamite-laden plane into the V-1 launching bunkers on the

Belgian coast. The plane blew up far short of the target, instantly killing Joe and his copilot, Wilford J. Willy.

"I'm about to go into my act," Joe Jr. had told a friend, "and if I don't come back tell my dad—despite our differences—that I love him very much." After the priests left, the Ambassador "went into a low and dangerous emotional ebb. He would not work. He stayed in his room with the shades drawn. He ate only enough to keep him alive, and he became so immersed in grief that he stopped speaking." The servants heard Wagner and Beethoven on his phonograph, day and night.

When Kennedy did emerge, the pain was simply too raw. He inveighed against "the kikes around Roosevelt." He convinced himself that much of that ruinous talk of his defeatism had been planted by FDR and his enemies in the White House to undermine his dreams for his sons. In 1942, already nursing his grievance with Roosevelt, Joe Kennedy had backed his bubbling warhorse of a father-in-law, Honey Fitz, in the Massachusetts Democratic primary for the Senate and, by so doing, badly weakened the administration's choice, Joseph Casey. Henry Cabot Lodge waltzed back into his Senate seat. With Joe Jr. gone, Kennedy did not hesitate to round on Harry Truman at a meeting at the end of 1944: "Harry, what the hell are you doing campaigning for that crippled son of a bitch that killed my son Joe?" Watching closely, Arthur Krock picked up on something much deeper: "Joe, when he volunteered on this final mission, which was beyond his duty, he [wanted to prove] that the Kennedys were not yellow, and that's what killed the boy. And his father realized it."

These were the initial sacrifices to what the sensation-mongering press would label "The Curse of the Kennedys." They met the requirement that Joe and Rose bred into this emerging generation to *accomplish*, irrespective of their capabilities, to buck the odds with suicidal intensity. The family was already living in the tabloids as much as in Hyannis Port. To propitiate the god of "what people think you are," reality was under revision.

First to be edited out was Rosemary. A slow, pudgy, gentle, increasingly frustrated recluse starting to erupt with unpredictable rages, her father subjected her in 1941 to an experimental lobotomy which left her infantilized. She would be hidden away even from the family for eight years behind bars at Craig House, a hospital for the mentally disturbed in rural New York, then warehoused at St. Colletta's in Wisconsin for the rest of her life.

The spring of 1948 would cost them another sibling. Kathleen Kennedy, "Kick," the widow of the future Duke of Devonshire, Billy Hartington, had fallen for the tall, rather jaded Earl Peter Fitzwilliam, Peter Milton. Peter was still married to somebody else, and Rose rushed over to London to threaten her low-slung but vivacious daughter with disinheritance and worse, along with anybody else in the family that sided with her, if she should attempt to marry the notorious Protestant. The worried Joe Kennedy—"You are and always will be tops with me," he wrote Kathleen—struggled against Rose's absolutism. The whole transoceanic row was cut short when Peter and Kathleen cajoled their unwilling pilot into flying his DeHavilland Dove into a bank of thunderheads over the French Alps; the starboard wing separated and the plane went down.

Insisting on flying small airplanes into bad conditions would remain a problem for the Kennedys—besides Kathleen, John F. Kennedy Jr. and Ethel Kennedy's brother and parents would perish under comparable circumstances, and Ted Kennedy was permanently incapacitated. Lem Billings would paraphrase Rose as having determined that Kathleen's death was "a matter of God pointing his finger at Kathleen and saying no!" Joe, who put his faith in more compassionate deities, would be the only family member to attend Kathleen's burial on the Cavendish estate.

When it came to Kathleen's misbehavior, Robert Kennedy would stand with Rose. He'd remained the altar boy in the family. "I'll send my girls to Catholic schools and colleges to believe," Joe has been quoted, "but I'll send my men to the marketplace to know better." With Bobby, somehow, everything overlapped. Seventh of the nine, Robert Kennedy came along when even the punctilious Rose would admit that she was up to here with bedtime stories. Once private polls demonstrated that his own political prospects were dimmer by the month, Joe Kennedy had started to tell people that from then on "my work is my boys." "He was referring to Jack and Joe, not Bobby," Evan Thomas comments acutely. Joe Jr. was everything anybody could want, and while Jack seemed feckless and immature in many ways, he displayed an incontrovertible flair. While Joe was still enjoying the sunny side of his ambassadorship, the two older sons had helped out with diplomatic chores, roamed Europe from Russia to the Vatican with cutaways in their luggage to report firsthand to the impressed financier.

At that point Bobby was a clumsy, willing fourteen-year-old, sweet, still full-faced and unsure of himself, with too many freckles and overwhelming front teeth that made him look at moments like a demented woodchuck. With his family unavailable, Bobby had been tucked away for three years at Portsmouth Priory, a sort of convent school for boys at which he worked very hard to please his father but still did poorly. "I just got out of about 3 hours of praying in Chapel," he opens one letter to the folks, "and so feel like a saint. Our retreat starts Thursday so I'm certainly going to be doing a lot of praying this week." The double-edged, quick, self-abnegating humor which would become Bobby's hallmark when he was uncomfortable was already in evidence.

Implicated in a cheating scandal, Robert Kennedy moved on to finish his secondary education at Milton Academy. Solidly into adolescence now and increasingly sarcastic and feisty, this thin-skinned runt among the Kennedy brothers fended off Milton's disapproving environment and made one life-long friend, Dave Hackett, himself a townie and sports hero around the gen-teel Episcopalian boarding school. By then nasty rumors were sweeping the Milton campus that Bobby's father was a bootlegger and sucked up to Hitler while hiding from the Blitz. There were fights, Bobby exploding into the face of any kid who brought up any of that.

These were lonely years, desperate at times. Bob and obstreperous little Teddy, seven years younger and shuffled off to the Fessenden School nearby for safekeeping, scrounged around together during the breaks for holidays. Bobby kept the folks informed that Ted was still too fat. At one point, he rec-ommends that his little brother model the *before* in a weight-loss ad. "If you haven't got any other plans for Teddy for Thanksgiving," Bob wrote his mother, "he'll probably go to the Commissioner's [Joe Timility, a crony of Joe's] for Wed. night and then go over to Aunt Bunny's for lunch. I'm not quite sure what I'm going to do yet," Bobby noted, struggling for dignity, "but I'll probably go along with Teddy." He himself wasn't going to letter in football. His math teacher informed the class that "two great things had hap-pened to him; one that Rommel was surrounded in Egypt and 2nd that Kennedy had passed a Math Test." This was turning into a decidedly down-beat November.

Once in a while, he let it out. "It took me a little while to get over this small paragraph in Mother's letter," Bob wrote the parents. "quote:—

"'Teddy is coming down March 19 and Bobby expects to come down a little later. We shall certainly be glad to see Teddy,' etc. End quote.

"That was a little hard to take Ma'Ma', and I expect you to write in your next letter that you'll be glad to see me also because I'm still quite a nice lit-tle boy."

Before he moved along to college, Robert Kennedy was in and out of fourteen boarding schools, rarely long enough to begin to get oriented. His mother seldom visited such places or got mixed up in the educational process, beyond jerking him out of St. Paul's when it looked as though attendance at Protestant chapel was mandatory. Bob was unique among her boys in that he remained quite religious and served at mass a lot. His grades refused to improve. "Please get on your toes," Rose admonished him; she was very fond of showing the children her own perfect report cards. "I do not expect my own little pet to let me down." Favorite or no, Rose could be very quick to register her displeasure. Discipline was regularly enforced with whatever came to hand, from coat hangers to shoes. One biographer maintains that Rose once "slapped Bobby's face so viciously that she punctured his eardrum and split his lip."

During the glory years of the middle thirties, when rising dignitaries like William O. Douglas and James Landis came through for weekends and the important affairs of government and economics got bandied about at long, leisurely dinners, only Joe and the older boys were expected to contribute their opinions. Rose, friends, and the younger children would get ridden right over. "Conversation with the Kennedys, including the family, it was a shin-kicking contest," Fred Dutton would testify in later years. "A lot of practical jokes, put-down humor."

The origin of it all, where the money came from, was to remain a mystery. "We never discussed money in the house," Joe himself would emphasize. "Well, because money isn't important. . . ." Who knew where that discussion might lead? When one confederate wondered what Joe was going to say if the kids started asking the wrong questions, the financier was blunt: "If they do, I'll tell them to mind their own goddamn business!" Robert Kennedy himself stated later that their own wealth "was a subject that was taboo. If the subject would come up about the cost of something or relating to money, it would immediately be diverted." Charles Spalding, the sort of white-shoe company the Ambassador was willing to let Jack invite to the house, remarked that when the children "talked about business, they really were just naïve. Listening to them talk about money was like listening to nuns talk about sex."

Throughout their childhoods the parents came and went. Rose managed nine trips to Europe during one fourteen-month period, almost always to Paris to upgrade her expensive wardrobe. She was unable to motivate herself to return in time for Honey Fitz's funeral. Vacation planning was desultory. Upon converging in Hyannis Port, the children would drop off their duffel bags in whichever bedroom appeared vacant. If there were houseguests, some younger member of the family might well wind up sleeping on the rubbing table in the exercise room. These days were jammed with tennis lessons and sailing lessons and swimming lessons and running on the beach and the unavoidable touch football. Whenever the financier was in residence for the moment he oversaw virtually everything, from the rearrangement of the furniture to the selection of the menus. After a particularly fine dinner, especially if the crème brûlée was up to standard, he had a way of appearing in the kitchen to slip a bill into the apron pocket of the cook, Margaret.

Bromides around the dinner table were incessant. They were to stick together, take what they wanted, win at all costs. Leave it to him to back them up. What the children gathered, of course, was that without the financier's wherewithal and aptitude for intrigue they wouldn't really have amounted to much. It was a slam-bang life around the Kennedy compound, nobody picked up anything, breakage on every level was constant, servants decamped for their lives.

K. Lemoyne—"Lem"—Billings, Jack's roommate at Choate and the life-long butt of his inspired teasing, would remember his introduction to the patriarch: "Mr. Kennedy shook my hand and looked at me with a pair of eyes which I will never forget. I can only describe them as the strongest I have ever seen. When he looked at you, you felt he saw you as you had never been seen before. He had the terrifying ability to look at you as you look at yourself." The patriarch's attention overhung everything, as inescapable as the billboard eyes of Dr. T. J. Eckleburg in *The Great Gatsby*.

The outside world, the universe of practical affairs, seemed to be reserved to a great extent for the older boys. Especially at the Palm Beach mansion the children would glimpse Joe, slathered with coconut oil and sunbathing naked in his "bullpen" beside the pool, issuing orders or negotiating into the special cupped mouthpiece which was attached to each of his telephones so that others couldn't overhear. Robert Kennedy's apprehension that he was never to be allowed to join the adult males hung on for a long time. "I wish, Dad," Bobby wrote his father in 1945 from his ROTC program at Bates College, "that you would write me a letter as you used to Joe and Jack about what you think about the different political events and the war as I'd like to understand what's going on better than I do now." The resentment was awkwardly disguised. Robert Kennedy was already twenty.

"He was the least loved of all the Kennedy children," Lem Billings would state flatly, and Lem was in the room a lot. Partly it was Bob's position in the pecking order—lost among the girls—and partly it was his underdog personality. He frequently seemed emotionally disoriented. By the time Bobby came along, the family was dispersed so much of the time that a few weeks at home was like rejoining the cast of a repertory company that met onstage.

Even as a child, Bob seemed attuned differently from the others. Several of the neighbors around Hyannis Port remembered him as a sort of emotional ragamuffin, hanging out with the rougher, more disadvantaged kids in the village, sometimes blacks or Indians. Another remembered Bob as part of a rabble that liked to hide in the moonlight beside the jetty and spy on the wealthy summer residents dancing in a local "speakeasy" on the deck of a scuttled boat. Once a local fat girl lost her glasses while swimming and Bob kept surface-diving until he retrieved them. "He was," according to this report, "sensitive to the feelings of other kids, especially of the less privileged kids who hung around as a part of the gang."

He craved a normal life. He raised rabbits and attempted a paper route, dropping off the papers while the family chauffeur, Dave, carted him around the neighborhood in the family Rolls. But attempting to remain a Kennedy produced a constant awareness of social dislocation: exchanging stamps with FDR, then messing with those nasty-smelling bunnies, and then, a few months after that, at thirteen, dressed up for parties at Buckingham Palace as the escort of the prepubescent Princess Elizabeth. He called her Betty.

His life as a boy, Jack Kennedy later admitted to a friend, was "like living in an institution," with "all the toothbrushes lined up in a row." A woman who once visited Hyannis Port when the rest of the family was away was taken aback to watch Jack "go through the empty house like an intruder, peeking in his father's room and looking in his desk drawers, and picking up objects on all the surfaces as if he hadn't seen them before." Joe was a known quantity, and a complete mystery.

For Bobby's generation, the feelings of suppressed alienation were even worse. "I was shuffled off to boarding school at the age of eight," Jean Smith would note. "That's why I'm still trying to get my head screwed on straight."

The unremitting parental drills devoted to winning and punctuality and current events and picking your friends with discrimination and exploiting expert help when you needed it affected each child differently. Jack, bedridden anyhow much of the time, dawdled over history and cultivated the detached, humorously ironic style that permitted him to pink the overbearing Ambassador when he needed to without ever quite breaking the skin. Teddy teased. Bob, Billings saw, was easily "the most devoted observer of all the clan rules," the best-behaved, the most religious. Watching his middle son in action, aware that Bobby was the type to keep trying to run through a brick wall if he wanted something, the Ambassador counseled him, according to Justice Department colleague William Orrick, "to go around the wall rather than try and push through it." The founding father was already nursing reservations as to how fanatic he really wanted his brood to become. Bob once got badly cut crashing through a glass door in his hurry to get to lunch. Much later—Bob was already twenty-two—he jumped off his sailboat and abandoned his inexperienced neighbor to cope with the pitching tide while Bobby swam ashore to arrive on time.

Rose remembered how "spectacularly prompt" Bob was about appearing at dinner at the appointed moment. The far more lapidary, bemused Jack regularly infuriated his father by drifting in, frequently with friends, halfway through the meal. Around water, Bob never hesitated to dive off anything, into anything, swim out too far with anybody. He broke a leg during football practice at Harvard and scrimmaged on it until the session was over. To get his letter, he jumped in briefly in the Harvard–Yale game in a cast—a performance that delighted his surprised father, who had rushed onto the field years earlier to threaten the job of the Harvard coach when Joe Jr. never got the nod.

Of the four brothers, only Robert collected his two-thousand-dollar check from Joe for not drinking or smoking until he was twenty-one; characteristically, he lost track of it somewhere in the rubble of his dormitory room. Where Bobby truly deviated was in the company he preferred. His pal Dave Hackett would recall a schoolboy who was "slight and small and was way down in a huge family. His brothers were very successful. . . . Things were not easy for him. So I think he just had a natural connection to the underdog.

"I think he basically was an underdog, or I initially said he was a misfit. And I think he was a misfit at a school, and I think he was a misfit all the way through his whole career, in a way, in the best sense of the word." Sensing Bobby's instinct for martyring himself, as Rita Dallas, Joe's nurse, would write: "It was a running joke with the family that when they were growing up, Bobby always took the blame for everything, and I think that his tough reputation came as a result of this."

He was a mediocre student—C's, a few D's. Accepted into decent clubs—Hasty Pudding, Spee, and Varsity Club—Bob preferred to blow off free time at places like the Old Howard burlesque house with his roughneck buddies. He kept dragging back to Hyannis Port an assortment of oversized working-class rowdies and ringers on the GI Bill whom Rose especially found it distasteful to confront in the halls. In Jack's case, the parents had been outspoken about screening whichever friends he brought home. With Bobby, there were far fewer expectations. Picking over his associates didn't really seem worth the trouble.

Desperate to fit in, Bobby was taking on enforcement responsibilities, serving as his father's stand-in. One of the PT-109 wives who joined their husbands at Hyannis Port get-togethers as the war wound down, Kate Thom, later summed up Bob's role. "They only served one cocktail before dinner. But these were a bunch of Navy men. So when the cooks left, we'd sneak into the kitchen and get the Scotch. Bobby came home from Harvard. He was a scrawny little guy in a white sailor suit. He was very upset that we were sneaking booze in the kitchen. He was afraid his father might catch us and he knew his father's wrath. But Kathleen handled him. She told him to get lost."

Even then, if fitfully, Bob was smartening up. Shortly before Jack Kennedy came home from the Pacific, Bobby had written him a letter from the dorm at Bates, where he had signed up halfway through Harvard to prepare as a seaman's apprentice in a Naval Training Unit preliminary to shipping out on the destroyer *Joseph P. Kennedy Jr.*

Bob was a little apprehensive because "Pappy has finally got some angle of getting me out of college in the middle of the summer" and put on a ship "named after my brother . . . but I'll get your ideas upon your triumphal return to the East.

"Everyone evidently thinks you're doing a simply fine job out there, except mother who was a little upset that you still mixed 'who' & 'whom' up. Get on to yourself.

"The weather stinks and we've only had one sunny day for a month. So I suggest you stay out there for as long as possible. That staying away will also be good for keeping you a fair-haired boy around the house, for I know it takes you almost as short a time as it does me to finish yourself off when you're home."

As with the Kennedys, the arrival of peace in 1945 moved Hoover to unflinching self-examination. They'd have to outflank their setbacks and forge ahead. If there was anybody around town Harry S. Truman liked less than Joe Kennedy it was probably J. Edgar Hoover. The trim little haberdasher from Kansas City wanted no truck with "all that sexual crap," as he sometimes referred to Hoover's Official and Confidential files. Worse than that, with Bess in the picture nobody was going to catch Harry compromising himself. A visit to Joe Kennedy's estate at Marwood soon after he arrived as a senator in Washington had found the plainspoken provincial from Missouri bowled over by the décor but uninterested in the female company available. This much gratuitous purity left Hoover at a disadvantage.

Dealing with the FBI, Clark Clifford would write, "President Truman was in a trap. He did not like Hoover, but in 1947 the FBI director was widely regarded as an American hero, protecting the nation against gangsters and Nazis." It became a standoff. When Hoover, a member like Truman of the D.C. Scottish Rite, came up for the thirty-third degree, the nobility of the Shriner, Truman blackballed him. Unfortunately, Hoover was obviously flourishing due to what Clifford recognized as "skillfully manufactured public-relations myths, but they prevented the President from even thinking about getting rid of Hoover."

Under Franklin Roosevelt, the FBI had experienced exponential growth. From 391 agents in 1933, the Bureau swelled to almost 3,000 in 1942, then on to 4,900 at the height of the war. Bustling over to the Hill to justify his budget requests year after year, the self-assured Director explained to his rapt audience of Congressmen on the Judiciary Committee or the Appropriations Subcommittee that he, himself, undoubtedly more than anybody else, regretted that the Bureau had become so extensive. The last thing anybody in the Seat of Government desired was for their organization to morph into a National Police Force. He would have preferred to restrict the Bureau's functions, but so much was now expected, crime and subversion being on the upswing. . . . Then Hoover was fond of citing the automobile recovery statistics, and the deposits repatriated when bank robbers were apprehended, and the impressive kidnap numbers. . . . The truth was, any time you added it all up, it became quite evident the FBI *made* several times what it cost to run the place; it was a net plus for the Treasury. Then Hoover snapped off a confidential wink to Manny Celler or John Rooney or whomever was chairing the Committee that afternoon, and whatever added budget or expanded powers the Director was after got ratified, normally by unanimous vote. Nobody pretended to worry much about exercising the Committee's oversight function.

Celler himself groused in private that Hoover had dossiers on every member of Congress and routinely tapped many of their telephones. Yet Manny invariably succumbed too. "He was a master con man," as Hoover's personal nemesis, William Sullivan, would put it after he himself fell from grace. "One of the greatest con men the country has ever produced, and that takes intelligence of a certain kind, an astuteness, a shrewdness."

It may be that Hoover's most distinctive attribute was his surehandedness when it came to the hydraulics of power. Over Roosevelt's long presidency, Hoover had transmogrified from a file clerk with a night law school degree into the nation's Colossus of Rectitude. Any time a man—all agents were men—took the oath of fidelity to the Bureau, he forfeited Civil-Service protections. People survived by second-guessing the Director's mood. Hoover's infallibility was uppermost. A strain of macabre Bureau humor came into being, each anecdote based on something that had happened. "I have been looking over the supervisors at the Seat of Government," Hoover popped out of his office one day to announce. "A lot of them are clods. Get rid of them." A panel was formed, known as the Clod Squad, and the trick was to dope out in time which supervisors were clods, exactly. . . .

William Turner, for many years an agent himself, has written that during a shootout in New York, an agent's leg was grazed by a bullet and he was "taken to the hospital for observation. The report to Washington got garbled. The next morning, Hoover appeared as scheduled before a civic group. 'Gentlemen,' he began, 'I am with you this morning even though my heart is heavy, for last night in New York one of my agents was killed in a gun battle.' The Director's words got back to New York, and agents drew straws to see who would go to the hospital and finish off the wounded agent."

Much of Hoover's renown he owed to Louis Nichols, who after 1937 took over the Bureau's public-relations arm, Crime Records. Crime Records could produce a profitable, ghost-written book by the Director himself, unnerve Hoover critics by activating the Bureau's hectic kennel of newspaper columnists, or jam up badly any Congressman who presumed to question the Director's omniscience. A burly, outspoken veteran with the emotional heft to wet-nurse his idol, Nichols reportedly told Hoover that, had he but gotten word in time of an upcoming uncomplimentary story in the *Washington Post,* he would have "gone over there and hurled myself bodily into the presses."

Hoover himself ventured that "Nick may not be very smart, but nobody can doubt his loyalty." Top-level policy direction around the Bureau came out of the Executive Conference, meetings of the handful of assistant directors who oversaw the divisions. Clyde Tolson chaired these exchanges, but Hoover was a weighty presence. Egged on by the presence of familiars like Al Belmont, Milton Ladd, Sullivan, Alex Rosen, and Deke DeLoach, the Director continuously punctuated the caseload with hard-bitten wisecracks and insider put-downs. DeLoach remembers such sessions as very free and open, with Hoover attempting to tease out even the most contrary of opinions. Sometimes there was a vote—which Hoover would overrule whenever he didn't care for the outcome.

What he successfully radiated was control, an aura of absolute and total self-possession. After one extremely bumpy plane ride, the Director dismissed the whole experience as "fantastic. . . . Perhaps a little frightening at times. I'm a Presbyterian and believe in predestination, but I think Clyde was frightened."

By the time Harry Truman had settled in as president, the word was coursing through official America that J. Edgar Hoover was somebody it paid to know. John Rooney grew dependent on his armored limousine. People on the Director's Christmas list might find an FBI agent available to meet their planes in a crunch. With Hoover's people killing time in the satellite agency in Hyannis Port, Joe Kennedy had very little need of the local constabulary.

Hoover made it clear that he was not too uppity to accept gifts, and agents all up and down the line made sure to express their devotion. No compliment was florid enough. Over many years, teams of FBI employees rebuilt and expanded most of Hoover's antique-clotted residence at 4936 Thirtieth Place N.W. in D.C. An illuminated fish pond and a wealth of expensive landscaping touches, plus services that ranged from resetting the Director's clock to dealing with his tax returns, got written off at government expense. When Hoover's dedicated black manservant, James Crawford, underwent brain surgery and did not appear to be in any condition to manicure the lawn, the American taxpayers comped the aging autocrat a backyard of virgin Monsanto Chemgrass, something Hoover's two Cairns would have a harder time shredding.

Casting around for additional income, Hoover lent his name to another book. His earlier effort, *Persons in Hiding*, dealt with the Dillinger era, but it was so derivative that even the admiring *New York Times* concluded that "it is time that Mr. Hoover gave his ghost some fresh material." *Masters of Deceit*, a fairly straightforward anti-Communist tract ground out by as many as eight agents overseen by William Sullivan over six months, sold much better. Proceeds were laundered through the FBI Recreational Association, with Hoover, Tolson, and Lou Nichols pocketing 20 percent each tax-free.

Like him or not, even Hoover's many detractors had to admit that the man had *presence*. There were always worlds behind worlds. Visitors approached the icon by crossing through a series of trophy rooms, hung with Hoover's many plaques and citations. A gruesome plaster-of-Paris death mask of John Dillinger and a sailfish the Director claimed to have caught helped decorate the thirty-five-foot paneled conference room, with its FBI seal embroidered in the carpet. There was a giant desk at the far end, with two lamps made of upright pistols and American flags and patriotic props of every variety to impress the visitor. A brass desk plate was engraved: "Two feet on the ground are worth one in the mouth."

But it was in a small—twelve by twelve—room to the rear that Hoover actually worked. His well-worn government-issue desk had little on it beyond a blotter, a tattered bible inherited from his mother, a potted plant, and a framed photograph of his first dog, Spee De Bozo. Above the inner desk was suspended a wavering purplish bug light, intended to deal with anything that flew in uninvited—the Director had a pathological fear of insects; if a fly landed on him he would become close to unhinged. Anything slimy, unkempt, pestilential, disorderly made Hoover's gorge rise, provoked all those middle-class fight-or-flight impulses handed down by too many generations of anal-vindictive Swiss. Aroused, these phobias poured out of him, and he would label his enemies "flea-ridden dogs" or "lower than the regurgitated filth of vultures."

The black agent who attended Hoover during working hours, Sam Noisette, later calculated that he spent half of his twenty-five years in the Bureau handing the Director towels. This fear of contamination haunted every conscious moment and pursued him in his dreams of being chased. Projected, it made Hoover conceive of himself and the Bureau as all that guarded the purity of the nation, especially against the "vermin" who schemed to propagate "Commoonism" in America. By Hoover's unconscious logic, anything he conceived of as contributing to the dissolution of the social order—beatniks, war protesters, the Southern Christian Leadership Conference—had to be Communist in its origins, or, at the mildest, Communist-inspired.

Another anxiety that Hoover's office reflected was the Director's suspicion that he wasn't up to his mission, that he wasn't big enough. Literally. He had his desk mounted on a six-inch dais, and special chairs arrayed below in which the cushions deflated slowly, so that his visitors sank little by little as his large face—creeping over the years into a kind of papier-mâché mask out of which stared those angry little onyx eyes—swelled against the gleaming blinds while he gushed invective.

Ever fearful of finding himself looking up to somebody, Hoover kept a little box in his office on which he would stand whenever it was necessary to confront a visitor taller than his five-foot-ten. New arrivals were instructed never to call attention to the box, or the heavy English-lavender aroma of the Yardley brilliantine with which he attempted to give some body to his thinning, corrugated hair. Underlings were to carry a clean handkerchief with which to dry their right palms before receiving the Director's noble handshake—no symptom of panic was acceptable, no repellent moistness.

Needless to say, they panicked, especially the agents-in-training. Joseph Schott, perhaps as cynical—and funny—a recruit as ever passed through the Bureau, remembered the day when, having muffed his introduction, Hoover "looked me square in the eye and asked, 'are you loyal to me?'

"What did you say?

"What the hell do you think I said?

"I said, 'Yes, yes,'" Schott admitted forlornly, "babbling like an idiot. I would have fallen down on my knees and kissed his big toe if he had told me to."

Behind the neurotic manifestations, of course, was sex. Sex, or its absence—among Hoover's biographers, the debate rolls on and on. The first important distinction to be made is between Hoover on the road, in more indulgent climes, and Hoover upright behind his desk in Washington. Around the capital the Director was very dogmatic about keeping his distance even from favored subordinates, who might run into the Boss socially no more than once a year at some ceremonial event. Hoover maintained his presentation of puncture-proof celibacy around serious churchgoing staffers like the impressionable DeLoach, who continues to be aghast at charges of sexual impropriety that flared up once the icon passed away.

There is some suggestion that the schizoid Director was attempting to conceal his overriding impulses even from himself. Affixed with yellowing Scotch tape to the slide-out board next to the kneehole in Hoover's battered interior desk was a carefully typed quotation ostensibly from—yes!—the Beat novelist Jack Kerouac:

> There was a man who believed that the highest you/
> could get on this planet, straight or stoned,/
> was to rock your loins in the loins of a beautiful woman who
> adored you, who could share your/
> madness and even your sanity,
> and who could play your [unreadable], call
> your bluff, chase your blues, undo
> you. With that you could play table-stakes poker with
> Alexander the Great.

> —JACK KEROUAC
> *On the Road,* 1955

These verses are not to be found in Kerouac's book, yet they somehow provided a kind of apotheosis the world-weary Director obviously *wishes* was out there for him, a conventional domestic answer to a lifetime of maneuvering, overwork, and constant, grinding tension. Whenever he was questioned about why he never married, the long-suffering bureaucrat brought up his tired smile and explained gallantly that he would certainly have preferred that, but what with his life of combating nefarious criminals along with noxious foreign elements he was in constant, dreadful danger. No wife should ever be put through all the worry. . . . To suggest to visitors what he was sacrificing, he liked to point out his studio portrait of Dorothy Lamour, all sultry and blooming in a low-cut lace-trimmed dress. "To Edgar," the inscription runs, "With my sincere admiration and friendship—Dottie."

Like glossies of Gene Tunney and Jack Dempsey and Joe DiMaggio hobnobbing with the Director, the Lamour photograph was intended to reassure spectators—Hoover not least of all—that the Boss was absolutely normal. Visitors to the antique-jammed Dutch colonial at Thirtieth Place he moved into when Annie finally died in 1938 often remarked at the big, framed Marilyn Monroe poster overhanging the stairwell down to his recreation room. Few discovered outside, in Hoover's "secret garden," his collection of statues of idealized young nude men, the afternoon sun dappling their buttocks through the surrounding foliage. . . .

One prominent psychoanalyst has categorized Hoover as "a bisexual, with a failed heterosexuality. . . ." In 1946, the Director consulted a prominent diagnostic clinic in Washington and wound up in the hands of the well-known psychiatrist Dr. Marshall de G. Ruffin. Ruffin's widow would assure Robbyn Summers—interviewing for the blockbuster that seared into the world's consciousness the spectacle of Edgar in a ruffled gown—that Hoover "was definitely troubled by homosexuality, and my husband's notes would have proved that . . . everybody then understood he was homosexual, not just the doctors." Furtively, Hoover had consulted Ruffin over the years, the last time shortly before he died, in 1971.

In *Official and Confidential,* Anthony Summers comes up with witnesses (several identified, others anonymous) who insist that they watched Hoover disporting with boys. Most of the headlines came out of Summers's interviews in France with his principal source, Susan Rosenstiel, the divorced fourth wife of the Supreme Commander. Throughout her extended testimony before the New York State Legislative Committee on Crime, which remains sealed, Susan had elaborated on the extent of her ex-husband's chronic association with the premier underworld personalities of the era, from Meyer Lansky to Sam Giancana.

Along with a bevy of apologists and manipulators for the reactionary right from Roy Cohn and George Sokolsky to Francis Cardinal Spellman, most of the board members of the national criminal syndicate appeared at one time or another at parties and testimonial dinners sponsored by the heavyweight at Schenley's. Hoover showed up regularly, almost always without Tolson, and at some point during 1958 Susan Rosenstiel insists that she was dragged by her husband to the infamous get-together hosted by Roy Cohn in "a beautiful suite . . . all done in light blue" at the Plaza in Manhattan at which the Director of the FBI confronted her in false eyelashes and a black wig, his short legs crossed demurely beneath his fluffy hemline. A follow-up orgy allegedly featured the Director in a feathered boa, involved with a couple of sleek young street hustlers in a maneuver requiring—this *was* squeamish old Hoover, after all—*rubber gloves!*

Susan Rosenstiel's account of Hoover in his transvestite manifestation raised hackles even with inveterate Hoover detractors like Peter Maas, in part because as Summers indicates, Susan ultimately would be sent up for perjury. Summers notes that New York Crime Committee officials believed that the charge was instigated by the powerful Rosenstiel to obstruct the committee's inquiry. Hoover never appreciated risk, and the starchy Director crossdressing and chicken-hawking in a large party in a suite in the Plaza was hard to envisage. But sexual urgency is sexual urgency, and the years were passing.

Hoover scholars tend to discount allegations that Hoover was *flamboyantly* gay. Professor Athan Theoharis dwells on the ferocity with which the Director had his cohorts bullyrag the aristocratic Richmond-bred CIA officer Joseph Bryan III in 1952 when Bryan told guests at a dinner party that Hoover "had a crush on a friend of theirs and had made advances to him several times; when it was found out that no progress could be made," Hoover had "turned him in." Outraged, Hoover ordered that Bryan "be made to put up or shut up. I want no effort to be spared to call his bluff and promptly." After threats and counterthreats, Bryan reneged and the matter died. Every effort was initiated immediately to discredit all charges. Disinformation efforts survived Hoover. A summary of KGB files by Christopher Andrew and Vasili Mitrokhin would have it that all those crossdressing rumors originated with the KGB's Service A in Moscow.

Despite efforts at every level to explain away the scandalous stories, enough kept breaking loose to suggest that Summers was on to something. A feature by Murray Weiss in the *New York Post* of February 11, 1993 documents the 1966 probe of an extortion ring by Manhattan District Attorney Frank Hogan's Rackets Squad. "The Chicken and the Bulls," as the extortionists called themselves, sent young men into hotel and airport bars to proposition distinguished-looking male visitors and lead them to hotel rooms. Other members of the gang would burst in posing as police detectives and shake the victims down. Organized by Sherman Kaminsky and Edward Murphy, the gang entrapped a wide range of educators and entertainers, a lot of military brass—one admiral, William Church, killed himself rather than risk disclosure—and the prominent congressman Peter Frelinghuysen. A photo turned up of Hoover himself "posing amiably" with Kaminsky, while Clyde Tolson had reportedly "fallen victim to the extortion ring."

At some point the FBI jumped into the investigation. Hoover's picture disappeared from the files and Kaminsky went underground, subsisting for eleven years in Denver raising rabbits and distributing wigs. One of Hoover's gifts was for retrofitting reality.

One corroboratory sidelight turned up when New York attorney John Klotz began to investigate Roy Cohn on behalf of a client. Declassified New York government files and spadework by a private detective substantiated the allegation that there was indeed a "blue suite" at the Plaza, Suite 233. "Roy Cohn was providing protection," Klotz discovered. "There were a bunch of pedophiles involved. That's where Cohn got his power from—blackmail." Like scorpions investigating coitus, Roy Cohn and J. Edgar Hoover would continue to circle each other with wary fascination for decades.

Even during the Roosevelt administration, the feasibility of two middle-aged bachelors soldiering chastely together through the decades went down a little hard. This skepticism was augmented by Hoover's doggedness about getting the sexual goods on everybody else. Presidents starting with FDR could warm up the afternoon poring over Hoover's gleanings. Edgar was a smut-hound, but he was *their* smut-hound, and it was better to keep him out there nosing up his treasures.

Hoover's choicest discoveries were sequestered in his inner office and tended by the vigilant Miss Gandy. There was an elaborate punctilio of cross-coding and timed destruction by the dreaded field office inspectors of the carbons temporarily retained by the local agents, of blue flimsies and white flimsies, of periodic follow-up sanitization. Touchiest were the Symbol

Number Sensitive Source Index and the Surreptitious Entries file. The Obscene File dated back to 1925. The surviving 167 Personal and Official and Confidential file folders represented a remarkable distillation, the most precious, most world-shattering dirt.

After all the strutting, the sermonizing, the outright blackmailing and the clandestine peepshows, the crust of sexuality around Bureau headquarters got scraped exceedingly thin. Disastrous breakthroughs could occur at any moment. Norman Ollestad, a recent recruit, remembered bumping into Sam Noisette, the chunky black factotum who put in decades as the Director's receptionist. Away from Hoover, Sam left out the obsequious body language and darky locutions the Director expected. After a few words, Ollestad wondered whether, once he was assigned to the field, "Are they still going to be watching us in the head?"

Sam said they wouldn't. After determining that Ollestad probably was not a "torpedo," somebody entrapping the unwary for the headquarters insiders, Noisette divulged that Hoover was on the lookout for *queers:* "The truth of the matter is that the boss doesn't understand *queers,* but he's scared to death of them, and that's why they watch you fellahs in the head."

Bad publicity? Ollestad wondered. Security risks? Subject to blackmail?

"If you want the truth," Sam said, "the big thing is that *queers* are just like some colored folk—they been fightin' all their lives. Fightin' and hidin' so much that they've just given up and they ain't got nothing to lose any more so they aren't scared of nothin'. The boss can't mold people like that. And that's the thing that scares him most."

During daylight hours, Hoover's apprehension about "perverts" had a way of tincturing the reports he disseminated. They included, according to Curt Gentry's account, "allegations of the two homosexual arrests which Hoover leaked to help defeat a witty, urbane Democratic presidential candidate [Adlai Stevenson]; surveillance reports on one of America's best-known first ladies and her alleged lovers, both male and female, white and black [Eleanor Roosevelt]; the child molestation documentation the director used to control and manipulate one of his Red-baiting protégés [Joseph McCarthy]. . . ." Inevitably, there was a file drawer on the Kennedys.

Sometimes Hoover's floating animosity tended to attach itself to one of his victims. Increasingly alarmed that Eleanor Roosevelt's concern for the Negro was likely to churn up social disorder, Hoover tiptoed into the subject with FDR. "The president says the old bitch is going through the change of life and we'll just have to put up with her," Hoover sighed to one of his lieutenants afterward. At times he jokingly held up Eleanor Roosevelt as the reason he never married. Dropping in on the flustered comedian W. C. Fields, Hoover managed to extort from him three miniature cameos of Eleanor Roosevelt reversed, turned into anatomical caricatures of the female genitalia. Hoover liked to pull them out to break up selected visitors to his basement recreation room.

This sort of hypermasculine good time got refreshed by the category of literature that Hoover otherwise reviled as "public desecration of every sacred symbol." Deke DeLoach cites assistant director William Sullivan's charge that, rummaging through the Director's desk one night, he found "lurid literature of the most filthy kind . . . naked women and lurid magazines with all sorts of abnormal sexual activities." DeLoach attempts to detoxify this by insisting that "everyone who knew the two men were well aware of their interest in women, their locker-room banter, their enjoyment of a good off-color joke." But things went way beyond that. Deep in the printing section of Crime Records was a screening theater, the so-called "blue room," where Hoover, Tolson, and selected senior officials studied surveillance footage and pornographic films. Nearby, harvested by the Special Operations Group, incriminating still prints and film and audiotapes were looked after with great care.

An element of affectionate sadism conditioned even the Director's highly touted practical jokes. The butt of many of them was Julius Lulley, the proprietor of Harvey's restaurant. Ray Wannall, a lifer who wound up as head of the Intelligence Division, remembers an elaborate send-up which kept Lulley pinned down for days in the Ambassador Hotel in Los Angeles, euchred by a switchboard ruse into the notion that Hoover and Tolson were drifting around somewhere in the monumental hotel and eager to get together. Only when Lulley was standing in his room over an elaborate brunch of Hoover's favorites—"sausages, eggs, Nova Scotia salmon, and bagels"—did Hoover finally get on the line to cackle that brunch was out of the question, since "You are in Los Angeles and we are on the beach in Atlantic City."

Invited to the Lulley farm, Hoover arranged for posters with Julius's picture to be nailed to trees on all the approach roads printed WANTED BY THE FBI. Another time, Hoover—always the ostentatious gallant—listened while Mrs. Lulley begged her husband for a fur coat while Julius kept insisting that such a gift was out of the question, too much money, the restaurant wasn't having that wonderful a season. . . .

When Lulley was gone for a few minutes, his wife continued to complain to Hoover. "Leave it to me," the Director reassured her. The next time Lulley went to New York, Hoover had his agents shadow the restaurateur as he escorted his mistress to dinner and joined her for the night in her apartment. Just as the two were about to step through the door, Lulley embraced the woman and Hoover's agents sneaked pictures.

Since Hoover and Tolson usually ate—gratis—at Harvey's, it wasn't long before Lulley stopped by their table for a chat. "Is your wife still interested in that fur coat?" Hoover asked his host.

"Really, Edgar, I can't afford that."

Hoover handed Lulley the photographs of himself and his mistress. His wife got the coat she was after the next week.

Apart from putting everybody's adoration level to the test with stunts like these, Hoover's pranks suggest how unthinkingly he cast himself in the role of the Fates, those mythological goddesses who reached in and reordered human events. FBI veterans like Robert Maheu would revere Hoover for authorizing a long compassionate assignment to Maine when his wife was sick, while other favorites like DeLoach never forgot showing up at a hospital to face a crippling $1,800 bill, only to be told that he had nothing to worry about, "your bill was paid by J. Edgar Hoover." In time, with ever-augmented power, Hoover began to identify with—and assume responsibility for—the entire society. In that direction lay megalomania.

While technically a division chief within the Justice Department, by the Truman years Hoover conceived of himself and his FBI as the unmoved mover behind everything of importance in Washington. Attorneys general came and went—presidents came and went—but the FBI abided. By now, Hoover accorded himself a level of bureaucratic self-indulgence that would have made Harry Truman redden. Hoover's crochets were table talk around postwar Washington. The Director traveled like the tsar in *Dead Souls*. His armored Cadillac was flown out ahead of him, a platoon of agents met his plane and dealt with the luggage, in his hotel a basket of fruit and flowers and a fifth each for himself and Tolson of the appropriate whiskey was to be waiting in his suite, courtesy of the panic-stricken local special agent in charge, who passed the hat.

At one point the Director's chauffeur-driven limousine was rear-ended turning left and Hoover, traveling behind the driver, was severely shaken up. After that he insisted that nobody who drove him could make a left turn, a requirement that could make a trip in from the airport last an afternoon. This left Tolson sitting in what Hoover now referred to as the "death seat" with Hoover's fedora perched in the window behind him. If anybody took a shot, he was expected to plug Tolson.

* * *

With the Cold War taking on more gravity every month by then, Hoover found himself either way ahead of or way behind the curve. All through the New Deal, with FDR regarding Communists in and around the government as at worst a nuisance, Hoover pedaled very softly, planting informants and watching but keeping his head down and waiting for the wind to change. Most of the headlines on the Red Menace went to Martin Dies, whose House Un-American Activities Committee had deputized itself to poke into everything from local sit-down strikes to the federal theater program. Dies was a nativist showboater from East Texas with a big hank of yellow hair and a florid pig-farmer's face. When Dies first attempted to borrow investigators from the Bureau in 1938, Hoover turned him away and wrote Dies off as suffering from "great delusions of personal grandeur." By 1941, with war in the offing, Dies put the word out that he was compiling a list of people he wanted to see detained in case of hostilities. This was an FBI function. "Now that the hunt is on I imagine the OGPU agents will sit and wait for Buck Dies and his merry men to arrive," Hoover chortled in a memo.

FBI turf was endangered. Another threat was Wild Bill Donovan, the cosmopolitan Buffalo Irishman the British were promoting to hash together some sort of foreign intelligence capacity for Roosevelt. This was a role Hoover had in mind for the Bureau—there were already FBI listening posts in Central and South America—but Donovan's Office of Strategic Services (OSS) rolled straight over that. Hoover spread the word that it was rife with lefties and waged a low-grade war of attrition, stirring up a raiding party of newspapermen pounding along behind Walter Trohan of the *Chicago Tribune* to scare the rookie president, Harry Truman, with stories that Donovan intended to perpetuate an "American Gestapo."

Truman folded the OSS in September 1945, but two years later, desperate for intelligence coordination, he authorized the Central Intelligence Agency. As Hoover vociferously judged such matters, the CIA was the worst way to meet the emergency: a collection of ornate, amoral socialites who would be impossible to eyeball while they perpetrated their mischief abroad. Calling on his water-carriers in Congress, Hoover had been able to get authorization for a smattering of FBI "Legal Attaches" throughout many of the world capitals to coordinate with law enforcement abroad; but, consequent to the establishment of the CIA, further international ambitions would have to be maintained on hold. A story made the rounds in Washington asserting that CIA counterespionage maven Jim Angleton had picked up some snapshots originally in the possession of gangland braintruster Meyer Lansky which featured the Director being serviced by the ever-dedicated Tolson.

In any investigative organization the keys were obedience and oversight, and since the war Hoover had been stocking his Bureau with unimaginative stand-up Catholics, almost every reliable soul so dedicated, as Joe Schott put it, that "If the Director told him to eat a pound of horse shit, he'd just ask, 'Where's the spoon?'"

The headquarters in particular got a government-wide reputation for bringing on ulcers, early congestive heart failure, and colitis. With such unstinting troops one fought the long-deferred battle against the East.

Ever since he faced down the monster Emma Goldman, Hoover had been hardening himself for the inevitable confrontation with the collectivist Antichrist "Commoonism," as he habitually mispronounced it. In his divided spirit, everything he attempted was to protect the American heritage. He would look away while his second-story adepts violated the Fourth Amendment and broke into a suspect's house to install a bug, and yet he would also insist on the same suspect's Sixth Amendment rights to counsel and a speedy resolution. He felt that the incarceration of the West Coast Japanese in 1942 was ill-advised and unnecessary. He emoted behind closed doors against the dropping of the atomic bomb.

We must not become like them. What came to madden Hoover, certainly during Roosevelt's tenure and, after that, once Truman settled into office, was the seeming insouciance in Washington when it came to subversion even inside the government. That pudgy autodidact Whittaker Chambers had been conducted into FBI headquarters as early as March 1941 to recite his tale of a spy ring among the well-connected. The disillusioned—and all-loved-out—Elizabeth Bentley showed up in August 1945 with 150 names, 40 government employees. A month later, the Soviet cipher clerk Igor Gouzenko surrendered to the Mounties with specifics about the Soviet program to pilfer atom-bomb secrets. Washington was not alarmed. Hoover was in torment, and speeches he started making left no doubt. "By spreading its poison through young veins, gangrenous Communism is attempting to render the future generation of Americans a quadruple amputee," he rattled forth, "—a nation without freedom of speech, press, assembly, or religion. The youth of this nation, armed with the scalpel of truth, can and must cut this disease from the body of America!"

He himself certainly intended to cut. But he would require fresh allies.

Not long after that, Joe McCarthy reared up in the Senate.

5

Tail Gunner Joe

Jack Kennedy and Joe McCarthy both started in the Congress in the Class of 1946. A wan, hollow-cheeked freshman among the far-flung colleagues—"We were just worms in the House," he would sum it up afterward—Kennedy looked out where he could for the Massachusetts Eleventh District and hoarded his energy for the demands of private life.

McCarthy was something else. He had arrived in Washington while it was still raw from the upheaval of war, essentially a midsize Southern company town, much of it black. McCarthy stood out immediately because he was so young—at thirty-eight, he was the youngest member of the Senate—and because he was so crude. In Wisconsin McCarthy had barnstormed the state to snatch the Republican nomination away from Robert La Follette Jr., heir to a great progressive tradition. McCarthy built his image as a farm boy and an ex-Marine, a straight shooter and a plain talker. America's brawler. You would, observed Alice Roosevelt Longworth, "be glad to have someone like Joe McCarthy on your side if you were in a big row or a street fight. I think he'd throw paving stones very well—awful things."

As a political property, McCarthy was self-made—self-invented, really—with something of the appeal of the compassionate charlatan, the type who bluffed you out and then let you in on the con. He could be funny—irreverent, iconoclastic—and, when you expected it least, generous and forgiving. In rigidly stratified Washington, he always kept treats in his pockets for the community's mutts—ex-FBI types, newspapermen, and aides on the rise.

Because he was one himself. He was a fraud and he knew it—relished it, capitalized on it, inflated it until it became his style. Challenged, he counter-attacked, bullied, drowned every studied refutation in a dense spray of countercharges. As a personal tactic, this worked for a while, but as a strategy it was imbecilic. It destroyed him early, and undoubtedly he knew it would.

McCarthy lived his short life in rich, manic spurts. Playmates would remember Joe as a magnetic, hyperactive kid around the family farm near Appleton, habitually in the thick of things with no awareness of upshots or consequences. Poorly coordinated, he was forever fracturing an ankle or smashing up his nose, only to climb back on the motorcycle for another header or into the ring for one more round. Poor, distracted, he never bothered with high school, throwing all his energies into building up his chicken business until he was trucking two thousand laying hens and ten thousand broilers to the Chicago stockyards before he turned twenty. Suddenly, looking up, Joe decided he'd need an education and finagled a schedule that got him four years of high-school credit in nine months.

By then a muscular youngster with emphatic black-Irish looks, McCarthy arrived at Marquette University and made himself felt. Studying when he had to, he became a habitué of all-night poker games and the scourge of intramural boxing. His coach would remember him as slow but fearless, "not a particularly good puncher," and inclined to "charge an opponent with a flurry of blows, not worrying about a defense." Few could really deal with that, although a well-trained boxer could take Joe apart. Classmates remember the time his donkey balked during a donkey baseball game, and Joe hoisted the two-hundred-pound beast and carted it in his arms to first base.

He'd already discovered that getting talked about paid dividends. After two years in the engineering school McCarthy switched to law and graduated in 1935. He hung a shingle out on the main street of tiny Waupaca, thirty miles west of Appleton, and, finding clients both poor and scarce, attempted to save himself by partnering up with a local politico. But politics is contagious, and by 1936 McCarthy himself was running locally for district attorney. He mounted a slam-bam attack on the opposition riddled with misstatements which nobody bothered to challenge. By 1939 Joe had identified a vulnerable local circuit judge, converted to the Republican Party, and prevailed after a brutal campaign that kept Joe stomping around barnyards mounting an assault based on his opponent's age. McCarthy became a judge at thirty.

Recently opened records reveal that most of his cases involved divorce or domestic abuse. McCarthy was an understanding judge, if reduced, according to his colleague Urban Van Susteren, to bluffing through each case knowing "nothing of the rules of evidence." As World War II progressed, he sensed that service in the military might enlarge his political future and took a leave of absence once he was sure of a direct commission in the Marines. In time, his war record would come to dog McCarthy. He reached the South Pacific late enough to miss the critical opening waves of combat and served as an intelligence officer, first in the New Hebrides and later on Guadalcanal, six months after serious resistance ended.

Essentially, Captain McCarthy put in his months overseas looking after paperwork and debriefing a squadron of pilots out on scouting and bombing missions. But the obstreperous judge was popular with the troops and soon promoted a very profitable liquor-smuggling operation while cleaning up during off-hours poker games. McCarthy went at poker the way he boxed—wild, lying low as the cards were dealt, then pushing out huge bets for odd amounts that baffled the others into folding when McCarthy had picked up little or nothing. For Joe, in general, this strategy worked.

As the months passed, McCarthy befriended the squadron's gunnery sergeant and let him in on his thoughts of running for senator. His campaign was likely to benefit from photos and stories linking him to combat. The sergeant was glad to oblige with a little off-hours instruction for the judge in firing the "twin thirties" the squadron's two-man dive-bombers used. During one exercise Joe riddled the tail of the plane. After McCarthy went out no more than eleven times, exclusively on low-risk "milk-runs" to mop up after bombing raids, photographing sometimes and sometimes happily pouring through so much lead at everything below the horizon—although never the enemy, according to a fellow officer—that he was greeted on his return from one mission with a placard proclaiming: PROTECT OUR COCONUT TREES. SEND MCCARTHY BACK TO WISCONSIN.

Later McCarthy would insist that he had been involved in the hazardous air strikes over Rabaul, but he was much too inexperienced and clumsy on send-out missions like that. Like his insistence that a scar on his ankle covered several pounds of shrapnel—in reality, McCarthy had stumbled down a ladder during a goofy equator-crossing ceremony and snapped a metatarsal—the exuberant captain's war record got reformulated every day.

In 1944 he wrote himself a commendation on which he contrived to get Admiral Nimitz's signature extolling his "excellent photographs of enemy gun positions" although "suffering from a severe leg injury." By 1952, still applying for new medals from the Marines, McCarthy would assert that he had flown thirty-two airstrikes, and so was awarded the Distinguished Flying Cross along with the Air Medal and four stars.

After thirty steamy months McCarthy was back in Appleton, weeks before the April 15 Republican primary. Campaigning around the state, he explained his limp alternately as the result of a combat mission, "an accident while helping remove a pregnant woman off a submarine," and the result of a plane crash. He had arranged to exit the war months before the bloody, final engagement at Okinawa.

McCarthy's principal challenge was to unseat the Progressive Republican Robert La Follette Jr. in the primary. A flaccid campaigner, La Follette Jr. let McCarthy and his businessmen backers blanket the state with 750,000 copies of a brochure detailing the judge's amazing—if largely fictional—wartime adventures. Communist organizers were still influential in the Milwaukee CIO, and in their determination to free the state from the Bolshevik-detesting LaFollette dynasty its leaders withheld their blue-collar members, while McCarthy was quoted in the press as having asserted that "Stalin's proposal for world disarmament is a great thing and he must be given credit for being sincere about it." "Communists have the same right to vote as anyone else, don't they?" McCarthy responded to reporters when the issue came up.

In the ensuing general campaign McCarthy's ads swayed ordinary people with punchy, compelling copy: "Joe McCarthy was a Tail Gunner in World War II. When the war began Joe had a soft job as a Judge at EIGHT GRAND a year. He was EXEMPT from military duty. He resigned his job to enlist as a PRIVATE in the MARINES. He fought on LAND and in the AIR all through the Pacific. He and millions of other guys kept you from talking Japanese. . . ."

See Joe. See Joe fight. This is as rudimentary as politics gets, but in Wisconsin that fall it worked. One rainy day in December 1946 McCarthy got off the train in Union Station in D.C. and found his way to an affordable hotel. Somehow, he drew press immediately; McCarthy generated features in *Life* and *The Saturday Evening Post* as the farm boy slugger who brought the La Follettes down. Tail Gunner Joe was on the scene.

Joe McCarthy was not the only rogue in the Class of '46. What made him special was his demonstrated willingness to keep battering away in the face of facts. Before Joe McCarthy discovered Communism, potentates around the American power structure discovered Joe.

By March 1947 McCarthy was speaking up on the Senate floor on behalf of commercial sugar users, cosponsoring a bill to end all sugar rationing. Officers with Pepsi-Cola were after him to abrogate the quotas so the company could ramp up supply; one affiliate signed a $20,000, six-month note for Joe at an Appleton bank. Supported by the real estate lobby, McCarthy lambasted public housing as "deliberately created slums" and "breeding grounds for Communism." He took $10,000 from Lustron, a fabricator of overpriced prefab kit homes, for putting his name to a pamphlet written by company employees and bureaucrats at the Federal Housing Authority. Joe's door was open, as was his hand.

Most notorious—most full of portent for the years coming up—was a series of inflamed Armed Services Committee hearings over the sentencing of the seventy-three SS defendants from the "Blowtorch Battalion" adjudged to have machine-gunned upward of one hundred twenty American prisoners near Malmedy in Belgium on December 17, 1944, during the Battle of the Bulge. By 1949 most death sentences had been reduced, but several of the ex-SS prisoners now maintained to journalists that their confessions had been coerced. McCarthy, who exploited senatorial privilege to sit in on the hearings, thundered to the onlookers that "There will be testimony here to the effect that of the 139 men who were sentenced to die about 138 were irreparably damaged, being crippled for life, from being kicked or kneed in the groin."

As the testimony developed, it turned out that these rumors were entirely fallacious. Never intimidated by the evidence, McCarthy piled into the Army's top interrogator: "Is it true you couldn't have convicted a man unless you beat the hell out of him in a cell?"

"Wait a minute there."

"I am going to get this from you if I have to keep you here a week." .

Senator Lester Hunt of Wyoming, a bona fide member of the Armed Services Committee, broke in despite himself: "Let's be more courteous with the witness. Let's not attempt any browbeating."

Behind this display of pugnacity with the Army's lawyers, McCarthy was playing to his top industrial sponsor back home, Walter Harnischfeger, head of the giant industrial equipment and prefab housing manufacturer. A notorious, unembarrassed bigot, close to the German-American Bund, Harnischfeger had been lobbying for his Nazi counterparts since V-E Day. A leader among the seventy deep-pocketed businessmen who originally backed McCarthy, he continued to regard Tail Gunner Joe as his personal protégé. By 1947, already surviving on personal loans, McCarthy was writing his banker in Appleton that "I have made complete arrangements with Walter Harnischfeger ... to put up sufficient collateral to cure both our ulcers. ..."

Another experienced sharpshooter who had started to keep an eye on McCarthy was Joseph P. Kennedy. McCarthy's was a high-maintenance lifestyle; he would welcome support. By the midforties, Joe Kennedy was emerging little by little from the paralyzing depression brought on by the death of his namesake and heir apparent, Joseph P. Kennedy Jr. Leery of the postwar stock market, Kennedy took a tip from Archbishop Francis Spellman and entered into a long collaboration with the roistering, well-connected Manhattan real estate agent John J. Reynolds. A militant Republican, Reynolds handled the Church's property. Kennedy picked up at bottom-dollar wartime prices a wide array of midtown buildings, always highly leveraged and very often distressed, and within a few years cranked up his net worth from perhaps $20 million to $100 million.

In 1945 Kennedy bought Chicago's Merchandise Mart, the world's largest commercial building, twenty-four stories with ninety-three acres of rentable space. Risking little of his own capital, Kennedy arranged a mortgage through the Equitable Life Assurance Society and took possession of what was widely regarded as a gigantic white elephant, weighted down with government leases. It was to become the core family holding.

Kennedy turned the Merchandise Mart profitable by working every lever of power. Having purchased the gigantic property for just under $13 million, Kennedy was shortly to borrow $19 million against the valuation and, on James Landis's recommendation, laid off a quarter of the debt onto the Joseph P. Kennedy Jr. Foundation. Then he retained lawyer-lobbyist Thomas Corcoran—"Tommy the Cork"—to activate his insider contacts in Congress and around the Treasury Department to push through construction of an additional federal building in Chicago. With so much new space available, the government relieved Kennedy of his unprofitable leases, over a third of the valuable commercial footage. Kennedy's net worth jumped by many millions, although when Corcoran billed the ambassador $75,000 for his services he would receive a check for $25,000, take it or leave it.

Joe Kennedy had now decided to dump his liquor distributorship, Somerset Importers. Until 1944, Somerset had been run day to day by Ted O'Leary and Tom Delahanty, carryovers from the grand old hit-and-run bootlegging era. Kennedy had already started breaking in the Connecticut attorney Thomas J. Cassara, a smooth operator with wide experience owning and managing hotels around Miami Beach. But Cassara was unexpectedly shot to death in the Trade Winds nightclub in East Chicago in 1944, apparently attempting to pry open the market for Haig and Haig without permission from the Outfit.

The Kefauver hearings in 1950 would develop the awkward facts that Cassara had been a front man for the Mob all along, that one of his business partners on the side was Rocco DeStefano, Al Capone's cousin, and that he had been gunned down shortly after putting together a distribution deal with another Capone-gang alumnus, Joe Fusco. If any of this ever made it into the papers, it was not going to help Jack Kennedy's much-ballyhooed political debut.

Not without mixed feelings, in 1946 Joe Kennedy sold Somerset to Joe Reinfeld and Abner "Longie" Zwillman for $8 million. After twenty-five years in Kennedy's service, many of them on the exposed edge of the bootlegging business, Ted O'Leary found himself on the street with a $25,000 severance bonus. "I don't think the parting was too cordial," O'Leary's son told Ronald Kessler. The aging Horseman had apparently been given to understand that he would get a piece of the enterprise, since usually "Joe was off doing other things."

With Somerset went up to $1 million a year in profits and a warehouse packed with aging fine Scotch. Reinfeld was a semireformed rumrunner, but the New Jersey–based Zwillman was a gangster of national importance, with a seat on The Commission, an investment partner of Frank Costello and Chicago's Tony Accardo, a major hood with panache enough to keep Jean Harlow as a mistress. During the bootlegging years, Longie's thugs and Kennedy's thugs had repeatedly shot it out. But business was business.

Heavily invested in Chicago, Kennedy began to probe cautiously for the pressure points. In time, he would become so tight with Mayor Daley that His Honor could all but write checks on Kennedy's Chicago account. The heirs of Al Capone continued to dominate the rackets, and according to Sam—Mooney—Giancana's brother, at no stage was Joe Kennedy above making an appearance when he needed to ask a favor or take the heat off himself.

Joe Kennedy was rich enough now to capitalize on the fact that not only could elections be bought; influence could be bought. As the younger Kennedy began to find his way a little in Congress, Joe Kennedy looked over Jack's more susceptible acquaintances. Pious, nerved-up Dick Nixon had an office across the hall and liked to saunter over and bat around the issues of the day with Jack. The dapper George Smathers—who managed before long to eject Florida's liberal Claude Pepper from his Senate seat with much the sort of calculated Red-baiting that Nixon exploited against

Helen Gahagan Douglas—turned into an irreverent after-hours companion for Jack, a couple of unattached pols prowling for chicks. Joe Kennedy had a knack for involving himself with his sons' promising friends, and before long he came up with major donations under the table for each of them when they ran for the Senate—$150,000 for Nixon, according to Tip O'Neill, and $125,000 for Smathers.

Joe McCarthy couldn't help but catch the canny Ambassador's eye. Later, McCarthy would claim that he and Jack had gone for a PT-boat ride together and Jack had included him on night-patrol missions along the Bougainville coast and even let him shoot those irresistible machine guns. This doesn't seem likely—John Kennedy later denied having run into McCarthy that early—but reality for McCarthy had a way of filling itself in. What seems to be plain enough is that Joe Kennedy made contact quite soon after McCarthy arrived in Washington and started to pump important financial resources into his career.

Kennedy's logic is easy enough to follow. In many ways, Wisconsin remains provincial to Chicago; farsighted to nail down a senator he could talk to any time he needed a tax break on some appropriations bill or a rider helpful to the Merchandise Mart. Furthermore, McCarthy would guarantee entree, somebody inside the system. His performances for Pepsi-Cola and Harnischfeger demonstrated that he would battle for his supporters. For all McCarthy's show of rough-talking independence, Kennedy sensed how needy this free-swinging farm boy remained.

A lot of McCarthy's impact came out of his ability at close quarters to present himself as a warm-hearted Irish slob—yet at the same time a slob who could hurt you very badly if he decided to. "He was very alert, very smart, also mean and vindictive," Drew Pearson had soon concluded. "One time he threatened to mutilate me so I couldn't go on television." In the face of this, a lot of the colleagues had started to take Joe seriously. During one investigation, Stuart Symington discovered that McCarthy was about to frame one of his personal friends. "Joe, this is no good," the courtly Missourian warned McCarthy. "So I'm going to have to take you on."

"Don't do it, Stu," McCarthy recommended. "If you do I'll destroy you, and I'm fond of you."

McCarthy's mixture of goose grease and pugnacity appealed to Joe Kennedy. The aging Ambassador was evolving his own foreign policy. In speeches and articles, he urged the country to withdraw from the Cold War, let the Russians have Western Europe and whatever else they thought they wanted rather than succumbing to the temptation to "fritter away" our strength. We were not suited temperamentally for empire, and in the end the cost would prove "an overwhelming tax on our resources."

Meanwhile, Kennedy was plumping for a rabid anti-Communism at home. Drew Pearson unearthed evidence of one early strategy meeting in Hyannis Port attended by McCarthy, Cardinal Spellman, and the rebounding financier. The cherubic Spellman—already a key operative in the Postwar Papist Cominform—was in regular touch with J. Edgar Hoover and Ngo Dinh Diem, the devout Catholic Mandarin the church and the CIA were incubating at Maryknoll Seminary and later in Lakewood, New Jersey, in expectation of his return to Vietnam.

As early as 1945, Joe Kennedy had been inducted into the Vatican's Sovereign Military Order, the Knights of Malta, an elite organization of ten thousand superinfluential Catholic men, founded a millennium earlier and ranging from James J. Angleton to Nazi bigwigs like Hitler's one-time Soviet specialist and leader of Adenauer's secret service, Reinhard Gehlen, and Franz von Papen and Hjalmar Schacht. This membership gave Kennedy diplomatic immunity; his private papers bristle with plans to drop in on Konrad Adenauer and Francisco Franco along with the late Goering's top economist Helmut Wohltat and Irish prime minister Eamon de Valera.

At Spellman's urging, the monastic Diem himself visited the Hyannis Port residence and became something of a friend of the family. Tommy Corcoran—looking out tirelessly for Chiang Kai-Shek as he promoted Civil Air Transport in collaboration with CIA cutout Whitey Willauer—let Kennedy in the back door as the China Lobby took on proportion. Senate insiders insist off the record that Chiang, along with Generalissimo Franco, turned into important funding sources not only for the willing Right but also for the conservative-minded young Jack Kennedy.

Except for their disagreement on the need to defend Europe, Jack Kennedy's outlook was still disappointingly close to his father's. "In January 1949," Thomas Reeves has written, "more than a year before McCarthy's Wheeling speech, Kennedy had attacked the policies of 'the Lattimores and [China expert] John Fairbanks,' the Yalta accords, and George Marshall. In November 1950 he told a Harvard University class that he supported the McCarran Internal Security Act, that he lacked great respect for Dean Acheson, and that he was very happy about Richard Nixon's defeat of Helen Gahagan Douglas." Furthermore, young Kennedy knew Joe McCarthy "pretty well, and he may have something."

Jack Kennedy was sounding off from sheet music provided by the China Lobby. The cry was abroad to hunt the traitors down responsible for the collapse of Chiang Kai-Shek's government on the mainland, to make somebody pay for the loss of China. A pack of attack columnists, mostly for the Hearst publications and the *Chicago Tribune*—Westbrook Pegler, George Sokolsky, Walter Winchell, Walter Trohan, Fulton Lewis Jr.—now thought they knew which names to name, many handed over quietly to friendly press and selected members of Congress by Louis Nichols, J. Edgar Hoover's publicity bagman.

Congressman Kennedy's career so far wasn't picking up a lot of altitude. He'd been a foot soldier in the campaign to push through the Wagner-Ellender-Taft Bill, underwriting fifteen million new homes, mostly for veterans, even in the face of American Legion complaints. He opposed the Taft-Hartley Act by bullyragging leftist union functionaries, pressing for names and Communist affiliations, before Nixon closed in on Alger Hiss. But Kennedy's involvement was day-to-day, desultory; his secretary of the period remembers him as whiling away many of his afternoons passing a football back and forth with his administrative assistant, Ted Reardon, then loading her down on weekends with leftover work.

Kennedy had set himself up in a three-story rowhouse in Georgetown with his family's hulking cook, Margaret Abrose, and Billy Sutton, his off-the-streets aide-de-camp. The place was disorderly, yesterday's discarded clothes trailing along the halls and some lady's briefs peeking out from under a sofa cushion. He himself looked disconcertingly young, like a wasted adolescent who had to drag himself hand over hand up and down the stairs because his back was getting more agonizing every month. Dispirited, he hired George Thomas, a black retainer most recently in Arthur Krock's employ, as a personal valet.

Before long, Jack's sister Eunice had moved in. In part to keep an eye on her feckless brother for the Ambassador, Eunice had taken a post her father arranged as executive secretary of a Justice Department commission on juvenile delinquency. Another marginal survivor of the long forced march childhood turned into around the Kennedy household, Eunice—"puny Euny," among her heartless siblings—also suffered early from chronic stomach problems and no stamina, like Jack. Developing into something of a tomboy, she seemed excessively serious and grindingly purposeful, relieved by the family taste for whacko practical jokes. Before long in Washington she was bringing home a collection of teenage misfits for dinner; her brother ducked out the moment one showed up at the door.

Another dinner guest who had started to come around was Joe McCarthy. If worse came to worst, McCarthy sighed one day to his administrative assistant, he always could marry one of the Kennedy girls. There was an invigorating raffishness about Joe that had its appeal at times even to Jack, who picked his friends over carefully. McCarthy had a punishing, under-handed humor, he never minded absorbing a punch if he could land some-thing himself.

Flush sometimes with money, then broke, then handing it out until he'd lose it all one night on his knees in a crap game—McCarthy led a gypsy life through all his years in Washington. "He was like a stray dog," observed his boyhood friend Urban Van Susteren. "He'd stay three days at one place, three at another, four at another. He'd sleep on the couch, on the floor, on the porch—it didn't matter to him at all." At one point he rented a room from his AA, Ray Kiermas. Clothes meant little to Joe—he'd buy four cheap blue suits at a time off the rack, then wear them interchangeably, sweating through them on sultry days like shirts until they were all equally shiny and threadbare at the elbows.

He treated his body no differently. Increasingly flabby, short of breath, his thin lank hair receded early, whisky puffed his jowls up and sharpened his grainy features. Shifty anyhow, he became for a generation the personification of gimlet-eyed. McCarthy's sinuses rotted, his long, bumpy peat-trowel of a nose looked sharp enough to pry open anything. What had been once a lik-ing for a companionable beer or two turned into a drinking problem, dealt with by wolfing down a quarter pound of butter on his way out the door.

What exactly the Kennedys expected from their farmboy prodigy makes for interesting speculation. "I like Joe McCarthy," the Ambassador was frank to admit later. "I would see him when I went down to Washington, and when he was visiting in Palm Beach he'd come around to my house for a drink. I invited him to Cape Cod."

At least at first "I thought he'd be a sensation." But McCarthy overdid things, and often during weekends with the family his gusto and willing-ness to play along left him a setup for the raucous Kennedy lifestyle, a figure of fun.

Appearances were everything; nothing less than winning could satisfy the father—"A certain freezing stare from his steel-blue eyes over his wire-rimmed glasses," as one biographer put it, "was enough to make a child cower." During sailboat races on Nantucket Sound, the Ambassador would follow the older boys in his launch, "shouting out their mistakes." Yet he could also be so soliti-cious, so identified with their futures, that it was awful to let him down. No wonder that visitors as often as not helped pay the emotional price.

McCarthy got bounced around. He cracked a rib playing touch football;

after four quick errors at shortstop they threw him out of a softball game to shamble up the lawn, humiliated, and watch from the porch. His performance in the water was worse. "They gave him the boat treatment," Rose wrote Bobby Kennedy in 1950, "i.e., throwing him out of the boat, and then Eunice, in her usual girlish glee[,] pushed him under. To everybody's concern and astonishment, the Senator came up with a ghastly look on his face, puffing and paddling. The wonder of it all was that he did not drown on the spot because, you see, coming from Wisconsin he had never learned to swim. . . . However," Rose concluded, "I am sure they will never try anything like that on him again, although you can never tell."

Another weekend, "he went out on my boat," the Ambassador would remember, and "almost drowned swimming behind it but he never complained." McCarthy was "always pleasant, he was never a crab." At least, never to them. Another time, McCarthy got tangled in the painter of a sailboat; Jack dove in to try to save him. To one friend, after a particularly hectic weekend, McCarthy let a little of it out: "Christ, I came up there to rest!"

McCarthy amused Eunice—he was like junk food after the restrictive Kennedy diet—who dated him a few times, quite seriously at first. His personal tastes were simple throughout those bachelor years: a fast lay before he got too sloshed, often atop the bedroom coats. Eunice was a little too delicate for anything like that, so high-strung as an insomniac teenager that houseguests were alerted not to flush the toilet at night for fear of waking her up. Before long Eunice moved on to R. Sargent Shriver, a high-minded *Newsweek* editor who started out advising Joe Kennedy as to the publishability of Joe Junior's letters from Europe, then went on salary to consult with Eunice and help manage the Merchandise Mart. When they were married in 1953, McCarthy presented the couple with a silver cigarette box, inscribed "To Eunice and Bob, from one who lost." Meanwhile, McCarthy consoled himself with sisters Pat and Jean Kennedy. Jean remembered Joe's line of anti-Communist small talk, after which he "kissed very hard."

By then the old financier was calling, more often than McCarthy really liked, usually for a favor. "Remind me to check the size of his campaign contribution," McCarthy scrawled on a note to Roy Cohn during one conversation. "I'm not sure it's worth it." Other backers, less well known and far less demanding, were attracted now to McCarthy's noisy crusade.

One conservative who recognized McCarthy's potential was J. Edgar Hoover. Like the complicated Director, McCarthy was a self-made power player with a poorly disguised contempt for the Washington establishment. Tail Gunner Joe could come up with a string of rambunctious asides calculated to keep the starchy Director snorting. They met over lively dinners regularly at Harvey's. Both loved the ponies: By 1947 McCarthy was often the third passenger in Hoover's armor-plated Cadillac limousine headed out to Pimlico for the afternoon. When Edgar couldn't make it, McCarthy was free to use his box at Charles Town in West Virginia.

Whereas Hoover kept his betting under control, sticking with the $2 window unless one of Frank Costello's go-betweens like Walter Winchell passed along trustworthy Mob information, Joe McCarthy was one to get himself in very deep, fast. Gambling kept him broke. Acquaintances who ran into the senator at Laurel or Pimlico might anticipate that he would try and bum a fifty to keep the afternoon going.

Always helter-skelter financially, McCarthy had no hesitations when well-heeled supporters of Hoover came forward behind the scenes and offered to help out. Soon after the end of World War II, a cluster of super-rich, hard-right Texas wildcatters—Sid Richardson, Clint Murchison, Hugh Cullen, and H. L. ("Daddy") Hunt—had started to back political candidates and bankroll ultraconservative initiatives. Richardson and Murchison especially cultivated Hoover.

Another friend of Joe's was Lewis Rosenstiel. The bluff, imperious Rosenstiel (known to his entourage as the "Supreme Commander"), another ex-bootlegger gone legitimate to build a distillery fortune—Schenley's—had been introduced to Hoover by Joseph Kennedy and become an enthusiastic huckster for the FBI, coughing up the bulk of the capital to fund the J. Edgar Hoover Foundation. Rosenstiel was already patronizing the career of Roy Cohn when the cagey Manhattan lawyer was little more than a cocksure adolescent.

A 1953 photograph survives which features Hoover and Tolson in slacks and open shirts, vacation garb, leaning on their shuffleboard prods. It is August, halfway through the several months of summer vacation to which Clint Murchison sported the pair each year at his exclusive California luxury spa, Del Charro, near La Jolla. Del Charro was a short drive from Murchison's Del Mar horse track, where the wildcatter was introduced to Hoover in 1949. To justify these months, Hoover underwent his annual physical at the Scripps Clinic. Joe McCarthy, posing on the left, still has his necktie on and his hands in his pockets, sweat beading his temples, barely rolled into town.

At that point Del Charro was functioning as a sort of far-West neutral zone where important players of assorted reputations could put their feet up and transact business unobserved. Except for Jews—Roy Cohn was reportedly ushered out posthaste when McCarthy unknowingly brought him along—the rules of membership were loose. William Torbitt, a Texas lawyer who poked into the business dealings of the Murchison crowd, maintains in an unpublished monograph that visitors to the compound between 1953 and 1963 included Al Capone's sidekick Johnnie Drew, Boston racketeer Joe Linsey (a productive early contact of Joseph P. Kennedy), "John Connally, Joe Bonanno, Carlos Marcello and other Mafia officers," all of whom "met constantly" with Hoover. Nixon dropped in, as well as senators Goldwater, Clinton Anderson, and George Smathers. A Murchison corporation, Del Hi-Taylor Oil Company, allegedly picked up "over $40,000" of Hoover's personal bills.

All this in addition to the three to four thousand dollars that Murchison comped Hoover to cover his and Tolson's residence in a posh bungalow on the grounds from mid-June to early September. Affronted, Hoover could become a trial. When the maitre d' refused to seat Hoover one evening because he made his appearance too late, Hoover pitched a historical tantrum and ordered the San Diego Bureau to round up the entire dining-room shift and grill the staff down to the last busboy as to the extent of their patriotism.

Summer after summer, Hoover continued to suffer from that combination of naïveté and indifference that characterized him in the presence of influential gangsters. He liked to breakfast before his morning at the track with Dub McClanahan, the gambler and part-time oilman who was in partnership with Carlos Marcello, the Mafia goombah throughout the Gulf. Another occasional conversationalist was the ubiquitous Johnny Rosselli, Joe Kennedy's regular golfing companion, the Mob's principal interface with authority from Los Angeles and Chicago to Las Vegas and Langley, Virginia. "I knew Hoover," Rosselli would confess cheerily enough during the years coming up. "I'd buy him drinks, and we'd talk. It would be fun to be with the Director of the FBI like that."

Carlos Marcello settled in for more than casual conversation. However witting, Hoover now found himself lounging around inside one of the principal junction boxes of organized crime. Strolling the Del Charro grounds, Hoover picked up with borderline lobbyists like Rosenstiel protégé Arthur Samish, the uncrowned king of the California legislature and an intimate of Frank Costello, as well the deft, fast-moving publicist I. Irving Davidson, who over the years had enlisted as clients (along with Murchison, the Somozas and the Duvaliers) Trujillo and Jimmy Hoffa. It was through Davidson that Murchison, strapped for the moment between gushers, arranged for a tremendous loan from the Teamsters' Central States Pension Fund. Through Hoffa, Marcello, along with several key figures in the Chicago syndicate, started to tap Teamster accounts to bankroll their investments in Havana and Las Vegas. Already humiliated by Robert Kennedy during his Rackets Committee days, a number of senior Mafia bosses would find themselves apprehensive that vital financing could get choked off once Kennedy became attorney general and activated his Get Hoffa Squad. But that was yet to come.

As Murchison's spokesman in Washington, Davidson stretched to placate the glory-hungry Director. Mobsters started lining up to contribute to the J. Edgar Hoover Foundation, most notoriously Yonnie Licavoli, whose philanthropic inclinations had long gone unnoticed throughout a career devoted largely to dusting contemporaries for the Purple Gang. The Hoover Foundation was dedicated to eliminating juvenile delinquency. The publishing house Murchison had acquired, Henry Holt, put out Hoover's ghostwritten books like *Masters of Deceit,* a profitable arrangement for everybody involved.

For Hoover himself, who demanded a controlled environment, the hijinks around La Jolla could get heady once in a while. Twenty years earlier, an aide had described the Director as a fastidious dresser, with a penchant for matching shades of Eleanor blue. "He is short, fat, businesslike, and walks with mincing steps," the aide revealed to a journalist. Years later, another former Hoover aide insisted that while the Boss didn't mince, he had "the smallest feet I've ever seen on a man." Whenever Edgar came barreling down the corridors, employees and visitors scattered to the sides, although from behind "His bottom—well, it sort of bounced."

At certain of the unbuttoned, alcohol-soaked revels outside La Jolla, Hoover's air of overweening self-importance didn't orchestrate too well. "Edgar," the famously uncouth Sid Richardson reportedly demanded one summer evening, "get off your fat ass and get me another bowl of chili." The chili had been flown in hot that afternoon from Texas. According to the Charro's manager just then, Allan Witwer, Hoover struggled onto his feet and complied.

Hoover's reaction under stress was either to machine-gun all opposition with a barrage of language or appear to go along without ever really implicating himself. Attempting to enlist the FBI Director into collaboration with the British Secret Service in 1940, Ian Fleming discovered a "chunky enigmatic man with slow eyes and a trap of a mouth," who heard his delegation out before expressing himself "firmly but politely as being uninterested in our mission.

"Hoover's negative response was soft as a cat's paw." Those long, hideaway summers at the Del Charro, Hoover needed to remind himself from time to time that he'd better overlook an indignity or two.

The obstreperous Joe McCarthy fit in much better. When McCarthy returned for his second visit in 1954, Allan Witwer found him all but out of control, "virtually on Murchison's payroll," and bound to amuse them all. "McCarthy was just a good-time Joe," as Witwer would recall. "He'd get drunk and jump in the pool, sometimes naked. He urinated outside the cabana, flew everywhere in Murchison's plane."

By 1954 Hoover was cooling on McCarthy, whose stunting with the facts during crucial Senate hearings was starting to endanger the anti-Communist cause. His Dionysian performances in California didn't help. After McCarthy married his attractive, strong-minded assistant Jean Kerr in 1953, Hoover and Tolson began stopping by the McCarthy flat for a pick-up dinner from time to time. But soon after the McCarthys and Edgar returned from the summer of 1954 in La Jolla, Deke DeLoach found the Director ready to write the senator off once and for all. One night Joe got himself skunked beneath the flickering torches that rimmed the central pool. Hoover groused that Joe had picked the quarrelsome Jean up and heaved her into the water. Elaborately chivalric since boyhood, Hoover was sorely tempted to let slide all social connection with the unruly senator.

6

Roy

Historians tend to concur that Joe McCarthy's career as a major-league Red-baiter opened with his speech in Wheeling, West Virginia, before the Ohio Country Women's Republican Club on February 9, 1950. "While I cannot take the time to name all of the men in the State Department who have been named as members of the Communist Party and members of a spy ring, I have here in my hand a list of 205 . . . that were known to the Secretary of State and who, nevertheless, are still working and shaping the policy of the State Department." What McCarthy actually had in his hand was his laundry list, and the number 205 came from a 1946 screening of employees at State on whom "damaging information had been uncovered." These included a woman said to entertain "Negroes and whites, both men and women, in her apartment," while others may have been drinkers or gamblers. Of the individuals he did identify, a majority were not currently with the Department, and some had never been.

Within a day, alighting in Salt Lake City, McCarthy had cut his list to 57 "card-carrying members of the Communist Party." By then his Wheeling speech was turning into something of a media event. A few days later, he assured reporters: "I've got a sockful of shit and I know how to use it."

As matters developed, he did. McCarthy had made anti-Communism his issue a few years after it came into vogue, well after the House Un-American Activities Committee started raking over witnesses and Klaus

Fuchs confessed to spying on the Manhattan Project and Alger Hiss got sent up for perjury. In July 1950, Julius Rosenberg was arrested on espionage charges and he and his wife, Ethel, would be convicted and sentenced to the electric chair the following April.

Interestingly enough, when his opinion was solicited by sentencing judge Irving Kaufman, J. Edgar Hoover urged that, in that she was a mother and a woman without previous convictions, Ethel's life be spared, since frying her might produce "a psychological reaction on the part of the public that might reflect poorly on the FBI." Just as, a decade earlier, Hoover had tried to prevent the incarceration of the West Coast Japanese, arguing that such might imply that the Bureau hadn't already tagged and numbered potential troublemakers, Hoover now was apprehensive that public reaction might blow back and scorch his operatives, who had been baying after the Red Threat since the early thirties.

Hoover had been especially irked with Harry Truman. In February 1946, Truman had refused to intervene to prevent the Senate from confirming Harry Dexter White as chief of the International Monetary Fund, a new instrumentality that White—along with John Maynard Keynes—had pretty much invented. While he was serving as assistant secretary of the treasury, most of White's friends, Hoover insisted, were parlor pinks, at least, and out-and-out agents of the KGB in a number of cases. Truman let the appointment go through.

On June 25, 1950, the army of North Korea invaded South Korea, and the United States was again at war. Like gallows, the prospect of youngsters coming home in boxes tends to concentrate a citizen's mind, and quite quickly the grumbling on the Right about who lost China and the goals of the Bolsheviks began to command public attention.

McCarthy's moment had struck. A career devoted largely to special pleading on behalf of Pepsi-Cola bottlers and unrepentant SS triggermen hadn't paid off very well so far. By consistently arguing against appropriations for NATO and Point Four and the Marshall Plan to placate his isolationist backers, McCarthy had in effect supported the standard Moscow line. Joe had a reputation as an amusing galoot; men tended to like him, to appreciate that half-menacing joke surliness. Women didn't. After four years he hadn't made it onto any of the important committees. He needed a signature issue.

This J. Edgar Hoover provided, if indirectly at first. In 1947, the FBI had put together a hundred-page document which started with the disclosures of Elizabeth Bentley and Whittaker Chambers and filled in the structural details of the Soviet espionage networks in America, along with a list of important Party activists. For three years FBI contact personnel had been attempting to interest dignitaries in and around the federal government in their report. A G-2 officer in the Army came across the document in 1949 and circulated it among several senators; McCarthy was reportedly the last. Soon afterward, McCarthy—who had been lamenting to William Roberts, a prominent Roman-Catholic D.C. attorney, that he badly needed something with meat on the bone to restart his career—attended a little dinner at the Colony Restaurant which included, besides Roberts, the senator, Father Edmund Walsh, and Professor Charles Kraus of Georgetown University. The issue McCarthy was looking for, they all agreed, was the immediate threat of Soviet subversion inside the United States government.

McCarthy was no reader, and this was a subject it took some command of history to sort out. Just as McCarthy, while functioning as a small-town judge, had brought his verdicts down with very little awareness of the rules of evidence, he now unleashed the dogs on The Manhunt of the Century with almost no comprehension of what constituted meaningful quarry. Give Joe a name—in many cases, the wrong name—and the hunt was on.

Once McCarthy was back in town after the Wheeling tour, his comments on Communists in the State Department generated challenges from a number of his liberal colleagues to substantiate his charges. This he attempted on February 20 from the floor, relying for lack of better evidence on 81 from an original list of 108 cases an investigator for the House Appropriations Committee, Robert E. Lee, had stumbled on in 1948 while picking over the Department's neglected loyalty files. Here was a ragtag lot—X, who was cited during the *Amerasia* investigations and took the Communist Chinese side during a round-table discussion; Y, who inadvertently borrowed somebody else's raincoat which had some Russian-language papers mashed into a pocket. . . .

A few were legitimate suspects; most were, at best, peripheral, and a majority on McCarthy's list were out of the State Department by 1950. Only one case, number 54, led to the indictment of a State Department employee. Yet at that moment McCarthy was riding a wave, as was soon evident when a subcommittee of the Senate Foreign Relations Committee was made up, chaired by Maryland Senator Millard Tydings, to prod to the surface and wherever possible explode the Wisconsin senator's shoddy evidence. Where was the treason in such celebrated examples as those of Harlow Shapely, the wooly Harvard astronomer, and Owen Lattimore, a Johns Hopkins expert on Mongolian affairs who had consulted over the years with State?

Both were undoubtedly deluded as to Soviet intentions. But at that time, bad judgment was not against the law.

In 1950, fueled by $10,000 from Clint Murchison, matched behind the scenes by embittered reactionaries like Joe Kennedy and Alfred Kohlberg, McCarthy coasted to reelection in Wisconsin and proceeded to take down his primary assailants. "[Democratic Majority Leader Scott] Lucas provided the whitewash when I charged there were Communists in high places," McCarthy bellowed at a Maryland Republican rally. "[Brien] McMahon brought the bucket; Tydings the brush." A tabloid handout featuring a doctored photograph of Tydings juxtaposed beside a shot of Communist leader Earl Browder cut into the Tydings vote. Both Tydings and Lucas lost their Senate seats, and McCarthy's effectiveness as a political hatchet man was starting to unnerve his fellow senators.

Fortified, McCarthy brought ex-FBI agent Don Surine onto the subcommittee staff to investigate promising suspects. Surine had been flushed out of the Bureau for swapping a few favors with a tart from Baltimore he was attempting to bust during a white slavery investigation. Hoover admired Surine's moxie and recommended him to McCarthy—the first of what soon developed into an unbroken string of FBI veterans brought in to prop up McCarthy's database.

Egged on by hard-right commentator Fulton Lewis Jr., Surine unleashed his chief on Anna M. Rosenberg, a hardheaded little Hungarian immigrant who had been a White House favorite during World War II and was up for confirmation as assistant secretary for Manpower. McCarthy trotted through an extraordinary troupe of professional anti-Semites, but in the end it was plain that the posse was descending on the wrong Anna Rosenberg, and she was easily confirmed.

Hoover retained a certain affection for McCarthy—"I've come to know Senator McCarthy well, officially and personally," Hoover told reporters during an interview in La Jolla. "I view him as a friend and I believe he so views me"—but it already required all the dexterity those quick little feet could muster to step around some of Joe's more egregious blunders. The blame for the Rosenberg fiasco, Hoover informed Senator Mike Monroney, belonged to "Edward K. Nellor, leg man for Fulton Lewis, [who] planned and executed the Anna Rosenberg smear for Lewis and Sen. Joseph R. McCarthy." Hoover needed to shift the blame, at least in public. The gadfly columnist Drew Pearson was all over McCarthy's bogus war record, while a Senate investigation into the Wisconsin senator's finances would reveal that campaign money had been drained off into speculations in the gyrating soybean market. At a Gridiron Club dinner, McCarthy assured the much older and much smaller Pearson that "Some day I'm going to break your leg, Drew, but for the time being I just wanted to say hello."

After an exchange of threats soon afterward, the intoxicated McCarthy cornered Pearson in the cloakroom and kneed him twice in the groin as he reached for his coat check. As Pearson collapsed, McCarthy floored him with a brutal chop as Dick Nixon materialized to implore: "Let a Quaker stop this fight." It provided a historic off-camera Republican moment.

For Hoover, the involvement of columnists in the tug-of-war over McCarthy's soul had all the allure of an unswept minefield. Ever since his crime-fighter days with Walter Winchell, Hoover had been leaking raw information selectively and traducing influential commentators in return for tips and opportunities to propagandize. Hearst regulars like Westbrook Pegler and George Sokolsky amounted to the neocons of their day, the theologians of the Right, and powerful voices in the shaping of public opinion.

Sokolsky especially seemed to be connected in every direction. A plump little one-time Trotskyite with big hair and an early, disillusioning journalistic career in Moscow and China, Sokolsky maintained in his cluttered Manhattan apartment a kind of ongoing seminar on the seductive iniquity of Socialist ideals. Big corporations and special interests had been slipping meaningful retainers to George for decades. "He was," Ted Morgan sums it up, "close to J. Edgar Hoover and had a productive relationship with the FBI. He was practically an unpaid member of McCarthy's staff, sending him documents, writing his speeches, giving him advice, and flattering him."

By the end of 1950, professional anti-Communism was turning into bumper cars. In late January 1951, Don Surine and two footpads broke into a barn in rural Massachusetts and highjacked the stored files of the Institute for Pacific Relations, Owen Lattimore's think tank. The files were hauled to the Manhattan offices of J. B. Matthews, the Hearst empire's Communism maven, and photostated before being smuggled back. Within days McCarthy and his advisers were crowing about this felony. Sokolsky, who had been a participant in the Institute, tipped off its former secretary-general, Edward Carter; McCarthy, meanwhile, responded to a reporter in Racine with the droll admission that he "succeeded in—I don't like to use the word 'stealing'— let's say I 'borrowed' the documents."

Meanwhile, operatives for the House Un-American Activities Committee and staffers from Senator Pat McCarran's Internal Security Subcommittee were closing in. Then there were investigators from Harry Truman's new Subversive Control Board. . . .

From Hoover's vantage point, this looked like the convergence of the vandals. Communism was *his* issue; amateur sleuthing wasn't welcome. The fact was , the previous summer Edward Carter had offered the Institute's files to the FBI, following which a dozen FBI agents had spent the summer combing out the paperwork for leads. There wasn't much there. A few years earlier there had appeared under J. Edgar Hoover's name in *Newsweek* a list of imperatives for citizens hoping to "successfully defeat the Communist attempt to capture the United States." Hoover urged his readers not to "confuse liberals and progressives with Communists," to report Communist misdeeds "to your law-enforcement agency," and to avoid becoming "a party to a violation of the civil rights of anyone. When this is done, you are playing right into the hands of the Communists."

Hoover liked to indulge his nagging civil-libertarian conscience from time to time. But he was on the alert for claim-jumpers, apprehensive about being supplanted as the nation's senior anti-Communist watchdog. Two terms under Truman had been an ordeal for the FBI Director. "Tell them I don't authorize any such thing," the no-nonsense president from Missouri had replied when Hoover sent along a few pages of wiretap transcripts gleaned from the telephone conversations of the indiscreet wife of a White House aide. Franklin Roosevelt did nipups over bonbons like that. "We want no Gestapo or Secret Police," Truman wrote in his diary. "FBI is tending in that direction. They are dabbling in sex-life scandals and plain blackmail. . . . This must stop. . . ."

Hoover was like a spider without a web. This left him more dependent than ever on his status as Top Cop, defender of American Capitalism against the gathering Red Menace. The emergence of McCarthyism was good for Hoover—it kept the subversion issue right up there in the headlines—yet it was becoming vital that Joe get a handle on himself, that somebody tell him when to move and whom to target.

Booze was a danger with the driven McCarthy. Somebody would open a bathroom door along one of the corridors at the rear of the Capitol, and there would squat Tail Gunner Joe, chug-a-lugging a fifth of whiskey while interrupting himself from time to time to chaw down a handful of baking soda. The baking soda quieted a diaphragmatic hernia. Then, sweated through and rumpled, McCarthy would clamber out and lurch toward the Senate floor, where he would turn his anger against contemporaries even Hoover hadn't identified yet.

On June 14, 1951 it was George C. Marshall, as self-sacrificing and incorruptible a patriot as the twentieth century would produce. Marshall was a Communist patsy, McCarthy ranted. He all but single-handedly lost China. He was "a man steeped in falsehood," the principal in "a conspiracy so immense as to dwarf any previous such venture in the history of man." Even the Republican Right stood frowning, lost in thought.

In November 1952, Dwight D. Eisenhower won the presidential election and carried both houses of Congress. McCarthy finally got his important committee assignment: he became the chairman of the Committee on Government Operations, within which the prize from McCarthy's point of view was the Permanent Subcommittee on Investigations. The Permanent Subcommittee was authorized to prowl the entire federal bureaucracy searching out malfeasance.

It was like locking a very hungry pit bull in an overloaded meat wagon. It would become clear before the spring was out that McCarthy was putting his "mission" ahead of the new administration's interests. He raised a ruckus over the appointment of James Conant as German High Commissioner. The hard-liner McCarthy helped install as security chief in the State Department, FBI veteran Scott McLeod, attempted to block the selection of Soviet expert Charles ("Chip") Bohlen as ambassador to Moscow. Chip Bohlen had translated for FDR at Yalta; his brother-in-law Charlie Thayer had crossed a line or two during his own foreign service career; once Bohlen's nomination came up for confirmation, McCarthy was noisily demanding that Secretary of State John Foster Dulles subject himself to a lie-detector test. Before things got completely out of hand Vice President Dick Nixon jumped in, the first of his many services as the canny Eisenhower conducted McCarthy toward his doom.

As soon as the election was behind him, fortified by a $200,000 budget, McCarthy took steps to staff up preparatory to redressing "twenty years of treason." His most revealing selection was young Roy Cohn, Chief Counsel of his Permanent Subcommittee. Cohn was twenty-four at the time and looked even younger—a waxen beardless prodigy with slicked-back onyx hair, sleepy eyes, a deep, intimidating longitudinal scar on his formidable nose, and virtually no chin. His ultraconservative credentials were already intact—"Roy's idea of cutting down on welfare is to kill a beggar," one friend offered—and important people were watching.

Cohn may have looked like a stripling, but he had been making one important scene after another for a long time. The only child of New York Supreme Court Appellate Judge Albert Cohn and his wealthy, doting wife Dora, Roy had pushed easily through the available Manhattan curriculum—Horace Mann, Columbia College, Columbia Law School. He completed his legal training at nineteen, a year too early to take the New York Boards.

He liked the high life. Walter Winchell's biographer would memorialize the first time the columnist ran into Roy, "porcine, erupted in acne and hideously dressed, table-hopping at the Stork Club." Sherman Billingsley was about to throw him out when Winchell told the proprietor who Roy's father was. Cohn became a regular, reportedly a habitué of that famous table 50 reserved for the likes of J. Edgar Hoover and Joseph P. Kennedy and his older sons.

Roy Cohn began his political education, he later wrote, as a "typical college liberal, active in Young Democratic organizations, and founder of the Columbia Law School Democratic Club." Never one to waste time poring over the law books, Cohn was a very quick study in the uses of influence. Having passed the bar, he wangled a slot as Assistant U.S. Attorney and quickly demonstrated an aptitude for high-profile cases, the kind that paid off fast with headlines in the tabloids. He got a lot of indictments, if not too many convictions. Society columnists like Leonard Lyons discovered Roy, who joined them on their all-night scrambles around the Great White Way, where gangsters and big new postwar money hobnobbed.

Cohn cut his prosecutorial teeth helping bring down the "Communist Eleven," the senior figures in the Party's American apparatus, and really caught the eye of the informed Right as part of the team that tried the Rosenbergs and Morton Sobell. Cohn's boss, U.S. Attorney Irving Saypol, was Tammany Hall's choice and a regular associate of Frank Costello. Saypol was a distant relative of the Cohns; Roy became the office "pet." Cohn very quickly managed a certain precocious notoriety by persuading the vacillating Judge Irving Kaufman to sentence Ethel Rosenberg to the electric chair. "The way I see it," Cohn would remember telling the judge, "is that she's worse than Julius. She's the older one, she's the one with the brains . . . she was the mastermind of the conspiracy. . . ." The whole proceeding set J. Edgar Hoover's teeth on edge a little, but he was forced to admit that this young Cohn showed an enviable tenacity.

Cohn was already renowned for his knack for coming into court unprepared, glancing through an associate's paperwork, then mounting a two-hour presentation without recourse to a note. He had an authentic photoretentive memory and a genius for tactics. He was intense. By 1952, Cohn had helped try over two hundred cases, many on loyalty grounds. They ran from the cosmopolitan mystery writer Dashiell Hammett to the Commerce Department economist William Remington, whose conviction was overturned by the Circuit Court. Cohn maintained that Remington's movements permitted the court to impute Communist Party membership and got him sent right back to the penitentiary for perjury; there he was murdered, still a young man.

By cornering William Perl, who Cohn had decided was part of the Rosenberg ring, and attempting to badger a confession out of him before the Bureau was ready to bring down its own raid, Cohn spooked Perl and wrecked the Bureau's timetable. When another suspect showed up in FBI sights, its internal memo read: "no information concerning the result of the interview should be furnished to the United States Attorney's office or Roy Cohn without specific Bureau approval."

In August of 1952 Cohn relocated to Washington. He was to become a special assistant to Attorney General James McGranery. Before that job got serious, Cohn insists that he found himself summoned to a hotel suite in New York's Astor Hotel and propositioned: "My God I'm glad to meet you," Joe McCarthy supposedly told Roy. "But you can't possibly be one tenth as good as everybody says you are. I just want to find out what's public relations and what's real."

Much of the job negotiation from then on took place through George Sokolsky. Sokolsky was everybody's rabbi. A font of opinions, running over with enthusiasm, Sokolsky was a friend of Albert Cohn and attached himself to Roy as to a son. Roy moved in quickly as vice-president of Sokolsky's private political action committee, the American Jewish League Against Communism. As a reformed Trotskyite, Sokolsky felt that he was entitled to pick the cadre for much of the anti-Communist crusade, and Roy Cohn definitely looked like a kid to watch.

That late-morning meeting at the Hotel Astor haunted Roy. Amidst a swarm of overdressed people, McCarthy was sitting on a bed naked to the waist in suspenders, a kind of forthright, hairy embodiment of the era's Male Animal, its champion against the Antichrist. "Here was a man," Cohn later wrote, "with warmth, humor, loyalty, a man who loved people, who was forgiving almost beyond the bounds of reasonableness."

Not long after that, in Florida, Cohn heard from Sokolsky that McCarthy really wanted Cohn as chief counsel on his subcommittee, but Joe Kennedy, a substantial contributor, wanted *his* son, Bobby, for the post. Robert Kennedy's qualifications were limited. Sokolsky kept the process moving, and things were resolved finally once Bob Kennedy agreed reluctantly to sign on as assistant to Francis ("Frip") Flanagan, another FBI retread McCarthy retained, Cohn said, "to placate Joe Kennedy." Flanagan remained in place as general counsel to the McCarthy subcommittee. Bob Kennedy was expected to replace Frip once the subcommittee got organized.

"Hey, Frip, Joe Kennedy here," the holdover general counsel heard on picking up his telephone a week after taking Bobby on. "I just want you to know that by God you won't have any trouble with him. But if you do, I'll give you my private number." Surveillance was very close. But things never quieted down long enough to realign the staff, and even McCarthy himself could never quite figure out who ranked whom.

In January 1953 there was a party in Washington to greet Roy's arrival. Celebrants included Vice President Nixon, J. Edgar Hoover, twenty senators, and Albert Cohn.

Robert Kennedy was quite openly peeved at the way things were working out. He was soon aware that McCarthy was under pressure from Richard Berlin, who ran the media conglomerate for Hearst and was another mentor of Roy's. Bobby undoubtedly remembered how closely his father had worked with Hearst, reorganizing his damned empire for him at the end of the thirties, and here Joe couldn't get him a sniveling little staff appointment. These Jews were simply too tough. It was a revelation that there were doors even the Ambassador couldn't break down.

Into his sixties now, Joe Kennedy was well aware his omnipotence was overstated. Emotionally, Jack's struggle to remain alive was a continuing agony for his father, who lacked his whimsical son's hard-won fatalism. Final rites were said over Jack four times. Arthur Krock sat watching the Ambassador collapse into tears when the diagnosis came in corroborating the bad news about Jack's Addison's disease. At one point, there were strong indications of leukemia.

Much of the frenetic competitiveness Joe himself had promoted during the earlier decades now seemed unsettling, overdone, fraught with terrifying potential. Teddy, who came of age during a less-militant era in the family's history, remembers his father urging him to do his best and not upset himself unduly over winning or losing. To outsiders coming into the family, the Ambassador, while volcanic on occasion, especially about his children's spendthrift habits, came through as understanding, sympathetic. He liked to vie with his sons over their women, take their dates to lunch, their loose, knowing older brother. Unhappy initially when Pat decided to marry not only an Englishman but an actor who wore red socks, Joe drew an FBI report which informed him that Peter Lawford was a habitué of Lee Francis's bordello in Hollywood, a purveyor of specialty prostitutes. Nevertheless, Joe conferred his approval on the marriage. Given Peter's languid, hothouse personality, the voltage generated when the offspring got together was so disconcerting that Lawford later admitted that "When it was in full swing it was like a juggernaut. I used to find excuses not to go. The old man watched this, and later he said to me, 'I know what you are going through.'" A true transatlantic eccentric and semireformed surf bum, Lawford tended to duck out of Kennedy entertainments, especially touch football, and amuse himself getting drunk with Joe's chauffeur. He insisted on playing golf barefoot at the better country clubs.

For Jacqueline Kennedy, Joe provided an unexpected ally. Attempting to cope with the miseries of her marriage—"History made Jack what he was," she would conclude privately, "this lonely sick boy. His mother didn't really love him"—Jackie saw through the opinionated financier's corrosive mannerisms immediately. She teased his slangy, old-fashioned delivery and he attempted to reassure her as her expectations of Jack continued to collapse. He bought her her first pieces of "serious jewelry" and bankrolled her stupefying wardrobe. Jackie laughed with Joe at Rose's collection of dolls from around the planet while Joe enlarged on the specifics of Gloria Swanson's exquisite genitalia and her uncanny sexual preferences. They shared a great deal of mischief. Jackie's private secretary would recount one giddy episode when Jackie and the Ambassador vied in their attempt to bean an escaping housekeeper with their lamb-chop bones.

Rose's favorite sister, Agnes, had passed away unexpectedly from an embolism in 1936, and her husband, Joseph Gargan, died young a decade later. The three Gargan children spent summers as they were growing up in the Kennedy household in Hyannis Port. Joe Gargan Jr.—Joey—quickly became an inseparable pal for little Teddy. The Ambassador Joey would remember was a benign if quietly controlling presence—none of that "bellering" the older children recalled—who woke him up along with Teddy to go horseback riding early in the morning and never missed his swim with Rose before lunch. Never much on formal socializing, Joe preferred to sit alone in the sunroom and read while his crony, ex-Boston Police Commissioner Joe Timilty, escorted Rose to the Wianno Club dances.

The worst it got was when the patriarch loudly dismissed some notion as "a lot of applesauce," or conferred on Joey a long and severe look over the top of his glasses the day Joey mashed up his convertible. When Gargan consulted his uncle on a business proposition, what he heard was: "Joey, you shouldn't come to me for advice. If you knew how many mistakes I made you'd never be in here afterward." With supporting relatives like the Gargans, it really wasn't necessary to project an air of patriarchal infallibility. Once

Joey's sister Ann developed symptoms of multiple sclerosis, her uncle made sure to sit next to her at dinner so he could cut up her meat.

Letting word get around that he was something of a pushover wouldn't be advisable for either business or politics. Best to keep it quiet. When Franklin Roosevelt's full-time secretary and part-time other wife, Missy LeHand, suffered a series of strokes and retreated to her family in Massachusetts to die, three gentlemen who apparently enjoyed her favors away from the White House—Bernard Baruch, William Bullitt, and Joe Kennedy—picked up her medical bills. It happened that the classmate who took Ted Kennedy's Spanish exam for him at Harvard, Bill Frate, was an acquaintance of mine. Tossed out of Harvard, what got him through two terrible ensuing years was help and regular, reassuring telephone calls from Joseph P. Kennedy. Meanwhile, the financier was sending along funds to subsidize Mrs. Willy, widow of the copilot in the Liberator in which Joe Jr. perished. Kennedy's Park Avenue office was forever issuing subsistence checks and paying burial costs for indigent ex-retainers.

What touched Kennedy's family touched him. Yet by the early fifties, the financier was piecing together a kind of back-up ensemble, an assortment of cronies less dependent on the financier, more autonomous, than uncomplicated coatholders like Timilty and Judge Francis X. Morrissey and Edward Moore. One carryover was the popular singer and bon vivant Morton Downey. A lifelong witness to Kennedy's "strange, almost turbulent interest in more seemingly unrelated topics," as well as the occasional beneficiary of his business deals, Downey was a willing straw when investments came up in which the financier didn't care to have his name involved. Furthermore, a show-business stalwart like Downey ran into a great many exorbitantly endowed women, whom he never hesitated to pass along.

Another courtier who turned up regularly was Father John J. Cavanaugh, President of Notre Dame. The gregarious priest was after the financier for years to endow a graduate school at the university and recruited Kennedy onto the University's board for a time. Kennedy persuaded Cavanaugh to take in the West Point athletes expelled over the cheating scandal and paid their tuitions. Whenever Cavanaugh visited, the Ambassador's complement of models and "secretaries" tended to get whisked out of sight.

As close as anybody during the later years was Arthur Houghton. Another East Boston boy who worked the administrative side of the entertainment business, "Dad's most delightful and zaniest friend," in Ted Kennedy's judgment, "Huxie" met Joe in 1917 while he was managing "a New York musical show with 24 beautiful chorus girls," and remained a regular companion on the golf course and at the races. His golf shoes were forever scuffed, Ted remembered, from "kicking his ball out of the rough."

Huxie was a fixture at the bad-boys retreat over which the financier presided in the South of France. "I take it for granted," one of the other insiders wrote Joe in August 1957, "that Art is chasing the girls till they drop from exhaustion and that you are strolling by and helping them out as they lay [*sic*] prostrate on the ground."

This sort of heavy-duty raillery was typical of the back-and-forth between Kennedy and the author of the letter, Carroll Rosenbloom, the owner of the Baltimore Colts. The two had met—this is already a stretch, given Kennedy's well-advertised prejudices—at a meeting to form an interfaith committee in Palm Beach. Rosenbloom was a rangy, horse-faced Jewish businessman who once played halfback at the University of Pennsylvania and took over his family's work-clothes factory in the midst of World War II. After cornering the market for battle fatigues and parachutes, he emerged from the war with capital enough to grab off the enormous Blue Buckle Overall Company. Rosenbloom picked up 53 percent of the floundering Colts early in 1953, and his mercurial temperament left his fellow owners with "the feeling that if you crossed him, he was capable of slitting your throat, then donating your blood to the Red Cross blood drive." A second-generation buccaneer, much like the Ambassador, Rosenbloom's knockdown irreverence, devotion, and raw guts appealed to Kennedy, who was soon playing most of his golf in Florida at the Palm Beach Country Club, where he remained the only non-Jewish member. High-end private clubs like The Everglades had remained evasive when it came to conferring full membership on the unpredictable Kennedys.

Both inveterate needle artists and unabashed skirt-chasers, their fraternity-boy relationship survives in their correspondence. "Dear Chief," Rosenbloom writes in 1956, "Not having heard a word, received no more presents of money, food, or girls, I take it that you have been livid with envy since I took it upon myself to put a respectable man in the mayor's chair in Dublin.

"Some people just can't help being mean and small. . . ."

Kennedy responds promptly, exclaiming over the "horrible news that a tie vote had resulted in the election of a mayor for Dublin and that the choice was to be left to chance . . . for a poor, unsuspecting Irishman to take a chance with a Jew on drawing the winner out of a hat, almost kills me. Of course, the inevitable happened—the Jew palmed the right paper and became the winner."

Rosenbloom has a gift for this sort of badinage, and at one point ends his remarks: "I can see you in Hyannis, locked up in your money vaults, the wind sighing along the beach and the waves pounding, a perfect picture of Midas if I ever saw one.

"When you get hungry and need a meal or a new suit or a pair of shoes, I expect you will be along this way and I will as usual contribute.

"Regardless of all your faults, I love you still."

In his way, Carroll Rosenbloom incarnated the savvy, like-minded son Joe Kennedy never had—somebody he could genuinely be himself with. Like Kennedy, Rosenbloom was affiliated throughout much of his working life with the executive-level underworld. A longstanding acquaintanceship with Mike McLaney, a professional golf hustler who worked the Miami coast, brought Rosenbloom into contact with the notorious three-hundred-pound Toronto financier and gambler, Lou Chesler. Over the years, Chesler had maintained a productive business association with, and functioned as an "occasional bagman" for, the Lansky organization. In 1956 Rosenbloom committed capital to several Chesler-backed promotions: General Development Corporation, then underwriting three new Florida communities; Universal Controls, which leased pari-mutuel betting equipment for racetracks; a shell company which bought up the Warner Brothers film library under the eventual name Seven Arts.

In 1958 the visionary Cleveland mobster Moe Dalitz had decided to part company with his interest in the Hotel Nacional casino in Havana. McLaney brought this opportunity to Chesler and Rosenbloom, who, after taking back his five thousand finder's-fee shares in Universal Controls, cut McLaney in so that the three assumed an $800,000 position in the fortresslike Caribbean landmark. This left them partners with majority owners Jake and Meyer Lansky. The arrangement had barely been finalized before Fidel Castro and his hotheads poured out of the Sierra Maestras and liberated Cuba. The casinos were lost, and McLaney himself spent time in a Cuban lockup. In Mob annals, the event was devastating: Meyer Lansky himself was reported to have fled abandoning $7 million in cash. Within the month, Carroll Rosenbloom sold off the family clothing business.

The fact that people in his circle were getting banged around in Cuba seems to have preyed on the Ambassador. One social friend who lived a little down Ocean Beach from the Kennedys, Earl Smith, served as Eisenhower's envoy in Havana and put up Jack when he blew into town to crawl the brothels. At various times, both Santo Trafficante and Meyer Lansky himself would remember exchanging pleasantries with the charismatic senator, out scrounging for fun-loving professional females to enliven his holiday. The ultraconservative Ambassador Smith was well known as a devoted Batista supporter. While adamant overall about his Cold War isolationist principles, Joe Kennedy was coming to believe that it would be necessary to intervene in Cuba, and soon.

Neither politics nor business sullies much of the correspondence between the Ambassador and his buddy Rosenbloom. "How are your friends in Canada these days?" Kennedy wonders in 1957, an allusion no doubt to Chesler and the Lansky hangers-on. Mostly the exchange is personal. "With you out of the country women are beginning to find me rather attractive," one letter from Rosenbloom goes, although they do "seem most interested in knowing where you are and could I get your address for them—you would be amazed to know how many times mutual friends and I have been crying in bed talking about what a fine fellow you are." Another, in July 1953, winds up: "Hope this finds the lovely Miss Janet well and happy. Please tell her I haven't forgotten her blouses."

The lovely Miss Janet was Janet Des Rosiers, a demure but realistic personal assistant the Ambassador had engaged in 1948. Something of a looker, with splendid legs, an upbeat manner, and solid secretarial skills, Des Rosiers received the go-slow-but-no-way-out treatment which had ensnared Daye Eliot. When winter arrived, Kennedy installed her in what he referred to as "our house" in West Palm Beach, and their affair commenced. She was a virgin, Kennedy discovered. "He was marvelous, you know," she confessed to Lawrence Leamer afterward. "It would be very difficult for any woman not to succumb to his charm. . . . My God, you can't imagine. It's hard to fight off a man of his authority and experience and ability, so I was gone right from the beginning." Little by little, she traveled with him, spent nights in his New York apartment—but always in the guest room, for the sake of propriety—and helped manage the Hyannis Port estate during Rose's many extended absences. She took dictation from Rose.

Janet left Kennedy's employ in 1958, evidently put off by the prospect of Ann Gargan's return. Their passion was behind them. During the 1960 primaries, Des Rosiers helped out as stewardess and secretary on the *Caroline*, occasionally massaging the candidate's feet and hands.

Kennedy stayed in touch. "Your note indicates that you are still running high and handsome," Kennedy responded to one card. "It must be a great satisfaction to you to have such a congenial traveling companion. I am looking for one of those myself." In the spring of 1958 the Ambassador was attempting to select an airplane for Jack's campaign and added that "it is as hard to make a decision as it is to find a girl for Rosenbloom. I think he has raised his standards since the night you were out with him. I don't think his morals are any better, but maybe his standards are."

After Joe got sick Janet wrote, still addressing him as Mister Kennedy, assuring him that "You are always in my thoughts for so many reasons." "We are having a rather cold and sunless summer in Paris," Janet lamented from her job in the embassy, "but I always manage to bring a little sunshine into my life—I just think about you and the many laughs we used to have!

"Please take good care of yourself—so often I wish there was something I could do for you." She was reportedly the beneficiary of several productive oil leases. Engaging Janet Des Rosiers was probably the happiest move in Joe Kennedy's life.

Ted Kennedy once told me that even he and his siblings were not permitted to just pop in on the Ambassador without clearance in Palm Beach. That was particularly true at Villa Les Fal in Eze, in the South of France. Recuperation was more and more important throughout those postwar years. Furthermore, contacts from the Ambassador's business life tended to surface in Florida, people the children wouldn't understand.

Among his many investments, the Ambassador had picked up 17 percent of the track at Hialeah. One of his partners at the Florida raceway was Frank Costello. Kennedy liked to fritter away postwar evenings in Meyer Lansky's Colony Club in Miami. Another Miami haunt he favored was the Park Avenue Steak House, the proprietor of which, Bert ("Wingy") Grober, was a Lansky standby as well as a customer of Somerset Importers. Over time, the Kennedy boys couldn't help but run into a few of the Ambassador's more presentable gangland confederates. Murray the Camel Humphreys claimed to have actually introduced his wife and his daughter, Llewella, to Jack and Bobby. They were, the Camel concluded, "wimps," dominated by their father.

One contact Kennedy liked to bum around with over the years was the outrageous comedian Joe E. Lewis. Originally a nightclub singer, Lewis managed to get into a hassle over both a woman and a nightclub booking with Al Capone's favorite button man, Jack ("Machine-gun") McGurn. Three of McGurn's employees fractured Lewis's skull and slit his throat, severing his vocal chords. Still Mob-connected, Lewis got enough of his voice back to specialize in raunchy nightclub jokes and struck up an acquaintanceship with the older Kennedy that lasted until the end.

Another operator Kennedy continued to cultivate was Mike McLaney.

McLaney and Rosenbloom, both crack golfers, had been tight for many years, and naturally Joe Kennedy liked to show off his short, straight game and take them on, presuming always a decent handicap and favorable odds. But McLaney and Rosenbloom had fallen out over the debacle in Havana, and McLaney sued to recover the shares of Universal Controls he had unthinkingly surrendered. "He was a killer at heart," McLaney would ultimately say of Rosenbloom. "Everybody who did business with him hated him."

For all this scrimmaging between his erstwhile golfing companions, Joe Kennedy continued to enjoy the company of the suave, unprincipled McLaney, who took the Havana financial beating and moved along, under Meyer Lansky's direction, to subvert a government in the Bahamas and initiate serious gambling in Port-au-Prince. McLaney was polished enough to expose to the kids. Throughout the fifties he visited the Palm Beach mansion. "I had drinks at the home," he would subsequently tell congressional investigators. "I liked the President very much. I thought Bobby was a mess. . . ."

In 1948, after repeated interruptions for naval training and the months shot getting Jack into Congress, Robert Kennedy had graduated from Harvard College and was enrolled—if on a provisional basis given his spotty grades, and necessitating a word to the administration from Harvard Law School Dean James Landis—at the University of Virginia in Charlottesville. Like his older brother, he was obviously sheltered and immature, besides which he came over as insolent and short-tempered whenever anybody crossed him. Outsiders found him very much like the Ambassador—the worst of the Ambassador. "Bobby was," Joey Gargan saw, "in many ways a great admirer of his father. He obviously had an enormous love and affection for him, and admiration for him. And I'm sure he imitated him in many ways."

After the Ambassador arranged for a quick tour of Europe, the Middle East, and South America, with credentials from the *Boston Post,* Bobby settled in at University of Virginia with the bluff George Terrien, one of his roommates at Harvard. Like Lem Billings, Terrien, a Navy fighter pilot in the Pacific, came from a once-prosperous upper-middle-class family, which lost its capital in the Crash. "You couldn't live with him," Terrien commented later, "but we got along. He was a royal pain in the ass. He was a bulldog about certain things, but I tolerated him."

In Charlottesville, Kennedy was the bane of his landlord for pocking up fragile wood floors with golf cleats and stippling the antique mantel with cigarette burns. Not to mention the dogs. After two years, he married. "My fiancée followed me down here and wouldn't let me alone for a minute," Bob wrote his sister Pat in 1950. "Kept running her toes through my hair and things like that. You know how engaged couples are." His fiancée was Ethel Skakel.

A good athlete, no deep thinker, a slapdash, well-intended homemaker, Ethel adored Bobby with an intensity that truly beggars description. The two were married in Greenwich, Connecticut, in a vast society wedding, preceded by a bachelor party which tore hell out of the New York Harvard Club. The previous generation of Skakels had made a lot of money, fast, and operated very recklessly based in a mansion in the estate country of Greenwich. Robert Kennedy's feisty, brooding temperament tended to put the Skakels off. "Bobby's such a chicken-shit little bastard," Ethel's brother George allowed to one acquaintance. "I can't figure out what Ethel sees in that little prick." Kennedy returned the favor. "If I wasn't married to Ethel," he told Dean Markham, "I wouldn't give those micks the time of day."

The Kennedy newlyweds attempted to keep house in a whitewashed brick Colonial, which Ethel presided over in the blithe, haphazard style legions of future guests would recognize. An untrained English bulldog named Toby Belch soaked down the carpets and laid waste to the owners' carefully chosen furniture. Ethel's sole culinary success, according to one report, was "Cheese Dreams, which tasted like glue and raw dough." Weekends, a plane from the Great Lakes Carbon Corporation, the Skakel holding company, often dropped them off in Greenwich or Hyannis Port.

Academically, Bobby didn't star in Charlottesville either, although he did manage to place toward the middle of his graduating class. He would joke later about having won his sole prize for having the "fifth best sense of humor" among his classmates. What started to emerge now was a sneaking, irrepressible sympathy with the underdog, a kind of private rage at the more flagrant abuses of establishment power. In college, Robert Kennedy had complained to Archbishop Richard Cushing, a family retainer, about the demagogy of Father Leonard Feeny, a Cambridge Jesuit who railed that there was no salvation except "subject to the Roman Pontiff" and savaged Harvard as a "pest hole" for Jews and atheists. When Harvard played University of Virginia, Kennedy joined his teammates in demanding that the team's black tackle stay with the group at the hotel.

At the University of Virginia, Bobby organized a Student Legal Forum and picked the speakers, often family or friends. Family lawyer James Landis made an appearance. Justice William O. Douglas spoke, which provoked a thank-you note from Bob alleging slyly that "Ethel now has a case on you which I believe casts a few aspersions [*sic*] in my direction considering the fact we've been married only a few months." Joseph P. Kennedy demanded that the United States exit Korea and whatever positions in Asia "we do not plan realistically to hold in our own defense." Congressman John Kennedy disagreed a year later but complained that his recent fact-finding tour revealed a sluggishness around the Atlantic Pact when it came to contributing forces.

In the spring of 1951, the Forum invited the black diplomat Ralph Bunche, whose performance at the United Nations had already garnered him a Nobel Peace Prize. Officials at the University of Virginia had indicated that seating for the lecture would have to be segregated, which was intolerable to Bunche. In a letter to university president Colgate Darden, Bobby demanded open seating, arguing that there was no "problem calculated to embarrass the University, unless the University should decide that it is necessary to create the issue itself by invoking an educational segregation policy which . . . is . . . legally indefensible, morally wrong and fraught with consequences calculated to do great harm to the University." Darden designated the lecture an "educational meeting" and left it unsegregated.

Another controversial speaker was Joseph McCarthy. Even before McCarthy got to town, the *Virginia Law Weekly* ventured that, while he "advocates cleaning the house," his "choice of cleaning materials . . . appears to be the subject of a lively debate."

Once McCarthy's speech was over, Bobby and Ethel entertained for him. One guest was E. Barrett Prettyman Jr., just then the editor of the University law review and after 1961 one of Robert Kennedy's crack attorneys in the Justice Department. "That was one of the most astonishing evenings," Prettyman recalled recently. "Because I saw—that night—the rest of McCarthy's life. There was a kind of a den, and he sat on a couch, and he had a couple of the wives on either side of him. He asked for a drink right away. And we began to ask him questions. In the beginning, he was very sure-footed in his responses, but as he began to get sloshed, he began to get tangled up in his answers, contradicting himself, or forgetting things, or whatever. And we watched him disintegrate. He just went to pieces. And he began to *realize* he was embarrassing himself, so he would get more embarrassed, and drink more, and people began to slip out. And that was the rest of his life, right there. . . . Bobby couldn't have missed what was happening."

As the evening deepened, McCarthy reportedly pawed one of the women, and, in the end, Robert Kennedy helped him to bed. But Kennedy refused to make any excuses for this perspiring family minion, whose controlled desperation and stubborn outsider status provoked a complicated resonance in the Kennedys' neglected middle son. Still subservient to influences like McCarthy and his father, Kennedy wrote a senior paper castigating FDR's sellout to the Reds at Yalta.

After law school, consequent to a phone call from his father, who told friends that he'd been after Bob for six years to figure out what he wanted to do with his life, Kennedy took a job with the Internal Security Division of the Justice Department in Washington, prosecuting cases for Assistant Attorney General James McInerney. McInerney was another FBI graduate the Ambassador had his eye on; he would become Jack Kennedy's lawyer, the intermediary on whom the family depended for some of their hairier extractions. Coincidentally or otherwise, Bobby caught some choice assignments, including the loyalty investigation of Owen Lattimore.

Bobby liked the work, whenever he was in town, although he moved over to the Criminal Division after a few months. With no desk of his own, Kennedy poached space from fellow apprentices like Henry Petersen and William Hundley—both headed for senior posts under Bobby in the Organized Crime and Racketeering Section of the Kennedy Justice Department. Colleagues found Bobby agreeable if a little preoccupied at times, no legal scholar, best known around the Department for rarely bothering to cash his paychecks. He helped prepare prosecutions, most notably the corruption charges against Truman appointee Joe Nunan, the Internal Revenue Commissioner, much of which he presented to a grand jury in Brooklyn. He assisted with several investigations in Western New York.

The Ambassador, always watching, encouraged Bob to cover the San Francisco conference that produced the Japanese peace treaty for the *Post*. At his father's urging, the unenthusiastic Jack invited Bob and Patricia to accompany him on a junket to Israel and the Far East. Congressman Franklin Roosevelt Jr. went along. "I have finally solved the problem as to why the Jews did not accept Jesus Christ," Bob wrote back. "F.D.R. Jr. is what they have been waiting for." In Vietnam, he and his brother concluded that the French were cordially hated, and in any plebiscite Ho Chi Minh would win. Jack got so sick later in the trip that his temperature reached 106 and he received last rites.

In 1952, Jack ran for the Senate against Henry Cabot Lodge. The mainspring of the Eisenhower candidacy that year, Lodge would have seemed unbeatable. Bob himself recruited Kenny O'Donnell for Jack's campaign staff. The stony, congenitally pessimistic football star and captain of the Harvard varsity team had never particularly liked the Ambassador. "Why don't you tell him off once in a while?" O'Donnell challenged Bobby in Hyannis Port when the financier was stomping around in one of his Emperor Tiberius moods.

"Oh, you tell him off," Bob suggested. "I like it the way it is."

As the campaign developed, O'Donnell decided that the Ambassador's outdated, heavy-handed methods were about to doom the whole thing. "He [Joe] dominated everything," one campaign strategist admitted afterward, "even told everyone where to sit. They [were] just children in that house." Kenny pleaded with Bobby to come up and take things over. Unhappy, Bobby wheedled another break from the Justice Department and made his way to Boston. "He just broke his butt," Jack's future administrative assistant Ted Reardon would sum up. Within weeks, Bob had pretty much reinvented the entire Kennedy shtik—the Kennedy secretaries, tea with the sisters, Rose Kennedy and her cue cards.

Administratively, aides found Bobby extremely demanding yet lacking in follow-up. The established Massachusetts pols found him insufferable. Joe Kennedy quickly set to work mollifying the bosses and buttering up the press to keep the momentum going. Governor Paul Dever, struggling with high blood pressure and running largely as a favor to Joe, called the Ambassador and unloaded: "I know you're an important man around here, but I'm telling you this and I mean it. Keep that fresh kid of yours out of my sight from here on in."

When one aide found himself getting ripped by the candidate for printing billboards out of state and told Jack to "Blame that sonofabitch brother of yours," who "ordered me to do it so he could save a dime of your father's money," Jack came back at him with uncharacteristic savagery: "Oh, bullshit, everybody bitches about Bobby, and I'm getting sick and goddamn tired of it. He's the only one who doesn't stick knives in my back, the only one I can count on when it comes down to it."

Not that the Ambassador stayed out. He bankrolled the *Boston Post,* which reversed political direction until Jack got elected. The campaign itself reportedly cost the family half a million dollars. The financier made sure Joe McCarthy never came into the state to attack Jack. In his turn, Jack Kennedy refused to participate in a Democratic Party broadcast condemning McCarthyism.

Privately, Jack was obviously divided. "How dare you couple the name of a great American patriot with that of a traitor," he jumped up to challenge the speaker at a Spee Club reunion who commented that Harvard College had never produced either an Alger Hiss or a Joe McCarthy. But privately, he was telling friends that McCarthy was "just another shanty Irish" who wasn't making life any easier for politicians with his pedigree. Jack rarely saw just one side of anything.

Pillow Talk

After Jack was moved up into the Senate, Joe Kennedy had again gone to work on Bobby's behalf. "My father built his financial empire with a secretary and a telephone," Eunice later observed. McCarthy got the calls that November. "You haven't been elected to anything," the financier raged at Bobby, whom he caught resting. "Are you going to sit on your tail end and do nothing now for the rest of your life?"

Bobby joined Ethel at their house in Georgetown. Even casual friends could see that Bobby was depressed. In 1951 the first of their eleven children, Kathleen, had been greeted with a lot of enthusiasm around the family—Joseph P. Kennedy's first grandchild! As godfather, Bobby and Ethel selected Joe McCarthy.

Robert Kennedy's mood didn't improve in early 1953 once he began to report to the McCarthy subcommittee offices. Morton Downey Jr. remembered a softball game on the Cape at that time, during which a local kid, one Gareth Skenk, demanded to replay a slide into home. Bobby, who was playing catcher, insisted he had tagged the kid out. When Gareth stole home a second time, Bobby stepped up and scrouged the softball into his mouth, knocking out a tooth. While the boy lay writhing and spitting blood, Bobby leaned over him. "You're right, Gareth," Downey remembers Bobby murmuring. "You were safe."

At work, young Kennedy's resentment was palpable. Roy Cohn later recorded what he would recall as his single extended conversation with Bobby. Not long before, Frip Flanagan had taken Cohn aside and told the boy prosecutor than he "had a real enemy in Bobby Kennedy . . . first of all, he isn't crazy about Jews. Second, you're not exactly a member of the Palm Beach polo set. And thirdly, you've got the job he wanted."

Soon afterward, Cohn's door opened and Bobby Kennedy, quite hesitant, came in and stood there a few moments. "You know," Kennedy said finally, "you're a real mystery man."

"I am?"

"Yes."

"Why, are you investigating me or something?"

"No. But some people, like Morton Downey, think you're the greatest guy. Other people think you're a real danger to my career. I don't know who's right and who's wrong."

Cohn, for once, fumbled for a response. Kennedy stood measuring him for a little while, then turned and walked out of the office. The fact was, the luminaries Bobby needed to confirm his status as a Commie-buster at McCarthy's side—cronies of his father like Cardinal Spellman, J. Edgar Hoover, even so unshakable a family friend as Downey—were wild about Roy Cohn. One slot was open, and Cohn already occupied it.

Cohn would later reminisce about "the first time I met Edgar Hoover," in 1952, "when I was in charge of this runaway federal grand jury up in the Southern District of New York, investigating the infiltration of a substantial number of American Communists into the Secretariat of the United Nations." The problem was, since membership in the Communist Party was not a crime for the moment, the grand jury could find no basis to indict. This left the grand jury the option of preparing a report it could release— in legal parlance, a presentment—which identified these individuals and exerted pressure on the UN secretary general to fire them all. Cohn rammed this through, against the wishes of his superiors in the Justice Department in Washington.

Here was a maneuver to tickle Hoover's heart. The Truman administration, Hoover assured Cohn, was teetering and "if they fire you, they'll make a hero out of you, and I will publicly back you up." Hoover instructed Cohn to "call me directly" whenever he had something to divulge, since the Justice Department "gossips are worse than the perverts in the CIA," and were already monitoring Cohn's office telephones to tip Hoover off that "you were an insubordinate little troublemaker, and that I shouldn't see you." For many years after that, Roy Cohn and the FBI Director traded favors, effusive compliments, gifts, and elaborate private dinners. It quickly became "Roy" and "Edgar."

Then there was Roy Cohn's personality. He was a punk still, by his own recollection. "I was rambling, garrulous, and repetitious," he himself wrote later. "I was brash, smug, and smart-alecky. I was pompous and petulant." Robert Kennedy's press aide during the Racket Committee days coming up, Ed Guthman, quoted a Los Angeles columnist as characterizing Cohn as the sort of big dealer who could not "walk into a drug store and order a chocolate malt without telephoning a half a dozen people, telling the proprietor that he kept the malt and the ice cream in the wrong place, being over effusive in thanking the soda jerk and getting into a raging argument with half his fellow customers at the counter."

Journalists who dropped by saw what was happening fast enough. Murray Marder understood Kennedy's discomfort given "his father's relationship to Roy, which was really close . . . in addition to which Cohn is the guy with the legal reputation and Bobby's is zero. . . . Roy treats him as a gofer. Not as a lawyer, fellow counselor, or anything like that. As a kid. A rich bitch kid."

Ralph de Toledano noted that Bobby "went about his business morosely, almost sullenly. In the late afternoon, when the staff would gather in Joe McCarthy's office, waiting for him to return from the Senate floor or from some appointment, Roy Cohn would sprawl out on his boss's chair, feet propped up on the desk. There would be a certain amount of horseplay, of loud humor, but Bobby would sit by himself, aloof and uncommunicative. No one paid very much attention to him, and this undoubtedly rankled."

Roy Cohn was tempting fate, literally. "By asking the Kennedy kid to refill the coffee cups," Nicholas von Hoffman concluded, "Roy had invited Nemesis into his life."

The winter and spring of 1953 found Bob Kennedy at his worst, his rawest and most unpredictable. As Flanagan's assistant, he was kept busy with a secondary project within the subcommittee, an attempt to track down which Allied ships were trading strategic materials with the Red Chinese. His brother Jack, well aware of what a bugbear McCarthy had become even in conservative Massachusetts circles, argued against his signing up with McCarthy, for reasons, Ted Sorensen saw, more political than ideological. Joe Kennedy felt otherwise. "Oh, hell, you can't fight the old man," Jack erupted to one friend. Over on the glory side, Cohn clutched his baton and threw himself and McCarthy into investigations, Bobby later wrote, "instituted on the basis of some preconceived notion by the chief counsel or his staff members and not on the basis of any information that had been developed."

They were winging it. Much of the truncheon work was done in executive sessions, no press or public allowed, where McCarthy attempted to beat up on anybody associated with colleagues who questioned him—Wayne Morse and Margaret Chase Smith were favorites, and Edward Morgan, the erstwhile chief counsel on the Tydings Committee. McCarthy attacked the State Department filing system and the personal habits of Eric Kohler, a senior government accountant and part-time homosexual. By mid-February, McCarthy and Cohn were all over the Voice of America, a subsidiary of the State Department. G. David Schine had joined the staff as "chief consultant."

What began as a witch hunt was developing into a romp. Schine was a tall, languorous recent Harvard graduate with hyacinth locks and limited intellectual firepower. "He always wanted to be somebody," his father Meyer Schine later epitomized. Meyer Schine was one of the great up-from-nothing success stories of his generation. Born in a dirt-floored hovel in Lithuania before the turn of the century, the ambitious immigrant made his way from slaving in a mill to candy butcher on a train to the acquisition, with his brother, of a string of third-rate local theaters. By the early forties, Meyer had started to pick up prestigious hotels in Florida and on the West Coast. Before long, Hoover and the unavoidable Tolson were basking in Meyer's generosity at the Gulfstream Apartments on Miami Beach and the Ambassador Hotel in Los Angeles.

As the Kefauver Committee discovered, part of Schine's cash flow stemmed from Mob payoffs in return for gambling operations in his hotels. Frank Erickson, alleged to tip Hoover off whenever a race was a sure thing, haunted lobbies on both coasts. Erickson set racing odds for the syndicate at tracks country-wide.

David Schine was remembered at Harvard primarily as a would-be big shot. In and out of a hodgepodge of courses on government and economics, he seemed to spend most of his day floating around Boston in his Cadillac, valet at the wheel, attempting to wow his few friends by calling them from his on-board telephone. A secretary attended courses for him and took notes; Schine insisted on maintaining an office in his suite in Adams House and was outraged to discover that even his secretary would have to come and go according to the parietal rules. The one book he read with enthusiasm was *The Fountainhead* by Ayn Rand, which confirmed his worship of power as well as the moral superiority of greed.

At college, Schine dated, conspicuously, starlets and airline stewardesses. Out in the business world, Schine reached the top at twenty-six on his promotion to general manager of Schine Hotels. He composed an eight-page pamphlet, *Definition of Communism,* and made sure no hotel room throughout the Schine empire lacked for a copy.

Most of the history in *Definition of Communism* was muddled and inaccurate, but nobody worried too much about the words when the music was so intense. In 1952, Roy Cohn met G. David Schine at Meyer's Roney Plaza in Miami Beach. "Both of us were about the same age," Cohn later wrote, "and both of us were close to Walter Winchell. We hit it off immediately." Cohn showed *Definition of Communism* to his boss, and McCarthy took Schine on as an unpaid adviser.

Psychohistorians ever since have been attempting to make some sense of the relationship among the three. Lillian Hellman, still steaming over the way the subcommittee had treated Dashiell Hammett, let it be known that she liked to call the Cohn-Schine-McCarthy association Bonny, Bonny, and Clyde. It probably went deeper than that. Before 1953 was out, McCarthy had become fixated on Cohn, regarding him as magical, indispensable. He hired Cohn originally, McCarthy later told friends, to dissipate the aroma of anti-Semitism of which he was uncomfortably aware after the fiasco with Anna Rosenberg. But Cohn was so bright, so much focused belligerence, not tenderhearted like McCarthy, that he had become the backroom driver of the operation.

Meanwhile, Roy Cohn was snakebit; he adored the handsome, insouciant David Schine. Cohn had become overnight the painfully brilliant little loudmouth in awe of the big, dumb Hollywood blonde.

Their partnership was highlighted during the misbegotten tour on which they embarked on April 3, 1953. Ostensibly to ferret out books by Communist-leaning authors in the overseas libraries of the United States Information Service, this five-star rampage through the embassies and consulates of Western Europe exposed these conspicuous McCarthy spokesmen to press conferences, at which they took a shelling. Challenged to explain his justification for including Schine, variously described as "good-looking in the style one associates with male orchestra singers," and disposed to brag to reporters about his collection of discarded cigar bands, Cohn defended his sidekick as having "written a book on the definition of Communism," and, a few stops later, "During the war he wrote a psychological warfare plan for the entire Navy."

The pair roamed widely, outraged to come across a copy of *The Thin*

Man in Rome or incensed when the latest edition of the *American Legion Monthly* wasn't on the rack in Vienna. Ridicule in the media mounted. McCarthy quickly convened follow-up hearings, and seasoned civil servants like Theodore Kaghan, who made the mistake of labeling the pair "junke-teering gumshoes," and Samuel Reber, the acting high commissioner in Germany, were hounded out of government service.

Were Cohn and Schine lovers? A bug the High Commissioner's Office planted in their hotel in Bonn produced a lot of "pillow talk," State Department patois for homosexual badinage, and the Frankfurt paper reported suspicious horseplay in the lobby, Cohn batting Schine over the head with a rolled-up magazine, after which they repaired to Schine's room and upended the furniture and tossed the ashtrays around.

Cohn, as long as he lived, denied that hanky-panky was afoot. But he was exposed. If there was "one thing I'd do different," Cohn would write, "I sure as hell wouldn't have taken that trip with my friend G. David Schine in the spring of 1953."

With McCarthy thundering away at lefties from Langston Hughes to the befuddled Earl Browder, Democratic members of the subcommittee tended to skip the sessions. It really wasn't much of a surprise that the foreign edi-tor of the *Daily Worker* espoused Marxist opinions. Braced by reporters, Bob Kennedy would concede that "Okay, Joe's *methods* may be a little rough. But after all, his goal is to expose Communists in government." He remained a believer. "At least we can say," he insisted to one listener, "that Senator Joe is one of the greatest senators we've ever had." Privately, Kennedy told McCarthy that he was "going out of his mind and was going to destroy him-self" if Cohn and Schine stayed on.

In early May, Bobby presented his breakdown of trade between Western Europe and the Communists. "It developed that Kennedy had discovered an amazing wealth of detail, all carefully documented, concerning the move-ments of ships involved in trade not only with Soviet bloc countries," the *Boston Post* correspondent wrote, "but with Red China itself." One hundred and ninety-two flag vessels, British mostly, but some from places like Norway and, of course, Greece, where the important shipowners were heavily involved, were even carrying cargo for several of the departments of the U.S. government. At one point, Kennedy severely cross-examined Aristotle Onassis.

The home countries of all the carriers were recipients of Marshall Plan aid. As the hearings rolled on, it became clear within a few hours that the Eisenhower administration had not been keeping track of any of this; that, as Acting Deputy Assistant Secretary of State for Economic Affairs John Leddy stated, "We might hurt our allies' feelings if we pressed them on the matter now"; and that despite the administration's ban on Western trade with the Reds, economics was more than likely to trump politics, as ever.

For Robert Kennedy, it was a few good days in an increasingly troubled season. John McClellan of Arkansas, the senior Democrat on the Government Operations Committee, liked what he heard. Even Roy Cohn conceded that Kennedy "did a good job."

Yet by midsummer, McCarthy was conniving with Dick Nixon, by now his designated handler in the administration, to scuttle Robert Kennedy's embarrassing disclosures. Kennedy showed up at the White House to present a letter demanding action and was artfully fluffed off. When Kennedy turned his report in, McCarthy sat on it. Meanwhile, on June 18, under pressure from J. Edgar Hoover to install somebody with a lot more fire in his guts when it came to grubbing up Commies, McCarthy let the phlegmatic Frip Flanagan go and took on J. B. Matthews as executive director of the subcommittee.

A onetime Methodist clergyman, Matthews had been preening his credentials since the thirties through service with the House Un-American Activities Committee and as the resident expert on Marxism for the Hearst conglomerate. But Hoover detested Matthews, whom Westbrook Pegler had termed a "self-confessed female impersonator," and in any case struck the Director as a competitive publicity hog. Matthews was about to publish an article in *American Mercury* that identified the Protestant clergy as "the largest single group supporting the Communist apparatus in the United States today." All three Democrats on the subcommittee—John McClellan, Henry "Scoop" Jackson, and W. Stuart Symington, none of whom were consulted in advance of this inspired selection—were on the point of boycotting the hearings.

Then Matthews was let go, replaced by the hefty Frank Carr, a recent FBI agent. But McCarthy never cleared Carr with his Democratic colleagues or, amazingly, with Edgar; Hoover was immediately alarmed that everybody would think "Carr was a pipeline" between the subcommittee and the Bureau. By now the Director was genuinely apprehensive about McCarthy's runaway subcommittee; all three Democrats quit. When Jean Kerr, the quick-witted and personable office assistant Joe was halfheartedly courting at the time, dropped in on Hoover and floated the suggestion that Robert Kennedy might make a workable replacement for Matthews, the Director let the air out of that one by remarking austerely that he "did not know anything about Mr. Kennedy." Other McCarthy staffers blackballed Bobby. McCarthy abruptly put Cohn in charge of day-to-day operations.

This left Kennedy stranded, unhappily contemplating the pleasures of constant subordination to Roy Cohn. One FBI memorandum refers to a contretemps during which Kennedy "braced Cohn on an administrative matter and brought it to a head by stating that it was either he or Roy Cohn. The matter was resolved in Cohn's favor. . . ." Kennedy resigned on July 29.

At this point, Hoover was beginning to bruit it about that he would not be helping McCarthy and his crew with leads from the Bureau's files. Typically, Hoover locked one door in public and opened all the windows. Ex-FBI agent William Turner would observe how "FBI agents put in long hours poring over Bureau security files and abstracting them for Roy Cohn. . . ." Lou Nichols, the assistant director and presiding oligarch in Crime Records, who had long handled publicity and liaison with Congress, was regularly overheard taking calls from Cohn, directing him to whichever special agent happened to be tracking some promising ex-Communist or unrepentant left-winger. While not technically "files," Cohn received, as he later admitted, "copied-over or synopsis reports," summaries loaded with anything that might advance the cause.

Nichols coached McCarthy in techniques like releasing a story just before newspaper deadlines, to cut off negative rebuttals. Once McCarthy had turned in desperation to his final, self-destructive assault on the U.S. Army, and the Army put its own technicians to bugging McCarthy's telephones, they reported conversations between Hoover and Roy Cohn "two, sometimes three times a day." "We were the ones," the renegade FBI assistant director William Sullivan later confessed. "We fed McCarthy all the material he was using. . . . I worked on it myself. At the same time, we were telling the public we had nothing to do with it."

Shortly after Bobby left, McCarthy announced his intention to probe the CIA. As the successor to the OSS, the Central Intelligence Agency had become a perennial source of agitation to Hoover. McCarthy would fasten on William Bundy, the well-born younger brother of McGeorge Bundy and Dean Acheson's son-in-law. An Agency analyst, Bill Bundy had contributed $400 to a defense fund for Alger Hiss.

When McCarthy summoned William Bundy, Agency Director Allen Dulles blithely stonewalled; to save some face all around, Richard Nixon smoothly arranged for Bundy to be subjected instead to an internal CIA review. McCarthy steamed. He hired another FBI veteran, Jim Juliana, Carr's number two on the New York "Red Squad," as the new chief investigator. The subcommittee was starting to look like an FBI alumni roundup.

Very much the odd man out, Robert Kennedy attempted to occupy himself that summer and fall as his father's assistant on the Commission on the Reorganization of the Executive Branch—the Herbert Hoover Commission. Robert Kennedy now found himself trapped in the midst of a cluster of touchy, squabbling septuagenarians, each incensed when one of his suggestions got turned down. Joe Kennedy, of all people, had emerged as the peacemaker. "Now, Chief, let me handle this," Joe urged the eighty-year-old Herbert Hoover when the Democrats on the Commission raised an objection. "I'll line up these fellows for you."

For Bobby, the situation was beyond enduring. "Working under the old man who still considered him a child," Lem Billings saw, "he felt he was getting nowhere. He was angry and got mad at people all the time. A lot of people thought he was an asshole."

Kennedy's vision of his own prospects undoubtedly took another hit in September 1953, when John Kennedy married Jacqueline Bouvier in Newport's most lavish social event of the season. The bride was beautiful and wide-eyed, brimming with good taste and effortless in all the Latin languages. Sensing Bobby's admiration, the rough-and-tumble Ethel disliked her instantly. "With those feet, kiddo, you should have been a soccer player," Ethel jibed when the breathy Jacqueline divulged her childhood dreams of the ballet. Jackie dismissed Ethel as a "baby-making machine."

Bobby radiated discontent. Attending the Yale game together that year with Kenny O'Donnell, Bob lost it and started bellowing in public when the hard-bitten O'Donnell berated him about McCarthy. When nearby baseball players lofted flies into his touch football game in Georgetown, Bobby stepped in between Ted and the biggest of the offenders and engaged in a bare-knuckle brawl that left him extravagantly banged-up at dinner. "That must have been a rough game of touch," Ethel said, looking over the bruises.

"Yeah," Bobby muttered. There really wasn't much to say.

In the early winter of 1954, Robert Kennedy caught a break. John McClellan, the starchy old segregationist from Arkansas who had admired Kennedy's work on the strategic shipping problem, got enough appropriations leverage to negotiate terms with McCarthy that would permit the minority members to have some influence on the selection of staff should they return to the hearings. Bob immediately called his father, who initiated "a few discreet inquiries," arranged for another job and a substantive payoff for the ranking applicant for the position, and locked up the Minority Counsel slot for his son. According to Bobby Baker, Joe's undisclosed $50,000 deposit into a McClellan bank account in Little Rock hadn't damaged Robert Kennedy's chances.

Even during the few months that Bobby had been gone, a good deal had changed. Stories had been circulating on and off for years in Washington's journalistic underworld to the effect that McCarthy himself could be tempted, especially when he drank, to mix it up with another man. In 1952, a letter had been forwarded to Attorney General J. Howard McGrath from a Lieutenant David Sayer claiming to have been rendered drunk and brutally sodomized by McCarthy at the Wardman Park Hotel. Under pressure, unwillingly, Hoover conducted a perfunctory investigation; his approach with McCarthy, according to an in-house FBI memo, was to lament in his exchanges with the senator that individuals with "unusual moral proclivities" got government jobs so easily. McCarthy was "quite concerned regarding this entire picture. . . ."

The snoop they both feared was the indefatigable Drew Pearson. The columnist kept a "tail" on the burly senator and had been compiling affidavits from individuals claiming to have been molested by McCarthy. During the autumn of 1952, campaigning in Nevada, McCarthy misspoke and accused the hard-boiled publisher of the *Las Vegas Sun,* Hank Greenspun, of being an ex-Communist. Pearson sent his paperwork along to Greenspun, who published a sweeping exposé in his column. He cited McCarthy's involvement with Charles Davis, a former Communist and confessed homosexual, and the arrest of Ed Babcock, an administrative assistant, for "solicitation of a lewd and lascivious purpose." Reporters at the *Capital Times* in Madison had slipped Pearson eyewitness accounts of McCarthy having spent the night in a Wausau hotel room with a prominent Young Republican "engaged in illicit acts with each other." Milwaukee insiders gossiped that "Sen. Joseph McCarthy has often engaged in homosexual activities" at the notorious White Horse Inn.

In September 1953, McCarthy and his lovely, obstinate assistant, Jean Kerr, finally got married. They reportedly argued all the way to the altar—"I was fired three times," she later admitted. The event was mounted at St. Matthew's Cathedral in Washington, attended by the Nixons, Allen Dulles, Hoover and Tolson, Sherman Adams, Secretary of the Army Robert Stevens, and John and Robert Kennedy. The Pope sent blessings. Willard Edwards of the *Chicago Tribune*, one of McCarthy's sympathizers in the press, "thought that Joe, nearly 45, consented to marriage only to quash stories that he was homosexual."

The pair would set up, visitors said later, in a kind of permanent pandemonium. The telephone rang constantly, newcomers wandered in and out amidst the mountains of unopened wedding presents months after the event, Joe bought a Doberman Pinscher and hung a huge poster of Jesse James in his study. With Cardinal Spellman's help, they adopted an Asian child. Hoover, who socialized very little, "used to love to come up and have Mrs. McCarthy, Jeannie, do the cooking," Roy Cohn later reminisced. "He used to come up with Tolson and there would be just four or five people and everybody could let—could exchange confidences and just sort of have a relaxed evening."

At one dinner, McCarthy won a bet with Cohn that he could get the Director to take his jacket off by charging him with wearing a wire. McCarthy could be amusing, in the straight-faced, hair-raising style of the confirmed drunk. Asked whether he'd like another round, McCarthy would present his slow smile and concede, "Well, you can put it this way— Yes." He would offer to show bystanders his abdominal scar "for a quarter." "Let me show you what I have here" he would whisper to admirers gathered around. He'd open his briefcase and slowly withdraw a large, loaded revolver.

The newlyweds were close, Cohn later wrote, but "both were strong-willed and Joe was difficult to domesticate." They squabbled over other women. At one point, Jean exerted her influence with Hoover to arrange for the transfer of an FBI agent to Alaska. The agent's attractive wife was one of the secretaries in McCarthy's office, and things were threatening to go too far.

A bureaucrat before anything else, Hoover sensed McCarthy slipping and now had seriously begun the dance of withdrawal. FBI records note that the Director saw Robert Kennedy on January 28 and February 15 and again in the late spring, "apparently on a personal matter." Eisenhower himself, the Director could see, was a very punishing inside politician. With war in Korea behind the country, the lust for hunting down subversives had started to abate. McCarthy was noisily rolling the artillery up for the spring campaign by early 1954. He would be pounding on the Army.

If Hoover was deserting, Joe McCarthy would be the last to figure it out. Meanwhile, Cohn's chronic emotional finagling was starting to leave the regulars around the Seat of Government seasick. A series of FBI Office Memoranda survives, somewhat censored, with enough left in the clear to indicate the gathering discomfort. "I advised _____ that Roy Cohn does not have a pipeline to the Bureau," one January 18, 1954 memo from Al Belmont to Milton Ladd opens, emphasizing that "information from our files is not made available to the Committee. I advised him that we do have contact with Cohn, inasmuch as matters on which the Committee has been working are pertinent to our jurisdiction. . . . I pointed out that Roy Cohn is very adept at bluffing. . . .

"In our contacts with Mr. Cohn, I think we should be very careful not to betray any confidence concerning information _____ has furnished to us."

Hoover's flat, emphatic script brings down the Director's concurrence: "Right. Cohn gets nothing from us and anyone having contact with Cohn should be most circumspect so he (Cohn) can't enlarge on it."

A few days later, a memo from Lou Nichols to Tolson expands on the problem, "since so far as I know, I am the only person who has contact with Cohn, I might perhaps be a little sensitive. . . . I certainly hope that Mr. Belmont is not laboring under any false assumption that I am engaged in the practice of furnishing the identity of our information from confidential sources to Cohn, as I am not."

Nichols goes on to insist that he has "never been under any illusions about Cohn's propensity of [sic] talking. Certainly his comments about the Director's sending him ties for Christmas is absolutely uncalled for, and I wish there were some way we could hop him on this without divulging the source of our information; obviously, we can't. I have tried to be circumspect in my dealings with Cohn and at the same time not precipitate any blow-up because Cohn is temperamental. . . . I think we have got to get along with him as long as he is in his present role.

"Cohn is smart beyond comprehension," Nichols continues, sketching out how he himself is being put in the middle between the McCarthy Committee and movers around the CIA. "On the evening of January 21, Roy Cohn called me from Florida. He has been down there for two days now and is apparently getting lonely." Cohn has been approached to arrange a meeting with a key official for McCarthy, but "If he sees Senator McCarthy, Senator McCarthy might get all excited."

"As a matter of fact," Nicholas ends the memo, rather plaintively, "I did not know that the Director had sent Roy two ties for Christmas . . . Roy sent me a tie. I sent him a New Year's greeting card with a thank you note."

A month later, Nichols again memos Tolson, explaining that he had underlined to Cohn that "we were getting sick and tired of former Agents going out and taking jobs wherein they are hired solely because of the fact they might have some knowledge. . . . Cohn stated he didn't think he was a stupid man, but he just could not understand the position I was taking."

Both Tolson and Hoover weighed in with reaction to these comments. "The main difficulty is that Cohn, if he hires enough ex-agents, will get access to our complete security set up, as well as knowledge of individual cases and informants," Tolson wrote. Hoover agreed: "That is exactly the point and that is the reason I originally opposed Carr's appointment both to McCarthy and Cohn. Ex-agents trying to make good on the Committee job are not going to drop an iron curtain on their past knowledge of Bureau cases, informants, etc."

The adroit Cohn had somehow maneuvered himself into a position from which he could play McCarthy and Hoover off against each other. "Roy Cohn called me this morning," Nichols memoed Tolson on February 26, "and stated he is thoroughly disgusted with the Senate Investigating Com-mittee and with Senator McCarthy" for agreeing to a scenario according to which six Communists in the Army would get called before the subcommittee and plead the Fifth Amendment. By allowing Secretary of the Army Stevens to so distance himself from the proceedings, Cohn complained, he was "having the ground cut out from under him; that he was fed up with it and told McCarthy so this morning. . . ." "Cohn stated that he is completely disgusted, not only with McCarthy in this instance, but is disgusted with Bob Kennedy who wants to bring back the girl," an ex-employee of the subcommittee who worked there "for some seven years and Cohn has flatly stated he had fired her before and the day she comes back on the committee staff, that day he walks out."

Meanwhile, "Roy stated that he is very fond of McCarthy personally; that McCarthy is coming to New York this afternoon and is going to stay at his house and probably McCarthy will persuade him to continue. . . ."

Chick business, in essence: a politics of tiffs and reconciliation. For Bob Kennedy, back as the minority counsel, this whiff of the seraglio could turn the stomach. Still impatient with his career, according to Morton Downey Jr.: "I think he made a lot of Irish mistakes, all of the venomous, vituperative things that people can do." Besides which "You had to have hair growing out of the corner of your shoulders with Bobby not to be a faggot. Bobby was extremely homophobic."

Called back to lawyer for the Democrats on the Committee, Kennedy wasted very little time before going to work on Cohn. Proceeding down his surviving list of military leads at the end of February, Cohn had fastened on one middle-aged woman, Annie Lee Moss, whose name an undercover FBI employee thought she remembered spotting on a list of Communist Party members ten years earlier. Annie Lee Moss was a forthright, naïve black lady who had been promoted from service in the Pentagon cafeteria to tending the Teletype machines. She first remembered having heard the word "Communist" a few years earlier, when the Hiss case hit the papers. A reporter picked up on the fact that the Communist Mr. Hall the FBI informant recalled as working with Moss was white, but the Mr. Hall Annie Moss knew was black. The reporter got word to Bobby.

Robert Kennedy had started passing notes to John McClellan—there were anomalies here—so Scoop Jackson sent Kennedy over to the Department of Justice to find out whether the FBI could provide better follow-up on Moss. This led to "rather a major dispute with the FBI . . . particularly with Lou Nichols," Kennedy would remember, "because they lied to me about some documents they made available to the committee [i.e., Cohn]. They were making information available to the committee, and they were telling me they weren't."

Cohn would portray Kennedy as having "stormed" into Hoover's offices and demanded Annie Moss's file. But Cohn had telephoned ahead, and Hoover instructed the staff to observe "absolute circumspection in any conversation" with Kennedy. According to Cohn, the Director now regarded Kennedy as "an arrogant whipper-snapper." "Robert Kennedy has got to be watched," Hoover memoed Nichols. "He is a dangerous fellow." This was the first skirmish in a campaign that would absorb a great deal of the rest of both men's lifetimes.

It was already apparent that the subcommittee might well have the wrong Annie Lee Moss—there were three in the D.C. directory alone, and they were quite possibly catechizing an innocent witness—again. By then, the Bureau was attempting to cover its tracks by funneling information to the subcommittee either through sympathizers in military intelligence or in Civil Service Commission background summaries. But independent journalists like Drew Pearson or Martin Agronsky knew, and were beginning to write, that most of what McCarthy had came from the FBI's raw files, often poorly vetted and dependent on hearsay.

While Hoover was playing out an increasingly coy hand with Cohn and McCarthy, he was bustling around reinsuring himself at command levels through the Eisenhower administration. Toward the end of 1953, Hoover briefed Attorney General Herbert Brownell on an "alleged conspiracy." Hoover's source had disclosed that "a group of Catholics in the United States led by Cardinal Spellman" was working "to undermine the Eisenhower administration and to eventually bring about the election of McCarthy as president." To this end, McCarthy was allegedly receiving the support of many wealthy Catholics, including "prominent individuals such as ex-Ambassador Joseph P. Kennedy. . . ." "The 'conspiracy' group is sending to McCarthy all sorts of individuals, which included émigrés who are passing out fabricated information."

As with Franklin Roosevelt, Hoover sold Joe Kennedy out to the sitting president without a noticeable qualm. The financier probably never knew. When Walter Winchell announced his support of Hoover for president in 1955, the Ambassador wrote Hoover that such an eventuality "would be the most wonderful thing for the United States" and guaranteed the Director "the largest contribution that you would ever get from anybody and the hardest work by either a Democrat or a Republican." Hoover framed the note.

By bringing Cardinal Spellman into the cross-hairs as a potential traitor, Hoover was attempting to establish himself at a safe distance from Roy Cohn and his backers—Cardinal Spellman, Lewis Rosenstiel, William Randolph Hearst Jr., Alfred Kohlberg, William F. Buckley Jr., George Sokolsky, Fulton Lewis Jr., and the entire self-important spectrum of Café-Society alarmists. At least for this round, the wail of the China Lobby was fading. Dwight Eisenhower was not interested in a land war in Asia.

Robert Kennedy's motives were easier to follow. By 1953, keyed in by Drew Pearson, reporters were beginning to ask why Cohn and especially the strapping David Schine seemed to have escaped military service. Cohn asserted some National Guard cover for the moment, but Schine was vulnerable. Although he alluded at times to a slipped disc, Schine had arranged things so that he disappeared into the jurisdiction of a malleable Los Angeles draft board. A reporter for the *Baltimore Sun*, Phillip Potter, needed inside help to trace the specifics of Schine's background, and this he got from Robert Kennedy. "Bobby wanted to get Cohn, and I wanted to get McCarthy," Potter said later on. "And we made a perfect team." The draft board reclassified Schine as fit for service.

Schine expected a direct commission, but now he ran into the chief of the Senate's Office of Legislative Liaison, Major General Miles Reber, the brother of Samuel Reber, whom Roy had driven out of the State Department. So David Schine remained a private. Once Kennedy was back on the Committee's payroll, he made a point of tracking Schine's performance at Fort Dix, and by the winter of 1954 was tipping off reporters to look into the way Private Schine was being treated during basic training. Before long, the life-style of this high-profile inductee was meat for the columnists—Schine's special fur-lined hood, his propensity to sit out target practice in the communications hut impressing the officers, while the rest of the battalion was training in the driving rain. Weekends, a chauffeur-driven Cadillac rushed Cohn and Schine to joints in Philadelphia or the Cub Room of the Stork Club. A high-level Department of Defense document survives in which the chauffeur alleges that the two "engaged in homosexual acts in back of car." KP was out of the question.

Cohn simply couldn't help it; he'd lost his heart. "Schine seems to have the dominant influence," one insider noted, "even though Cohn outranks him in everything intellectual. He seems to be fond of humiliating Cohn in front of strangers, quick in putting him into his place. He is most outspoken in his criticism of Cohn's mannerisms and acts generally as if Cohn were his inferior." McCarthy anticipated the damage that running publicity about Schine's privileged life might do. "For God's sake," McCarthy implored Secretary of the Army Stevens soon after Schine was inducted, "don't put Dave in service and assign him back to my committee. If he could get off weekends—Roy—it is one of the few things I have seen him completely unreasonable about. He thinks Dave should be a general and work from the penthouse of the Waldorf. . . ."

Playing as they did throughout the Army–McCarthy hearings, Schine's escapades suggested corruption that the common reader could understand. Robert Kennedy did everything he could to ensure that Schine received the attention he deserved. McCarthy opened his main assault on the Army in January 1954. Robert Kennedy led off the inquisition, aggressive to the edge of brutal. The target selected was Major Irving Peress, an openly leftist dentist filling teeth at Camp Kilmer, New Jersey. Peress had been permitted to resign his commission with an honorable discharge.

David Schine had just been assigned to eight months' service at Camp Gordon, in Georgia. Cohn proclaimed himself incensed at the inconvenience and struck back by demanding that McCarthy be allowed to interrogate six members of the Army loyalty board. Before long, McCarthy was bullyragging the commandant at Kilmer, General Ralph Zwicker, who objected to the way McCarthy seemed to want to impugn his intelligence.

"Either your honesty or your intelligence," McCarthy had growled. "I can't help impugning one or the other."

Eisenhower had had enough. "This guy McCarthy is going to get into trouble over this," he told his press aide, Jim Hagerty. The president had been reading his advisories from Hoover. "He's ambitious. He wants to be president. He's the last guy who'll ever get there if I have anything to say."

By April, the way had been cleared to close McCarthy down. On *See It Now,* Edward R. Murrow had panned in on McCarthy's style and cut and spliced a presentation calculated to chill the Wisconsin senator's most unthinking admirers. What once seemed forceful on the evening news—"the look of perspiring sincerity on his face," as Jack Anderson wrote, "the awkward, ringing delivery, the heavy first pounding on the rostrum"—it all verged on insane, criminally menacing, when juxtaposed to the small screen. Handlers for the president had quietly pulled J. Robert Oppenheimer's security clearance, forestalling a McCarthy headline-grabber. Hoover had worked up a wide-ranging dossier on the physicist and his far-left friendships and associations.

On April 22, the long-awaited Army–McCarthy hearings opened. Ostensibly, the hearings were convened to give McCarthy a forum to substantiate his charges against the military. But as McCarthy's support continued to crumble even among the Senate's Republicans, the burden of the proceedings soon became the effort to establish whether McCarthy had been abusing the Army or the Army McCarthy. McCarthy's main assault went in behind a two-and-a-quarter-page letter from J. Edgar Hoover to General Alexander Bolling, chief of Army Intelligence at the time, dated January 26, 1951. The letter contained the names of thirty-five Fort Monmouth employees suspected of subversion.

The Army had hired as its attorney the crafty, homespun old Boston lawyer Joseph Welch. While pitted against the offstage Edward Bennett Williams, McCarthy's hired legal gun, Welch easily established that most of the individuals cited, down to the last doddering thirties Marxist still humping in the laundry, had long since been cleaned out by a decade of loyalty boards. The more important questions, which now arose, were what McCarthy was doing with a document like this, and why, once he procured it, he had not turned it back to the executive branch for action. Attorney General Brownell immediately ruled it an unauthorized use of classified information. Hoover himself was irate, especially when he discovered that Walter Winchell had a copy first, and attempted to disown the letter; on further investigation, it turned out to be a boiled-down summary of Hoover's fifteen-page original, no doubt condensed years earlier in Lou Nichols's shop and passed along to Cohn before the Director started to find the hairs standing up across the base of his neck each time his pal from Wisconsin began waving a document.

Under the TV lights, the demagogue was melting down hour by hour. "He came into American homes as humorless, demanding, dictatorial, and obstructive," Cohn himself later wrote. "With his easily erupting temper, his menacing monotone, his unsmiling mien, and his perpetual five-o'clock shadow, he did seem the perfect stock villain." It wouldn't be long before McCarthy would attempt to pillory one of Welch's uninvolved junior associates, and Welch would come back with the words that effectively finished McCarthy: "Little did I dream you could be so reckless and so cruel as to do an injury to that lad." McCarthy had met his master at sanctimoniousness, and he had lost.

Military lawyers had prepared a forty-page Schine Report, which itemized exactly what favors Cohn and Schine had extorted from the Army and what qualifications Schine had, or didn't have, even to pretend to advise the subcommittee. Bob Kennedy sat next to Scoop Jackson and handed him note after note as he drew out McCarthy himself. Kennedy's snide questions at one point pertained to the "Schine Plan," a pretentious set of proposals through which to wage "psychological warfare" against the Communist world. Schine proposed a "Deminform" of the capitalist nations to counter the Reds. Each phrase made the onlookers erupt into fresh waves of laughter.

Cohn, furious, attempted to defend the plan, but Jackson kept gaveling him down. Once the hearing ended, Cohn made straight for Kennedy. "Tell Jackson we're going to get him on Monday," Cohn erupted, jabbing a file folder toward Kennedy's face. "We've got letters he wrote to the White House on behalf of two known Communists."

"You tell him yourself," Bobby came back. "Don't you make any warnings to us about Democratic senators. You've got a fucking nerve, threatening me."

Cohn blared out that it was unfair to have Kennedy serve with the inquiry in view of his "hatred for one of the principals"—himself.

"If I have a dislike for anyone in the case," Kennedy said, "it certainly is justified. Don't warn me, you won't get away with that, Cohn. You tried it with the Army; you tried it with the Democratic senators. Now you are trying it with me. Don't try it, Cohn."

"Do you want to fight now?" Cohn demanded, moving toward Kennedy.

"Do you think someone who has a personal hatred of someone in this case can continue to sit there and advise senators? Do you think you're qualified?"

But Robert Kennedy was moving off into the crowd.

"Aw, we got a cute kid here," Cohn explained to the converging reporters.

If Kennedy seemed vindictive, Cohn gave him cause enough. Perhaps a month before the blowup, Cohn had confided to Drew Pearson's legman Jack Anderson that FBI reports had disclosed that links to a group of "pinkos" had kept Bob's kid brother, Edward Kennedy, out of the Army's radio school at Ft. Holabird, Maryland. Informed in time, Joe Kennedy called Louis Nichols and unloaded on the assistant director. Joe would not tolerate his son's being "victimized."

There was no investigation, Nichols assured Joe, and this was one more instance of McCarthy's staff "throwing the name of the FBI around." Joe killed the item.

For Robert Kennedy, the incident provided one more humiliating example of the way his father insisted on breaking in time after time to straighten up the wreckage. Every job he got involved some FBI has-been his father probably knew through Hoover. Hoover, characteristically, cranked down the flow of information to McCarthy and Cohn but kept the association alive. An FBI memo of June 14 passes on a promise from Roy Cohn to Walter Winchell after "the blowup last Friday with Robert Kennedy" that Cohn "has made his last mistake." Hoover would remain Cohn's *consigliere*.

McCarthy continued to socialize with the younger Kennedys, and there were reports of Joe at lunches with Jean Kerr and Pat Kennedy and Peter Lawford, with Roy Cohn sitting in. Eunice and Sarge Shriver joined McCarthy in Chicago sometimes, although Sarge was known to be cooling. "I'm sorry you and Bobby are always at each other's throats," Cohn claims John F. Kennedy remarked when the two met at C. Z. Guest's April-in-Paris ball at the Waldorf. "I think you've got a great deal of ability and I like this job you've done against Communism. The fight between Bobby and you hasn't carried over to us."

For McCarthy, the rest of the year went straight downhill. On June 19, too hot to handle around the clubby Senate, Roy Cohn was forced to resign. He returned to his mother's house in Manhattan. Bureaucratically, McCarthy was eviscerated from then on: Roy had always handled everything: scheduling, contacts, information, tactical moves, political scheming. Both were hit-and-run artists, disorganized, quick studies and dependent on that. After a miserable summer and much stalling, the Republicans lost the Senate that fall and the survivors voted to censure McCarthy 67–12 on December 2. Jack Kennedy was recuperating in Florida from another back operation that nearly killed him the day the motion to censure reached the floor, and he refrained from voting either way or having his vote paired. Hard liberals like Eleanor Roosevelt would never forgive him. Ideologically, Jack was already walking a very fine line: by withholding his vote for the confirmation of rightist witch hunter Robert Lee, Kennedy knew that "John Fox and McCarthy are going to be wild about this." Aides of the period describe McCarthy as "the *other* type of Irishman that Jack tried so hard to dissociate himself from." Jack was fairly open about his distaste for McCarthy's "excesses" while purging the State Department. Still, as John Kennedy himself observed, with that bulletproof diffidence that saved him over and over, "I was rather in ill grace personally to be around hollering about what McCarthy had done in 1952 and 1951 when my brother had been on the staff in 1953. That is really the guts of the matter."

McCarthy was ruined. Roy Cohn, who looked in often, came upon his champion sunken into his chair at home, staring into the fire, beaten. Robert Kennedy was staggered to find his mentor "looking terribly. . . . Couldn't stand straight and often appeared to be in a trance." By 1956, as Ted Morgan sums it up, McCarthy had become a "commuter to Bethesda Naval Hospital, leaning on his wife's arm and slow in movement, suffering from back trouble, heart trouble, elbow trouble, stomach trouble, knee trouble, hernia trouble, and, above all, drink trouble . . . he drank a bottle a day, which takes serious application."

McCarthy died on May 2, 1957. He was forty-eight. When Robert Kennedy got the news, he put his head down on his desk and wept. He joined the small party that attended the burial next to the McCarthy parents in Appleton, Wisconsin. This death, Bobby admitted, "was very difficult for me as I felt that I had lost an important part of my life." By then it might have occurred to Bob that, by energetically undermining Cohn, he had brought down Tail Gunner Joe.

Later he would characterize McCarthy's career as a toboggan ride "so exciting and exhilarating as it went downhill that it didn't matter to him if he hit a tree at the bottom. . . .

"I liked him and yet at times he was terribly heavy-handed. He was a very complicated character. His whole method of operation was complicated, because he would get a guilty feeling and get hurt after he had blasted somebody. He wanted desperately to be liked. He was so thoughtful and yet so unthoughtful in what he did to others. He was sensitive and yet insensitive. He didn't anticipate the results of what he was doing. He was very thoughtful of his friends, and yet he could be so cruel to others."

Afterward, reading that, it would be hard for Bobby's intimates not to suspect that he had caught at least a glimpse of his own private demon reflected in the tortured McCarthy.

8

The Taste of Blood

With Cohn gone and McCarthy in no shape to rattle the colleagues, the Permanent Subcommittee on Investigations of the Government Operations Committee came largely under John McClellan's control. Bob Kennedy was chief counsel, the survivor of his first big-league blood feud. He remained restless.

The Subcommittee disposed quietly of whatever seemed worth mopping up after—the Peress case and the purported Ft. Monmouth subversives. Kennedy was more attracted to a spate of conflict-of-interest leads turned up by outside sources. Charles Bartlett, a journalist friend of Jack's, had discovered that Secretary of the Air Force Harold Talbot solicited government business for a firm in which he still held half the ownership. Talbot, a golfing partner of Joe Kennedy in Palm Beach, was a popular socialite with a good many boosters in the Senate, and even the fading Joe McCarthy spoke out to implore that the Secretary "does not get an unfair deal and a smear."

But Kennedy, largely unsupported except for what Bartlett got into the *Chattanooga News,* kept up the cross-examination; as the facts surfaced, Eisenhower demanded Talbot's resignation. As with the strategic cargoes, politics and favoritism were anathema to Kennedy once he had tasted a little blood.

While Kennedy was winding up the hearing on Talbot up in July of 1955, he got a letter from his father. "Just a quick note," the Ambassador wrote from his villa at Eze. "Heard from Mother that Talbott [*sic*] had said that his activities were no different from mine when I bought Haig and Haig while in government. I should say they were!" Joe points out that he acquired the franchise for Haig and Haig before he went into government service, and did no business with the government, ever. There is no mention of favors for Jimmy Roosevelt, of the thousands of cases of Scotch headed west across the Atlantic in precious cargo space in 1940, or of the insider speculations against Czech currency. Above all, let the children remain uncontaminated.

Hours after he wound up the Talbot inquiry, Robert Kennedy caught a plane via Paris to Teheran to meet his father's close friend William O. Douglas, by then the senior liberal lion on the Supreme Court. The pair were off on a hiking and climbing expedition through Soviet Central Asia. Challenged by his wife of the period, Mercedes, as to why he had agreed to take along this touchy, provincial middle son of the Ambassador, Douglas minced no words: "I have to do it. Joe wants me to do it. Joe thinks it would do him some good." The elder Kennedy, after all, had persuaded FDR to appoint Douglas to the Supreme Court. Rose found Bobby "loath" to go and "rather depressed" at the prospect, but Joe had decided the boy's "ego needed boosting and he needed to feel he was interesting to other people."

The two rambled widely throughout the Moslem South, Douglas making friends everywhere while Bobby proved a trial to his Intourist keepers with his bumptious anti-Communism. He found the caviar too dirty to eat and distrusted the Soviet medical facilities, although in the end he developed a fever in Omsk, which it took a great brute of a female physician and a colossal injection of Russian penicillin to get him through. He wrote his children, of which there were by now four. "Say your prayers," one card recommended, "and get to bed on time and you won't grow up to be a juvenile delinquent like your mother."

KGB records of the trip characterize the thirty-year-old Robert Kennedy as a "dangerous opponent" of socialism who repeatedly asked his interpreter to "provide him with women of loose morals." Such requests were by no means unusual. He was blooming late.

But he caught on. During Jack's first run for the Senate, for example, one of JFK's aides would allude to several nights Bob spent with Elizabeth Okrun, a debutante apprenticing with the campaign. Even that most unremitting of Kennedy loyalists, Arthur Schlesinger Jr., was reported by Anthony Summers to have admitted that "Bobby was human. He liked a drink and he liked young women. He indulged that liking when he traveled—and he had to travel a great deal."

Back in Washington, Bob Kennedy stopped by at the Department of Justice to report on his trip to J. Edgar Hoover. A rather terse memorandum of the visit survives. The Director had been watching closely as this impertinent young careerist disassembled Roy Cohn, and Hoover could already see that Robert Kennedy might get very troublesome to handle.

The Investigations Subcommittee returned to prying into East-West trade. Special interests were at work, and the Eisenhower administration now refused to release to Congress even the *lists* of strategic goods it was pretending to embargo. But this was now Bobby's bone, and he continued to worry it.

In 1956, he attended the Democratic National Convention in Chicago. By now, Jack Kennedy was making the columns as a future presidential nominee. Once Adlai Stevenson secured the nomination, he threw the vice-presidential choice open to the convention. An impromptu assemblage of Kennedy shock troops—family, mostly, with a handful of political allies and Ken O'Donnell and Larry O'Brien—began to canvass frantically. At an early juncture—Jack had arranged things to step out of the room in time— Bobby got a call through to the vacationing Ambassador, lying low on the French Riviera. Joe now was convinced Stevenson was political dead meat: "Jack's a total fucking idiot and you're worse!" Avoid this ticket!

"The Ambassador's blue language flashed all over the room," O'Donnell wrote later. "Whew. Is he mad!" Bobby expired as the line went dead.

Jack Kennedy narrowly lost the nod to Estes Kefauver, who had sent the delegates Christmas cards, and for several months the mood in the Kennedy camp was not elevated. Jack himself went sailing in the Mediterranean with his brother Teddy and George Smathers, and while he vacationed Jacqueline lost the baby she had been carrying. Robert Kennedy, unfailingly attentive, arranged for its burial. Bob himself remained embittered. On the plane back to Boston after the convention he flailed away at the delegate sitting next to him to the effect that Jack "should have won and somebody had pulled something fishy and he wanted to know who did it."

Bobby now had a new subject: the mechanics of presidential politics. Joe Kennedy donated heavily, and Bob joined the Stevenson campaign, bumping down from whistle-stop to whistle-stop and sitting in on strategy meetings. This was Bobby's first extended exposure to important figures in the liberal Democratic brain-bank like Ken Galbraith and Arthur Schlesinger Jr. Two years before, Kennedy had responded to a Schlesinger letter to the *New*

York Times by resenting Arthur's "personal attack on my accuracy if not my truthfulness," and demanding that the self-assured savant make "the necessary public apology." Now, traveling together, the pair proved compatible.

Eugenie Anderson, another politico just learning the ropes, remembered Kennedy as "always sitting in a corner and acting rather uncomfortable." Always making notes. The entire effort, Kennedy concluded, was "ghastly. More important, my feeling was that he [Stevenson] had no rapport with his audience . . . no ability to make decisions." "He spent all day long discussing matters that should have taken, at the most, a half hour," Kennedy commented in retrospect. "I was learning what not to do." In November he voted for Eisenhower.

Back in the Permanent Subcommittee on Investigations, the purpose of the inquiry had started to shift even before the election intervened. An attempt to run down the cost of uniforms opened the way into the broad subject of labor racketeering. Even Robert Kennedy could see that month after month tracking down subversives in federal book binderies and petrifying retired fellow-traveler librarians might be a waste of the taxpayers' money. J. Edgar Hoover still insisted that the handful of dues-paying Communist Party members left after the Soviets invaded Hungary constituted the tip of the iceberg. As things developed, a remarkable percentage of the surviving faithful were FBI informants, and Edgar himself admitted during an off-guard moment that, without dues from his spies, the Party might soon go belly-up.

They needed an electrifying issue, something the newspapers could follow. A tough, sophisticated reporter Bobby was talking to, Clark Mollenhoff of the *Des Moines Tribune-Register,* started chewing on him about the iniquities of labor corruption, the extent to which certain union leaders were selling out the rank and file through sweetheart deals with hoodlums. Mollenhoff had his sights on the Teamsters.

This was a radioactive subject, no matter which tongs you picked it up with, since organized labor was the molten core of the Democratic Party. Around Joseph P. Kennedy, with his buried associations, the air was likely to explode at even the mention of such an initiative. Robert Kennedy broached the matter over the Christmas recess of 1956 in Hyannis Port, and the upset Ambassador brought down the worst intrafamily brawl Jean Smith could remember. The whole thing was a "terrible idea," her father felt, he was "deeply, emotionally opposed," and Joe and Bobby had "an unprecedented furious argument." "The old man saw this as dangerous, not the sort of thing or sort of people to mess around with," Lem Billings later testified. Bobby was a donkey; if anything went wrong, any chance Jack Kennedy ever had as a contender for the presidency would disappear overnight—Bobby had already approached Jack to sit on the Subcommittee and back him up. The unions were vital, why look too closely into the perversities of *that* universe? Connections were everything in politics. . . .

Coming on the heels of the brothers' ill-advised scramble in Chicago to grab the vice-presidential nomination, this was the second time his sons had flatly opposed the Ambassador's fiat when it came to an important career decision. The father habitually courted risk, but it was *controlled* risk, situations in which he himself could rig the outcomes. An assault on labor racketeering could quickly drive both Jack and Bobby into raging political waters, too high and dangerous for even Joe to calm. As in Chicago, Bob was driving the initiative.

Bobby faced his father down. Estes Kefauver had led the big, splashy hearings into organized crime in 1950, and then he beat Jack at the convention. Joe asked Bill Douglas to talk some sense into Bobby. Douglas didn't get anywhere. "He feels it is too great an opportunity," Douglas informed his wife.

The dilemma for Joe Kennedy, of course, was that he could give the boys advice, but he really couldn't begin to tell them the whole story. At his age, he needed backup: in 1955 he had named Robert, who already oversaw the Joseph P. Kennedy Jr. Foundation, as executor of his estate. Control was inexorably shifting. "We have met the enemy," as Pogo rephrased Admiral Farragut, "and he is us." From this point on, the past of the Kennedys would come to consume their future.

By fits and starts, Bob Kennedy had started to edge out from beneath his father, whose apprehension about the wrong publicity kept him behind the scenes despite his own misgivings. So far Bob's immediate bosses had been handpicked by the financier, seasoned FBI veterans like McInerney and Frip Flanagan, undoubtedly vetted by Hoover himself and available for day-to-day telephonic liaison. The volatile Joe McCarthy could be kept at heel by hints of a diminished campaign contribution. Once the so-called Rackets Committee started staffing up, the Ambassador made sure to keep one hand on the rudder—the committee's chief accountant, Carmine Bellino, broke in with the FBI in 1934 and participated in the capture of John Dillinger. Carmine ran the Bureau's bookkeeping section until 1946, then opened his own office, serving Joe Kennedy as "both his personal accountant and private gumshoe," according to Robert Maheu, who split the rent on the

premises. Bellino pitched in often to straighten out a variety of congressional committees.

Bellino was a virtuoso, a talent who could spread out the most over-
cooked set of books along with a shoebox of scribbled check stubs and the
remains of a ledger and divine within a few hours where all the assets went.
A low-keyed good-government buff himself, he understood within a week or
two that his new boss was not to be compromised. "Bob is the only man I've
met in government who is willing to go all the way, all the time," he conceded
by 1958. His sister-in-law, Angela (Angie) Novello, came on as Kennedy's
personal secretary.

But Joe Kennedy's writ ran out increasingly in the face of Bob's day-to-
day mentoring by Senator John McClellan. McClellan was a low-keyed self-
righteous hardscrapple Arkansas small-town judge and attorney, part of the
oligarchy of largely self-taught legal scholars determined to protect the vulnerable South from the race-mixing industrial future. Having covertly
accepted Joe Kennedy's $50,000, McClellan paid the Ambassador due defer-
ence. "He was a bible-belt Jew hater," Roy Cohn judged later on.

McClellan's long, hard-working life had been potholed with domestic
disasters. One way or another, nearly his entire family had been wiped out by
the time Bob Kennedy came into his life, and in 1958 his remaining son died
in an auto wreck; Bob accompanied him to Little Rock for the funeral.
Despondent much of the time by then, drunk many evenings, McClellan
came to depend on Bob to sit with him and, often enough, to carry him back
to his apartment and spend the night while the tormented senator sobered
up. The carbuncular legislator discerned and approved in Kennedy a set of
moral bearings as inalterable as his own. Month by month, Kennedy became
a surrogate son.

To JFK's annoyance, Bob quickly borrowed Ken O'Donnell from his
brother's Senate staff and turned him into his administrative assistant. The
pudgy, cigar-chomping San Francisco muckraker Pierre Salinger, author of a
series of *Collier's* exposés of Teamster malfeasance, joined La Verne Duffy
and another fallen-away FBI investigator, Walter Sheridan, to track down the
juke-box cash slips and itinerant knuckle-dusters the committee needed to
make its cases. William Lambert and Wallace Turner, two implacable
reporters from the *Portland Oregonian* who had been closing in on Dave
Beck, were on and off the staff and would develop into key crusaders for
Bobby as they moved their bylines to *Life* and the *New York Times*. Before
long Kennedy's employees, in D.C. and around the country, totaled 104, the
largest Senate committee staff in history.

* * *

Nationally, Bobby was coming into view. In early 1957 his brother Jack sold him Hickory Hill in McLean, Virginia. A vaulting, sprawling near-Georgian manor house from which General George McClellan once ran the Union Army, its five and a half rolling acres provided plenty of space for the stables and rabbit hutches and chicken coops and hog sties that Kennedy's fast-compounding family seemed to demand. There were tennis courts and an enormous—and notorious—swimming pool.

Ethel was the presiding sprite. Enthusiastic to the edge of madcap, Ethel hired and fired help nonstop—at one point, there were seventeen in service—and ran a household for her boys like *Lord of the Flies* on uppers. No impulse ever thwarted—Ethel greeted an unsuspecting European royal with a face-full of shaving cream and pushed Andy Williams's head into the icing of his birthday cake when he didn't blow out the candles fast enough.

In time, exotic animals were everywhere underfoot. Ethel instructed one of the maids to spray the light bulbs throughout the manse every day with *Arpege* to sweeten up the air, undoubtedly a wise precaution, since creatures like the ill-tempered coatimundi were wont to shit under the dining-room table. Money meant very little, as Joe Kennedy strenuously pointed out. When one of Steve Smith's accountants called to tell Ethel that her checking account was overdrawn, her well-tanned features registered simple astonishment. "It can't be," she assured the clerk. "I still have some checks left."

Bobby seemed to like it just that way. He put in long hours, often driving home alone along the winding Chain Bridge Road at ten or eleven. The years of strain had already started to register: He tended to walk hunched forward a little, shoulders pulled back, as if into a perpetual headwind. Still fundamentally withdrawn, Bob regarded people he didn't really know from under those sloping epicanthic folds with a quizzical, skeptical glance, often pulling speculatively on his hooked and bony nose. Even that toothy grin, if it ever arrived, looked more like a gesture than a statement of the heart, a presentation of too much failed orthodontry. The world was not to be trusted. Much of the time, underneath the hearing table, his hands would shake so violently that he needed to grip one with the other to keep things under control.

Bobby was well aware that he was venturing onto perilous ground. To coordinate with the Committee Hoover assigned Courtney Evans, a heroically diplomatic attorney from the FBI's Criminal Division. But Kennedy intended to bring in other resources and was soon dependent on a number of well-placed newspapermen around the country as well as investigators from the Internal Revenue Service and the Federal Bureau of Narcotics. As defensive of the Bureau's prerogatives as everybody knew Hoover to be, the fact that the McClellan Committee was pulling in tips and disclosures unsanctified by a trip through the Bureau's censorship filters riled up the thin-skinned Director. McClellan—and Kennedy—were clearly threatening to the FBI.

This showed up promptly in the Bureau's internal paperwork. A file search on John McClellan on February 6, 1957 takes note of a charge against McClellan's father for taking a bribe for helping a well-heeled country boy evade the draft. In 1954 Joseph McCarthy had quoted McClellan as disparaging Hoover as a "little bureaucrat." Hoover scrawled at the bottom of the advisory: "This McClellan is certainly a cheap politician." When Senator McClellan and Robert F. Kennedy requested an appointment with the Director in September 1956, "A mutual convenient time for the meeting could not be arranged." The rundown cites news reports that both McClellan and Senator Irving Ives of the Labor Committee had put in rival resolutions in January to "conduct an investigation of labor-union racketeering and its underworld tie-ups."

It wasn't the union abuses so much as the "underworld tie-ups" that were unsettling Hoover. In November 1957, the constabulary of Apalachin, in upstate New York, raided Joe Barbara's country house. Sixty-three management-level thugs from gangs everywhere east of the Mississippi were arraigned, while dozens more lumbered out the kitchen door or scraped through the nearest window and bolted for the surrounding woods. Sam Giancana shredded a twelve-hundred-dollar suit on barbed wire making his escape and chuckled later about "some of the guys slippin' and slidin' down on their asses, splittin' out their pants" as they forded the autumn streambeds in their alligator shoes.

After such a sighting, even Hoover was hard-pressed to question seriously the existence of the Mafia. Kefauver hearings or no Kefauver hearings, Hoover had continued to maintain that there was no such thing as national organized crime. When deputy FBI director William Sullivan and his assistant Charles Peck put together a report on the Apalachin get-together and its known attendees and distributed twenty-five copies to law-enforcement officials around the government, Hoover termed the entire document "baloney" and recalled and destroyed every copy. There was no Mafia, period. Local hoodlums, yes. The responsibility of local police. But no Mafia.

Apart from his determination to keep the trust of his friends in the "underworld," Hoover was largely disinclined to jaundice his carefully protected relations with rainmakers in the Democratic Party like Congressman John Rooney, who looked after appropriations for the Justice Department. More even than the limousine service the Bureau provided, Rooney appreciated the fact that Hoover did not trouble the important Democratic bosses throughout urban America, who depended on their own sweetheart arrangements with the paymasters of the syndicate. It took a regular application of grease to make the wheels go round.

Hoover was openly irked at McClellan's attempts to interest Congress in a National Crime Commission, an overriding entity to coordinate all federal agencies and deal with the Mob in an effective way. The Director objected that this approach amounted to one more backdoor scheme to turn the FBI into a national police force, an American Gestapo. This would be as deleterious as the recurrent talk of subjecting the Bureau to Civil Service requirements. Critics were already charging that the FBI's vaunted indictment statistics resulted from its success against unimportant criminals, adolescents on a spree in stolen cars and hillbilly bank robbers and the occasional demented child-snatcher. Most of the sleuthing, as well as the arrests, originated with local cops.

Each time some sorehead in Congress even hinted at reforming the FBI, Hoover rustled those Official and Confidential files of his. Like the rattle of a rattlesnake, they immediately made folks step back. If that didn't work, as Max Lowenthal, a friend of Truman, wrote in 1950, "Friends and relatives of Congressmen were frequently placed on the FBI rolls whenever it wanted larger appropriations or special favors from Congress." Hoover lambasted critics in speeches to well-disposed audiences, covering onlookers with an acid foam of rhetoric within which he termed skeptics "the perennial sob-sisters of both sexes," "fiddle-faced reformers" and "swivelchair criminologists," often guilty of "actual affiliation with the criminal element." These "nitwits and porous-brained sentimentalists . . . seek to undermine the foundations upon which we must stand if we are to protect the American home."

So long as Truman was in the White House, the Director depended on his legendary ability to dance convincingly on both sides of the same issue, at times on both sides of a single fact. By 1953, for example, Hoover was tarring the exiting Truman presidency with charges that in 1945 he, Hoover, had warned Truman off Harry Dexter White, Henry Morgenthau's gifted popinjay of an assistant secretary of the treasury during the Roosevelt administration.

When key Soviet defector Igor Gouzenko maintained during his debriefing in 1945 that White had not been among Moscow's contacts, Hoover seemed to be convinced enough to scribble a note to the retired Henry Morgenthau as late as 1948 which confirmed that he had looked over the aspersions against White's loyalty, and there was "nothing to it." Yet Hoover simultaneously proceeded to get word to the McCarran Committee, homing in on "Un-American Activities," implicating White. A 1947 grand jury refused to indict White based on insufficient evidence. Both Deputy Director Sullivan and William Turner, seasoned FBI managers of the period, agreed with Truman that the White case was a "red herring." But by 1953 Eisenhower's new attorney general, Herbert Brownell, was on a tear to damn Truman as "soft on Communism," and Hoover, Turner saw, was "swinging with the apes," testifying before the Senate Internal Security Subcommittee. Hoover was especially frosted because Truman had let the story out that he had promoted White to executive director of the International Monetary Fund to protect an FBI investigation.

White himself had expired unexpectedly of a heart attack in 1948, but his controversy lived on. Nowadays, factoring in the Venona decrypts, the Mitrokhin documents, and White's apparent inability to get through the afternoon without a ping-pong game with Soviet agent handler Nathan Silvermaster, Hoover could most likely clinch the argument. However witting, White was a very dubious choice to make economic policy at the top levels.

Especially striking year by year was Hoover's unique ability to shift his ground, those agile little dancing feet. While Truman was president, Hoover attempted to behave himself—"Cut them all off," Harry Truman gruffed to an aide when transcriptions of Hoover's latest wiretaps came through. "Tell the FBI we haven't got time for that kind of shit." But Truman and Hoover shared one confidant, George Allen, and in time Truman did weaken enough to look over the phone conversations of Thomas ("Tommy the Cork") Corcoran, slid across the transom by Harry Vaughn. The president was starting to worry about the China Lobby.

As organized crime rose under the Congress like a whale about to sound, Hoover scrambled to adjust. What deserves particular scrutiny here is the way Hoover gerrymandered, the selectivity with which the Bureau proceeded to map organized crime on a national scale. Basically a loyal man, Hoover kept an eye out on behalf of valued acquaintances. By the middle fifties, the Director's nose for the high life was occasionally leading him and Tolson to a few stolen days in the fleshpots of Havana; Sirio Maccioni, the proprietor of Manhattan's fashionable Le Circe, remembers spotting them both in their tropical worsteds presiding over their worshipers at one of the glitziest of the new Mob casinos, the Tropicana. As Hoover's reluctance to deal with organized crime head-on became undeniable, apologists like Ralph de Toledano explained Hoover's complaisance away by declaring that he "knew that it was futile to take on the crime which is entangled with legitimate business or local politics until the community—national or otherwise— was ready for it."

Meanwhile, play along. When Truman's independent-minded Attorney General J. Howard McGrath backed legislation to ban slot machines from every state but Nevada, where gambling was legal, Hoover fought the idea on the ground that it would embroil the Bureau in something better left to local police. The Director never mentioned that his secret compadre in the barber's chair, Frank Costello, was heavily invested in the machines and was deeply committed to new territory around New Orleans with *his* sawed-off protégé, Carlos Marcello. With prohibition a memory, gambling was the oncoming big thing.

Reacting to all the publicity thrown off by Apalachin, Attorney General William Rogers established a Special Group on Organized Crime within the Justice Department under Milton Wessel. The McClellan-Kennedy Racket Committee hearings were showcasing hoods on television like Joey Glimco, hog butchers of the American language who seemed to have survived the Jimmy Cagney era intact. Hoover, contemplating unhappily the prospect of being swamped by the competition, mandated the FBI's Top Hoodlum program.

The Top Hoodlum program provided the Bureau a major shove in the direction of confronting organized crime. The use of taps and bugs preceded even Hoover's time, but there was always a certain skittishness about such an aggressive form of electronic eavesdropping because so little of it was admissible in court. If a defendant's lawyers could prove that a case was built on wiretap evidence, the whole thing was likely to be thrown out, as happened most embarrassingly with the Communist courier Judith Coplon. If even national security cases were likely to be tainted by questionable surveillance techniques, what was the hope with powerfully connected Mob bosses, flanked by battalions of attorneys and terrifying to jury members?

The FBI approach was limited. Hoover refused to plant his own people in situations where one of them might be tempted to take a bribe. Nobody went undercover. The Director wanted his special agents in dark suits and snap-brim hats and shoes you could see your lantern jaw reflected in—not an easy disguise for anybody prowling the waterfront. Informants, peddling hearsay, filled up the raw files with whatever they ran across, but very little of that was of much use before a judge.

Accordingly, the Top Hoodlum program evolved quickly into a drive to *gather* information, although the methods used to assemble the files made them quite likely to invalidate any future prosecution. As "SAC of a field office whose territory included Nevada," the late-stage Hoover favorite Mark Felt wrote, by 1956 "I was under continual pressure from the Seat of Government to move against Mafia infiltration of the gambling casinos in Reno and Las Vegas." Lacking "adequate laws such as the Congress enacted in the Sixties, we could do little more than gather information through the use of informants and electronic surveillance. . . ."

These same years, special agents like William Roemer, a hard-fisted ex-boxer with an itch to upset the Chicago Mob, started directing the placement of microphones as big as Coke bottles ("Little Al") behind radiator grilles and top-shelf soup cans in places like the Armory Lounge. Sam Giancana and his designated hoods liked to debate who would go up on the meat hook next at one of the shadowy tables toward the back.

Before too long, the experts at the Bureau pieced out a fairly coherent picture of what certain members of the syndicate were up to. Naturally, they couldn't use it. While tapping telephone lines was sometimes authorized, usually on national security grounds and generally requiring either a bench warrant or the signature of the attorney general, the planting of bugs, "microphone surveillance," rolled forward administration after administration in a kind of legal limbo. Don't ask, don't tell. Unfortunately, the placement of most bugs involved an unequivocal violation of the law, breaking and entering: illegal trespass. Again, whatever anybody learned that way was inadmissible in court, and might even get a case built on solid evidence thrown out.

So where the Mob was concerned, the Director was doing very little more than betraying a kind of late-blooming prurient interest. Almost nothing the FBI picked up regarding the so-called Top Hoodlums was turned over to Justice Department lawyers for prosecution. Richard Ogilvie, who ran the Midwestern office of Milton Wessel's Justice Department crime-fighting wing, later commented that "Hoover was very cool to the whole idea of the Attorney General's Special Group. He ordered that the FBI files, containing the very information we needed on organized crime, were to be closed to us. . . ." Meanwhile, Hoover took a liking to the amiable Attorney General William Rogers and made a rare social appearance piano-side to join the Rogers family sing-alongs at holiday time. Hoover cut the Top Hoodlums program in half as soon as the heat was off. Thus ran bureaucratic ambivalence during the Eisenhower administration.

The Rackets Committee hearings were intended to expose the bad eggs in and around the labor movement. They were also intended to offer some exposure to John Kennedy, whose lackadaisical performance as a lawmaker since 1947 hadn't left a lot to run on for president. Bobby was very meticulous about scheduling the showier, more widely televised hearings when his brother could make it.

The Senate Select Committee on Improper Activities in the Labor or Management Field—the Rackets Committee—threw out a wide net and in the end dragged in very little. Unquestionably the biggest catch came early. The Teamster president, Dave Beck, was an entrenched pasha who lived so lavishly that it was no challenge at all to prove that Beck had drained $370,000 of the union's money into lifestyle purchases for himself. Ultimately Beck was jailed for keeping $1,900 from the sale of a union Cadillac and evading income taxes. He was a big, soft target.

Beck's mind worked slowly during the hearings. "Well, let me answer it this way," Beck responded to Bobby during one exchange. "I don't know where you are going or where you intend to go. . . ."

"Yes, you do, Mr. Beck," Kennedy cut him off.

Kennedy was still learning, unfortunately under the lights. "As a committee counsel," Russell Baker would write, "he was clearly incompetent. He stammered, got confused in his questions, blushed, got angry, lost his poise, seemed childish, a boy trying to do a man's job. Except for the famously rich father, I thought, he would be lucky to find work as a file clerk."

A good part of Kennedy's problem was his indifference to what was politically feasible, what the system would bear. Shortly before the 1956 election he had again tweaked Hoover's famously oversensitive tail. This might be the moment, Kennedy put the word out, to direct the Committee's operatives into a thorough investigation of wiretapping around the nation's capital. Aghast, Hoover responded immediately through James Juliana, an ex-FBI attorney now functioning as the Republican minority counsel. Quash *that* idea. Kennedy let it go, but now he had Hoover's interest again.

Whenever organized crime came up, Hoover wouldn't walk the walk. When Kennedy asked for background information on a hundred Apalachin participants, the FBI produced nothing on forty of them and little beyond newspaper clips on all the rest. Committee lawyers made the identical request of the Federal Bureau of Narcotics, the predecessor of the DEA, and received a dossier on every single hoodlum. Thus began what William Hundley would refer to as Bobby's "romance with the Bureau of Narcotics."

The director of the Bureau of Narcotics was Harry Anslinger, a hulking, egg-bald powerhouse who looked a lot like the Swedish Angel. Anslinger ran a squad of 240 street agents, mostly in New York City, who terrorized the dealers and pushers of the period catch-as-catch-can. One of Anslinger's agents, Howard Diller, asserted on a noteworthy series of interviews with C. David Heymann, "many of us were college graduates but at heart we were cowboys and renegades. In those days you didn't need a subpoena or search warrant to enter a house in which you suspected the use of drugs, you just went in with guns drawn. We'd push the people against the wall, arrest them and confiscate the drugs. We did a lot of wiretapping, too, all of it illegal."

In short order, Kennedy turned into a narc buff. "The notion that Anslinger had," in Diller's opinion, "and that was consistent with what Robert Kennedy ultimately stood far, is that as long as you got the bad guys, it didn't matter how you did it. So you commit some crimes, you kick a little ass, you have a little fun, you kill somebody—in the end, good would be achieved. . . .

"Pretty soon, he began participating in some of the more illicit aspects of these drug busts, which might involve opium, heroin, hashish and/or cocaine." Other agents "would purportedly come back with reports of him seizing bags of coke for his own use, or, more probably, for distribution among his buddies." When hookers were on the premises, "Bobby thought nothing of fondling these women or having intercourse with them. Or he'd force them to engage in fellatio. Then, afterward, he'd brag about it, just like the agents. . . . He struck me as basically schizophrenic, a man capable of great good and, at the same time, incredible evil." A call girl Jack Kennedy frequented, who specialized in moderate S&M, allegedly turned away Jack's suggestion that she book a session for Bobby because "I heard he was an out-and-out sadist."

Another Manhattan contact of the period, Mel Finkelstein of the *Daily News*, who covered the night beat on crime, let Bobby Kennedy ride with him sometimes when he chased down incidents blaring out of the police frequencies. Finkelstein claimed to remember the night Kennedy stood there while three cops picked up a black man who had been molesting a two-year-old girl and threw him out the window of a six-floor Harlem walk-up. Then Bob attempted to console the toddler's mother. On other nights, Kennedy might extort a free tumble out of some street harlot, then drag a couple of bums into La Caravelle, in which the financier retained an interest, and buy them dinner. "One of the most unusual men I've ever known," Finkelstein decided.

Unavoidably, Hoover heard about these forays. "I knew about it," Kennedy's FBI liaison Courtney Evans told C. David Heymann, "and I was amazed by it. To actually become involved in the knocking down of doors! These were the kind of madcap antics that always made the Director suspicious of RFK's character, and probably for good reason. He resorted to many of the same ploys after he became attorney general."

For Bobby, law enforcement required a kind of frontier justice. The white hats went out to hunt down the black hats, and then you string 'em up. That wasn't Hoover's take. Stung early in his career by the excesses of the Palmer raids, the Director would remain apprehensive about the fallout from unconstitutional searches and seizures. "He was a great civil libertarian," Deke DeLoach says flatly. "FBI agents were required to read people their rights long before the Miranda decision."

Chroniclers of the period were quick to contrast Bob Kennedy with his new mentor, John McClellan. Stephen Fox compared McClellan with a deliberate old Baptist mastiff, wise in the law and funereal in tone as he castigated these "characters who come here from other lands . . . human parasites on society." The parade of gangland witnesses and crooked union organizers hauled before the committee were Italian, mostly, many immigrants.

At his elbow, "the younger and smaller Kennedy, sarcastic and needling, an excitable terrier occasionally brought to heel by his boss, yapped at the witnesses in his flat, nasal Boston Irish voice." Observers commented on the fact that Kennedy's methods owed a great deal to his months with Joe McCarthy. "Bobby doesn't care how he wins," Joseph P. Kennedy would declare flatly. Another time Joe told Oleg Cassini: "Bobby is tough. Had he lived in Germany, he would have joined the Gestapo and been sincere about it."

With friendly witnesses especially, Bob liked to extract the answers he wanted during executive—closed—session, then read them back before the national audience, rephrased slightly as questions. This amounted to leading the witness to dramatize the results Kennedy wanted.

With adverse witnesses, Kennedy sometimes piled on with "a great mass of what may be the truth, but which appears often to be simply hearsay, slander, or malicious invention." No witness could confront the source of anything he heard. Accordingly, reputations could be ruined, jobs lost, self-respect shattered, and there was absolutely no recourse.

The Kennedy brothers were establishing themselves, but constitutionalists had started to watch. Privately, Justice William O. Douglas was "not too happy." A widely noted piece in *The New Republic* by Yale Law School professor Alexander Bickel accused Kennedy of embarking on "purely punitive expeditions" and indulging in the "relentless, vindictive battering" of witnesses. "No one since the late Joseph R. McCarthy," Bickel judged, "has done more than Mr. Kennedy to foster the impression that the plea of self-incrimination is tantamount to a confession of guilt." Kennedy did himself no good by admitting that "although the Fifth Amendment is for the innocent as well as the guilty, I can think of very few witnesses who availed themselves of it who in my estimation were free of wrongdoing."

Such absolutism is a guaranteed eyebrow-raiser. However clean his fingernails, Hoover was a survivor of the bright-light and rubber-hose era of American criminal justice. He knew where Bobby's approach led.

Hoover was lying back at this stage, but within the Eisenhower Justice Department his displeasure was felt. Attorney General William Rogers refused to attempt to indict in case after case on the basis of the committee's findings. Partly it was politics, but there were other, more substantive reasons. After he had requested that twenty of his witnesses in a row be tried for perjury, and Rogers refused them all, Kennedy announced that he would be sending no more recommendations along.

William Hundley, head of Justice's Organized Crime Section, later concluded that most of Kennedy's cases were not solidly made. He bucked a few to the FBI and the IRS. No one, Hundley said, was "breaking their back trying to make cases for Bobby Kennedy."

Where the justice system failed, national exposure sometimes succeeded. Publicity drove senior officers from the Bakers' Union, the Butchers' Union, the United Textile Workers' Union, and the Operating Engineers' Union. The Kennedy brothers emerged as stars. The pursuit of James R. Hoffa was now becoming Bobby's obsession.

BOOK TWO

POWER

◆

"The three most overrated things in the world are the State of Texas, the FBI, and mounted deer heads."

—JOHN F. KENNEDY, from *Hoover's F.B.I.* by WILLIAM W. TURNER, p. xiv

"A good lie is better than the whole truth in most cases."

—J. EDGAR HOOVER

"History is a set of lies agreed upon."

—NAPOLEON

Hoffa

James Riddle Hoffa first came to Bobby Kennedy's attention in the winter of 1957. Almost from the start, Hoffa incarnated the evil Kennedy took it as his mission to vanquish in America. God knows the chemistry between the two men couldn't have been worse. Hoffa was an unrestrained prole, short (five foot five), stumpy (180 pounds), and radiant with concentrated power. At forty-four, he was approaching maximum clout inside the labor movement. He still made it a point to wear off-the-rack suits and white wool sweat socks so that his counterparts from the business end of the trucking industry would make no mistake about his coal-mining origins. Like Dave Beck, he was a grade-school dropout. Unlike Beck, Hoffa betrayed little interest in strutting like a sultan around the Marble Palace, the luxurious new Teamster headquarters in D.C., or in limousines, or in expensive men's cologne.

He made a unique impression. A dab of brilliantine was never able to restrain his short glossy black hair, so that feathers of it tended to stand up all around his scalp. His mood was normally a kind of caustic good humor, but should Hoffa become genuinely angry, as Paul Jacobs wrote, "his gray-green eyes get incredibly cold and menacing. It's then that his ruthlessness, his obvious belief in physical violence as an instrument of power, shows through. . . ."

Bobby met Hoffa at an impromptu little dinner that a lawyer-publicist named Eddie Cheyfitz arranged in February 1957 so that the two men might come to appreciate each other before the labor hearings got everybody dug in. Cheyfitz hoped to convince Bobby that Hoffa was, at heart, a reformer. The fact was, Hoffa knew that Kennedy was going after Dave Beck, the corrupt president of the National Teamsters at the time, and Hoffa was more than willing to supply—through Cheyfitz—the Rackets Committee with whatever its investigators might need to bury Beck. Hoffa was next in line for Beck's job.

Cheyfitz's law associate, Edward Bennett Williams, a social friend of Bobby's, was Jimmy Hoffa's lawyer. The evening did not go well. Hoffa met Kennedy with his meaty handshake and lost no time in emphasizing that he was a very tough operator. "I do to others what they do to me, only worse," Hoffa assured Kennedy, and Cheyfitz bemoaned the extent to which Beck, now a rich man, had spoiled and overcontrolled his son, leaving him a "jellyfish." The parallel was presumably not lost on Kennedy. Bob tried to fend Hoffa off with a little of the fey, self-deprecating humor the Kennedy brothers favored whenever they were uncomfortable. Hoffa was not amused.

After dinner Cheyfitz himself brought up the problem areas they all might expect during the upcoming hearings. Before long "Bobby kept peppering Hoffa with questions," La Verne Duffy heard, "until Hoffa finally said to him, 'what is this, the Inquisition?'" They were soon heatedly discussing the "paper locals" in New York City, fictitious subdivisions of the union with charters and officers but no members. A number of officers in these locals were thugs on the payroll of top Manhattan-area gangsters like Johnny Dio (Dioguardi) and Tony (Ducks) Corallo. Hoffa brushed the whole subject off—this was a device to preempt the no-raiding pact they would have to sign once the pending AFL/CIO merger got finalized. Furthermore, that's how the world was evolving, and Jimmy Hoffa was a devout capitalist. "Twenty years ago," he would tell an interviewer, "the employers had all the hoodlums working for them as strike-breakers. Now we've got a few, and everybody's screaming." Several versions of the dinner have Bobby and Jimmy arm-wrestling, Hoffa putting Kennedy down again and again.

What to Hoffa seemed the normal intestinal life of the American economy gave Bobby a severe cramp. As it happened, barely a week before Cheyfitz hosted his dinner party a reactionary New York lawyer named John Cye Cheasty showed up in Kennedy's office and laid out what proof he had so far that Hoffa, acting through Meyer Lansky's intermediary Hyman Fischbach, had tried to hire him to sign on with the Rackets Committee. Cheasty would be well paid to keep Hoffa informed. For perhaps a month,

Cheasty, working with the FBI and supervised by Hoover himself, passed carefully selected committee papers pertaining largely to Dave Beck to Hoffa and brought back Hoffa's reactions. The hearings would peter out by spring, Hoffa expected, so Kennedy could enjoy the summer on Cape Cod. Hoffa's detectives were unearthing rumors that Bobby had dressed in girls' clothing as a child and had a history as a homosexual.

On March 13, on the street at Dupont Circle, Cheasty handed Hoffa a large manila envelope of fresh documents and Hoffa pressed on Cheasty two thousand dollars in a wad. FBI cameramen were filming the entire transaction. Minutes later the FBI picked up Hoffa by the elevators in the Dupont Plaza Hotel on charges of bribery and conspiracy.

Alerted by Hoover, Robert Kennedy and Ethel contacted reporters before going down to the courthouse after midnight personally to watch Jimmy Hoffa get booked. "He kept looking at me, his eyes full of disdain," Kennedy reported to La Verne Duffy. Hoffa told Kennedy to run along home to bed. "I'll take care of things, Bobby," Hoffa assured Kennedy. "Don't let's have any problems." But Kennedy wouldn't leave, and after a few minutes Hoffa challenged Kennedy to a push-up contest. Hoffa could do fifty, one-handed.

If Hoffa were to be acquitted, Kennedy promised the press a few days later, he would "jump off the Capitol." That was a mistake, because defense counsel Edward Bennett Williams staged one of his bravura courtroom performances. First he presented Cheasty as a labor-hating grudge-bearing McCarthyite bigot. After this, he put Hoffa on the stand and let him rant through one of his finest up-from-the-loading-docks cadenzas as a champion of the working man. Then he called Kennedy to the stand and impeached his competence as committee counsel, demonstrating that he regularly played to public opinion through leaks to favored reporters. If Kennedy could pass around the committee's secrets to the working press, what was the point of jumping all over Cheasty? Furthermore, Kennedy had violated professional ethics by going to dinner with the defendant a few weeks earlier.

Eight of the twelve jurors were black, the result of Williams's adroit challenges. Williams hired a black attorney to sit conspicuously at the defense table. Near the end of the trial, Williams brought in Joe Louis, who had grown up with Hoffa in the slums of Detroit. Before the jury, Hoffa squeezed the great fighter's shoulder. Nobody in the courtroom knew that the perennially broke boxer was being carried on the payroll of a Chicago trucking firm and had received a loan from the Teamsters' pension fund.

To explain everything, Hoffa took an oath that whatever money he had given Cheasty was a legal fee—Cheasty was his legal adviser. What was this supposed connection with Kennedy?

The jury acquitted Hoffa. "I'm going to send Bobby Kennedy a parachute," Edward Bennett Williams informed the press. Kennedy was now spoiling for revenge. Privately, he laid a lot of the blame for this embarrassment at the feet of the FBI. They had claimed to have an airtight case, and Williams shredded it. The fumbling Justice Department prosecutors couldn't stand up to Hoffa's far-fetched defense. The government had failed Bobby. Hoover had failed him.

With Dave Beck out, Hoffa was slated to be voted in overwhelmingly in 1958 as the president of the Teamsters' Union. Hoffa's primitive temperament and his contempt for the gentility were nothing but welcome to the million and a third over-the-road drivers and freight handlers and loading-dock roughnecks who paid their dues and drank up their paychecks. Under Beck and, increasingly, Hoffa they were emerging into real job security, with solid welfare benefits and a generous pension plan. Employers, having struggled for years with a work force of unreliable transients, appreciated the discipline the union leadership was bringing to this tumultuous industry.

With this many members, the flow of income from the dues was stupefying. If Hoffa could come up with a dense roll of cash for Cheasty, or Joe Louis took out a loan from the Teamsters he knew he'd never repay, well—there was plenty more, almost a quarter of a billion by then, and back at the Marble Palace the bookkeeping was casual.

How unwelcome these Senate investigations were became clear when Pierre Salinger and Carmine Bellino showed up with subpoenas. "You can tell Bobby Kennedy for me that he's not going to make his brother President over Hoffa's dead body," the Teamster leader fulminated. When the Committee investigators finally got a look at the records, they found the names and sometimes the numbers ripped out of checks and hotel bills. Key witnesses disappeared or refused to talk. Hoffa was trashing evidence, fast.

Kennedy would be pressing hard for how precisely Hoffa exploited such a wide array of middle-level thugs to control the locals. But the squat, incisive Teamster chief was probably more concerned that Rackets Committee investigators be kept as far as possible from the ambitious loans his pension fund was contemplating. The Teamsters Central States, Southeast and Southwest Areas Pension Fund, run out of Chicago, was already one of the great unpublicized honeypots in financial America. It had the virtue of remaining largely unsupervised. There were eight representatives of management and eight of labor in place as trustees, but Hoffa exerted such intimidating leverage that oversight was never contemplated. Approximately 60 percent of the assets were sunk in risky real estate ventures, entirely at the discretion of Hoffa and his cronies.

Over the years, Teamster assets went out to underwrite everything from the million dollars Richard Nixon squeezed out of the Central States Fund to defray the costs of the Watergate cover-up to an estimated $300,000,000 plowed into Las Vegas by way of the Sunrise Hospital conglomerate and the Paradise Development Company. Having erected the main strip of casinos and hotels with Mormon money, the Mob shrewdly bought up enormous tracts of surrounding land with 6 percent notes from the Teamsters. Clint Murchison tapped Teamster assets to bankroll his more flamboyant wildcatting ventures. Carlos Marcello habitually involved the pension fund in his elaborate and extremely lucrative insurance swindles.

At this point, Bob Kennedy was not merely bloodying a few frequently broken noses around the wiseguy circuit; his probe now threatened to impinge on important business arrangements, tacit agreements of importance where the overworld met the underworld. In this limbo, Jimmy Hoffa and J. Edgar Hoover—not to mention Joseph P. Kennedy—would recognize a universe of collaborators. A lot of damage could come out of this. Joe Kennedy had good reason to explode Christmas 1956.

As the hearings matured, party differences among the senators on the Rackets Committee produced rising rancor. Besides McClellan, Patrick McNamara of Michigan and Sam Ervin were joined by John Kennedy, who modestly explained his presence as a way of fending off the intransigent Strom Thurmond, still a Democrat in 1957. The Republicans included what was left of Joe McCarthy, the snappish prairie conservative Karl Mundt, Irving Ives, and Barry Goldwater. When McCarthy passed on, he was replaced by Homer Capehart of Indiana, an intractable reactionary who did not forbear during executive session to refer to Robert Kennedy as "that little snotnose."

The Republicans were increasingly concerned that Bobby was browbeating witnesses and skewing the proceedings so as to whip up a maximum of good publicity for himself and his brother. McClellan continued to depend on his protégé, but after a few months he found Bobby's press releases so outspoken that he insisted on clearing them personally before they went out. Bob tended to get carried away. "When the going would get rough," Goldwater remarked afterward, "John McClellan was likely to take over the questioning, thus saving Bobby from embarrassment."

Edward Bennett Williams, by now on retainer for the Teamsters, responded to a show of shock by Kennedy with the soul-destroying comment: "I'm not surprised you don't understand it, Mr. Kennedy, but I hope the lawyers of the committee will." Another attorney who matched wits with Kennedy during the hearings would observe that "Time and again . . . I saw him march a witness right up to the brink of what looked like a really hot disclosure—only to fluff it." Pitted against the brainy Teamster vice president Harold Gibbons, "the verdict of most who looked on was that Mr. Gibbons, no lawyer, tied Mr. Kennedy in knots." Kennedy himself would term Gibbons "a tall, thin man with a cold, superior look" who "lives expensively and well."

The sessions got painful at times for John Kennedy, watching his strident little brother work the witnesses over, frequently badgering his subjects, or resorting to hearsay police testimony, or shutting a witness up before he could defend himself. Jack and Sam Ervin were collaborating in the Labor Committee on a piece of legislation intended to help reform the labor movement without riling up the AFL/CIO bosses so much that they'd sit on their hands in 1960. At times, Bobby's charges seemed to indict the labor movement wholesale. "We have only one rule around here," Jack Kennedy declared during one hearing. "If they're crooks, we don't wound 'em, we kill 'em." That meant, decoded, that uncontaminated labor officials need not worry.

Red meat to Bob were characters like Joey Glimco, a thug the head strategist of the Chicago Mob, Murray "Curly" Humphreys, had anointed in 1944 to manage the fifteen Teamster taxicab locals. Glimco was to pave the way for Hoffa to consolidate power throughout the Midwest until he exerted control, at which point the Mob would call in its chits. The burgeoning Central States Welfare Fund was to supply the capital for the Mob's projected enterprises in Nevada and elsewhere. The son of Curly Humphreys's murderous sidekick Paul ("Red") Dorfman, head of the Waste Handlers Union, Allen, was to administer the loans.

A shakedown artist who would kneecap his mother if she fell short on her vigorish, Glimco remained quite tongue-tied beneath the committee-room lights and embraced the Fifth Amendment. This peeved Bobby, who was already annoyed with Glimco's "heavy, sickly-sweet smell."

KENNEDY: "You haven't got the guts to [answer], have you, Mr. Glimco?"

GLIMCO: "I respectfully decline...."

MCCLELLAN: "Morally you are kind of yellow inside, are you not? That is the truth about it?"

GLIMCO: "I respectfully decline...."

When it was Sam ("Mooney") Giancana's turn, Kennedy characterized him as "chief gunman for the group that succeeded the Capone mob." This understated Mooney's role in Mobdom by quite a lot. By the later fifties, the great wheelman and rubout artist was essentially the don of the Chicago Mob. A compact, balding Italian-American of middle years, Giancana affected Panama hats and very wide, very dark shades. He was a man who could silence a casino merely by walking quietly through the entrance. Among his closest friends was Frank Sinatra, and he and Joe Kennedy tended to meet from time to time, if rarely in a public place. Robert Kennedy took sport with him:

KENNEDY: "Would you tell us if you have opposition from anybody that you dispose of them by having them stuffed in a trunk? Is that what you do, Mr. Giancana?"

GIANCANA: "I decline to answer because I honestly believe my answer might tend to incriminate me."

KENNEDY: "Would you tell us anything about any of your operations or will you just giggle every time I ask you a question?"

GIANCANA: "I decline to answer because I honestly believe my answer might tend to incriminate me."

KENNEDY: "I thought only little girls giggled, Mr. Giancana."

Hoffa took up five days. He rarely seemed perturbed, refusing to take the Fifth but regularly referring the committee to one of the other witnesses, whom Hoffa knew he could depend on to bury the subject. Cornered, he parried with phrases like: "To the best of my recollection, I must recall on my memory, I cannot remember." Deferential to the senators, he made a point of addressing the chief counsel as "Bob," or "brother." "I used to love to bug the little bastard," Hoffa admitted years later. "Whenever Bobby would get tangled up in one of his involved questions, I would wink at him." Hoffa found it "ridiculously easy to get him to lose his temper." Occasionally, for minutes at a time, the two would attempt to stare each other down. "His face seemed completely transformed with this stare of absolute evilness," Kennedy wrote afterward.

An acquaintance of the period slowly turning into a friend, the peerless journalist Murray Kempton, explained to Jean Stein that "Bob, who had an underlying distaste for the kind of people his father used to buy, recognized the devil in Hoffa. . . . A general fanaticism for evil that could be thought of as the opposite side of his own fanaticism for good . . . and, therefore, involved direct combat."

A representative cross-section of organized crime floated through the committee's hearing rooms. Typical of the flotsam was "Crazy Joey" Gallo, an enforcer for the unions around New York who threw Kennedy off by assuming a solicitous, even a protective attitude toward the chief counsel. In Kennedy's outer office, Gallo knelt down and fingered the rug, pronounced it excellent for a crap game, then rushed over to frisk a casual visitor since "if Kennedy gets killed now everybody will say I did it." When JFK ran in 1960, Gallo wrote Bob asking what he could do to help get his brother elected.

"Just tell everybody you're voting for Nixon," Robert Kennedy wrote back.

One very big fish Kennedy dragged out of the deep was Carlos Marcello. Marcello, who presided over an astonishing list of criminal activities across the Gulf States, was very short (five foot two), very cunning, and psychologically unbudgeable. The eldest of six sons of an immigrant Sicilian peasant couple, Carlos had been born in Tunisia and never naturalized when his parents crossed over to New Orleans and settled in as vegetable farmers. At nineteen, Marcello began a three-year stretch in the Louisiana State Penitentiary for putting a pair of younger boys up to a series of grocery-store and bank robberies. Upon emerging, the ambitious parolee finagled control of a bar called "The Brown Bomber," in which hard drugs and marijuana went along with the booze and hookers. "We had nuttin' but colored people in dere," Marcello explained later in the subliterate Cajun patois inquisitors like Kennedy found, at the very least, intriguing, "and man did dey drink."

Marcello was a realist. At twenty-five he became a soldier in the Louisiana Mafia, a loosely structured alliance of unusually tolerant thugs, which permitted Carlos and his brother Vincent to branch out into the distribution of jukeboxes and pinball machines, pool tables and gambling paraphernalia. When the New York reform mayor Fiorello La Guardia decreed during the early thirties that slot machines were to be prohibited throughout the city, the suave gangster who controlled the slot-machine franchise, Frank

Costello, struck a deal with the "Kingfish," Senator Huey Long, to accept Costello's warehouses of slot machines in return for a 10 percent rakeoff.

The New York Mob was decentralizing. At Meyer Lansky's direction, a national underworld communications center and a clearinghouse for money laundering was started up in New Orleans, one of the gateways to Cuba and the Caribbean. A trusted Costello flunky, "Dandy Phil" Kastel, moved south and struck a deal with Marcello according to which the Marcello brothers' Jefferson Music Company ran 250 of Costello's slots and kept two-thirds of the gross.

Like Costello, Marcello was very openhanded and discriminating when it came to payoffs around the political and law-enforcement establishment of midcentury Louisiana. In 1938, an undercover FBI agent bought 23 pounds of marijuana from Carlos. He served nine months of a one-year sentence. After that Marcello was regularly charged with robbery, IRS violations, and violent assaults on individuals who crossed him, from cops to investigative reporters; all charges were quickly dropped, while records of the arrests disappeared. Impressed, in 1944 the New York mob brought Marcello in for 12 1/2 percent when the syndicate opened its first casino in Jefferson Parish, the Beverly Club. Costello, Lansky, and Kastel divided up most of the remaining equity. More slots and a racetrack wire service appeared in 1947.

That same year, the Immigration and Naturalization Service finally deported the head of the Mafia in New Orleans, "Silver Dollar" Sam Carolla. In a heated backroom conclave at the Black Diamond nightclub in New Orleans, Marcello got the nod. The little man's freehanded ways, his promise as a land speculator, and leakage from an FBI report which specified that a hoodlum the New York syndicate wanted eliminated wound up beaten to death by Carlos and his accomplice, then dissolved in lye and dumped into the swamp behind the Marcellos' Willswood Tavern—the whole package manifestly qualified Marcello for senior leadership. At thirty-eight the neckless, uneducated little Sicilian-Creole had a chair on the Commission.

One unmistakable bit of evidence that Carlos Marcello had hit the big time was his unwilling appearance before Senator Estes Kefauver's traveling road show in 1951. Kefauver was chairing the Senate's Special Committee to Investigate Organized Crime and held extensive hearings in the Jefferson County courthouse. Marcello pleaded the Fifth 152 times. In 1953 the U.S. government issued a deportation order against him.

The same year, Aaron Kohn showed up in town. Kohn was a soft-spoken ex-FBI agent who quickly determined that while New Orleans' corrupt mayor DeLesseps ("Chef") Morrison supposedly governed the place,

Marcello and his six brothers all but owned it. Hired by the privately funded Metropolitan Crime Commission, Kohn established that Marcello had pieced together a 6500-acre swampland property known as Churchill Farms, which communicated by way of a patchwork of bayous and lakes with the Gulf of Mexico, a perfect, unpoliceable drug destination. Kohn traced at least three gangland-style murders to Marcello and tracked his ownership of the huge New Southport Club casino, an assortment of "Venus-trap" strip joints in the French Quarter. Most important was Marcello's implication in the national gambling wire service now centered in the business district. All this barely began to hint at the empire the stocky, bustling Mafia kingpin managed out of his crude cinderblock office behind the Town & Country Motel. A plaque on the door suggested the mentality of the man:

THREE CAN KEEP

A SECRET

IF TWO ARE DEAD

Far beyond the bayou country, Marcello was feared and appreciated. Long afterward, Carlos bragged to an FBI agent that he slipped one local police chief "$50,000 in cash every few months. I used to stuff de cash in a suitcase and carry it over to his office. . . . I took care of everybody."

Kohn, sorting all this out, got very little help. The mayor's office and the police department withheld their own records. Earlier, the FBI had kept a weather eye on the ascending little gangster, but now that Marcello had reached rarefied air he seemed too big, too connected to touch. His Mafia responsibilities extended throughout Louisiana, Alabama, Mississippi, and Texas, with ventures in Arizona, Nevada, and California coming into prospect. Between the racing wire and a call-girl ring that encompassed the South, very little escaped Marcello's appreciation. A Louisiana native, Joe Civello, a close associate of Jack Ruby, ran a full spectrum of rackets in Dallas for Marcello.

One tipoff to Marcello's eminence by then was his appearance in respected Mob watering holes. He showed up to joke around with the other hoods and politicians at Clint Murchison's Del Charro resort, like J. Edgar Hoover, a cosseted guest. That might or might not be germane, but Aaron Kohn, attempting to pin down Marcello's holdings, got no help from the FBI and in fact had to put up, according to John Davis, with "the constant ridicule of his former FBI colleagues." The Bureau was making no effort to bug or tap Marcello. When Robert Kennedy requested Marcello's FBI file, all that was available was a memorandum from the special agent in charge in

New Orleans, Regis Kennedy, which dismissed the Caesar of the Gulf as no more than a local "tomato salesman" (the Pelican Tomato Company was one of the myriad of Marcello family investments).

Marcello's appearance before the McClellan Committee on March 24, 1959 served to replay his performance before Estes Kefauver. Kohn fortified Kennedy mightily. Flanked by his adroit attorney, Jack Wasserman, Marcello sought refuge from every question in the Fifth Amendment. The judicial Senator Sam Ervin confronted Marcello with the best question of the session: "I would like to know . . . how a man with this kind of record can stay in the United States for five years, nine months, twenty-four days after he is found to be an undesirable alien. . . ." Marcello referred the question to his attorney. Robert Kennedy was listening, closely.

The months of emphasis on Teamsters and mobsters had started to pique the Rackets Committee's Republicans. Hoffa, after all, was a dependable contributor to Republican Party campaigns. What about the United Automobile Workers, whose leader, Walter Reuther, Hoffa cheerfully referred to as "the leader of Soviet America?"

Prodded hard by Barry Goldwater, the Republicans hired investigator Jack McGovern. McGovern dropped out of sight for a while, then rejoined the committee with a doctored National Labor Relations Board report and a number of examples of spot corruption around the UAL. Most egregious perhaps was the case of Richard Gosser, the head of a Toledo local with a long record of indictments for burglary and car theft and a conviction for armed robbery. While operating his local, Gosser padded his income with kickbacks and property speculations underwritten by the union treasury. There were tax problems. A union member who demanded an accounting, John Bolman, got hit hard enough while introducing his motion in the union hall to crush a bone in his face. Called before the Rackets Committee, Bolman found Bob Kennedy breaking into his testimony and grilling him hard as to his motives in coming forward against the leadership.

Compared with Hoffa's backroom alliance with Cosa Nostra luminaries, whatever revelations McGovern brought to the surface seemed provincial, penny-ante. But Goldwater and Mundt and Curtis were heartened and demanded that the committee go after the Reuther brothers and the bloody Kohler strike in Sheboygan, Wisconsin, by 1958 well into its third year. Kennedy himself flew out and found an industrial war zone. Illegal picketing and vandalism were met by scabs and the company's own army. Dozens and dozens of workers had died. Inside the huge, antiquated brick buildings it was like revisiting a nineteenth-century industrial gulag. Temperatures in the enamel shop ran well over 100 degrees, and workers gobbled down lunch in a couple of minutes with their visors up, perspiring into the glowing ovens.

In Washington, Walter Reuther finally took the stand. A lean, earnest figure of stunning articulateness, Reuther was authentic, compelling. One arm had been shattered by a shotgun blast through the window of his modest home. Even Goldwater was at a loss for words. "You were right," he conceded to Kennedy. "We never should have gotten into this."

To the annoyance of the Republicans, as month followed month, the whole show was turning into a brother act. Insiders labeled Bobby "a one-man firing squad for Jack." The hearings were televised, which conferred on the Kennedys a new level of national celebrity. His years in Hollywood had left the Ambassador quite expert in studio legerdemain. Determined to sell Jack "like soap flakes," Joe Kennedy spent money and called in favors from every direction. Picture spreads in *Life* and *Look* and the *Saturday Evening Post* portrayed the senator fading wide to wing a pass, or bronzed and devil-may-care at the tiller of the *Victura*. Crutches were never visible. Jack's first child, Caroline, materialized, round-faced and irresistible.

A spare, adenoidal-looking Robert Kennedy was often in the frame. Perhaps for the first time, he was being taken seriously. Russell Baker, returning to the hearing room after some months, found that the Racket Committee's chief counsel had "grown-up, and done it very quickly. Now his questioning was calm, shrewd, and to the point. He had picked up the self-confidence needed to keep him in control of touchy situations in the hearing room. Surprising in a daddy's rich boy, he had a sense of irony, a sharp wit, and the gift of humor. . . ."

By now the Kennedy brothers were starting to angle their spotlights. One early and carefully calculated probe was the attention paid by Bob Kennedy's investigators into the dealings of Murray Chotiner, the pudgy, effective Mob lawyer who masterminded Richard Nixon's rise in California and now found himself accused of "influence-peddling" for having initiated calls to clients from the White House. Right-wing commentator Ralph de Toledano would write that all this Rackets Committee static served to force the worried Chotiner to keep a very low profile during the 1960 campaign, helping produce the Nixon loss. With this investigation pending, Robert Kennedy had stopped by Bureau headquarters to explore what Hoover might have on Chotiner and Alger Hiss; Hoover blew off this brash middle Kennedy brother with his personal recommendation that "before any such move was made it should be given very careful study and evaluation. . . ." Slow down!

The brothers were refining their material. Joseph Rauh, sitting in as Walter Reuther's lawyer, observed later to Arthur Schlesinger Jr. that "Bobby must have had some form of communication with his brother Jack or there really is a thing called extrasensory perception. Every time we were getting into trouble Jack would enter the Hearing Room, take his seat on the Committee dais and help us out. It got to be a joke inside our crowd as Jack walked down the aisle each time Mundt, Goldwater or Curtis was scoring points against us."

Jack was the money player, but Bobby was calling the plays. He already accepted fully that in politics, as in touch football, it can be advisable at times to slip somebody the elbow, to rethink the goal line. On discovering that Hoffa had a wiretap expert on his payroll, Bernard Spindel, to track his fellow Teamsters and intercept FBI surveillance reports on Hoffa, Kennedy began to explore the intricacies of clandestine surveillance. The distinctions between bugging and tapping and the admissibility of either, whether under the law or before the courts, appeared to slide right by the glowering young prosecutor.

Having decided that the Mob was well into the process of taking over the country, Kennedy concluded that "if we do not on a national scale attack organized criminals with weapons and techniques as effective as their own, they will destroy us." The emergency was uppermost, and civil liberties represented to an afterthought. Confronting the evasive Hoffa through hearing after hearing, Kennedy attempted to startle the stolid Teamster chieftain by playing him recordings of his recent telephone exchanges with notorious hoodlums. It would be assumed, later on, that most of these thought-provoking tapes were borrowed from Frank Hogan, the New York district attorney.

It developed that Kennedy had instigated an electronic surveillance program of his own, complete with a committee "investigator," Edward Jones, a Kennedy family employee. Thus, Bob could later write that "our Committee staff never used wiretapping equipment or a listening device." For some months, Jones conducted an assortment of wiretap operations, and on at least one occasion the committee investigators planted a wire on one of its informants. There was no thought of exploiting anything they discovered in court—that was clearly illegal—but Kennedy rarely scrupled to break out these tapes during open committee sessions or pass the material on to selected journalists. This sort of unauthorized leakage was very often more than enough to sully a reputation or undermine a career. Bob Kennedy had obviously learned plenty from Joseph McCarthy.

Trading information with, and leaking inside information to, carefully chosen columnists and/or media representatives has been a tradition in government since Benjamin Franklin. Hoover became a virtuoso early. By now Robert Kennedy was cultivating a following of his own among the Capitol reporters who moved in and out of the Rackets Committee hearings, coming up with unusually straight—for a politician—answers to most of their questions and inviting a delighted few to soirees at Hickory Hill.

Kennedy already liked to play around with trial balloons. Early in 1958 he indicated that the Rackets Committee was about to follow up on rumors that large corporations were amusing clients with "call girls." That produced a headline or two but no serious committee enthusiasm. A year later, the *Washington Post* quoted him as stating that he had received offers of financial support for his brother's imminent presidential effort if he would take it easy on certain of the witnesses. He had, Kennedy was quoted, "dismissed" any such approaches. They "never affected the work of the staff." Karl Mundt was noisily indignant and demanded names, while an alarmed McClellan called the committee into executive session and disavowed the whole brewing scandal.

The responsibility for picking up after Kennedy's blunder fell to Kenneth O'Donnell. When the FBI closed in, O'Donnell had to confess that the entire fiasco was more a matter of "innuendoes" than any outright offers. FBI assistant director Alex Rosen wrote up the incident for Hoover. A characteristic note appeared in pen on the bottom of the report: "Re: Robert Kennedy—this is what happens when the prodigal son gets too far away from home and papa."

As the months passed Kennedy had indeed become crisper, better organized, less likely to find himself in shouting matches with evasive witnesses which John McClellan was forced to cut short, rephrasing Kennedy's question to take the edge off. As the ubiquitous Lem Billings commented: "For the first time in his life he was happy. He'd been a very frustrated young man, awfully mad most of the time, having to hold everything in and work on Jack's career instead of his own. I think he found himself during the Hoffa investigation."

Bob's foreboding at having taken his career onto a tangent of which the Ambassador disapproved so wholeheartedly was starting to lift. Not that the old financier had budged. "All you're doing," he railed at both his middle sons once the hearings had started, "is jeopardizing future votes. One of you on such a panel would have been too many. But both of you—forget it. You're committing political suicide."

Sometimes the financier insisted on attending the hearings personally. The committee's chief clerk, Ruth Watt, acknowledges that "You knew when he was there. Bob was a little keyed up, a little tense and so on. There was a strong paternal influence over all the Kennedys."

Perhaps the greatest satisfactions came from Robert Kennedy's manifest gifts for handling this very large staff. Telephones were ringing constantly, unsorted documents rose in piles between the desks, and investigators rushed in and out with tattered union financial records, tips from disgruntled members of the locals, eyewitness accounts of beatings and intimidations, of acid-throwing and selective arson and murder. La Verne Duffy, who put in twenty-five years on the Government Operations Committee, would reflect that "There was no one like him. He had an uncanny ability to get people to do more than they thought they could do. He didn't do this by bringing pressure on them. It was because they wanted to please him. He gave people a sense of personal interest in themselves, their work, and their families. This was his secret. He never got mad except when someone lied to him. He couldn't stand that."

Along with John Seigenthaler, Ed Guthman—still reporting for the Seattle paper, their specialist on Dave Beck—became an unpaid adviser to the committee. Guthman appreciated the way Kennedy had protected Guthman's sources in the Teamster union as well as "the skill and tenacity with which he and his investigators went about their work. But it was more than that. I enjoyed being in his company. Though he was sometimes withdrawn or laconic, I usually found him easy to talk to. When he was working, he was very serious, but his sense of humor, wry, needling and often self-deprecating, was never far below the surface."

This ability to size up a complicated undertaking and organize and run it quickly and effectively was very reminiscent of his father's. Like Joe, he could be brutal and undiplomatic when that served his purposes. Also like the Ambassador, he had the acumen to select capable staff and the solidity of character to enlist their loyalty. He was a born chief, and now he had a tribe.

With outsiders, he maintained a reputation, as Harris Wofford would later write, as "an arrogant, narrow, rude young man. . . ." Then teaching at Notre Dame Law School and attempting to help out the liberal wing of the Democratic Party, Wofford first approached Bobby for advice on what Congressman Chester Bowles should look out for when he visited Muslim Asia. Wofford found Kennedy seated "at one end of a long cavernous office in the basement of the Old Senate Office Building." Wofford was directed to a chair at the other end and spent the best part of an hour watching Bobby eat lunch from a tray a black attendant brought him, talk on the telephone, pick through some paperwork. As Wofford was about to leave, Kennedy indicated that he might approach. He had "nothing special to suggest," Wofford would report, after which "he went into a diatribe against the Soviet regime, which he explained was a great evil and an ever-present threat, and [bade] me goodbye."

If Bob Kennedy seemed preoccupied to the point of surly much of the time, it may have occurred to him that, while he was raising a lot of dust, there really wasn't that much likely to emerge. The Eisenhower administration remained disinterested in revelations like the fact that the Teamsters had helped senior gangster Paul ("The Waiter") Ricca out of his problems with the IRS by acquiring his pretentious home. As in many of the examples in the volume Bob ground out just after he retired from the Rackets Committee, *The Enemy Within*, the Waiter's culpability had more to do with Kennedy's viscera than with the law. Hoffa and his principal lieutenants might "have the look of Capone's men. . . . Sleek, often bilious and fat, or lean and cold and hard. They have the smooth faces and cruel eyes of gangsters; they wear the same rich clothes, the diamond ring, the jeweled watch, the strong, sickly-sweet smelling perfume." One witness was "so repulsive that I could not stomach the thought of calling her to Washington to testify." But style ain't substance. "When you admit to me that there's obvious wrongdoing here and you tell me on top of that that you can't make a case out of it, it makes me sick to my stomach," Kennedy complained to William Hundley, chief of the Organized Crime Section of Eisenhower's Justice Department.

"I can't be responsible for your gastric juices," Hundley shot back. Kennedy hung up on him.

Working on *The Enemy Within*, Kennedy attempted to suppress his gathering suspicion that, for his father at least, justice was selective. Pressure was exerted on Bobby through Arthur Krock, who wrote the preface, to excise a negative reference to Edward Bennett Williams, the well-connected lawyer for several senior hoodlums, most prominently Frank Costello. The Ambassador himself stepped in and forced Krock to ease off on his criticism that the book was loaded to favor union extremists over crooks. Nothing escaped the old man's eye.

After meandering for years through the sociological garbage dump that constitutes Mob America, Robert Kennedy found himself stumbling over unanticipated coincidences, developments good for a laugh until you thought about it. Committee investigators, Kennedy wrote, digging into the records on a building in Manhattan being leased by various presumably crooked labor unions, suspected that "the building was owned by a racketeer or perhaps even by The Mob! .... They were shocked to learn who owned the building.

"It was my family."

One committee senator who disliked Bobby all along was Arizona Senator Barry Goldwater. Something of a pal of Willie Bioff, the Las Vegas hood who had gone to prison alongside Johnny Rosselli for extorting too many movie producers, Goldwater divulged to one friend that "Bobby struck me as a mean little asshole, with his high voice and his uncombed hair." Once in place as chief counsel, Kennedy "informed us about the mandate of the Committee as if he were reading a prescription off a bottle of medicine." Goldwater sensed that Bobby was driving Jack deeper than he really wanted to go; "he pushed Jack, was tough on him." As Bobby's own investigators began to turn up evidence of his father's persistent dealings with organized crime, Goldwater would remember, "it just killed him."

At one point, Al Capone's attorney, Abraham Teitelbaum, was summoned to appear before the Rackets Committee and reportedly got word to Bobby that he, Teitelbaum, would have to reference Joe Kennedy as complicit in certain Mob transactions were he actually forced to appear. Bobby nevertheless pressed the subpoena and Teitelbaum backed off, now suggesting that Jack's campaign might expect a major contribution from him if he emerged undamaged. It was Teitelbaum's hint of a bribe—Bobby was already scouting up cash for Jack—which reached the chaste ears of Karl Mundt and produced the flurry in the newspapers which Ken O'Donnell and John McClellan were put at pains to stifle.

By then Bobby was out for bigger game. In pursuit of Paul Dorfman, Hoffa's principal go-between with the Outfit in Chicago, Kennedy found him "closely linked with such underworld figures as Tony Accardo, who became the head of the Chicago syndicate after the death of Al Capone, and with Abner (Longie) Zwillman—a top gangland leader in the United States. (Longie Zwillman committed suicide shortly after being subpoenaed by our Committee.)" The Ambassador apparently omitted to mention to his son that Longie Zwillman had been a factor in his own career since the rum-running skirmishes of thirty-plus years earlier, or that it was onto Zwillman and a partner that the financier off-loaded Somerset Importers. Murmuring into the mouthpiece of that special privacy-receiver on his telephone in

Hyannis Port, or locked away naked in his elaborately wired bullpen sunning and rapping out instructions from Palm Beach, Joe Kennedy was in touch with a shadow universe he never anticipated would impact his children.

Ultimately, what was intended to be John Kennedy's signature accomplishment as a legislator, a bill to reform labor without infringing on its enormous influence, got slid out from under him. After passing the Senate overwhelmingly, the Kennedy-Ives Bill got butchered in the conference. A piece of harsh, Republican-inspired legislation was reported out and passed quickly. It required union officers to file annual financial reports, denied convicted felons a shot at union office for five years, and closely regulated union elections. This was the much-ballyhooed Landrum-Griffin Act. After a few weeks of futile behind-the-scenes lobbying to modify the final language, both Kennedys ducked for cover. Jack had taken his name off the bill.

Never one to let an opportunity slip, Jimmy Hoffa proclaimed that "the two rich Kennedy boys are trying to get a law passed that will destroy the entire American labor movement." Joe, offstage but tireless, kept after the media, and within months the family was reemerging as champions of legitimate labor (Jack)—a play for the industrial states—and hell on labor abuses (Bobby)—a welcome note across the South and throughout the border states.

It was beginning to look as if those bitter Rackets-Committee years might have been worth it all along. Their father had been right about one thing: "It's not what you are that counts, but what people think you are."

The Gas in the Room

John Kennedy became president in 1960 as a result of three simulta-
neous campaigns. Everybody is familiar with the first—the candidate's
own exhausting performance, highlighted by his crisp reminder to the
Greater Houston Ministerial Association of the proper separation between
church and state and his face-off in debate with Richard Nixon, whose jowls,
powdered up with "Lazy Shave," became mottled within minutes by furrows
of descending perspiration.

Bobby's role was more complex. As campaign manager, he led the delegate hunt. This involved a year of round-the-clock days which started with a
closely calculated division of the country into precincts and personalities
and the assignment of the dozen or so key Kennedy lieutenants—Ken
O'Donnell, Larry O'Brien, Ted Sorenson, Pierre Salinger, Steve Smith, Ted
Kennedy, Connecticut boss John Bailey, and all the secondary hopefuls—to
charm and wheedle and promise and intimidate convention delegates to lock
the nomination up for Jack. Bobby would be watching, pushing, encourag-
ing, and chewing ass every minute as the situation warranted.

The third—and perhaps the most important—of the campaigns would
get as little publicity as possible. This required the critical involvement of
Joseph P. Kennedy, who ran from place to place, from leader to leader, with—
Hubert Humphrey got it exactly right—"a little black bag and a checkbook."
The states that won the thing for Jack, the big industrial states—New York,

Massachusetts, Pennsylvania, Illinois—came on line early because the Ambassador understood the value—and the price—involved in wooing the leadership. "I just got a telegram from my father," John Kennedy liked to joke with crowds toward the end of the ordeal. "It said, 'don't buy one more vote than is necessary. I'll be damned if I'll pay for a landslide.'" Each time he tossed this out, the old financier exploded.

As with most Kennedy humor, the rocks lay inches below the surface. They all knew from the beginning, as Teddy White put it shortly after the election, that many outcomes would depend on "the private resources of Joseph Kennedy." These resources were not a figure of speech. Tip O'Neill once confided in me about having been summoned in 1960 to Cleveland by the financier, who met him on a street corner and pulled a wad of thousand-dollar bills bigger than his hand out of a topcoat pocket. "This goes to Mike DiSalle," the patriarch grunted and peeled off twenty or thirty thousand for O'Neill to slip to the Ohio governor, who controlled the delegation. Bobby had attempted to elbow the imperious DiSalle into line one time too many, and the financier wanted to smooth things out a little.

All through the later fifties, Joe Kennedy had been pouncing on largely Irish-Catholic old-line political bosses who ran the big-city machines. One of their own could aspire to the presidency, the Ambassador kept insisting, and that would of course be Jack, with his Ivy-League polish and his well-publicized wartime heroics. Joe remained very dogmatic about never writing anything down, but money and favors of every variety changed hands, and one after the next the bosses fell into line—Charles A. Buckley in the Bronx, the widely connected and endlessly accommodating Congressman Eugene Keogh, Peter Crotty in Buffalo, the potentates of Tammany Hall so sensitive to Frank Costello's feelings. John McCormack, majority leader in the House, worked on William Green in Philadelphia and Pat Brown in California. Mayor Richard J. Daley in Chicago, whom Kennedy had brought along since he was a county clerk, was dependable early, while Governor David Lawrence of Pennsylvania found himself attempting to stall Kennedy in Harrisburg, then fending off his own big-city delegates, whom the Kennedy organization was breaking out one by one.

On February 29, 1960, Joe Kennedy started calling in another, rather more shadowy set of "resources." These were the associates Kennedy had in mind when he observed that he kept his business life quiet because he didn't want "my children to inherit my enemies." At Joe's bidding, his occasional golfing partner Johnny Rosselli rounded up the dignitaries of the

Chicago Outfit, Joe Accardo, Sam Giancana, and "Curly," Murray ("the Camel") Humphreys, for a meeting at Felix Young's Restaurant in Manhattan. A scattering of East Coast hoods sat in, including envoys from the Bonnanos. Kennedy scarcely bothered to ingratiate himself with these battle-scared veterans of the Capone era. He would need—and expect—a substantial cash contribution from the assembled. He looked to them to make available the Outfit's many thousands of worker ants in the crusade for Jack.

Murray the Camel spoke up to object that Bobby seemed to be on some sort of racket-busting tear with the McClellan Committee. Joe brushed that off. "The elder Kennedy replied that it was Jack who was running for president, not Bobby," according to an onlooker's account, "and that this was 'business, not politics.'"

That seemed to persuade Kennedy's uneasy dinner guests, few of whom were logicians. Joe Kennedy later bragged to his son-in-law Steve Smith that he alone among the campaign strategists had "the balls to go straight to the Mob themselves." Not that the financier was breaking virgin ground. A willingness to tap the assets of the hoodlum community goes back a long way in American politics. United Artists boss Joe Schenck funneled mob money to the New Deal for years before the IRS bagged him for collusion with labor racketeering in the film industry. A key figure in Franklin Roosevelt's reelection machine, Sidney Hillman, widely dubbed "Labor's Statesman" as a cofounder of the CIO, maintained Lewis "Lepke" Buchalter, the ranking hitter of Murder, Inc., on the union's payroll until 1937. Lepke terrified union holdouts and recalcitrant businessmen equally and backstopped industrial peace. Democratic National Committee Chairman Robert Hannegan and Hillman managed to double-team the faltering FDR into agreeing to take on Harry Truman as vice president in 1944. Widely regarded as a toady to Kansas City Boss Pendergast, Truman appealed to gangland as somebody who understood their needs.

Through George Smathers, whose bonds to Richard Nixon were at least as close as to Jack Kennedy, the Kennedys remained well aware that cash and assistance greater than anything Joe was likely to raise would pour through from organized crime into the Nixon campaign. Nixon's involvement with the underworld began with his 1946 entry into politics when, turned down by the FBI, the ungainly Navy veteran responded to an ad in an Orange County newspaper and found himself maneuvered into Congress by attorney Murray Chotiner, a dirty-tricks specialist who with his brother represented 221 Mafia functionaries between 1949 and 1952, almost invariably with success. Meyer Lansky's top lieutenant in California, Mickey Cohen, agreed to finance Nixon's early career in return for help keeping his bookmakers out of jail.

Once ensconced in Congress, Nixon wasted very little time before establishing a durable and rewarding friendship with Charles ("Bebe") Rebozo, an elementary school classmate of George Smathers's deeply involved in Florida and Cuban real estate speculations. The unseen mover all up and down the Caribbean basin remained Meyer Lansky, in league with Santo Trafficante and Carlos Marcello running drugs and controlling a booming empire of hotels and casinos. By 1956 Howard Hughes was buying into government and contributed $100,000 to Nixon's handlers to help stymie the dump-Nixon campaign, along with an additional $205,000 for Nixon's brother Donald, purportedly "for a hamburger restaurant." Nixon was filling in as the anti-Castro action officer everywhere in the Eisenhower government. As the 1960 campaign shaped up, Joe Kennedy was aware of rumors that Jimmy Hoffa and his Teamsters had assembled a war chest of $1 million for Nixon, this to be matched by another $1 million Marcello was soliciting among the Eastern gangsters.

For Joe Kennedy *not* to offset the syndicate's obvious bias toward Nixon would probably doom his son's already-chancy prospects. He'd better revitalize, quickly, his longstanding connections with the underworld. In 1954, to Joe's annoyance, one of his middle daughters, Pat, had married Peter Lawford. Lawford looked more and more like an indiscreet alcoholic of tortured sexuality. One of his running buddies by the later fifties was Frank Sinatra, whose career had started to recover after a postwar slump. Sinatra was quite shamelessly on the social make. Joe Kennedy was well aware that Sinatra had arrived at a kind of mascot status among the dominant mobsters and that he was particularly close to the dreaded Sam Giancana, now the ramrod of the Chicago organization.

Sinatra's mother, Dolly, was regarded highly around Hoboken as both a kitchen-table abortionist and a midlevel ward heeler with ties to the Jersey City machine. Joe approached her directly. Little Frank had broken in running political errands and venerated successful politicians. Once Lawford joined the Kennedys, Sinatra helped the family out however he was asked. Joe advised Frank on his IRS problems, and Frank provided girls for Joe. There developed a pecking order. "I was Frank's pimp," as Peter Lawford didn't mind confessing, "and Frank was Jack's. It sounds terrible now, but then it was a lot of fun."

By the later fifties, John Kennedy was in and out of Los Angeles quite a bit, staying over at the old Louis B. Mayer mansion in Santa Monica his sister and Lawford had bought, or weekending in Palm Springs with Frank. Jack remained a cheerful participant in the "debauched hotel parties" Sinatra liked to throw and continued to indulge his hit-and-miss flirtation with Marilyn Monroe. Inevitably, old Joe showed up from time to time to rummage among the spoils.

Forever on the move, the Ambassador had dropped in on Sinatra at the crooner's Palm Springs estate, where Frank's black valet took offense at Joe's racial slurs and referred to an incident during which one of the circulating hookers got burned by the financier's cigar. Plans were laid. Detectives the financier had retained were running down the rumor that Richard Nixon had been consulting Dr. Arnold Hutschnecker, a New York psychotherapist, so Sinatra could leak the story to his newspaper outlets.

The well-informed Ambassador had years before picked up on Sinatra's standing with the Mob. Joe Kennedy auditioned Sinatra in 1959, when Lawford and the crooner were flown into Palm Beach. They agreed that Frank would direct a reworking of "High Hopes" as a theme song for Jack's campaign, and recruit his friends to impart a heightened Hollywood glamour to the candidate's entourage.

Toward the end of the year, the patriarch again summoned Sinatra, this time to Hyannis Port. "I think you can help me in West Virginia and Illinois with our friends," Kennedy informed the dazzled star. He meant the Mob. "You understand, Frank, I can't go. They're my friends too, but I can't approach them. But you can." Characteristically, Joe was vacillating between anxiety about his Mafia antecedents and his presumption that only he—certainly not his overprotected children—could steer the touchy negotiations intended to propel Jack into the presidency.

The scrawny, explosive Sinatra had been raised by the Mob. Gangsters like Willie Moretti underwrote his career as a band singer, and as early as Christmas of 1946, when the deported Lucky Luciano was sneaked into Cuba for a homecoming bash at the Hotel Nacional, Sinatra dropped by with top Chicago gunsels Joe Accardo and the Fischetti brothers, Al Capone's nephews. Reported to be favored with a member such that at romantic moments it all but towered over him, Sinatra's eagerness to entertain his friends captivated the executive-class personalities around the Cosa Nostra. Sam Giancana and the crooner exchanged star-sapphire pinkie rings.

* * *

As Joe Kennedy sized the situation up, once backroom dealmaking had locked in the industrial states, the six or seven open primaries his son would enter were crucial to their chances. Wisconsin would be important in that it would demonstrate Jack's appeal compared with Hubert Humphrey, the populist senator from neighboring Minnesota. Then West Virginia, a predominantly Protestant, rural state, would lay to rest the apprehensions of the party bosses about a Catholic candidate.

Once the presidential primary season loomed, the Ambassador was racked by another of his characteristic seizures of nerves. Jack was running for the presidency too early, Joe divulged to Red Fay and Charles Bartlett. He was too young, the economy wasn't bad enough, there was the Catholic issue. "He won't have a chance," the patriarch concluded. "I hate to see him and Bobby work themselves to death and lose." Joe told Charles Lewin that he "got down on his knees every night and prayed Jack wouldn't have to take the job." Joe's confidence was guttering again.

The financier's apprehensions sharpened further once the Harris poll the family had commissioned convinced Jack to go into costly West Virginia. "It's a nothing state," Ben Bradlee would remember Joe protesting, "and they'll kill him over the Catholic thing." According to Bobby Baker, a lot of undeclared cash was moving toward the Kennedys from Taiwan and Madrid, but overcoming West Virginia's religious bias was going to take prodigious expenditures, a vast pattern of artfully distributed statewide bribes. Cardinal Cushing reminisced in later years about sitting with Joe Kennedy and breaking the recalcitrant state down parish by parish. Buying off the preachers of every color was vital. At a preliminary meeting to file the necessary papers, Kenny O'Donnell would remember, officials "actually shrank up against the wall, as if such a Catholic might be contagious." Ashen, Bobby telephoned his brother, who countered with the Harris poll. "The people who voted for you in that poll," Bob told Jack, "have just found out that you're a Catholic."

The fundamental problem with West Virginia was West Virginia. A chronically depressed moonscape of worked-out strip mines and backwoods hollows, what organization there was seemed to involve tradeoffs among law enforcement officials and the occasional local run-down clubhouse. It kept coming back to one unwelcome fact: If you wanted West Virginia, you had to buy it.

Which simplified the process. Once the Chicago Outfit—Curly Humphreys dissenting—decided to help Jack, Mooney Giancana and Sinatra arranged things with Paul ("Skinny") D'Amato, the connected proprietor of the lush 500 Club in Atlantic City. An initial $50,000 was transferred from the Las Vegas skim and earmarked for "desks and chairs and supplies for politicians around the state." Joe Kennedy met briefly with Skinny and agreed that his son, once elected, would authorize the return of deported syndicate overlord Joe Adonis. D'Amato had a broad acquaintanceship around the thickly ethnic Northern Panhandle of West Virginia as well as outlying New Jersey, particularly among the powerful local sheriffs, many of whom frequented his casino, and D'Amato now toured the state tearing up gambling markers to entice wavering lawmen and county officials. A compliant New Jersey lawyer, Angelo Melandra, disbursed additional cash to the well-connected needy.

The financier couldn't leave the details alone. When Vincent ("Jimmy Blue Eyes") Alo, Meyer Lansky's sidekick, refused during the early weeks an approach from Kennedy coatholder Phil Regan, an entertainer who traveled with Jack in 1960, to help Kennedy bring Giancana into this fight, the financier approached the "rising star" in the Illinois state attorney's office, Robert McDonnell, through circuit court judge William J. Touhy. McDonnell was in time to marry Giancana's daughter, Antoinette. A deal was struck which stipulated that if Jack made it, his administration would ease off on the Mob, especially its promising Las Vegas ventures. By July of 1960 the Outfit's primary fixer, Murray the Camel, was holed up in the downtown Hilton working the phones for weeks to politicians and renegade Teamsters, endeavoring—against his own better judgment—to sew the race up for Jack. Mob stalwarts across the country were manning phone banks and running voters to the polls and paying off poll watchers.

Sinatra had long since arranged a powwow between Kennedy and the urbane Teamster official Harold Gibbons, whom Bobby had termed "as ruthless as Hoffa . . . a tall thin man with a cold superior look," corrupt and self-serving. Joe received Gibbons warmly at the Palm Beach residence. "Well, Mr. Gibbons," the financier opened, "I don't think there's much of a war going on between the Kennedys and Hoffa. I hardly hear the name Hoffa in our house any more." Jack himself followed up with a mollifying call to Jimmy Hoffa personally, during which he touched Hoffa up for a donation; Hoffa pitched a tantrum over Bobby. By then, Hoffa had secretly committed the Teamsters to their million-dollar pledge to the Nixon campaign, matched by another million from Carlos Marcello and the New Jersey and Florida wiseguys.

Not that the candidate was apprised of everything. Even before Jack announced, according to Walter Trohan, the patriarch was importuning John L. Lewis, the czar of the United Mine Workers. Union miners mucked coal throughout much of West Virginia. Lewis supposedly assured Kennedy that the state was already a lock, in view of "the agents Joe Kennedy had dispensed throughout the state," as Gus Russo writes, "dispersing cash to county assessors, judges, party chairmen, etc. The average payoff was said to be $4,000 to $5,000. It was understood that much of this was undertaken without Jack Kennedy's knowledge." Ted Kennedy was reportedly dispatched early to grease the Democratic county committeemen.

The West Virginia primary foreshadowed the way the Kennedys worked, their collective reflex for calculated deniability. Nobody must draw attention to Joe Kennedy's moves as he tenderized the place politically, the deals he cut with racketeers as well as hundreds of pipsqueak dignitaries from dogcatchers to black Protestant ministers, all thirsting for a payoff. Once details drifted back, Bob Kennedy was heard to "snap feistily at his father" for "clumsy missteps" which threatened Jack's status as the idealistic candidate. Joe brushed Bobby off.

Bobby was more autonomous every day, oblivious to the niceties even politicians expect. Fred Dutton, on leave from California to reinforce the Kennedys, judged Bobby a "power creature," who, like Joe and JFK, "always wanted to do serious, heavy, major things and weren't afraid of losing a bit of their soul to do it." Confronting the demands of a reformer in New York, Bobby had "pushed up his shirtsleeves and replied, 'I just want my brother to be elected president. I want you all here in New York to help. Once he's elected we don't give a damn if blood runs in the streets of New York.'" After such a blast, even Joe Kennedy came over to the pols as tender-hearted, comprehending of their needs, a balm. Away from the publicity, the Ambassador continued to repair whatever he could.

In hopes of capitalizing on FDR's huge following, Joe expended a chit and flew Franklin Roosevelt Jr. to Palm Beach. Roosevelt had lost a gubernatorial primary to Averell Harriman in 1954, brought down by Carmine De Sapio. "You know, Franklin," Kennedy announced by way of greeting, "if it hadn't been for that guinea, you would have been elected governor, and now we would all be working for you." Kennedy himself was rankled still by De Sapio's unwillingness at an early meeting to commit to Jack on the condition that he racked up as little as 35 percent of the turnout, a hesitation the Tammany leader shared with the other New York borough chieftains. Charles Buckley and Eugene Keogh, both in the financier's pocket, would drag the organization over the line for Jack at the state convention and subsequently in Los Angeles.

A big, florid, splendidly barbered man with much of the juice that put his father over, FDR Jr. was paraded around the West Virginia hustings while Bobby pored over the susceptible county slates. Where should their money be spent? In West Virginia, historically, cash under the table was standard operating procedure; Larry O'Brien unabashedly handed the filthy stuff out, maintaining afterward that "Neither Jack nor Bobby knew what agreements I had made—that was my responsibility." Trapped in this earthquake, Hubert Humphrey felt the ground opening. "Kennedy is the spoiled candidate and he and that young, emotional, juvenile Bobby are spending with wild abandon," he shrilled.

Already losing a pound a day and manifestly troubled by the sight of unemployed miners lolling around the stoops of their blackened shanties feeding lard on stale bread to their rickets-ridden children, Robert Kennedy was in no mood to coddle a hysterical Humphrey. Hubert had been 4-F during the Second World War, and Bobby pressured Roosevelt to turn this into an issue, guaranteed to resound throughout the piney scrublands, where patriotism was a religion. "There's another candidate in your primary. He's a good Democrat, but I don't know where he was in World War II," Franklin roared one day to a startled crowd, and then it was too late to take it back.

In the aftermath, John Kennedy was reported to be disgusted, and Roosevelt remorseful. For all the money—millions, by some reports—the Kennedys poured into West Virginia, the outcome remained in question until the last backwoods precinct sent through its numbers. Bobby, as always, was left to smooth things over in Charleston while the candidate himself recovered at his ease in the District, diverting himself with a risqué movie. Later, after Kennedy swamped Hubert, Bobby gritted his teeth and visited the Humphreys in their hotel room. Muriel Humphrey couldn't look at him.

As Jack Kennedy's chances improved, the Director of the FBI decided he had better look over this rising politico. As a social contact of Joe's, Hoover made it his business to demonstrate some interest in the glamorous if ineffectual senator. "It was with great regret that I learned of the suffering occasioned by your recent operation," Hoover wrote Jack in 1954. "You have the heartfelt prayers and hopes of your many admirers and friends, and I hope that this thought, as well as the gallant courage and determination which you have displayed in the past, will give you the fortitude you need."

As early as 1956, Hoover instructed the faithful DeLoach to update him on the candidate. The next day Deke presented the Bureau's gleanings, pointing out the file on Inga Arvad "and other sexual escapades. And that, frankly, while he was somewhat of a bright individual, he had a very immoral background. Hoover told me, 'that is not right. You have misinterpreted the files. You're talking about the older brother of John F. Kennedy. . . .'"

This was, at minimum, disingenuous, since Hoover, whose memory was prodigious, had meddled from first to last in the Arvad imbroglio. The Director was acting out for DeLoach a role quite recognizable to students of his divided personality, that of the high-minded civil libertarian, the chaste, noble guardian of the nation's values, so often the last to know when people of consequence were letting him down. In fact, agent reports were continually flowing across his desk attesting to such trivia as the framed sailing photograph the senator kept on his desk, with Kennedy at the tiller and a pair of naked bimbos nudging at his elbows. DeLoach would remember well the afternoon the Director drifted back from lunch with Joe Kennedy during the later fifties. A few of Jack's more celebrated sexual peccadilloes had taken up the conversation. "I sometimes think I should have had that boy gelded at sixteen," the Ambassador had confided to the amused Director, who shared the mot with DeLoach. Hoover's memory was famously selective. The Director knew well enough that Joe Kennedy's namesake, Joe Jr., had perished fifteen years earlier.

The Director was never in doubt about the origins of the family fortune. "Mr. Hoover was familiar with Joseph Kennedy's history as a bootlegger," DeLoach admitted recently. The Director maintained a voluminous file on the subject. Kennedy had, after all, introduced Hoover to Lewis Rosenstiel, the imperious distiller who bankrolled the J. Edgar Hoover Foundation and had been implicated decades earlier in state and federal investigations. Then there were Hoover's off-the-clock exchanges with the courtly "Prime Minister of the Underworld," Frank Costello, who liked to croak out references to Kennedy as one of his ex-partners as well as a fellow shareholder in Hialeah. Even for the quick-footed Director, all this would have been impossible to step around.

After 1957, press fallout from the Apalachin meeting compelled the disgruntled Hoover to institute his Top Hoodlum Program, if only to stay abreast of Harry Anslinger's Bureau of Narcotics and the Justice Department's fledgling Special Group on Organized Crime. FBI gunslingers like Bill Roemer in Chicago started agitating to wire up gangland. In March 1960, the SAC in New Orleans advised the Director of the involvement of "Dandy Phil" Kastel, Costello's plenipotentiary to Carlos Marcello, with a group featuring Joe Fischetti "and other unidentified hoodlums . . . financially supporting and actively endeavoring to secure the nomination for the Presidency of . . . John F. Kennedy." Evidence was that "FRANK SINATRA is going to campaign for KENNEDY," supplemented by Sinatra's songwriter, Jimmy Van Heusen. Kennedy's brother-in-law, Peter Lawford, "has a financial interest in the Sands Hotel in Las Vegas," purportedly controlled by Joseph ("Doc") Stacher, Meyer Lansky's alter ego in Las Vegas. Sinatra himself had been given 9 percent of the Sands.

Hoover's informant had "occasion to overhear a conversation which indicated that senator KENNEDY had been compromised with a woman in Las Vegas, Nevada," during the time *Ocean's Eleven* was being shot, while he was roistering for a few days with Sinatra, Dean Martin, and the regulars of the Rat Pack. Then there were airline stewardesses in Miami. He "would hate," Hoover's informant observed," to see a pawn of the hoodlum element such as SINATRA have access to the White House."

Two weeks after that, Hoover's Los Angeles SAC was passing through a tip from a "representative of *Confidential* magazine" about "some sort of indiscreet party" in Palm Springs attended by Kennedy, Lawford, and Sinatra, backed up by "affidavits, allegedly from two mulatto prostitutes in New York." Kennedy's campaign manager was apprehensive and "bewailed Kennedy's association with Sinatra. . . ."

Concerned as he declared himself to be about the feckless senator's morals, the Director was equally alarmed that Sinatra—and by extension Kennedy—was falling into the hands of "subversives" in the movie industry. FBI teletypes of March 22 and 23 sound the alarm that Sinatra proposed to hire blacklisted screen writer Albert Maltz to produce an antiwar screenplay, *The Execution of Private Slovik,* and that John Kennedy persuaded Sinatra to hold off announcing the contract until after Kennedy had won the New Hampshire primary. Whipped along by the Director's disapproval, the Hearst press went after Sinatra. Joseph P. Kennedy himself delivered the crusher: "It's either Maltz or us," the Ambassador instructed Sinatra. "Make up your mind." The crooner dropped the project.

* * *

On official levels, both Kennedy brothers and the Director made sure their exchanges would reflect a mutually beneficial appreciation. "Dear Bob," Hoover observed in a short letter during the Rackets Committee days, "I have just learned that you were the recipient of the 1958 Lantern Award, and I wanted to drop you this note to extend my hardiest congratulations. I was certainly pleased that you were afforded this recognition, which was richly deserved. Sincerely, Edgar."

Robert Kennedy came back immediately: "Dear Mr. Hoover: Thank you very much for your kind note regarding the Lamp [sic] Award in Boston.

"I was highly honored—particularly because I had the privilege of following you."

Well aware of Hoover's fondness for lavish compliments, Robert Kennedy had begun years earlier to kowtow to the aging authoritarian. "Dear Mr. Hoover," he wrote the Director in 1956, "Just a note to tell you how much I admire your fine work in the Brinks, Weinberger and Riesel cases. You have established a record of which the whole country is very proud.

"I hope the United States continues to enjoy your leadership for a long period of time."

In his turn, Hoover made sure in 1959, as Kennedy stepped out of the Rackets Committee, to "express my heartiest congratulations upon the outstanding accomplishment you made while serving in this important assignment. Certainly, the work of the committee under your leadership stands as a shining example of what can be achieved by perseverance and determination. I feel that your efforts have contributed materially to the security of our country and to great progress and advancement in this field. . . ."

All traditional Washington boilerplate. Yet beneath these stroke exchanges, the skepticism of Hoover and his band of senior lieutenants as to the judgment of this brash, single-minded runt among the Kennedy brothers comes through in repeated memos. A backgrounder as early as July 1955 reiterates the Director's view that Kennedy's attitude in the Annie Lee Moss case "clearly shows need for absolute circumspection in any conversation with him." FBI informants inside Kennedy's subcommittee had disclosed that Kennedy's staff "was conducting inquiries on wire tapping in the District of Columbia and that they had contacted officials of the telephone company in this connection"—normally a procedure reserved for the FBI once the attorney general signs off. An ongoing Bureau probe into transgressions by the Harry Lev Company, a supplier to the military of caps and hats, was blocked by Kennedy until Lev had testified, a maneuver Hoover explained by noting that "Kennedy was completely uncooperative until after he had squeezed all the publicity out of the matter he could."

In 1959, the gist of another wrapup suggests that Kennedy continues to require adult supervision. The Director is quoted as remarking, with a certain asperity, that "Mr. Kennedy has returned from Russia with a rather dim impression of its economy and alleged liberties." There was the 1956 meeting in Hoover's office to ward off Kennedy's moves to subpoena Murray Chotiner. Nobody had forgotten how, when FBI officials were about to scoop up Jimmy Hoffa near the elevators of the Dupont Plaza Hotel, the overeager Bobby kept after the Director for permission to move in alongside the agents, but "was not permitted to do so and following the arrest informed a representative of the Bureau that he then realized the rashness of such a request and hoped it would not be held against him." Then there was the time Bobby and Ethel popped up when Hoffa got booked.

The Robert Kennedy reflected in these memos remains restive and puerile, addressing Hoover at once with both the ostentatious respect and the ill-concealed resentment he displayed on occasion toward the demanding patriarch. Intimidated by the Bureau, Kennedy pretends to deflect his impatience on the Department of Justice, a dodge Hoover pretends to second by pointing out that "a number of memoranda prepared by the Bureau for Kennedy's Committee had not been cleared by the Department and that Kennedy's attitude possibly resulted because of the Department's refusal to accede to requests made by Kennedy's Committee for information."

Kennedy was indeed steaming because most of the evidence the Rackets Committee was dredging up got dismissed by William Hundley and the Eisenhower litigators as far too flimsy to generate indictments. The Bureau's in-house review of Bobby's *The Enemy Within* notes that "relative to the bribery case against Hoffa here in the District, Kennedy relates that although he was convinced that FBI had given the Government an air-tight case, he credited Hoffa's acquittal as being due to the effective work of Hoffa's attorney, Edward Bennett Williams, together with 'the unpreparedness and ineffectiveness of the Government attorneys who prosecuted the case.'" Carmine Bellino had "furnished the U.S. Attorney . . . information as to Hoffa's whereabouts which was pertinent to the trial," but the U.S. Attorney neglected to read Bellino's memorandum and so "had not been able to get his dates and places straight." The Bureau is off the hook.

However profusely Kennedy thanked Hoover, he was well aware that the stodgy old bureaucrat was himself the source of a lot of the gas in the room, the reason so few of his cases were getting made. Kennedy understood what it meant when the Director kept deciding to cancel, at the last minute, coordination meetings with himself and Senator McClellan, and professed himself unable to reschedule them on days no delegation of Camp Fire Girls would be denied a handshake. As close as Hoover had positioned himself to Attorney General William Rogers, he continued to claim that there really wasn't much he could do, as one FBI summary stated, about the stubborn fact that the Department had not cleared a number of memoranda. Increasingly adept at government work, Robert Kennedy knew by now when he was getting the pipe.

Another grievance Hoover was starting to nurse with Bobby centered on his espousal of a National Crime Commission, a body which would coordinate operations against organized crime. Having ducked this mission himself, Hoover was increasingly apprehensive that a competing body would drain off media voltage. Weeks after John Kennedy was elected president, an internal FBI report on Robert Kennedy's appearance on *Meet the Press* quoted him as having quipped that "sixty of the Nation's top hoodlums met at Apalachin and yet not one Federal agency was aware of the meeting." The report concludes, with evident relief, "There was no mention of FBI, a federal clearing house for crime or National Crime Commission."

Two weeks later, another memo summarizes a *Los Angeles Mirror* interview with Chief William Parker, "possible head of a new national crime commission," who was quoted as remarking that "The FBI are fine firemen but the house is burning down." Parker "admitted to the *Mirror* reporter that he had been in touch with Robert Kennedy in Washington." JFK had announced Bob's nomination as attorney general one week earlier. Hoover was already feuding with Chief Parker before Bobby started blotting out the sun. It wouldn't be long before the unsinkable Ethel, after a passing tiff with Hoover at a Justice Department get-together, deposited a note in the FBI suggestion box recommending "Chief Parker in Los Angeles for Director."

On November 9, 1960, Jack Kennedy woke up president. Carroll Rosenbloom and assorted Kennedy family members were tearing one another up in a touch football game down on the Hyannis Port lawn. It had been a long night, with votes in critical precincts shifting back and forth. The Democratic National Committeeman from Illinois, Jake Arvey, once identified with Adlai Stevenson but all along a close collaborator of Sam Giancana, telephoned Frank Sinatra every half hour. Richard

Daley kept Hyannis Port informed. Illinois was a "must" state, and political organizers in both parties played peek-a-boo with their final returns, releasing the latest count around Chicago only after the momentary total downstate was out, then starting the count again. By morning JFK had carried the state by 8,858 votes, and nationally Kennedy triumphed by 118,550 votes out of a total of 68,832,818 cast.

Joseph P. Kennedy was exultant, but he was also worried. More than anybody else, he'd exerted his influence from his command post in Marion Davies's mansion to snag Lyndon Johnson the vice presidential nomination, shrugging off both Johnson's attack on him early in the convention as a Nazi-lining "umbrella man" and the horror Robert Kennedy could not suppress at the prospect of the outlandish Texan prominent in his brother's government. The patriarch had accepted the fact that this election was going to wind up very close-run, that they would need every redneck Lyndon and Sam Rayburn could muster, and that if and when they won it would be very important to keep the details of how they brought it off to themselves. Beyond all that, he plainly nursed reservations about how well the boys would do with so much unaccustomed power.

One observer they'd have to hedge in was J. Edgar Hoover. The votes were barely counted before the Director started multitracking, furiously. On election day, Hoover dispatched one of his signature mash notes to the president-elect—"Permit me to join the countless well wishers who are congratulating you on being elected President of the United States. . . . America is most fortunate to have a man of your caliber at its helm in these perilous days. . . ."—after which he immediately summoned Phillip Hochstein, editorial director of the Newhouse newspaper group, and mounted a tirade accusing the Kennedys of having stolen the election in a number of states, including New Jersey and Missouri, where the Newhouse chain published. Would Hochstein join the effort to reverse the election results? Deke Deloach would fill Hochstein in on John Kennedy's shameless womanizing.

Soon after Kennedy took his oath, the FBI's Chicago SAC sent through the Justice Department his report on the Illinois election: "the fact that it was stolen was brought to Robert Kennedy's attention," recalls Robert Blakey, a lawyer in the Department. No action was taken.

For Hoover, obviously, there wasn't any choice. Since he arrived in Congress, Nixon had been integral to the hard-core Right, repeatedly bumping around Alger Hiss with documents Hoover provided and functioning inside the Eisenhower administration as its lifeguard to the drowning Joe McCarthy. Nixon dropped by Murchison's resort in La Jolla periodically to butter up his wealthy like-minded supporters. Jack Kennedy, meanwhile, continued to woo the liberal wing of the Democratic Party. And as for Bobby? He had been unruly all along, brutal in the way he scuttled Roy Cohn and hell-bent after publicity at everybody else's expense.

The rumor that Robert Kennedy would move in shortly as his boss, however nominally, disquieted Hoover, already phobic about his job. By the later fifties, FBI headquarters was as thick with sadomasochistic counter-rhythms as a Sussex boarding school. In 1957 the bumptious Lou Nichols had moved on to a senior position that Roy Cohn invented for him at Schenley, organizing the place for Lewis Rosenstiel. Deke DeLoach, a presentable Georgian, was fighting it out as deputy director for the spot closest to the throne with William Sullivan, a short, opinionated scholar of the Communist Menace. The ten other assistant directors kept those memos churning, while Hoover administered discipline day and night, alternately censuring and rewarding merit up and down the line while jerking the roughly eight thousand field agents in and out of the fifty-odd stations according to the results of incessant surprise inspections. The standards kept changing: At one point, getting caught wearing a red necktie—Hoover thought red betokened insincerity—could ruin a career. At the executive conferences, "adverse publicity" was the bugbear, and blame got passed very freely down the line. Agents in the field labeled the headquarters crowd "the greatest assemblage of Monday-morning quarterbacks in the world."

At the very apex of the Bureau, Hoover continued to preside and Clyde Tolson continued to administrate according to his loveless, surgical principles. Clyde was slowing down—he was getting cranky and unpredictable—and now was struggling to maintain his normal two-step distance behind the Director each morning when the limousine let them out and they bustled the last few blocks to the Justice Building. This was their appointed exercise; the Director insisted on it, like the cottage cheese at lunch.

The idea that Bobby had better step in as attorney general began and ended with the patriarch, who was understandably concerned that the family plant somebody they could rely on inside the boiler room of the government to short-circuit inquiries into the election results. Both Jack and Bobby himself were slow to warm to the notion. Jack had been toying with the prospect of installing Bobby at a civilized distance, in Massachusetts as governor, to "clean up the mess in the Legislature and the Governor's Council." Much as he admired his brother's organizational talents and celebrated bite, the question remained: How close did Bobby have to be before he jeopardized everybody's comfort level? "Do you realize that high-pitched, grating voice is going to be dinning at me night and day for the next twelve months?" Jack Kennedy had muttered to an aide a year earlier, shortly before the primaries began. The old man depended on Bob, but at parties Bobby was "always the kid brother who was deadly serious and the butt of jokes, the natural fall guy as opposed to JFK, who was witty and urbane," as Igor Cassini recalled. In response, Bobby could be rude, tactless, insufferably self-involved. "I sometimes wish that Bobby, because he is so wonderful, had been an amoeba and then he could have mated with himself," Jacqueline Kennedy commented not long after she found herself trapped in the family.

Robert Kennedy himself had forebodings about taking on the attorney generalship. "In the first place, I thought nepotism was a problem," he told Arthur Schlesinger Jr. "Secondly, I had been chasing bad men for three years and I didn't want to spend the rest of my life doing that." Joe Kennedy would later insist that Bob "fought this nomination, fought it until he drove Jack and me crazy."

Drove Joe crazy, at least. Never insensitive, Bob had picked up on what Jack was attempting to hint at over Christmas when the president-elect presented him with a leather-bound copy of his own book inscribed: "For Bobby—the Brother Within—who made the easy difficult." Jacqueline, sensing that her husband was extracting blood a little close to the bone, added, "To Bobby—who made the impossible possible and changed all our lives."

Assorted personages around the capital attempted to head off this appointment. Drew Pearson wrote that he feared that Bobby would go after "controversial questions with such vigor that your brother in the White House would be in hot water all the time." The august Clark Clifford, who looked after the touchier legal situations for both the father and Jack, was delegated by JFK to go talk the patriarch out of his insistence that Bob go in as head of the Justice Department. "Thank you very much, Clark," the founding father opened when Clifford was finished. "I am so glad to have heard your views." Then "pausing a moment," Clifford later wrote, "he said, 'I do want to leave you with one thought, however—one firm thought.' He paused again and looked me straight in the eye. *'Bobby is going to be Attorney General.* All of us have worked our tails off for Jack, and now that we have succeeded I am going to see to it that Bobby gets the same chance that we gave to Jack.'"

The financier was immovable. When Jack's worldly stablemate over the Congressional years, George Smathers—like Clifford, a friend of the family with very little use for Bobby—interrupted the financier perusing the morning paper at one end of the pool in Palm Beach and suggested that Bobby was well suited to fill in as assistant secretary of defense, the old man barked "Jack! Come here."

The president-elect obeyed. "I want to tell you," the head of the family opened up on his cowed son, "your brother Bobby gave you his life blood. You know it and I know it. By God, he deserves to be attorney general and by God, that's what he's going to be. Do you understand that?"

"Jack said, 'Yes sir,'" as Smathers remembers it. "And so Bobby became attorney general."

Bobby would shortstop trouble, the old man's agent-in-place should the infighting turn ugly. Aware of the thinness of his margin and prompted by his father to propitiate conservative sentiment as quickly as he was able, days after the election Jack Kennedy reappointed Allen Dulles as Director of the CIA and renewed J. Edgar Hoover's mandate at the FBI. Robert Kennedy was telling his brother that he personally opposed the crusty Hoover's reappointment, judging Hoover "out of date" and "likely to block Justice Department initiatives against organized crime."

Resigned now to the prospect of bringing Bob in as attorney general, JFK telephoned Hoover under the pretense of sounding him out. Joe had already called, along with Cardinal Spellman—now on Joe's shitlist for having supported Nixon and interested in redeeming himself by vouching for Bobby. The Director was well aware of which way the wind was blowing, and told the president-elect, according to DeLoach, that Kennedy would "need one person in your cabinet who will be loyal to you, who will give good advice to you. . . ." Go ahead and pick Bobby.

Making the rounds that day with Bobby, John Seigenthaler remembers, both Harry Truman and Justice William O. Douglas had strongly advised Robert Kennedy to turn down the attorney-general appointment. Hoover was the last stop. Kennedy showed up in a shriven mood and performed another ritual obeisance before the nation's Symbol of Rectitude. Take the post, Hoover recommended, although the phrasing he used suggested to Ken O'Donnell afterward that he was less than enthusiastic. "Bobby's read on Hoover's reaction," Seigenthaler recalls, "was that he didn't mean it."

"I didn't like to tell him that," Hoover confided to William Sullivan, "but what could I say?" Within months, as Bobby, in DeLoach's phrase, "tried to run roughshod over the FBI," Hoover lamented to George Sokolsky that waving Bobby in as attorney general was "the worst damned piece of advice I've ever given anybody in my life."

It's Bobby!

Early in 1961, a few days after the snowy inauguration, Hoover memoed Tolson, assuming a hopeful note: "On January 13, 1961, I saw the Attorney General and presented him the mounted badge of the FBI making him an honorary Special Agent.

"The Attorney General was most appreciative of this honor which had been conferred upon him."

The mounted badge of the FBI: What could better exemplify the tone of the status games, the boys'-club one-upmanship around the hermetic Bureau? Guardians of public order, noses in everybody's secrets. For Robert Kennedy, just then preparing himself to launch one of the great adrenalin burns in American history, his mounted FBI badge was about as significant as a mail-order Texas Rangers certificate.

Not that they took Hoover lightly. "All the Kennedys were afraid of Hoover," admitted the *Washington Post*'s Ben Bradlee, an intimate of the incoming president. Edgar would remain a figure of fun around Hickory Hill, but none of the Kennedy brothers underestimated the Director's unscrupulousness when it came to culling the information in those dreaded raw files, his paranoia, his willingness to kidney-punch anybody with a word to the media, his puncture-proof public relations. Whatever else he did, John Kennedy admonished his single-minded brother, "you have got to get along with that old man."

Much of the rub between Hoover and Robert Kennedy originated with their opposed conceptions of what the Justice Department—and especially the FBI—ought to be doing. Hoover's America amounted to a kind Christian-pageant fantasy of the System, where Mom's pie was forever cooling on the windowsill and lovable old bootleggers who had matured into philanthropists watched over right-thinking toddlers who already yearned to validate their lives as tomorrow's G-men. Commies and beatniks and race-mixers glowered along the fences, hell-bent to eradicate this utopia if only Hoover would give them any kind of opening.

Robert Kennedy saw things differently. Since childhood an outsider, he couldn't help sneaking a glance, as he sweated to elect his brother, at the squalor of millions of American lives, at the brutalizing results when yesterday's gangsters undermined the unions and ate away at corporate America. In 1961, Robert Kennedy's comprehension of what had gone wrong remained spotty. He did understand that feeding this corruption was not the most exalted purpose of government.

The ambivalence both brothers felt at following through on their father's demand played out, as usual, in humor. "Well, I think I'll open the door of the Georgetown house some morning about 2:00 A.M., look up and down the street, and, if there's no one there, I'll whisper, 'It's Bobby!'" JFK responded when Ben Bradlee asked how he intended to break the news that Bobby would be attorney general. When the day came, his older brother had sent him upstairs to clean up a little—"I said it was the first time the President had ever told the Attorney General to comb his hair before they made an announcement," Robert Kennedy noted in his journal. Once they were about to confront the press, Jack muttered, "Don't smile too much or they'll think we're happy about the appointment." This chafed on sensitivities dating back thirty years.

The first wave of objections was predictable. Robert Kennedy had never tried a case. He was thirty-five, a galvanic eel slithering into a tank of bottom-feeders. Liberals disliked Bob especially; the new administration's mandate was shaky enough. Almost half the budget—and the manpower—of the Department went to J. Edgar Hoover, a very dogged infighter who even his sometime pal Roy Cohn once slipped enough to characterize as a "killer fruit."

The Justice Department was huge—seventeen hundred lawyers all told, thirty thousand civil servants. Apart from the FBI, the Department of Justice maintained divisions responsible for Civil Rights, Criminal, Tax, Lands and Natural Resources, Civil and Anti-Trust, and Internal Security, along with the Solicitor General. It included Immigration and Naturalization, the

Bureau of Prisons, and the Border Patrol. The FBI itself maintained a liaison officer to report back on each of the other divisions, usually an FBI assistant director, attached like a commissar so that nothing the counterparts did might take the Director by surprise.

Information flowed one way. With 41 percent of the budget and 42 percent of the manpower in the Department, the FBI was the elephant in the broom closet. Its Director was never that delicate about edging his counterparts out of the picture, stamping along the perimeter to redefine his turf. "We are not going to inject ourselves into any 'domination' of the Dept.," Hoover scrawled at the bottom of a long memo from one of his SACs, who had just completed an extended exchange with Ed Guthman, the incoming attorney general's public relations coordinator. Guthman had been filling Hoover's man in on longstanding "difficulties between the Attorney General and Congress" with which the Bureau might lend a hand. "If we are asked a question," Hoover concludes, as ever from Olympus, "then we may answer it." May, certainly not will.

This memorandum came through a month after Robert Kennedy took over, and reflects the impunity with which Hoover expected to conduct Bureau affairs. "They all have the same problem—the control and management of J. Edgar Hoover," the longtime chief of the Justice Department prison division responded when asked to pinpoint the greatest single roadblock any attorney general might anticipate. This Robert Kennedy understood going in.

The Bureau would continue to run up its statistics against the nation's car thieves and bank robbers and kidnappers and the occasional befuddled Trotskyite, but, even after public pressure had forced the FBI to put in place its Top Hoodlums Program, organized crime was nursed along like an unsightly relative panhandling around the back. The collection process—hearsay, mostly, an increasing percentage originating with "microphone surveillance," bugs—still involved illegal trespass. Hoover himself kept reiterating that the FBI was not bodyguards, not prosecutors, in no way a "national police force." Their job was investigating, period. Investigating, and stashing the secrets they needed to entrench themselves further.

Robert Kennedy's first shrewd move in office was to button in staff all across the Department with stature enough to fend off Hoover. As deputy attorney general, reportedly "on his brother's instruction," Bob installed Byron ("Whizzer") White. Jack Kennedy knew White when White was a Rhodes Scholar at Oxford in 1939 and Jack and his Harvard roommate Torbert McDonald were woolgathering around the Continent, picking up whatever impressions they could for the deskbound Ambassador. The young Kennedy remembered White from an embassy reception when they bumped into him again in the Hofbrauhaus in Munich, after which the three sported around town in Whizzer's car, which attracted a rain of bricks at one point from a clutch of storm troopers. Four years later the big, somber, brainy one-time All American and ex-professional football player turned up as a naval lieutenant at Tulagi in the Solomons, where the disheveled and normally shirtless and ravaged-looking Jack Kennedy had a reputation as a PT-boat commander who drove his frightened crew out beyond the limits of common sense as well as the sparkplug in the scrub football games around the base, a problem even for the experienced Whizzer. After the war, the two remained in contact. Joe Kennedy threw business to Whizzer's firm in Denver, and White ran the Kennedy-for-President effort in Colorado.

The incoming president expected White to help make up for what his brother lacked. "I can't see that it's wrong to give him a little legal experience before he goes out to practice law," JFK cracked vis-á-vis Bobby in front of the Alfalfa Club. Robert Kennedy did not think that was very funny. A dry, ultracompetent strict constructionist who had clerked for Supreme Court Justice Fred Vinson and retained splendid connections with his fellow recent Yale Law School graduates, White ushered into the Justice Department as division heads a killers' row of sober-sided fellow savants: Nicholas Katzenbach, also a Rhodes Scholar, plucked off the University of Chicago law school faculty as head of the Office of Legal Counsel; the cryptic Burke Marshall, a partner at Covington and Burling, would run the Civil Rights Division; Louis Oberdorfer oversaw the Tax Division; William Orrick, the Civil Division. All Yalies. Harvard Law School professor Archibald Cox, the pedantic workhorse who had directed Jack's research staff during the recent campaign, came in as solicitor general.

To relieve this all-starch diet of Ivy Leaguers, Bobby hired the tall, deliberative contrarian Ramsey Clark—whose more loosely constructed pol of a father, Tom, was still sitting on the Supreme Court—to lead the Lands Division while the head of the Criminal Division was Herbert J. (Jack) Miller, a smooth young Republican Bobby had gotten to know as a recent appointee to the Board of Monitors intended to scrub up the Teamsters. Miller was another lawyer the Ambassador had been retaining for specialized work. By degrees, Kennedy sought to spare Hoover's feelings yet phase out the antiquated Internal Security Division.

As personal staff, Kennedy carried over a trio of dedicated newspapermen from the Rackets Committee. John Seigenthaler came on as administrative assistant, and Ed Guthman dealt with the media. Joe Dolan worked on relations with Congress. All this amounted to a very heavy bench, hopefully enough to balance Hoover.

Overall, Kennedy did very well with most of these handsomely credentialed personages, but the very accomplishments of so many pillars of the law threw a dense collective shadow. The attorney general in most administrations is expected to function as a kind of political troubleshooter for the beleaguered president. This often meant that legal corners would have to be rounded, if not exactly cut. That got no easier with all those deacons standing there watching.

"Kennedy knew he was obviously not qualified to serve as attorney general," Katzenbach, who would succeed him, concedes right away. "He perceived that what he did in Justice would be viewed with a jaundiced eye, and he wanted to do everything right. Over time I really came to admire and love him—he had a sardonic sense of humor." Family responsibilities outdrew everything else. "The Kennedy boys certainly feared their father," Katzenbach could see. "He was a giant, they feared him in the sense that they did not want to go against him. Bobby adored his father. Bob always started from the proposition that his brother was always right, and if there were mistakes JFK was misled.

"Bob was a better lawyer than people have often given him credit for—he understood what you had to say." But there were obvious, deep insecurities. "I'd explain my reasoning to him on something and he'd say 'Shit, why don't you come over and explain that to my brother yourself?' You wouldn't have any other A.G. doing that without sifting through it on his own. He'd get us all out to Hickory Hill and he'd say, 'I've got this problem, you guys are all better lawyers than I am. I need your advice. I'll just make the decision. . . .'"

Robert Kennedy had barely emerged from his long stint on the Rackets Committee, and now he saw no choice except to saddle up the Department with a maximum of publicity and tearass after the Bad Guys. Virtually Kennedy's first move was to borrow Narcotics Bureau Director Harry Anslinger's punch list of the forty most pernicious thugs in America, and start assigning aggressive Department attorneys to gouge them out of America's body social.

Part of the problem was, most of these hoodlums had managed to entangle themselves at deep—indispensable?—levels within America's body politic, and not a few, like Murray the Camel, contributed importantly to John Kennedy's election. With so many Ivy League proctors in attendance, Robert Kennedy could not show favoritism even had he been so inclined.

Overall, he wasn't, at least at first. He needed to cast himself as the scourge of his generation, to relieve his apprehension that the nation was about to collapse into kleptocracy.

One of the first moves Kennedy came to regret was his decision to replace William Hundley, a hardscrapple Pittsburgh parochial-school type who stepped on so many of Robert Kennedy's requests for prosecution during the Eisenhower years. Hundley had been the chief of the small, rather ineffectual Organized Crime Section within the Criminal Division under Attorney General William Rogers. Kennedy was farsighted enough to keep the street-wise Hundley around—the pair had had a brushing acquaintance during the early fifties when both apprenticed under James McInerney. As a special assistant, Hundley showed a pool hustler's aptitude at certain of the touchier undertakings, projects Bobby didn't want his high-minded division chiefs anywhere near. For Hundley, all this amounted to a de facto demotion, but his contacts outside government were such, as he would admit freely afterward, that "If I'd had a job to go to, I woulda gone."

His replacement, Edwyn Silberling, was a balls-up Brooklyn prosecutor who fortified a Harvard education with an extended stint in the Air Force, practiced trial law in Manhattan, then banged his way along over five bruising years as a senior litigator with District Attorney Frank Hogan, cracking down on felonies from waterfront racketeering to baby black-marketing. Unlike J. Edgar Hoover, Hogan believed in the real-world existence of the Mafia and regularly locked up goombahs from around the boroughs.

By 1960 Silberling was collecting headlines as the special prosecutor for the governor of New York. When John Kennedy ran for president, Silberling spoke in his behalf at rallies. Robert Kennedy invited Ed into the administration as chief of the Organized Crime and Racketeering Section, where, Silberling noted later, he was repeatedly assured he would have "carte blanche in the hiring of the attorneys who would be in the program . . . this program would be beefed up and the spearhead of a national drive."

Silberling brought to Kennedy's entourage the kind of hands-on legerdemain when it came to busting mobsters that was in embarrassingly short supply during Kennedy's Rackets-Committee years. Ed understood how to build a case. He had broad experience when it came to the technology of entrapment. A lithe tennis-playing Jewish professional with a lot of Ivy-League polish, Ed seemed to style himself as a kind of counterpart to his boss. He acquired a palatial home in McLean close to Hickory Hill and reportedly was not shy at all about requisitioning the Kennedy family plane for a pressing errand.

One of the activists Silberling hired, Jay Goldberg, remembers him as "Wonderful, on a scale of one to ten a ten. Courage, personality, wonderful: He was a crime-buster. Everybody to a person loved Silberling. He stood up for you, he was a man, there was no politics. . . ."

In short order, the head-count of the section rose from 10 to 50. They brought in Wyn Hayes, a brawny, wisecracking New York City Narcotics Department veteran, and let her integrate the files from everywhere in the government. Starting out with Harry Anslinger's forty reigning hoods, Wyn pieced out a compendium of crime-related personalities that ran to several thousand secondary gangsters and ultimately several hundred thousand troubled spirits connected to the underworld. Anything to keep it going, anything to satisfy her "babes."

Whatever the locals couldn't handle, Silberling's lawyers were gunning to investigate for themselves, then prosecute. These projected "strike forces" of Silberling's, often replete with specialists borrowed around the government, from the IRS to Immigration and Naturalization, were intended to stick with individual cases until the guilty verdicts came down. They were well aware that their intrusion might trigger resentments among regional U.S. Attorneys, but during the break-in months the attorney general was confident he could sort things out as they mashed along. Silberling would be "reporting to Bob Kennedy and be working directly with him," according to the directive. Silberling carried over as his deputy Henry Petersen, another lawyer Kennedy rubbed elbows with in 1951 as an apprentice in the Justice Department.

Several months after Ed Silberling had set up shop in Washington, Jack Miller came into the Department. Miller is a fellow who can tell you almost nothing at considerable length and with great geniality, and for quite a while Silberling somehow failed to focus on the rather large fact that Miller had been appointed head of the Criminal *Division* while he himself was running the Section. Miller was an assistant attorney general while Silberling was a special assistant attorney general, another distinction that Silberling somehow missed. Miller ranked Silberling, but Silberling obstinately ignored the fact.

Acute jurisdictional dislocations came out of this. From Silberling's angle, the more the regional legal establishment, including local U.S. Attorneys, got involved in any case affecting people of influence, the more skewed the prosecutorial outcome was liable to be. As Silberling saw it, "Bob

Kennedy's primary concern was the results to be obtained. . . . But he did not want to antagonize local political leaders . . . organized crime, the business of crime, can't operate without effective links between public officials and the racket operations; and local political connections are likely to affect who's going to be prosecuted and how they're going to be prosecuted." To get the convictions Kennedy claimed he wanted, logic demanded that Silberling and his task forces go in from outside and clean up any substantial criminal enterprise, and parochial politics be damned.

Often that didn't happen. Miller ushered young lawyers Silberling judged to be incompetent into the Section, and Silberling promptly washed them out. Silberling would be particularly rankled by one major narcotics bust, built up from evidence supplied by Anslinger's troops, the Sûreté, the Sala de Finanza from Italy, and the Mounties, during which Miller allegedly pulled rank at an inopportune moment and without warning turned the whole mess over to the regional U.S. Attorney. The prosecution fell apart, and recognizable names stayed out of the news.

Slowly, excruciatingly, Silberling found his circumstances shifting from reporting to Bob Kennedy to reporting to Jack Miller. During the early months, Kennedy liked to pass out the Heinekens among the attorneys in Silberling's section and bat the cases back and forth and pump up morale. He got the IRS involved, spurring Commissioner of Internal Revenue Mortimer Caplin's people to devote as much as 50 percent of their audit time to reviewing the tax returns of racketeers. The stumbling block that first year was largely the FBI.

Dependent as he found himself on fact-gathering from around the government, Silberling was effectively stymied each time he went to the Bureau. Apprehensive that his own men might succumb to temptation while dealing with "crimes where there were substantial amounts of ready cash constantly on tap, gambling . . . or narcotics," Hoover insisted that his paragons maintain at best an arm's-length relationship with votaries from the Mob. Snoop, don't talk. Undercover work by FBI street agents was absolutely forbidden. While selected FBI reports were on occasion available to the Organized Crime Section, the identity of the "confidential informants" from whom the reports were derived would be routinely withheld. To think about basing a prosecution on hearsay from T-5, who could turn out to be a gossip columnist from Palo Alto, or T-2, quite possibly a prison guard retailing the errant buzz floating up and down the cellblock, was maddening for Silberling's hungry attorneys. At one point, Silberling's men stumbled on the cover sheet for one of the reports, which helped to decode key symbols. This too was discouraging—one vital source, for example, was a bank official passing on the scuttlebutt overheard between depositors, nothing likely to survive thirty seconds in open court.

Yet Silberling persevered. Certain investigations held up; several of the cases his lawyers were starting to make were incontrovertible. Before long Kennedy authorized Silberling to start up an investigative unit inside the section.

The summer of 1961, profiting from the administration's surprising rebound in the polls following the Bay of Pigs, Robert Kennedy broke precedent and appeared before the House of Representatives to—"ad nausea," Jack Miller recalls—lobby through the controversial mixture of antiracketeering proposals the Justice Department was sending up. They passed so quickly, Justice official William Geogheghan later gloated, that "nobody had a chance to read them." Cloakroom rumors persisted that Bobby got the chairman of the Judiciary Committee, Senator James Eastland, to ram the Department's proposals through during a groggy after-hours session in return for appointing Eastland's vociferously bigoted college roommate, Harold Cox, to the Court of Appeals for the Dixie Fifth Circuit. Bobby's five new bills forbade the transmission of gambling information by wire in interstate commerce and gave the FBI jurisdiction over interstate gambling and particularly the transportation of policy numbers or gambling paraphernalia, including slot machines, across state lines. The Fugitive Felon Law was expanded. Gambling—the colossal and alluring mirage into which several generations of syndicate kingpins from Meyer Lansky and Frank Costello to Sam Giancana and Johnny Rosselli had long since committed their futures—now passed under federal control. Only a proposal by Kennedy to regularize wiretapping hadn't passed.

Hoover steamed. In one undefended legislative thrust, Robert Kennedy had executed a flanking action that blindsided the Bureau. To be responsible for the logistics of gambling was to be responsible for the Mafia. Not that there was a Mafia—just, here and there, a "bunch of hoodlums," the voluble Director told everybody he could buttonhole, something for the local cops. In New York City, the Bureau had four hundred agents assigned to the Red Menace and four watching crime. Not that Hoover intended to shirk his responsibilities. Always the conscientious bureaucrat, he intended to meet this obligation—selectively.

Part of Hoover's problem was the way Kennedy had impudently

sauntered in and absolutely taken over the place. Most attorneys general understood that they might expect to oversee the Justice Department for so-and-so-many months, creatures of the sitting administration; Hoover had positioned himself to go on forever. Between the unpredictable contents of those Official and Confidential files and the Director's paralyzing clout with Congress, Hoover was like a gigantic toxic sea urchin; nobody swam too close. After forty-plus years, the Director obviously regarded the entire Department of Justice as an extension of his region of authority, an appendage of his beloved Bureau.

Behind closed doors, J. Edgar Hoover was starting to register his age. By now Clyde Tolson, for so long the trim, quick-witted exemplar of the model Bureau personality and the snappy first-baseman on the headquarters softball team, was suffering a series of blood clots along with ever more alarming symptoms. At times, working at his desk, his right eye would begin spontaneously to hemorrhage. He dragged his left leg. Even Hoover's greatest boosters inside the Seat of Government were finding Tolson insufferable, his clean-desk, office-disciplinarian crispness now curdled into a habitual rigidity, a nit-picking fussiness.

Sometimes it taxed even the self-assured Director. "Leave him alone!" Hoover commanded one support agent at the Del Mar Track. Tolson had stumbled badly. "Let the dumb asshole get up by himself." Emotions involving other people had always been infuriating for the Director. DeLoach remembers Hoover dragging himself into the offices during the middle sixties after one of Tolson's increasingly severe attacks. "My God, Deke," the panicky Hoover breathed to his deputy. "I almost lost him last night."

He himself remained in wonderful shape, Hoover insisted, but he was in fact slowing down. After lunch he accepted no appointments until three o'clock, ostensibly to deal with the afternoon's paperwork. In fact, Hoover napped, stretched along his office sofa. "Mister Hoover had had prostate surgery," DeLoach recalls, "and I think he had several small strokes. He was slurring his words. . . ."

Barring presidential exception, the mandatory retirement age within the federal bureaucracy was seventy, an age the Director would reach during the first year of John Kennedy's second term. He lived now riddled with apprehension at the prospect of finding himself dismissed; one of his favorite monologues dwelt on what stepping down might be expected to cost a man accustomed to authority. He'd seen it too many times: people dry up, they rot, they die inside. . . .

He'd have to do whatever was necessary to protect his position. It was quite clear within weeks how unfortunate it was that the new president's brother was also his attorney general. At least, *this* brother. It was a mark of the hubris Robert Kennedy was bringing to the post that he immediately abandoned the standard-sized office in the back of the attorney general's suite and chose to conduct his affairs out of what was normally the Department's reception area, an enormous vaulted chamber regularly compared with a gymnasium. It filled up quickly with furniture groupings and watercolors by his children taped to the exquisite walnut panels and mementos of the sporting life—not Bobby's—from a mounted musket to a sailfish above the mantel to a stuffed tiger next to the vast marble fireplace.

Robert Healy, then running the Washington Bureau for the *Boston Globe,* had been a pal of Jack's throughout his years in Congress. Tracking down a story, Healy arranged to interview Bobby in his office during his first weeks as head of the Department. "And, Christ, what an office it was," Healy still remembers. "Enormous, as long as a football field: It dwarfed anything around the White House. He sat and watched you approaching, making your way toward his desk. I'd known him, of course, since he was a punk kid working on Jack's House campaign in 1946. So there he was, and I sat down, and I asked him a question.

"He'd developed a technique of not really looking at you—looking away, out the window, and then he'd make you repeat your question two or three times. So I asked him something, and he turned away and looked blank, and didn't say anything. This was supposed to unnerve reporters, as I understood it.

"So I got mad when he didn't answer, and I got up and started out without saying anything. And all of a sudden he was trotting up behind me, all apologetic, you know . . . saying, 'Look, Bob, we've been friends a long time, I didn't mean anything by that.'

"After that, things were okay between us."

The columnist Stewart Alsop, a Roosevelt descendant whose brother Joseph had socialized with JFK for years, also found the empowered Robert Kennedy a trial. "You would go and see him in his office," Stewart Alsop later said, "and you would ask him a question, and he'd respond either with that enormous grin of his and no words at all, or he'd just laugh. Sometimes you'd have a carefully prepared question, and all he would say was, 'Yes,' or 'No,' or 'That's what *you* think,' or something like that."

Partly this was insecurity, of course, altitude sickness. A poorly chosen response could do a lot of damage. The alternative form Kennedy's evasiveness frequently took, ruthless self-assertion, could not have been better calculated to set the slipping old Director's teeth on edge. Doubtful about his own legitimacy, Kennedy now compensated by scrambling to exert control up and down the corridors, starting with the barricaded FBI.

Bob sent word over to the worried Hoover that from then on all communications the Director might care to have with the White House would have to be routed through the attorney general's switchboard, hostage to Bobby's approval. Announcements of important arrests, changes in Bureau policy, leaks to the media—the red meat of Hoover's venerable publicity apparatus—were all subject to Justice Department clearance. Hoover would be expected to operate in accordance with his civil-service status—a third-level bureaucrat.

One early decision that especially grated on Hoover was Kennedy's directive to place a buzzer on Hoover's desk so Kennedy could startle him with the touch of a finger. "Shall I get Hoover over here?" the attorney general asked William Hundley on one occasion, plainly intending mischief. During previous regimes, the attorney general always stepped across the hall to confer with the legendary Director, by appointment. "I was curious more than anything else," Hundley said, "so I said 'Jesus, yeah.'" Kennedy mashed the button, and after a few minutes the FBI Director bustled in, red-faced and upset. "They started arguing about something. Bobby put it to him, how are you coming with hiring minorities and women? He was tough. Hoover said, I can't find any qualified. They jawed at each other. . . ." The fact was, "No General had ever done that to Hoover. I couldn't believe it."

Even more alarming was Kennedy's tendency to brush by the sputtering Miss Gandy and demand the Director's attention without any warning. Once—humiliation!—Kennedy burst in on Hoover profoundly into his nap. Another time Kennedy invited the Director to lunch, then escorted the touchy autocrat, who clearly expected at the very least the Metropolitan Club, to adjacent stools at the nearby People's Drug.

This inclination to presume on the protocol-worshiping old man peaked on the day the attorney general brought a troupe of his older children (as undisciplined a lot as ever horrified the nation's property owners) to visit the Director's office at a time when Hoover himself had stepped out briefly. The safe was open, Robert Kennedy Jr. recollects with no small glee, and he and his siblings jumped in and started pulling out documents by the handful. Just then Hoover himself appeared, and the younger Kennedy has still not quite gotten over the tantrum the enraged FBI Director mounted.

Formally, both Bob Kennedy and the Director endeavored to maintain good relations. In February 1961 Hoover called the attorney general and offered to let one of the agents in Richmond pick up Kennedy's law school degree, which Bobby never bothered to collect. A month later Hoover sent a note to Robert Kennedy Jr., recuperating in the Georgetown University Hospital, assuring the seven-year-old that Hoover himself felt "certain, however, that you have already made many new friends among the doctors and nurses at the hospital" and enclosing two packets of FBI postcards to "make the hours go a little faster."

An early memo survives entitled ATTORNEY GENERAL'S EFFORTS TO GET INTO BUREAU GYMNASIUM TUESDAY EVENING, 1/31/61. Kennedy, Byron White, and two other unidentified staffers had shown up after seven P.M. with intentions of putting to use the FBI gym. The night supervisor in the mechanical section had refused to let them in, even after a round of introductions. "This certainly proves the point we have been stressing—our employees should always be busy; engage in no horse play; and be properly attired. No one knows when and where A.G. may appear," Hoover added in pen. There is no suggestion of a reprimand for the employees who denied Hoover's boss access to the sacred FBI territory. In time, over the ensuing months, gym rights were negotiated.

Kennedy's tendency to roam the building, as often as not in shirtsleeves with his tie yanked down, shaking hands and introducing himself around from the mail rooms to the support attorneys paging through documents on every floor to the FBI's own Print Shop and Photostat center— Kennedy's hands-on methods obviously made the acutely territorial Director uneasy. His realm did not need a glad-handing demagogue.

In late March, Bobby appeared on a television program during which he was interviewed by Senator Kenneth Keating. Resolutely, according to an in-house memorandum, Kennedy toed the FBI line—he himself has changed his mind as to the desirability of a National Crime Commission, he "sees eye to eye with the Director on all of the matters," and "thinks their relationship is of the best and they get along extremely well." The "threat of Communism in this country is as serious as it was 5 or 10 years ago" and "the FBI is doing excellent work in this field." Kennedy "stated that the Director has made many major contributions and that he hopes he will continue to have a long and worthy service in the Federal government."

It would be hard to come up with a more abject sellout of Robert Kennedy's private opinions on any of these subjects, but there are compelling bureaucratic reasons. Even Tolson is impressed—"I don't think better is required," he scrawls at the bottom of the memo—but Hoover shows no enthusiasm beyond agreeing to send a copy to the attorney general.

A few days later another memo lands on the Director's desk which reiterates, although indirectly, so that nobody in the Bureau can be held to account, that there is a vulnerable side to the private life of the Kennedys, material similar to the Sinatra allegations of the previous year. Hoover is cautiously stocking his arsenal.

That spring Bob Kennedy was negotiating with producer Jerry Wald and screenwriter Budd Schulberg preparatory to signing contracts for a screen version of *The Enemy Within*. The contract was seemingly finalized when Joe Kennedy telephoned the studio to revisit the terms. But Bobby had already signed, Joe was told. "What the hell does he know about it?" the patriarch barked and improved the results considerably.

The prospect of a bombshell movie glorifying the war against organized crime and Kennedy's vendetta against Jimmy Hoffa was less than enticing to Hoover. The memo compounds unverified charges against Wald and Schulberg, supposedly originating with "several members of the Screen Writers Guild," who alleged that Schulberg was a member of the Communist Party.

All this mixed in with references to an anonymous letter received by studio boss Jack Warner—a well-established champion of the status quo, and a collaborator of long standing with Frank Costello and assorted filmland mobsters—which lambasted JFK as "a sex maniac and a sex pervert." When Wald died abruptly and Teamster lawyers threatened that the union would refuse to deliver the prints, the project collapsed. Rumblings from the FBI helped undermine the project.

Once Ed Silberling's organized-crime task forces were starting to home in on individual racketeers and corrupt local machines, Kennedy made it a point to bounce around the country to check out progress in the field. He tended to travel in a small party, usually including John Seigenthaler, Bill Hundley, and Courtney Evans, the likable and politically deft ex-liaison to the Rackets Committee whom Hoover had now promoted to assistant director in charge of special investigations, thus making him senior administrative staff and eligible to partake in all the executive conferences. Apprehensive as they remained at the prospect of those ulcer-perforating inspection raids from the Seat of Government, local field agents now discovered that a visit from Bobby Kennedy turned into an invigorating, morale-boosting opportunity to toss impressions back and forth. Off came the jackets and ties, out came the cold beers, and, supplemented sometimes by their counterparts from the IRS or the Narcotics Bureau, they found themselves hashing out a collective plan of attack on criminals the local SAC had during earlier years been given to understand he was to accord a very wide berth.

For Hoover, obviously, the prospect of having his own people preempted was torture. The versatile Evans, who quickly perfected the technique of explaining the same situation one way to Hoover and another to Kennedy, came under deepening suspicion. The question arose: who was whose commissar? Evans remained under pressure to salt heavily his memos to the Director with aspersions directed at Kennedy's competence—and as a legal mind, certainly, most of the hotshots in Kennedy's shop had their own doubts—yet Evans obviously liked Kennedy and relished his friendship.

Kennedy's lapses of judgment continued to trouble Evans, not only the raids on hookers and drug dealers during the Rackets Committee years but occasional night forays afterward. Kennedy's insistence on moving around totally without security worried Evans, who quietly made sure Kennedy "had a lot of protection at times, but he didn't know about it. Plainclothesmen any place where I thought there might be an incident."

"Both sides believed in me," Evans would insist, although at one point Evans remarked to Mark Felt, a rising Hoover protégé, that "Last night, I told my family I was sure I was going to be fired, but I didn't know whether it would be by Hoover or Kennedy."

Afterward, Evans drew his own conclusions. "They were too much alike. When I looked at Bob Kennedy operating in 1961, I figured that's the way Hoover had operated in 1924 . . . same kind of temperament, impatient with inefficiency, demanding as to detail, a system of logical reasoning for a position, and pretty much a hard taskmaster." Privately, Evans saw his mission as primarily to keep Kennedy "from running wild."

Risk-taker that he was, Kennedy could not resist the occasional sortie into the fastness of the FBI. Aware of Hoover's methods, in situations where a target was promising and Kennedy had reason to believe the Bureau was holding out on him, he developed the habit of turning up at the Justice Building on Saturday, when it was reasonable to assume that Hoover and Tolson were amusing themselves at the races, to demand of the FBI duty officer whatever paperwork existed pertaining to the cases at hand. This approach in effect short-circuited the FBI's elaborate vetting and censoring procedures, and dossiers came through without the customary maddening inking-out of names and connections and the concealment of confidential informants behind letter and number symbols.

To defend his perimeters, the unhappy Hoover decided to forgo his precious Saturdays at the track and show up himself at the headquarters offices. Once, when Bobby had come in with a pack of those obstreperous children of his, he got a call from the White House: You better get right over here. On his way out the attorney general bolted through the Director's chambers and charged the nonplussed Director of the FBI with responsibility for keeping an eye on the fast-moving youngsters. Hoover reportedly ranted on for weeks about those rampaging "brats," and the whole idea broke up agents in the field.

Internecine warfare now started in earnest.

Panther Piss

Kennedy hadn't been attorney general long before he found himself getting badly scraped battering across the narrows between corruption and politics. One very early exposure involved Bernard Goldfine, the New England textile manufacturer whose gifts of hotel rooms and a vicuña coat to Eisenhower's chief of staff, Sherman Adams, had come to light and forced Adams out. A failure to file tax returns had drawn the attention of the House Committee on Legislative Oversight, which was surfacing evidence that Goldfine had probably passed out several hundred thousand dollars illegally to deserving politicians. One of JFK's priorities immediately following the Bay of Pigs humiliation was to not brown off ex-President Eisenhower, who remained devoted to Adams.

With the ubiquitous Edward Bennett Williams as his lawyer, Goldfine had come forward and was attempting to trade information as to whom he had paid off and when and how, if that would keep him out of the penitentiary. Goldfine was at once cunning, sclerotic, and a little bit senile. He became a challenge.

Robert Kennedy assigned William Hundley to manage the Justice Department's interests in a situation that could soak down everybody's parade. Now one of several special assistants to the attorney general, the street-smart Hundley, with his serviceable ties to the previous administration, turned very quickly into Kennedy's go-to guy whenever circumstances required careful behind-the-scenes handling.

The danger with Goldfine was that he was liable to burst a leak in the wrong direction. Kennedy arranged with Hundley to look Goldfine over in Ed Williams's opulent new offices. A few years earlier, after Williams defended Hoffa from Rackets Committee bribery charges, the Teamsters put Williams on a $50,000 annual retainer. "Am I responsible for all of this?" Bobby wanted to know as he got off the elevator.

Bernard Goldfine came prepared to confess to payoffs to Sherman Adams and the two New Hampshire senators, Styles Bridges and Norris Cotton. The key to Goldfine's manipulations over the years turned out to be his assistant, Mildred Paperman, a wily, aging spinster whose involvement with Goldfine merged the personal and the professional. Mildred kept the petty-cash box, where Goldfine normally stored several hundred thousand dollars, and every time he had a payoff in mind he would instruct her to "Give me ten thousand dollars; I'm going to meet Adams." Mildred claimed to record these substantial transactions by scrawling the totals on the inside covers of packets of matches.

Hundley took a hard line: "Look, you know, Mildred, one of two things happened. I mean you either made this up or there is documentation and you have it, see, in which case tell me which it is. Otherwise there's no point in continuing with this thing." Mildred started to cry.

A few days later Williams called and arranged to meet Hundley for lunch at the Metropolitan Club. Mildred had kept a diary, as things turned out, in which she maintained a record of every dollar that changed hands. She worried that Goldfine might be losing interest in her and might at some point accuse her of embezzling some of the money.

Just as Hundley suspected, the diary listed contributions to "Democrats, Republicans, labor leaders, internal revenue agents." Prominent Democratic politicians along with several judges were implicated. When Hundley started going down the list with Kennedy, the attorney general would break in—"There. I know this guy. I'm sure it was just a political contribution."— but then the same recipient would turn up month after month. Bobby studied the diary. "Oops!" he burst out after several all-but-overlapping payoffs.

Early in the investigation, Kennedy hit the buzzer and summoned the unhappy Hoover. "Even then it wasn't a cordial relationship," Hundley remembers.

"What do you want, Mr. Attorney General?" the Director demanded, stiffly.

"I want something done on this Adams case."

"I'll look into it," Hoover said and left.

But Hoover's modus operandi was to keep an eye out for the politicians who dealt with appropriations for the Bureau, not drag them into court. He maintained a watch on Hundley's efforts to prosecute Goldfine—a contact man from the FBI, Tom McAndrews, had been assigned to stay with Hundley and keep the Director informed—but Hoover evidently made no serious attempt to run down the names on Mildred Paperman's list.

As the weeks passed, Hundley kept chewing away at the evasive Goldfine, pressing him to supply enough details about all those judges and IRS personnel and politicos to give Hundley's investigators leads they could turn into evidence. Goldfine was willing enough to rat out Adams and the New Hampshire senators, whom he regarded as having sacrificed him to the investigating committees once the vicuña-coat story turned into headlines, but he was not willing to discuss in any depth most of the other names in Mildred's diary, people he was well aware had ties to the current administration.

As Hundley turned up the pressure, Goldfine began to hint that he might be inclined to talk more freely, but only to "number one," the attorney general. An impatient Bobby flew in late one Sunday evening from Chicago to give Goldfine his opportunity to cleanse his soul. Williams produced his client and he and Goldfine and the annoyed attorney general faced off in Byron White's office. It quickly became clear that Goldfine was there to haggle, demanding, over and over, "What's in it for me?" before he would open up at all. He indicated he might take into his confidence his new "number one," JFK. Beside himself, Robert Kennedy blew up at the slippery old influence peddler. Goldfine regarded him wearily. "Huh," he observed to the embarrassed Williams. "He doesn't have any class like his brother."

To build a federal case against anybody on Goldfine's list it would be necessary to trace the cash Goldfine was handing around, and cash is very hard to monitor. Sherman Adams was always careful to convert his handouts into money orders, thus frustrating any efforts to track down serial numbers, and pass along the money orders to pay rent and cover expenses. The biggest break Hundley's investigators got occurred when they were able to prove that Goldfine had presented Cadillacs to a pair of influential U.S. senators.

But Hoover was following the twists and turns as the case wound through the moils of the Justice Department. The Director's weary dark eyes rarely blinked. Before the prosecutors could perfect their evidence, Hundley remembers, "Hoover goes up and tips 'em, they give the Cadillacs back, we got no case. He had their votes for the rest of their lives. He never sent it over for indictment; he just put it in his file. And he had the effrontery to tell me he *always* did things like that. Hell, it was my case, Jesus.

"He was a super bureaucrat, I'll say that. He was a law unto himself."

Saddled still with tax problems, Goldfine plea-bargained his way down to a year in the penitentiary at Danbury, assisted by a lukewarm endorsement from the Justice Department. Manifestly ill, Goldfine served very little time. What might have been a huge bipartisan scandal got effectively suppressed.

From Kennedy's angle, the Goldfine case worked out. Goldfine did a few months for dereliction vis-à-vis his tax obligations, but those charges came out of Congress: Eisenhower couldn't blame Bobby for that. Adams was never indicted. Those well-placed officials and politicians, Democrats mostly, whose names turned up in Mildred Paperman's diary would remain anonymous. It was a resolution straight out of the J. Edgar Hoover playbook.

More upsetting by far were the cries of outrage arising from the Keogh brothers, the head of the New York Irish political machine and a sitting Congressman, Eugene, and a justice on the New York State Supreme Court, Vincent. Eugene Keogh was a stalwart in the national Democratic Party, a key driver on the House Ways and Means Committee and a crony of long standing of Joseph P. Kennedy. Along with Charles A. Buckley, and in the face of vociferous misgivings expressed by Carmine De Sapio and the Tammany Hall regulars, Keogh had maintained discipline across the New York delegation in Los Angeles in 1960 and stampeded the Empire State early enough—and solidly enough—for John F. Kennedy to assure his selection on the initial ballot. Another round, and it had started to look as if the nomination might escape the front-runner.

So the Kennedys owed Eugene Keogh. Furthermore, Jack Kennedy held Keogh in high regard. Once the scandal broke, four days before Vincent Keogh was indicted by a federal grand jury, JFK would make a point of attending the Army-Navy game with Eugene Keogh. Months before, when word reached the president that Bob was considering indicting Vincent Keogh, John Kennedy had erupted, "My God, I hope he doesn't. Gene Keogh is my friend, and, if there's any way I can honestly help him, I'd want to help him."

The problem was that enough publicity had gotten out ahead of any attempt to litigate to make it awkward for the administration to look away. The item in the *Wall Street Journal* early in 1961 that kicked the whole thing off alluded to "a routine investigation into a Maryland jukebox racket" by the

FBI which "stumbled on the rumor that a New York justice had taken a bribe to fix the sentence of Sanford Moore, the operator of a jukebox company who had been convicted of bankruptcy fraud." Information about ongoing Bureau investigations never seeped into newspaper columns like this except when the Director expected it to fortify his own situation—or damage his enemies.

Sanford Moore was the principal in the Continental Vending Machine Company and a business associate of the Teamster-related mobster Tony "Ducks" Corallo, a heavy on Robert Kennedy's to-get list since Racket Committee days. The "Ducks" stemmed from Corallo's knack for ducking subpoenas. Both Moore and Corallo were very familiar to Ed Silberling as fixtures of the eastern syndicate. Silberling sent one of his Organized Crime Section bloodhounds, John Lally, to New York to squeeze Moore. During Lally's third interrogation, Moore happened to spot Assistant U.S. Attorney Elliot Kahaner ambling through the detention station of the Eastern District with one arm lapped over the narrow shoulders of the attorney general, out consorting with the grunts.

Moore snapped. Out came his admission that he had slipped Kahaner a $35,000 bribe, which he intended to divide with Supreme Court Justice Vincent Keogh. The trail quickly led to a sometime business partner of Moore's, Dr. Robert Erdman, a wealthy orthopedic surgeon from the Bronx, who broke down under questioning and conceded that he had indeed presented half the money to Vincent Keogh, who thanked Erdman warmly by postcard for "the package."

All this looked like plenty of grounds to indict and produced an increasingly fired-up grand jury. Meanwhile, Silberling arranged to fill his bosses in on the scandal. "You've got to prosecute this," Byron White told Bob when Silberling finished laying out the evidence.

Kennedy was devastated. "Bob Kennedy put his head between his hands and said, 'I told my brother I didn't want this job,'" Silberling later reported. Kennedy "sat there looking miserable. A number of weeks went by, I would say, before that investigation was continued. . . .

"My own impression was that if it were at all possible to avoid going ahead with this case he would have avoided it. And it was only because he was persuaded that there was a greater danger involved if he did not go ahead with it . . . there were leaks that there was such an investigation taking place. . . . Local newspapers had picked up something on it. . . ."

Among Silberling's attack attorneys, there was the widespread suspicion that Kennedy was riding the brake. Victor Navasky quotes one witness at a

White House judicial reception who overheard a freewheeling discussion of the Keogh situation. "O'Donnell was in favor of having Judge Keogh resign and dropping the whole thing. Then Byron said something. I think it was a joke about Bob's dragging his feet—and Bob's face lost color. 'How can you say that?' he asked. He was really upset. He thought Byron was accusing him. I think Byron was just wisecracking. Anyway, Bob walked away shaking."

The problem with operating in the shadow of incorruptible personalities like White is that they are incorruptible. Kennedy didn't dare waver. "What this administration needs more than anything," John Kennedy decided once Bobby's agenda started to come across his desk, "is an attorney general that we can fix."

With the Keogh proceedings starting to heat up, Robert Kennedy brought in William Hundley to fine-tune the Justice Department's involvement. Bobby made his own hopes clear, if indirectly. If Vincent Keogh were actually indicted, Kennedy observed at one point, the judge would be ruined, and "I'd hate to have that on my conscience." References to Bobby Kennedy's conscience were something new.

"I don't want to interfere in your case," Kennedy assured Hundley, but what about asking Keogh and Erdman to take lie-detector tests? Hundley got in touch with the FBI in D.C. Essentially a one-witness case, "backed up by a lot of circumstantial evidence," as Hundley saw it, "I knew I had to try this sucker." The Bureau could help.

Word came right back. "The Bureau had refused to do it," Hundley remembers. "But you know the Bureau; it isn't that unusual."

"I think you misunderstood me, Al," Hundley told the assistant director who delivered the news. "You know, the attorney general wants it done."

Hoover himself was following this exchange. "Sherlock Holmeses must have their fun," he scrawled on one memo authorizing the polygraph. When Erdman blanked out and Keogh showed up guilty, if not conclusively, Hoover penned in, "This proves I was right." Still dug in, no matter what.

The whole thing went to trial in May 1962. Days before that, Erdman's lawyer called Hundley to demand immunity. "Go back and tell your client there will be no trial of Keogh on Monday," Hundley responded. "We'll be prosecuting *him*."

There were five defendants. Two pleaded guilty; the others were convicted. Keogh, Kahaner, and "Ducks" Corallo each got two years.

Word quickly got around that Robert Kennedy had emphasized that Hundley was to keep Eugene Keogh out of the proceedings "at whatever cost." "Every time Eugene Keogh's name was mentioned," Department lawyer Henry Ruth would recall, "the phone rang and it was the attorney general."

Lured into this quagmire by FBI leaks to the papers, the Kennedys thrashed hard to limit the damage. Hoover watched with amusement, obstructing where he could. When the traditional letters of congratulation were prepared for the attorney who won the case, Bobby couldn't get himself to put his signature on any of them.

As Silberling's investigations took on a life of their own and threatened the administration itself, Robert Kennedy had less and less time to contend with the fallout. The distracted attorney general himself, the high-riding Silberling later commented, "did not have a quick grasp of the legal implications. . . . Part of the problem is that he was accustomed to getting reports—you know, here's John Doe, evil man, and he's supposedly doing evil things; well, why can't he be prosecuted . . . ?

"Bob relied on Byron White for the running of the department, for deciding structurally or organizationally who was going to be doing what."

John Kennedy himself knew what was going on. "I said I wanted a legal opinion," the president broke out when Bobby volunteered to satisfy his brother on some point of law. "Don't *you* get on it. Get Archie Cox on it."

Jack needed Bobby elsewhere. One assumption shared by a generation of liberal historians has been that Jack Kennedy rushed unawares into the Bay of Pigs invasion and that Robert Kennedy was largely left out of meaningful tactical planning. Once that misadventure collapsed, the president faced up to the inevitability of involving his nut-cutting little brother in the treacheries of clandestine warfare. This perception needs revision. The fact is, the liberation of Cuba was turning into a preoccupation among the Kennedys many months before Jack became a candidate and scored heavily off Richard Nixon in debate for Nixon's supposed indifference to Castro.

Along with the outrage endemic among their Palm Beach Society cronies like ex-ambassadors to Cuba Earl E. T. Smith and William Pawley and the Charles Wrightsmans and Allen Dulles and George Smathers at the presumption of the Castro regime as it nationalized foreign assets, Joe Kennedy and his family were subject to the poolside carping of Lansky-organization affiliates like Mike McLaney and Carroll Rosenbloom. Hundreds of millions vaporized overnight when Castro grabbed the casinos.

Tangentially, the financier had been keeping an eye on Cuba for forty years, since Rose's important position in the Atlantic, Gulf and West Indies Line left her the beneficiary of the big Hayden, Stone carrier's extensive Cuban sugar plantations. Like everybody else, Joe took the island for granted, part of the American hegemony.

More immediately: Joe Kennedy and Morton Downey turn out to have been seriously invested together in Cuba's lucrative Coca-Cola franchise, which had been confiscated along with everything else once the Bearded One absorbed foreign holdings. For Castro to collectivize this wonderfully corrupt and universally receptive playground which sat a tempting ninety miles off the Miami coast, this colony of self-indulgence for the flighty East-Coast rich—this was an affront, this was unacceptable!

Conservative forces were quick to gather. Shortly before JFK's inauguration, as the CIA had begun to nail down staging areas prior to its projected move against Havana, General Anastasia Somoza, the brother of the president of Nicaragua, flew into New York for a meeting with Joseph Kennedy in his new offices high in the Pan American Building. A counter-revolution was brewing. The Vatican was following everything closely. Wealthy, expropriated Roman Catholic Cubans had agreed to help with the financing. Joe Kennedy himself accompanied Somoza to New York to sit in on talks with Dulles at CIA headquarters.

By 1961, as executor of his father's estate, Robert Kennedy was picking up on enough of his father's connections to worry about implicating Joe. Shortly after the inaugural, the abstracted attorney general was already on record helping out with the support logistics for the upcoming assault of Cuba. One important resource was the Agency's long-standing partner in subterfuge, the United Fruit Company ("The Great White Fleet"). The vice president of United Fruit would later pass along the corporate impression of the president's brother, from his "arrogant and demanding attitude" to his "dirty long hair," as Bobby requisitioned a couple of freighters to transport guns, men, and material for the anticipated assault on Castro.

So Bobby was in on the details even during the planning stages. Testimony before the Church Committee would reveal that, on the morning of the landing of the doomed brigade, Jack Kennedy's unreliable back was flaring up, and Bobby was lumbered with the decision to withhold the critical air strikes. Richard Goodwin, throughout those inaugural months the driver and shaper of the green administration's policy toward Latin America, was described by one aide to McGeorge Bundy as having "danced around the White House, demanding that we . . . call out the fleet . . . send in the goddamn

Marines!" Meanwhile, Joe Kennedy telephoned the Oval Office a reported six times on the day of the landing. "The old man wanted to go in on air strikes," George Smathers would tell one interviewer. Many years afterward, with the detachment of the memoirist, Goodwin himself would conclude that "the most serious misjudgments of his [Kennedy's] presidency—the Bay of Pigs, growing involvement in Vietnam—emerged from secret, incestuous councils unrestrained by political debate and public temper." Among the Kennedys, incestuous definitely means family.

After the debacle, a lot of history got rearranged. "I was brought in on the Cuban situation about four or five days prior to the actual event," Robert Kennedy dictated in a memorandum of June 1. "I should have had Bobby in on this from the start," JFK conceded to Kenny O'Donnell. As it happened, Jack Kennedy's historic incapacity to either commit or renege once Brigade 2506 started breaking up on the coral reefs of the Bay of Pigs was hard to explain away. The president assumed responsibility in a very manly style, but enough was leaked to lay the real blame on the joint chiefs, or Adlai Stevenson, or Dean Rusk, or the CIA, which in fact *had* misled not only the chief executive but its own Intelligence Directorate to assure the go-ahead for the invasion.

A fiasco this impossible to spin depleted even JFK's reserves of self-possession. Joe complained to Rose that Jack had been on the telephone to him much of the day following the collapse of the beachhead, virtually "crying with despair. He was blaming Allen Dulles and the CIA for getting him into this mess." Joe told his wife he was "dying," trying to improve Jack's morale. "You lucky mush," the old financier lied, this was the best thing that could have happened. Jack was getting his administration's inevitable come-uppance behind him early in his tenure.

But after hearing Jack blame the world for far too long, the disgusted Ambassador leveled with his son: "Oh, hell, if that's the way you feel, give the job to Lyndon!" Once emotions leveled off, the Ambassador would greet his son in Palm Beach with a characteristic outburst: "You blew it!" Johnson might have stood up. At some level, the skeptical financier's fallback position kept sliding into view, his half-conscious motive behind insinuating the mas- terful Texan into his disease-ridden son's government.

Robert Kennedy as well lingered on the telephone with his father. With Bob it was mostly about getting even. "He's a hater, like me," the Ambassador was fond of observing about his middle son, by which he meant that Bob was a realist. After bickering with Khrushchev in Vienna, Jack had groaned that it was "like dealing with Dad—all give and no take." Bobby alone among the children, Ken O'Donnell saw early, "could handle the father." They traded calculated digs: Bob was very cheap, and so his father sometimes made it a point in one of the very expensive restaurants he frequented to order lavishly from the a la carte menu, then sign Bob's name to the check. Loosen the boy up.

More fatalistic and aggressive by nature than his older brother, at first Bobby ascribed his brother's miserable failure of nerve in Cuba to exhaustion and overwork—"You know, we've been through a lot of things together. And he was just more upset this time than he was any other"—while flaring out savagely at subordinates, especially the few like Chester Bowles who had openly advised against the ill-prepared Cuban invasion. Bowles pronounced Bobby "emotional and militant," and, like most of the other genuine liberals around the administration, soon found himself either banished or sidelined.

As with their father, the prospect of failure remained psychologically intolerable to the sons. Cuba—which, kept to proportion, would have amounted to no more than a bedbug in the political covers—turned into an engulfing many-armed monster which all but consumed the Kennedy presidency. Anything less than "winning" upset the sensitive president—he raged and sulked when Ken O'Donnell shot a deer on Johnson's ranch before *he* managed it and tended to overturn a checkerboard when he was about to lose or to caution Jacqueline not to keep trouncing him at Scrabble. Failing to replace Castro was not to be endured. Bobby, their Galahad, was appointed to slay this apparition overshadowing the family's self-respect.

While instinctively remaining a little out of reach personally, the president saw no workable salvation from then on except to involve his brother completely in the subversive-warfare response to Castro. Bobby could live with blame. The "Robbie and Johnny" phase of their relationship now deepened. Bob was "absolutely incorruptible," JFK told key aides. "Then he has terrific executive energy. . . . Bobby's the best organizer I've ever seen."

Whenever organizing was involved, there persisted a certain confusion in the case of both the Kennedys between planning over the long haul and reacting to the day's events, improvising. Like many staff-dependent rich, Robert Kennedy was constantly losing vital letters and documents; he refused to carry money around; he habitually blamed underlings when some proposal he himself mislaid hadn't evoked the desired response. Both Kennedy brothers came alive in a crunch. They liked the play-action pass much better than strategizing the game.

Behind this ever-increasing shift of responsibility was John Kennedy's health, undoubtedly the administration's best-protected secret. The truth was, the president was out of commission a great deal of the time. The ill-advised use of primitive steroids to palliate his ulcerative colitis, dating back to Kennedy's adolescence, along with a congenitally short leg, helped bring on the premature osteoporosis which wrecked his lower back and seems to have triggered the Addison's disease which left him several times the recipient of last rites. During public appearances he employed a hip-to-neck body corset. His father stockpiled in safe deposit boxes around the world pellets of desoxycorticosterone acetate (Doca), which had to be implanted in the muscles of his back and thighs every few months. As president, he was making do with adrenals the size of flyspecks and appeared more and more puffy from cortisone while he exhibited ever increasingly the classical symptoms of grandiosity, invulnerability, and recklessness. According to CIA Section Chief Cord Meyers, the president was now experimenting with grass, coke, and poppers. Other writers mention acid. To navigate without crutches he required, every six hours, massive injections of procaine across the lower back and buttocks. Amphetamines cranked up his charm level through many a reception. He napped much of every afternoon. He was lactose-intolerant and had an underactive thyroid and a 350 cholesterol reading. His prostate was giving him trouble, and he continued to contend with a nasty, incurable drip from chlamydia and gonorrhea, which were under constant treatment with heavy antibiotics. Migraines plagued him. Otherwise he was fine.

It is a testimony to the raw force of John Kennedy's will that he was available so much of his presidency. Most days he swam laps in the White House pool before lunch and dinner. Protracted flirtations with beauties like Judith Campbell and Mary Meyers diverted him, supplemented by interludes in the pool with press aides Fiddle and Faddle. He remained an incorrigible campaigner, racketing around the country—and Europe several times—to proclaim Western values and inspire the allies. Vigor was the watchword.

Behind guarded doors, much of the time John Kennedy was hors de combat, down, too sick to function. Bobby took his place, often justifying the initiatives he took, the orders he gave around the government, with the phrase "my brother wants," or "my brother thinks. . . ." Senior bureaucrats found this offensive, this spontaneous takeover of authority based not on Bobby's office but on his blood. It wasn't Robert Kennedy's choice. The co-presidency was thrust upon him.

Bob attempted to improve things, insofar as that seemed possible. In June

1962 he had an assistant drop off "a small bottle, about one-quarter full of an orange-colored liquid" for analysis by the FBI laboratory. It originated with Dr. Max Jacobson of New York, alluded to by the president's Secret Service contingent as the "bat wing and chicken blood doctor." The FBI technicians were, as usual, not particularly helpful, establishing only that the contents were neither barbiturates nor narcotics. The active ingredient was evidently amphetamine, for the abuse of which Jacobson ultimately lost his license. Robert Kennedy attempted to persuade his brother to give up injecting himself with speed, but Jack felt that he needed it. "I don't care if there's panther piss in there," Jack reportedly said, "as long as it makes me feel good."

So day-to-day responsibility continued to shift. "Management in Jack's mind," Undersecretary of State Chester Bowles once remarked to Arthur Schlesinger Jr., "consisted of calling Bob on the telephone and saying, 'Here are ten things I want to get done.'" Maxwell Taylor would observe that JFK barely recognized his cabinet members, or military, or understood the sweeping governmental machinery: "Where you put in the gas, where you put in the oil, where you turn on the throttle." Bobby was paying attention. In crisis after crisis the public would see pictures of the brothers pondering a decision together, their elegantly clippered necks inclined toward one another, experiencing mind-meld.

Forty years of special handling was wearing on Jack at times. Just before the dinner at the extravagant Bouvier wedding in Rhode Island, Joe had taken George Smathers aside and cautioned him that, since he would be speaking for the groom, "I want you to be funny, to make Jack look good. I don't want the Bouviers to be outshining us." Which meant: give Jack the choice lines. Periodically, Jack writhed at too much micromanagement. "I guess Dad decided that he's going to be the ventriloquist," he once lamented to Lem Billings, "so I guess that leaves me the role of dummy."

Yet, for the most part, John Kennedy accepted—without questioning the details—the financier's intimate involvement in every phase of his life. Even in the White House, the father continued to pay almost all of his son's wide-ranging personal and office expenses. Emotionally, Jack Kennedy seemed to require the old man's gusto and approbation. As late as election day, when he found his son showing signs of bridling internally at the responsibilities of the presidency, the Ambassador spoke up: "Jack, if you don't want the job you don't have to take it. They're still counting votes in Cook County."

The founding father's hesitations about the competence of both of the boys obviously continued to run deep. He made sure that he had access to even the most incidental interplay among the White House offices. Ex-Harvard

Dean James Landis, who had been receiving discreet checks from Joe for nearly thirty years, was planted quietly in the White House as a special assistant. Offices were found in the White House as well as the Department of Justice for Carmine Bellino, the FBI-hardened, all-seeing accountant to whom the Ambassador had recourse whenever a financial crisis threatened. Anthony Gallucio, a family friend who worked in several of the campaigns, ventured that "the father pays people right on Jack's staff to con Jack into doing things the father couldn't persuade him to do . . . the father manipulates things, pays for things, goes ahead with plans without Jack's knowledge. Jack simply lacks the backbone to read the old man the riot act."

JFK's personal secretary Evelyn Lincoln later revealed that there was a telephone on her desk with a direct line to Joe, wherever he was. At times, wearing thin, Jack would joke with his staff that he wished his father would just disappear over the ocean somewhere so he could be free of the old man's incessant opinions and demands.

Bobby remained Joe's surrogate. Even the famously detached young president could not help resenting at times the extent of his dependency. He told his old friend Charles Spalding that he was increasingly of the opinion that Bob was "overly ambitious, hard-nosing it." As for speculation that Jack himself might wind up the secretary of state in some future Robert Kennedy administration: "Let's not dwell too long on the prospect of taking orders from Loveable Bob." Later on, Harris Wofford would quote Arthur Schlesinger's aside that "Robert was not often asked to the White House on purely informal occasions, after working hours," since "at the end of a long day he was often too demanding, too involved with issues. Teddy made the President laugh. Bobby was his conscience."

As if to compensate, Bob and Ethel Kennedy pumped up the schedule around Hickory Hill. They were already notorious for their big, noisy parties, balloons squeaking and a band blaring forth and their Noah's Ark of pets meandering among the tables, grazing off of everybody's plates. The Robert Kennedys attracted headlines when Arthur Schlesinger Jr. found himself, bow tie and all, floundering around the pool, and Ethel wound up in court for attempting to rustle a spavined old horse she spotted a neighbor abusing. At a St. Patrick's Day dinner she alternated place settings with glossy plump green bullfrogs. Robert Junior's menagerie now came to include hawks and snakes and falcons and iguanas, many dogs of assorted breeds, a honey bear that squeezed into the bookcases by day and emerged to forage in the refrigerator at night, a sea lion who attempted to take over the swimming pool, and several dwarf ponies.

Bedlam was the norm. Except for Ena Bernard, a square-set black woman from the Caribbean who arrived at Hickory Hill as a nursemaid and saw Ethel through all eleven children, the seventeen or so regular servants got hired on and quit or got bounced out by the dozen, unable to adjust to Ethel's demanding and capricious ways. The children were already more than anybody could hope to manage, high-spirited and destructive and arbitrarily disciplined, if at all. A sign on the front lawn announced "Trespassers Will Be Eaten." For Ethel, obedience was unenforceable; she struggled to amuse this tumultuous brood by releasing a greased pig in the formal dining room. If a visitor seemed stuffy, she rarely squelched the impulse to toss a drink into the offending features or overturn a salad bowl on too elaborate a coiffure. An unsuspecting European royal walked into a face-full of shaving cream.

Ethel was devoted to her many children, but Bobby remained her priority. Her one reliable meal with the family was breakfast, described as "lots of greasy bacon, eggs cooked in lard, glazed doughnuts, and ice-cold milk popped in the freezer for fifteen minutes before being served." Enlisted to come up with a snack one night late, Ethel clattered ineffectually amidst a welter of pots and pans. Bobby looked on dolefully. "Mother of the Year," he offered, sotto voce.

Robert Kennedy, when he was there, attempted to hold things in focus a little. His many offspring listened to him, and at his insistence—Rose and Steve Smith were forever sending notes emphasizing that Ethel was going through too much money—he kept the heat around the mansion turned low, so that visitors were chilly in winter. He encouraged roughhousing; gangs of the children would greet him once he finally turned up at the door—prematurely humped over, white with fatigue—and jump their father, setting off what they all called a "tickle-tumble" as everybody piled on amidst peals of laughter and yelps of pain. He chased them all over the house and joined in their pillow fights.

Yet once in a while he showed them his other side. In the midst of a frolic, unexpectedly, Bobby would slap one of the boys, hard. Children "have to get used to being hit," and "learn to take it and go on," he told one bystander, until "there is no surprise, no shock they can't sustain." If one of them wept, Bob warned that Kennedys never cry.

Like Rose, Ethel attempted to infuse the household with a strong Roman-Catholic presence. She converted the reprobate Paul Corbin, a bare-knuckled political odd-jobs man whose prior infatuations had ranged from Communism to McCarthyism. No unmarried couple was welcome at Hickory Hill, nor would the Robert Kennedys attend a gathering where the unsanctified were expected. God would look after her own family's future. Like Bobby, Ethel depended on a hard Celtic fatalism.

If the Robert Kennedys were rarely invited to the White House, the president and Jacqueline seldom swung by Hickory Hill. Other White House eminences attended at their peril. Ethel's brothers James and Rushton Skakel passed along their memory of one incident. "After the party got rolling pretty good," Jim Skakel recounted, "Ethel got up on a chair and she was feeling pretty good and she said, 'I'm giving a toast to the second most important man in the Western World.'" Before Lyndon Johnson could sidle toward the microphone, Rushton concludes, "Bobby rushed up to claim the number-two spot. LBJ was so shocked he couldn't believe it."

JFK was not captivated by the idea either. When *Life* characterized Bobby as the number-two gunslinger in town, the president offered his opinion: "That means there's only one way for you to go, and it ain't up." For anybody as thin-skinned as Bobby, there had to be a warning somewhere in that.

One constant in Bob Kennedy's life just then was Brumus, the enormous, phlegmatic Newfoundland that sat up behind his chair at dinner and took it hard when Kennedy went anyplace without him. Brumus had a personality even seasoned dog-lovers came quickly to abhor. Eyes faintly aglitter behind his rufflike shag of lusterless black hair, Brumus's breath was horrible and he was a champion drooler.

The Kennedys had acquired him as a gift from the humorist James Thurber, a connoisseur of the demonic in all its manifestations. Despite his constitutional lethargy, Brumus had a talent for making himself both unwieldy and repulsive. At dinners laid in tables around the pool Brumus tended to wake up, to a certain extent. If he spotted something desirable, he tended to reach out with one giant paw and scoop it up. "Once was enough for me," one worn-out ex-dinner guest announced afterward. "That damned dog was all over me, and Bobby seemed to think my objections were pretty stuffy if not downright unmannerly. Brumus got most of my meal and left paw marks all over my clothes."

"Brumus was always a big problem at the pet shows at Hickory Hill," Art Buchwald would testify, "because he was ready to eat the pets and bite the children." The first year, "Brumus went up to these two women having their lunch on the lawn, and he lifted a leg and peed on their backs. Bobby saw this happen, and he ran into the house. I accused him of having a questionable profile in courage."

Brumus had feelings, too; at least Bobby said he did. Whenever Brumus nipped a child or tore apart somebody's roses, and the landowner registered annoyance, Kennedy became very sharp, very protective, worried that his pet might be psychologically scarred. A neighbor once cornered Brumus ripping up his flower bed and hung a sign around the monster's neck: VOTE FOR NIXON! The dim-witted Newfoundland hauled it back to Ethel, no doubt preoccupied with plotting his next outrage.

It should not come as a great surprise that J. Edgar Hoover didn't like Brumus either. By the spring of 1961, Kennedy had started to accord Brumus an early-morning shot at joining him at the office. Brumus, who normally lay sprawled and semicomatose across the top of the central staircase at Hickory Hill, somehow understood when Kennedy appeared in his pinstripe suit with his briefcase that, if he were to have any hope of going along, he would have to arrive at the car first. The attorney general and the Newfoundland would tumble together down the wide stairs and barrel toward the car. If Brumus managed to hurtle by Bobby and land in the passenger seat in time he got to come along to work.

On the FBI side of the fifth-floor corridor, Brumus was an unwelcome addition to the complexities of the day. It was quickly brought to the Director's attention that Brumus had been marking his territory all around the red pile carpet of Kennedy's mammoth office. The ultimate affront came when the languorous beast took a calculated dump immediately outside Hoover's suite. Furious, Hoover convened an executive conference, at which the Director and the dozen top professionals in the FBI debated with great heat for hours the feasibility of bringing the attorney general up on charges for violating the federal code banning dogs from government buildings. It was gradually concluded that it might be just as well to delay prosecution.

Soon after Robert Kennedy was installed, the Director and Tolson came by the attorney general's office by appointment to find Bobby cocked back in his massive red cordovan-leather swivel chair, behind his six-foot-square mahogany desk, shirtsleeves rolled up and his undone necktie dangling in two strips down his narrow chest. Kennedy was tossing darts at a target across the room. As Hoover and Tolson attempted to open up the subject at hand, Kennedy continued to peg dart after dart, pocking up the celebrated walnut paneling each time he missed and interrupting their disjunctive exchanges whenever he climbed out of his chair to recover his darts. An inveterate gum-chewer, Kennedy's reedy, singsong voice could be very difficult to understand.

Tolson was profoundly disgusted, and Hoover was enraged. The old autocrat understood his status inside the Kennedy circle—Art Buchwald had written a column in which he maintained that Hoover wasn't real, he was a mythical creature concocted by *The Reader's Digest*—and Edgar now became half-unhinged whenever he attempted to describe the dart-throwing incident. This was, at minimum, the "most deplorably undignified conduct . . . ever witnessed on the part of a Cabinet member," Hoover sputtered, "like a child playing in a Dresden china shop. It was pure desecration, desecration of public property." Privately, Hoover had started to refer to Kennedy as "that snot-nosed kid," or "that hippie intellectual."

It was as if, within a few months, this upstart scion of the self-indulgent Kennedy family intended to dismantle the entire Cold War apparatus Hoover had intrigued so long to jockey into place. The Director attended one staff luncheon at the Justice Department, after which he either sent along his apologies, or detailed Courtney Evans to take notes for him, or ignored future planning sessions completely. The Internal Security Division of the Justice Department, to Hoover's fury, was melting away week by week; most of whatever talent survived had been diverted into Bobby's war on what he referred to as "organized crime." The neophyte attorney general, Hoover remarked in a memo, had big ideas about the penal system, similar to those of that imbecilic ex-Director of Prisons James Bennett, a pair of "misguided sentimentalists" whose "maudlin proposals" went so far as nattering about closing Alcatraz.

Bobby pushed his brother to commute the seven-year sentence of Junius Scales—"your friend, Junius Scales," as Bobby jibed liberal *New York Times* columnist Tony Lewis. Scales was the only individual jailed under the Smith Act. He had admitted freely to having belonged to the Communist Party yet refused to "name names," identify everybody he knew who joined over the years—not that the Bureau didn't have every one of the bastards numbered and tagged. But humiliating Scales was important to the Director. It sent the right signals.

Robert Kennedy's lurking egalitarianism became even more evident to the Director when he quit the stodgy, establishmentarian Metropolitan Club, to which he was admitted in 1955 with the endorsement of Arthur Krock. By 1961, irritated because the club still refused to admit blacks even as luncheon guests, Kennedy wrote the manager a reproving note and included his resignation.

More alarming day-to-day, as Hoover saw things, was the extent to which Kennedy appeared to be piecing together those "strike forces" of do-gooder lawyers inside that Organized Crime and Racketeering Section, unmistakably intended to supplant the Bureau any time Hoover didn't feel like cooperating. Kennedy played this very cute—whenever he wanted something the FBI didn't have, or wouldn't give him, he acted as if he could simply pretend the Bureau was already on top of whatever it was, and he would demand whatever he thought he needed. All this was squeezing the Bureau in directions it soured Hoover to think about.

If there was anyplace the Director hated to venture, it was that no-man's land where high-rolling entrepreneurs, municipal politicians, and limousine-class retired bootleggers got down to the practical business of staking out the future. Why the insufferable Bobby remained so intent on raking all this up was baffling. As with the Keogh incident, by pressing too close the Kennedys risked collapsing their own party around their future.

Take the Chacharis investigation. Bobby's Rackets Committee probers had turned up a frenzy of illegal land speculation and insider favor-trading that extended from the Carpenters Union to Teamster local 142 in Lake County, Indiana. Lake County featured Gary, a tough, no-bullshit steel-making town churning with unassimilated ethnics.

Wyn Hayes's ramifying index of hoods suggested that midlevel syndicate gangsters like John LaRosa and Frank Rizzo were part of the mixture. To nose around western Indiana, Robert Kennedy sent out a newcomer to his bullpen, Jay Goldberg. Goldberg was tall and young, prematurely balding, an absolutist from Frank Hogan's Parris Island for prosecutors. A little bit fevered with self-righteousness at times like his polished and unapologetically cocksure mentor Edwyn Silberling, Goldberg remained pretty much oblivious to the political by-product.

Goldberg was an easy kid for Midwesterners to underestimate. His emotions spoke for him. He shoved language out at people in a warm, rich Borscht-Belt delivery that the Gary establishment hadn't experienced. Until he arrived in Gary, "I had never been further west than Lakewood, New Jersey," Goldberg muses now, "with my parents. If you carried the mantle of the Kennedys it was the biggest." Goldberg went directly to the head of the local FBI and "I asked, 'What's doing up here?' And he said, 'Nothing, no crap.' So I said, 'What about the Hobbs Act—threats against commerce, extortion?' But they were hostile."

They suggested that Goldberg should move on downstate, "where the big-time operators are, and when I got back to Washington, the FBI had sent back a report that I left classified documents unattended in my room. . . ." After that, day to day, "I never had contact with the FBI—they had disappeared off the face of the earth."

But Goldberg was not to be fluffed off easily. Even on that first visit, "You know what I learned? In the Midwest there are towns that are *owned* by people. They control the sheriff, the district attorney, and the people are serfs." Goldberg's next stop had been the headquarters of the North-West Indiana Crime Commission, a citizens' protest group set up in the wake of the Rackets Committee disclosures and led by Frank Lynch, a former FBI man himself. Filled in by Lynch at first, Goldberg began to prize up a pattern of entrenched graft so pervasive that gravel contractors were forced to pay off three or four councilmen to deliver a load of sand. One company, Goldberg relates, "had done municipal work for 43 years, and never once had they failed to pay corrupt politicians the price of doing legitimate work."

IRS Commissioner Mortimer Caplin, a tax-law professor of Bobby's at the University of Virginia, stood ready to put a large contingent of the IRS's huge corps of tax examiners at the disposal of Silberling's organized-crime strike forces. After he returned to Gary with his wife, Goldberg recalls, "I meet a person from heaven, Oral Cole, like a real rube. And he's a genius for the IRS. And he tells me this entire story, and he becomes part of my body."

Silberling authorized a federal grand jury. Cole supplied the exhilarated prosecutor everything he needed—ultimately four hundred items in evidence. Goldberg took to extracting testimony from the principal culprits in the gloomy, intimidating grand-jury room. Hunched over in a high-backed chair, his back to the witnesses, Goldberg gestured each awed official under investigation to a nearby seat. No one was permitted to view his face. "Look," their Grand Inquisitor might open. "You're standing in 150-degree water. It's in your power to cool that water off to about fifty degrees, or make it much hotter. . . ."

By now, the Indiana newspapers were bannering each indictment. Goldberg was a celebrity, worshipful citizens hounded him for autographs in the nearby lunchrooms. There were rumors circulating that the powerful mayor of Gary himself, George Chacharis, was increasingly under suspicion.

Chacharis took preemptive action. Goldberg got a call from the attorney general directing him to confront Chacharis: "The Mayor wants to offer his cooperation. Call him and set up a meeting."

Real trouble over Chacharis would mean a major political dustup for the Kennedys. George ("Cha-cha") Chacharis was a plump, highly emotional Greek-American who had built his machine in Gary out of decades of perspiration supplemented by graft while remaining approachable and living very modestly. He had been an early supporter of John Kennedy's candidacy; without Chacharis, Kennedy would never have won Indiana, which might have meant the presidency. Predictably, George Chacharis was already penciled in as the next U.S. Ambassador to Greece.

With Chacharis's grand-jury appearance pending, Goldberg found himself badgered by calls from Jack Miller, the head of the Criminal Division, Silberling's boss. Ease up on Chacharis. But when Chacharis did keep his appointment in the grand-jury chambers, Goldberg laid it on him. The evidence against the mayor was overwhelming, Goldberg assured Chacharis from the shadows, and, unless he confessed, "a ten-ton truck bearing the markings 'Federal Government'" would be bearing down on the culpable politician. Goldberg welcomed his cooperation, but "If you lie, it will be as if you placed yourself in the path of this oncoming truck. . . ."

Within days Goldberg received another call from Kennedy. By now Ray Madden, a power from Indiana on the House Rules Committee, was threatening to block passage of the Kennedy farm bill if Goldberg didn't drop the charges.

Robert Kennedy was very explicit. "I want you to show the mayor," he told Goldberg, "the list of witnesses and all the evidence."

"Well," Goldberg said, "I can't do that."

"Well," Kennedy said, "I'm directing you to do that."

"Well," Goldberg said, "I just won't be able to do that."

"And he put his hand on the phone," Goldberg recalls, "and I could hear him saying to that archcriminal: 'George, you won't be able to see the exhibits.' You know, like a child. Because Robert Kennedy was more than just a prosecutor. He was a politician."

In tears, Chacharis now protested that Goldberg was about to lock him up before the grand jury could convene, that Goldberg had in fact threatened to run him over with a truck. Kennedy instructed Goldberg to return to Washington at once. A contingent from the local FBI was dispatched to drive

Goldberg to O'Hare outside Chicago, but "Their argumentativeness was so horrendous," Goldberg maintains, "that I said, 'I wonder who owns this town.'" That tore it; the agents stopped the car.

Goldberg's epiphany was nothing new: that FBI professionals from top to bottom were demonstrably more interested in buttering up the local power structure than collaborating with "reformers." The Bureau existed primarily to prop the system up, not to purify it. It would continue to be up to elements of the Department of the Treasury—the IRS; Alcohol, Tobacco and Firearms; Harry Anslinger's Narcotics door busters—to back up honest district attorneys and send away hoodlums.

Goldberg reappeared in Washington beneath a tidal wave of Indiana support. MAYOR'S INCOME TO BE INCLUDED IN INVESTIGATION, ran one headline, while another asserted BOB KENNEDY KEY MAN IN FATE OF BIGSHOT POLITICIANS IN GARY. A billboard went up that read: GOLDBERG, LEAD ME TO YOUR TAKER. As Kennedy's Justice Department brain trust assembled to hash out what exactly to do about their splashy, perverse shit-stirrer, a shipment of one hundred coconut shells arrived at the Department from Gary with HELP carved into every one, a JFK memory aid.

With Goldberg and his documentation about to appear, Chacharis rethought his position. He couldn't help acknowledging that perhaps he *had* taken a certain amount over the years, but "some of that money was for Jack." He might even have exaggerated what Goldberg said. John Seigenthaler was in the room when Bobby told Chacharis that he would have to pay the price for having broken the law, and Seigenthaler never forgot the way Chacharis laid his head down on Bobby's desk and wept. Within minutes, Bob had Secretary of Labor Arthur Goldberg hotfooting it to the White House to scotch Chacharis's ambassadorship.

Goldberg was a hero in Gary, but around the Justice Department the pros were scuttling for cover. His bosses let Jay present his indictments, and virtually every allegation he made held up and produced a guilty verdict. Chacharis and his cohorts went to jail. Despite Silberling's objection, Treasury lawyers were sent in to try the cases. Back at the Department, Bobby Kennedy toyed with the notion of sending Goldberg along to Las Vegas, but Kennedy decided that "I think you'd run into trouble with Frank Sinatra."

"That was to me an amazing commentary on the power of a hoodlum," as Goldberg construed it. He was under bombardment. "You've got to *listen* to what the attorney general says," Henry Petersen told him. "How would you feel if someone was locking up *your* friends?" Jack Miller asked him when Goldberg complained about being underappreciated by the boss.

Finally Bobby himself remarked to Jay, in that arctic tonality the Kennedys reserved for tight corners, "You know, my brother said to me that if we don't stop locking up Democrats he's going to have to put me on the Supreme Court. You know, to get rid of me—"

It wasn't only Goldberg. By 1962, with all those hundreds and hundreds and hundreds of auditors and tax examiners and narcs and special agents out there churning up the hustings, ugly situations were hitting the papers. Labor unions and big-city machines constituted the nervous system of the Democratic Party, they supplied the troops. In 1958, both Robert Kennedy and his brother had stepped in when the Rackets Committee conservatives, Senators Goldwater, Curtis, and Mundt, attempted to rough up Richard Gosser, the Toledo honcho for the United Automobile Workers and one of Walter Reuther's most productive vice presidents. In *The Enemy Within*, Kennedy inferred that Gosser's worst offense had been to maintain, many years earlier, "an interest in a hardware store that sold goods to the union." During the McClellan hearings, Robert Kennedy had jumped to the defense of a UAW official who took the Fifth Amendment rather than admit to kickbacks to Gosser. Kennedy—who had repeatedly assaulted witnesses who pled the Fifth as cowardly, and brought down upon himself the condemnation of civil libertarians—now justified his tactics by characterizing the Fifth Amendment as "an important safeguard written into the Bill of Rights."

As attorney general, after 1961 reality rolled back over Bobby. Throughout John Kennedy's presidential run, Richard Gosser had steamed together northeastern Ohio for the Democrats. His cadre of twelve thousand labor organizers clinched the local Democratic victory. Once convicted of armed robbery, he remained a grifter. Aware that the IRS had started to audit his affairs, Gosser planted a secretary in the Toledo offices of the Treasury Department.

The investigation highlighted Gosser's collaboration with the flourishing Mob-controlled "policy" runners around the auto plants. The FBI moved in. What could gratify Hoover more than taking down a key lieutenant of pink-hued Walter Reuther? No less than thirty-five agents descended upon Toledo. They caught the secretary passing documents dusted with fluorescent powder, along with an assortment of wiseguys that extended all the way to the Licavoli mob in Detroit. When it was over, Silberling's lead attorney Jake Tanzer concluded, "We'd essentially destroyed the Democratic organization in that area."

* * *

Robert Kennedy greeted each of these spoiling operations with nervous stoicism. "Great. But can't you guys come up with a steel company president once in a while?" he joked as the Gosser case broke. Overbooked, Kennedy often found out about the Organized Crime Section's latest gesture of political suicide during late-afternoon updates with Silberling's rampant attorneys. While two black orderlies in livery handed coffee around, and Brumus snoozed loudly, the lawyers would brainstorm whatever was new and diverting. Bobby and Whizzer White were fond of passing the football back and forth. Nobody brought up political repercussions with the immaculate Whizzer present.

Certain of the cases woke everybody up better than the coffee did. One centered on George Ratterman, a strapping football star at Notre Dame who quarterbacked for the Cleveland Browns and returned to Newport, Kentucky, to build a following as an investment adviser and sportscaster. Immediately across the Ohio River from god-fearing Cincinnati, Newport had established itself as a sinkhole of "brothels, saloons, and bust-out gambling joints" at least since the Civil War. Of recent decades, it had emerged as a clearinghouse for the national betting syndicates, important to the system of horse parlors and bookmaking wire lines devised by Meyer Lansky.

A talky, hands-on Catholic with eight children, Ratterman volunteered as an independent in the race for sheriff, pledged to extinguish vice. In mid-April 1961, the startling story broke on the wires that three of Newport's finest had been summoned to an upstairs room in the venerable Glenn Hotel to discover Ratterman naked and incoherent on a hotel bed with an exotic dancer billed as "April Flowers." A local photographer had happened by and emerged with pictures of the entire tableau.

April was naked, too. According to her original story, the hotel manager, Tito Carinci, had tipped her off that there was a party upstairs. Interviewed by one of Silberling's hot dogs, Bill Lynch, April explained that, having just finished her turn on the runway, she was "kind of hot," and needed to undress.

Lynch pointed out that all she had on when she made her entrance was "these two sequined pasties on your breasts and this tiny sequin-studded g-string."

"Well, Mr. Lynch," April explained earnestly, "you have no idea how itchy those sequins can get to be."

All this was news to Ratterman. He'd knocked back eleven highballs, if memory served, with Carinci, a buddy from his football-playing days, and was finally persuaded to cross the river and have a meal in Carinci's suite at the Glenn. Everything after that got blurry, and subsequent blood tests revealed that Ratterman had absorbed a serious dose of chloral hydrate, a Mickey Finn.

The scandal was a set-up, obviously, and within hours the national press arrived. At trial it became evident that lots of the hanky-panky around the event was being orchestrated by the local top-forty Mafia functionary Frank "Screw" Andrews, née Andriola. With the exception of the Lexington-based FBI agent Frank Staab, according to the primary chronicler of the Ratterman story, Justice Department attorney Ronald Goldfarb, "The local FBI agents not only were not helpful, but some were also reluctant to do what we asked of them. I learned the facts of life: The agents' bread and butter were stolen-car cases, and the local police helped make their jobs easy. Because this was how FBI agents accumulated their case statistics, they weren't happy about our going after their sources."

The foot soldiers, as usual, were supplied by the IRS. There was a huge "commando-like" raid on a gigantic betting parlor in the outlying Sportsmen's Club. April Flowers recanted, and Goldfarb successfully prosecuted Screw Andrews and seven other numbers operators and sent them away for extended stretches. Newport as a gambling center was largely closed down. Ratterman got in as sheriff. The Glenn Hotel burned to the ground, undoubtedly a "friction fire," Ron Goldfarb decided, "which occurs when you rub the mortgage against the insurance policy."

The price this string of prosecutions carried was clear to Robert Kennedy, never allowed to forget that his brother would come up for reelection in 1964. Yet one by one he went along with most of them, if bitterly at times. There was a medieval element in Robert Kennedy's makeup, much satisfaction from looking down a long line of politicians burning at the cross.

But as the administration settled in, Kennedy's dream of pulling talent together from across the bureaucracy to converge on organized crime was producing a compounding interdepartmental dissonance. As the premier exponent of the "strike force" concept, Edwyn Silberling had remained Robert Kennedy's point man throughout the early, gung-ho months. Silberling simmered to find his counterparts around the law-enforcement community pulling against him, resisting encroachments on their turf. His attempt to exploit the FBI in his dynamite-laden probe of the Keogh brothers had resulted in "a holdup of four to six weeks and no investigation by the Bureau," Silberling couldn't help wailing afterward.

Hoover himself was unabashedly antagonistic, and regarded Silberling as an unsophisticated interloper, the stooge in Robert Kennedy's plot to throw together a kind of proxy FBI. Lou Oberdorfer resented Silberling's bid to "take the criminal tax prosecutors away from the Tax Division on the theory that tax cases were just one more criminal case and they should be used to punish criminals." Even Kennedy enthusiast Ramsey Clark brooded over the ethics of identifying an evildoer, then ransacking his life in the hope of stumbling on grounds to incriminate.

A number of Silberling's successes point up a tendency to let his lawyers career out there a lot wider than the law allowed, to experiment with harassment. Silberling bagged Louis Gallo for false statements on a VA loan, admitting later that "The U.S. Attorney told me they'd be laughed out of town on a horse shit charge like that," except that Gallo pleaded guilty. When Chicago goombah Moses Joseph neglected to list two convictions on an FCC application, Silberling's sharpshooters dropped him on a perjury proceeding. Soon after investigators for the Park and Wildlife Service found 563 mourning doves, 539 over the limit, in the freezer of Outfit underboss Joseph Aiuppa, Silberling jumped on the case and eked out a conviction under the Migratory Bird Act. The complaint was enlarged to cover an ornithological massacre of 1,400 birds perpetrated by Aiuppa's soldiers in Kansas, prompting an exhilarated Robert Kennedy to fly west to savor the sentencing. Aiuppa emerged with his nickname, "Joey Doves," although the conviction would be overturned eventually on the basis of illegal search and seizure.

Silberling's hope of rounding up the Five Families at the top of the Greater New York Mob dissipated quickly in the face of competing claims by the U.S. Attorney for the Southern District, Robert Morgenthau. A close-mouthed Navy veteran with expressionless eyes and the bearing instilled by three generations of prominence in public life, Morgenthau remained immovable when it came to fending off IRS examiners as well as Silberling's eager lawyers. Methodically, Morgenthau ground up a wide assortment of white-collar criminals along with heretofore-untouchable flunkies the Mob was grooming to supervise its widening gambling commitments.

Until the Nixon administration pushed him out, Morgenthau prosecuted successfully almost half of the organized-crime cases credited to the Justice Department during the nineteen-sixties. Tracking Meyer Lansky, whose syndicate by then was—according to Lansky himself—"bigger than General Motors," Morgenthau's auditors were able to establish that the Exchange and Investment Bank of Switzerland had been chartered primarily to launder money for the syndicate and that characters who consistently bobbed up on the wrong side of the stock-registration and bankruptcy laws or patrolled crap tables from Las Vegas to the Grand Bahamas for Lansky—Max Orovitz, Ben Sigelbaum, Ed Levinson—were meeting Cosa Nostra payrolls.

In time, Morgenthau even managed to indict Mike McLaney, the high-stakes New-Orleans-born golf hustler who gambled his future alongside the Lansky interests in the Hotel Nacional in Havana. Unsettling enough—the ricochets were getting harder to dodge every month—McLaney remained very tight with Joseph P. Kennedy.

A pending indictment of officials in the Electrical Workers Union in Puerto Rico brought James Carey, the president of the union and quite a prominent figure in the Democratic Party pantheon, to the White House to upbraid both Kennedy brothers for "vindictive prosecutorial tactics." He was boiling over with "shock and resentment," as he promptly informed the press. The indictments came down nevertheless.

As late as the autumn of 1963, at the suggestion of the attorney general, the Section began to "look into public officials" in Philadelphia, "with the idea of tax investigations." Before long, Congressman William Green, another pal of Joe's and a wheelhorse in the Party, called Bobby directly to remind him that "It's October and you have an election coming, and I hear you're looking into tax returns—my tax return." Bobby told his probers to hold off until December.

John Kennedy was only too aware of what exactly drove his brother. He liked to joke that Bobby was a cop at heart, and some day when nobody else turned up he'd slap the cuffs on Rose. The runt of the litter was claiming his own. Early in the administration, when Robert Kennedy told his brother that appointing Joe Kennedy's durable stoolie, Frank Morrissey, to the federal bench was out of the question, the president looked up. "What shall I tell Dad?"

"Tell him he's not the President," Robert Kennedy said.

Nevertheless, as totems across the party fell, the question did arise as to how incorruptible is too incorruptible. Everybody knew that a lot of the fur was flying because of the single-mindedness of Edwyn Silberling. At least as bad, Silberling, accustomed in New York to running his own shop, remained in substantive denial of the fact that he was subordinate to Miller. He refused to attend Division meetings. "I had little or no regard for Jack Miller's capacity,"

Silberling confessed afterward. "I felt he was inexperienced, not knowledgeable in the field of prosecution." Accordingly, "in fact, I never did seek to obtain prior approval from him for any prosecution that was mounted, or proposed prosecution, which left us a fairly vulnerable target for Hoover and the FBI."

For his part, Miller could not miss "a semi-reluctance on the part of some of the lawyers in the Organized Crime Section to talk frankly and candidly with me." One aspiring prosecutor in the Section, Mike Fawer, calls up his impression that "Ed Silberling didn't know how to surprise people, he seemed to get into turf struggles with people. Miller was a tough son of a bitch, a fast study, and in the end he kicked the shit out of Ed."

What success Silberling had required keeping some distance from most of the regional United States attorneys, "who were there on a patronage basis," and did not "want to overstep the bounds if it means that it's going to antagonize the people who have been responsible for their appointments"— in other words, the local power structure. The FBI was playing Hoover's usual double game, sanitizing whatever documents Silberling's staff saw and refusing strike-force attorneys access to FBI interrogations.

Hoover personally was scrutinizing every move they made, in part by bugging their conference rooms and elevators and partly in the form of Courtney Evans, Hoover's liaison with RFK. "[I]f there was a conference taking place among Courtney Evans, Jack Miller and myself, I would have the feeling that here was Miller and myself," Silberling later explained, "who should have been on the same side of the fence because here we are defending the Department with the toughest nut it had to work with, the FBI, and it wasn't that way at all. It was Miller and I opposed, and then Evans picking and choosing, and inevitably and consistently picking Miller's position."

So Silberling found himself in charge of an unacknowledged guerrilla operation inside the Criminal Division, able to enlist fierce loyalty among most of his younger attorneys, while the older lawyers, many holdovers from the Eisenhower and Truman era, preferred Miller's play-it-safe approach. The key to getting something under way, plainly, was to pick up on a situation like the *Wall Street Journal*'s leak that pointed at Vincent Keogh, or Oral Cole's suspicions about "Cha Cha Chacharis," or Ratterman in the altogether, and get the Section to jump on its own. The next round of publicity made unavoidable a federal grand jury.

As political losses mounted, even Robert Kennedy had to admit that this situation was insupportable. Courtney Evans, Hoover's envoy, undoubtedly reflected the Director's distaste for peeling away working arrangements of long standing around the country in return for this week's headlines. "I guess

I was as much a part of the campaign to get rid of Silberling as anybody," Evans will now concede. "He was out of his depth. I didn't think he had any concept of what organized crime was, the machinations they went through to buy off public officials." Jack Miller, Evans's future law partner, was running out of patience, and Nick Katzenbach was openly critical.

"Silberling was a terrible problem," Katzenbach is frank to concede. "He wanted to go after people in a half-baked way, bring cases that weren't ready to be brought, use wiretaps all over the place. Jack Miller wasn't prepared to go anything like as far as Silberling." In the end—characteristically—Bob Kennedy called Silberling in and took his office away without exactly firing him. William Hundley, by now Kennedy's clean-up hitter, was eased back into his old job.

The faithful Jay Goldberg bewails Silberling's demise. "They moved him from an office the size of Yankee Stadium to a stall. And I would look out the window and I could see that he was shunned—nobody would walk with him. The Department of Justice, like all of Washington—it's founded on backbiting, it's horrible to survive. When you've been deposed nobody walks with you, you're alone in the room, you're doing crossword puzzles, and you have no work. He was very distraught."

Goldberg departed soon afterward. He would remember Kennedy as a "wiry, attractive sort of person," but in the end "a politician, an imposter [*sic*]." Political investigations went on, if now with much more sensitivity to repercussions. The regime was maturing.

The Little Man

f **Robert Kennedy glanced over** his shoulder each time his ferrets dug anywhere near politics, nothing was supposed to inhibit him when one of the Mob's senior gonzos ventured into range. The example that keeps coming up is Carlos Marcello, the squat, burly Creole-Sicilian from New Orleans who had stiffed Kennedy during the Rackets Committee hearings. A Lansky protégé since the thirties, Marcello's primitive swampland manners belied the cunning that had permitted him to build a two-billion-dollar empire in gambling, drugs, and agricultural commodities. He was without challenge the wealthiest and best entrenched of all the senior Cosa Nostra Commission members, the likeliest strike-force target.

That needs a second look, too. Marcello himself tipped off a journalist for *Newsday* that Robert Kennedy had dropped into the Crescent City early in the 1960 primary season in search of a political handout. Politely, Marcello told Bobby no: His allegiance for many years had been to Lyndon Johnson, whose career Marcello helped underwrite by way of his organization's bagman in Texas, John Halfen, in return for help beating back any legislation relating to slot machines and wire-line gambling.

Marcello showed up at the Democratic Convention in Los Angeles that year, and Bobby reportedly sought him out and implored him to use his influence with the Louisiana delegation to help assure a first-ballot victory for his brother. Marcello turned him down again. Meanwhile, the bantam don

contributed $500,000 to Richard Nixon. JFK won, narrowly, on the first bal-
lot, and Bobby wasn't about to forget that Marcello had humiliated him twice.

Bobby wasted no time in making his unhappiness felt. Shortly after the
inauguration, Marcello got word that a major tax case against him was under
way and he would again face deportation proceedings—a lifelong problem
for Marcello, who had been born in Tunis and neglected to undergo naturalization. By April the first bill from the IRS had arrived—federal tax liens
totaling $835,396. A *New Orleans States-Item* news story of December 28,
1960, quoted Bobby Kennedy as stating that he "would expedite the deportation proceedings pending against Marcello after Kennedy takes office. . . ."
An FBI surveillance tape recorded a Mob exchange during which a major
capo, Angelo Bruno, remarked that Marcello had contacted Sam Giancana in
Chicago and Santo Trafficante in Tampa urging them to send in Frank
Sinatra, known to be friendly with "the President's father."

Nothing helped. Scarcely weeks in office, Robert Kennedy now started to
pressure various Division leaders around the Department to take some
action in the Marcello case. Hoover remained intractable. After advising
Kennedy to leave Marcello alone, the Director sent over a much-redacted file
on Marcello which the Justice Department lawyers concluded was pretty
largely useless.

There was some indication of Hoover's having directed the New Orleans
agent assigned to Marcello, Regis Kennedy, authorizing the use of "unusual
investigative techniques" and "a microphone surveillance"—a bug. But none
of the subsequent FBI memoranda show signs of anything productive;
beyond following the Mafia kingpin around in unmarked cars and taking
note of the occasional nooner with his beautician mistress, Lucille, very
little of any real pertinence in court came through. Regis Kennedy would
continue to maintain that Marcello was simply a very successful "tomato
salesman," and suspicions gathered that Regis—like virtually everybody else
within reach of the open-handed Marcello—was probably on the pad.

Ed Silberling's lawyer on the case, John Diuguid, quickly established that
Marcello had already taken steps—reportedly ten thousand dollars each to
key members of the Parliament in Rome—to avoid being deported to Italy,
the traditional dumping ground for fading American gangsters. One of
Marcello's flunkies during the later fifties was a perennial jailbird with very
fluttery nerves, Carl Irving Noll. Marcello had dispatched Noll to Guatemala,
already a stopover on Marcello's drug-delivery itinerary, with $25,000 to
locate a village with a public ledger with blank space enough on the day of
Marcello's birth to doctor in the specifics of Carlos's origins. Conducted to

San Jose Pinula by a local government attorney and heroin mule, Antonio Valaderes, the pair did indeed arrange to bribe a clerk to scribble in Marcello's original name, Calogero Minacore, after which Noll flew a photostat of his ersatz birth certificate North to the worried don.

As 1961 opened, Noll was doing time at the penitentiary in Lewisburg, Pennsylvania. Pining for an early release, Noll revealed to prison officials that he had helped manufacture Carlos Marcello's fake birth certificate. Word of Noll's revelation reached the Immigration and Naturalization Service, which copied it to both the Justice lawyers and the FBI.

Since "The FBI had refused—all the way up to Hoover—to pursue leads about these activities in Guatemala," Ron Goldfarb later wrote, "Silberling said, 'OK, if they won't do it, we'll do it.'" He sent John Diuguid to Guatemala to round up witnesses able to testify that Marcello had falsified his documents.

Diuguid would compare those days to an episode in a James Bond fantasy. Conducted from point to point in a long black embassy sedan, Diuguid was trailed constantly by unidentified operatives in equally long black automobiles. His room was tossed and searched. A few steps behind him all through his visit was David Ferrie, the multifaceted ex-Eastern Airlines pilot who suffered from alopecia, Marcello's sinister odd-jobs man in the outlandish brick-red wig and paste-on mohair eyebrows who haunted Oliver Stone's *JFK*.

Diuguid pinned down a witness who admitted that he'd forged the certificate, and an FBI chemist took a scraping of the yellow ink of the entry and pronounced it inauthentic. Now Kennedy had something.

Able at last to demonstrate beyond a doubt that Carlos Marcello had no claim whatsoever to repatriation in Guatemala, Robert Kennedy decided to misrepresent this forgery as valid and ship the Mafia boss to his bogus birthplace at once. The opera-bouffe sequence which was to follow is unique in the annals of the federal bureaucracy, an episode even Goldfarb, by now a Kennedy loyalist, would label as a "grossly illegal deportation." Others not so finicky referred to it as a kidnapping.

The job of snatching this dangerously well-connected little bull of a mobster off the street and shipping him to the tropics was not something many in the bureaucracy were in a hurry to embrace. In early March, Kennedy evidently made it plain to General Joseph Swing, the head of the Immigration and Naturalization Service, that he was up for this fatigue duty. Like any apprehensive bureaucrat, Swing craved company and reached out to Hoover, contacting FBI headquarters and indicating that he "wanted some help from the Director and the Director's personal advice." "It is possible," reads the FBI memo, "that General Swing is under pressure from the AG to deport Marcello and is seeking the Director's advice as to how this could be accomplished."

Typically, Hoover ducked a meeting with Swing and passed him through to Courtney Evans. Memoing back, Evans indicated that arrangements were under way to dump Marcello off in Guatamala, and soon, to forestall Marcello's lawyers. Swing expected the FBI to help out by alerting him to whatever it knew of Marcello's "current activities" and "daily movements. . . ." Swing's intention was to grab Marcello without warning when he showed up for his quarterly immigration check-in on April 4, a procedure in clear violation of a Supreme Court ruling mandating that a seventy-two-hour notice be given any alien subject to deportation. Furthermore, everyone involved was well aware that the entry permit for Marcello the Justice Department had squeezed out of the Guatemalan government was based on fraudulent documents. Perhaps it is not that surprising that Hoover was meticulous about distancing himself.

The relocation of Marcello came off with brutal efficiency. When the unsuspecting gangster showed up at the INS offices in the New Orleans Masonic Temple Building, he was abruptly informed of his pending deportation and handcuffed and hustled to the Moisant International Airport in a three-car convoy, sirens blaring, and loaded at once onto an empty Border Patrol passenger aircraft waiting on the tarmac, engines already roaring. "You would have thought it was the President going in instead of me going out," Carlos attempted.

No contact was permitted with his deportation lawyer, Jack Wasserman, no change of clothes or money, no toothbrush, no telephoning his wife. There was no food available to him on the plane throughout the 1,200-mile flight. In Guatemala City, his plane was met at the military airport by a Colonel Battery, of the local constabulary; since there were no other arrangements in place for this titan of organized crime, he wound up going home with Colonel Battery's secretary, Miss Jinks, who spoke English and indicated to Marcello that he might as well sleep on the other half of the king-sized bed in her apartment. "I didn't have no pajamas," Marcello would recollect. "I was ashamed. But she turned out the light and turned her back to me."

Meanwhile, Attorney General Robert Kennedy announced that Marcello had been deported "in strict accordance with the law," a statement Ed Silberling pronounced dubious at the time in a letter to Jack Miller. Kennedy himself, as he informed the press, was "very happy Carlos Marcello is no longer with us."

In darkest Guatemala, Marcello's trials were just beginning. At first, Marcello contrived to bring several of his family members down from the United States and set up in considerable style in the Biltmore Hotel in Guatemala City and even started holding conferences with local commercial types in the hospitality, shrimping, and slot-machine trades, just in case. But the important paper in town, *El Imparcial*, began to run editorials emphasizing how bogus Marcello's claim to citizenship was; President Miguel Fuentes promptly expelled Carlos.

Marcello's family returned to Louisiana, and he and his lifelong friend, the attorney Mike Maroun, started toward San Salvador in a battered station wagon. They soon ran into marauding soldiers, abandoned the station wagon, and after a six-hour ride on a rickety bus through the ragged, desolate mountain country between El Salvador and Honduras these two pudgy, aging men in silk Shantung suits were reduced to wandering, the $3,000 they had left between them stuffed into their crumbling alligator shoes, starving and increasingly desperate to come upon some vestige of civilization. Fearful that two Indian boys they picked up to guide them were about to murder them with their machetes, Maroun and Marcello plunged down a thorn-ridden ravine, where Marcello tumbled through the boulders and bayonet grass with their guides in hot pursuit and broke three ribs. "If I don't make it, Mike," Marcello instructed Maroun, "tell my brothers when you get back, about what dat kid Bobby done to us. Tell 'em to do what dey have to do." It amounted to a blood oath.

But the two kept going and, after a long, agonizing haul down the Honduras side of the divide, sighted a provincial airport where they were able to hire a flight to the capital, Tegucigalpa. There, Marcello later insisted, he procured a forged entry permit and a ticket to Miami and reentered the United States on May 28.

There is compelling evidence, compiled by Robert Blakey while leading the investigation for the House Select Committee on Assassinations, that Marcello was actually reinserted into the United States aboard a Dominican Republic Air Force jet. By late May, Marcello's friends were marshalling. Alongside his perennial colleague Santo Trafficante of Tampa, Marcello had been a large factor for decades in the narcotics traffic throughout the Caribbean. A personal favorite since the thirties of the all-seeing Meyer Lansky, Carlos reportedly controlled a third of the drug franchise in Cuba. The compliant Dominican dictator Rafael Trujillo had been the recipient of payoffs from the Marcello organization all along, and the key intermediary between the two was frequently I. Irving Davidson, the elusive, cosmopolitan Washington public relations specialist for both Marcello and Trujillo. Davidson lived around the corner from, and socialized constantly with, J. Edgar Hoover, and like Marcello was a regular guest at El Charro, Clint Murchison's exclusive California hideaway.

An inveterate heavy borrower, Murchison had been financing his far-flung oil-leasing gambles with cash from the Vito Genovese crime syndicate and now was moving on to the Las Vegas casino owners and Jimmy Hoffa. Hoover himself had promoted his one-time administrative assistant, Thomas Webb, onto Murchison's payroll, where he became "the fixer for the Murchisons, the bagman," as Bobby Baker later put it. Davidson and Hoover usually dropped by the get-togethers before the Redskin games at Tom Webb's place.

Davidson stuck a hand in commercially every once in a while. While he would deny having been a partner with Jimmy Hoffa in a gunrunning side-line to Castro before the Communist takeover, Davidson was free to admit that "I sold a tremendous amount of tanks and whatnot to Batista in 1959." Davidson had a feel for dictators.

As soon as word got around that Marcello was gone, Davidson dealt himself a hand. He contacted the FBI with information that Carlos's broth-ers had chartered a plane headed for Guatemala to pick him up. By then, it was way too late for that. Davidson seems to have rechecked his Rolodex, and from then on it is not too hard to imagine how a phone call or two from Washington to Santo Domingo led to a black pickup outside Tegucigalpa.

Furthermore, a June 16, 1961, FBI report maintains that "a high-ranking U.S. government official may have intervened with the Dominican Republic on Marcello's behalf," noting that "Senator Russell Long of Louisiana, who had received financial aid from Marcello, had been very much concerned with the Marcello deportation case and was sponsoring a Louisiana official for a key INS position from which assistance to Marcello could be rendered."

It appears that Marcello called in his chits in the nick of time. Weeks after Marcello's abduction, the Bay of Pigs exploded under the untested administration. Jack Kennedy had not done well. Robert Kennedy was con-verted overnight to his brother's eyes and whip all across the military/intel-ligence complex. At virtually the same moment that Marcello's jet was pur-portedly headed north toward Miami, the Dominican dictator Rafael Trujillo was gunned down. In his definitive biography of Marcello, John H. Davis notes, parenthetically: "(In 1975, the Senate Intelligence Committee discovered that the CIA had been plotting the assassination of Trujillo for months with the blessing of Robert Kennedy, who knew that the elimination of Trujillo was a necessary move in his war against organized crime.)" Across the Caribbean, from the Mob's standpoint, key enablers were blinking out. The underworld was beginning to understand what it had on its hands.

Whatever else came over the transom, Kennedy's priorities weren't changing. "My first love is Jimmy Hoffa," Bob admitted freely enough, and Hoffa felt the heat. Kennedy intended to incarcerate Hoffa, as Jimmy's devoted wireman Bernard Spindel put it, "whether it be for spitting on the sidewalk or hanging a picture crooked." Attempting to dismiss Kennedy as a "parasite" and a "spoiled kid," the cagey Teamster president struggled for the psychological upper hand by telling one journalist "If this kid don't get away from this, he'll crack up. I talk to people who go to parties with him, to his home, and they say that he's got one topic of conversation. Hoffa. He's got to flip." The story went around that, spotting the lights on in Hoffa's suite in the Teamster Headquarters on his way home, Kennedy returned to the Justice Department to slave through the evening. When Jimmy Hoffa heard about that, he started leaving the lights burning all night.

No doubt a key reason Kennedy brought in Jack Miller to head the Criminal Division was his familiarity, as lawyer for the recently defunct court-appointed Teamster Board of Monitors, with most of the gangland hangers-on as well as the shell game Hoffa was conducting with the books of the Teamsters' Central and Western Pension Fund. Yet as a corporation attorney with almost no involvement with the criminal side, Miller would leave ensnaring the likes of Jimmy Hoffa to Bobby.

To carry this fight into the field, Kennedy rehired as a "confidential assistant" his senior Rackets Committee investigator, thirty-five-year-old Walter Sheridan. An exceedingly dogged, deceptively soft-spoken Fordham graduate, Sheridan was a wartime submariner with four years in the FBI and a stint in NSA Counterintelligence. "His almost angelic appearance hides a core of toughness," Kennedy had written. Sheridan might be depended on to bring to bear everything the law allowed and—like Hoffa—whatever else the situation required. Bystanders who knew them both have in fact compared them—stocky types in monotone suits straight off the rack at Sears, up from the bricks, impatiently shouldering aside obstacles. Sheridan did not scruple to inform a potential witness that he might get the witness's wife tucked away in jail if he didn't open up, but he could also display, as one of his trial attorneys put it later, "a wonderful, persuasive ability to get you on the team, to give you the sense that you were involved in a righteous crusade."

Sheridan, no lawyer, headed a kind of informal subunit within the organized crime section known as the "Get-Hoffa Squad." Culls from all over the Department along with promising litigators from the staffs of regional U.S. Attorneys and the D.C. legal establishment, the Squad was augmented quickly to twenty-plus lawyers, Sheridan's "Terrible Twenty." "It burned my ass," Ed Silberling later conceded. "I had to justify my budget requests by work produced, but half of the jobs were Hoffa Squad jobs. They used up a lot of the top grades, which interfered with my hiring and, besides, I didn't have control over them."

Among Silberling and his own team of largely Manhattan-bred prosecutors, the feeling was general that the Hoffa Squad was embarked on to a kind of vigilante free-for-all, as likely to result in years of split juries and reversals on appeal as anything resembling justice. Most of Sheridan's cadre was knock-down, drag-out Catholics, with Nathan Lewin on hand as the "intellectual-in-residence." The idea was to balance off Hoffa and his top hoods, predictably fronted by an army of crack criminal attorneys, with Kennedy's army, his gumshoes and electronic experts and tough courtroom virtuosos.

Five years of spadework by the Rackets Committee had produced rooms full of files, chockablock with depositions and formal complaints and local court transcripts. What it had not produced was convictions. Two trials of Hoffa in 1958 for having hired his electronic wizard Bernard Spindel to tap the wires of other Teamsters he suspected of disaffection (the Justice Department's case was in good part dependent on the government's own wiretaps) resulted in a hung jury and a not-guilty verdict. The alleged conspirators were proven to be out of town when the plotting supposedly occurred; Bobby blamed the sloppy preparation of Justice Department attorneys and illegal FBI procedure. A month after the November elections in 1960, lame-duck Attorney General William Rogers indicted Hoffa and two associates on twelve counts of mail fraud consequent to Hoffa's involvement with a huge land promotion in Titusville, Florida, Sun Valley, not far out of Orlando. To secure a $395,000 loan by a local bank to underwrite the scheme, $400,000 from the Teamster Central States Pension Fund had been put on deposit in the bank at no interest.

One of Hoffa's two associates in this scheme, Henry Lower, was an escaped convict and narcotics dealer alleged to maintain productive relations with the Tampa Mafia chieftain Santo Trafficante. The initial Sun Valley subdivision had occurred in 1954, funded by Hoffa's local, and involved a tract big enough to encompass eight thousand lots. The $395,000 follow-up loan was to begin to provide, belatedly, long after nearly two thousand lots had been sold, paved roads and a rudimentary water hookup. There was no sewer or water to any of the thousands of lots peddled to gullible Teamster members. Hoffa and his up-from-the-ranks Detroit sidekick, Bert Brennan, ultimately vice president of the Michigan Conference, retained a hidden option to buy up 45 percent of the tract at the token 1954 price.

That William Rogers, during the terminal weeks of the Eisenhower administration, would land an indictment on Hoffa after the Teamsters had slipped Nixon a reported million dollars in campaign funds—this hit Jimmy hard. Hoffa blasted his go-between to Nixon, Irving Davidson protégé Allan Oakley Hunter, outraged about the "big double-cross" by the outgoing vice president, who in fact eventually pulled enough strings to quash the indictment. Robert Kennedy's appointment as attorney general had already been announced by then, and Hoffa was jittery.

A born field general, Kennedy deployed his shock troops. Shortly after the change of administration, some fifteen grand juries had been convened around the country to sift through Teamster affairs. By early July 1961, while Hoffa contrived to get himself elected president of the Teamsters during a stupefying blowout at the Deauville at Miami Beach, cases were taking shape against senior mob personalities only Jimmy Hoffa would have the cojones to invite into union office. Hoffa himself was reinflating, fast: shortly before the convention, the mandate for the Teamster Board of Monitors had been allowed to lapse, and, a week after the convention, a federal judge ruled that the Sun Valley grand jury had not been empaneled properly and dismissed the indictment.

Hoffa's freshly elected board of officers was not so lucky. As the decade unfolded, his barely christened international vice president, Anthony Provenzano ("Tony Pro"), whose overnight rise in the trade-union movement paralleled his elevation to caporegime in the Genovese flowering of the Cosa Nostra, was on his way to seven years for extorting payoffs from New Jersey truckers. William ("Big Bill") Presser, a Teamster trustee and reputed "gunrunning buddy" of Hoffa's during those rumored side trips to Cuba, caught a Contempt-of-Congress conviction. Barney Baker, Hoffa's notorious 380-pound Central States "organizer"—read enforcer—would look at a long stretch in the penitentiary for shaking down a Pittsburgh newspaper publisher. Johnny Dio (née Dioguardi), a senior soldier in the Luchese family and Hoffa's top organizer of paper locals around New York, was indicted for hiring the thug who, apparently at Hoffa's bidding, threw acid in the face of labor columnist Victor Riesel and blinded him. Johnny Dio was tucked away in the end for stock fraud.

Puerto Rican muscleman Frank Chavez went down, and Hoffa's secretary-treasurer in Detroit, Frank Collins, and even the unwary telephone operator in a favorite Teamster haunt, Mrs. Sally Hucks, for destroying subpoenaed telephone records. It was an artillery barrage.

Kennedy's Criminal Division push overlapped a campaign by the Narcotics Bureau that bagged Vito Genovese himself, Carmine Gallante of the Bonanno gang, and top mobsters in Gambino's group. The Corsican Connection was eroded. Frank Hogan's tough prosecutors put the lot away.

Kennedy's first attempt as attorney general to pin Hoffa's wings back in court played out in Nashville, Tennessee, starting on November 22, 1962, at the height of the missile crisis. The government's complaint went back to 1948, when the Commercial Carriers Corporation, a Cadillac haul-away trucker around the Middle West and into the border states, found itself struck by the Teamsters. Commercial Carriers arranged to solve its labor problems by leasing some of its equipment from a new company it helped create called Test Fleet, Inc. With an initial payment of $4,000, Hoffa's wife Josephine and the wife of Hoffa crony Bert Brennan, then head of Detroit local 337, under their maiden names, invested in the dummy corporation and made a net profit of $155,092 in eight years. By 1962 the take approached a million dollars. Government lawyers had long regarded the Test Fleet sweetheart deal a violation of the Taft-Hartley Act.

At worst, the Test Fleet infraction amounted to a misdemeanor, exposing Hoffa to a year of jail time, tops, and in real life no more than a few months, if not a suspended sentence. Edward Bennett Williams, watching the trial unfold from his eminence as a $50,000-a-year general counsel for the Teamsters, observed that "Jimmy is just like Joe McCarthy. If he beats this case, he'll be like the guy who jumped out a sixth-floor window and survived. He'll take the elevator up to the eighth floor and jump again. . . . He's just like Joe. He's a jumper."

The trial in Nashville provided Hoffa his initial leap. Walter Sheridan himself has written an exhaustive chronicle of the ins and outs of this landmark proceeding, where cosmic forces gathered to fight through a set of ultimately trivial charges. As formidable a purveyor of influence as I. Irving Davidson, Hoover's pal and Carlos Marcello's godfather in Washington, made it a point to sit up front with the Teamster notables when important witnesses testified. Egged on by Teamster lobbyist Sid Zagri, key senators from both parties—Hiram Fong, Homer Capehart, Edward Long of Missouri—along with at least a dozen loud voices in the FBI claque in Congress went public with their outrage that such a statesman of the labor movement as Jimmy Hoffa should be subjected to this public humiliation. The ever-testy William Loeb of the Manchester (N.H.) *Union Leader*, a pension fund beneficiary, compared Robert Kennedy with Caesar.

From the first day he attempted to empanel a jury, the federal judge in the case, the unreachable William E. Miller, was already uneasy about the reliability of the existing pool. Several prospective jurors informed the judge that they had received calls from a "Mr. Allen," a reporter for the Nashville *Banner*, asking questions in preparation for a story he was allegedly preparing. There was no Mr. Allen at the *Banner*, and all the jurors contacted were excused.

Then one of the jurors who had already been tentatively empaneled, James Tippens, reported to the judge in chambers that a neighbor had approached him with $10,000 in hundred-dollar bills if he would vote for Hoffa's acquittal. Tippens was dismissed. Then an informant the Get-Hoffa Squad maintained in the Hoffa camp, Edward Grady Partin, told Sheridan that *another* of the jurors, Mrs. James Paschal, the wife of a local highway patrolman, had now been approached through the head of Teamster Local 327, Ewing King, with promises of a promotion for her husband if Hoffa was exonerated. There was a black female juror the Hoffa fixers had their eyes on, and Mr. Gratin Fields, a retired black railroad employee was approached through a black Teamster business agent, Larry Campbell, who sent word back to Hoffa, Partin reported, that he intended to vote for acquittal but would not accept any money.

Edward Grady Partin himself was a Teamster leader from Baton Rouge, Louisiana, with an overloaded rap sheet and a number of reasons to rat out Jimmy Hoffa if that was what it took to remain on the outside. The agenda for Sheridan was to substantiate as many as possible of these efforts to reach individual jurors with the prospect of hanging Hoffa high for jury-tampering.

Although the increasingly paranoid Hoffa was convinced that Robert Kennedy had authorized limitless bugging and tapping of the Teamsters, the Get-Hoffa lawyers were only too conscious that even the smallest provable infraction by Sheridan's team of the federal privacy laws could get vital convictions thrown out on appeal. Nevertheless, a few years later Robert Kennedy himself countered one journalist's observation that "You were too smart to bug Hoffa" with a sneer and the ambivalent response, "If you think *that*, there's no point in talking with you." FBI sources later specified that Sheridan was tapping Hoffa with the aide of the Kennedy family wireman Eddie Jones, temporarily on an Immigration and Naturalization payroll.

This left the FBI leadership looking on. No doubt the likes of Hoover and Tolson back at the Seat of Government were skeptical—fundamentally disapproving—of Robert Kennedy's determination to corner as influential a powerhouse as Hoffa. Hoffa had a lot of friends in Congress, he passed a lot of money around. Furthermore, as Get-Hoffa lawyer Charles Shaffer put it, "The FBI hated Walter. It looked like we were going to do things historically reserved to the Bureau. . . . As a result, the Bureau would never help us. We'd request stuff and it would never come."

Yet Hoover was still too astute a bureaucrat to unilaterally refuse, in writing, requests from the top of the Justice Department. Furthermore, Kennedy's drop-in visits to field offices around the country had helped him break out a number of the special agents in charge, who had autonomy enough to respond to a direct order from the attorney general without reporting back too many details. By 1963, aggressive agents like William Roemer and Neil Welch were planting microphones and orchestrating the kind of big-store sting operations and undercover penetrations against important mobsters it would have horrified their Director to have to acknowledge. This did not mean that Hoover intended to be overtaken by events, and a few years later a Tennessee technician, Benjamin David ("Bud") Nichols, with whom the Director was already in the habit of outsourcing touchy surveillance work, signed an affidavit to the effect that, under FBI orders and subject to Walter Sheridan's guidance, he had tapped Hoffa and thoroughly bugged the hotel room of the sequestered jury.

So events in Nashville played out on seemingly unconnected tracks, with deniability uppermost. "We got very little cooperation from the top of the FBI," recalls James Neal, the Hoffa Squad attorney who prosecuted the Teamster boss in Nashville and again in Chattanooga. "We got great cooperation from two local agents here in town. A man named Ed Steele and Bill Sheets. They were terrific. But their efforts on our behalf were not appreciated by the head of the FBI. I think they were ultimately censured in some way.

"The local agents, who were doing a terrific job, would let me know that they were sort of put out there on their own. Hoover didn't like to get out there where things got messy, he didn't want to get down and dirty." So Hoover looked away while Sheets and Steele followed Ewing King and watched him switch cars to throw his pursuers off track as he sneaked out of town to lean on patrolman Paschal, or ran a tight chronology of Larry Campbell's toll calls.

Overhung by the missile crisis, the Hoffa trial in Nashville ended, most disappointingly for the prosecution, with a hung jury, 7–5. Every session had been supercharged—at one point, a lunatic drew down on Hoffa himself with a pellet gun as Hoffa flattened him with one punch—with overtones of a political *crise*. Judge Miller was particularly disgusted with the way things went. "I have signed orders," he announced during his summation, "to convene another grand jury soon after the first of the year to investigate fully and completely all of the incidents connected with this trial indicating illegal attempts to influence jurors by any person or persons whomsoever and return indictments where probable cause therefore exists." Having escaped the frying pan, Hoffa was now plummeting straight into the fire.

After all those years of battering his way up through the trade union movement, Hoffa had no doubts about which way was down. "During my first year as an organizer," he wrote later, "I'd had my scalp laid open six times wide enough to need stitches. I'd been beaten up by police, company guards, goons, and strikebreakers two dozen times in one year. My brother Billy had been shot in the stomach by a company official and I'd seen a union business agent beaten to death by company goons. You get so you're always ready to take an eye for an eye."

Between the Test Fleet trial in Nashville in November 1962 and the jury-tampering trial in Chattanooga in February 1964, Robert Kennedy's universe had collapsed. With the assassination of his brother, Lyndon Johnson took control in the White House, Johnson's long-time neighbor and crony J. Edgar Hoover recovered his untouchable status inside the Justice Department, and Robert Kennedy became overnight, as Hoffa himself phrased it, "just another lawyer." But by then the evidence against the chief of the Teamsters had taken on a momentum of its own.

Getting anything on Hoffa was never easy. Showily unpretentious, the bouncy Teamster leader still lived in the modest brick-faced $6,800 blue-collar residence he'd owned throughout his rise. He normally used cash; most of his calls seemed to originate from pay phones in unpredictable locations; every once in a while he ordered all recent financial records and correspondence destroyed. Even Carmine Bellino, that most penetrating of auditors, who now worked in the White House but kept a satellite office near Bobby in the Justice Building, had run across very little documentation it made any sense to take to court.

Sheridan himself operated out of an interior office with a blank door, so situated that informants could be smuggled in and out unobserved. His primary job remained to track Jimmy Hoffa, minute to minute, anywhere in the country. Whatever Robert Kennedy was doing, wherever he happened to be, he remained in close touch with Walter Sheridan.

It would be difficult to exaggerate how visceral the struggle between Kennedy and Hoffa had now become. In the aftermath of the Nashville trial, Hoffa and several of his attorneys put in an appearance at the Justice Building to inspect relevant documents in preparation for the follow-up trial in Chattanooga. One of Hoffa's lawyers, the Florida criminal specialist Frank Regano, has written of Hoffa's gathering fury while waiting around with the custodian of records for forty-five minutes until the General, as Bobby liked to be called, finally made his appearance.

When Kennedy finally meandered in with Brumus on a leash, Hoffa was beside himself. "Where the hell do you get off keeping me waiting while you're walking your fucking dog?" Hoffa erupted. Kennedy merely "smirked," Regano records.

"'You son of a bitch,' Jimmy snarled," as Regano, tells it, "lunging at Bobby, knocking him against the wall. He started choking Bobby with two hands and hollering, 'I'll break your fucking neck! I'll kill you!'"

"He had," Regano writes, "a killer's look in his eyes." While the phlegmatic Brumus wandered over to a corner, the three lawyers strained to pry Hoffa's powerful fingers loose from Kennedy's windpipe before Hoffa could finish him. Flushed, silenced, Kennedy wobbled out of the room, followed by his disinterested Newfoundland.

"The son of a bitch deserved it," Hoffa gasped. "Keeping me waiting."

Kennedy had an airtight case of assault, but embarrassment and self-discipline inclined him to let the whole incident go and dispatch Hoffa through the courts. The Nashville proceedings, whatever their frustrations, had opened the way to nail Hoffa. What this incident demonstrated—apart from the fact that Brumus was as worthless as everybody suspected—was how profoundly panicked the trial in Nashville had left the normally self-possessed Teamster president. He'd set himself up, and he and Kennedy both knew it.

Hoffa was obviously cracking beneath the full weight of the federal government. Shortly before the Nashville trial, Hoffa had rounded on Sam Baron, a scruple-ridden Teamster field director who had been in touch with Sheridan for several years, when Baron attempted to explain to Hoffa a sticky negotiation and caught a left hook followed by another knock-down and a shove that sent Baron sprawling over a chair. Baron brought charges, which invited some weeks of heavy breathing whenever he answered his telephone or inquiries like "Hoffa wants to know what kind of coffin you want."

Hoffa's morale didn't improve when flunkies like Joe Franco brought word back in 1963 that the local rep of the Get-Hoffa Squad in Detroit, Tom McKeon, had sent four FBI agents to break into Franco's house and haul him in handcuffs to the local lockup for neglecting to pay a $32.50 liquor stamp. A recent widower, Franco found himself summoned to the federal building by McKeon and jaw to jaw with Kennedy himself, backed up by Carmine Bellino. "I want information from you," Franco quotes Kennedy; "I don't care whether it's hearsay or fantasies or what. I want anything you can give me that I can use to bring Hoffa to trial." Hoffa, or Frank Fitzsimmons, or their lawyer William Bufalino. For anything leading to a conviction, "I'll give you five years of federal immunity." Otherwise, "I'll have you in jail in the next two weeks," and "what I'm going to do is take your four children away from you and put them in an orphanage and have you declared an unfit father." Kennedy gave Franco the two weeks to make up his mind.

On hearing all this, Hoffa reportedly decided to let his electronics whiz, Bernard Spindel, insert a microphone beneath the skin of Franco's chest. They would get Kennedy's offer on tape. But time ran out, and the idea died.

"Everyone in my family forgives," Joe Kennedy had assured Harold Gibbons in Palm Beach just prior to the 1960 primaries, "except Bobby." Each hour proved that out more dramatically. Shortly before the Chattanooga trial, the Teamster brain trust discovered that years earlier Sheridan had put on his payroll an ex-con named Frederick Michael Shobe, convicted of burglary, forgery, and armed robbery in Michigan and in danger of having his probation revoked when the authorities discovered that his job on the docks put him in contact with other ex-convicts.

Under threat of more and extended jail time, Shobe agreed to roam the country on the government's tab and function as what he himself called an *agent provocateur*, "inciting riots and fomenting trouble within the Teamsters union." Perhaps Hoffa might overreact, and give the Hoffa Squad its opening.

Another live wire central to the Hoffa prosecution was Sheridan's informant, Edward Grady Partin. A massive, intimidating presence with just enough wavy-haired charm to turn an interviewer's head, Partin was tough enough to agree to come forward when the moment was right to testify against Hoffa, yet agile and persuasive enough to inveigle himself onto Hoffa's retinue before the Nashville trial. While *Life* magazine—a sounding board for Kennedy since his campaign to undermine Roy Cohn—would note that Partin had caught Sheridan's eye doing time in Baton Rouge "because of a minor domestic problem," the fact was that Partin had a lifetime history of involvement with the law, and remained very poor at staying out of trouble.

Originally a Mississippi boy, as early as 1943 he had drawn a fifteen-year sentence in Washington state for breaking into a restaurant, escaped from the lockup twice, then joined the Marines and was dishonorably discharged. By 1961, having drifted up in Baton Rouge and established himself as the president of the Teamster local, he had been charged by dissidents with embezzling union funds and trashing the local's records and dumping its empty six-hundred-pound safe in a nearby river as well as implication in the savage beatings of his primary critics. One died soon afterward, crushed by an overloaded truck.

By June 1962, Partin was under intense investigation by both the FBI and local authorities. A recent traffic accident subjected him to manslaughter and leaving-the-scene charges, and not long after that Partin got picked up for colluding in the kidnaping of a sidekick's two children. By now he was looking at colossal fines and quite possibly the rest of his life in prison.

Ed Partin was the kind of organizer to whom Jimmy Hoffa was drawn naturally—not faultless, for sure, but rough and ready. The two had evidently collaborated during Hoffa's efforts to run guns to Castro, purportedly to hedge all bets for his Mob contacts. Partin later claimed, "I was right there on several occasions when they were loading the guns and ammunition on the barges. Hoffa was directing the whole thing." Furthermore, as Partin himself later remarked, "Hoffa always assumed that since I was from Louisiana I was in Marcello's hip pocket."

By 1962 Carlos Marcello and the Teamsters Central States Pension Fund, which Hoffa controlled directly, were deeply interinvolved. Partin had been dropping by to kibitz with Jimmy since 1957, and so in August 1962, with indictments in Baton Rouge in the works for Partin and the Nashville proceedings a few months out for Hoffa, it was no surprise when Partin turned up to support the Teamster president in Hoffa's D.C. headquarters.

A month later, Partin was in jail in Baton Rouge, awaiting trial. One day he requested an audience with the local district attorney and unloaded his conscience. On his recent trip to Washington he had found Hoffa in a surly mood, apprehensive. Furious with Bobby Kennedy, Hoffa told Partin that he had been trying to choose between two methods of eliminating his nemesis, one involving the firebombing of Hickory Hill to incinerate Kennedy and "all his damn kids." The other would require a sniper competent to take out Kennedy, "always riding around Washington in that convertible with that big black dog." Hoffa "had a .270 rifle leaning in the corner of his office," Partin told the authorities. Obviously hoping for the right response, Hoffa directed Partin's attention to the weapon, remarking, "I've got something right here which will shoot flat and long. . . ."

It took no time at all for that lively scenario to reach the Justice Department. Days later, one A. Frank Grimsley, a lawyer on the Get-Hoffa Squad, rushed down to Baton Rouge, and shortly after that somebody paid Partin's bail, he submitted to an FBI polygraph test to confirm his credibility, and he was back on the street with Walter Sheridan's confidential telephone number written down on a slip of paper in his billfold. By October 22, Partin had talked his way onto Jimmy Hoffa's entourage in Nashville, where he served throughout the trial as the Teamster boss's doorman, sergeant-at-arms, and confidant.

With Edward Partin in place, the prosecutors had very little need for a lot of electronic surveillance. Jim Neal remembers hanging around Sheridan's temporary office in Nashville when a call came in with instructions on where to meet from "Andy Anderson," Partin's nom de guerre. Even the lead prosecutor didn't know who that was; Sheridan listened carefully to his message and "scurried right out," Neal recalls. With Courtney Evans in Washington doing as much as he could get away with to mollify Hoover (known to be a stickler on Sixth Amendment matters relating to court procedure), Sheridan broke out as many FBI agents as the situation would tolerate to log in the movements of everybody in Hoffa's camp who might be implicated in Teamster efforts to fix the jury.

The government's case against Jimmy Hoffa for jury tampering was tried starting on January 20, 1964, before federal judge Frank W. Wilson in Chattanooga. Hoffa flew in Bernard Spindel with a thousand pounds of electronic monitoring equipment to forestall government eavesdropping. Except for a steady stream of pedestrian blather picked up from exchanges among the FBI radio cars, Spindel's efforts were never productive. Hoffa's lawyers would maintain that it was the government that stacked the jury this time, loading up the pool with white-collar professionals and senior military against a few clerks and two truck drivers.

The heart of the Hoffa defense involved the claim that Sheridan and his lawyers had tried to coerce the compromised jurors into testifying against Hoffa with threats to indict them or their wives and that the imaginative Walter Sheridan, collaborating with his provocateur Frederick Michael

Shobe, had plotted to unhinge Tom Parks, the implicated uncle of black Teamster Larry Campbell, with theatrical voodoo rites and horrific schemes of abduction. The term of his parole having expired between the trials, Shobe had now decided to take his chances with Hoffa.

In the end, it came down to Partin's testimony, which recapitulated Hoffa's day-to-day oversight of the repeated efforts to corrupt the jury. One of the jurors told Jim Neal afterward that after the first day of cross-examination most of the jury agreed that Hoffa's lawyers destroyed Partin by harping on his criminal problems. But then they left him up on the stand for six more days, and Partin's stolid, unemotional responses had won the jurors over little by little.

The accuracy with which each furtive telephone call or back-alley exchange of information with Partin led the FBI field agents to critical rendezvous or unexpected links in Hoffa's support system shored up a body of testimony that even Hoffa's battery of top-flight lawyers could not shake. Outcries from the Hoffa bench that somebody had rifled their files in the Patten Hotel, that Partin's ex-wife had been receiving $300 a month from government sources, that Hoffa had only let Partin hang around in Nashville so he could Dutch-uncle the hapless Louisiana organizer, whose local was falling apart—none of this helped.

On March 12, 1964, Jimmy Hoffa was sentenced to eight years' imprisonment, along with a $10,000 fine. Ewing King, Larry Campbell, and Tom Parks each caught three years and $5,000.

Two defendants got off. Both arrived in Nashville on October 20, 1962, and ran into Ed Partin in the coffee shop of the Andrew Jackson Hotel two days later. One was Nicholas Tweel, a Lebanese-American cigarette distributor from West Virginia out angling for a commercial loan from the other man, Allen Dorfman. Partin recognized Dorfman, by then a personage around those anterooms of the business community where the labor-union movement connives with the Mafia. A handsomely groomed ex-physical education instructor who administered the ever-mounting portfolio of loans for the Teamsters Central States Pension Fund through his family's Union Casualty Agency, Dorfman represented a lot of financial clout. The stepson of Paul ("Red") Dorfman—for years a Capone sidekick, acknowledged wherever earnest men spoke out of the sides of their mouths as a "hood's hood"—Allen Dorfman was unapologetically in town to backstop Hoffa in any way possible.

Edward Partin promptly reported to Sheridan that Tweel and Dorfman had invited him back to Tweel's room and confided that they were "fixin' to get at the jury," in Partin's words. Exactly why a prince of the Mob like Dorfman would incriminate himself in such an offhand way in front of a roustabout like Partin did not become at all clear over the course of the Chattanooga trial, and accordingly the jury let both of them off. What does come over is the fact that Hoffa and his fate had now become very important to the power brokers at the top of the Chicago Outfit. They were watching over their investment.

Many of these cross-connections got dragged into the light over the thirteen weeks of Hoffa's next trial, which began in Chicago on April 27, 1964. By then the Sun Valley land promotion in Titusville was deep in bankruptcy after Henry Lower emptied out the till, and Hoffa had been struggling to maneuver Pension Fund clients into coughing up enough collateral to bail out the $400,000 loan from Local 299 in Detroit while defending himself against allegations that he had maintained a covert financial interest in this big, soggy development. A previously undisclosed trust agreement was entered into evidence in Chicago, which demonstrated that Hoffa not only had a 45 percent option on the property but also owned 22 1/2 percent outright.

Many of the manipulations it took to keep Sun Valley from disappearing into the swamp were left up to a fast-moving ex-furrier named Benjamin Dranow. Dranow seems to have been delegated by Hoffa to shop around access to the rapidly compounding Teamster pension treasury. Mobsters turned out to be as interested as anybody else in cheap money, and before too long Pension Fund customers included Zachary A. Strate Jr., a close associate of Carlos Marcello, who borrowed $4,675,000 to put up the Fontainebleau Hotel in New Orleans, and Ed Levinson, Bobby Baker's discreet backer, the manager of the Fremont Casino in Las Vegas, on whom the Chicago Outfit was depending to realize its dreams in Nevada.

By 1964, employers were shoveling $6 million a month into Hoffa's pension fund, the assets of which now exceeded $200 million. Distrustful of government bonds, not to mention the stock market, Jimmy Hoffa so dominated the pension fund's board of directors that he alone decided where to put out capital, normally at below-market interest to guarantee a maximum of political and commercial leverage. Over 60 percent was in real estate, most of it speculative. The fund's portfolio had migrated from Florida to Nevada.

* * *

The most substantial borrower was Moe Dalitz, the urbane gangland proprietor of the Desert Inn as well as the Stardust in Las Vegas. Hoffa had been on kitchen-table terms with Dalitz for many years, ever since Hoffa's one-time mistress Sylvia Pagano O'Brien brought around this sharpest member of Detroit's murderous "Purple Gang" to meet the gutsy, rising Teamster organizer. A regular and, at times, a very dangerous business contact of Joe Kennedy's during the rumrunning twenties, Dalitz had moved on to Cleveland to oversee the Mayfield Road Gang before his makeover into semilegitimacy as a Lansky partner in the Hotel Nacional Casino. During the second-round Nevada gambling boom, Teamster money went into The Dunes directly and into a lot of the other buildings along the Strip by way of Webb and Knapp, Del Webb's huge if shaky development arm. Webb remained a major Hoover supporter and a Del Charro regular.

There were a number of sizable loans to Clint Murchison Sr. and Jr., starting with the Truesdale Estate in Los Angeles. The innovative I. Irving Davidson borrowed $5 million for a D.C. hotel. The diminutive lobbyist with the clown's nose and the perpetual elfin grin was infamous for skipping in and out of backroom Washington politics like "a cat on eggs," by one description, privately implicated in everything from wholesaling Israeli staghorn tanks to Nicaragua to pleading the CIA's case around Congress. J. Edgar Hoover relished the tidbits Davidson produced, and Davidson and Murray Chotiner, the mob lawyer who masterminded Nixon into the presidency and wound up with a White House office, were linked by longstanding bonds to Carlos Marcello.

Jimmy Hoffa, Carlos Marcello, and the Murchison family were all valued clients of the enterprising Davidson. Already in legal peril after the jury-tampering verdict, the decision in Chicago the following July left Hoffa convicted on four counts for conspiring to defraud and soliciting kickbacks while granting fourteen loans. Hoffa received a five-year sentence, to run consecutively with the eight years awaiting him for jury tampering. Hoffa's future now hung on whatever results his lawyers could get in the appeals courts.

This meant discrediting Edward Grady Partin. In March 1965, Hoffa himself dissuaded Frank Chavez, head of the Puerto Rican Teamsters, from gunning down Partin, Walter Sheridan, and Robert Kennedy himself. By then the syndicate had decided that the wisest approach would be to persuade Partin to repudiate his own testimony. Marcello recruited the Louisiana governor's administrative assistant to bribe Partin. Santo Trafficante made the effort. Carlos Marcello's son-in-law, D'Alton Smith, invited Partin over to his house and promised that, if Partin would admit that the Get-Hoffa Squad had wiretapped Hoffa, "the sky's the limit. It's worth at least a million bucks. You'll be put in charge of all loans in the South." Smith telephoned Allen Dorfman, assuring Partin during an aside that "Dorfman's controlling this thing—he's running it. The 'little man' [Marcello] is holding the money."

Partin understood that he would probably stay alive as long as the Mob had any reason to hope that he might yet sell out the Get-Hoffa brigade. At that point Audie Murphy, World War II's most decorated soldier, showed up in Louisiana as an employee of D'Alton Smith and attempted to coax Partin into signing a deposition according to which, Partin maintains, "they were accusing me of everything, including being involved in the Kennedy assassination." In Mafia circles, rescuing Hoffa was getting a lot of priority. "We own de Teamsters," Marcello asserted a few years afterward. "We" meant mostly himself, Santo Trafficante, and the Chicago Outfit.

After Lyndon Johnson became president, Bobby Baker recently confessed, he was himself contacted by an intermediary close to Louisiana Senator Russell Long. "I need a personal favor," Long's friend confided. "I cain't tell you what it is, but I'll buy you a first-class ticket on the Eastern Airlines. . . ."

The two wound up in "some little ol' restaurant" in Jefferson Parish, sitting across from Carlos Marcello. "I'm trapped out there," Baker recalls; and once they settled in, Marcello "says, 'Mister Baker, our mutual friend tells me that Lyndon Johnson is your dear, great friend.'

"I say, 'Yes, although he was a coward at my trial.'" Baker had just taken a nasty fall for a tax delinquency.

Marcello wasted little time: "'I have a million dollars in cash that I would love to give to him or whoever he assigns, to get a presidential pardon for Jimmy Hoffa.'

"And I said, 'Mister Marcello, the biggest coward in America when it comes to something like this is Lyndon Baines Johnson.'"

"But the end product," Baker concludes, "was that Chuck Colson got the million dollars. . . . He put the hooker in. Nixon would have given the total pardon, but I think Colson put a sentence in the pardon that he had to wait five or ten years before he could be active in the Teamsters."

With the Kennedys sidelined, Partin discovered that he would have to contend with forces beyond the Mob. Local politicians were infuriated; Teamster money was vital. "The federal government seemed to get after Edward Grady Partin the moment Hoffa was convicted," James Neal says. Both directly and through Bobby Baker, Johnson owed Marcello. A minimum of $50,000 a year from the race-track and wire-service take from Marcello's huge profits in Texas had worked their way via Marcello bagman John Halfen to Lyndon Johnson throughout the fifties, in return for assurance that the Majority Leader would ward off any serious antiracketeering legislation in Congress. Only when LBJ had been effectively immobilized, sulking through his honorific role as vice president, was Robert Kennedy able to pull off his dead-of-night antigambling coup and squeeze into law the bills that pressured the FBI into the forefront of the assault against organized crime.

Once Johnson became president, key prosecutors under Bobby quickly found themselves conducting what rearguard actions were possible. Out of residual loyalty to Kennedy and Sheridan, Neal, by then in private practice, defended Partin against a series of indictments, starting with one in Houston that charged Partin with attempting to murder a witness. Neal got Partin off; next to come along was an action in Atlanta alleging violence on the job site, for which Partin was convicted but the judgment was subsequently dropped. Resentments remained highly personal.

The Get-Hoffa Squad got Hoffa, and in the end secured 190 indictments and 115 convictions of Teamster officials and their associates before Robert Kennedy resigned. Yet inside the Justice Department, the suspicion that the Squad was doing its business by fair means or foul made many of its counterparts pull back. "We didn't feel it had the prosecutorial ability to achieve convictions," sniffed Tom McBride, one of Ed Silberling's Organized Crime Section attorneys. Victor Navasky concluded that Sheridan and his protégés absorbed too many resources and became "a demoralizing factor in a department which generally tended to treat the Get-Hoffa Squad like a bad joke." Ramsey Clark, then assistant attorney general for the Lands Division, muttered that "you don't stake a jury-fixing case on the word of a man like Partin, who has a twenty-year criminal history," and, when Hoffa's case reached the Supreme Court, the dissenting Earl Warren echoed Clark's opinion.

Bobby Kennedy had singled out for persecution primary notables in the burgeoning netherworld of organized crime, individuals on whom millions of law-abiding citizens depended. Quaint, burly little Carlos Marcello ran a webwork of undertakings already estimated to pull in several billion dollars a year. Hoffa ran the country's largest union, whose drivers serviced everybody, and at the time of his conviction presided over a gathering hoard of capital on which the senior statesmen of the nationwide criminal syndicate were depending to bring them back after Castro grabbed off their casinos in Havana.

* * *

Hoover understood all this and watched with some concern. Apart from the fact that senior water carriers for the Bureau in Congress like Missouri Senator Edward Long (later proved to have pocketed a $100,000 payoff from Hoffa) were incensed by Kennedy's hounding of the Teamster president, Hoover had no doubt at all that Jimmy had gotten it right when he insisted to his biographers Ralph and Estelle James that "underworld forces lie just beneath the surface in most American cities, uncontrolled by the ineffective or cooperative police." Hoover's decades of off-the-books exchanges with Frank Costello, who had been greasing public officials for the Mob since the nineteen-twenties, left him in no doubt. For Teamster locals to survive and resist the thugs local industrialists routinely hired, as Hoffa had discovered when he rescued Harold Gibbons in St. Louis in 1951, they needed a concordat with the major players.

Without question his associations had coarsened Jimmy's character. But what about these types Bobby Kennedy was trafficking with under the covers? "The Bureau didn't want anything to do with Partin," Walter Sheridan would tell Victor Navasky. "They were afraid of him. . . . The Bureau's inclination was to leave him alone because he might be a double agent." Hoover continued to be leery of Sheridan's cavalier approach to due process, his scorched-earth methods when it came to softening up witnesses. In Nashville, under Sheridan's guidance, a moonlighting policeman had helped entrap Hoffa's respected lead local attorney, Z. T. Osborn. Osborn had agreed, within range of a minifon the FBI taped to the small of the cop's back, to bribe a juror. Afterward, Sheridan procured $3,000 from Kennedy brother-in-law and manager of the family accounts Steve Smith to help tide over the undercover snitch. Osborn killed himself.

To Hoover's way of thinking, bruises the Bureau sustained going along with Sheridan's power plays would be slow to heal. Once the noisy trials were forgotten and the Get-Hoffa lawyers disappeared into private practice, the Bureau would still be hung out there around the local communities, dependent on regional law enforcement, catering to the power structure.

Even inside the Kennedy camp there were eventually second thoughts. Government auditors were forced to conclude that for all Jimmy Hoffa's seventh-grade education, the pension fund investments he selected did extraordinarily well. Sheridan himself later remarked that he believed "to a certainty" that Hoffa used the money he siphoned from the deals he made "to pay off Congressmen," not riotous living or the padding of Swiss bank accounts. Before the Chicago trial, Robert Kennedy allegedly attempted to arrange a plea bargain for Jimmy, to assure that the Teamster president would not subject himself to a follow-on stretch in the slammer; Hoffa turned that down, with indignation. After 1967, his appeals exhausted, the smoldering Teamster boss moved into a very small cell in the federal penitentiary in Lewisburg. Every time he ran across some ex-colleague from the Justice Department, Bob Kennedy tended to ask with obvious concern how Jimmy was doing.

Not that he softened up completely on the subject. In 1968, Ted Kennedy passed along to his mercurial older brother, relaxed and brooding in the tub, the offer an intermediary had now brought to *him* of a million dollars of Teamster money for help springing Hoffa.

"If I get to be president," Robert Kennedy said, "Jimmy Hoffa will never get out of jail and there will be a lot more of them in jail." Certain obsessions never die.

If Robert Kennedy suffered even momentary afterthoughts consequent to his vendetta against Jimmy Hoffa, Hoffa's primary sponsor on the Commission of the Cosa Nostra had long been cherishing his own fantasies, centered on the Kennedys. In one of the great unavoidable set-pieces of assassination literature, one humid September afternoon in 1962 a pop-off private detective with time in service as a publicist for the Riviera in Las Vegas, Edward Becker, happened to sit in on an exchange over a table of cold cuts and warm Scotch in the kitchen of Carlos Marcello's primitive farmhouse deep in the swamp around Churchill Downs, the 6,400-acre Marcello holding in the Louisiana grassland.

"Man," Becker reportedly said, "isn't it a fuckin' shame the bad deal you're getting' from Bobby Kennedy? I've been reading about it in the papers. All that deportation stuff. What are you goin' to do about it, Carlos?"

Leaping to his feet, the stumpy, bull-necked Mafia boss, still smarting from his abduction the previous year, broke out in Sicilian: "*Livarsi 'na pietra di la scarpa!* (Take the stone out of my shoe!) Don't worry about that little Bobby sonovabitch. He's going to be taken care of . . . I got—"

"But you can't go after Bobby Kennedy," Becker put in.

"No, I'm not talkin' about dat. Ya know what they say in Sicily. If you want to kill a dog, you don't cut off the tail, you cut off the head." As Marcello explained breathlessly, the president was the head.

This was an exchange that was going to reverberate through a lot of history.

14

Jack's Hair Would Have Turned White

Justice Department publicists liked to circulate the statistic that, prior to Robert Kennedy's takeover in 1961, there were nineteen indictments of organized crime figures. In 1964, there were 687. Other number-crunchers were quickly asking: Who? Who were they actually rounding up, and who would remain in business?

The fact was, in something over three and a half years as attorney general, Kennedy never incarcerated any of the Cosa Nostra kingpins. Another four years might well have remedied that. But Kennedy drew a blank.

His luck with Carlos Marcello suggested how thankless it was. On June 5, 1961, raging, Kennedy responded to word that Marcello had found his way back into the country by dispatching twenty federal agents to Shreveport, Louisiana. It was already too late; Marcello's lawyers and Lyndon Johnson's undisclosed associates had thrown up obstructions, which made all subsequent deportation efforts a great deal harder. Around the Kennedy administration, Bobby's abduction of the New Orleans mobster had become an in-house joke. As late as January 1963 Kennedy continued to summon the disgruntled Hoover to his office to pound on him about getting some electronic surveillance on Marcello. The FBI reports never changed: Marcello was a "private businessman," a salesman for the Pelican Tomato Company.

They did no better with Santo Trafficante Jr. In dealing with the Tampa mobster, it soon was borne in on Kennedy, they'd better remain wary, because Trafficante was an indispensable figure in the CIA program to murder Castro carried over from the final months of the Eisenhower administration. The misleadingly unobtrusive Santo, who drove old cars bleached colorless by the tropical sun and meandered around Tampa and Miami weighted down by rolls of quarters so he could do his business entirely on untapped pay phones, receded naturally on close approach into the heat and shadows.

Low-keyed and wary, as befitted a second-generation member of the Mafia's ruling Commission, Trafficante's casino properties in Havana had rivaled those of the Lansky syndicate. He remained the preeminent importer of cocaine and heroin to North America, with worldwide sources and contacts dating back to the hallowed French Connection introductions arranged by the don, his father, in back rooms around Corsica and Marseilles. Even Harry Anslinger's Narcotics Bureau bravos were hesitant to work too close to Santo. Informants disappeared quite easily. Besides, Miami was Hoover territory.

Miami remained the jumping-off point in the gathering crusade against Castro, the Casablanca where so many volatile elements were coming to a bubble. In Miami, the Mob, the CIA, and the fratricidal émigré Cubans were all chaotically attempting to identify their own forces and sort everybody else's out. Everything required a second look. One man's thug could blossom overnight into another man's asset.

An outstanding example of how complex the thing had gotten was the repeated attempt to deal with Mike McLaney. The suave, New Orleans–born golf hustler had regularly been entrusted by no less discriminating a connoisseur of criminal capacity than Meyer Lansky with obligations that ran from attending the cage at the Nacional to overturning the Bahamanian government. Moving down his list of Lansky lieutenants, before long the implacable Robert Morgenthau would move to indict McLaney.

What made this collar especially awkward for Bobby was the fact that McLaney was all but an intimate of the patriarch. "We used to golf together two or three times a week at the Palm Beach Country Club," McLaney later maintained, and one of Mike's attendants remembered how "Joe, Jack and Bobby used to sit with Mike on the veranda, where they could have private conversations." Bobby was, McLaney admitted, "the only one I didn't like."

The Palm Beach Country Club was Jewish; Joe Kennedy golfed there, he was fond of remarking, largely as a matter of convenience; others would interpret it as a gesture of contempt toward the more exclusive WASP establishments. McLaney first met Joe through Carroll Rosenbloom.

Another golfing buddy of McLaney's was Florida Senator George Smathers, Jack Kennedy's rooting buddy through many an abandoned bachelor party and by 1961 perhaps the leading exponent in Congress for the Liquidate-Castro-At-Any-Price contingent. By now an affiliate member of the Nixon-Rebozo-Chotiner claque, Smathers kept at Jack Kennedy to jump in and straighten out these bandits in Havana.

After the acute disappointments engendered by the Bay of Pigs, "Gorgeous George" Smathers's welcome at the White House was starting to wear thin, especially when he belabored Cuba; one evening the president cracked a plate bringing his fork down too hard when Smathers wouldn't stop. Not that the Kennedys intended to neglect El Maximo Lider. Robert Kennedy personally picked out the membership of the Taylor Commission, chaired by Maxwell Taylor, a specialist in antiguerrilla warfare, and went on the record with the "general feeling that there can be no long-term living with Castro as a neighbor." By then, Bobby had been designated "the untitled overseer of the intelligence apparatus in the Kennedy administration" and chaired the Special Group Augmented (SGA), which would preoccupy itself largely with "the Cuba Project." Under the policy direction of an overtouted ex-public-relations executive, Brigadier General Edward Lansdale, Operation Mongoose was to be run out of the Agency's vast installation in Florida, JM/WAVE, and wreak as much havoc—"bang and boom," in Bobby's lingo—all across the island as upward of $100 million a year could buy.

The CIA's outspoken Sam Halpern backstopped the flamboyant William Harvey as desk officer on Task Force W, which integrated those night landings and sugar-refinery detonations and treetop overflights. Halpern reflected the mood around Langley: "Everyone at CIA was surprised at Kennedy's obsession with Fidel. . . . It was a personal thing. The Kennedy family felt personally burnt by the Bay of Pigs and sought revenge."

Mongoose never really worked—Castro had the island sewed up—but all the noise and harassment the gringos kept bringing down on the island's shaky infrastructure, those flaming canefields and toxified banana groves and hot-wired jungle transformers, quickly undermined any hope of reconciliation with Washington and alarmed the Soviets, who interpreted this programmatic hellraising as preliminary to a second invasion. Moving missiles in began to seem an option. Yet whatever the United States did, the irredentist Cuban hotheads and out-of-pocket businessmen and gamblers and tinhorn adventurers who had been bankrupted when Los

Barbudos came storming out of the hills still clamored for nothing less than full recovery, now.

Throughout the remaining $2^1/2$ years of the Kennedy presidency, American policy with respect to Cuba turned into a continuous display of neurotic administrative ambivalence. Robert Kennedy got deeply involved in the innumerable morale-boosting and financial wet-nursing requirements of hundreds of permanently aggrieved Cuban popoffs of every political inclination. Some were high-minded reformers, and some remained under the sway of Batista, and some were developing fast under CIA instruction into paramilitary contractors increasingly adept at dusting competitors and running drugs. The Agency itself, with Robert Kennedy's permission whenever he was agreeable and behind his back when that was what it took, persisted with its plotting to murder Castro.

Obsessed with the fantasy that the Kennedy administration was not pursuing their interests with enough dedication, the deserving rich around the Palm Beach/Greater Miami circuit were turning the bombardment of Cuba into another of their private charities. Ex-ambassador to Cuba William Pawley, an oil industrialist and longterm Nixon backer as well as an experienced right-wing troubleshooter, persuaded concerned friends like Clare Boothe Luce to sponsor a boat each to raid the Cuban mainland; ever open to experience, Mrs. Luce took to mothering her wards, referring to them as "my three Cubans."

Another high-energy onlooker determined not to be left out was Joe Kennedy's sharklike companion on the links, Mike McLaney. He remained bitter about losing his stake in the Nacional as well as time served in a Cuban jail. In middle age an urbane, fine-featured charmer with a permanent oxblood tan and a distinguished clubman's receding hairline, McLaney still dropped in regularly to have a drink with Joe at La Guerida.

Well connected in aviation circles, McLaney propounded a scheme to firebomb the huge Cuban oil refineries of Esso, Shell, and Texaco in conjunction with the Bay of Pigs landings. McLaney's plans were maturing fast when Robert Kennedy showed up at a critical meeting on a houseboat at Surfside to make it very clear to McLaney and his friends—witnesses remember Kennedy driving a forefinger into the genial hustler's chest—that there would be no saturation bombing of the refineries. The FBI had tipped Bobby off, and the U.S. majors were horrified at the prospect of losing the choicest of their installations, which they expected to recover.

McLaney never liked Bobby—"he was a mess," McLaney repeatedly reflected in later years—and increasingly felt the shadow of the vindictive attorney general slide across his projects. On the last day of July 1963, the FBI raided a pink cottage just north of Lake Pontchartrain in Louisiana owned by William McLaney, Mike's brother and another opportunist active in the gambling business in Havana during the Batista heyday. The raid netted "a ton of dynamite, twenty 100-pound aerial bomb casings, bomb fuses and striker assemblies, a 50-pound container of Nuodex, and all the stuffings to make Napalm." Two weeks before, customs agents, evidently alerted by the FBI, had intercepted a Beechcraft about to take off from an abandoned airfield outside Miami with two 250-pound bombs and a full complement of heavy-duty explosives.

On hand to attend the loading of the aircraft near Miami was Sam Benton. Like many others implicated in the Cuban-Mafia underground, Benton amounted to a pretentious, upscale gofer. Benton had put in time as Mike McLaney's key aide at the Hotel Nacional Casino. That ubiquitous giant Gerry Henning, working training camps for Cubans in both Florida and Louisiana, insists that "Benton knew Bobby Kennedy too. Bobby sent him up and down the east coast in a sting operation involving a stolen securities fraud investigation being run by the Justice Department." Other sources identify Benton as essentially a "Marcello operative" who "introduced Bobby Kennedy to Johnny Rosselli."

Benton was among the eleven conspirators, mostly Cubans, who got picked up by the FBI in the McLaney cottage near Lake Pontchartrain with enough big-league explosives to take out much of Havana. Everybody involved got let off immediately. At this point, Mongoose had largely been abandoned in the wake of the Missile Crisis, and Jack Kennedy, through William Attwood and others, was exploring some kind of back-channel decompression of the crisis over Castro. Simultaneously, intriguing with his friend Enrique (Harry) Ruiz-Williams, Robert Kennedy was later alleged to be bringing along the so-called "C-Day" coup scheduled for December 1963 to invade Cuba from Nicaragua and Guatemala, wipe out Castro, and install another progressive revolutionary less likely to subordinate the island to the monolithic Soviets.

The enterprising Mike McLaney continued to offer a presentable liaison between the Kennedys and a wide range of syndicate personalities. One aide of Mike's who called himself Steve Reynolds would maintain that, after the ceremony welcoming the freed Cubans of Brigade 2506 in the Orange Bowl in 1962, the president dropped by to look in on Mike. Jack Kennedy had played a round or two of golf with McLaney over recent years, although the debonair hustler never let the wagering get serious: Jack's back put limits on his drive, McLaney saw, and in any case—this was the president, after all— "that wouldn't have been right!" After his historic speech to the returned prisoners, Jack Kennedy stopped off at McLaney's villa across Indian Creek "to sit on the back patio, where they were joined by an emissary of Sam Giancana's. They spoke for about twenty minutes." The emissary himself, Reynolds indicates strongly, was Johnny Rosselli.

Rosselli's availability any time Joe Kennedy needed him hadn't flagged. "Mister Smooth," as he was widely tagged around the circuit, was temperamentally suited, like Frank Costello, to mediate a turf war or select an out-of-state contractor or spread the necessary amount of currency around before the machine guns came out of the violin cases. Rosselli had achieved a great deal of status during the thirties everywhere in the movie colony. As Chicago's man on the Coast, Rosselli's silver mane and manicured deportment were recognizable around Musso's or the Brown Derby or Hillcrest Country Club, very often in company with film moguls like Harry Cohn or Joe Schenck. Schenck let Johnny in for a percentage of Agua Caliente, Schenck's Tijuana track. Flawlessly tailored and spit-shined and perpetually smelling of the barbershop, Rosselli could maintain his composure and keep the peace even while dividing up the local rackets with spitfires like Ben— "Don't call me Bugsy!"—Siegel. He could be pushed too far—Rosselli reportedly had a hand in making sure sixteen slugs took malcontent Les Bruneman out of local bookmaking.

Except for a short, unworkable marriage to the starlet June Lang, things were moving along nicely for the Outfit's showboater in Los Angeles until Joe Schenck of Twentieth-Century Fox cracked in front of a federal grand jury and admitted to a $100,000 extortion payoff to Willie Bioff of the gangster-controlled International Alliance of Theatrical Stage Employees. When the Outfit attempted to silence one of Bioff's accomplices by brutalizing, then incinerating, his blonde card-dealer of a girlfriend, the enraged Bioff blurted to the federal prosecutor everything the government needed, and in enough detail to send all the principals involved, Rosselli included, to prison. Plucked out of infantry training, Johnny Rosselli spent 1944–1947 in the grim federal facilities in Atlanta and Terre Haute, Indiana. To avoid the pen, as tough a nut as Frank Nitti, Capone's top enforcer, got drunk and shot himself through his brown fedora.

Even three years in prison were an ordeal for a bon vivant pushing forty with incipient pulmonary tuberculosis as well as compounding arthritis in his major joints. Back in Los Angeles on parole, Rosselli adhered with great scrupulousness to his cover identity as an "insurance broker" and even held a sort of job with the maverick filmmaker Bryan Foy as an associate producer, grinding out such low-budget nailbiters as *He Walked by Night.* When Mob gambling became a very big thing in Havana, Rosselli slipped out from under the parole board's spotlight and broke in as a troubleshooter and senior manager in Trafficante's San Souci.

By the early fifties, the volatile Sam Giancana was the operating head of the Chicago Outfit. Rosselli was to put that smooth, liquid, convincing inflection of his to arguing for whatever projects Chicago favored. Rosselli preferred to operate as a singleton, avoiding the responsibilities and expenses of the traditional capo. In 1955, the Outfit's Joe Accardo financed the Riviera Hotel in Las Vegas. Willie Bioff, cleaned up by now and part of Barry Goldwater's entourage while introducing himself under the name Al Nelson in hopes of a fresh start, turned up to contribute whatever he could and promptly got distributed across much of greater Phoenix by a strategically placed bomb beneath his pickup. Rosselli was personally of the opinion that taking out a veteran with Bioff's contacts and managerial promise was excessive. "Us fucking Italians ain't human," the genial mob strategist deplored. "We remember things too long, hold all those grudges inside of us until they poison our minds."

Next came the Stardust. By 1957 Johnny Rosselli had brokered into being the Tropicana, a $50 million carpet joint the principal investors behind which, along with the Outfit, included Meyer Lansky, Frank Costello, Carlos Marcello, and "Dandy " Phil Kastel of New Orleans and—in for ten percent, a much bigger position than made sense for an entertainer of Downey's circumstances—Morton Downey. Downey's piece supposedly came out of Frank Costello's percentage. It was universally assumed that Downey was a straw for Joe Kennedy.

What with those worldly, insinuating Mediterranean eyes and classic aquiline features, at ease in anybody's club or resort, Johnny Rosselli was automatically serving the Outfit's purposes, whether pulling together the syndicate's heavy hitters at Felix Young's restaurant in Manhattan for Joe shortly after Jack Kennedy announced or breakfasting at Del Charro with J. Edgar Hoover. He helped distribute cash during the West Virginia primary. It was Johnny Rosselli who smoothed over Frank Costello's feathers and convinced him to cancel the contract he had put out on Joe Kennedy after the financier shorted the mobster on a real-estate deal. Dark, glossy, accommo-dating, the Outfit's don-at-large had become indispensable in many worlds.

Rosselli's client list by the later fifties was upgrading fast. Rosselli's most versatile contact man during this period, Robert Maheu, seems to have maneuvered him into a position to see after certain "business func-tions" for Maheu's top client, Howard Hughes, and Rosselli was starting to appear at dinner parties in Hughes's corporate fortress on Romaine Street in Los Angeles.

Dade County (Florida) police records turned up a file detailing a sur-prisingly personal exchange between the dapper gangster and the founding father in 1960. The financier was getting a little alarmed about his sons' irre-sponsibility with women. In fact, well before Robert Kennedy resigned his attorney generalship, Rosselli had been delegated by "the family" to put the arm on a Los Angeles private detective about to name the president as a core-spondent in an unseemly divorce action. Rosselli remained an adroit opera-tor and maintained vital connections during the difficult years coming up with important syndicate contacts, from Marilyn Monroe to Jack Ruby.

All through the runup to the 1960 primaries, Joe Kennedy milked his abun-dant mob connections. "How much can I count on from the boys in Las Vegas?" ran the note from JFK that Frank Sinatra kept framed in his recre-ation room in Palm Springs. In fact, the Las Vegas muchachos were rumored to have thrown in $15 million. The financier put together a fund-raiser on a ranch in Arizona to hit up the New York don Joseph Bonanno and his pro-ponents across the organization, and his son Bill was dispatched to Manhattan to try and sell the New York Mob on Jack. As the Las Vegas FBI reported, the candidate himself attended Mass with Smiling Gus Battaglia, an underboss in one of the New York families, who showed up at a Phoenix fund-raiser for Jack in 1959. JFK himself was probably unaware of how deeply obligated his campaign was getting. Kenny O'Donnell, who found himself handing out cash in many an obscure precinct, was in hourly touch with the Ambassador. "If Jack had known about some of the telephone calls his father made on his behalf to Tammany Hall–type bosses during the 1960 campaign, Jack's hair would have turned white," O'Donnell wrote afterward.

Joe Kennedy dispatched a mutual acquaintance to Vincent "Jimmy Blue Eyes" Alo, Meyer Lansky's alter ego. There is some evidence that the cunning Lansky, who got cleaned out for a total of $17 million in cash and property in Havana, liked Jack's aggressive anti-Castro pronouncements during the

debates and rerouted additional Las Vegas money into the Kennedy excheq-
uer. It hadn't come easily; since 1927, when Lansky's gunsels intercepted a
convoy of Joe Kennedy's whiskey coming ashore and wiped out eleven
guards, Lansky confederate Doc Stacher had nursed the conviction that the
Kennedys were "thirsting for my blood" and regarded Bobby's rampant
crime-busting as the outcome of "a personal grudge."

Such suspicions were nonsense, so far as Joe was concerned. The Chicago
heavyweights featured in Joe Kennedy's prayers. One day in 1960, when
Murray "the Camel" Humphreys was struggling to coordinate the Illinois
unions behind Jack, his annoyed wife asked after the whereabouts of Sam
Giancana, who dumped all those hours of telephoning on her overworked
husband.

"He's taking care of his end, Blondie," the preoccupied Camel muttered.
"He's with Joe Kennedy in California."

The patriarch did not present himself to the Mob primarily as a suppli-
ant. By nature a player, with golf bets sometimes running to $10,000 a
round, the financier could assess for himself the cash flow predictable from
institutional wagering. So he was more than an interested party when the
long-awaited Tropicana opened on the Las Vegas Strip on April 3, 1957. It
was the biggest, splashiest casino anywhere, the embodiment in concrete of
the syndicate's breakthrough into national legitimacy.

While owned on paper by Indiana insurance executive Ben Jaffe, a carefully drawn trust subsequently pinpointed the true backers of the Tropicana.
Downey was the real surprise. "I wouldn't be surprised if he was fronting it
for Joe," Morton Downey Jr. said flatly years afterward. "That's how they
worked."

A few months later Frank Costello took a bullet in the lobby of his apartment house on Central Park West from Vincent "The Chin" Gigante. The
bullet grazed Costello's head and spun around his skull, and, while he was
stretched out in the hospital, city detectives came upon an itemization in the
hand of the Mob's manager at the Tropicana, Lou Lederer. It detailed the skim
for the month, the cash the Mob was draining off prior to sending its figures
along for tax purposes.

The notoriety this incident generated would have enduring consequences. The staid Mormon bankers to whom the Mob had so far been able
to go for capital to develop Las Vegas closed their cashier's cages, which left
the mobsters dependent on Chicago money—increasingly, the Teamsters'

Central and Southern Pension Fund, Allen Dorfman. Not very many months later, Robert Kennedy moved in as chief counsel to the McClellan Committee and did his damnedest to roast like weenies beneath the committee-room lights most of the grandees of organized crime in America. And not too long after *that*, the Mob's overextended position in Cuba abruptly collapsed along with Batista. Then, to top everything off, once JFK won the presidency, Bobby unleashed his Get-Hoffa Squad to put away Jimmy. On whom the wiseguys had come to depend financially.

The Kennedys were presenting the organization with a very substantial problem.

It has been said that Joe Kennedy's many holdings touched organized crime at a hundred points. If the Tropicana was one, another was the Cal-Neva Hotel. It was the hard-driving financier's pleasure to drop out from time to time, to refresh his nerves, and among his off-the-record destinations California had always been a favorite. Around 1928 he had discovered the idyllic hunting and fishing compound. Well up a circuitous road and over-hanging Lake Tahoe's stunning Crystal Bay, the Cal-Neva's entertainment rooms straddled the California/Nevada line. Any time state cruisers from either jurisdiction pounded into the dooryard, it was a snap to slide the gaming paraphernalia across the well-waxed floor and into another state.

Along with the bracing air and the ten-foot Christmas trees Joe Kennedy shipped back to Hyannis Port every fall, the Cal-Neva recommended itself for its atmosphere of luxurious privacy. The place was well calculated to gratify its rich, shadowy clients. Secret tunnels connected the bungalows. Hustlers long inured to every imaginable appetite stalked the Alpine galleries. The Cal-Neva afforded a chance for the patriarch to try his luck at the tables, and, needless to say, there were always the women. "He may be old," Walter Winchell remarked of Kennedy's deportment around the public rooms, "but he's still in there pinching."

Typically, if Joe Kennedy took a liking to something, he wanted to possess at least a piece of it, whether it was a Broadway show or a racetrack or an actress or a restaurant or a seat in Congress. The Cal-Neva was no exception. The ambassador had been a denizen of the place since it was acquired by Norman Biltz—the "Duke of Nevada"—and watched a succession of owners, mostly Mob-connected, strain to make it pay. In 1955 a battered Lansky subordinate from Miami, Bert "Wingy" Grober, took over the management. A restaurateur and bookie the financier had patronized for decades, Wingy, whose left arm was congenitally shriveled, was presumed to be keeping an eye on the premises for Joseph P. Kennedy.

By the later fifties, the FBI was starting to keep track of arrivals and departures at the resort, and resurfacing Bureau paperwork specifies that Kennedy was "visited by many gangsters with gambling interests." "He had considerable experience in the bygone era of smuggling," Hoover's top aide, the courtly Deke DeLoach, will admit at this point. "And that's how he made his fortune, according to Mr. Hoover." In time, the Bureau ran up 343 case files on the financier, most of them intended to disappear quietly into the Director's Official and Confidential archives.

The aging patriarch's fascination with young, available women hadn't deserted him. Meyer Lansky would reminisce about Joe Kennedy's postwar visits—"four or five times a week"—to the Colonial Inn on Miami Beach, which Lansky and Frank Costello co-owned. The financier would normally arrive with a date and put a menu up to keep from being snapped by the club photographer while ogling the exuberantly nude floorshow. Were any of the girls free later? By then, one of Costello's minions observed, Kennedy tended to exhibit something of the furtive, helpless air of "a priest on the cheat," world-weary and disapproving beneath his mechanical bonhomie.

Throughout reactionary Palm Beach, stories continued to make the rounds about the patriarch's attachment to Françoise Pellegrino, the gamine who had been caddying for Kennedy in Antibes since she was eleven. The demands of too many grandchildren had driven their grandfather to lie low for much of the summer in the South of France, and Françoise was often-times at his side when he returned briefly to scrutinize the books.

As the fifties ended, the Ambassador was beginning to fend off mortality. In 1956, at sixty-eight, Kennedy had stopped over at the Hotel Raphael in Paris with the demure young woman who had been his personal assistant, confidante, and mistress for eight years, Janet Des Rosiers. Excruciating pain along his lower abdomen frightened him, and the pair flew back at once to Boston. Doctors at New England Baptist found indications of cancer, and performed a prostatectomy. On the pretext of a strep throat, Kennedy arranged to check Des Rosiers into the hospital with him; she later reflected that "the thought of being alone in the hospital was more than he could tolerate." Rose never stopped by, although J. Edgar Hoover dispatched a get-well note.

The confidence and vibrancy that had marked the Ambassador's long, many-faceted career was now threatened more and more by premonitions of abandonment. Janet Des Rosiers returned one night later than she had expected to her little apartment in Hyannis Port to discover the financier on her bed, weeping, crying out "Why did you do that to me? Why did you do that to me?" For all the children, the ambitions fulfilled, the celebrated charities—the wind still blew with an increasing fury out there, the portents of death and failure drafted across his dreams.

Not that the children would ever be allowed to penetrate the bluster. The financier was consolidating. Part of the horse-trading that pulled the Mob in behind Jack involved the Cal-Neva. With Joe involved, here was more leverage Giancana and his crew might exert on the presidency. A follow-up FBI memo would specify that "Before the last presidential election," and consequent to the arrival of the "many gangsters with gambling interests" at the Cal-Neva, "a deal was made which resulted in Peter Lawford, Frank Sinatra, Dean Martin and others obtaining a lucrative gambling establishment, the Cal-Neva Hotel, at Lake Tahoe. These gangsters reportedly met with Joseph Kennedy at the Cal-Neva. . . ."

What appears to have happened was the transfer of 49.5 percent of the Cal-Neva stock to the Sinatra group (represented, according to the deed, by Sinatra, his manager Hank Sanicola, and Dean Martin) while Wingy Grober—Kennedy—hung on to 50.5 percent: control. The cash to underwrite Sinatra's end of the partnership, $350,000, came directly through Sam Giancana. Skinny D'Amato took over the active management.

The investment was troubled, almost immediately. Sinatra and Giancana got into a poisonous wrangle after Sinatra chewed out Edward Olson, the head of the Nevada State Gaming Control Board, labeling him "a hunchback and a crippled idiot" for complaining about catching Giancana on the premises—the Windy-City wheelman was near the top of the list in Nevada's Black Book, its index of mobsters barred from statewide gambling establishments. Olson was further incensed when Skinny D'Amato persisted in slipping hundred-dollar bills into the pocket of the Nevada Control Board's inspector. The Cal-Neva abruptly lost its gaming license. Because of Sinatra's big mouth, Giancana moaned into FBI microphones, Chicago was out $470,000.

While it lasted, the Cal-Neva's ownership arrangement, to quote the penetrating Gus Russo, produced a situation in which "in essence, Bobby Kennedy's nemesis, Mooney Giancana, was now in partnership with Bobby's father." Ushering the starstruck Giancana into the resort was what it took, apparently, to get Jack elected.

* * *

Joe Kennedy was again haunted by his existential "itch," those unpredictable fits of nervous irritation because things were slipping, that, whatever they accomplished, the "nice people," in Rose's phrase, weren't going to like them any better. His exertions for the Hoover Commission hadn't really brought much recognition. Allen Dulles, something of a hanger-on around the Palm Beach estate of his friends the Charles Wrightsmans, arranged to appoint Kennedy to the predecessor to PFIAB, the President's Foreign Intelligence Advisory Board, mandated by Eisenhower's advisers to oversee the rampaging CIA. The financier signed up to keep an eye on the intelligence picture in the South of France as well as Italy, where his seasoned contact Count Enrico Galeazzi was alarmed because the Vatican's own intelligence system had obviously been penetrated. Kennedy promptly got into a tiff in Rome with William Colby, the Agency's soft-spoken but obstinate station chief, who refused to turn over the names of the CIA's local agents to this tempestuous old reactionary, and after a frustrating six months Kennedy dropped off the review panel. Existing documents would suggest that Kennedy was briefing J. Edgar Hoover personally when anything he ran into looked interesting to the Bureau.

At that stage Kennedy was more and more interested in clearing the way for Jack. This would require indirection; he'd somehow have to keep his famous profile down. When somebody brought up the Catholic issue with Harry Truman, the scrappy ex-president volunteered: "It ain't the Pope, it's the Pop." The public's perception that a notorious presence like Joe Kennedy might overhang the break-in months of Camelot forced the financier to lie low, holing up in Eze and avoiding the White House. But staffers of the period remember his unremitting attempts to track the internal process. "The sun never set but that Kenny O'Donnell had to deal with at least two very lengthy telephone calls from the Old Man," one insider recalls with a laugh. Many of these exchanges concerned the financier's determination to grab off Jack's old Massachusetts seat in the Senate for Teddy, a display of hubris the hard-bitten O'Donnell particularly disparaged.

Wherever Kennedy found himself, the burden of his investments got heavier every month. By 1960 the financier's twenty Park Agency employees, overseen by CPA Tom Walch, were scrambling to remain abreast of the cascading paperwork, yet most of the substantial decisions rolled back onto the principal himself, as often as not on the run or over the telephone.

Along with the Merchandise Mart and his Kenoil and Moheen petroleum exploration companies, there was a Coca-Cola bottler and distributor, worldwide real-estate speculations, a smattering of securities. The charitable foundations took time; by 1965, $17 million had reportedly been distributed. Only Joe could grasp it all.

Financial analysts of the period had started to revise downward the 1957 *Fortune* assessment of Joe's net worth from $250 million to perhaps half that, "and it was not invested wisely." When Rose Kennedy upbraided her husband for not letting her in on the extent of the family's assets once inflated estimates appeared, Joe blew right back: "How the hell could I? I didn't know myself." But he knew. Clerks at a handful of desks at the Park Agency offices functioned essentially as a clearinghouse, updating accounts and dealing with the torrent of family bills as they poured through.

Between the exorbitant life styles of the children and the heavy, hidden costs of the political campaigns, Kennedy's capital was eroding. This ate at Joe. Once, galled by her extravagances, he had unloaded on Ethel at a family gathering; she ran out, deeply upset. When she finally returned, it took a quip by JFK to save the situation. "Dad," he informed the financier, "we've talked it over and decided there is only one solution. You'll just have to work harder." Like so many of the diffident president's asides, the effect was hilarious and, after a moment, heartbreaking.

Joe continued to work, perhaps too hard. For years, specialists at the Leahey Clinic outside Boston had warned Kennedy that he was overtaxed, his blood pressure was up. They prescribed exercise, a low-fat diet and anticoagulants. Members of his household were skeptical about whether he ever bothered to have the prescriptions filled.

By the autumn of 1961, after a summer away and a quick trip West to check on the ailing Marion Davies in Palm Springs and play a little golf with Tony Curtis, he'd joined the family over Thanksgiving in Palm Beach and moved on quickly to check out several real-estate deals in New York and pick over the books at the Merchandise Mart. On December 10, 1961, prompting family members to remark at how played-out he looked, the patriarch reappeared in Florida.

For all the financier's seemingly ageless snap, his ability to spring out of a chair to greet somebody he needed for the moment (those outsize teeth gleaming with the ferocity of his reception)—Joe Kennedy was kidding himself. He wasn't the same. Sudden dizzy spells overtook him now, and he had fallen from his horse. He had to exert whatever strength he had to manage a couple of laps in the pool. Nine holes of golf was a strain. The protocol of brittle respect between himself and Rose had left him emotionally sapped, dependent on his lonely niece Ann.

Two days after Joe Kennedy started to pull himself together in Palm Beach, Hoover sent the attorney general a distillation of the transcriptions the FBI's Chicago office had garnered from their microphone surveillance of the local gangsters. Most of the threats and all the raw language were processed out, but the gist was clear: "information has been received indicating that Samuel M. Giancana, a hoodlum figure, has sought to enlist [Chicago Special Agent William Roemer would later indicate that the name blanked out here was Frank Sinatra] to act as an intermediary to intercede on Giancana's behalf with the Attorney General. In this regard, consideration was allegedly given to making such overtures through the father of the Attorney General. However, [blank] is reported to have rejected this idea.

"Information has been received that Giancana complained bitterly concerning the intensity of investigation being conducted of his activities and that he made a donation to the campaign of President Kennedy but was not getting his money's worth."

Sinatra had in fact already approached the Ambassador several times to intercede for Giancana. The singer also suggested to the president that Giancana was feeling a precariously high level of heat. JFK had characteristically sloughed Sinatra off on Bobby, who was reportedly "really insulting to Frank and very unreceptive." When Sinatra brought the problem up again with the president, Jack recommended that he "go see Dad," because "Joe was the only one who could talk to Bobby."

The volatile patriarch had counseled Sinatra about his financial problems, helping cut his income tax one year from $1 million to $65,000, but when the warning about Sinatra came in from Hoover, Joe ordered footage of Sinatra removed from the inauguration coverage, then reinstated it, then invited Frank to visit him on the Côte d'Azur, then sent word that there was "no room" for the crooner at the villa. Again, panic was setting in.

What no doubt alarmed both Bobby and Joe about the FBI report on Giancana was the implication that *Hoover* was now about to take a hand in this potentially cataclysmic game the Kennedys were playing with the Mob. There is a lot of evidence that Jack Kennedy, largely on his own or through the intermediation of Judith Campbell, had himself developed a working relationship with Giancana and his managers. An FBI wiretap picked up Rosselli going into details about the president and Campbell. If any significant part of this got through to the public—and Sandy Smith of the *Chicago*

Sun-Times was one of the Director's favorite outlets—the details could blow the Kennedys out of the White House.

It would be hard to evaluate how heavily Hoover's summary weighed on the financier. "I get awfully blue sometimes," he confided to one old friend during a walk on the strand that winter. On December 19, 1961, having ridden out to Palm Beach International Airport to drop Jack off at Air Force One, Joe and his niece Ann Gargan decided to play the back nine at the Palm Beach Country Club. On the sixteenth hole he complained of feeling a little ill and sat down. Ann got him back to the mansion and led him to his bedroom. Rose looked in later and found him stretched out on his bed, still in his golf shoes. When Bobby telephoned after a while, Ann went to alert her uncle and found him "just lying there. . . . He couldn't pick up the phone."

When, ultimately, they got Joe to Saint Mary's Hospital, the stroke that would leave the patriarch grotesquely twisted and largely incommunicado for the next eight years had established itself. Throughout recent months, Rose had been reassuring people that Joe was "in wonderful condition for his age," and showed no alarm when Ann Gargan brought him back to La Guerida. When, after several hours, a doctor came and Joe was hustled off to the hospital, the chauffeur, Frank Saunders, was dispatched to pull Rose off the golf course so she could sign the necessary medical releases. Before she went over, she insisted on a swim at home. By the time the Saint Mary's emergency room personnel were permitted to intervene, the damage was too extensive to be reversed.

Confronting this horror, Rose Kennedy broke down for once and covered her face with her fingers. "My son, my poor, poor son," she got out, apropos of the president. "So much to bear, and there is no way now for his father to help him." As ever the least deluded when it came to Kennedy reality, Rose perceived at once that without her husband the safety margins between the family and all the encroaching power centers were gone. For all his brash, slangy, demanding mannerisms, the aging financier could deal with the world.

Rose's shock resonated widely. "Why, oh why," Frank Sinatra's valet George Jacobs overheard his boss wail when the extent of the financier's disability became evident, "did Joe get that fucking stroke?" Joe was the Mob's last hope, their way around Bobby. If the attorney general persisted with his scorched-earth campaign, who was there out there now to call him off?

Much of the same reasoning pertained to Hoover. More dangerous, if anything, as his mind began to wander at times and his paranoia about losing his job became paramount, the Director put up with what he attempted to dismiss as Robert Kennedy's puerile efforts to steal away the loyalty of his agents and embroil them in an institutionally dangerous flank attack on organized crime, interinvolved as it remained with politics at every level. The old financier's laudatory—even worshipful—tone toward Hoover and their long history of conniving together gave Edgar a fallback contact, a number to call when Bobby got unmanageable. Now nobody was available to answer.

Lyndon Johnson was another factor. Assiduously cultivated—and funded —by the Ambassador all through the middle fifties, Johnson understood that, even in the face of all those "Chamberlain-umbrella-man" insults the Texas delegation tossed around at the convention, the Kennedy founder was looking to Johnson to help ground Jack's unproven, eclectic government. When Bobby raised welts, Joe Kennedy was understanding. That channel had closed, too.

Perhaps most aggrieved was Jacqueline. As first lady, she found herself "appalled by her father-in-law's hold on the president," yet she, too, had succumbed years before to his comforting, protective presence, "a tiger mother," Jackie later observed, "swatting his cubs when they were out of line, and drawing them in with his paw when they were troubled." Presidential aides remember the father dropping by the West Wing to distribute gallons of fresh ice cream from a factory he happened to own while the First Lady "danced down the halls arm in arm with him, laughing uproariously at his teasing." Now there would be no open draw account at various couturiers, no more "important jewelry," nobody she dared hope could speak to Jack when his extramarital rampages got totally out of hand. Their center could no longer hold.

What made the Giancana connection so dangerous for them all was Giancana. Judith Campbell—Judith Campbell *Exner,* as she would be referred to by historians, her married name in later years—the statuesque brunette who secured the lead in the upcoming sexual farce, would memorialize Sam Giancana as a calm, low-key widower with a ruddy complexion and "penetrating, dark eyes." Judy was a known broad among members of the Western Mob since 1951, when Johnny Rosselli had picked her up "hanging around the studios" while she was still Judith Immoor and before she married the actor William Campbell.

Famously "pushy and reckless," irresponsible on the telephone, Judy Campbell was introduced to Giancana at a big cast party in the French Room at the Fontainebleau in Miami by Frank Sinatra in March 1960. Giancana manifested an interest in Judy right away, yet he was patient to the point of martyrdom when she explained that her affair with presidential candidate Jack Kennedy required that she reserve her favors. Exner was a woman with stern California standards.

Sinatra, who broke Exner in himself before passing her around, had included Judy in a little Kennedy family party at the Sands in Las Vegas early in the primaries. Things started up that evening with Jack. When Giancana began to attempt to court Exner, Sinatra undoubtedly told him that she was Jack's girl. That same winter Giancana had run into Phyllis McGuire of the Singing Sisters and fallen hard for her, to the point of obsession.

Sam Giancana was well known to be a mobster with a short fuse and a hungry wolf's disposition when it came to cornering whatever appealed to him. His restraint, month after month, with the idealistic Exner was utterly out of character, unless what he was after wasn't primarily dictated by his glands. With Joe and JFK unable to rein Bobby in, Giancana, with the help of Sinatra, could smell an angle.

Another advantage Giancana was already cultivating while dealing with the "G," as Giancana often referred to the federal government, was his complicity in the CIA's efforts to eliminate Castro. In August 1960, the Agency's operations chief, Richard Bissell, had authorized a $150,000 expenditure to look into the "executive action" route to removing Fidel Castro from power. The Agency was already subsidizing an FBI veteran, Robert Maheu, who kept pitching his all-purpose firm, Maheu Associates, as essentially a "problem solver" rather than merely another shoe-leather detective agency. Castro was increasingly a problem.

The deputy director of the Agency's Office of Security, James O'Connell, dropped by to meet Johnny Rosselli at a cocktail party Maheu arranged. Rosselli was a familiar name to the Agency after having imported some Mob muscle to Guatemala a few years earlier and bailed the CIA out of an impasse that had developed between United Fruit and Standard Fruit, in which the Mob had an interest. O'Connell explained the situation; Rosselli seemed to like what he heard but added that "he'd have to check it out with someone in Chicago."

This would be Sam Giancana. Giancana, too, seemed ready to go along, although, according to the CIA inspector general's report, Sam was "flatly opposed to the use of firearms," as in "a typical gangland-style killing," because "the chances of survival and escape would be negligible. Giancana stated a preference for a lethal pill that could be put into Castro's food or drink." It must be tasteless, and undetectable afterward.

Dick Nixon would later suspect that, by requiring the slow-moving CIA to come up with so sophisticated a drug, Giancana was attempting to stall the plot against Castro until after the election, denying the Nixon campaign any reflected glory for sidelining the bearded dictator. Other onlookers had their doubts. Little Al and similar FBI microphones planted around Celano's Tailor Shop and the Armory Lounge picked up within weeks on Giancana boasting that Castro was about to be eliminated, with "a girl" scheduled to drop "a pill" into something he ate or drank.

The third stooge in this hapless cabal was Santo Trafficante Jr., the senior Florida Mafioso whose restrained, often absentminded manners had lulled many a rival into fatal mistakes. Now into his middle forties, Trafficante might have passed, according to his attorney Frank Ragano, for "a bank executive or an Italian diplomat," what with his spreading tonsure and the gold-accented horn-rims. Trafficante spent a lot of time in Havana, where his Tampa family was heavily invested in five casinos and hotels, operated in uneasy coordination with the Lansky interests. A second-generation fixture on the Commission, Trafficante had been sent by his father to apprentice around New York with the Luchese and Profaci families and undergone his graduate schooling in Corsica and Central America and Mexico alongside the most promising narcotics traffickers anywhere in the profession.

Trafficante was a virtuoso at extracting whatever he wanted from both sides of a situation. He was a prime collaborator in selling out Albert Anastasia in 1957, the morning the brutal overboss got his beneath a hot towel in the barbershop of the Park Sheraton. Anastasia had his eye on Havana. During the months Fidel Castro was gathering strength in the Sierra Maestra, Trafficante smuggled him explosives and machine guns while over the same period supplying Batista with heavy armaments. After Havana fell, Trafficante was cut off and passed several months in one of the revolution's jails, Trescornia Camo, although he appears to have remained reasonably comfortable even there, and received visits from soldiers in Carlos Marcello's army, Lewis McWillie and Jack Ruby. Marcello and Trafficante together still controlled most of the drug business around the Caribbean.

Looking back, Johnny Rosselli, perhaps the only sincere patriot of the three, told Jimmy "The Weasel" Fratianno: "Remember when Santo was jailed and they grabbed his money when Castro came to power, and then suddenly he was released with all his money? He was probably reporting everything to Castro's agents, and Miami's full of them." CIA files document insider reports that Trafficante expected to nail down "gambling, prostitution and dope monopolies" in the event Castro fell. But in the meanwhile, Mob sources indicate, Trafficante made a deal with Castro to retain his existing drug network, on the island and around the Caribbean. Castro exacted a kickback, and the dope pipeline would remain an important source of dollars for the Communist dictator.

With Trafficante functioning as a mole, Rosselli ultimately realized, the Agency's plan to eliminate Castro, ZRRIFLE, couldn't possibly go anywhere. One effort to infiltrate three sharpshooters wound up with the would-be assassins "captured and tortured until they told all they knew about our operation," Rosselli admitted. "All these fucking wild schemes the CIA dreamed up never got further than Santo." Meanwhile, with U.S. involvement in Vietnam heating up, Trafficante was not above utilizing his new compadres in the CIA to help establish himself as a top dealer around Southeast Asia.

Personally, the fastidious Trafficante wasn't that high on the Kennedys. He recalled rather somberly the time in 1957 he had run into John Kennedy on a visit to Havana and offered to arrange a "private sex party" for the senator at one of the Trafficante hotels, the Commodoro. Watching Kennedy through a two-way mirror disporting with three ripe hookers had amused him at the time, but in the end, Trafficante told Ragano, he "lost all respect for him."

According to the ancient Sicilian code, respect trumps everything. Sam Giancana, absorbing bedroom details about the president from Judith Exner, was equally put off. Meyer Lansky's widow would reveal that, as a senator, Jack himself had approached the criminal mastermind in Havana and solicited his advice on where the girls were liveliest. "Throw him a broad," Giancana remarked in 1959, "and he'll do anything." At home or offshore, an assignation with Kennedy was all about servicing Jack, quickly. "It was the most memorable forty seconds of my life," another of Kennedy's squeezes, Angie Dickinson, was fond of joking, and, especially in Mob circles, word got around.

Giancana was a slim, elaborately dressed fellow, not too tall even in his toupee. Peter Lawford described him as a man with "the face of a gargoyle and the nose of a weasel," and his had been a life to nurture that drop-dead look. Old enough to have been a legendary wheelman and occasional enforcer for the Capone generation as well as a participant in the St. Valentine's Day Massacre, Giancana had done time for homicide, assault, bombing, burglary, and contributing to the delinquency of a minor. Police records would link him with two hundred torture-murders, including the command performance the FBI recorded and played for Bobby which left a three-hundred-pound juice collector named Action Jackson dying for three days on a beef hook after many hours of severe rectal violation and the electrification of his penis.

But this was by no means boudoir talk, and when the mood was right Giancana could bring to bear a "beguiling, lilting charm" that overcame a great deal. Judith Campbell Exner was a rather stately bourgeois party girl with big, black, well-coiffed hair and an appealing—if faintly bovine— receptivity. She relaxed men, and, for some months, for Giancana that was enough. He had a hook into the president by way of his patronage of Judith, whom he would refer to sometimes as a "business contact," and another into the "G" for having agreed to snuff Castro. Not to mention the Cal-Neva.

Sam Giancana *was* serious about Phyllis McGuire. An earlier boyfriend of Phyllis's was Dan Rowan, the straight man in the comic Rowan and Martin TV show, *Laugh-In*. To test his new powers, in October 1960 the suspicious Giancana pushed Maheu to arrange for the CIA to bug Rowan's hotel room in Las Vegas. A private investigator named Arthur Balletti went in to set the mikes but left his equipment around when he decided to take a break. A maid appeared to make up the room, discovered the gear, and called the sheriff, who arrested Balletti and alerted the FBI.

Maheu himself eventually leaked the news to his former FBI colleagues that the Agency was behind the break-in, and it was soon apparent that Giancana was behind the Agency. A March 8, 1961, FBI report places the bugging "at the time that subject Giancana was romantically interested in Phyllis McGuire. This situation is being explored in view of the fact Giancana possibly the prime moving force in having the installations made against Rowan."

How early either Kennedy brother became aware of the Agency's plotting to liquidate Castro remains a subject of debate. Richard Bissell made it plain to me during several interviews that he briefed candidate Kennedy fully as regarded the parameters of what turned into the Bay of Pigs. The working assumption in every informed quarter was that Castro was to be taken out of the picture before the brigade came ashore to facilitate the indispensable popular uprising. On the early suggestion by the renowned CIA floater, Hans Tofte, that Castro had to be removed ahead of the invasion, Jack Kennedy allegedly responded, "That is already in hand."

Exactly when the Kennedys were told that Giancana, Rosselli, and

Trafficante were integral to all this is harder to pin down. With Chicago wired, Hoover himself was plainly picking up on the outlines months before Jack Kennedy took office. Bureaucratically, the shoving contest began in March 1962, when the FBI prepared federal indictments against Balletti and Giancana on trespass grounds in the Rowan case and Sheffield Edwards, James O'Connell's boss at the Agency, was reduced to an appeal to Sam Papich, the FBI liaison to the CIA, to let it alone in the national interest.

By March of 1962 the uneasiness between the FBI Director and the Kennedy brothers was seeping into the press. Drew Pearson predicted in a column that Hoover was on the way out, and rumor had it that his replacement would be the director of State Department Security, William Boswell. Frightened, Hoover sent the attorney general and Kenny O'Donnell a memorandum specifying that the Bureau's investigation of "John Rosselli, a West Coast hoodlum," was producing a wealth of astonishing details concerning the regular contact between a Judith Campbell and Sam Giancana, as well as Campbell's suprising exchanges with the Oval Office. On Rosselli's tapped telephone, the indiscreet Campbell was blabbing her head off. Subsequent commentators would speculate that Rosselli had knowingly set the whole thing up.

At midday on March 22 the FBI Director arrived in his armored limousine and planted himself in the executive-mansion dining room for luncheon with the president and O'Donnell. Pointedly, Bobby was not invited. Even the understated O'Donnell would characterize the ensuing four hours as "bitter." The Old Man had the goods, and the unhappy president was compelled to agree. Hoover would stay on. To make very sure the president kept in mind just how many ways the Director was capable of exploiting such information, Hoover got word to Roy Cohn's schoolboy crony Richard Berlin, the top Hearst honcho in New York, and arranged to insert a brief reference in Walter Winchell's nationally syndicated column. "Judy Campbell of Palm Springs and Bevhills," the squib ran, "is Topic No. 1 in Romantic Political Circles." Here was an item designed to rumble through John Kennedy's innards like shit through a Strasbourg goose.

The entire imbroglio had been taking shape for almost a year. According to the official histories, Robert Kennedy was first let in on the assassination plotting against Castro on May 7, 1961; by then the Cuban invasion was a smoking ruin. "If you have seen Mr. Kennedy's eyes get steely and his jaw set and his voice get low and precise," CIA counsel Larry Houston would remark, "you get a definite feeling of unhappiness." Furthermore, as Bobby is invariably quoted, "If we were going to get involved with Mafia personnel again he wanted to be informed first."

This was in all likelihood intended to establish Kennedy's outrage for the permanent record. During those early months, Justice Department officers told the *New York Times*, "Bobby pushed to get Giancana at any cost," and expectations were high. Yet Maheu insists that the Kennedys were aware of the Mafia involvement all along, which leaves them compromised from the start. On May 9 Bob Kennedy advised Hoover, according to the Director's memorandum of conversation, that he had been "considerably disturbed" by this initiative, and agreed with Hoover that it reflected "horrible judgment in using a man of Giancana's background for such a project." He had "issued orders to CIA to never again in the future take such steps without checking with the Department of Justice."

A day later, expertly spinning his web, Hoover circulated a memo among his top staff dealing with his exchange with the attorney general in which "I stated as he well knew the 'gutter gossip' was that the reason nothing had been done against Giancana was because of Giancana's close friendship with Frank Sinatra, who, in turn, claimed to be quite close to the Kennedy family. The attorney general stated he realized this and it was for this reason that he was quite concerned when he received this information from CIA about Giancana and Maheu. The attorney general stated that he felt notwithstanding the obstacle now in the path of the prosecution of Giancana, we should still keep after him."

Having made it plain to the attorney general in his arid, poisonous style how vulnerable this administration might find itself should the dogs of publicity unearth the Kennedys' involvement with Giancana, the Director resumed his aloof stance while under his direction, out in meat-eating Chicago, his army of FBI special agents went frenetically to work. One of Hoover's most effective bureaucratic techniques was to oppose some precipitous course of action by his superiors, then, while continuing to present himself as above the battle, let word flow down to his knucklebusters on the bricks to tear apart anybody the politicians demanded. This produced great resentment, loudly trumpeted, and usually left Hoover looking sage and farsighted. Such tactics worked brilliantly, for example, when JFK got all worked up about the nation's steel executives, who resented being jerked out of bed by FBI agents almost as much as the business reporters who covered them.

Dogging Giancana offered Hoover the perfect opportunity to embarrass the Kennedys while presenting them with what they said they wanted. In

Chicago, once the heat from Apalachin was off, the FBI contingent dealing with the Bureau's Top Hoodlum Program had fallen from ten to five, and even these survivors were routinely sent out on mundane investigations. Within a year after Kennedy became attorney general the Chicago THP was keeping seventy agents busy.

By now the density of the endeavor made everybody itchy. All across Cook County the word was out that Sam Giancana had stepped up and become the overboss of the Outfit, subject to the occasional intervention of Joe Accardo, Murray the Camel, and Paul "the Waiter" Ricca, who had collectively grown fatigued with too many day-to-day responsibilities. Giancana's tendency to flash it around in Las Vegas and California admittedly made the directorate nervous, but Sam still had the energy, he was a whiz with numbers, and none of them could bust those kneecaps forever.

Life's Mob expert Sandy Smith would write that "Giancana rules the First Ward like a Tartan warlord. He can brush an alderman off the city council with a gesture of his hand—as he did in 1962." At Giancana's elbow waited the burly, glamorous Richard [Scalzetti] Cain, by 1962 a made man within the Mafia while simultaneously performing as chief investigator for the Cook County Sheriff's Office, a regular informant for the FBI, and the principal recruiter for the CIA around Chicago's West Side. The Agency wanted Spanish-speaking punks to beef up the Mongoose forces outside Miami. *Time* magazine later reported that Cain's services sucked up $100,000 of Agency funds, after which the Outfit threw in $90,000—"ice," protection money, a given, as Mooney tended to dismiss such matters. An experienced wireman, Cain had installed taps for President Prio in Havana before the Castro takeover and assisted the CIA with important bugs throughout Mexico City.

So Sam was obviously well-fortified, yet he remained prepared for concessions to pacify the new administration. After painful reflection, in 1962 Giancana told his personal representative to the U.S. Congress, Roland Libonati, that despite seven terms he was all through. Robert Kennedy had snarled at Libonati his assurance that if the Congressman returned to Washington he would wind up in the penitentiary. The "frail, gnomelike" Moe Giancana had unmistakably decided to throw Bobby a living public sacrifice.

Nothing seemed to do much good. The trio of special agents the Bureau hung on Sam Giancana were every one big, nervy galoots of the sort that appealed to Hoover. With word already down from the Director to get as close as possible to the leadership of the Outfit, Special Agent Bill Roemer helped direct the installation of many more taps and microphones, some in the Las Vegas properties, and coordinated squadrons of Bureau vehicles to buzz alongside Giancana wherever he went. None was particularly discreet. Roemer, four times the Notre Dame heavyweight boxing champion and a very long hitter, made sure his surveillance team followed Giancana's foursome on the golf course and peppered them with drives. Giancana's game collapsed. Nine-man groups of agents stayed busy around the clock to keep Giancana in "lock-step" mode. "If he went to dinner," Roemer wrote later, "we went with him. If I was on the shift and he got up from the table to go to the men's room, I'd get up and be at the next urinal. I found that really bugged him. He had shy kidneys. He couldn't do it when I was right there."

Roemer met Giancana's planes, led away Phyllis McGuire to be interrogated, and accused the don of being a "fairy" because he was looking after Phyllis's purse while the other agents grilled her. "He put his head right up under my chin," Roemer remembered, "and said, 'You fuckin' cocksucker! Who do you think you are talkin' to? I could have Butch [Blasi] come out here with his machine gun and take good care of you right now!'" After a superheated exchange centered on Hoover and the Kennedys, Giancana shouted: "Fuck John Kennedy. Listen, Roemer, I know all about the Kennedys, and Phyllis knows more about the Kennedys, and one of these days we're going to tell all."

Ultimately, Giancana had to secure a court order requiring the Bureau to back off. But he was obviously cracking, and when he blew, Hoover had good reason to anticipate, the shrapnel would fly inside the Kennedy administration.

Meanwhile, Hoover would keep his eye on the principals. It was an established rationalization around the Bureau that its agents only stumbled across the indiscretions of decent citizens in the course of scrutinizing criminals. Accordingly, in time the Bureau put out an explanation to the effect that only "by checking the long-distance phone bills of Johnny Rosselli," a legitimate target, did the FBI's Los Angeles office discover that he was making calls to Exner. This led to the discovery of many she made "to Giancana and the Oval Office."

In *The Dark Side of Camelot*, Seymour Hersh pieces out a very credible scenario, which establishes that the Bureau was pulling together a file on Exner by early 1960. Hersh plots the logistics of the many meetings that Exner claims she and Jack Kennedy had, and those that she and Jack Kennedy and Sam Giancana had, and concludes from White House logs and the presidential traveling schedule and FBI and Secret Service interviews that Exner's version—which, admittedly, shifted quite a lot over the years—fits.

Scrupulously underplaying the extent of his information, Hoover had already dropped a shoe by February 27, 1962. He sent Courtney Evans with a memo to Robert Kennedy and others at Justice and around the White House noting that someone in contact with Rosselli and Giancana, Judith Campbell (Exner), had called the president's secretary, Evelyn Lincoln, twice within a week. "The relationship between Campbell and Mrs. Lincoln," Hoover added coyly, "or the purpose of these calls is not known."

There was a message here, nothing either Kennedy brother was likely to misinterpret. According to Justice Department insiders, along with Johnny Rosselli's, Hoover had been tapping his attorney general's line, and he had heard Bobby laughingly assure his friends that, as big a pain in the ass as the Director had become, it really would not matter for a whole lot longer because he was on his way out. At worst, he would be seventy in 1965, and Jack would dump him then.

Hoover—to whom his position and his existence were interidentifiable —panicked. The stage was set for that very grim executive-mansion lunch. Watching both autocrats, Courtney Evans could imagine a head-on collision that would obliterate them both. "I figured I had one mission," Evans maintains with all the conviction his ninety years can muster. "Keep the Kennedys from firing J. Edgar Hoover. I thought that was a blow they'd never recover from politically. Hoover had such connections on the Hill, such a reputation for having all the gossip in Washington stored away. . . ."

Still mindful of his brother's determination that he accord this dangerous gaffer the deference any national monument expected, Robert Kennedy couldn't suppress from time to time his acute annoyance as Hoover manipulated situation after situation to thwart Bobby's will. While brooking no explicit disrespect of the Director among the lawyers in the Department, coming off his day with longtime friends and close colleagues Kennedy sometimes vented his exasperation and homophobia.

"J. Edna," he observed to Kenny O'Donnell during the early months, was "the kind of guy we can deal with," discounting for the time being those ancient, pendulous jowls and Bobby's private suspicion that Edgar had to "squat to pee." When Tolson went into the hospital, the attorney general could not help wondering, "What was it, a hysterectomy?" As his frustrations deepened, Kennedy confided to O'Donnell that Hoover "had gone mad. He's a fucking cocksucker. Any day now I expect him to show up at work wearing one of Jackie's Dior creations. And then there's that sheer nonsense about the Communist Party. What a supreme and utter waste of time."

Even more grating was Bobby's inability to nail up a dossier of his own to threaten the Director as those Official and Confidential files looked about to avalanche. The worried attorney general instructed William Hundley, the once and future chief of his Organized Crime Section, to come up with *something.* "We tried to prove that Hoover was homosexual," Hundley now confesses. "We had all that information that came out later about him runnin' around the hotel in a dress. . . . That was all bullshit. You can never be sure, you know what I mean, but I think he was some sort of a eunuch. . . ."

Bobby's latent animosity took on an edge as Hoover's remorseless army of wiretappers and surveillance gumshoes started closing in tighter every week on the Kennedys themselves. What made it particularly maddening was Hoover's astuteness when it came to trapping Bobby into signing off on measures calculated in the end to implicate his father or Jack. By 1962, the Bureau had been tapping Judith Exner's line for quite a period, Evans says, and presumably over Robert Kennedy's signature. The Director smelled paydirt. It was the executive conference crowd at the top of the FBI, Evans now admits, who, after so many years of looking away, found themselves chiming in with the Director to agree that Giancana was "a bad guy," and "decided to make his life miserable. This was renegade FBI activity as far as I'm concerned. Didn't produce anything. Just got us bad publicity."

During the initial months, Robert Kennedy was obviously a little slow to catch on to what Hoover was up to in Chicago, and excited by all the action. Sam Giancana was, after all, now advertised in law-enforcement circles as the premier crook in America, the worthiest of trophies. Roemer describes an early inspection visit during which Kennedy, his press aide Ed Guthman, Bill Hundley, and Courtney Evans descended on the FBI field office in Chicago. When the special agent in charge, Marlin Johnson, greeted them with a prepared statement, Kennedy cut him off: "Mr. Johnson, I didn't come here today to hear a canned speech about how magnificent you are. I didn't come here to hear from *you* at all. Now why don't I just step around there and take your desk. You can just sit over there in the corner and we'll listen to the agents who are out on the street, the men who are doing the work you think is so great."

Vintage early Bobby. By dissing Hoover's supervisor in Chicago, Kennedy was putting the Director down, hard, while demagoging the street agents. The attorney general soon had the men who had been running their full-court press on the Chicago Outfit falling all over one another to share their secrets with this young, charismatic boss. "I was surprised he knew so much about one guy in particular: Giancana," Roemer would write. Kennedy made the rounds, pounding members of each team with questions about the mobster he was tracking, ultimately settling on Roemer himself, who had a presentation demonstrating the de facto alliance between the Outfit and local politics. The *piece de resistance* was several key surveillance tapes.

"To lay the groundwork for him," Roemer writes, "I explained that this was a tape of a conversation we had procured by placing a microphone in the headquarters of the Regular Democratic Organization of the First Ward."

The tape caught segments of a conversation between Pat Marcy and two Chicago police department vice cops. Marcy was a "made guy," a confirmed Mafioso installed in the regular Democratic organization "to run the ward for the mob." As the tape ran, Marcy could be heard distributing the monthly envelopes from the Outfit to the vice-squad policemen and making sure the pimps and loan sharks themselves were kicking in. One vice officer refused to be bribed; the three now decided that he would have to be taken out.

Here was the raw evidence of which a young prosecutor dreams, and Kennedy kept calling for more, apparently oblivious as to how they got this stuff. Worse, criminal prosecution could shut down Giancana's vital river wards, on which John Kennedy's reelection might again depend. The seasoned William Hundley looked on with deepening alarm, and before they got into more specifics was able to get Kennedy out of the room, away from all this information these agents could only have obtained by recourse to criminal trespass.

It was already too late. As soon as Hoover got word of the presentation, he rounded up every agent present and in a position to swear that Kennedy had been listening and exacted sworn affidavits attesting to the presence of the attorney general.

The Director would bide his time.

In June 1963, having proclaimed to anybody who would listen that "This is like Nazi Germany and I'm the biggest Jew in the country," the frazzled Giancana appeared in federal court in his determination to end the FBI's maddening "lockstep surveillance." By then, Jack Kennedy had stayed away from Judith Campbell for over a year and changed his travel schedule to avoid overnighting with Frank Sinatra, which Kennedy explained to Peter Lawford was impossible, "while Bobby's handling the [Giancana] investigation." A measure of sanity was overtaking the White House. Robert Kennedy, as usual, would catch the blame once Sinatra was dumped off the presidential agenda, but years later Kenny O'Donnell admitted that he had been the one to force the issue. "Bobby, the Justice Department isn't arranging this trip," O'Donnell told his old roommate.

"Oh, all right, have it your way," the attorney general groused. By then he was beginning to comprehend more fully the history between his family and the Outfit and the sort of fallout openly humiliating a pepperpot like Sinatra might release.

Receiving word of the presidential change of plans, Sinatra promptly threw Peter Lawford down a flight of stairs and demolished his own helipad with a sledgehammer. By that time, Operation Mongoose had developed into an even greater—and more expensive—flop than the Bay of Pigs. Any Mob effort to dust Castro had been reduced to an inside joke—"I'm not in it," Giancana confided to Rosselli; "Maheu's conning the hell out of the CIA."

In court, Giancana gave organized crime in America a very tense moment when, queried by the U.S. attorneys as to whether he had ever broken any laws such as would justify FBI surveillance, Giancana answered—no. By answering at all, he had waived his immunity rights and opened himself up to detailed cross-examination. The file on Giancana's lifetime of felonies would probably have filled the courthouse.

But Bobby Kennedy had lost his nerve. On the far-fetched ground that the Justice Department did not wish to legitimize the judicial branch's authority over the executive, Kennedy instructed U.S. Attorney John Lalinsky not to cross-examine. Chicago Special Agent in Charge Marlin Johnson, who had suffered enough, was humiliated at finding himself required to refuse to respond to all questions "on instructions from the U.S. attorney general, order number 260-262."

In Hoover's judgment, the hook was set. The Director would tell Nixon officials that, by the time the Bureau was ready to arrest Giancana on racketeering charges, an alarmed Robert Kennedy had burst into his office and blocked the initiative. "He knows too much," Kennedy had blurted. By that stage, Kennedy knew too much, too.

After two harrowing years in office, Robert Kennedy had genuinely come to understand that Mob history intersected all along the fault lines of Joe Kennedy's career. In March 1962, Byron "Whizzer" White went onto the Supreme Court. Around the Justice Department, the starchy, intimidating White—who as deputy attorney general had found himself looking after the Department more and more of the time as Bobby got spread ever thinner— had functioned as conscience and proctor whenever touchy investigations arose. He had been instrumental in selecting Edwyn Silberling and backed him up in conflicted situations like the Keogh tangle. White's departure would finally permit a shift of emphasis.

Close observers could not mistake a heightened sensitivity to nuance in Bob Kennedy's treatment of the senior gangsters. One writer remarks, "FBI records show that Attorney General Kennedy seemed to be more concerned about the incestuous marriages in the Gambino blood family than he was about Carlos's criminal activities." By then the godfather of New York crime, Gambino was something of a protégé of Frank Costello, the long-term associate of both Joe Kennedy and J. Edgar Hoover.

FBI records detail a meeting at the Brown Derby between Johnny Rosselli, who asserted that he was representing the interests of Attorney General Kennedy, and Fred Otash, the sleazy but effective private investigator who seemed to find himself crawling in and out of so many of the Kennedy family's peccadilloes. In March 1961, presumably as a favor to Joseph P. Kennedy, Rosselli darkly informed Otash that "Fred was in trouble because he was about to name John Kennedy as a corespondent" in a divorce action, the extraordinarily messy Robert Westbrook/Judi Meredith breakup. Before the details could hit the tabloids, Otash would receive a check for $15,000 and Meredith an "under-the-table settlement" for $35,000 "to avoid any big scandal or derogatory publicity."

Early in 1963, openly demoted and humiliatingly sidelined, Edwyn Silberling gave up his cubicle and retired from the government. William Hundley moved back into his old slot, chief of the Organized Crime and Racketeering Section. A hard-working and tolerant soul with a good Irish appreciation for the preposterous, Hundley was able to reestablish working relations with the Bureau and its thin-skinned master, whom Silberling had consistently antagonized.

Silberling drew his own conclusions. Years later, reflecting on the Giancana embroilment, Silberling told an interviewer that "Bobby took me off the Chicago investigation just when I began to come up with information, the reason being that his father was often mentioned in connection with the Mafia. He was interested in crime-busting only to the extent that his family wasn't involved."

15

First Ethel, Now Us

All through the Kennedy presidency, while the front lines of Bobby's war on crime rolled back and forth, one national-security crisis after the next threatened to swamp the White House. The president's uneven health made coping with all this a lot more perilous. Dr. Jacobson's "miracle tissue regenerator" contained, according to better laboratory analysis than the FBI could provide, a mixture of vitamins, painkillers, addictive amphetamines, and human placenta as well as primitive steroids, quite close to the pepper-uppers with which Doktor Morell kept Hitler going. Along with the massive injections of cortisone and procaine, this many experimental compounds left even the strong-willed president either zonked or unable to sleep a good part of the time. His doctors prescribed Tuinal, which left him groggy, confused, hypertense, and/or depressed, so that an extremely strong antidepressant was sometimes indicated.

But the demands of statecraft are incessant, and Bobby was available. "The two of them shared the presidency," Eunice Shriver would observe. Bob Kennedy didn't deny it. "Isn't it exciting?" he joshed reporters. "I couldn't have done it without my brother."

Much as he appreciated the backup, Jack Kennedy was more than aware of Bobby's rough edges and stepped in from time to time to mitigate. Early in JFK's term, apparently prompted by the ferocity with which the Eisenhower Justice Department had gone after Truman appointees like T.

Lamar Caudle, Bob pushed a tax evasion case against a top Eisenhower aide, presumably Sherman Adams. Republican Leader Everett Dirksen stopped by the White House to suggest that Bobby drop the case. Jack telephoned Bob, urging his brother to "Place it in the deep freeze."

"This will destroy us politically," Bob responded. "To grant a special favor to a tax evader."

The exchange got heated. "I'm the president," JFK ended it. "If you can't comply with my request, then your resignation will be accepted."

It got down, often enough, to principle versus politics. "Tell him to get his dumb fuckin' brother to quit opposing my friend Ross Bohannon for a federal judgeship in Oklahoma," Senator Robert Kerr told one intermediary for the president, who could not understand why Kerr was blocking the administration's investment credit tax proposal. JFK quoted Kerr verbatim to the attorney general, complete with questionable Southern accent. Bohannon got his judgeship, and Jack Kennedy got his legislation.

Historians would ask afterward why Robert Kennedy was able to generate such intense and uncompromising loyalty throughout most of the Justice Department while churning up something close to revulsion around the rest of the government. It played out much like those touch football games: Bob was a truly inspired improviser, who stopped at nothing up to and including moving the goal posts if that was what it took to win. Opponents got battered, while people on his team shared his rush of adrenalin. "He was not a systematic organizer," Nick Katzenbach admitted afterward. "His method was to create a little bit of a madhouse by picking people rather than organizing." Never one even to pretend to read briefs or position papers, "He was inclined to trust people and give them broad authority until they proved they didn't merit it."

These were government employees under the attorney general's control, of course, people he could hire or fire. Officials in the other departments, outsiders, too often got pushed around or humiliated, especially when they disagreed. A CIA briefer never forgot the incident, during the worst of the missile crisis, when JFK, seeking broad bipartisan support, asked his brother to usher in Robert Lovett, the prestigious Republican financier and secretary of defense during the Truman years. Bobby reportedly stuck his head out the Oval Office door and signaled Lovett with a sharp "Hey, you!" After Lovett disdained to respond, Bob followed up with another "Hey, you!" When Lovett, affecting confusion, pointed to himself, Bob erupted "Yes, you! Come here."

"The president," the aide would later record, "slammed his pen to the desk, ran his hand across his brow and, thoroughly disgusted, screamed out, 'Goddamn, Bobby!'"

Robert Kennedy's us-versus-them mentality raised contusions all across the bureaucracy. As the months passed he seemed to be micromanaging everything, up to and including the thousands and thousands of patronage jobs available to the Post Office Department. Memories would remain rawest around the CIA. Jack Kennedy was badly stung by the humiliation consequent to the Bay of Pigs and attached his brother to the rattled Agency to let its survivors understand that he did not intend, again, to be misadvised.

The high-minded but ineffectual California industrialist John McCone was moved in to replace the disgraced Allen Dulles late in 1961, and both brothers Kennedy were resolved that the old crowd out at Langley had to be brought under discipline. By then Jack Kennedy was discovering the advantages of containing his own exasperation and sitting there in apparent composure tapping the metal band of his pencil against his front teeth while his infuriated brother tore bureaucratic ass. In a late interview, CIA operations chief Dick Bissell would remember his own largely fruitless efforts to get compensation for the widows of the pilots whose B-26s had been shot down during the preliminary raids on Castro. This would risk deniability. "Bobby was like a wounded animal, while the president just sat back and let him attack," Bissell said afterward.

It was the familiar Kennedy family blame game, with Bobby in place as the designated goat. "I'm afraid, Mr. President," one of the Southern archons warned JFK while he was receiving a small delegation of senators on the White House porch, "that I'm going to have to attack you on those civil rights."

"Don't do that," the president came back. "Can't you just attack Bobby instead?"

So Bob was spending mornings at CIA headquarters to drive Mongoose and head off another disaster in the making. What his restive subordinates thought about their new, de facto intelligence boss comes through in a bumper sticker that showed up in the parking lot at Langley: "First Ethel, Now Us." Impressed at that point by the proposals of Maxwell Taylor to develop flexible response techniques against wars of national liberation, the Kennedys brought him back from retirement to serve as chairman of the Special Group for Counterinsurgengy (CI), soon to be renamed simply the Special Group Augmented (SA). Taylor was bumped up to chair the Joint Chiefs before replacing Henry Cabot Lodge as ambassador in Saigon.

Taylor was the chair, but Bobby expected to call the shots. Thomas

Parrott, a crisp, seasoned CIA professional who functioned as the secretary for the group, didn't leave his feelings in doubt: "Bobby, in my view, was an unprincipled sinister little bastard." Parrott would remain annoyed at the way Kennedy would blow into a meeting and cross his ankles on the edge of the conference table and make everybody else strain to see his face beyond the soles of his shoes.

Parrott remembered how subservient the other members of the committee, McGeorge Bundy included, became once Kennedy spoke up and expressed a preference. Once, after Kennedy indicated that he would like the acute but wordy Arthur Goldberg to join the Special Group and all the others were quick to go along, Taylor himself stepped in to veto the recommendation. "Oh, shit, the second most important man in the country loses another one," Bob exploded and rushed out of the meeting, slamming the door behind himself.

Taylor himself—after whom Bob Kennedy named one of his sons—was frank about Kennedy's immaturity at that point: "I don't think it occurred to Bobby in those days that his temperament, his casual remarks that the president would not like this or that, his difficulty in establishing tolerable relations with government officials, or his delight in causing offense was doing harm to his brother's administration." With supporters like Taylor, who needed the critics?

The situation didn't improve, for the most part, as Kennedy got closer to the clandestine battlefield. In the autumn of 1961, the legendary senior CIA operative William Harvey was brought in from Berlin to take over Task Force W. Artfully buried in Task Force W's mission description was the resuscitation of ZRRIFLE, Boris Pash's feckless program to assassinate foreign leaders. Like the Mongoose program under Edward Lansdale, this endeavor was low-percentage, expensive, and in the end enormously damaging to American prestige.

The gruff, bug-eyed William Harvey was used to working with very little administrative oversight. Tossed out of the Bureau for alcoholism in the fifties, the suspicion would persist that Harvey had been planted by Hoover as a mole in the early Agency. By 1961 William Harvey had matured into "a pyramid of flab, frank enough to characterize himself as a reliable consumer of three martinis at lunch—'two doubles and a single.'" He was an anomalous presence among the trim, hard-edged New Frontiersmen.

Habitually, Harvey secreted a number of revolvers around his disheveled person, a snub-nosed .38 crammed into the cleavage of his rump. He liked to manage all operations close to the vest, and it took whatever control he could muster not to shoot Robert Kennedy the day Harvey waddled into his own office to find the attorney general riffling through the papers on his desk. Harvey stormed up and grabbed the papers away from Kennedy, roaring forth an oath. Privately, Harvey referred to Kennedy simply as "that fucker."

Just about the greatest asset Mongoose had, Harvey decided, once his doubts about collaborating with gangsters cleared up, was Johnny Rosselli. Quickly dubbed "the colonel" by CIA insiders, Rosselli could work closely with the violent David Morales—("the Indian")—the Agency's most accomplished field specialist at busting underclass insurgencies like the Tupemoro guerrillas in Uruguay. Both men relished bar stories afterward which featured them jumping ashore beneath coastal machine-gun fire, their boats breaking apart as they waded onto the soggy Cuban beaches with fresh supplies.

Rosselli in turn handed off a lot of administrative responsibility to the temperamental exile Tony de Varona, Cuba's prime minister under Carlos Prio. Heavily primed to take down Castro by himself if necessary, Varona exploited his contacts to collect several generations of poisons along with detonators and boat radar and dynamite by the truckload. Under Ted Shackley, Harvey's protégé in Berlin, the JM/WAVE station topped four hundred agents. Not that many reached their targets alive.

Bob Kennedy would subsequently characterize the CIA of the period as "not very good" and accused it of intending "to send sixty people into Cuba right during the missile crisis." *It* meant Harvey. Yet Agency survivors recollect that most of the pressure came from above, not below. The Kennedy brothers "were just absolutely obsessed with getting rid of Castro," insists Sam Halpern, the durable executive assistant to several operations directors. "I don't know of any senior officer that I talked to who felt, aside from the pressure from the Kennedys, that Castro had to go." After decades of holding his tongue, questioned yet another time about who gave the orders to do away with Castro, Richard Helms finally erupted on television: "There isn't any doubt as to who was running that effort. It was Bobby Kennedy on behalf of his brother. It wasn't anybody else!"

With regular civil servants unable to respond as satisfactorily as they demanded to the requirements of the Kennedy brothers, Bob brought in assets of his own, family resources. He directed the Agency to provide him with an experienced operative, Charles Ford, whom he personally intended to run. A big, powerful, glad-handing clandestine-warfare boomer of the sort Hoover might have put to use, Ford was rechristened "Rocky Fiscalini" and introduced to a variety of underworld personalities. "Bobby was absolutely convinced that the mob had a stay-behind system in Cuba," Halpern says,

A turn in the semitropics—Rose and Joe as newlyweds. *(Kennedy Library)*

P. J. and Joe Jr. kill an afternoon at the shore. *(Kennedy Library)*

Rose and the dazzled Robert prepare for the Court of St. James. *(Library of Congress)*

A knowing Hoover at four.
(National Archives)

Hoover and Tolson at the top of
their game—whatever that was.
(National Archives)

Clyde Tolson and the rising Hoover hit the Manhattan nightspots. *(National Archives)*

Joe Kennedy busses the bride—JFK's wedding. *(Kennedy Library)*

Joe Kennedy absorbs instruction
from Eugenio Pacelli (Pope Pius
XII). *(Kennedy Library)*

Roy Cohn registers alarm at hearing the day's outrage from his indulgent boss, Senator Joe McCarthy. *(Library of Congress)*

Jimmy Hoffa (below) cocks an ear toward his wiretapper, Bernard Spindel. *(Library of Congress)*

Carroll Rosenbloom conducts business. *(Library of Congress)*

Bobby Baker warms up to actress Dorothy Malone. *(Courtesy of Bobby Baker)*

Judith Campbell Exner during an appreciative moment. *(National Archives)*

Ellen Rometsch, Jack Kennedy's final odalisque. *(Wide World)*

Younger and Older Brother. *(Kennedy Library)*

The inimitable Brumus. *(Library of Congress)*

Sam Giancana and Phyllis McGuire sample a little wine. *(Associated Press)*

The luminous Marilyn Monroe establishes a point with Frank Sinatra at the Cal-Neva. *(Dordero Photo Collection)*

Johnny Rosselli (right) doesn't much like what his lawyer has to say. *(Library of Congress)*

Flanked by attorneys Jack Wasserman (left) and Mike Maroun (right), Carlos Marcello waits to refuse to incriminate himself. *(Library of Congress)*

JFK, an attentive Hoover, and the ever-skeptical Bobby endure a rare White House visit. *(Kennedy Library)*

Martin Luther King Jr. (second from left), not happy in Bob Kennedy's shadow. *(Kennedy Library)*

The ultimate Robert Kennedy wades through his new constituency. *(Library of Congress)*

"since they had so many assets left there. There were casinos and gambling dens and prostitution rings and God knows what else." In Halpern's opinion, "The concept was crazy." Security on the island was too tight.

Ford was under orders to go in "naked" and report back only to Bobby. The Kennedys had apparently put Ford in touch with Joe's contacts around the Lansky organization. Once Mike McLaney got out of jail in Havana he seems to have made his own underlings available, starting with his right hand man at the old Nacional, "Sam Benton."

McLaney is said to have offered a competent explosives man $90,000 to bomb Castro; then, after a fervid meeting at the Kennedy Palm Beach estate at which "They were all there—Joe, Bobby, the President," when the gamblers asserted that "We could have had him [Castro] killed in ten minutes," one participant recalls, "Mike was against it. He knew it would destroy the White House if it got out."

Another layer of backup that Robert Kennedy infiltrated to keep check on the CIA was overseen by the indispensable Walter Sheridan. He and three other Get-Hoffa Squad veterans had formed the "Five Eyes" investigative agency ("International Investigators Incorporated, of Indianapolis, Indiana") and were intermittently on retainer to the Kennedy family for special projects. Along with Bobby's friend John Reilly, the head of security at State, the "Five Eyes" were apparently brought in to monitor and ultimately wire-tap Otto Otepka, the holdover State Department security official the Kennedys resented for having lodged his objections to the much looser hiring practices around State in front of Eastland's Internal Security Subcommittee. Otepka hoped to blackball top liberal academics like Walt Rostow.

What drove Robert Kennedy was his impatience with the bureaucratic establishment, his need across the board to back himself up with some kind of shadow apparatus, people beholden to *him*. Like his father, he was never hesitant to raid an available staff or commission for talent. Like Joe, he had a knack for arousing in his most talented discoveries powerful and abiding loyalties.

Kennedy interacted least effectively with entrenched bureaucracies, starting with the FBI. He loved to manipulate external to the system. Determined to begin to efface the administration's early record by ransoming the 1,150 prisoners Castro had rounded up on the beaches of the Bay of Pigs, Kennedy entered into unofficial negotiations with the bearded dictator through a private attorney, James Donovan.

When enough private-sector cash had been raised and the deal was down, Kennedy dispatched the respected E. Barrett Prettyman Jr., whom he had known since law school, "to deal with Castro over some of the goods that he was getting. . . . I was primarily in charge of getting transportation for some of the goods coming into Florida and then going on to Havana. Getting planes, trains, trucks, and then a ship" for the many tons of pharmaceuticals and crated farm implements the Communists demanded. "As a result of that, Bobby got the mistaken idea that I was this great expert on transportation.

"It was ridiculous—I hardly knew a truck from a plane. In any case, he had a problem at the Justice Department. The ICC lawyers were hardly talking to the anti-trust lawyers at Justice, and there were a lot of things going on in the transportation field, and he asked me if I would come in to get that straightened out. . . . So I came over as his special assistant, and did the job in three months. It was mainly a matter of getting people together and cracking heads. Well, now he was really convinced."

Prettyman wound up in the White House as the president's expert on transport mergers and dealt with problems which ranged from keeping people in school to building new playgrounds. Whenever an hour came free, Kennedy liked to grab Prettyman and go fire up some neighborhood school children. Prettyman remembers the day they stopped by a local school where the indoor pool wasn't working. When it was, the crime rate in the neighborhood dropped. It would take $30,000 to fix the pool. "Bobby turned to me and said; 'get the money.' So I called a priest and some Jewish groups and we got the money immediately. We had Chuck Connors come in for the opening of the pool. That's the sort of thing that Bobby was so good at."

No forms, no wait, no haggling. He brought the same short fuse to affairs of state. From the early days of the administration, Bob Kennedy had cultivated a spirited back-channel friendship with Georgi Bolshakov. On paper the Soviet embassy's press attaché, the peppery Bolshakov was presumed by intelligence professionals to be KGB. The many Kennedy meetings with the uninhibited Russian, who loved to bate Kennedy by pointing out the authoritarian reflexes of the ruling elite in America, provided a pipeline to Khrushchev. These fifty-plus meetings served to defuse crises from a face-off of tanks at the Brandenburger Tor to escalating civil war in Laos.

All this behind the backs, not only of the State Department, but also the FBI. Hoover had been introduced around the offices to Bolshakov as merely another information officer posted to the Soviet embassy and was startled when JFK summoned the Director to a rare conference in the Oval Office in August 1962 and instructed him to order tight surveillance on the Russian. The FBI was reportedly ordered by the president to nail down Bolshakov's sexual preferences and entice him into a compromising situation, so he remained vulnerable to blackmail.

By then the intelligence community was swarming with rumors of Soviet missile ramps under construction in Cuba. The backstage details of the Missile Crisis have been covered in a raft of books and articles, not least Robert Kennedy's own, *Thirteen Days*. Simply thinking about preemptive air strikes, Robert Kennedy would observe in a note to Ted Sorensen, "I now know how Tojo felt when he was planning Pearl Harbor."

By stubbornly levering the originally hawkish assortment of military and diplomatic personages on the Executive Committee of the National Security Council (ExComm) from a plurality for saturation bombing of the missile sites to agreement on a phased blockade in the face of which the Soviets could withdraw with at least a semblance of self-respect, Robert Kennedy may very well have saved Western civilization. The president had gone about his usual unhurried rounds throughout those two critical weeks, while the exhausted Robert Kennedy forced into place the consensus that averted, in his own words, "a catastrophic war."

Many years later, at dinner in Moscow with several of the senior KGB and military officials of the period, men in the room with Khrushchev, I myself was given to understand that the Soviet leadership was resolved, should their bases in Cuba be bombarded, to send their nuclear-armed bombers and missiles against the important population centers throughout NATO. Not many of us would have survived.

Not that Robert Kennedy was squeamish, particularly, about tossing foreigners into the maw of *Realpolitik*. How far that went became apparent once Congress surfaced the details behind the Trujillo assassination. The Dominican Republic's dictator Raphael Trujillo was regarded as a bloodthirsty tyrant even by the Eisenhower administration, and plans were afoot inside the CIA to move him out well before the Kennedys took over.

With the Alliance for Progress pending, Trujillo remained a geopolitical eyesore. The boys at ZRRIFLE now had him on their short list. Weapons the Dominican dissidents could put to use to solve their problem came onto the island under the direction of Henry Dearborn, the U.S. deputy chief of mission, who stayed in place as consul general after diplomatic relations were cut off. Here, as with Patrice Lumumba or Salvador Allende or Ngo Dinh Diem, acceptable tradecraft necessitated that the Agency move the flats around and prompt the principal actors without actually pulling any triggers. Deniability would be uppermost.

In March 1961, according to an account by L. Gonzalez Mata, Trujillo's chief of security in 1960, Johnny Rosselli and the CIA's ever-industrious E. Howard Hunt Jr. came ashore on the island. By then, to the consternation of the White House, there was a complication. One of Joe Kennedy's regular golfing partners, the playboy columnist Igor Cassini (Cholly Knickerbocker), a popular contributor to Hearst, had arranged for his own small public relations firm, Martial, to profit indirectly from a $150,000 annual contract with the Dominican Republic without complying with the Foreign Agents Registration Act. Cassini had apparently misled Joe Kennedy as to where he expected to come out financially, and JFK approved a secret meeting between Trujillo and Robert Murphy, the agile diplomat who wound up the top State Department professional under Eisenhower. Cassini went along to look after his own interests. Documents which soon leaked indicated that Cassini was aware "from confidential talks with the eldest Kennedy that the President had already decided to act favorably in the Dominican case, even going over the heads of the adverse opinion in the Department of State."

Then Senator J. William Fulbright announced hearings into influence-peddling foreign lobbyists, and the investigative reporter Peter Maas began to ask around. Cassini's assurances to Joe Kennedy looked more and more dubious.

The Kennedys had plainly been conned, and they took it hard. After George Smathers failed as an envoy from JFK to convince the dictator to leave on his own, on May 30, 1961, Trujillo was gunned down from ambush. Bobby was irate to discover that his father had been implicated. Earlier in the process, Cassini—Ghighi to his friends—had evidently assured Robert Kennedy that he had no vested interest in the survival of Trujillo. FBI wiretaps gave that the lie and passed through one of Igor's exclamations about the patriarch himself: "That self-righteous bastard! I know the redhead he's sleeping with."

When Cassini lawyer Louis Nizer went by the Justice Department, Bobby unloaded on him: "Ghighi has not come clean with me. You're on the level, but your client is a son-of-a-bitch blackmailer."

Robert Kennedy had nursed his distaste for the Cassini brothers over some years. He even blocked on their names—"Which one is Igor and which one's Oleg?" he kept asking—but their breed of defunctive polo-playing aristocratic exile obviously aroused the slum rat never buried that deep in Kennedy's temperament. At Palm Beach parties, Igor would remember Bobby as "deadly serious and the butt of jokes," a "natural fall guy" as compared with the "witty and urbane" JFK.

Both brothers were lunching partners of the patriarch. Once Oleg began to supply Jacqueline Kennedy with those trim, pink suits and pillbox hats during the White House years, Joe told him, "Don't bother the kids with the bills. Just send them to me. I'll take care of it." He warned Oleg to stay away from Jacqueline—at least in public. When Oleg brought Grace Kelly, whom he was courting, by La Caravelle, the financier startled the couturier by remarking, "You know, Grace, I know this donkey. He's a pretty good boy, but you'd be making a terrible mistake to marry him." After which, predictably, he pitched the actress himself.

The Ambassador had once tried to get Igor fired by Hearst over a column he didn't like but then thought better of it and invited him to lunch. They played golf. "If he couldn't beat you he became your friend," Igor realized afterward. A notorious womanizer, Cassini favored Joe regularly with introductions to the local trade. Igor was the source of the story that Joe offered Jackie one million dollars not to divorce Jack.

One Narcotics Bureau contact with whom Bobby ran the streets, Howard Diller, would find it "interesting that Robert went after some of John's close friends, and some of his father's close friends, and maybe there was an anger." Disapproval nobody around Hyannis Port dared vent toward the father or the brother could be absorbed by the cronies. Even Morton Downey Jr. acknowledged that, with the Kennedys, "Friendship only went as far as the front door"; they would always protect their own turf first.

Rose Kennedy was fond of Igor's young wife, Charlene, and anticipated Bobby's attitude. Once details of Cassini's attempted coverup—obviously leaked with Bobby's encouragement by Hoover—broke into the news, Rose dreaded the rest: "Cassini had to be made the scapegoat to save Joe from public revelations that might kill him," Rose's biographer Charles Higham observes. "By destroying Igor Cassini, Bobby could get the whole family off the hook."

Before long the FBI was all over Cassini, federal charges came down, he lost his column, and what with the legal fees Louis Nizer extracted, ruin threatened. Igor's wife, the thirty-eight-year-old socialite daughter of the Palm Beach stalwart Charles Wrightsman, wrote JFK that she "cannot tell you how surprised and shocked I have been by Bobby's harsh and punitive attitude." Soon afterward she swallowed thirty sleeping pills and died at Lenox Hill Hospital from a weakened heart. Now left with three motherless children to raise, Cassini pleaded nolo contendere and accepted a six-month suspended sentence and a $10,000 fine.

From Hoover's vantage point, here was a dilemma he could exploit, however it turned out. Bobby apparently signed off on telephone taps not only on Igor but also on his couturier brother Oleg ("Oli"). Agents ransacked bank records and grilled Martial employees "down to the last typist and cleaning lady" and made Igor's mistresses account for every stolen moment. Each incriminating statement, every overheard indiscretion, went straight to the Kennedy brothers. Treated properly, Hoover loved to demonstrate, the Bureau could easily turn into a very beneficial ally.

It would be hard to establish afterward how much of Bobby's reaction to Cassini's bad judgment stemmed from the columnist's tendency to brush off Joe's middle son as an overearnest twit at cocktail parties around the Palm Beach circuit. Igor reproached himself later on for not having taken his own brother's advice and kowtowed before the attorney general.

Part of the problem, Kennedy kept insisting, was that law enforcement was his job. If he started bending the rules for everybody his family knew, the press was guaranteed to demand his innards on a spit. The price of consistency could get high.

Another supporter who wound up overboard was Paul "Skinny" D'Amato, the supercool wiseguy who had helped Joe Kennedy out in a big way in West Virginia. D'Amato was the leading spirit in the celebrated 500 Club in Atlantic City. The Ambassador had taken $50,000 from Skinny and the boys and accepted their guidance to determine which sheriffs and county commissioners were worth the greasing. D'Amato was an intimate of several generations of Sinatras. Skinny thought he had an arrangement with the Ambassador which would permit the deported senior mobster Joe Adonis to return if Jack got elected. By 1961 it was plain that Bobby wasn't going along with anything like the return of a gangland celebrity like Adonis. FBI wiretaps picked up Skinny D'Amato sounding off about moving cash from Las Vegas to solidify the election for JFK.

Sniffing blood, Hoover himself rushed transcripts of the wiretaps across the corridor to Bobby. On the spot, the attorney general agreed to authorize heavy coverage of D'Amato; before long the government indicted Skinny for failing to file a corporate tax return for his club. As it happened, the 500 Club had lost money the year in question so no return was required. The purpose was to discredit D'Amato, in case he continued to shoot his mouth off about helping the family, and load him up with IRS interest and penalty requirements he could never discharge.

What was all this about "Skinny being indicted on bullshit charges?" Sinatra's lawyer, Mickey Rudin, demanded of Steve Smith, the Kennedy brother-in-law who wound up looking after the money.

"Well, you don't understand politics," Smith said.

By then, Sinatra had retained D'Amato as his de facto resort manager and auditor at the Cal-Neva, and so the affable gangster the Justice Department was grinding underheel worked indirectly for Joe Kennedy. Skinny had become disposable, a fish the overworked attorney general abruptly found himself embarrassed enough to throw to the smug, expectant FBI Director.

Bobby's brother the president, watching chunks of helpful, long-standing friends of the family fly by the windows as the attorney general proved there would be no fear or favor, attempted in his way to mitigate. JFK pointedly inquired of Nevada Governor Grant Sawyer: "What are you doing to my friend Frank Sinatra?" He was privately horrified at the tragedies which befell Igor Cassini's family. He arranged for Bobby Baker to deal with his IRS problems by retaining Kennedy family lawyer James McInerney—who, as it happened, died a few hours before their scheduled appointment, run down by a teenager on Sixteenth Street.

Hoover kept careful track of the compounding carnage. He was very selective about whom he helped, whose interests were undercut and whose were protected. If there absolutely had to be a war on crime, Hoover intended to identify the criminals.

Closer to home, Bobby found himself caught in the crossfire between Joe's old stablemate Carroll Rosenbloom and Mike McLaney. There had been rumors around the NFL for years that Rosenbloom, often through Lou Chesler, was betting as much as a million dollars a game, both for and against his Baltimore Colts, and affecting the point spread with decisions he was sending down to his coach through the general manager. One case in question was allegedly the 1958 Colts–Giants championship game—known among bookies everywhere as "the greatest fix ever made"—because Rosenbloom supposedly refused to authorize the field goal which would have guaranteed the game for the Colts. He reportedly held out for a touchdown, which meant a victory by more than the 3½ point predicted spread, and accordingly won big not only in the field but also in the betting parlors. One Rosenbloom hanger-on insists "Even Joe Kennedy had a piece of the action."

McLaney included in his lawsuit against Rosenbloom depositions his longtime gumshoe Sam Benton had pulled together accusing Carroll of rigging a number of the outcomes. By late 1962 many of these charges against Rosenbloom had come to the attention of the carbuncular Senator John McClellan, who announced that his Permanent Subcommittee on Investigations was about to scrutinize closely this unconscionable business of game-fixing.

Like Hoover, Robert Kennedy had privately started to regard the righteous McClellan as something of a nuisance, another would-be reformer circling for headlines. Their father-son relationship had cooled. But enough was left to permit Bobby to refer the problem to league commissioner Pete Rozelle, with instructions to "get tough." The attorney general "simply told the old man to back off," one of Bobby's aides of the period revealed later. "McClellan trusted Bobby and did just that." Rosenbloom slipped through.

Everybody took a step back. By 1963, Rosenbloom, Chesler, et al. were building their $23 million casino, the Monte Carlo, in the Bahamas, part of the Lucayan Beach Hotel in Freeport. Later on a government witness would testify that "Meyer Lansky had given one Michael McLaney one million dollars and Mr. McLaney was going to turn this money over to . . . [Bahamanian Premier] Lyndon O. Pindling for a gambling license."

McLaney would wind up with a 50 percent interest in the Cat Cay Club, also in the Bahamas, and his witnesses abruptly recanted their affidavits against Rosenbloom. In years to come, despite his having contributed the use of "three airplanes, a boat and a helicopter" to Pindling's election campaign, The Premier's Royal Commission termed Mike "an unscrupulous individual" and threw the soigné hustler out of the islands. He landed in Haiti, where he would attend, for Papa Doc Duvalier, to the Casino Internationale in the Royal Haitian Hotel in Port-au-Prince.

No doubt the most painful was the case of James M. Landis. A brilliant jurist who proceeded from an informative stint as Joe Kennedy's understudy on the Securities and Exchange Commission to the deanship of the Harvard Law School, Landis served for decades as the financier's better angel. The two wrote a short book justifying the decision by King Leopold of Belgium to surrender to the Nazis and collaborated on Joe Kennedy's unpublished memoirs of his ambassadorial years. Landis advised Kennedy with respect to taxes and trusts, refusing to bill him, and wound up a special assistant to the President in JFK's White House.

During the middle fifties, not certain as to the basis of a block of stock he had sold to pay for his daughter's polio rehabilitation, Landis put the approximate payment due in escrow and neglected to submit federal tax forms for the next five years. During his FBI security check, the discrepancy was picked up. IRS Commissioner Mortimer Caplin decided he had to press the issue, and the increasingly unstable jurist Bobby characterized as "the best friend the Kennedys ever had" wound up in the Public Health Service's equivalent of Bedlam on Staten Island. Landis was disbarred in early 1964 and drowned himself before the end of that year.

The exchange of cash and concessions between officeholders and favor-seekers is probably inescapable. Watchful as Bobby was, outright corruption was rare while JFK was president. Still, even the most idealistic politician prefers to reward his friends.

In 1964, fighting for his seat in the Senate from New York against the carpetbagging Bobby, Kenneth Keating charged that the Kennedy Justice Department had "made a deal" while settling the General Aniline and Film (GAF) holdings in America which led to the return of $60 million to Interhandel, a cloaking entity in Switzerland for the "former Nazi cartel owners" of the I.G. Farben complex. The charge was undoubtedly valid, but lawsuits, which involved the various Farben properties in the United States, had been in process since just before World War II, when the Alien Properties custodian originally grabbed them off. For many years, the interests of the ex-Nazi litigants were looked after by John Foster Dulles.

Administration after administration, these confiscated shells had served as a device to remunerate individuals close to the seat of power. Shortly after the Kennedys went in, Carmine Bellino was appointed a consulting account-ant to the Farben holdover, a sinecure was established for Lem Billings, and one of Joe Kennedy's lawyers, William Paxton Marin, became vice chairman. This smacked of payola, and Bobby decided to close it down rather than risk a public furor.

Ultimately, closeted in the attorney general's vaulting chambers with two Swiss bankers, an Interhandel attorney, and the impatient Kennedy him-self, Nick Katzenbach jockeyed through a compromise which split the pro-ceeds of a sale. Interhandel would then remit $40 million in tax claims and penalties to the U.S. government. Throughout the long, tense negotiation, penned into the anteroom and lonely for his master, Brumus continued to hurl his enormous bulk against the massive office doors.

One of the more puzzling revelations emerged from Seymour Hersh's unearthing of the testimony of several FBI veterans who haunted Judith Campbell Exner once she fell out of favor. A pair of footpads who evidently worked for General Dynamics pried open the balcony doors of Exner's Los Angeles apartment and went after something incriminating inside. Subsequently, the General Dynamics TFX jet fighter beat out the competition from Boeing. Connect the dots yourself.

Much more dangerous, allowing for official Puritanism as well as the public's irrepressible appetite for oversalted tabloid fodder, would be the cause célèbre involving Marilyn Monroe. Aides of the period deny that Robert Kennedy was involved with Marilyn, although Jack might perhaps have had something to do with her. Courtney Evans comes closest to acknowledging what was going on, having observed that "the only place he [Robert Kennedy] ever went out alone at the end of the day was when we were in Los Angeles. I had my own suspicions at the time that he was seeing Marilyn Monroe." Evans remembers in particular stopping by the Lawfords' for cocktails, after which he found himself excused while Bobby disappeared into the night. John Seigenthaler recalls an evening party at the Lawfords' when he and Bobby both danced with Marilyn. But that was all.

Years ago the evidence was overwhelming that that was not all. A friend of Pat and Peter Lawford all through the Rat-Pack era, Marilyn had been canoodling with JFK whenever his travel schedule permitted, normally in Manhattan or Los Angeles but also, on one well-attended occasion, at Frank Sinatra's palatial spread just outside Palm Springs. Along with her legendary pulchritude, Marilyn brought an eyelash-batting display of adoration to important men, not to mention an unexpected flash of wit from time to time.

Jack appreciated her company, but in the end she amounted to one more beguiling piece of tail after a demanding day. He refused to factor in how much damage a burst of exposure that annealed him to a megastar like Marilyn Monroe could do to his standing with much of the nation. Joe Kennedy was concerned and instructed his troubleshooting lawyer, James McInerney, to get out to the Coast and run down anything he could establish about the president and Marilyn. No detective, McInerney sounded out his fellow Fordham graduate Edward Bennett Williams as to where to begin.

With Joe Kennedy's stroke late in 1961, there really wasn't anybody like the founding father out there flying wing. The family would be particularly vulnerable were Bobby to compromise himself. As if on cue, Robert Kennedy now found himself teetering along the edge the spring of 1962.

At that point the thirty-six-year-old Marilyn was ripening fast, from an aging starlet with a touch of nymphomania and a neurotic disinclination to show up regularly on the set into an out-of-control sleeping-pill addict whose power trips bordered on the deranged. Were she not such a valuable cinematic property, she might very well by then have been locked up, like her mother, in a public sanitarium. She was a very poor selection for the role of girlfriend to the President of the United States.

Or the attorney general. Their first meeting on February 1, 1962, took place at the Lawfords'. Bobby and Ethel were stopping over prior to a fourteen-nation goodwill tour. Bob got Marilyn to simper a few words over the phone to the paralyzed Ambassador, and it was immediately after that that Jean Smith wrote Marilyn thanking her for her get-well note to the founding father and joking "Understand that you and Bobby are the new item! We all think you should come with him when he comes back East." Like the sisters' giggled warning to Oleg Cassini about the dreaded Bobby—"He's going to put your brother in jail"—Kennedy humor comes laden with demonic premonition.

Warned by the tight-lipped Hoover, the president resigned himself to winding down his flirtation with Hollywood. He rescheduled his desert stopover in March from Frank Sinatra's hacienda to Bing Crosby's hacienda, where Marilyn put in an appearance in one of her signature terry-cloth bathrobes. In 1983, C. David Heymann wrote, Peter Lawford, dying of a destroyed liver, reminisced to the biographer about those "madcap fantasies" in which Marilyn indulged. Having decided to displace Jacqueline and bear the rest of Jack's children, Marilyn managed to reach the First Lady by telephone and inform her that she would be moving into the White House any time. "For all her romanticism and masochism," Lawford concluded, "Marilyn could be a mean little bitch. Everybody wrote her up as being the poor, helpless victim, but that wasn't necessarily always the case."

By May, when Marilyn Monroe came east to serenade the president on his forty-fifth birthday, the actress and Bobby *were* an item. James Spada's biography of Lawford has Bobby stopping by Monroe's dressing room in Madison Square Garden for a quickie before her couturier, Jean Louis, stitched the tipsy star into the legendary "skin and beads" creation (nude underneath) and she wobbled onstage to croon "Happy Birthday" to JFK before millions. Arthur Schlesinger remembers Bobby "dodging around her like a moth around a flame." "Boy, what an ass!" the President of the United States murmured appreciatively. Jackie missed the birthday party, preferring to ride that day in Virginia. Afterward, in what would be the final stand between them, Jack and Marilyn made love in the Hotel Carlyle. Bobby reportedly took her later that night.

Hollywood is no nunnery, but these are not the moves associated with a rational woman. Early in 1961 Marilyn had signed herself into the Payne Whitney Psychiatric Clinic in New York in search of help with her addictions. She wound up strapped into a straitjacket until her unshakably loyal ex-husband, Joe DiMaggio, arranged for a transfer until she was capable of dragging back finally to California and her ever-choppier career. By now her days centered on her daily session with her Freudian psychiatrist, Ralph Greenson. Needy, culturally insecure, ridden with insomnia, she bought a house in Brentwood while clinging for security to her Doheny Drive apartment.

By the spring of 1962 the distraught Marilyn Monroe was hanging on the telephone to Evelyn Lincoln, threatening to go public with details about her affair with Jack. Hoover himself sent over word to the president that both the Lawford houses and Marilyn's residences were bugged (on his authority, as it turned out, and against the attorney general's orders). Mobsters had been seen entering and leaving.

JFK dispatched his brother to alert Marilyn that there was no way Jack and the actress could continue their affair. Attempting to reassure the depressed star, Bobby himself succumbed. "It wasn't Bobby's intention," Lawford would report, "but they became lovers and spent the night in our guest bedroom. Almost immediately the affair got heavy. . . . It was as if she could no longer tell the difference between Bobby and Jack."

This involvement turned very quickly for Bob into the lark of a lifetime and a cascading worry. On the telephone to George Terrien, Bob Kennedy's Harvard roommate and the husband of Ethel's sister, the exhilarated attorney general cackled that George Skakel, Ethel's promiscuous brother, "would keel over if he knew who I was screwing. . . . Just tell George I've had Marilyn's pussy. . . . You know, the woman Jack used to jack off over." The Skakels were incredulous. "She wouldn't fuck him even with *my* dick," George Skakel announced.

But she was. "Oddly enough, through some admirable quirk, Bobby was the one Kennedy male who cared about how women felt," Igor Cassini had to concede. "He was there and was nice when they needed it." Marilyn needed it very badly that summer. Marilyn's "sleeping pills buddy," a neighbor in her Doheny Drive apartment building, Jeanne Carmen, remembers answering

Marilyn's door to confront an astonished Robert Kennedy. Suddenly, Marilyn "came out of the bathroom with her robe on and her hair wrapped in a towel and she jumped into his arms and they kissed . . . they were kind of like two kids in love."

On stolen time, Marilyn donned a wig and attached a fake beard to her famous boyfriend, and off they went for an afternoon on the nude beach north of Santa Monica. For Marilyn, whom the omnipresent Dr. Greenson had been coaching in orgasm techniques to help her achieve a breakthrough, Bobby was a wonderful surprise. Marilyn told Jeanne Carmen that her newest Kennedy was "marvelous in bed—sweet and loving as no man had ever been. She often said, 'He's my little love.'"

This couldn't go on, needless to say. One regular visitor to the Lawford house, Peter Dye, remembers Bobby as playing "sort of a macho role" around Marilyn. "He was never animated, never cracked a smile. . . . I think she was turned on by the idea of mental genius. She liked that type, instead of being pushed around like a piece of meat." For Bobby—whose peers around the Justice Department will admit that he was "no great intellect. But quick, quick"—this was a welcome turnabout. When Bob caught Marilyn taking notes on something, writing in her diary, he bristled unexpectedly, lashed out at her and threw the diary across the room, demanding that she "get rid of this at once." Everything they said or did was OFF THE RECORD!

Like so much else, Marilyn's overloaded little red diary was to disappear when she passed on. One bystander who had been given access to Marilyn's most intimate musings was Robert Slatzer. Slatzer had been in and out of Marilyn's life since 1946, when the star-struck greenhorn magazine writer from Ohio helped Marilyn pick up a strew of clippings from the twenty-year-old actress's scrapbook after she stumbled in the lobby of the Twentieth Century-Fox studios. Slatzer became a lover, when that helped, and a confidant the rest of the time.

When Marilyn's clandestine romance with Robert Kennedy started to gutter, she had gotten in touch with Slatzer and taken a drive with him up the Pacific Coast to Point Dume. As they lounged on the beach, Marilyn told the journalist that "Bobby Kennedy promised to marry me. What do you think of that?" Riffling through the pages of her diary, Slatzer noticed entries like this quote from Kennedy: "I want to put that S.O.B. Jimmy Hoffa into jail, no matter how I do it." Another note specified "on the day of the invasion [Bay of Pigs] the President, suffering back pain, had let Bobby run the operation, and it was Bobby who had refused to lend air cover. This, in fact, infuriated certain CIA factions."

Marilyn told Slatzer she was "frightened and confused" at the fact that the attorney general had "all those gangster connections." Bobby had maintained "that he was powerful enough to have people taken care of if they got in his way." The diary mentioned Giancana and Rosselli and alluded to "CIA participation in the assassination of Raphael Trujillo in the Dominican Republic." The United States was going to refuse sanctuary to Ngo Dinh Diem. Kennedy was determined to make sure Sinatra lost his Nevada gambling license "because of his alleged associations with underworld figures."

Jack, Marilyn assured Slatzer, was able to "mesmerize" her by leading her into discussions about "paintings, sailing, literature," what she called "the nice things in life." Bobby, brimming over with vitriol, "boasted about whom he was going after in his fight against crime." He'd left her profoundly upset.

Shrugging off Hoover's heads-up, the technologically challenged attorney general seemed largely uninterested in how intensely his enemies might be watching and listening. When Fred Otash, the best-known of the Hollywood private investigators, got commissioned to wire up Peter Lawford's home, purportedly at the behest of Joe DiMaggio, he discovered a working bug already in place, courtesy of Howard Hughes, who had no scruples when it came to helping out Nixon. The ever-accommodating Otash had already been hired by Marilyn Monroe to install electronic surveillance in her own apartment so she would have plenty of documentation should she need it later to deal with the Kennedys. Meanwhile, Hoffa's highly regarded wireman, Bernard Spindel, had infiltrated both of Marilyn's residences in California as well as her New York apartment on East Fifty-seventh, along with the Lawford properties, and set in place a galaxy of hidden microphones, reportedly on a contract that originated with the FBI.

Spindel, who anticipated a seller's market for the dozens and dozens of giant reels his subordinates would accumulate, allegedly peddled copies of the tapes not only to Hoffa but also to the CIA, Carmine De Sapio, and Carlos Marcello. To demonstrate his matchless technical legerdemain, Spindel divulged to one assistant that important information about Marilyn and Bobby arrived by way of a microphone he managed to implant in the baseboard of Kennedy's office in the Justice Department, transmitted through conductive paint. Before too long, the leakage of secrets set off a witch hunt around the Criminal Division.

The surviving FBI FOIA dossier on Marilyn Monroe is skimpy, rumors floating to the surface months after events. Hoover kept other files. One, which is evidently intended to summarize Bureau findings of recent years, refers to papers found in a taxi which "tied in BOBBY KENNEDY with the

COMMUNIST PARTY" and "sex parties" in Jack's penthouse suite at the Carlyle Hotel which included the Kennedy brothers and "MARILYN MONROE." By early 1962 Hoover was getting more intense every month. He and Courtney Evans were looking at microphone transcripts indicating that Hoffa and mob boss Sam Giancana expected to blackmail the Kennedys over their association with Monroe and other women.

An outside technician whom Hoover entrusted to back Spindel up on the West Coast and bug the Brentwood house and the Lawford estate would remember the Old Man "sitting alone in a car," rasping out "This needs to be done. Could you get this done? If you could do it, it would be greatly appreciated. I will not be obligated. I will owe you no favors. But I will remember." Hoover's off-the-books specialist was waiting in Los Angeles minding his sensitive equipment on the night Marilyn Monroe died.

For months, remarked one FBI onlooker, Robert Kennedy plainly "couldn't have given a shit less" when it came to who was watching or listening. On quick visits, he drove up in an open convertible borrowed from the FBI SAC for Los Angeles. But, as one warning followed the next, the awareness crept up on him that he was playing out this infatuation on a soundstage presided over by his enemies. Tipped off that Marilyn was bugging her own premises, Kennedy scrambled from room to room hunting down microphones, demanding "Where is it? Where the fuck is it?"

Incredulous at reports that Bobby was involved with the celebrated sex bomb ("I don't believe it could have happened. . . . Bobby was always so *sanctimonious*."), Rose Kennedy warned her son sharply to break it off. Furthermore, it began to dawn on Bob that Marilyn, for all her aging-nymphet act, could be a very shrewd, impulsive, obstinate, self-promoting woman. As in his own case, most issues were black or white to her; recently steeped in New York radicalism and allegedly primed by recent conversations in Mexico with Communist sympathizer Frederick Vanderbilt Field, she had trouble accepting his assurances that he and his brother couldn't fire J. Edgar Hoover because they simply did not consider themselves strong enough. She told friends that Bob was giving up Ethel for her. The years in orphanages, a childhood spent straining to gratify a succession of foster parents, had engendered in the emotionally battered Norma Jean insatiable urgencies. When Marilyn wanted something, there were no excuses.

That spring, she wanted Bob. Several biographers refer to an unintended pregnancy, a miscarriage, or a Mexican abortion. The film on which she was purportedly at work, *Something's Got to Give*, was in the process of being abandoned because Marilyn's involvement was simply too desultory for

George Cukor to tolerate. George Smathers (as in the Trujillo imbroglio, the final emissary from the Kennedys before the firing squad) showed up to "see what I could do . . . by talking to her." Marilyn had lost all control.

On June 26 Robert Kennedy reappeared in Los Angeles and the following day stopped by Marilyn's house for perhaps an hour. After he left, the actress was desolated. Two weeks later, the Lawfords took Marilyn to the Cal-Neva Lodge for a few days to cheer her up. She passed out in her chalet from too much champagne and an overdose of sleeping pills and had to be rushed to a Los Angeles hospital in Frank Sinatra's private jet to get her stomach pumped.

The last week of July, Marilyn was back at the Cal-Neva, operating out of one of the complimentary chalets, number 52. Peter Lawford flew up with her, and Frank Sinatra had a surprise guest—Sam Giancana. Meyer Lansky's sidekick, "Jimmy Blue Eyes" Alo, happened to join the party, and it was rough even by Mob standards. "They kept her drugged every night," Alo would recall. "It was disgusting." Sinatra took some pictures which "showed a nauseated Monroe on all fours being straddled by Giancana, then kneeling over a toilet, then covered in vomit."

"Mooney thought she was a pig," one of Giancana's henchmen divulged. "I had her once and I got lost in her. And I got a big schmoke." Soon afterward, the FBI microphone behind the radiator in the Armory Lounge in Chicago picked up the unmistakable voice of Johnny Rosselli admonishing Giancana: "You sure get your rocks off fucking the same broad as the brothers, don't you?"

While never insensitive to the fact that Giancana remained his primary boss, her degradation triggered complicated emotions in the guardedly compassionate Rosselli. He himself had become a devoted, but platonic, friend to Marilyn Monroe, reintroduced by the Lawfords years after having picked her up around Twentieth Century-Fox in 1951. Rosselli could judge for himself by 1962 how deteriorated she was, how many powerful people she was in a position to destroy if her mental state got any more precarious. He knew how adept the Outfit was when it came to cauterizing its problems.

Another self-appointed guardian to the shaky actress had haunted the Cal-Neva that week. Marilyn's ex-husband Joe DiMaggio was a long-time pal of Sinatra's manager, Skinny D'Amato. It happened that Joltin' Joe, too, turned up that tortured final week in July, a spectral disapproving presence who stood there frowning while Marilyn was herded from one locked chalet to the next.

Depleted, Marilyn was dumped off outside Los Angeles "stupefied and barefoot" by Sinatra's pilot. On Monday, July 30, 1962, she placed her final call to Robert Kennedy in Washington. She evidently did not get a lot of satisfaction, because Peter Lawford passed along her ultimatum that unless Bobby Kennedy "explained to her face-to-face why their relationship was over, she would hold a press conference and reveal their affair." Floundering now for self-respect, Marilyn suddenly challenged her masseur as to whether he had heard any stories about her and Bobby Kennedy. "Well, it isn't true," Marilyn burst out. "He's not my sort. He's too puny."

The weekend of August 4, Robert Kennedy was scheduled to address the American Bar Association in San Francisco. He would be arriving with Ethel and four of their children and staying at John Bates's ranch, sixty miles south of the Bay Area. The bar association had reserved a large suite for the Kennedys at the St. Francis Hotel, where Marilyn finally reached Bob and evidently badgered him into sneaking away on Saturday afternoon, August 4, ostensibly to award the Kennedy Cup at Angel's Park for the first Tri-International Soccer Match. Marilyn demanded a "face-to-face" confrontation. Peter Lawford awaited his brother-in-law's helicopter at the Twentieth Century-Fox lot and drove him out to Brentwood.

Marilyn had been up most of the night before, hectored by telephone calls from an anonymous woman who kept screaming "Leave Bobby alone, you tramp. Leave Bobby alone." When Kennedy did appear around three in the afternoon, he found a spicy Mexican buffet Marilyn had ordered in for him. The actress had been drinking most of the day and again threatened a press conference during which she would ventilate everything she knew about both Kennedy brothers. "Marilyn presently lost it," Peter Lawford told C. David Heymann, "screaming obscenities and flailing away at Bobby with her fists. In her fury she picked up a small kitchen knife and lunged at him. We finally knocked her down and managed to wrestle the knife away."

They summoned Dr. Greenson, Marilyn's psychiatrist. According to Heymann's interview of the actor, Lawford believed that Greenson, too—like so many of the males and certain selected females in Monroe's circle—was sexually available to the unstable star. If she talked freely, he, too, would probably be ruined. By 4:30 P.M., Greenson had given Marilyn an injection to calm her down and Kennedy and Lawford left.

Around seven, Lawford called Marilyn and invited her to his house for some Chinese takeout and poker with a few friends. His wife was in Hyannis Port. Marilyn, evidently feeling the effects of an indeterminate number of sleeping pills she had taken along with a lot of champagne and Dr. Greenson's sedative, decided to stay home.

* * *

This compounding Hollywood tragedy turned out more multilayered than Troy. According to *Double Cross*, the rendition by Sam Giancana's brother and nephew of the Chicago Outfit's unwritten history, other predators were watching. Through Giancana, the CIA had ostensibly been exploiting Marilyn as sexual bait to compromise susceptible Third-World leaders like Sukarno, and Agency officers were starting to fret as Marilyn kept threatening to take her story to the press. Bureau veteran Guy Banister in New Orleans was keeping Mooney up to speed as concerned the FBI's interest.

When the Chicago don discovered that Bobby Kennedy was scheduled to return to California he allegedly installed a four-man team of assassins led by Leonard ("Needles") Gianola and James ("Mugsy") Tortorella near Marilyn's new home in Brentwood to listen in with Bernie Spindel and pick the ideal moment to intervene. If everything went smoothly, the world would pin it on the Kennedys. They overheard Marilyn's tiff with Bobby, understood that Greenson had given Marilyn a potent injection of phenobarbital to calm her down, slipped into Marilyn's bedroom shortly before midnight, and, "with all the efficiency of a team of surgeons, they taped her mouth shut and proceeded to insert a specially 'doctored' Nembutal suppository into her anus." Spindel's wireman later insisted that one tape picked up the sounds of Marilyn being slapped around and a male voice asking, "What do we do with her body now?" The suppository had been provided by the same chemist who concocted the lozenges with which the Agency intended to poison Castro, also developed to leave no trace.

It was Giancana's intention to implicate Bobby, to let the evidence compound that the attorney general and the frightened psychiatrist conspired to murder the distraught actress. A number of the autopsy findings confirm the *Double Cross* version. There were very few unabsorbed capsules in Marilyn's stomach and nothing to speak of in her lower passages, definitely not enough to kill her. Dr. Greenson himself later remarked on the presence of chloryl hydrate in her system, a drug he himself never prescribed for Marilyn, although her housekeeper Eunice Murray later admitted that Marilyn sometimes took enough chloryl hydrate with milk to get to sleep; the mob version emphasizes "the suppository's massive combination of barbiturates and chloryl hydrate" which instantaneously entered her bloodstream. The autopsy report would note that "The colon shows marked congestion and purplish discoloration."

As recently as August 2005, the Los Angeles County Prosecutor of the period, John Miner, broke a forty-year silence to render his judgment that the actress had been heavily plied with chloral hydrate—knockout drops—then flooded with barbiturates "of a massive amount that entered her body ... through the large intestine": in Mob parlance, a "hot shot." Like the coroner Dr. Thomas Noguchi, along with bruises, Miner "noticed a discoloration of the large intestine. . . ." Marilyn had been murdered.

In time, what had in all probability occurred became clear to Peter Lawford, who retained an arm's-length acquaintance with Sam Giancana. "Marilyn took her last big enema," Lawford confessed to his third wife.

That night, the panic was general. Anthony Summers's painstaking reconstruction of Marilyn's final hours suggests that her housekeeper, Eunice Murray, claimed originally to have discovered her recumbent body, still gripping the receiver of her precious telephone and summoned Dr. Greenson at 3:30 in the morning. Hours earlier, around 7:30 P.M., Peter Lawford, already in his cups, had gotten a call from a despondent Marilyn informing him that she was about to kill herself. This was a familiar routine for the volatile actress; in mordant good humor, Lawford suggested that "my God, whatever you do, don't leave any notes behind." But the call stayed with him, and by the end of the evening Lawford had apparently alerted Marilyn's two doctors, Dr. Hyman Engelberg and the psychiatrist Ralph Greenson along with her publicist and lawyer, Arthur Jacobs and Milt Rudin.

Both medical men probably arrived at Marilyn's house before midnight. Then, according to the statements of the ambulance attendants and technicians who found themselves involved, an ambulance arrived and the rescue workers oversaw Marilyn's trip to the Santa Monica Hospital; Marilyn died either en route or shortly after arriving at the hospital. "We'd hauled her before because of the barbiturates," insisted the chief of the ambulance company. "We'd hauled her when she comatosed." But this time Marilyn had virtually nothing in her stomach to pump. Nobody had any doubt that the entire scenario would be awkward to explain to the press, especially in view of Robert Kennedy's visit shortly before; once they were sure that Marilyn was dead, whoever accompanied her to the hospital seems to have decided to turn the ambulance around and lay her out in her bedroom.

Having supposedly dropped Robert Kennedy off to climb aboard his helicopter, Lawford returned to Brentwood and subsequently reported having been awakened with word of Marilyn's demise around 1:30. He hurried to her house to tidy up the bedroom and destroy Marilyn's suicide message.

At 4:35 A.M., Sergeant Jack Clemmons, the weekend watch commander in the West Los Angeles Police Station, received a telephone call from Dr. Engelberg informing him of the death of Marilyn Monroe. Clemmons found the actress's nude body on its side on a sheet, a telephone receiver still in her hand, with no indication of the violent choking and vomiting or the convulsive thrashing around associated with death from an overdose of sleeping pills. Her water glass was dry—the plumbing in her bathroom wasn't working—and there was no sign of the bra and earplugs and eyeshade she normally wore to bed. She was quite rigid, her state of ashen-gray morbidity suggesting to the experienced policeman that she had been dead for four to six hours.

At about 2 A.M., Peter Lawford showed up at the Hollywood office of private eye Fred Otash—by now collecting fees on every side of this escalating scandal. Lawford looked, Otash later said, "half-crocked and half nervous," and retained Otash to send one of his operatives to comb belatedly through Marilyn's records and remove anything that could possibly link her to the vulnerable Kennedy brothers. By the time Otash's man showed up, "the place was swarming with people. They were incapable of sweeping the place or anything." Sinatra's lawyer, Milt Rudin, seemed to be in charge. Within hours, Peter Lawford had joined his wife for a breather in the security of Hyannis Port.

Transported by helicopter on his round-trips to Culver Field, Robert Kennedy is presumed to have arrived back at the Bates ranch at some point during the very late evening or early morning. He got up in time to attend Mass, ride one of the horses, and play a little touch football. He addressed the bar association. The news of Marilyn's demise reached the group Sunday afternoon. Kennedy didn't react much, Bates observed. "It was really taken rather lightly," discussed "in sort of an amusing way."

Whatever mood he affected, Robert understood that Marilyn's death was no joke. If his brother-in-law and Fred Otash did their jobs, only the telephone records would be available to link the attorney general to the unraveling actress. Kennedy representatives apparently reached the sympathetic Captain James Hamilton of the Los Angeles Police Intelligence, who turned up quickly on the scene and made sure such telltale souvenirs as a crumpled scrap of paper with a telephone number at the White House disappeared from Marilyn's night table. Hamilton was reportedly able to prevent the transfer from the telephone company of the vital tape, which specified which calls Marilyn had made during the last forty-eight hours of her life.

To make very sure that none of this leaked, Robert Kennedy was apparently forced to appeal directly to J. Edgar Hoover. While Hoover would subsequently deny this, according to General Telephone Division Manager Robert Tiarks a squad of FBI agents from out of town descended on the company offices and appropriated the vital tapes before they could disappear into the vastness of the accounting system. As in the Ellen Rometsch case a year later, both Kennedys were hostage to the discretion of the unbudgeable Director.

Los Angeles Police Chief William Parker reportedly told one source that he kept copies of the telephone records from that August night in his garage, and that they were "my ticket to get Hoover's job when Bobby Kennedy becomes president." Years later, Deke DeLoach would remember the massive flow of "communications coming in from the Los Angeles Division," including "the Kennedy phone number on the nightstand," and G. Gordon Liddy, backing DeLoach up in Crime Records, remarks at how intense the scrutiny was: "The stuff on the brothers and Monroe was very, very closely held."

Unaware of the purported visit by Giancana's snuff artists Needles Gianola and Mugsy Tortorella, Robert Kennedy had to assume that he, alongside Dr. Greenson, had been some kind of factor in ending Marilyn's life. What forgiveness was possible, how could he avoid damnation? Years later a remnant in the otherwise shredded FBI file on Spindel cites a source as saying that "Senator [RFK was New York Senator from 1965 until his death in 1968] Bobby Kennedy was present at the time Marilyn Monroe died and _____ wanted to 'get' Bobby off his back—could do so by listening to the various recordings and evidence concerning Bobby's presence there at the time."

Worse, Sam Giancana—with whom Kennedy's father was invested in the notorious Cal-Neva Lodge—was guaranteed to have picked up the high points of Jack and Bobby's involvement. All hope of prosecuting the most notorious hood in America disappeared over that nightmare weekend. "He knows too much," Robert Kennedy had blurted out to Hoover. Directly or indirectly, Giancana's poisoners had accomplished their purposes.

Playing with studied malice to the altar boy in the brash attorney general, Hoover made it his business to pink the scab of this horrible, ineradicable episode. Days after Marilyn was laid to rest in a private ceremony which Joe DiMaggio refused to permit the Kennedy entourage to attend, FBI surveillance microphones picked up an exchange between Meyer Lansky and his wife in which the gangster referred to an affair between Robert Kennedy and somebody in El Paso. Hoover passed the intercept along to Kennedy.

Reporting back to Al Belmont, Courtney Evans informed the headquarters that Kennedy maintained that he "had never been to El Paso." Then, gratuitously, Kennedy had added that "being in public life, the gossipmongers just had to talk. He said he was aware there had been several allegations concerning his possibly being involved with Marilyn Monroe. He said he had at least met Marilyn Monroe since she was a good friend of his sister, Pat Lawford, but these allegations just had a way of growing beyond any semblance of the truth."

One confronts reality, and then one fabricates the record. Hoover would not let it slide. Almost two years later, he informed Kennedy directly of the publication of a short paperback by Frank Capell, *The Strange Death of Marilyn Monroe*, in which "Mr. Capell stated that he will indicate in his book that you and Miss Monroe were intimate and that you were in Miss Monroe's apartment at the time of her death." At that point, Kennedy was about to relinquish the attorney-generalship, and the Director made sure to leave him with something to think about.

The Glamour Preacher

By 1963, Arthur Schlesinger observed of Robert Kennedy, "civil rights had displaced organized crime as the issue of law enforcement closest to his heart." Given that his pursuit of senior mobsters led Bobby into such a minefield of unexploded family revelations, perhaps this is not surprising. But civil rights, too, would have its booby traps and suicide missions. Not the least of them involved Hoover.

It started with politics. To produce in Congress, John Kennedy was depending on the Solid South. In the Senate especially, most of the vital Democratic committee chairmen—James Eastland, John Stennis, John McClellan, Sam Ervin, William Fulbright—were unshakable segregationists. Never much of an ideologue, Jack Kennedy had kept it cordial with the Southern wing of the party all through his years in Congress. Several of the archons had supported him for vice president in 1956 against Estes Kefauver, himself a border Southerner.

Neither Jack nor his scrappy little brother were perceived as unacceptably progressive on race issues. "Jack Kennedy had been privately scornful of what he called the 'real liberals,'" Ted Sorenson would write, "and he knew comparatively little and cared little about the problem of civil rights and civil liberties."

After Dwight Eisenhower sent federal troops into Little Rock in 1957 to enforce a Supreme Court school desegregation decision, Lyndon Johnson had wriggled through Congress the first significant civil rights measures since Reconstruction, in 1957 and 1960. Jack Kennedy went along with both of them but also voted for amendments that the Southern bloc attached which all but neutralized them. They were written off as political gestures of limited impact, an exercise by Lyndon to broaden his appeal in preparation for the presidential campaign of 1960.

Jack Kennedy had come into office preoccupied with Cold War issues, and throughout his two terms in the Senate the importance of lunch-counter sit-ins or the prerogative of some tidy black seamstress whose feet hurt to keep her seat in a bus in Montgomery, Alabama, were for the most part lost on the self-involved young aspirant. For all his aplomb, Jack Kennedy was privately transfixed by the prospect of mutual nuclear annihilation.

Bobby took his cues from Jack. "I did not lie awake at night worrying about the problems of Negroes," the attorney general would concede later. All through his brother's abbreviated presidency, Kennedy tended to regard civil rights agitators as unwelcome, maddening much of the time. Harris Wofford, the administration's civil rights adviser, observed that "Each major decision was made hurriedly, at the last minute, in response to black pressures, with no overall strategy." It took Kennedy a long time to comprehend the rage and desperation and outright denial of humanity that spurred the emerging generation of Negro leaders. In years to come, Bobby would understand.

For J. Edgar Hoover, the dilemmas that arose from "too many niggers in the streets," as Bureau-speak sometimes put it, seemed easier to resolve. Stay out. "Hoover didn't want to be involved in anything that was controversial," comments Courtney Evans, the assistant director who found himself the intermediary between Bobby and the Director. "Hoover dragged his feet as much as he possibly could not to make an effort in civil rights cases. He was brought up in D.C. when it was segregated, and his political power came from the chairmen of the committees, all from the South." Put simply: "He was a Southern bigot all his life."

While Hoover had not lost his sensitivity to the national mood, he was not inclined to turn the country over to "vociferous firebrands." The threat of black extremists had concerned Hoover from the onset of his career. By 1919, when the stripling bureaucrat was beginning to demonstrate his promise as "the most dangerous file clerk in America," his General Investigative Division of the Department of Justice was already attempting to cope with the "Negro Question," and he himself had concluded in a report that "the Reds have done a vast amount of evil damage by carrying doctrines of race revolt and the poison of Bolshevism to the Negroes." As riots broke out, he emphasized "the numerous assaults committed by Negroes upon white women."

When Jamaican-born Marcus Garvey emerged to champion economic independence for the country's downtrodden black citizens, Hoover hired four black operatives to come up with something they could take to court on this flamboyant troublemaker; they nailed him in 1923 for ostensibly exploiting the mails to defraud while soliciting for his Black Star Steamship Line. Meanwhile, though reconciled to the fact that juries in the South were disinclined to indict even self-confessed race murderers from the Ku Klux Klan, Hoover did manage to bring down the Imperial Kleagle in Texas on white slavery charges. When nothing else worked, Hoover could already see, in Bible-Belt America sexual transgression would get it done.

Eleanor Roosevelt's hectoring demands that the Bureau *do* something about the abuse of colored citizens particularly irked the Director. Fortunately, her worldly-wise husband tended to wave aside the First Lady's vaporings. Truman, who integrated the armed forces, was inclined to leave well enough alone. When civil libertarian Joe Rauh prodded Attorney General Tom Clark to get the Bureau to investigate a murder attempt on U.A.W. president Walter Reuther, Clark reported back that "Edgar says no. He's not going to send the FBI in every time some nigger woman says she's been raped."

Paradoxically, it was under the seemingly immobile Dwight Eisenhower that race relations in America began their historic shift. Eisenhower's first attorney general, Herbert Brownell, an adroit politician from the Dewey-Rockefeller wing of the Republican Party, lobbied through a measure to confer on the Justice Department the capacity to initiate civil suits in support of voting rights, instituted a civil rights commission, and elevated the Civil Rights Section in the Justice Department to Division status. Combined with the 1954 *Brown vs. Board of Education* Supreme Court decision ending the legal segregation of schools and Lyndon Johnson's 1960 Civil Rights Act, which provided for injunctive relief whenever voting registration was impeded by "threats, intimidation, or any other form of coercion," the activists in Washington were finally in a position to go after Jim Crow.

Hoover personally was skeptical and fought to undermine every proposal. At a cabinet-level presentation in 1956, the Director inveighed against "the specter of racial intermarriages" and "mixed education" and insisted that it was "the leading citizens of the South . . . bankers, lawyers, doctors, state legislators and industrialists" who comprised the White Citizens'

Councils. Most of these dignitaries were easier to recognize without their hoods. Emmett Till had recently been found in the Tallahatchie River in Mississippi with a cotton-gin fan tied around his neck and the perforation from a .45 slug passing through his crushed skull.

Hoover's impulse to justify segregation was rooted in his distaste for change. He commented to one Justice Department aide that "Everybody knows that Negroes' brains are twenty percent smaller than white people's," a factoid which influenced his policy that black people in his employ remain supporting personnel, menials.

Paradoxically, Hoover appears to have shared the traditional Southerner's distaste for being tended intimately by whites, so that his domestic entourage was all black—his close-mouthed housekeeper, Annie Fields, his chauffeur and houseman, James Crawford, an additional body-servant, Worthington Smith, and the indispensable Sam Noisette, who spent his decades ushering visitors into the Director's inner sanctum and handing Hoover lavatory towels every few minutes. Hoover arranged to insulate the help from military service all through World War II by arranging for special exemptions, in time promoting the men to special agents. His two black drivers in Miami and La Jolla were also elevated to special-agent status, and until Bob Kennedy came along these five were the only agents of color in the Bureau.

Hunted down by the renegade FBI author Norman Ollestad, Sam Noisette gave up a wealth of clues. By then a heavy-set man in advanced middle age with a heroic comb-over who had clung with care to the rich darkie idiom which authenticated him to Hoover, Noisette was a competent painter and a piercingly adroit appraiser of his employer's mentality. It had been Noisette who, after warning that "the walls of Justice got ears," explained to Ollestad exactly why the boss was so nervous about black people and "queers."

Aborigines, iconoclasts, beyond control! How profoundly the Director felt when it came to blacks broke through in an interview he authorized once the Kennedy era was over. "He wanted me to lower our qualifications and hire more Negro agents," Hoover told a reporter. "I said, 'Bobby, that's not going to be done as long as I'm director of this bureau.' He said, 'I don't think you're being cooperative.' And I said, 'Why don't you get a new director?'"

Bureaucratic chicken at this level was a deviation for Edgar, who filibustered his way through several extremely tense confrontations when presidents were attempting to fire him, and suggests how absolute was his revulsion at the thought of a significant admixture of black faces among his handpicked elect.

* * *

Cartha ("Deke") DeLoach, the ingratiating Georgia native who served as Assistant to the Director of the FBI through the later sixties, and so amounted to the third man, along with Tolson and the Director, to preside over senior administration, maintains that Hoover was well aware of the advantages of enlisting black men to serve in his army. "Mister Hoover assigned me to go to black colleges and law schools in the 1950s," DeLoach remembers. "We needed black agents in New York, Los Angeles, etc. Most of them told me they could get better salaries in private firms than from the FBI, a number didn't want to carry guns or put in the long hours of overtime. . . ."

During Kennedy's tenure, once the attorney general began to poke the issue at Hoover to keep him off-balance, a few black agents materialized. "We got an assistant attorney general from New Jersey," DeLoach recalls, "and four Notre Dame football players. There was a father and his son on a bank-robbery squad.

"By 1970 there were 122 black agents."

Bobby's attorneys were skeptical. "We thought Hoover was shipping the same black agent around the country along with a picture of Jack Kennedy" whenever the attorney general was on the road, John Reilly would comment. One issue the lawyers at Justice were inclined to sidestep even under Bobby was the fact that there were no blacks above the GS 11 level, the grade level at which serious decisions get made, serving in the Department itself.

While 122 agents beat five, out of an FBI agent roster which ran in excess of eight thousand, the enlistment of 117 black recruits during the sixties does not betoken in the Director a tsunami of the heart. What it does suggest is J. Edgar Hoover's unrivaled capacity to give as little ground as humanly feasible while compelling the rest of the government to operate by his rules. In his seminal study *Kennedy Justice,* Victor Navasky compares the extra-FBI divisions of the Justice Department with transients passing through the federal system, tenants, leaseholders. Each may very well "complain to the landlord and he will try to exploit his lease (although he doesn't want to risk having his water turned off) but essentially he *assumes* the terms of his lease in his dealings." Hoover would continue to write the leases.

The Director would also continue to decide what anybody outside the FBI might get to examine, how much was inked out, when speculations from the raw files ought to be fed to the press to advance the Bureau's purposes. Hoover would not permit his darlings to risk their lives as bodyguards, to be pushed into confrontations where, if anything went wrong, the upshot might annoy key Congressmen or reflect poorly on the Bureau.

"The General had yielded to the Director on the one thing that counted:

control," Navasky summed it up. "Mr. Hoover's price for reluctantly going along in civil rights was that he have control of his own troops, that the FBI oversee its own men, use its own systems, follow its own rules, provide parallel rather than integrated services. This seemed a reasonable enough bargain at the time and Kennedy cavalierly traded control (which he never exercised anyway) for cooperation."

Hoover's unabashed disinclination to involve his boys in all this civil-rights skirmishing was not entirely uncongenial to the Kennedys, at least behind closed doors. Unwelcome demands were building on the new administration. The head of the Civil Rights Division during the last six months of the Eisenhower incumbency, Harold Tyler Jr., had been a rawboned reform-minded veteran with seven years as a federal prosecutor in New York. He had pressed Hoover to help the Department out with the new civil rights guidelines; when Hoover remained inert, Tyler dispatched a division attorney, John Doar, to hunt down evidence on his own. Doar roamed the South and spent a lot of time with sharecroppers; he reportedly "obtained more evidence in West Tennessee with a $19 camera than the whole Bureau," which evoked in the Director a rare outbreak of undisguised chagrin.

Doar would stay on into the Kennedy administration as the right arm of his Exeter schoolmate, Assistant Director for Civil Rights Burke Marshall, and work in close conjunction with Harris Wofford, who had been backgrounding candidate Kennedy on the politics of race and started out with a desk in the White House as special assistant for civil rights, an abruptly created post lacking any discernible clout or responsibility. Hoover sent along a report "insinuating that Wofford had Communist sympathies." Wofford was a raffish young Notre Dame law professor who had been the first white man to graduate from Howard University Law School and went at the conundrums of race with a deep commitment to the struggle and a firsthand acquaintanceship with the emerging black interest-group leaders.

Wofford's mentor at Notre Dame had been its president, Father Theodore Hesburgh, a crusty, highly principled priest who really didn't care much for Joseph P. Kennedy and so never expected anything remarkable from his self-aggrandizing sons. Hesburgh had stepped up to serve on the original U.S. Civil Rights Commission and functioned as spokesman for its chairman, John Hannah. Wofford filled in as counsel for Hesburgh on the commission until he moved up to the White House and promptly found himself scooting back and forth like a bear in a shooting gallery in which the corks were coming in simultaneously from the Kennedy brothers, the Civil Rights Commission, impatient leaders around the black community, and J. Edgar Hoover.

The most immediate problem for the Kennedy administration was that the black leadership and the bleeding hearts on the Civil Rights Commission seemed to expect a social revolution overnight; both Jack and Bobby were persuaded that, if changes came too fast, the political backlash would flatten them all. The administration's choice for staff director on the Commission, Berl Bernhard, started out non grata with Hoover for having panned the Bureau for unconvincing civil rights enforcement while sitting on a panel at Catholic University. The Director made a phone call and got Bernhardt hauled before Jim Eastland's Internal Security Subcommittee—a kind of Star Chamber the reactionary Eastland kept available for the Director—to answer to his scathing committee counsel, Jay Sourwine.

Sourwine wasn't Bernhard's only problem. When the Commission's 1961 report came out for fresh hearings and much more trenchant and sweeping legislation, Bernhard announced that he "had never seen anyone so angry at the Commission as Robert Kennedy, not even John Patterson or George Wallace." Hoover managed to hang an FBI "liaison officer" on the Commission, who made sure the Bureau found out first what the Commission was up to and mainlined rumors to Bernhardt calculated to undermine the movement.

To get himself reelected in November 1964, John Kennedy was going to require not only the nonwhite vote but also a preponderance of the South, a hard enough finesse even without summers of devastating racial upheaval. Candidate Kennedy had been talking up his intention to issue an executive order barring discrimination in federally assisted housing "with the stroke of a pen," but President Kennedy wouldn't quite sign the paper, and in time the pens started pouring into the White House. Kennedy had them boxed up and deposited on Wofford's desk, something to distribute among "your constituency," as the president termed the top African-Americans.

Even moderates were getting antsy. Clarence Mitchell, the NAACP's man in Washington, asserted that the New Frontier looked "suspiciously like a dude ranch with Senator James O. Eastland as the general manager." As Chairman of the Judiciary Committee, the Mississippi senator was in a position to bury a lot of legislation, and if Bobby intended to get his antigambling proposals out of committee he'd have to deal. To assure Thurgood Marshall a seat on the Second Circuit Court of Appeals, Eastland made it plain enough, he'd expect the administration to go along with the appointment of his avowedly segregationist college roommate, W. Harold Cox, to the Fifth Circuit, accountable for the Deep South. "Tell your brother," Eastland instructed Robert Kennedy when he ran across him in a Senate corridor, "that if he will give me Harold Cox, I will give him the nigger." Like several other justices Eastland was able to install around the Fifth Circuit, Cox remained in character. "Who is telling these people they can get in line [to register] and push people around like a bunch of chimpanzees?" Cox erupted at one point, nailing down his footnote to history.

In company with Cox, the Kennedys went along with the appointment of four additional hard-core seggies to judgeships around the Fifth Circuit, including Long protégé E. Gordon West of Louisiana and the notorious J. Robert Elliot of Georgia, a Talmadge bootstrapper. By 1964 the court was more reactionary than during the Eisenhower years.

As late as June 1963, civil rights–oriented journalists like Jack Newfield continued to write off the Kennedys as feckless when it came to race, quite cheerful about indicting "nine civil rights workers in Albany, Georgia, on conspiracy charges, while white men who burned down Negro churches, and shot at civil rights activists, went unpunished. We saw Negroes trying to register to vote in Greenwood, Mississippi, urinated upon by a white farmer, while lawyers from the Justice Department calmly took notes destined to be filed and forgotten."

This is a blanket indictment, and probably not fair. Both Kennedy brothers sympathized with the predicament of blacks in the South, but the problem remained changing anything. Very few Dixie juries were likely to send anybody to jail for burning a cross in the weeds in front of some sharecropper's hovel. The way to long-term justice remained the franchise. Get blacks on the voting rolls.

Even with the recent legislation, this was a forbidding project. It required a massive, county-by-county effort to educate and encourage black voters, litigate suits, nullify poll taxes, upgrade eligibility lists. "Each case," Victor Navasky wrote, "depended on painstaking investigation—analysis of voting rolls, compilation of demographic statistics, comparison of handwritings, careful interviews with registrars and a statistically significant sample of black and white failed registrants, successful registrants and others." It took the specialized manpower only the FBI could provide. But enlisting the Bureau meant giving "the FBI effective veto power over each and every civil rights activity in which it was a participant."

For Robert Kennedy, the effort to collaborate with the Bureau was like seducing a porcupine—you had to proceed with extreme caution, and establish with great precision what you were after. As Burke Marshall would note in retrospect: "You could not say to the FBI 'Infiltrate the Klan.' But you could ask for a 'preliminary,' 'limited,' or 'full' investigation of particular Klan activities. These were terms of art."

Hoover was warier yet. Culturally, desegregation was an abomination to the Director; administratively, it was slowly becoming the law of the land, and Hoover was never entirely oblivious to the fact that he was a federal employee. By way of Courtney Evans, Hoover indicated that his people would help, subject to his own judgment. The Bureau was thin all across the South, and it was those cantankerous county executives and sheriffs and deputies and public safety commissioners who shook his hand at the FBI Academy who plumped up the Bureau's precious car-theft statistics and bank-robbery-recovery numbers.

A lot of the tumult arose around the stocky, infuriating figure of the Reverend Dr. Martin Luther King Jr. King might have been assembled to work on Hoover's most atavistic fears—a stumpy black hobgoblin of a preacher whose slanted almond eyes and crude, puffy West-African-Negroid features, accentuated by a drummer's mustache, made him a menace to white maidenhood everywhere. His lips were extraordinarily expressed, meaty. Still in his twenties, King's lugubrious, turn-the-other-cheek manner masked a barely suppressed megalomania, a taste for incidental lechery, and a nasty cigarette habit. There was an impudence. To Hoover he looked like the undertaker of civilization.

First publicized as the guiding spirit of the Montgomery, Alabama, bus boycott in 1955, King had gathered to himself a disputatious rabble of like-minded activists and opportunistic jitterbugs, other Baptist clergymen mostly, the Southern Christian Leadership Conference. It was their strategy to identify communities around the old Confederacy in which discrimination was rampant and convulse them enough through allegedly peaceful means to force their power structures to drop the color bars.

This was a noble concept, although it seldom worked. What ended the Montgomery boycott was Supreme Court intervention; what worked best overall was fanning up a firestorm of national publicity, which compelled the federal government to intercede. The Kennedys were treated to a trial run of this high-stakes racial gamesmanship when Martin's wife Coretta telephoned Harris Wofford during the autumn of 1960 and pleaded with

Wofford to convey to candidate Kennedy that, after a bogus arrest for carrying an expired driver's license, her husband had been hustled into Reidsville Penitentiary, where Coretta was convinced the rednecks were about to finish him off. Jack called Coretta; Bobby (privately out of joint because Wofford hadn't contacted *him* first) called the sentencing judge and sprang the shaken preacher. The Kennedys promptly leafleted the nation's black churches with a brochure headed "No Comment Nixon Versus a Candidate with a Heart, Senator Kennedy," and on election day the African-American vote swung hard from Republican to Democrat.

From then on, King appeared to presume a certain entitlement; the Kennedys backed away. King was not invited to the inauguration, nor did Bobby include him in a comprehensive meeting of civil rights personages at the Justice Department. The hope continued to be that Justice Department lawsuits and private-foundation–backed initiatives like the Voter Education Project would erode the mechanisms of segregation.

Black America—especially younger Black America—was not impressed. By April 1961, busloads of Freedom Riders, black and white, were racketing around the South attempting to integrate every washroom and diner into which they swarmed. A representative of the Freedom Riders had called on Robert Kennedy at the Justice Department before the provocations began and even evoked from the preoccupied attorney general the aside that "I wish I could go with you"; later on, Kennedy insisted that he had been blindsided by the elaborately staged convulsions.

On May 14 a mob turned over a bus full of demonstrators from CORE and burned it in Anniston, Alabama. King's SCLC had bought the tickets. When a second bus reached Birmingham, a delegation of Ku Klux Klan was waiting with bicycle chains, pipes, and baseball bats. Birmingham's pragmatic police commissioner Eugene ("Bull") Connor had struck a deal with the Klan to keep his troopers away from the bus station for twenty minutes so that the Klansmen could work the Riders over "until it looked like a bulldog got a hold of them." By the time police did arrive, the faces of the Riders were unrecognizable beneath the blood.

Tipped off to Connor's arrangement by a Klan informant, Gary Rowe, FBI agents were spotted "taking movies of the beatings." Connors explained that his men put in a late appearance because he had let them off for Mother's Day.

A similar melee broke out when the bus pulled into Montgomery. By then Bob Kennedy's administrative assistant, John Seigenthaler, was on hand to represent the federal government. "I'd go in," Seigenthaler and his boss expected, "my Southern accent dripping sorghum and molasses, and warm them up." JFK was off at a retreat for the weekend, and Robert Kennedy himself was eager to calm things down, and responded with annoyance to King's call from the basement of a besieged church. When King shrugged off Kennedy's request for a "cooling-off period" and alluded to the possibility that hundreds of thousands more were waiting to join the invasion, Kennedy snarled, "Don't make statements that sound like a threat. That's not the way to deal with us" and added that, without the feds, "you'd be as dead as Kelsey's nuts."

Out on the swarming streets, attempting to drag one bull-headed female Rider into a car to escape the rampaging mob, Seigenthaler was clubbed from behind with an iron pipe and lay unconscious on the sidewalk, his skull fractured and his ribs cracked, for twenty-five minutes until local police hauled him to the hospital. The word in the station house was that "every white ambulance in town" was "broken down." Before he passed out, Seigenthaler caught a glimpse of several FBI agents across the intersection, meticulously taking notes.

Advised well in advance of the Klan's intentions by its informant in the KKK, the FBI, which was exchanging memos all along with the bigot-heavy Birmingham Police Department, refused to pass its information to the Civil Rights Division in time to forestall these homicidal mobs. Here was the selective cooperation they might expect from the Bureau, the Director's sly way of letting nature take its course. Of updating this bumptious, untried attorney general to what he might expect, taking on the power structure.

Interestingly, Robert Kennedy stepped around this potentially lethal assault on one of his closest aides. Placate "that old man," Jack Kennedy had told his brother; Bob resumed his role in what Taylor Branch would call "an Oriental pageant of formal respect, beneath which played out a comedy of private insults and mismatched quirks." Hoover was already turning Martin Luther King into one of his obsessions, a "vociferous firebrand" he wanted his men to "expose, disrupt, misdirect, discredit, and otherwise neutralize."

Robert Kennedy kept sending King and the Freedom Riders advisories to stop embarrassing the administration, especially while his brother in Vienna was attempting to restrain Khrushchev from grabbing off Berlin. Periodically, it occurred to Bobby that the FBI could help. "Edgar," he buzzed the Director on the hated intercom, "how many agents do we have in Birmingham?" Hoover ducked that. "We have enough," he informed his boss. "We have enough." And then he let loose such a blizzard of language that Kennedy never had the opportunity to ask again.

Once the tumultuous summer was over, the attorney general prevailed on the Interstate Commerce Commission to end segregation in interstate bus facilities, more evidence to King and the movement that incitement paid. Success in either camp kept ushering in the next crisis.

Throughout the Old Order, exasperation was on the rise. "There's nobody in the whole country that's got the spine to stand up to the Goddamned nigger except me," Alabama Governor John Patterson, the first Southern governor to endorse Jack, had railed at Bobby's envoy John Seigenthaler during the Freedom Rider crisis. "Look, Governor, why don't you just let this be Mississippi's problem, we'll provide the protection to get these agitators over there," Seigenthaler proposed, but Patterson "bucked at that." When his safety commissioner Floyd Mann indicated that he *could* convoy the agitators over the state line, Patterson "started to tin-can a little. 'What will Bull think?'" he asked finally, half-conceding. But the Freedom Riders stayed on schedule.

It seemed more likely every day that King and his imitators were in the process of running the table, breaking up the arrangements the Kennedys were depending on to continue in power. "There goes the South," Robert Kennedy expired once the Freedom Riders' appearance in Montgomery turned it into a "teeming anthill of violence" and National Guardsmen had to be dispatched to rescue the federal marshals.

Bobby didn't want much more of that, and Hoover didn't want it either. King was the crux of the agitation. Between his amazingly steep learning curve and that Old-Testament mahogany baritone, King was like a loud-mouthed five-year-old with a taste for picking fights, serene in his confidence the playground monitor would break it up in time. The whole thing was becoming intolerable.

Hoover was settling on an angle.

From Emma Goldman to Owen Lattimore, it had been Hoover's tactic to identify somebody close to any disruption to scapegoat. The focus for Hoover's attack on King would now be Stanley D. Levison. Levison was of a type which had worked out well for Hoover. A dedicated, somewhat naïve social meliorist from a millennial Jewish tradition, Levison was a New York attorney with a comfortable personal fortune built up after decades of in-and-out business speculations, from artillery fuse manufacture to laundries to real-estate manipulations and automobile dealerships. He now seemed conscience-bound to dabble in desperate liberal causes. Close up, he registered as bland mostly, unobjectionable, a nondescript do-gooder contemplating the confusion of the world with equanimity from behind his formidable, dark-framed glasses.

Levison's presence in the King entourage must have been flagged for Kennedy early, because, shortly after the Bay of Pigs, Harris Wofford put together a combined White House/Justice Department luncheon at the Mayflower with King and a pair of aides. When Robert Kennedy got up for another pass at the buffet table, Wofford fell in behind him. "You remember that fellow you were worried about my having associations with, that I didn't remember?" Harris prompted the attorney general.

"Who's that?"

"Stanley Levison," Wofford said. Kennedy looked blank. "Well," Wofford said, "you better remember him now, too, because that's him you're sitting next to."

The heads-up on Levison in all probability originated with Hoover, who had been tracking Stanley through much of the Fifties. A Bureau informant code-named "Solo"—two brothers, actually, Jack and Morris Childs, both long-term functionaries in the American Communist Party—had started to supply the FBI with operational details in 1952. One name they turned over early was Stanley Levison's, whom the Childs brothers credited with having involved himself since 1945 or 1946 in business schemes to finance the Party apparatus, launder money, and set up fronts for the Amtorg Trading Corporation, the Soviet purchasing commission.

From 1953 to 1955, the Childses maintained, Levison promoted himself into administrative control of the Communist Party's indispensable reserve fund. Then Levison's interest shifted. His involvement in Party affairs slacked off, and he began to direct his contributions and his organizational savvy to In Friendship, a civil rights fund-raising group in Manhattan. There he met Bayard Rustin, the bony, itinerant hobo pacifist with the West Indian accent, a devout Quaker and an unapologetic homosexual, who would become the first outsider from the cities of the East to bounce in on Martin Luther King during the Montgomery busing boycott. Rustin had arranged for Levison to meet King in the summer of 1956. It was commitment at first sight, both ways.

The FBI had been surveilling and even bugging Levison throughout the middle fifties; by 1957, its internal security experts had deleted Stanley from their "key figures" list of important Party operatives while taking note of the occasional informal get-together with secondary apparatchiks like Lem Harris. Early in 1960, a couple of agents from the New York field office had approached Levison in the hope of persuading him to reactivate his involvement in Party activities and report to them. Levison turned them down. He'd fallen in love with another cause.

In 1956 King was twenty-seven, a word-smitten pup preacher a year out of graduate school, and modest enough to welcome whatever Levison might offer. "[Levison's] skills," David Garrow would observe, "lay in exactly those areas where King's were weak: complicated financial matters, evaluating labor and other liberal leaders who sought to be of assistance, and careful, precise writing about fine points of legal change and social reform programs." Levison labored over King's book about the Montgomery protest, *Stride Toward Freedom,* negotiated with his publisher, prepared his tax returns, and helped the preoccupied preacher stave off a groundless Alabama income tax–evasion lawsuit.

When King offered to remunerate Levison, the New Yorker wouldn't hear of it. His capacities, he explained, were acquired "in the commercial jungle" and therefore were "always abhorrent. Hence, I looked forward to the time when I could use these skills not for myself but for socially constructive ends. The liberation struggle is the most positive and rewarding area of work anybody could experience."

Levison's disgust with the system resonated with the idealistic King, who even during his years in the Crozer Seminary had found himself brooding over the words of Social-Gospel advocates like Walter Rauschenbusch. Rauschenbusch condemned America as a "mammonistic organization with which Christianity can never be content." Yet Marxism—"cold atheism wrapped in the garments of materialism"—appalled King even more, especially joined with Lenin's dictum that any means was justified by some dimly perceived but glorious future, which King correctly guessed would turn out to be a "crippling totalitarianism."

Ideologically, King probably influenced Levison more than Levison King. But day to day, Levison provided the mature, lawyerly oversight; King trusted his judgment completely as Levison helped staff out the SCLC with Wyatt Walker and Andrew Young and, in New York in the autumn of 1961, Hunter Pitts "Jack" O'Dell. "Stanley was this seemingly loyal, mousy, ever-willing-to-do-work guy around Martin," Harris Wofford remembers, the gray competent presence straightening out the books.

Part of King's dependence on Levison arose from King's furtive recognition that, as national acclaim broke over him, he was struggling at times for intellectual footing. While dazzling the ladies or overwhelming some country congregation, King liked to throw out references to the Jansenists or Nietzsche or St. Thomas Aquinas. But with the world watching, he fretted in private about his own tendency to cut corners, to inflate his language or demagogue complicated issues. Since the deeply disturbing day he had discovered as a freshman at Morehouse College that he was reading at an eighth-grade level, it would be King's reflex to cover himself. Finishing up his doctoral dissertation, he evidently panicked and pirated text from a former Boston University student. He was not above delivering an unacknowledged sermon by Harry Emerson Fosdick to impress some up-market congregation. Levison, by vetting a great deal of the voluminous body of material King either delivered or wrote, helped reassure the preacher—secretly quailing beneath his air of phlegmatic self-possession—that he was authentic, that things would be all right.

Hoover could smell fear across the four intervening states and made sure his people kept tabs on this mouthy little social revolutionary. King inflamed the public; he presented a danger to the established order, the national security monolith.

Bureau officials later maintained that they had missed for years the connection between King and Levison. This is unlikely. Harris Wofford saw Bureau cables indicating that the FBI was tapping both King's phone in Montgomery and Levison's in New York while Harris helped edit *Stride Toward Freedom* in 1958, an interlude when Stanley and Martin engaged in long, rambling, soul-searching telephone conversations several nights a week. Levison had taken to referring to King as his best friend. FBI reports pertaining to A. Philip Randolph's 1959 Youth March on Washington noted that King spoke—"Do you realize what would happen . . . if three million Negro voters were added to the rolls in the South?"—and that Randolph thanked Stanley Levison for his logistical help. A memo suggested that Levison's contribution "may have been at the direction of the CP as we do know that the CP was extremely interested in the demonstration." A follow-up document specified that Levison was "closely associated" with King, "one of the motivating forces behind this demonstration."

Hoover waited. By the end of 1961 the Kennedys were still binding up their political wounds after the mayhem of the Freedom Rides. Each time they rescued King it cost them in the South. This firebrand preacher wasn't sympathetic when the rueful attorney general attempted to sketch out for him certain of the administration's dilemmas. "Some of these problems you have created yourself," King told Bobby, "by appointing these segregationists federal judges."

The astute Director sensed how susceptible they were. On January 8, 1962, Hoover sent a letter to Robert Kennedy stating that the Bureau had discovered that "Stanley D. Levison, a member of the Communist Party, USA . . . is allegedly a close advisor to the Reverend Martin Luther King Jr." A "reliable informant" inside the Party had passed along the word that Isadore Wofsy, a senior Party official, reported that Levison wrote the speech that King delivered in Miami in December to the AFL-CIO convention. Jack O'Dell, the New York head of SCLC fund-raising, had clear Communist ties. Memos to follow.

Hoover exploited the scraps of gossip he overheard promiscuously. When Charles E. Whittaker reigned from the Supreme Court the spring of 1962, Hoover's wiretaps on Levison produced another utterly contrived backroom fandango. King was after Stanley for guidance as to how to handle the rumored appointment of the first black to the Supreme Court, circuit court judge William Hastie. Hoover jumped in immediately in the hope of alarming the attorney general with word that Hastie had been "connected" with "ten organizations cited as Communist fronts on various lists of subversives. . . ."

Meanwhile, Chief Justice Earl Warren remained, Robert Kennedy later commented, "violently opposed to having Hastie on the Court" because he was "not a liberal," while William O. Douglas lamented to his erstwhile traveling companion that Hastie would be "just one more vote for [the ultraconservative] Frankfurter." Katzenbach called Hastie "pedestrian," Bobby noted, which "just killed him with President Kennedy." So Deputy Attorney General Byron White, who had been holding Robert Kennedy's feet to the fire when it came to prosecuting Mob-connected politicians, relieved the pressure by moving along to the Supreme Court and quickly proved himself perhaps the least liberal Democratic appointee of his generation.

The possibility that King might have become a Communist tool engendered panic at the Justice Department. After a mid-January meeting with civil rights leaders to sketch out strategies to assure voter registration, Robert Kennedy told John Seigenthaler to find a way to draw King aside and broach this touchy business. "As I took him down to the car after that meeting, I did," Seigenthaler remembers. "I was somewhat indirect in explaining the problem. I mean, this was sensitive, delicate. Obviously I didn't have to mention the Bureau, or Hoover, for him to understand about whom I was talking. The memos on Levison and O'Dell were couched in terms that would make you believe that there was some informant whose life might be at risk or whose role might endanger them. This was at a time I thought I could read the metaphors and decide whether he was talking about a wiretap or a human source. But my recollection is that he had somebody inside.

"Hoover plainly identified Levison as actively involved in the CPUSA and O'Dell as well." But Hoover took it further. "He identified Levison as with the KGB. Later there was one memo, to my recollection, that identified him as a colonel. Hoover's memos were very, very persuasive. You would think Levison was evil incarnate, guiding the movement on a direct line from the Kremlin. . . ."

That January day on the curb in D.C., Martin Luther King had stood there in his black suit and taken in Seigenthaler's warning with his customary mandarin ponderousness, the reserve he displayed for Whitey. "He got it right away," Seigenthaler remembers, "and expressed appreciation, and said in effect that his interest in people who helped in the movement was whether their chief and primary motivation was in advancing the movement. He didn't look at their political backgrounds or pasts in determining whether the commitment was real.

"And I clearly separated the attorney general from others in the government who might want to see the movement less than successful."

Others in the government. Hoover's implication to the divided attorney general was that Levison—and, accordingly, King—were acting under direct orders from Moscow. One scorcher was the imputation that Levison himself had been a colonel in the KGB—a *colonel* in the *KGB,* a level of rank and importance even the legendary Kim Philby never truly attained! The truth was, as the Bureau well knew when it attempted to inveigle Levison into taking up where he left off as a financial adviser to the American Communist Party, Levison was little more than another pinko dupe who ultimately figured it out. The Bureau had never even managed to come up with the number on his Party card.

Working another favorite channel, Hoover sent along Levison's dossier to James Eastland, chairman of the Senate Internal Security Subcommittee, who turned Levison over to the mercies of Jay Sourwine on April 30. "To dispose of a question causing current apprehension," the unruffled Levison opened, "I am a loyal American and I am not now and never have been a member of the Communist Party." Then he took the Fifth.

* * *

At that point, the FBI's own Atlanta field office sent up an extended analysis, which concluded that there was no significant Communist influence at work on King. Hoover sent it back and demanded results consonant with the Bureau line. William Sullivan, the peppery assistant director who ran the Fifth, or Domestic Intelligence, Division of the Bureau for Hoover, would admit years afterward that he had *never* seen compelling evidence indicating that Levison was a Party member. When Byron White got his back up after the initial warning about Levison and demanded of Courtney Evans Levison's FBI case file, the Director coldly refused to surrender any substantiation and scrawled on the request, "King is no good anyway. Under no circumstances should our informant be endangered."

Hoover continued to stonewall his superiors and run his bluff. In March 1962 he extracted Kennedy's permission to install a national-security wiretap on Levison's office telephone. FBI "suicide squads" had been breaking into Levison's premises for quite a while by then, planting microphones which kept the Bureau informed of offhand statements like Levison's aside that King "probably hasn't looked at a book for twenty years" and was a "born sucker," and at one point praised the Bureau for "terrific work" against the Klan. No Communist plotting, ever. One bemused underling suggested after some months that somebody should copy to the attorney general a summary that concluded that Levison was not involved in anything subversive; in fact, King's personal opinions came over as decidedly anti-Communist. Hoover stepped on that, fast.

The rest of 1962 played out on complementary tracks, while King—quite unsure underneath, straining to maintain his prominence in the movement, full of foreboding—announced his participation in nonviolent insurrections in community after community, and both Kennedys—and Hoover—kept attempting to damp King down.

Overlapping much of the year was the ordeal known as the "Albany Movement," the effort to desegregate Albany, Georgia, by means of round after round of marches and picketing. The Albany police chief was shrewd enough to keep the static level below the publicity threshold. Local bus service was suspended for the duration, anonymous benefactors kept bailing King out of jail, nobody was egged on to club anybody else. U.S. District Judge J. Robert Elliot, one of those sops the Kennedys threw Jim Eastland, came up with an injunction which forbade civil disobedience. It took all Robert Kennedy had to persuade King to obey the injunction. The injunction was overturned; Albany's blacks rioted; when several attempted to boycott the store of a white juror, FBI agents were out there "as thick as hogs," with eighty-six involved in the investigation that led to the prosecution of Albany's primary black activists for "obstruction of justice."

King's long-established counterparts in the movement were losing patience. To Roy Wilkins and most of the other, statelier veterans around the Urban League and the NAACP, who had themselves worked hard over the decades to maintain a level of civility with Hoover, King and his messiah complex portended disaster. King was, the baby-faced Julian Bond of SNCC now decided, "a very simple man" who "sold the concept that one man will come to your town and save you." He hadn't saved Albany.

On November 18, 1962, the frustrated King spoke up for attribution. "One of the greatest problems we face with the FBI in the South," he intoned, "is that the agents are white Southerners who have been influenced by the mores of their community. To maintain their status, they have to be friendly with the local police and people who are promoting segregation. Every time I saw FBI men in Albany, they were with the local police force."

Important newspapers featured King's remarks, and they hit Hoover very hard. Was he to gather that this pompous little preacher was accusing the Bureau of corruption? Forever willing to commit to the extra mile on paper, Hoover ordered DeLoach to talk with King, to "set him straight." The FBI called the SCLC offices twice; King never returned the calls. The Bureau was covered. "It would appear obvious that Reverend King does not desire to be told the true facts," DeLoach established in a memo on January 15, 1963. "He obviously used deceit, lies, and treachery as propaganda to further his own causes." King was a "vicious liar," and subservient to the Communists.

"I concur," the Director noted in the margin.

From then on, King was not to be warned of any assassination rumors. Hoover would ultimately divulge that Robert Kennedy, Martin Luther King Jr., and Quinn Tamm, the independent-minded executive director of the International Association of Chiefs of Police, were the only three people in the world he genuinely despised.

Within the Justice Department there was an awareness that the Bureau now intended to deal with King once and for all. For the Kennedys, Jack's presidency was turning into a continual crisis over civil rights, shattering set-piece engagements like the face-off with governor Ross Barnett of Mississippi in September 1962 over the admission of James Meredith to Ol' Miss. Before that was settled the U.S. marshals ran out of teargas, two bystanders were killed and 375 wounded, and the president had been forced to order the army mobilized against a sovereign state, never a politically profitable option.

JFK, Bobby remarked, was "torn between an Attorney General who had botched things up and the fact that the Attorney General was his brother." When John Kennedy tried to explicate his motives during a follow-up television address, King made few friends around the White House when he announced that the Kennedys "made Negroes feel like pawns in a white man's political game." Bobby's efforts that May to enlist Jimmy Baldwin and convene a rap session of Negro writers, activists, and intellectuals in a family apartment at Central Park South exploded into recriminations and unbottled racial fury.

Another bloodbath threatened in June of 1963, when newly elected governor George Corley Wallace, a pompadour with a sneer, threatened to position himself in the schoolhouse door indefinitely to prevent two black applicants from registering for the University of Alabama. It took weeks to choreograph the scenario that would permit Wallace to back off without denting his machismo, starting with the nationalization of the Alabama Guard.

This tense, long week of bumper cars with George Wallace occurred against the backdrop of Martin Luther King's months-old effort to crack open Birmingham. Between the risible Bull Connor and hair-trigger Al Lingo, the Director of Public Safety, King was guaranteed headlines. Connor came up with a "special superforce water cannon that could blast bark off trees a hundred feet away" and "blow marchers back like rag dolls. . . ." By May, out of troops, King was marching children, and the sight of one of Connor's attack dogs mauling an eight-year-old girl produced lively TV. "Who better to prick the conscience of the country?" King's wildest strategist, James Bevel, demanded of the alarmed preacher.

At a cabinet meeting on June 11, the day of the schoolhouse-door standdown by Wallace, John Kennedy threw out the possibility of presenting his long-deferred civil rights bill to Congress. The administration's poll numbers were collapsing, from 60 to 47 percent. Much of the Great Heartland was unhappy with the chaos. There was a vote taken among the cabinet; only Bobby favored attempting to jump-start the civil rights agenda.

"The more he saw, the madder he became," Burke Marshall said later. That night, John Kennedy spoke, dwelling on the "moral issue . . . as old as the Scriptures and as dear as the American Constitution. The heart of the question is whether all Americans are to be afforded equal rights and equal opportunities. . . ." The administration was about to send down a civil rights proposal with teeth.

* * *

However elevated their consciousnesses, neither of the Kennedy brothers wanted King to bulldoze their agenda. When did nonviolence invite violence? "School children participating in street demonstrations is a dangerous business," Robert Kennedy remarked. "An injured, maimed, or dead child is a price that none of us can afford to pay." By then the relationship between Bob Kennedy and King was "strained but friendly," John Seigenthaler recalls. "He was a pain in the side of the administration because he was basically in the streets, and Kennedy was trying to keep the whole damned thing in the courts."

It had become important to the Kennedy brothers to rein King in, but he was hard to harness. King "held no public office," as Taylor Branch put it, "displayed no personal ambitions that could be traded on, succeeded by methods such as going to jail, and thrived on the very upheavals that most unsettled the Administration." Beyond that, "at first sight King would be mistaken for a waiter at most Washington establishments. . . ."

Hoover thought he had the answer. The previous autumn, a few weeks before King chastised the FBI for inertia around the South, the New Orleans *Times-Picayune* had broken an unsigned story which charged that Jack O'Dell was "a Communist who has infiltrated to the top administrative post in the Rev. Martin Luther King's Southern Christian Leadership Conference," and, as a "concealed member" of the CPUSA's national committee, had been "carrying out his Communist party assignments" under the guise of civil rights employment.

By 1963, King was long aware that O'Dell had once put in an appearance before the House Un-American Activities Committee, to whom Hoover routinely passed off anything that struck him as redolent of subversion. Confronted by King, O'Dell, a black man, protested that he was not a Party member but that he had indeed attended meetings and written for Party publications. The Kennedys were squeezing King to dump anybody with Communist associations. John Seigenthaler was again dispatched, this time to lean on his Nashville contact, the Rev. Kelly Miller Smith, a member of the SCLU board, to prevail on King to let O'Dell go. "Remember, we were all living in the backwash of the Red Scare," Seigenthaler says now.

King authorized a misleading press release, which specified that O'Dell functioned "purely as a technician" concerned with "mailing procedures," and that he had now resigned "pending further inquiry and clarification." In fact, O'Dell ran the all-important fund-raising staff for the SCLU throughout Greater New York. He had resigned and been cleared and rehired simultaneously and so had never really abandoned his post.

Still fuming over King's November challenge, Hoover authorized a full-scale campaign against King and deployed Deke DeLoach to plant the *Times-Picayune* smear of O'Dell in four other newspapers. Rumors smoldered through the winter. King was already planning his March on Washington. On June 22, 1963, determined to protect his White House from any vulnerability-by-association, John Kennedy exploited the private audience for which King had been lobbying to strong-arm the evasive little rabble-rouser.

Bobby softened King up first. After subjecting him to a few sobering minutes with the incisive Burke Marshall, Robert Kennedy went to work on King with a directness only he could muster. The attorney general was fortified by a detailed FBI briefing on some of the dangers King and his cohorts presented. The truth about O'Dell and Levison was worse than anybody suspected. They both were "paid agents of the Soviet apparatus," key operatives, guided hour to hour by Moscow. Just how the Bureau was so sure about all this would have to remain classified, even from the Kennedys.

Hoover was in fact developing very prolific sources. How reliable they were would come under scrutiny. The Childs brothers, whom even the head of the American Party, Gus Hall, assumed to be independently wealthy, judging from their sumptuous lifestyles, were not only luxuriating in their substantial stipends from the Bureau but also embezzling about 5 percent of the monies the Kremlin sent along to keep the CPUSA viable. Their reports drew heavily from the offhand remarks of the unstable James Jackson, the American Party's secretary for "Negro and Southern Affairs," who hinted that "most secret and guarded people" were "guiding" King.

Reinforcement came from Victor Lesiovsky, the notorious "Fedora," a KGB officer working as special assistant to UN Secretary-General U Thant. The Bureau had turned Fedora in March 1962, and he had agreed that Levison was one of theirs. The problem with Fedora's disclosures was that CIA counterintelligence had already concluded that Fedora was a double agent, sent over in part to help discredit King and slow the movement down. Jim Crow weakened America, a long-term advantage as the Soviets saw things. Lesiovsky made a point of striking up an acquaintance with the gullible Levison, forever "a goodhearted and undiscriminating liberal," in Arthur Schlesinger's phrase, "for whom there was no enemy to the left."

From these soggy informants the Bureau pulled together the inspired conjecture they used to alarm the Kennedys. As Robert Kennedy hammered away at him about the world-threatening malevolence behind this nonentity on whom King depended to correct his spelling and gossip with him long-distance whenever he couldn't sleep, King manifestly had a terrible time keeping a straight face. Kennedy remembered King as "always sort of dismissing the whole idea." "Well," Kennedy concluded in retrospect, "he's just got some other side to him. So he laughs about a lot of those things, makes fun of it."

When worlds collide. Running down, Bobby turned this perverse, unmanageable black visionary over to his brother. Jack led King out of the Oval office and into the Rose Garden. "I assume you know you're under very close surveillance," the president told his guest. Dramatically placing one hand on King's shoulder, Kennedy half-whispered his conclusion that King must "get rid of" both O'Dell and Levison. "They're Communists," the president said.

When King rejoined that Hoover regarded a great many folks as Communists and asked for details, Kennedy responded that Levison's position in the Party was of too exalted to permit him to get into specifics, but Levison was O'Dell's "handler," and *O'Dell* was "the number five Communist in the United States."

It is easy to imagine King's almond-shaped eyes bugging out a little with that one, taking on a gleam. "I don't know how he's got time to do all that," King ventured after a moment. "He's got *two* jobs with me."

The president was not amused. King asked for proof. But Hoover was not about to compromise his sources, even to JFK, and they both knew that. Kennedy turned the conversation to the Profumo scandal, consequent to which British Prime Minister Macmillan "is likely to lose his government because he has been loyal to a friend." King "must be careful not to lose your cause for the same reason." Furthermore, "if they shoot *you* down, they'll shoot *us* down, too."

To a man who for five years had rarely stepped into the street without the near-certainty that sometime soon he was going to get his head blown off, the fall of somebody else's government does not constitute the most electric of motivations. Not that many months earlier in New York, a zealot had plunged a letter opener into Dr. King's chest at a book signing, so close to his heart that if he had sneezed he would have burst his aorta. Existentially, Reverend King and President Kennedy were operating on different planes.

What did impress King was the way Kennedy conducted him out into the Rose Garden before opening the conversation. "I guess Hoover is buggin' him, too," King observed to Andrew Young afterward. As for the charges against O'Dell and Levison? "I checked him on that," King said. "I told him that can't be true, and he just turned red and shook." The president then assured King that Burke Marshall would turn over to Andrew Young proof that Levison was "a secret party muckamuck." Marshall met Young in New Orleans. When Levison came up, Burke muttered about some vague analogy with KGB agent Colonel Rudolf Abel. "Burke never said anything about any evidence they had," Young would recall. "He always quoted what the Bureau said it had. I didn't feel this was conclusive. They were all scared to death of the Bureau; they really were."

Hoover really didn't need to justify anything. It was like standing before the Oracle at Delphi, the place reality began. Furthermore, both Kennedy brothers had to consider the successive updates the Director kept sending over to Bobby relating to Judith Campbell (Exner) and Sam Giancana. Along with the fact that, on Robert Kennedy's orders, the late Marilyn Monroe's telephone records had been confiscated by the FBI. . . . Hoover's grip on the brothers was getting tighter every day.

King, recovering from his Rose-Garden euphoria, slipped into another mood, a condition more common with the overstressed clergyman every month. When Harris Wofford reached him, "King seemed dumbfounded and depressed, and said he had far more reason to trust Levison than to trust Hoover." Reluctantly, King released O'Dell on July 3, writing him that "the situation in our country is such . . . that any allusion to the left brings forth an emotional response. . . ." When King filled Levison in on the president's misgivings, Levison stepped back on his own: "I induced him to break," he would recollect. "I said it would not be in the interests of the movement to hold on to me if the Kennedys had doubts." A mutual Manhattan friend, the black uptown attorney Clarence Jones, would pass information back and forth and Harry Wachtel, a founder of the Gandhi Society, an SCLU fund-raising arm, would back him up with legal advice.

Forever his brother's scorekeeper, Robert Kennedy had been particularly affronted when King seemed to fluff aside the president's express demand that King jettison O'Dell and Levison. On June 30, a story obviously pieced together out of FBI files and planted before King had made up his mind about O'Dell tore into the beleaguered fund-raiser in the *Birmingham News.* "The reporter," James Free, comments Hoover's biographer, "was known to be especially close to the attorney general."

Even after O'Dell was out and Levison—who never had a job with the SCLC—slipped into semibanishment, Robert Kennedy's determination to hound King and his cronies continued to shadow his judgment. When Clarence Jones dropped by the Justice Department to alert Burke Marshall that Dr. King was not prepared to get along totally without Stanley Levison's good offices, but intended to stay in touch with Levison through Jones, and would be gratified were the leadership in the Civil Rights Division to let him know which telephones around the SCLC circuit might *not* be tapped, Robert Kennedy blew up. Already under pressure from Hoover over the Ellen Rometsch incident, the whole idea that Jones seemed to be leaning on *him* to collaborate with this perverse preacher to deceive the FBI was so infuriating to Kennedy that on that same day Kennedy passed word to the FBI that he had decided to augment the Levison surveillance with wiretaps on Clarence Jones *and* Martin Luther King.

This was a switch. Normally, wiretap requests went up from the Bureau to the attorney general, who signed off without too many questions being asked. "We were against putting a wiretap on King," DeLoach insisted years later. "We told him that it would be wrong to do that, an embarrassment if it were ever found out." Courtney Evans emphasized that the Bureau "was not at all acquainted with Jones," and technical surveillance on King's home or office was of doubtful effectiveness, since "he was in travel status practically all the time."

Accordingly, Hoover now requested from the attorney general written authority to tap King "at his current residence or at any future address to which he may move"—hotel rooms, the guest quarters of friends, anyplace. By then the furor in the right-wing press about Communist "influence" on King was dying down. Evans seems to have tipped Kennedy off about the trapdoors implicit throughout the authority Hoover wanted and emphasized that the surveillance which did go forward on Jones should keep the Justice Department up to speed as regarded Levison. Courtney Evans helped debunk the charge that King was a Bolshevik because he had spoken once at the Highlander Folk School, a meeting place for egalitarians and lefties across the South. Robert Kennedy, backing down, released a statement to the effect that no top black leader was Communist or "Communist-controlled." No authorized tap on King—yet.

As planning went forward preliminary to the March on Washington, sponsored by the entire spectrum of nonrevolutionary black advocacy groups, a kind of unannunciated solidarity set in across the Justice Department. This thing could flame up, get completely out of hand, and jeopardize the administration's pending civil rights bill. Well before the day of the giant rally, August 28, a series of measures was put into place to keep King responsible and Civil Rights Division strategists as close as possible to the details of the planning.

When SNCC chairman John Lewis released an advance draft of his speech recommending that blacks refuse to support the administration's breakthrough civil rights legislation, since "There's not one thing in the bill that will protect our people from police brutality," Burke Marshall recruited UAW chief Walter Reuther, Archbishop Patrick O'Boyle, and King himself to beat on Lewis until he toned that down. Justice Department technicians were stationed by the public-address system, on hand to pull the plug if things got out of hand. Troops waited by their M-14s throughout the city, prepared to move in fast. Malcolm X had already dismissed the entire day-long exercise as the "Farce on Washington."

The March proceeded peacefully; once it was over, the principals filed into the cabinet room at the White House, where John Kennedy greeted King with a grin and the passing reassurance that he, too, had a dream. Hoover was not mollified. On July 25 the Bureau's Crime Records Division had arranged for a sweeping, fallacious attack on King in the Atlanta *Constitution,* as liberal a paper as could survive in the South. "Onetime Communist Organizer Heads Rev. King's Office in New York" ran the lead, three weeks after King fired O'Dell. The *Constitution* piece probably could not have run without a nod from the Civil Rights Division.

King could read the tea leaves. Without the Justice Department, ultimately, to ride to the rescue, his kind of orchestrated provocation couldn't possibly work. King's mood swings were becoming more pronounced; after so many months and years of hitching up his guts and presenting to the world that podgy, unthreatening, oracular visage, he now needed more and more of what Taylor Branch calls the "opposing release of instability, fury, wanton merriment, and profane despair."

As transcriptions from the Clarence Jones wiretaps reached the Director's desk, a sunburst of possibilities broke over Hoover and his lieutenants. The feed from the Levison surveillance over the years had never proved especially revealing. Somber pronouncements, long stretches of gentle line-editing whenever a King speech or a book was in the offing, a dig or two at loafers on the staff, even the occasional lament from Stanley about how "disenchanted" he was becoming with liberals these days. King remained the paragon: dreamy, mild-mannered, and hard to budge.

With Jones, King came alive. Like the Rev. Ralph Abernathy and Young and Wyatt Walker, Jones was another of the "road buddies" who traveled with King whenever he was out there organizing, which amounted to most of the time. They saw King's other side: the ribald outcries, the mistresses marking time in suburbs around the country (frequently somebody else's wife), the bouts of noisy, exultant grab-ass on nights when the mood was sky-high and tomorrow was dependent entirely on the reflexes of some drunken cracker with a rusty handgun.

That summer's FBI intercepts played to a lot of this. With Jones and his friends the talk switched around, interspersed with hoots of laughter and exchanges that without warning turned shockingly blue—a shock to Hoover, at least, who took to referring to King as a "tomcat, with obsessive degenerate sexual urges." Those last weeks before the March on Washington the talk drifted regularly to the extravaganza's organizer, Bayard Rustin, with his decades of browsing the hellpots of the left along with those morals arrests.

"I hope Bayard doesn't take a drink before the march," one conversation ran.

"Yes," King replied. "And grab one little brother. 'Cause he will grab one when he has a drink."

These exchanges went straightaway to Robert Kennedy, who sent the choicer selections along to Jack. "I thought you would be interested in the attached memorandum," the attorney general commented dryly.

"I'm away from home twenty-five to twenty-seven days a month," King confided to one friend. "Fucking's a form of anxiety reduction." Beyond that, he was the glamour preacher in the Negro community of the era, when certain of the livelier ladies *expected* their spiritual leader to undertake a raid on the choir every once in a while. According to the noble Coretta, the whole subject never came up.

Nevertheless, it troubled King, who preached with great heart about the Dr. Jekyll and Mr. Hyde in all of us. A "guilt-ridden man," as Coretta later admitted, he knew that roistering made him vulnerable. Hoover knew it, too.

A Wall-Banger of a Date

By the autumn of 1963 the March on Washington was finally behind the administration, the long-delayed civil rights bill was in the hopper, yet Martin Luther King remained unmanageable. Robert Kennedy, sympathetic to the cause, treated King as an irritant, at the very mildest. For J. Edgar Hoover, King had become an obsession.

Around the Justice Department, senior staff people were discriminating, Taylor Branch has noted, between "the Director's 'good days' of crisp, brilliant efficiency and his 'bad days' of cartoonlike lunacy." More and more, the increasing percentage of bad days seemed to be associated with Hoover's phobia about King, on whom every incidental exchange, every rant, tended to expend itself.

Now that he had resolved to rid the country of this outlandish troublemaker of a preacher, Hoover lost no opportunities to twit the worried brothers by reminding them that John Kennedy's prospects for a second term might depend on the Director's forbearance. He was the custodian of their secrets. Chance favors the prepared mind, and by the summer of 1963 the buildup of paperwork detailing John Kennedy's indiscretions overflowed Hoover's desk.

Times had begun to change. Traditional restraints on the media were loosening; the scandal over Christine Keeler's affair with British Minister of War John Profumo, who was sharing the leggy call girl with Yevgeny Ivanov, the deputy Soviet naval attaché with unmistakable links to the KGB, was in the process of bringing down the Macmillan government. John Kennedy was markedly uneasy, as evidenced by his pained reference to the Profumo mess while escorting Martin Luther King Jr. around the Rose Garden. It could happen here.

Until that summer, the cerebral young president appears to have regarded his own performance as a sexual omnivore as a kind of *divertisse-ment*. Like those daily injections of steroid-laced amphetamines from the indispensable Dr. Jacobson, a variety of partners was therapeutic. "I get a migraine headache if I don't get a strange piece of ass every day," Kennedy conceded to Harold Macmillan. Macmillan hadn't blinked.

Raw information bearing on Jack Kennedy's incessant romantic foraging had started to reach Hoover long before the inauguration. FBI files indicate that Robert Kennedy was detached briefly from the 1960 campaign to work with the damage-control team Joe had hired to turn over to Alicia Darr Purdom a half million dollars to drop her breach-of-promise suit against Jack. The candidate had supposedly agreed to marry her in 1951 once he discovered she was pregnant.

Another rumble came through with the discovery of the Blauvelt family tree, first printed in 1957, which recorded the aftermath of a drunken post-war Palm Beach party. Jack Kennedy and the tiny but strong-minded socialite Durie Malcomb allegedly stood up before a justice of the peace, after which, a friend of the family would summarize, "the Old Man had a shitfit and got it nullified."

Accurate or not, these stories were starting to edge into the columns and unsettle the president. Worse, the Director had no compunctions about carting in those dreaded raw files of his and spreading them around the Oval Office. Judith Exner would recollect one occasion when the normally unflappable Jack Kennedy referred to Hoover as a son of a bitch and attacked him for having "tried to use, you know, this information as leverage." The president resented "'the gall of the man,' to try to intimidate *him*. He was absolutely livid."

Some of this Hoover couldn't avoid. In 1959, an incensed Georgetown housewife named Florence Kater went so far as to picket candidate Kennedy for carrying on with her tenant, Pamela Turnure. Florence had the snapshots and the tapes and kept after local reporters as well as the FBI to *do* something. Even the hardened Kennedy crisis manager James

McInerney couldn't hush her up. Turnure joined the White House staff as Jackie's press secretary.

The upheaval over Profumo forced Jack Kennedy to consider the possibility that all those rumors might one day actually break the surface of the legitimate media. Even the conservative *Washington Star* had buried the Kater charges. But sooner or later, the more influential enemies of the administration—and J. Edgar Hoover no doubt ranked among them—could get a lot of this out.

Hoover was watching closely. In early June 1963 he had memoed the attorney general advising him that a prominent wiretapper, probably Hoffa's standby Bernard Spindel, had information to sell either Hoffa or Republican Senator John Tower pertaining to Robert Kennedy's role as bagman in the Purdom payoff. The FBI legal attaché in Rome had already filled in the Seat of Government with background details concerning Alicia Darr Purdom. Born Barbara Maria Kopczynska, she had entered the United States as a displaced person and "reportedly operated a house of prostitution in Boston. In 1951 or thereabouts she moved to New York City, where she was blackmailing people involved in the 'Jelke case.' In California she allegedly was the mistress of Johnny Myers," the agent building Marilyn Monroe. Joe Kennedy had opposed Jack's involvement with Purdom on the grounds that she was merely another no-class "Polish Jew." The old man clearly hadn't picked up on the half of it.

By July 23, 1963, the attorney general was made aware of an FBI memo from W. A. Branigan to William Sullivan concerning "Bowtie," the code name for the Profumo/Christine Keeler earthquake that was rippling through London. Courtney Evans followed up within a day to advise that he had alerted Robert Kennedy that a prominent British pimp, Harry Allen Towers, tipped Scotland Yard that he himself "had lived with Simon McQueen, a New York City call girl, and that one of her clients was alleged to be the then presidential candidate John F. Kennedy. He was further informed that Marie Novotny had gone to New York to take McQueen's place, as she was traveling on pre-election rounds with the presidential candidate. . . ."

Robert Kennedy had responded, "It did seem preposterous that such a story would be circulated when a presidential candidate during the campaign travels with scores of newspapermen." Keep him in the loop.

A month earlier, the Bureau's Domestic Intelligence Division passed along an advisory: "Marie Novotny is a woman arrested for prostitution in New York City along with Harry Towers in 1961. In previous interview

Novotny claimed she was never involved with U.S. Government officials. Attached cable reflects Novotny acquainted with Peter Lawford."

By then the president was genuinely interested. Two of the hookers in the Keeler ensemble getting featured billing in the London tabloids, the sleek Suzy Chang and Marie Novotny, were trollops he knew by more than reputation. Novotny had a dedicated following in England and was the sparkplug of an alleged Soviet vice ring that worked the United Nations. Both were personal favorites of the needy chief executive; Peter Lawford had arranged the introductions, and Jack had been especially diverted on visits to Manhattan when the Czech-accented Novotny and a friend dropped by to entertain him with their nurse-doctor specialty.

Very little of this was likely to help Kennedy politically if it ever got out. Instructions went down from the White House demanding that both the FBI and the CIA keep ahead of this story. "Stay on top of this case," Hoover cabled his legal attaché in London. On June 29, a Hearst sheet, the *New York Journal American,* broke a story in its afternoon edition, which connected "a man who holds 'very high' elective office" to "a Chinese girl" implicated in the Profumo scandal.

Hoover "already knew of the accusations," historian James Hilty has written, "and may have had a part in getting the story to the *Journal American,*" in all probability tipped off by Roy Cohn, who had a client among the Profumo defendants. The Kennedys endeavored to kill the story after one edition, and Bobby broke up his July 4 weekend to pull in the two investigative reporters who wrote the story, James Horan and Dom Frasca, and squeeze them for the name of the "very high" elected official. It was his brother. They had gotten their scoop from the English tabloid *The News of the World,* to which Novotny was selling her most newsworthy reminiscences. Horan and Frasca were alarmed to find Courtney Evans of the FBI sitting in, and his memo reports "a continuing apparent reluctance to volunteer information." The attorney general was intimidating, cold, "just looking at him" with "those steel blue eyes," Horan remarked afterward, and Evans noted in his memo to Hoover "almost an air of hostility between the Attorney General and the reporters."

Hoover routinely planted stories throughout the Hearst system, relying most of the time on Deke DeLoach and his Crime Records contacts like George Sokolsky to get a rumor started or call in a favor from Roy Cohn and his career-long sponsor Dick Berlin, who ran the communications conglomerate. But something this sensational, especially if it exploited the national security slant, had the potential to bring the presidency down. Joe Kennedy had cultivated intimate ties to the Hearst family for forty years, and Bobby apparently went directly to the chairman of the Hearst Corporation, William Randolph Hearst Jr., who quashed the allegations before they developed legs.

For Hoover, by then, it was a question of survival. Deep in the FBI file on Robert Kennedy is a reprint of a July 2, 1963, editorial from the Danville, Virginia *Register* asserting that "Bobby and his big brother want to retire J. Edgar Hoover as FBI Director and bring in a young man who will eagerly turn the respected agency into an enforcement arm—ready to enforce Bobby's orders—everywhere . . . the Kennedys are seeking to obtain the civil rights legislative package so that it will give the Attorney General such powers and use the FBI in such a manner that Mr. Hoover's wishes or his presence or absence will not matter to them." The piece was entitled: "The Police State—Right Now?"

Hoover initialed the bottom. In Hoover's position, survival meant believing the worst. Then the Director caught a break. The wife of a German army sergeant stationed in Washington, Ellen Rometsch, got mentioned in a Jack Anderson column as a habitué of the Quorum Club, a kind of alcohol-soaked hideaway for legislators and their friends in the Carroll Arms Hotel, the homey if dilapidated hostelry adjacent to the Capitol. One of Rometsch's more durable recent relationships, Anderson emphasized, had been with a Soviet embassy attaché. Delaware's puritanical Republican Senator John J. ("Whispering John") Williams noticed the item. So did J. Edgar Hoover.

On July 3, 1963, Courtney Evans sent Alan Belmont a memo specifying that he had alerted the attorney general to the fact that a Bureau informant had "received allegations from one ELLEN ROMETSCH to the effect that she has had illicit relations with highly placed government officials." Rometsch "is alleged to be from East Germany and to have formerly worked for Walter Ulbricht," the head of the Communist government in the "East Zone." Hoover, smelling something with meat on it, had marked up one early memo about Rometsch "Press vigorously and thoroughly."

Ellen was a call girl. A good-sized, slender woman with a voluptuous figure and, according to her FBI tail, a "rough" complexion and a penchant for "heavy makeup," she had a reputation at both ends of Constitution Avenue as a wall-banger of a date. She would be linked in future FBI investigations with the August 1963 suicide of Philip Graham, publisher of the *Washington Post*. According to several historians, she was another in John Kennedy's string of Elizabeth Taylor lookalikes, but with her sloe-eyed, come-hither manner and the blood-red lipstick glistening on her full mouth and the glossy upswept ebony hair she looked more like a big pink Teutonic houri, bred for the trade. Washington was too small a town for her and John Kennedy to have stayed away from each other, and they hadn't.

Between the rich promise of a personal scandal and the national-security implications of a story like this, the chances of containing it indefinitely weren't wonderful. Robert Kennedy was well aware that his brother had been availing himself of Rometsch's services from time to time. It happened that one of his top investigators during the Rackets Committee days, La Verne Duffy, had drifted into a very serious love affair with Ellen. La Verne was a bachelor, and the two were talking marriage. On August 21, 1963, Ellen found herself on a U.S. Air Force transport with Duffy, deported abruptly to Germany. Duffy was along to calm her down and, back in Washington, sent regular large payments in deutschmarks, by every report from the Kennedys, to help her remember to keep her mouth shut.

This might have passed under the bridges of history had not the Bobby Baker investigation erupted. A child of the Senate, Baker had started out as a page and built himself a powerful insider position as secretary to the Majority. An inspired flunky and protégé to Lyndon Johnson and Robert Kerr, Baker had an aptitude for carrying water—and cash—from one power center to the next as each cloakroom crisis demanded. By the early sixties, Baker was out to make himself at least a little bit rich and had allegedly begun to trade political access for contracts with a vending machine company in which he held $28^1/2$ percent of the stock, Serv-U. Two of Meyer Lansky's top casino managers, Ed Levinson and Ben Siegelbaum, were Baker's partners in the company. An insurance broker complained to John Williams, who by senatorial courtesy was sitting in on executive sessions of the Senate Rules Committee, that with Baker's connivance he had been strong-armed into buying useless radio advertising time on the vice president's stations in August and presenting Johnson with a television set and a stereo to get Johnson's insurance business.

Once the Rules Committee probers began to dig, Robert Kennedy's teeth started grinding. Under normal circumstances, the opportunity to let the dirt rise to the top and smear Lyndon Johnson would have been welcomed by the attorney general, whose distaste for the vulgar, demonstrative Texan was very poorly hidden. Here was the chance to bump him from the ticket.

But probing into Baker's excesses was likely to lead the press straight to Ellen Rometsch, a raw nerve. In October, once Baker was attracting headlines, Hoover briefed the attorney general on Rometsch and five other alleged prostitutes "involved and all tie in with Bobby Baker," who were observed moving in and out of Baker's house, his office, and the Quorum

Club, which Bobby Baker founded. Kennedy expressed his concern to the Director that, should the hypermoralistic Williams find out about Rometsch's origin, he was likely to play the "security angle."

Bobby could smell brimstone. His risk-loving older brother, with his studied, feline gestures and the rich, Palm-Beach brush of chestnut hair that required professional styling every day, was closer to a tabloid expose than any of them would admit. The attorney general had recently gotten into a nasty face-off with the phlegmatic Pierre Salinger when Bob demanded that Salinger get rid of the two cute press aides, Fiddle and Faddle (Priscilla Wier and Jill Cowan) with whom the president was inclined to amuse himself during schedule breaks. Salinger had his orders; the girls stayed.

His face more lined from extracurricular responsibilities every day, Robert Kennedy was well aware that his brother was entangled with Ellen Rometsch. One of Jack's bird-dogs, railroad lobbyist Bill Thompson, maintained a suite in Washington's Fairfax Hotel which the president and George Smathers occasionally put to use. Jack Kennedy had long since leased private quarters in the Mayflower in which to conduct his more established dalliances, but the Fairfax offered the excitement of the illicit. One evening Thompson was having drinks at the Quorum Club with Bobby Baker and several of the call girls in his stable. Ellen Rometsch was particularly staggering.

Thompson turned to Baker. "Who is that one?" he wanted to know.

"She is a lady of the town. She is married to a sergeant who works at the German embassy. She's a Nazi, she's in commerce, she was broke at the end of the war and she wanted pretty clothes, etc."

"Do you think you could set her up to have dinner with the president?"

The dinner was arranged. The next day Bobby Baker got a call. "Mister Baker," the chief executive opened, "That was the best blow job I ever had in my life." Baker luxuriated in the thrill of the successful matchmaker, and there were evidently a number of subsequent get-togethers. Gratification seems to have gone both ways, because Rometsch reported back to her tickled sponsor that "Jack was as good as it got with the oral sex. 'He really was a satisfier,' she told me, in her broken English. 'Made me happy. . . .'"

Unfortunately, Whispering John Williams was on Rometsch's trail. His investigators had followed up and passed on a lot of whatever he had discovered to the senior ferret for the Cowles publications, Clark Mollenhoff. Years earlier, Mollenhof had badgered Robert Kennedy into taking an interest in Jimmy Hoffa. A huge, blunt good-government fanatic and one of Hoover's well-worked press contacts, Mollenhoff had started to nurse increasing doubts about the Kennedys and listened hard when Williams let him in on certain of the details the committee investigators were picking up as they interviewed their way into Bobby Baker's operations.

On October 26, 1963, a piece over Mollenhoff's byline appeared in the *Des Moines Register*. The Rules Committee had plans to call witnesses prepared to testify as to the reasons for Ellen Rometsch's unexpected departure from the United States. Both "Senate employees" and "members of the Senate" were implicated, and "evidence also is likely to include identification of several high executive branch officials as friends and associates of the part-time model and party girl. . . . Those acquainted with the woman class her as 'stunning,'" the article observed and revealed that, along with compromising "congressional leaders," there was a risk of security breaches, even espionage here "because of the high rank of her male companions," several "New Frontiersmen."

Here was a cat already more than halfway out of the bag; both Kennedy brothers knew they had to get it back in, somehow. The attorney general dispatched La Verne Duffy to West Germany at once to smooth down Ellen Rometsch, who was now irate. Then, with many a step and slow, Robert Kennedy took the long walk across the corridor to speak with J. Edgar Hoover.

This was, the severely humbled attorney general explained to the delighted if stone-faced Hoover, a situation with the makings of a disaster for both political parties. Ellen Rometsch had distributed her favors in a nonpartisan manner, compromising Democrats and Republicans equally. If Williams pushed ahead with his hearings, the integrity of the United States itself might well be compromised. Only he, Hoover, could be depended on to have the clout inside the Congress to approach the leaders of both parties in the Senate, Mike Mansfield for the Democrats and Everett Dirksen for the Republicans, and convince them to expunge the whole matter from the Rules Committee's agenda.

Hoover toyed with his tortured attorney general, proposing blandly that, since his men had already come up with a memorandum concerning these distasteful matters, he ought really to send the report over and let the facts speak for themselves. Perhaps the attorney general personally might like to read it aloud to the senators? When Kennedy looked stricken, Hoover admitted that he had in fact been made aware of a telephone message from Senator Mansfield, and would in all likelihood consent to speak to him and Dirksen.

Mollenhoff's story had already broken loose a feeding frenzy among the capital's reporters. To avoid leaks, Mansfield, Dirksen, and Hoover met quietly in Mansfield's unpretentious home, where Hoover convinced Dirksen and the openly disgusted majority leader to prevail on Williams and delete the Rometsch inquiry from his upcoming hearings.

Hoover's October 28 memo to his assistant directors reflects the old man's barely suppressed pride at single-handedly stemming the deluge. "I called Kenneth O'Donnell, Special Assistant to the President," Hoover opened, "and told him about my meeting with Senators Mansfield and Dirksen and that everything is well in hand. I advised Mr. O'Donnell that the Senators assured me that they would say nothing; that statements by Senator Williams of Delaware"—hours earlier, Williams had put out a press release to the effect that the "Iowa story" was off the committee's agenda—"seemed to pull the rug from under Mollenhoff's story."

The Director went on to the effect that he had briefed the senators on the Bureau's findings and "Senator Mansfield was surprised as to the activities which had been going on." Furthermore, "I informed Mr. O'Donnell that we had made a thorough investigation and no security element was involved and that we had in writing that no contact with the White House was made by the woman in Germany." Both senators had assured Hoover personally that they would not talk about this with the press or go beyond "what they had seen in the newspapers."

Finally, significantly, "Mr. O'Donnell extended an invitation from the President for me to have a luncheon with the President on Thursday, October 31, 1963, at 1:00 P.M., which I accepted."

It had been over a year since Hoover and JFK had enjoyed a lunch together; the Director had taken great satisfaction in his gossipy monthly lunches with other, better-disposed chief executives, like FDR and Ike. But John Kennedy found the old fellow "an awful bore," what with his nonstop harangues, and invited him rarely, and always included Bobby, which tended to chill what little exchange of views there was. This invitation clearly registered the extent to which, as the summer ended, power had shifted.

Hoover followed up immediately with a memo, which recapitulated his assurances to the attorney general, emphasizing that "Senator Mansfield and Senator Dirksen were perfectly satisfied and willing to keep quiet," and that "the statement issued by Williams . . . gave them . . . nothing concrete to work on." A day later Hoover had moved to lock in his advantage by advising Robert Kennedy of "a rumor circulating on the Hill that I was being replaced . . . predicated upon the fact that I had not issued a statement adjudicating the Bobby Baker affair. The Attorney General made the remark that when Hoover's replacement came in, he was going out." Hoover then claimed to have reassured Kennedy: the Director would stay on, notwithstanding this flurry of rumors, which Bobby dismissed as "unfounded and vicious."

Now that Bobby Kennedy was his new best friend, Hoover kept a hammerlock on the administration by secretly coaching his claque in the House, led by the likes of Congressmen Sam Devine of Ohio and H. R. Gross of Iowa, to express their outrage that "the current Administration is applying pressure on the Director to make statements or take action which is not within the proper functions of the Bureau," and, worse, that "the AG demanded the Director make a statement, or furnish a letter, to the effect that the White House officials are absolved from any connection with the Ellen Rometsch–Bobby Baker story. Allegedly, the Director told the AG flatly he would not furnish such a statement, and the Administration is 'burning.'"

Meanwhile, over at Crime Records, Deke DeLoach was spiking repeated demands from the attorney general's office that the Bureau cut off the spread of the Mollenhoff material into the *New York Daily News* and the Associated Press. On hearing that "the President was personally interested in having this story killed," DeLoach "explained . . . on each occasion that it was not within the province of the FBI to kill the story. . . . I told Guthman he should make his own statements to the press without dragging the FBI into this matter."

Characteristically, Hoover was willing to step out and save the president —for a price—but he wanted no responsibility, in case the whole thing soured. This was already one of Edgar's greatest bravura turns. His prestige was such that he alone could step in and convince the top dogs of the Senate that the Rometsch scandal stopped short of the White House and in any case had no national-security aspects—both assurances doubtful at best, as Hoover well knew. Yet at the same time, he wouldn't go public to exonerate the White House and permitted the whole mess to pile up, a tangle of unresolved combustibles smoldering at the margin as the government built its corruption case against Bobby Baker. Hoover could at any moment arrange to leak classified material from a follow-up investigation guaranteed to barbecue the president. Or not. It would all depend on how cooperative Bobby Kennedy and his brother turned out to be on issues that were important to the Director.

From Hoover's perspective, the manipulations beneath the surface of the Rometsch entanglement could not have come along at a better moment. The same weeks the Rometsch affair was impending, other events kept exploding into the news to keep the Director scrambling to regain control. Joe Valachi, a soldier in the Genovese family serving time in the Atlanta penitentiary, who had beat to death another inmate he concluded was sent to silence him, agreed to a wholesale debriefing by the Federal Narcotics Bureau. Valachi's revelations produced the floor plans for the entire Cosa Nostra. After years of dismissing the notion of a nationwide system of organized crime as "baloney," Hoover had shouldered in to force his own interrogators on Valachi to extract the remaining details, only to be preempted that August by Robert Kennedy, who leaked this sensational story as a Justice Department coup before turning Valachi over to the McClellan Committee so that the politicians could share a tasty meal of worldwide publicity.

Inside the Bureau itself, a kind of ideological brushfire had broken out which threatened the entire rationale of the place. Preliminary to the March on Washington, the Director had tasked his assistant director for Domestic Intelligence (Division Five), William Sullivan, to produce a study that demonstrated the extent of Communist infiltration in the civil rights movement, with special attention to M. L. King.

Sullivan was widely regarded as the odd bird around headquarters, "something of a bantam rooster," in the judgment of Deke DeLoach, his most conspicuous rival among the senior Hoover lieutenants. Regarded—especially by himself—as the FBI's senior intellectual-in-residence, this small, rumpled, fiercely opinionated Massachusetts Irishman—and Kennedy supporter—with the perpetual spatter of gravy stains on his twisted necktie was the house expert on the international Communist conspiracy. He was already starting to evidence, the lordly DeLoach would later write, "more ambition than was good for a man, combined with a slight deficiency in principle."

Sullivan's study shocked Hoover. Finally submitted to Hoover on August 23, for sixty-eight pages it wove its bureaucratic way toward the unwelcome admission that Communists were not a decisive element in the civil rights movement. "The Party views the struggle for equal rights as part of the Marxist concept of the never-ending class struggle and not, as most Negroes see it, an attempt to solve a racial issue. Thus, the Party would involve the Negro in a much broader struggle than the already titanic one in which he is now engaged." Communist influence was "infinitesimal." The biopsy was in, and the results were negative.

Hoover's whole position depended on the notion that Communism remained the primary threat. While only a few thousand members survived in the apparatus itself, and a large percentage of them were paid FBI informants, as Hoover saw it the danger was now even *more* acute, since that meant that the masses had gone underground and would be harder to identify and control. Worse, as the Director was overheard to observe during one unguarded aside, "How am I going to justify our appropriation in the House if this gets out?"

"A few months went by before he would speak to me," Sullivan later wrote. "Everything was conducted by exchange of written communications. It was evident that we had to change our ways or we would all be out in the street."

"This memo reminds me vividly of those I received when Castro took over Cuba," Hoover snapped when he deigned finally to take cognizance of his captive intellectual. "You contended then that Castro and his cohorts were not Communists and not influenced by Communists. Time alone proved you wrong."

Whipped, Sullivan recanted. On August 30, he groveled his way through an apology on behalf of Division Five, which conceded flatly that "The Director is correct. We were completely wrong . . . the Communist Party, USA, does wield substantial influence over Negroes which one day could become decisive." King's "I have a Dream" speech was "demagogic" and King himself was "the most dangerous Negro leader of the future in this Nation from the standpoint of Communism, the Negro and national security." They must now concern themselves with "the many Negroes who are fellow-travelers, sympathizers or who aid the Party, knowingly or unknowingly, but do not qualify as members." From then on, it would be "unrealistic to limit ourselves as we have been doing to legalistic proofs or definitely conclusive evidence that would stand up in court or before Congressional Committees."

With a nod from Hoover, they'd operate outside the law. The whole thing reads like a midnight diatribe by Dr. Goebbels.

As October opened, Hoover had his pieces in position all across the chessboard to corner Martin Luther King. Typically, the Director made sure that the impetus to tighten up surveillance on King appeared to originate from elsewhere in the headquarters. On October 4, William Sullivan, avidly seeking redemption, produced a memo requesting permission from the attorney general to install a wiretap on King's residence in Atlanta. "I hope you don't change your mind on this," Hoover scrawled on Sullivan's recommendation, careful to tear enough skin off to keep this mercurial bookworm alert.

According to Hoover's subsequent memo on the subject, after reneging in July 1963 Kennedy agreed in October to permit the broadscale tapping of King's telephones. "On October 7, 1963, a request for authority to place a telephone surveillance on King's residence was sent to Mr. Kennedy. On October 10, 1963, he authorized this surveillance, and surveillance on any future residence of King, by his written signature.

"This telephone surveillance was installed on November 8, 1963 and was discontinued on April 30, 1966." What Hoover does not mention in his memo of record was the fact that tapping King's telephones was specifically authorized by Kennedy "on a trial basis," for a month or so. "Bobby thought it was absolute blackmail," Nicholas Katzenbach later observed, "but he felt he could not, with all of the flood of memos about all his [King's] Communist associations, then turn the Bureau down on a tap. . . ."

Two weeks later, Kennedy had registered his irritation to Evans at the government-wide circulation of the FBI report "Communism and the Negro Movement," an unabashed smear of King. By then all recipients had had the chance to peruse these largely unsubstantiated charges. His wiretapping permit in hand, the Director agreed to pull back the reports. "I have talked to A.G. and he is satisfied," Hoover wrote below Evans's description of Kennedy's annoyance. Hoover would take whatever he wanted. Before anybody thought to review the permit, Jack Kennedy was dead.

Two questions would arise which haunted Robert Kennedy for the rest of his life. Did he knowingly okay heavy surveillance on King, whose status just then approached that of a savior among the Negro masses? And if he did, had he understood fully the scope of the document he signed?

The evidence seems undeniable that Kennedy in fact did authorize what quickly turned into the wholesale exploitation of "technicals," as wiretaps were referred to inside the Bureau. Both Kennedys were quite peeved that, whatever King told them, Stanley Levison was still around, involved in the ghosting of King's new book about the Birmingham protests and patiently advising the SCLC. With the 1964 presidential election coming up, it was more important every day to tone down this randy, publicity-hungry preacher, keep him from inflaming many more communities across the politically fragile Black Belt. It could be that enough of the Bureau's unobtrusive little green Plymouth sedans with their two-way radios parked carefully behind the motels which King and his repertory company favored for their bacchanalias might have a proctoring effect.

The Kennedys needed badly to placate Hoover. The Bobby Baker hearings were breaking into a rolling boil in the Rules Committee; one move to irk this crazy old man and Ellen Rometsch was liable to flop right out of the cauldron and merchandize her client list to the tabloids. Partisans around Bob Kennedy would explain that he was only attempting to prove that Hoover was wrong or that the tap was a quid pro quo for the Director's restraint with the administration's civil rights legislation pending in committee. Kennedy knew better. Once, off guard, he confided that he had *had* to give King to Hoover or "there would have been no living with the Bureau."

Another excuse that made the rounds was the justification by ignorance. A rich man's son, Kennedy had no mechanical background, his aide Joe Dolan would observe. "He couldn't tell a spark plug from a generator." A July 6, 1961, memo survives in which Courtney Evans is attempting to alert Al Belmont as to what their greenhorn attorney general does and does not understand about the use of "electronic devices," which he has been pushing his Organized Crime and Racketeering Section to put to use against mobsters and their supporters like Jimmy Hoffa's mouthpiece, Haggerty. Furthermore, in 1961 the incoming attorney general had put his signature to a Bureau request to the New York telephone company to lease certain of the city's lines for low-voltage juice to power long-term hidden microphones.

"He is, of course, aware we do have some coverage of this type because of the nature of information that has been supplied to him, particularly in connection with the activities of leading hoodlums in Chicago," Evans reports. "There is a serious question as to whether he has any comprehension as to the difference between a technical surveillance and a microphone surveillance. . . . Obviously, this is the field which should be closely controlled by the Bureau." Courtney contrived to keep Kennedy away from it.

But there is a lot of reason to believe that Kennedy—whose family, after all, was known to keep a wireman on retainer at times—wasn't all that naïve about bugging and tapping. One friend of the family remembers how Bobby gestured him into that cavernous attorney-general's office and played him a tape of a conversation in a car between Raymond Patriarca, the boss of the New England Mafia, and Sonny McDonough, a statehouse power around the Commonwealth of Massachusetts. To intercept an exchange like that required an extremely sophisticated bug. Ed Silberling, still nursing his bruises, would declare in 1967 that Kennedy was well aware of electronic surveillance and "particularly where Jimmy Hoffa was concerned, he encouraged it."

Evans, solicitous of Bobby's legend, attributed some of the disagreement to Kennedy's lapses. "In some situations there were probably facts which would lead one to believe that ordinarily a person would understand . . . " he would remark years later in connection with the electronics. "Many a time I would talk to him and after five minutes I would stop and say, 'Robert, you didn't hear a word I said.' And he would readily admit that his mind was off on some other important problem and he hadn't heard what I said. . . ."

For all of that, by signing that release which permitted the Director essentially unlimited rights to pursue King, Kennedy crossed a line. He knew it. Hoover had him there, too. He had lost control.

He would never recover. In June 1968, days before he died, Robert Kennedy was prepping himself for a debate with Gene McCarthy in a San Francisco hotel. A few close advisers were tuning him up. Having held back key files for five years, Hoover provoked an open confrontation with Robert Kennedy in the press and leaked the Bureau's documentation specifying that it was *Kennedy* who agitated to slap the wiretaps on the late, recently martyred Martin Luther King. This disclosure in all probability had cost Kennedy the Oregon primary.

John Seigenthaler was in the room. "As I recall," Seigenthaler says, "Dick Goodwin put the question to him. And his answer was—it sounded evasive— it was basically: 'The FBI was seeking to establish that there were subversive ties to the movement and in order to prove that there were not I discussed the matter with the Director. . . .'

"And Dick said, 'Bobby, that's not enough of an answer.'"

"And he said—he was rather cross about it—'Well, that's all the answer you're gonna get. That's all the answer anybody's gonna get.' And that ended it."

Unshackled, Hoover's legions spread across the Southland, sniffing for evidence. A Division-Five conference in Washington stressed the importance of "neutralizing King as an effective Negro leader. . . . We are most interested in exposing him in some manner or another in order to discredit him." A unique communications center all but impossible to trace to the FBI went in at Peachtree Towers in Atlanta to service the wiretap lines. To supplement its electronic snooping, in 1964 the FBI would insert one of its own paid informants, James Harrison, into the SCLC's executive staff as comptroller. Now, once the freshly authorized taps were installed, Bureau eavesdroppers could keep ahead of Martin Luther King's unceasing travel schedule, with enough warning to allow their "sound men" to implant "misurs," bugs for microphone surveillance, inside walls and behind the fretwork of dressers and sideboards, where they were hard to detect. At one stage, the Bureau specialists were running fourteen misurs simultaneously on King, which produced a huge transcription overload.

It would become a joke with Abernathy and the others to feel behind the drawer-slides of desks and along bedboards and rip loose those sensitive little microphones by their delicate filaments and make speeches—"Hey, there, Ol' Edgar . . . "—blaring with humor and bravado. But after a day spent heading up a march beneath a steady rain of rocks and bottles, constantly on the alert for the glimmer of a gun barrel, this awareness of untiring, unseen auditors was no help.

A dragnet this pervasive was unlikely to come up empty. On January 6, 1964, after a long and harrowing morning spent working with their D.C. lawyers preparing a defense against trumped-up libel charges by the State of Alabama for alleged misstatements in a 1960 money-raising ad, King and several of his staff and a few women of assorted hues had repaired to the Willard Hotel near the White House. After eleven reels of nondescript, informal chatter and glasses chinking and heavy-duty ethnic jokes, just as the festivities were reaching their height, auditors for the Bureau caught King ripping loose, his rich voice unmistakable above the soft, wet sounds of fatigue and abandonment. "I'm fucking for God!" he broke forth. "I'm not a Negro tonight!"

For Sullivan and Hoover, coming into this inch or two of tape was like dropping a twelve-point buck. "This will destroy the burrhead!" Hoover was overheard to exclaim. Sullivan and his technicians were soon at work piecing together a compendium of this and a few other highlights of the unremitting King surveillance, suitable for media distribution. They already had enough, as Sullivan noted, to knock King "off his pedestal and reduce him completely to influence."

These tapes recording King on the rampage would turn into one of the hot potatoes of Bureau history, thrown back and forth and vigorously disowned by every survivor who got anywhere near them. "The fact that King and twelve acquaintances of his went to a hotel and hired a hundred-dollar-a-night call girl and most of them had something to do with her while they were drinking Black Russians—that was the subject of that tape," Deke DeLoach is willing to respond in his earnest basso when cornered on the subject. "None of us ever played that tape to any reporters, I only heard fifteen to twenty minutes of that tape when Sullivan brought it to my office. I told him to shut it off; I wanted to hear no more. But Sullivan had a fetish for doing things against Dr. King. He got Lish Whitson, the retired head of the old espionage section, to fly to Miami and mail it to Coretta King. Mr. Hoover was horrified when he found out about it."

In his posthumously published expose of the Hoover FBI, *The Bureau,*

William Sullivan insists that *Hoover* was behind the entire travesty. The Director, who "had always been fascinated by pornography," arranged through Alan Belmont to have a box dropped off which contained a compilation of Martin Luther King's greatest hotel-room hits as well as a letter intended for Coretta King which Sullivan claims he never saw. The letter urged King to "look into your heart. You are a complete fraud and a great liability to all of us Negroes . . . a dissolute, abnormal moral imbecile. . . .

"King, there is only one thing left for you to do. You know what it is. You have just 34 days. . . . There is but one way out for you. You better take it before your filthy, abnormal fraudulent self is bared to the nation. . . ."

The package had been opened in January 1965, in Atlanta, days after King returned from Oslo, where he had just received the Nobel Peace Prize. "The purpose of the tape," Sullivan wrote, "according to Belmont, was to silence King's criticism of Hoover by causing a break between King and his wife which would reduce King's stature and therefore weaken him as a leader.

"I had not heard or seen the tape, and I did not know about the unsigned note until it surfaced in the press."

But Sullivan is gone, shot dead in 1977 by a teenaged deer hunter, and the survivors who honor Hoover's memory are quick to defend their Director. "Sullivan prepared a letter in the Martin Luther King case which was available to the Church Committee, which was termed by them a letter which urged King to commit suicide, which wasn't the case," says Ray Wannall, the head of counterintelligence for the Bureau during the last Hoover years. The original was discovered in Sullivan's office files after Hoover fired him abruptly and changed the locks in October 1971. When Sullivan wrote that King had "so many days to redeem yourself," Wannall says he meant "from then to Christmas day. He often said that Martin Luther King was a man of the cloth." It is important to realize, Wannall has written, that Sullivan "had a knack for symbolism. He was a devout Catholic and as such must have considered King's inordinate sexual desire one of the seven deadly sins—lust."

Sullivan composed the letter himself, Wannall said recently, "and had it mailed to Martin Luther King without anybody in the Bureau knowing about it." What keeps coming through is how *guilty* anybody anywhere near this wholesale persecution of King now feels, how important it is to recast the history a little, establish some distance from the scene of the crime. Keep salvation open. "Since World War II the FBI recruited heavily at Jesuit schools," Kenneth O'Reilly has noted, "and by the 1960s Protestant agents considered themselves a distinct minority, members of a 'PU'—a Protestant underground."

While mailing this so-called "suicide package" to SCLC headquarters in 1964 was most likely the heaviest sin to carom around the Seat of Government, it amounted to one among the many racked up attempting to repress the irrepressible reverend. There apparently were other, preliminary tapes. Berl Bernhard had persevered as staff director of the Civil Rights Commission until early November 1963. Not long before he left, the FBI special agent who had been assigned to commissar duties with the commission, who had been hanging around outside the door inspiring, Bernhard remembers, "this eerie feeling that everything you did he was watching," approached Bernhard with a wrapped parcel in his hand.

"Mr. Hoover sent this to you so you would have a better understanding of your friend Dr. King," the agent said. "You don't understand what you are dealing with."

Inside the parcel were two tapes. One turned out to record a long, rambling telephone conversation between King and Stanley Levison. "They were talking about having some demonstrations somewhere," Bernhard recalls. "What I was told was that Levison was some kind of Communist agitator, but it sounded to me like a hundred other calls or comments. Like, I think we would get more out of going to one city or another. This was to show me that he had some basic influence on Dr. King."

The other tape is still hard for Bernhard to discuss. "It was what you would expect if you really wanted to nail someone, if you'd been waiting for that perfect time when a massive indiscretion was occurring, of a prurient nature. It was so unpleasant, vile, that they should be recording that kind of stuff. But it wasn't surprising—there was so much animus by Mr. Hoover toward Dr. King and the whole civil rights movement, it was palpable."

This in the autumn of 1963, more than a year before Hoover inaugurated his concerted campaign to discredit King. What seemed to gall the Director most was the worldwide acclaim in which this cheeky black minister had succeeded in mantling himself. Hoover fumed—"They had to dig deep in the garbage to come up with this one"—when *Time* magazine selected King the 1963 Man of the Year. Hoover succeeded in preventing Marquette University from granting King an honorary doctorate, only to discover that *Yale* intended to dignify the reverend. The Director turned to his long-time ally Cardinal Spellman in his unsuccessful effort to keep the Pope from receiving King, a kind of worldwide sanctification which could easily open the way to the Nobel Peace Prize, a distinction the Director was privately convinced he himself deserved. King should have gotten instead the "top alleycat" prize, Hoover groused on a memo.

The deteriorating Hoover appears to have perceived in King a kind of malevolent antipode, a version of himself in an alternate universe, a force for cultural degradation he personally must contest and obliterate. It did not matter much how. On November 18, 1964, Hoover summoned a contingent of the Women's National Press Club and, after rambling through chapter and verse to repudiate the notion that the Bureau had done nothing in the civil rights field, referred to Martin Luther King's complaints in 1962. "In view of King's attitude and his continued criticism of the FBI on this point," Hoover said, "I consider King to be the most notorious liar in the country." When the startled DeLoach passed Hoover notes urging him to tone this down, keep everything off the record, Hoover brushed him off and waded in deeper by calling King "one of the lowest characters in the country," "controlled" by the Commoonists. The ladies had their scoop.

Vacationing in Bimini, King responded with a press release that revealed a bloodcurdling level of media sophistication: "I cannot conceive of Mr. Hoover making a statement like this without being under extreme pressure. He has apparently faltered under the awesome burden, complexities and responsibilities of his office. Therefore, I cannot engage in a public debate with him. I have nothing but sympathy for this man who has served his country so well."

It was against the repercussions of this exchange that the "suicide package" went out to Atlanta. Alarmed bystanders—Nicholas Katzenbach, Bob Kennedy's recent replacement as attorney general, Lyndon Johnson—attempted to patch things up; King and his advisers attended an inconclusive meeting with Hoover and his staff, but both antagonists were beyond that. "If King wanted war, we certainly would give it to him," DeLoach told Roy Wilkins. Walter Jenkins in the LBJ White House evidently urged DeLoach to get the story out.

While DeLoach continues to deny having taken any part in a coordinated effort to defame King, at least eight of the most highly regarded editors and reporters in the trade—from Ben Bradlee at *Newsweek* to *Los Angeles Times* bureau chief David Kraslow to John Herbers at the *New York Times* and Ralph McGill at the *Atlanta Constitution*—maintain that they were all shown pictures, transcripts, and/or recordings by spokesmen for the FBI's Crime Records Division documenting King's performance in an orgy or leaving a hotel with a Caucasian prostitute or chasing other white women around motel rooms, photos snapped through one-way mirrors. None of this appeared in print.

To Hoover's astonishment, nothing worked. For the Director, much of whose appeal to repressed America came out of his ability to project his image as a snappy, no-nonsense Puritan, their Holy Abstinent, the realization that the upcoming generation of his fellow countrymen didn't really care that much whether Martin Luther King Jr. liked the ladies or not came as a shock.

Bureau attempts to float rumors that the Kremlin was underwriting King and that the preacher was embezzling from the SCLC treasury to pad out a bank account in Switzerland got laughed off by reporters. It was apparent to anybody who covered the movement that King had absolutely no interest in worldly goods and was embarrassed even by his own modest house in Atlanta and simple lifestyle at a time when so many others were hungry. The problem for the public-relations spinners in the Bureau just then was the fact that King was in fact a dedicated and godly man, pretty much the martyr-in-waiting millions thought he was.

When his headquarters brain trust advised the Director to ignore King's more-in-sorrow-than-in-anger response when Hoover called him a liar, Hoover went along reluctantly: "Okay. But I don't understand why we are unable to get the true facts before the public. We can't even get our accomplishments published. We are never taking the aggressive, but allow lies to remain unanswered." It sounded like an old man's complaint.

Yet Hoover had not defended his unique perch near the top of the American government for going on forty years without attending public opinion. It couldn't be plainer by 1963 that Bull Connor and his ilk were perceived as grotesques by the preponderance of the American people. Old-fashioned, breast-beating Anglo-Saxon supremacy was out of style. By July 2, 1964, after a winter and spring of grabbing lapels and gripping shoulders and trading political favors with a ferocity unapproached even during his heyday as Leader of the Senate, Lyndon Johnson had hustled into law John Kennedy's Civil Rights proposals. Seated together in the East Room of the White House for the signing ceremonies were Robert Kennedy and Everett Dirksen, George Meany and Martin Luther King and J. Edgar Hoover.

While regarded through much of his career in Congress as something of a Yellow-Dog Democrat, with well-wrought allegiances to Dixie's Bourbon committee chairmen, Johnson had an unexpected side. His hardscrabble upbringing in the dust bowl of West Texas had inculcated in him an ineradicable prairie populism, tempered after his arrival in Washington by the idealism of the New Deal. Furthermore, he harbored a lifelong distaste for the

Ku Klux Klan. As a boy of thirteen, he had been herded with the women and children into the cellar of the family farmhouse while his father and uncles roamed the porch with shotguns. The Klan had threatened to kill his father.

The perception that foulmouthed rednecks were free to stave in the skulls of protesters or dynamite their way across the Old Confederacy, confident that white juries would let them off—this weighed on Johnson. In mid-September 1963, a blast tore a giant hole in the façade of the Sixteenth Street Baptist Church in Birmingham, reducing to blood-soaked body parts four girls in early adolescence, milling around the lounge in their fresh white usher surplices before the eleven-o'clock prayers. This was the twentieth unsolved explosion in "Bombingham" and got a lot of play in newspapers throughout the world. Important power centers in America had had enough; the labor unions quickly raised $160,000. Hoover was listening. As far as he was concerned, money always deserved a vote.

The epidemic of atrocities left the Director in a quandary. Whatever his racist inclinations, open violence like this reflected poorly on the Bureau. Despite the decades of walking their dogs together and impromptu Sunday night suppers, once he became president, Lyndon Johnson was starting to find the Director's endless bursts of logorrhea taxing and contrived whenever he could arrange it to do his FBI business through Deke DeLoach. For somebody who craved a lot of face time with the chief executive to mitigate his chronic paranoia, the awareness that Johnson, like JFK, was starting to leave him out of things was painful for the aging Director.

As Hoover approached the mandatory federal retirement age, seventy, Johnson had pointedly sidestepped the question of whether the Director might expect to go on forever, extending Hoover's tenure "for an indefinite period of time," which could mean not even the remainder of his term. In November 1964, *Newsweek* printed a story alleging that the president was about to replace Hoover. Tolson wrote the magazine himself, charging "a new low in reporting."

One important aide to Johnson remembers the day Johnson attempted to fire Hoover. "Hoover walks in with an armload of files, smiling," the aide recalls. "Twenty minutes later he walks out, still smiling, and LBJ is white as a sheet. 'He's got everything, the son of a bitch,' the president tells me."

Wily as Lyndon was, Hoover knew his dossiers wouldn't protect him indefinitely. Ellen Rometsch wasn't relevant to LBJ's career. Robert Kennedy hung on as attorney general for almost a year following the death of JFK, first stupefied by guilt and sorrow and then resolute about following through on his vendetta against Hoffa and, more and more, concerned with the empowerment of Southern blacks. With his brother gone, keeping the Solid South in the Democratic column made very little difference to the lame-duck attorney general, especially since the 1964 candidate would undoubtedly be Lyndon.

After he moved into the Senate, Bobby prevailed on Johnson to replace him with his deputy, Nicholas Katzenbach, less of a hippy as Hoover saw things but equally a short-sighted, race-mixing liberal. When Katzenbach got shunted off into the State Department, Johnson created a vacancy on the Supreme Court for Abe Fortas by trading Tom Clark's seat away in return for putting in Katzenbach's deputy, Ramsey Clark, Tom's boy, as attorney general. Hoover soon wrote Ramsey Clark off as a "spineless jellyfish," in part because he routinely turned down Hoover's requests to reinstitute taps on Martin Luther King. Both Katzenbach and Clark, unfortunately, did not carry the sort of personal baggage the Director hoarded on the Kennedy brothers and so were harder to maneuver. This continuity at the top of the Justice Department was reinforced by the fact that Burke Marshall and his deputy John Doar continued to preside over the Civil Rights Division, in Hoover's eyes a hotbed of fanatics forever truckling to King and his like.

The problem was that by now the country, as well as the government, was moving toward desegregation; the process was probably irreversible. Hoover was a realist. As "Freedom Summer" broke across the South in 1964, the Ku Klux Klan was out there burning crosses—sixty-one in one night in southwest Mississippi—and firebombing black homes and churches and murdering blacks at random. When appeals from the Civil Rights Division to the FBI to "come down and shoot the lion" seemed to be ignored, Bobby Kennedy bypassed Hoover and dispatched Walter Sheridan and a half-dozen live ones from his "Terrible Twenty" to "get something on the Klan."

Sheridan's operatives had just taken down Jimmy Hoffa. They were a power to be reckoned with. Hoover at once memoed Burke Marshall about "a man in Mississippi named Walter Sheridan who claims to be doing investigative work for the Department of Justice. This is to inform you that he is not a member of the FBI." The Director sent over an agent to lecture John Doar: "Either the Bureau is going to be *the* investigative agency of the Department or it's not. Either it's going to do all of it or none of it." At this point Kennedy and Marshall recommended to Johnson that he urge the Director to get the FBI to put to use in Mississippi some of the "spectacularly efficient" methods with which the Bureau had undermined the Communist Party.

This approach gave Hoover enough running room to redeem himself.

He could oppose integration, but he could also take a stand against hood-lums, lowlifes, disturbers-of-the-peace. Furthermore, the Klan's traditional fulminating against the Pope would motivate the Director's heavily Roman-Catholic troops in the field. The South was difficult for his men, Hoover once remarked informally, filled as it was with "water moccasins, rat-tlesnakes, and red-necked sheriffs, and they are all in the same category as far as I am concerned."

What kept coming through was the fact that Hoover hated to expose himself. Like penetrating organized crime, desegregating the South looked formidable and dangerous. This was not car thefts or small-town bank rob-bers, situations in which the local police would expend the shoe leather and the Bureau agents in the field offices would step in afterward and rack up credit for the statistics.

This was hard.

"I really don't think the black community knows or appreciates the work the FBI did," a field agent who worked the South, Roger Depue, com-mented afterward, "If you arrested a Klansman there were certain parishes [counties] where the sheriff wouldn't take the prisoner. You had to take the prisoner in the back of a bureau car, and you would have to drive through several parishes before you found one that would take him. Sometimes you had a parade of pickup trucks following you. There was a tremendous effort to intimidate agents."

Hoover played this very cute. Succumbing to Lyndon Johnson's cajoler-ies, Hoover agreed to open the first FBI field office in Jim Eastland's home state, which the natives were already starting to advertise as Occupied Mississippi. On July 10, 1964, Johnson flew the Director down to Jackson on Air Force One. Received by local politicians as a hero and a sympathizer, Hoover emphasized that the Bureau "does not and will not give protection to civil rights workers" and refused to repudiate the governor's statement that "the state should refuse to comply with the new Civil Rights Law."

Having established his bona fides as a sho-nuff bigot, Hoover returned quickly to D.C. and, before the month was over, shifted responsibility to William Sullivan's Domestic Intelligence Division, the same Division Five that was already out there honeycombing Martin Luther King's world with microphones. Referred to behind his back around the management suite as "Crazy Billy" because of his unpredictable, high-voltage mood shifts and his lack of street sense, Hoover's bantamweight Domestic Intelligence maven took on all responsibilities for bringing under control this resurgence of race-baiting below the Mason-Dixon line.

Across the South, within a year, 2,000 Klansmen, 20 percent of the membership, were paid informants for the Bureau. The others would be subjected to "interviews" from agents "just to let those individuals know," in the Director's words, "the FBI knew who they were and had an eye on them." The total number of Bureau agents in Mississippi jumped from three to upward of 150 in a state with 480 Klansmen, every one accumulating a file of his own and now carefully watched.

By September, Sullivan had authorization to create a new Counter Intelligence Program—COINTELPRO—"COINTELPRO—White Hate Groups." Like the anti-Communist COINTELPRO, these units were intended to enter into a kind of no-holds-barred subversive warfare against the Klan, developing techniques of harassment and disruption to unnerve and in the end pulverize the Klaverns across the South. Incoming Attorney General Katzenbach subsequently approved the Bureau's wide-ranging attacks on the Klan as "hard, tough, and outstandingly successful" and boasted that "I authorized them. . . . I would do so again." Robert Kennedy himself later termed the Bureau "very effective" under circumstances like these. What Sullivan and his people were into was a kind of secret government-sanctioned vigilante operation, much of it outside the law.

A coordinated vendetta like this relieved the Director's frustrations after years of attempting to drag a feckless assortment of barnyard dynamiters and juiced-up backwoods bullies before sympathetic Southern juries, likely to let them off. The rest of the Justice Department, with its thousand-plus nit-picking, procedure-crazed attorneys, was never to be informed. COINTELPRO—White Hate Groups went forward now with amazing efficiency. It was, without a doubt, utterly unconstitutional.

From the beginning, having felt his way into a role within the federal bureaucracy as a kind of deus ex machina entitled to restructure anything he liked, Hoover was always happier to avoid the courts. You ultimately brought down a miscreant like Dillinger with a hail of bullets, not one more prison sentence. If a leak to the newspapers or the threat of getting hauled before a Senate subcommittee could slow some social-betterment nut down—fine, better than litigation.

By now Hoover was permitting some of his more imaginative SACs surprisingly long leashes. Bill Roemer alludes to one operation during which a Tucson agent "formed a vigilante group" and bombed the winter homes of Joe Bonanno and the Detroit capo Pete Licavoli in "an attempt to get something going between the two families of the Cosa Nostra." Hoover undoubtedly appreciated this, so long as nobody connected the Bureau. Besides, Livacoli had made a substantial contribution to the J. Edgar Hoover Foundation.

The methods of the COINTELPRO squads turned out to work so well that they would be integrated into standard FBI operating procedure and permit the Bureau to take on elements in society before which the Director had long been privately apprehensive, in particular the extremists of all races and the leadership of organized crime. By hounding Hoover into these unwelcome arenas, Robert Kennedy permanently altered the FBI.

"The Klan did push us to the limit," Deke DeLoach admits. "Several Klansmen had a black coffin, six of them all told, and they walked up to the front door of this agent's house. When his wife came to the door they said, 'Your husband's been involved in an automobile accident.' Then they dropped the coffin and left. The woman almost had a heart attack. There was another instance when they put rattlesnakes in the driver's side of an automobile. . . . They wiretapped our phones in Mississippi. They would walk along the sidewalk and bump agents. . . . We did reply in kind. One Klansman told an agent, 'If you walk into my store, I'll kill you.' So two agents showed up at this Klansman's farm, one armed with a shotgun, another with a .38 revolver.

"They said, 'Okay, we're on your property. Kill us.' And the man looked at 'em, and he sank to his knees and he started crying. One time we spread rumors that the Klansman who was the treasurer of the Klan was embezzling money. That caused such a furor in the Klan that they kicked him out. Another time we indicated that the head of the Klan was sleeping with another Klan officer's wife. . . . They almost had a duel in connection with it. It helped break up that entire chapter of the Klan."

According to ex-SAC Neil Welch, the Bureau took it a great deal further than that. Alarmed that *his men* were threatened now, the Director instructed them to stop watching the action from the courthouse porticos. Hoover negotiated an accord with the governor to purge all Klansmen from the Mississippi state police. Another, less cooperative governor reportedly came around when the FBI burned a cross on his lawn. Near Natchez, a team of G-men responded to death threats by forming up in the street outside the Klansmen's favorite saloon and methodically shooting out the windows.

More ominously, Welch has written, "The Agents had full discretion . . . a number of men previously involved in Klan violence around the state seemed, by remarkable coincidence, to experience misfortune. Some disappeared from the area. Some were forced to leave Mississippi for health reasons. A few took unplanned trips to places like Mexico and seemed to lose all interest in the Klan upon their return." By then, the Bureau was running its own informants, protectively colorated in bib overalls and pickup trucks, which meant that "much of what they were doing was invisible, and as a consequence civil rights workers insisted that the FBI was not doing enough."

Rumors, possibly authenticated, were passed among nervous small-town tradesmen donning sheets, which warned of "nighttime FBI raids to shove condom-wrapped shotgun shells into the rectums of hostile Klansmen, daring them to complain, and of Mafia informants secretly imported to extract information by old-fashioned torture." Money changed hands. A $25,000 payoff produced the bullet-ridden bodies of civil rights activists James Chaney, Andrew Goodman, and Michael Schwerner beneath an earthen dam, but even after the Bureau arrested the Klansmen responsible, nobody in the state, including Fifth Circuit Judge W. Harold Cox, was interested in any serious effort to convict.

Hoover himself remained conflicted. On March 25, 1965, four Klansmen passed a car driven by Mrs. Viola Luizzo, who was shuttling marchers into town for Martin Luther King's demonstration in Selma. One Klansman took a shot and severed her spinal cord, which killed her instantly. The teenaged black barber riding with her jumped free after the crash. One of the Klansmen in the shooter's car, Gary Rowe, was a Bureau informant. When the shocked LBJ inquired of the Director after the background of Mrs. Liuzzo and her husband, Hoover stated that Mr. Liuzzo "doesn't have too good a background and the woman had indications of needle marks in her arms where she had been taking dope; that she was sitting very close to the Negro in the car; that it had the appearance of a necking party." Sociologically, the Director hadn't budged.

By Hoover's lights, to bring the Klan under control did not mean endorsing desegregation. The trick was to guide the process from behind the scenes while keeping the rest of the government, and especially the "fiddle-faced reformers" around the Justice Department, off-balance and away from anything important.

That first summer, the Director was annoyed at the way Bob Kennedy kept sending his people into the upheaval of Birmingham to buffer the Freedom Rides. Worse, when they got back they had the gall to complain about the Bureau to its civil rights liaison, Assistant Director Alex Rosen. With that, an attack was mounted on the Department's civil rights chief, the scrupulous and unassuming Burke Marshall. As late as 1964, irked by word that Marshall had remarked that the Bureau knew the Klan was waiting but neglected to inform the rest of Justice while continuing to smear King, Rosen called Marshall to announce, "The Director wants you to know that you are a goddamned liar!"

Marshall took the brunt of Hoover's wrath all along. Shortly after the last of the Freedom Riders went home, Hoover designated one of his operatives to telephone Marshall, who had complained to the Bureau about being underinformed, literally day and night, and pester him with irrelevancies. There were a series of 3:00 A.M. reports to Marshall detailing such incidents as a nasty exchange in a Shreveport, Louisiana, diner, gleanings mostly from the local newspapers.

When anything substantial came in Hoover bided his time, holding back the choicer items to exploit at a time of his own choosing. On a memo describing King's January 1964 performance at the Willard, concerned that the treacherous Kennedy might just tip King off as to the extent of Bureau surveillance, Hoover entered in the margin: "No. A copy need *not* be given A.G." Hoover hoped that Kennedy would first find out about this shocker from the newspaper stories Crime Records was attempting to plant.

Robert Kennedy had his own sources when it came to Reverend King's exuberant one-night stands. "If the country knew what we know about King's goings-on, he'd be finished," Kennedy muttered to one aide. Frank Mankiewicz remembers that by the later sixties, when King's name came up, "We'd make a face." But King's personal vagaries were beside the point.

A few months after the effort to circulate the Willard material, Hoover's electronic wizards secured a tape of King in a motel room watching a rerun on television of John Kennedy's funeral. Registering their poorly disguised distaste for King to the last, the Kennedys had neglected to invite the celebrity preacher to the last rites. Nevertheless, King made his way from Atlanta to the capital on a train, alone, and waited morosely in one of the crowds watching the cortege go by. He was still bitter because the administration had done so little in September when the Klan bombed the Sixteenth Street Baptist Church.

As the televised rerun of the funeral reached the moment when Jacqueline Kennedy and her children knelt by the president's coffin and the widow inclined her head to say good-bye, FBI technicians caught King muttering, "Look at her. Sucking him off one last time."

That was too good, and Hoover sent Courtney Evans over with a transcript for Robert Kennedy, deploring this "vilification of the late President and his wife." All that winter Hoover had been cold to Kennedy, refusing any direct exchange and ignoring Kennedy's rather forlorn notes to the effect that it might be well were they to speak on occasion. Kennedy read the transcript and handed it back to Evans. It made him too sad to deal with for the moment. Still too emotionally depleted most days to talk, Kennedy observed that this memorandum was very helpful.

By then the terms of the struggle were shifting for Bobby, forever.

Roy Cohn Redux

Hoover's intervention in the Rometsch incident left the Director a lot less worried. The FBI had obviously weathered those maddening early months, when, as Assistant to the Director Mark Felt later wrote, Robert Kennedy regarded the Bureau "not as a law-enforcement agency but as an arm of 'his' administration . . . a kind of private police department, with Hoover as its desk sergeant." Felt registered Hoover's "scorn of JFK's philandering." Furthermore, "Personality differences set up a barrier with Attorney General Robert F. Kennedy," along with "Hoover's refusal to accept the alleged affair with Marilyn Monroe. . . ." But by the autumn of 1963, the FBI had recovered its "independent status." It was again totally Hoover's creature.

Ideologically, Bobby continued to meander. Long after Joe McCarthy folded, the short, doughty Hearst columnist George Sokolsky soldiered on as the leading druid of the unreconstructed Right. "Sokolsky would call me twice a week," DeLoach recalls. "We would talk over many things. He was afraid he was gonna die, quite concerned about his age and his health. Whenever he'd come to Washington I'd have an FBI agent sleep in his suite because he thought he was going to go during the night."

Soon after Kennedy became attorney general, Sokolsky requested an interview. Bob looked into Sokolsky's apartment on his next trip to Manhattan, and after that Kennedy made it a point to drop in on the depleted old anti-Communist, still rapping out three columns a week while attempting to cope with diabetes, cancer, and heart problems. Hoover watched. George might well provide a fresh way to get at Bobby.

Cohn had been Sokolsky's prodigy all along. The columnist had babied Cohn since assuming his place in Dora Cohn's animated salon at 1165 Park Avenue. When Roy returned from the glory years with McCarthy, Sokolsky touted him up. Cohn—like Bobby, a soft touch for any loyalist—chipped in with his schoolboy chum, the travel-agency magnate Bill Fugazy, to provide George a refurbished taxicab and a driver.

Barely thirty, Roy Cohn soon laid his spoor across Manhattan, reconfirming his reputation as the Western World's second most sinister mama's boy. His gift for outrageous business practices and high-wire finagling in the courts attracted a following from the start. The banjo-eyed postteen wiseacre with the patent-leather hair and the manic self-confidence was giving way to the big-spending, middle-aged insider, quick-witted and irreverent yet solicitous of his friends and clients, with a natural reserve of back-street legal moves that made it easy for Roy to slip virtually any punch. He prided himself on never stepping out his door without a pocketful of judges. Roy was to assert that the fact that it took Attorney General Robert Kennedy three years to indict him came as rather a disappointment: "I mean, part of my mystique depended on people thinking that I was getting away with every kind of shady deal." "I'm kidding, of course," he wrote later, "but I think only my mother knew that I was honest."

But was he kidding? Along with half the hoods in the Five Families and Carlos Marcello and a wide spectrum of the semireformed wiseguys laboring to justify Teamster money in Las Vegas just then, Cohn's clients would include Donald Trump, the Roman Catholic Diocese of New York, Samuel Lefrak, Cardinal Spellman, and even Aristotle Onassis once he had faced the inevitability of cutting loose the spendthrift Jacqueline. You went to Roy Cohn if you were in a corner.

Roy Cohn's backers around Manhattan were formidable, not merely opinion-makers like Walter Winchell and Sokolsky and Leonard Lyons, but also media powerhouses like Richard Berlin at Hearst and Si Newhouse, heir to the Conde Nast fortune along with magazines and papers across the republic, both cronies since Horace Mann. For Hoover, Cohn provided a deniable cutout to skeptics about the Kennedys from Winchell to the Edwin Weisls, Sr. and Jr., bankers and king-makers since FDR.

Roy inherited solid Tammany connections, which brought in resources from Frank Costello to Carmine De Sapio. He matured quickly into more than a son to Lewis Rosenstiel, the grandiose old bootlegger and master of Schenley Distillers; with Sokolsky's help, in 1957 Cohn secured a choice berth for Lou Nichols, Hoover's top assistant director at the time, as the $100,000-a-year executive vice-president in charge of corporate development and public affairs. A beetle-browed slugger dating back to the Dillinger era, as the impresario of Crime Records Nichols had generated the media adoration on which Hoover's legend rested. While Cohn was still an anti-Communist prodigy, Nichols fed Roy documents. Top Bureau officials were staggered by what Roy Cohn could do for somebody.

With John Kennedy president, Cohn sensed a hardening of the atmosphere. He rang up Jim Juliana, who had worked for him on the McCarthy committee before signing on with Bobby. Should Cohn be concerned? Let's put it this way, Juliana warned him, "Hoffa's number one. You're number two. Get out of town."

Antennae bristling, Cohn faked subservience. When Morton Downey—no doubt at Joe Kennedy's urging—took Cohn to lunch at "21" to request that he write Judiciary Committee chairman Eastland a letter espousing Bobby's appointment to attorney general, Roy promptly did that. Still a nominal Democrat, he sold $10,000-a-page ads to help repay Jack's campaign expenses. To Bobby's annoyance, the White House staff recruited Roy to convince Si Newhouse to instruct one of his newspapers, the New Orleans Times-Picayune, to ease up on Congressman Hale Boggs, a Kennedy ally.

Bobby raged against soliciting any favors from Cohn. "Listen, is your hard-on more important than your brother's program?" Kenny O'Donnell demanded of the truculent attorney general. Nothing did any good. Before long Cohn heard that a ten-man team of tax investigators had been detached from the IRS to dig through Cohn's affairs, the "Get-Cohn Squad." It was soon evident to Cohn that an extraordinary barrage of covert methodology—mail cover, wiretaps, undisguised physical surveillance—was starting to pound in, coordinated by the U.S. Attorney for the Southern District Robert Morgenthau. As sere a prosecutor as New York had ever seen, Morgenthau was on a rampage making cases against untouchable Mob figures.

Cohn ascribed Morgenthau's relentlessness to generational payback. The tall, dry, sharp-featured U.S. Attorney was determined to even the score for the role the callow boy wonder had played during his Red-hunting days in humiliating Robert Morgenthau's father, FDR's secretary of the Treasury. Henry Morgenthau Jr. had released occupation plates to the Soviets so they could flood postwar Germany with American-backed dollars. Cohn blackened the reputation of Henry Morgenthau's closest and most controversial aide, Harry Dexter White. A gut-fighter himself, a measure of revenge was understandable to Cohn.

What baffled even Bob Kennedy's Justice Department colleagues was the exaggerated dedication, willy-nilly, of scarce Justice Department resources to accommodate a grudge. Ramsey Clark, who ultimately served as Lyndon Johnson's attorney general, recalls admonishing Morgenthau about dragging out a witch hunt: "I asked him to personally review anything involving Roy Cohn. I said I would be very distressed if we were to use the power of the office because we didn't like somebody. I didn't say it in an accusatory sense, but I was worried about it."

John Kennedy himself was uncomfortable all along about giving Bobby too long a leash. The president understood well enough how rabid New York politics could get. Roy was broadly connected; even during the Rackets-Committee years, Senator Kennedy had made it a point to assure Cohn that "The fight between Bobby and you hasn't carried over to us." Jack Kennedy's impulse to smooth over Bobby's grievance with Roy carried into the White House. Edward Bennett Williams, like Roy a pal of Bill Fugazy, called Fugazy from the Oval Office one night to sound him out. The president was apprehensive, Williams told Fugazy, "worried that his younger brother would get burned dealing with the malevolent and elusive Cohn."

Jack's wariness about running athwart of Cohn was shared very widely. People came away persuaded that, for all his mild, milky, heavy-lidded blue eyes and that phlegmatic affability, this fast-moving little attorney could deliver a feral bite. He had not lost the talent to elbow himself into easy proximity with power. Before the fifties were over, Cohn was the miracle worker around the white-shoe legal shop at Saxe, Bacon and O'Shea, the representation you could depend on to extract you from an ugly marriage or arrange for an endless series of continuances on your case until the right judge, frequently enough a well-reimbursed intimate of Roy's, would toss the whole thing out.

More precariously, coming into his thirties, Roy seemed to fancy himself a sort of takeover artist, an entrepreneur. He was already arrogating to himself a lifestyle no law practice was ever going to support. This was the Go-Go era, the dawn of the Sex Revolution. Roy spent his days on the move, running up enormous bills at Le Cirque and Pavillon and with air-taxi companies and stretch-limousine franchises, few of which he actually expected to pay. Sue Roy Cohn? Much of his business he conducted out of the harem-scarem town house he picked up on East Sixty-eighth Street, overseen by his doting mother, "Muddy," or between orgies on a succession of yachts which culminated with the ninety-nine-foot, steel-hulled *Defiance,* the colossal operating costs of which Roy attempted to finagle with bad checks he wrote on banks he controlled temporarily in Illinois. When marina fees came due Cohn instructed his captain to exit the harbor at three in the morning. The atrociously maintained *Defiance* ultimately burned at sea, presumably scuttled, according to Coast Guard reports, for the insurance. The first mate died in the blaze.

It would not appear that anybody who conducted business the way Roy Cohn did would need the government's help with destroying himself. But Bobby was impatient. Cohn was politically entrenched and arranged things so that anything of substance he owned—his town house, the Lincoln limousine with the RMC vanity license plates and the mobile telephone, several generations of yachts—was either leased or technically the property of corporations supervised by his nominees. Everything was expensed to the practice. To hurt Cohn, it would be necessary to indict him on criminal grounds.

Or cripple him financially. In 1960 Cohn bought Rosensohn Enterprises, which originated as a device to legitimize the contract held by the gangster Fat Tony Salerno to mount the upcoming second heavyweight title fight between Floyd Patterson and Ingemar Johansson. The fight grossed $4,000,600; "by order of the Attorney General's office" federal agents stepped in and immediately confiscated both the live gate and the receipts throughout theater box offices. Before long the fighters and the hotels and Madison Square Garden got reimbursed, but word came down, according to Cohn's press agent, that "the promotion's money will be held and Uncle will take his cut out first, when he's ready. . . . It's no secret that Bobby is out to get Cohn. Now he's Attorney General and all he has to do is pick up a phone. He did."

Kennedy picked up the phone again in the autumn of 1962, when Cohn and his law partner, Tom Bolan, formed Championship Sports to present the Patterson-Liston fight. Floyd Patterson had barely been assisted off the canvas before the IRS attached the proceeds, subsequently paying off outsider expenses but stiffing the promoters for over half a million dollars. Cohn could readily identify the source of his troubles. "It's almost worth all the headaches," he told the *Wall Street Journal.* "Almost but not quite."

Cohn was not blameless. "Being anti-Communist does not automatically excuse a lack of integrity in every other facet of life," Kennedy assured their mutual friends. As one of the regulars in Lewis Rosenstiel's retinue, Cohn couldn't avoid rubbing elbows with the bumptious old rumrunner's personal following, perennials like the petite, understated Meyer Lansky. Once its casinos and hotels in Cuba came under gathering pressure with the imminence of Fidel Castro, leadership around the syndicate was preoccupied with Las Vegas.

Lansky's most trusted lieutenant in Vegas was Morris E. (Moe) Dalitz, the preeminent mobster first in Detroit and after that in Cleveland. Moe Dalitz had first befriended Jimmy Hoffa when Hoffa was an enforcer for the Detroit Teamster local. Dalitz turned up in Arizona subsequent to the execution of Bugsy Siegel in Los Angeles to look after the interests of the New York families while managing the Desert Inn. A seemingly mild, comparatively well-spoken business type, Dalitz was a great deal of help to Robert Maheu when Maheu was attempting to organize the gambling capital at the behest of Howard Hughes. By 1960, Cohn was Dalitz's guest of honor at a New Year's Eve dinner.

For all his politesse, Dalitz remained at base a gangster. When Sonny Liston in his prime got into an altercation with the aging Dalitz and raised a fist the size of a bowling ball inches from the gambler's face, Dalitz never blinked. "If you hit me, nigger," Dalitz told the heavyweight champ in low but definite tones, "you'd better kill me, because if you don't, I'll make one telephone call and you'll be dead in twenty-four hours."

A well-informed source places Cohn as Dalitz's lawyer in meetings in Havana as early as 1958, cutting up the stock of a Las Vegas hospital complex, the Sunrise. The Sunrise ultimately boasted 688 rooms and twelve hundred doctors on staff, the biggest facility west of Chicago. For years, the skim from the casinos left town somewhere on the person of a heavily bandaged patient in an ambulance. By 1958, the notoriety rising out of the Rackets Committee hearings compelled the Mormon-controlled Bank of Las Vegas to refuse to finance Mob projects. Jimmy Hoffa stepped forward, and from then on Allen Dorfman and the Teamsters' Central States Pension Fund took on the Las Vegas real-estate explosion.

Once shares of the resulting partnership, A&M Enterprises, got parceled out, Cohn—already invested in Desert Inn Associates—received a piece worth $76,000. Fugazy—hoping for the travel business—also reportedly participated. Dalitz cut *his* friends in—there were perhaps twenty partners, including the Chicago kingpins and the New York heavyweights—and lesser shareholders included rainmakers like Dalitz's accountant, Eli Boyer, a high-power Los Angeles dealmaker who put together a series of loans for Roy from Hong Kong and Panama banks. The Mob depended on Boyer to launder money. The same crowd scraped together backing for Cohn as he was rigging his takeover of the Lionel Corporation, an early raid good for a round of Manhattan headlines. Other participants in the proliferating Vegas boom included Sam Garfield, a Detroit schoolmate of Dalitz and an oil speculator who helped out with the Lansky-Dalitz casinos in Havana. Another Mob carryover was Allard Roen, the son of a thug Dalitz favored during his Cleveland period, who backed Moe up now at the Desert Inn.

It is quite possible that these were not the playmates that Al and Dora Cohn would have picked for Roy, but Cohn was a very astute lawyer, and in those pre-RICO days nothing he was up to was against the law. What started the landslide that very nearly buried Cohn was the involvement of the stately White Russian scam artist and gambler Alexander Guterma. In an effort to make good on an IOU for $500,000 he had given to Clint Murchison and several of the capos around the Genovese crime family (including Jerry Catena, one of Roy's regular drinking buddies), in 1955 Guterma had acquired a shell company, United Dye and Chemical Corp., and combined it with another dog, Handridge Oil. Without bothering to register shares with the SEC, the swindler adroitly drained what assets there were into yet another corporation, then foisted what little was left of the original shell onto the investing public for $5 million. Garfield and Irving Pasternak, also part of the management at the Desert Inn as well as the Stardust, conspired in the effort to pump these shares out at inflated prices by means of a classic high-pressure bucket-shop operation.

By 1958 the SEC was moving in on the United Dye crowd, and by the middle of 1959 a grand jury had been empaneled in the Southern District of New York. To limit his prison time, Guterma spilled his guts. Dalitz and his associates retained Roy Cohn. Cohn apparently told the gamblers that he would require $50,000 to make the necessary arrangements. This he would not collect if any of them were indicted. When the indictment was handed up in August, none of the Las Vegas group was implicated.

By the summer of 1961, the Kennedy Justice Department was combing through the detritus of the United Dye court proceedings in hopes of pinpointing Cohn's involvement. Irving Younger, at that point an assistant United States attorney for the Southern District of New York, would remember being summoned to the incoming U.S. Attorney's office. Robert Kennedy sat watching as he "fidgeted with a pair of heavy horn-rimmed glasses." "The Department," the plainspoken Morgenthau told Younger, between puffs on his cigar, "has a special interest in Roy Cohn." Ransack the files. Go anywhere. "Your job is to find out whether Cohn is guilty of something. The Department wants Cohn."

One lead came out of a securities fraud case involving a Liechtenstein entity called Brandel Trust, the promoter of which was believed to be talking with Cohn. On that flimsy rumor, Younger flew to Zurich and extorted Brandel's records from the Swiss banker in the case, Paul Hagenbach, whom Younger was able to lure back to New York. At Morgenthau's insistence, a squad of FBI technicians bugged Hagenbach's room at the Plaza. Nothing.

In June 1962 Younger resigned; soon afterward he ran into Bill Hundley, about to be reinstated as the head of the Justice Department's Organized Crime Section. "We've heard that you were forced out for being too tough on Cohn," Hundley greeted him.

Younger denied it.

"Well, if you say so, okay. But the Department thinks maybe Cohn got to Morgenthau."

"The Department" meant Bobby. Once it became clear that the Brandel investigation wasn't going anywhere, Morgenthau attempted to restore his true-believer status by poring over the United Dye evidence, hoping to substantiate his suspicion that Cohn might have endeavored to bribe Morton Robson, the assistant U.S. attorney in charge of prosecuting the Las Vegas gamblers. Once a grand jury was in place, Cohn underwent thirty hours of interrogation, 4,852 questions, in a titanic effort to catch him out in a misstatement, a tactic worthy of Joe McCarthy at his worst.

Before long not only the employees but also the clients and the friends of clients at Saxe, Bacon were getting dragged before grand juries. Teams of FBI agents were around the office so much that bystanders assumed they worked there. "When Internal Revenue came," Cohn protested to one radio interviewer, "they were in such a hurry to see who was going to come out with my head first that they actually served a subpoena on Mr. Morgenthau's office to try to get back some of the records which he had taken for their own use."

Cohn was already worried enough to send a wire to Walter Winchell for his *Daily Mirror* column: "Do not and never have represented any Las Vegas interest nor have I been asked to. As to Bobby Kennedy, there is no grudge or feud whatsoever. He is against Crime and Communism and so am I, and he has my complete support."

One acquaintance of Roy's attempted to persuade Morgenthau that Cohn probably was not dense enough to bribe a U.S. attorney, especially *after* the judgment had come down. Morgenthau got upset.

"What do you want to protect this fairy for?"

"Morgy," the intermediary protested, "he's still a human being and you can't go on the word of a liar like Garfield." By then, according to testimony from one of Cohn's partners, Garfield had admitted to Cohn at breakfast that "a lot of people are under an awful lot of pressure. They have sentences hanging over their heads and the only way out is to tell a story the Government wants to hear."

On September 4, 1963, Morgenthau got his indictment. A federal grand jury agreed that Roy Cohn and a second lawyer, Murray Gottesman, committed perjury and conspired to obstruct justice, both by blocking the indictment of Cohn's gambler clients in 1959 and later by attempting to intimidate them once they began talking. At a press conference immediately following the arraignment, Cohn laced into Morgenthau for retaining "an international confidence man on the Government payroll trying to pick up something, anything, on me." As for Robert Kennedy's hostility? "I think that history speaks for itself on that subject. I have never been invited to any of his swimming parties."

Robert Kennedy was following all this closely and in April 1966 offered to release Walter Sheridan and another top investigator from the Get-Hoffa squad for long enough to back Morgenthau up. Morgenthau waved Bobby off. The heart of the U.S. Attorney's case was Allard Roen's testimony that, on Roy Cohn's instruction, Sam Garfield had called him from Detroit in 1959 and directed him to lie low at the Desert Inn and hand over $33,333.00 in cash—Roy would keep a third for himself—to "Robson." On August 29, 1959, a man who represented himself as Morton Robson, the assistant U.S. attorney who had already put away Frank Costello and now would be prosecuting the Desert Inn crowd, allegedly met Roen by the bank of elevators in the lobby of the Desert Inn and accepted the money in a plain white Desert Inn envelope.

The case was harder to nail down than Morgenthau expected. Cohn accused the U.S. Attorney of "inspiring managed news leaks designed to hurt me and destroy me." Robert Kennedy had backed Morgenthau by feeding a reporter he had favored since the Rackets Committee days, William Lambert, enough to plump up an expose in *Life*. Another ally in the press, Wallace Turner, launched a five-part series on crime-ridden Las Vegas in the *New York Times*.

But the prosecutors were compelled to shift their ground once it became apparent that the real Morton Robson could demonstrate that he had not been anywhere near Las Vegas on that fateful August evening. Those allegations of threats to the unindicted coconspirators amounted to hearsay. At one point,

Morgenthau's lead attorney, Gerald Walpin, was dispatched to tea at Hickory Hill to keep Bobby abreast, embroidering on developments while the insatiable Brumus lapped milk out of the creamer of the silver service. Ultimately, the verdict depended on one unpersuaded juror, a black girl who worked as the secretary of the Liberal Party. Cohn's lawyers had sweated to get her excused, yet in the end she hung the jury.

Those hours before the verdict came down cost Roy a lot of composure. Early in the trial, Roy's mother Dora did not hesitate to phone the court to explain that her son had overslept, so could the judge reschedule for a later hour? Roy was a celebrity; the level of his hubris was such that, seated next to the ancient Winston Churchill at Lord Beaverbrook's chateau above Monte Carlo, Cohn never even bothered with a by-your-leave before finishing off whatever was left on the old hero's plate. But the yawning prospect of a decade in the penitentiary left Cohn uncharacteristically dry-mouthed until the mistrial was announced.

When the case was retried, the world had changed. Ed Weisl Jr., an intimate of Cohn, was close to LBJ. Cohn won easily. Until the Nixon administration jacked him out of office in 1969, Robert Morgenthau battered away at Cohn as the impatient lawyer acquired and unloaded properties, moving on from Lionel to what the *Wall Street Journal* called a "slashing legal attack" against the Manhattan bus company, Fifth Avenue Coach Lines, which left Roy in control and the previously flourishing bus company on the brink of bankruptcy. Cohn and his pals took over a small loan company and turned it into a holding operation, Tower Universal Corp.

Raking up the Fifth Avenue Coach transactions, in 1968 Morgenthau accused Cohn of, in effect, egging on his partner in the takeover, Larry Weisman, to bribe the New York City appraiser to pump up the settlement money that Cohn and his allies would extort from the City when it was forced to acquire the bus company. Cohn then allegedly blackmailed Weisman into selling Cohn his holdings cheap for fear that Cohn would tip off the authorities that Weisman had tendered the bribe. When Cohn's attorney suffered a heart attack just before the end of the trial, Cohn riffled through the stricken man's notes for a couple of minutes, then delivered a two-hour spellbinder of a summation. That way Cohn sidestepped cross-examination. Bystanders suspected the heart attack had been staged.

But one man's sleaze is another man's axle grease, and each time Roy again squirmed loose of Morgenthau's clutches, J. Edgar Hoover admired his dexterity more. "Roy and Hoover were very close," one of the lawyers at Saxe, Bacon observed. Roy kept the set of his own fingerprints that Hoover had the FBI mount for him on display in the firm's anteroom and remained on the short list to receive his Christmas box of Havana cigars from the Director. "They were old pals and allies," the lawyer noted. "I think he was getting information from Hoover during the government prosecution."

FBI files of the period highlight the Director at his most deft and equivocal. When Byron White insisted that the Bureau bug Hagenbach's room at the Plaza, the headquarters demanded assurance from Morgenthau's office that "there is full security and no entrapment is involved" as it pretended to help prove that Cohn and his associates "participated to a degree on the over-all [sic] scheme as hidden principals." Hoover, reading over the memo, scrawled in "Strange nearly 2 years have elapsed and not yet brought to trial." He smelled a frame. As luck would have it, the tape recorders of the Bureau technicians in the next room of the Plaza malfunctioned, so the exercise was useless. The special agent in charge in New York cabled crisply that "NORMALLY REQUESTS OF THIS TYPE ARE HANDLED BY THE AGENCY INVOLVED, IN THIS CASE SEC." The Bureau would cooperate as little as it could.

By now, Cohn himself had "heard numerous rumors that the FBI was investigating him" for the purported United Dye bribe and leaned on George Sokolsky, who called Deke DeLoach. "Obviously George was doing a little fishing for Roy Cohn," DeLoach reported to John Mohr, his counterpart on the administrative side. Meanwhile, attempts by the FBI to establish Morton Robson's whereabouts that fateful August night in 1959—normally a simple-enough matter for the ubiquitous Bureau—appear to have been beyond the FBI's capacity; when Morgenthau's man Gerald Walpin finally got Robson on the stand, he discovered that there were reliable defense witnesses to the fact that Robson was in New York while his Doppelgänger was getting paid off at the Desert Inn.

It would appear that Cohn was in a lot more jeopardy than he realized. A July 13, 1962, FBI memo notes a conversation between a spokesman for the Mob in Las Vegas and Jack Miller, Kennedy's head of the Criminal Division. "Miller was contacted to determine if he would be willing to trade [the "heavy pressure" on] Las Vegas for Roy Cohn and Miller said 'absolutely no.'" "Send memo to A.G. and Miller," Hoover writes below.

By July 1962, with the United Dye investigation starting to heat up, FBI General Investigative Division Supervisor A. C. Larson was memoing

McGrath inside the Seat of Government about an exchange between Sokolsky and one Special Agent Wick, during which Sokolsky lamented that the pending investigation was becoming "a harassment to Cohn. . . . Mr. Sokolsky said that he talked with Lou Nichols about the advisability of writing in a column, blasting the Department on the impropriety of questions asked in the grand jury." Sokolsky felt "the FBI was being used" and "could well get the reputation of persecuting people. . . ." Hoover lifts his skirts and backs away. "If he contacts us again he should be told it is entirely in hands of A.G.," he scribbles in between paragraphs.

DeLoach, back from a short leave by August, moved in to scotch this sudden threat from Hoover's ally of so many years. One of the Bureau's street agents had evidently told a woman who went to Sokolsky that "Roy Cohn is in great trouble," which Sokolsky felt he "had no right to say. . . ." DeLoach came back hard: "I told George . . . that it seemed to me that each summer when he went to Otis, Massachusetts, to his farm he did nothing but sit on the edge of the lawn with a 60 foot extension to his telephone and pontificate like the Pope. . . .

"George interrupted me at this point and stated one week ago the Attorney General had looked him squarely in the eye and told him he knew nothing about this case." DeLoach pointed out that two weeks earlier Sokolsky had told him that Kennedy had ordered Morgenthau to "arrange an appointment with Roy Cohn." Which was it? Sokolsky "then stated that I should know that he was pulling a bluff . . . he wanted to 'scare the hell' out of L. B. Nichols inasmuch as Nichols had been trying to take away certain prerogatives of his at Schenley Industries."

As long as Robert Kennedy was attorney general, the Director had to walk a fine line. Later on, during the heat of the Fifth Avenue Coach trial in 1969, three New York FBI field agents backed up Robert Morgenthau when Cohn insisted that the U.S. attorney's office had planted a convicted larcenist on Bacon, Saxe. Goaded by the furious Lou Nichols, Hoover transferred all three to the bureaucratic boondocks within a matter of hours. With Nixon in the White House, an excess of restraint wasn't required any longer.

By 1962, Sokolsky was getting old. As if to test Cohn beyond all reason, Robert Kennedy was busy now wooing Sokolsky away. Earlier in the year, after one of those instruction sessions in his cluttered apartment, Sokolsky had walked Kennedy to the elevator and confided, "I'm looking closer at Roy." "[J]ust as Cohn is extraordinarily gentle with his friends," Sokolsky conceded in a column his last spring, "he is often brash, unnecessarily quarrelsome and seems to set up an unpleasant personality. . . ."

Sokolsky died the following December. Both Cohn and Robert Kennedy were honorary pallbearers. Standing on the steps of the Central Synagogue of Manhattan before the service, Cohn spotted the attorney general, extended his hand, and stated, "George would have been glad that you came." DeLoach was there, too, and reported to headquarters that Cohn told him that Bobby had "greeted him very cordially outside the church and had mentioned don't worry about this case involving you. Just keep up the practice of law rather than 'maneuvering' so much."

By 1963, attempting to corner Roy Cohn involved a number of unintended risks for Robert Kennedy. Cohn's Las Vegas contacts tended to overlap Bobby Baker's Las Vegas contacts, and many of them received their marching orders from Meyer Lansky. With Baker's profitable sideline as a procurer for Jack Kennedy, and Lansky's artfully cloaked assistance in getting the president elected, the wrong witness shooting off his mouth before the wrong subcommittee could generate the kind of headlines even Hoover couldn't protect them from.

Ultimately, Robert Kennedy could no more resist the chance to root around in Bobby Baker's collapsing affairs that he could in Roy Cohn's. Like many others, the attorney general saw in Baker a surrogate for the vice president, "Little Lyndon." Spoiling as he was to drive Lyndon Johnson out of his brother's administration, anything that promised an excuse to drop Johnson from the ticket in 1964 was bound to enlist his covert support.

Baker was a country boy from Pickens, South Carolina, a friendly, tireless bootlicker scurrying up and down the corridors all day and half the night, a genius at accommodating his elders who started out at fourteen as a page in the wartime Senate and quickly made himself indispensable to the Democratic Majority. In time he ascended to the respected post of secretary to the Majority. While Jack Kennedy was maneuvering toward the presidency, Bobby Baker had matured into a sleek young functionary with famously indulgent eyes, unapologetically on the make. One of the legions of pages over whom he in turn bestowed would remember him as a "hillbilly version of Sammy Glick, with a Wildroot pompadour and pleated silk ties."

Sometime during the fifties, forever fetching and flattering and locking in plane reservations for the behemoths of the Senate, Baker married a comely young woman, Dorothy, who worked as chief of staff for Mississippi Senator James Eastland's Internal Security Subcommittee, J. Edgar Hoover's favorite Star Chamber. Children came right along, several, Lynda and

Lyndon John, named after his boss, whom Baker always addressed with an affectionate fillip as *Leader*. An indefatigable nose-counter, this self-made child of the Senate had entrenched himself as a confidant of the top players in both Houses.

Doing well for others, Bobby Baker concluded early that it was time to fatten up his own situation. He went to law school and took on an associate in a practice to whom he could easily direct applicants for something out of Congress. In his other role as secretary to the Democratic Campaign Committee, Baker quickly assessed for himself the unenunciated require-ments of the post. "When you been in the business of raising campaign funds," he says now, "the guy who's been the head of your local campaign committee wants you to get him a date. I would say 90% of the people who made campaign contributions want to see if they can't get laid."

There was a market here, and Baker stepped forward. As founder and majordomo of the Quorum Club, he supplied the legislators and their friends from his private stock of "play girls," as FBI memoranda referred to Baker's prizes, headlined by the ravishing Ellen Rometsch. Many would be spotted in the lounge of the forty-one-story beachside motel complex known as "Bobby Baker's Carousel" in Ocean City, Maryland, working its exclusive "gentleman's club" with its cachet "as a hideaway for Washington power brokers."

Most of the financing behind "Bobby Baker's Carousel" had come out of bank loans finagled by Oklahoma Senator Robert Kerr. A gargantuan, rough-spoken ex-wildcatter, Kerr controlled the Finance Committee and was "generally accounted," Arthur Schlesinger Jr. has written, "the most powerful and ruthless man in the Senate." Kerr took a shine to Baker. "I shouldn't tell you this," he confided to his lackey from Pickens, "but I real-ly love you more than my five children. Because you're so able and helpful to me."

It weighed on Kerr especially that Baker was not amassing a fortune. He talked from time to time about going partners with Baker raising Black Angus in Hutchinson, Kansas. When that looked impractical, Kerr put the arm on a lobbyist for whom he had recently done a lot of favors, Fred Black. As the Washington representative of North American Aviation in D.C., Black worked a deal with Kerr which got the Apollo Project awarded to North American so long as the enormous rockets got built near Tulsa, a twenty-thousand-job bonanza for Oklahoma even though it required a $2 billion, eighteen-mile canal to barge these monsters to the Gulf of Mexico.

There were inevitably quid-pro-quos, and one of the quos, as Kerr told

Black, was that "I want you to take care of Bobby." "So that's when Fred Black got into the vending business," Baker says now with a rueful laugh.

Both Robert Kerr and Fred Black were gamblers. For years, Kerr made it a point to sit down to a gin rummy game with Joe McCarthy every payday and clean him out. Black was seriously hooked. He earned a reported $500,000 annually, and everything went right out to the track or got frittered away around the tables in Las Vegas. This big roller was bound to attract a following in the gambling capital. Black fell in easily with the magnetic Johnny Rosselli and quickly found himself spending a lot of time with Ed Levinson, proprietor of the Fremont Casino, and Bennie Siegelbaum out of Miami, two senior Lansky lieutenants.

Kerr put together a $400,000 startup loan for Baker and his law partner, Ernest Tucker. Black, normally strapped for cash, interested Levinson and Siegelbaum in investing heavily in the resulting startup, a vending-machine distributor called the Serve-U Corporation. Within two years, Serve-U was booking $3.5 million annually in the California-based defense industry, much of it with North American. Too shrewd to register as an officer or even a stockholder of Serve-U, Baker in fact owned 28 1/2 percent of the corporation. The vending machines themselves were reportedly manufactured by an Illinois company controlled by Sam Giancana.

Baker's first real premonition of trouble brewing came when one of his Quorum Club buddies, Ralph Hill, who had recently slipped Baker $5,600 to lock up the business around the Capitol for his own vending operation, abruptly found himself under heavy buy-out pressure from the boys at the Serve-U Corporation and instituted a $300,000 civil suit.

Bobby Baker was scrambling by now in every direction. The enormous, shoddily constructed Carousel, battered simultaneously by a compounding array of building loans and unseasonable hurricanes, absorbed every dollar Baker could raise. His new associates lost no time in identifying new projects for him. "Bobby Baker a partner with Meyer Lansky?" he exclaims now. "It was a bigger shock to me than it was to you." Nevertheless, collaborating closely with Cliff Jones, the former lieutenant governor of Nevada who wound up working for Lansky at the Hotel Nacional in Havana, and sharing a suite on occasion with Levinson, Baker bounced in and out of the Caribbean to help wring casino concessions out of the Dominican Republic. Among his scattered business participations, Baker allegedly joined a seven-man syndicate which borrowed $105,000 from Hoffa's Teamsters to promote a shopping center that would never be built. He picked up $6,000 a year in legal fees from the Haitian-American Meat and Provision Company, S.A. for permits to allow the importation of meat from Haiti into Puerto Rico and the United States. Haitian-American was a Murchison holding.

Baker originally met Hoffa through Tommy Webb, the loose-jointed FBI veteran who, along with JFK's procurer Robert Thompson, looked after government business for the Murchisons. Webb had remained on a confidential basis with J. Edgar Hoover while cutting himself into lucrative deals with Levinson and Siegelbaum. None of them stayed out of touch long with the enterprising I. Irving Davidson, who handled public relations for Carlos Marcello.

This mélange of fixers and bagmen were quick to exploit the Quorum Club. Another watering hole was the palatial hospitality suite Fred Black set up at the Sheraton Carlton Hotel, adjacent to the galaxy of rooms the State Department had set aside in the hotel to divert foreign visitors. It provided a retreat to which Black and his friends—"and I was among them" Baker would emphasize—"repaired to conduct business, drink, play cards, and entertain ladies."

One of the ladies who showed up regularly to entertain and be entertained was Ellen Rometsch. Her tolerance and inventiveness comes through in the reminiscences of one of Ellen's colleagues, "Miss B," a festive soul who liked to perform attired solely in harem pants and a tambourine. One humid evening came to mind especially. Three of the regulars stripped down and "finished the party pouring champagne over one another in the bathtub." In time, "Three girls, still rosy from their champagne bath but drowsy too, elected to sleep together; but one woke up and in an unaccountable fit of annoyance bit an exposed portion of another's anatomy."

Ellen Rometsch was the bitee; fortunately, she was a wonderful sport. Talent aside, her resilience was enough to endear her to Baker, who counseled with Ellen in the three-level lavender-carpeted town house he maintained for his sultry girlfriend Carole Tyler and her roommate, Mary Jo Kopechne, a secretary in Senator George Smathers's office.

Bobby Baker was not alone in appreciating the professionalism at work in Fred Black's suite. Around the end of 1962, under pressure from Bob Kennedy to expand the Bureau's Top Hoodlums program and crack down seriously on the Overlords of the Mob, Hoover was giving his attorney general plenty of rope by authorizing extensive surveillance programs in Las Vegas. Ignoring Nevada law, the FBI's Las Vegas wireman had slipped in and bugged Cliff Jones as well as the executive offices at the Desert Inn (Moe Dalitz) and the Fremont Casino (Ed Levinson). The take was rewarding, and Hoover and his brain trust were only concerned that certain of their discoveries seemed to be playing back through the Justice Department, where they suspected Levinson had positioned a mole. The reinstated chief of the Organized Crime Section, Bill Hundley, was suspiciously close to Edward Bennett Williams, the power-hitting criminal attorney whose client list at that stage had come to include Levinson, Jimmy Hoffa, Fred Black, Sam Giancana, and ultimately Bobby Baker.

The entente between Fred Black and Levinson promptly came to light. By December 28, 1962, the FBI Field Office was circulating paper to "determine the feasibility of installing a misur" in Black's D.C. office in the Riddell Building and "Suite 438-40" in the Sheraton Carlton Hotel, which Black maintained "for entertainment purposes." The request alludes to the sweetheart arrangement between Black and Bobby Baker and their "joint interest in the Serv-U-Corporation," as well as the "close association between highly placed Government officials and Las Vegas casino owners." The memo to authorize these bugs proceeded from Courtney Evans, Attorney General Kennedy's liaison with the Bureau and, at this point, unmistakably his friend, to Al Belmont, an assistant director. In view of Baker's longstanding identification with Lyndon Johnson, and Robert Kennedy's undisguised distaste for Johnson, this wasn't at all promising for the vice president.

Insinuating his supersensitive spike microphones into Black's infamous hideaway produced an overnight triumph for Hoover. "The FBI had on their tapes," Bobby Baker will confide now, setting aside for a moment his persona as the star-struck innocent prancing alongside the Dark Gods of History, "that they had siphoned off about sixteen million dollars in cash. Siegelbaum lived in Miami, and he would take the money to Nassau, to Credit Suisse." Recording Black, the FBI had stumbled onto the primary evacuation route of the Las Vegas skim. "So after all," Baker concludes, "the reason they all went crazy over me was that Meyer Lansky was in on it."

By now, that looming journalistic gumshoe Clark Mollenhoff was after Ellen Rometsch. Supplying him with leads initially was not only Hoover but also, according to Bobby Baker, the attorney general, presumably still unaware that his brother headed Rometsch's client list. Bobby glimpsed an opportunity to undermine LBJ. Robert Kennedy backed up Mollenhoff's exposés by shoveling through information to the task force *Life* magazine put together under his durable ally William Lambert to dig out the specifics.

All this publicity predictably attracted Delaware Senator John J. Williams, casting about to recover his renown as "The Watchdog of the Senate" by conducting a preliminary investigation. One fish he netted early was Don Reynolds, a Silver Spring, Maryland, insurance broker with whom

Baker had a kickback arrangement and whom he sent to Johnson when the vice president was hard-pressed to find term insurance after his 1955 heart attack. Reynolds was still upset because Johnson had extorted $1,208 in the form of useless advertising from Reynolds along with a television set and a stereo before he would write the policy.

The aggrieved Reynolds was also willing to go before the Senate Rules Committee in November 1963 and testify that he had seen a suitcase full of money which Baker himself told him contained a "$100,000 payoff for Johnson for his role in securing the Fort Worth TFX contract," a $7 billion award to General Dynamics for the controversial fighter. The Secretary of the Navy, Fred Korth, had been forced out in October over the TFX contract.

Afterward, in oral histories and comments for the record, Bob Kennedy consistently denied that he had plotted to bounce Johnson off the ticket in 1964. Not that he ever totally warmed to Lyndon. "He's mean, bitter, vicious," Kennedy remarked to one interviewer. "An animal in many ways." There was no pleasing him "unless you want to kiss his behind all the time." Among the Hickory Hill elect, the laughter erupted easily once stories started around about "Uncle Cornpone." While JFK was president, Bobby never hesitated to dart into the Oval Office and break up a conversation between Jack and Lyndon or stride ostentatiously out of a meeting just as Johnson was hauling himself to his feet to speak. "That little shitass" was the term the vice president normally applied to the attorney general.

For all the denials, the evidence is compelling that Robert Kennedy *was* scheming to dump Lyndon. Responding to an interviewer's question about "Robert Kennedy's role in the Bobby Baker case," Kennedy's press aide during his last years, Frank Mankiewicz, admitted that "I have a feeling that that was one of the things he didn't want me to know about. Every once in a while he'd say, 'Well, I'll tell you about that some other time.' By which I understood, and I'm sure he meant, that he didn't want my mind cluttered up with a lot of facts that I might have to reveal."

Phil Brennan, a staffer on the House Republican Policy Committee and a clandestine columnist for the *National Review,* picked up on Ralph Hill's scrap with Baker and brought Hill to Whispering John Williams. "A few days later," Brennan recalls, "the attorney general, Bobby Kennedy, called five of Washington's top reporters into his office and told them it was now open season on Lyndon Johnson."

Kennedy had been preparing his case. Well-substantiated rumors flew around the capital for years linking Johnson to Billie Sol Estes. Estes was in prison by 1963 for cashing in on huge government contracts for the storage of nonexistent grain; some of the payout was reportedly recirculated to Johnson. Walt Perry, an IRS investigator, maintains that Estes told him that he passed $10 million in bribes to LBJ. Estes also claimed to have turned down Bob Kennedy's offer to let him out of prison if he would testify against Johnson. Meanwhile, FBI documents indicate that Kennedy was after a list of Texas politicians on the take compiled by Carlos Marcello's bagman, Jack Halfen.

Baker rolls his eyes at talk like that. In his experience, Johnson was always "a coward when it came to money." By September 1963 any attempt to get at Lyndon by way of Baker looked dicey, partly because the attorney general had to confront the president's own entanglement with Rometsch and partly because there were so many politicians of both parties at risk for their careers—and marriages—if Baker ever talked. Earlier, when Justice Department prosecutor William Bittman approached Hoover for help in entrapping Baker by attaching a body recorder to Cliff Jones's boy in Washington, Wayne Bromley, Hoover blew up and tossed Bittman out of his office. Bittman found a technician in the Narcotics Bureau.

Characteristically, although stonewalling the Department, Hoover managed to compromise the family friend who kept the books for Baker enterprises, Georgia Liakakis, reducing her to a Bureau informant and forcing her to sell Bobby out through methods even the faithful Clyde Tolson found unstomachable. Whichever way this promising scandal broke, the Director intended to keep the Bureau ahead of the headlines. The opportunity to save the Kennedys by misrepresenting what he very well knew and quashing the Rometsch rumors with Senators Mansfield and Dirksen had reinstated J. Edgar into control.

By autumn of 1963 the whole mess required a scapegoat. Once indictments started to come down, the attorney general telephoned Baker to assure him that "my brother is fond of you and remembers your many kindnesses. I want you to know that we have nothing of any consequence about you in our files. . . ." The president himself recommended James McInerney, the Kennedy family troubleshooter, as the best criminal tax lawyer around. Then McInerney got killed.

After November of 1963, reportedly threatening Hoover directly with "revelations of the assassination conspirators," Fred Black hired Edward Bennett Williams and was able to get his tax-evasion conviction reversed by the Supreme Court on grounds that the FBI technicians had illegally compromised his lawyer-client confidentiality at the Sheraton Carlton. Solicitor General Thurgood Marshall supported Black's brief. Hoover appeared before the Court himself to admit error but insisted that all this bugging occurred at the insistence of Robert Kennedy. This issue rolled back and forth over Kennedy for the last two years of his life.

Bobby Baker had long regarded himself as a secure personage among Washington's "untorturable classes," in Graham Greene's phrase, but before long he, too, was forced to reconsider. Baker was much too famous—and disposable—by then, and in 1967 he went along to Lewisburg penitentiary on seven counts of theft, fraud, and income-tax evasion. Political insiders were especially aghast at evidence that he had pocketed payoff money turned over in good faith to "influence" various senators. Not long before he died, ex-President Johnson confided to Bobby Baker that he had often touted Baker as "Like a son to me, because I don't have a son of my own." As to why exactly he had let Baker swing, he would confess: "You know, J. Edgar Hoover came to me shortly after I became president and said he had electronic evidence that you were mixed up with a bunch of Las Vegas gamblers. He warned me against lifting a finger to help you."

Hoover remained a court from which there was no appeal.

The Patsy

Throughout the midday break on November 22, 1963, while John Kennedy was having his head blown off in Dallas, his brother the attorney general and the U.S. Attorney for the Southern District of New York, Robert Morgenthau, along with his tough-minded chief of the criminal division, Silvio Mollo, were sitting over chowder beside the pool at Hickory Hill, strategizing ways to bring down Roy Cohn. An extension telephone rang, and Ethel carried it around to Bob. Hoover was on the line. He said the president had been shot. A few minutes later, Hoover called back to report that JFK's wounds were critical. "You may be interested to know," the attorney general replied, "that my brother is dead." Hoover did not seem particularly excited, Robert Kennedy would remember, or in any way upset, "not quite as excited as if he were reporting the fact that he had found a Communist on the faculty of Howard University."

Over on Capitol Hill, all through these same midday hours, a closed session of the Senate Rules Committee presided over by B. Everett Jordan of North Carolina but sparked by the unappeasable Whispering John Williams of Delaware was evoking well-documented testimony from the acutely panicked Don Reynolds. It implicated the vice president. Billie Sol Estes was leaking the news from prison that he had paid off Johnson in a very substantial way, and references to all this were starting to break out in the newspapers. Porous as Washington was, some of the evidence against Johnson that

John Williams was extracting was likely to wind up in the next news cycle, perhaps the following morning, and give the Kennedys what they needed to bump Lyndon.

As things worked out, the Jordan-Williams hearings were aborted. Word swept the capital that Jack Kennedy had been murdered; nobody could be sure that a vast plot against the entire government was not about to engulf everybody; business for the day was over. Reynolds never formally presented his testimony; and, needless to say, once Lyndon B. Johnson was sworn in as president that afternoon, nobody stepped forward to bring up these extremely awkward charges of corruption. The Lyndon Johnson presidency was about to begin, with its amazing array of legislative accomplishments and the endless slough into Vietnam.

Across the historiography of twentieth-century America the assassination of John Kennedy provides the Dismal Swamp. Insight comes in flashes, riddled with conspiracy theories and pain and lingering foul suspicions. Virtually hour by hour, this acute if complaisant young president was catching on to the authentic requirements of our troubled postwar society. Then came the gunshots that knocked us onto a tangent and dumped Kennedy's brains into his terrified wife's lap.

It would be easier to endure if we knew what happened. Part of our malaise arises from the public's awareness that it quickly became the victim of a sloppily executed magic trick, a government-sponsored attempt to stuff a giant wardrobe of incongruous information into a pitifully small valise. Facts kept hanging out, bald inconsistencies and ugly, suppressed relationships. The vehicle for this farce was the Report of the Warren Commission, a treatment of Kennedy's murder issued a matter of months after the horrible event and dependent for its facts and conclusions largely on a rushed, scrambled investigation by the FBI.

The Commission's preordained conclusion was simple in the extreme: The assassination of John Kennedy began and ended with the performance of Lee Harvey Oswald. A quixotic misfit with grandiose pretensions, Oswald had acted alone while shooting the president from the sixth floor of the Texas School Book Depository overlooking Dealey Plaza in Dallas. Still keyed up, Oswald killed Officer J. D. Tippit later that afternoon and was arrested by the local police in a neighborhood movie theater shortly after that. Within the hour, Hoover had reached Robert Kennedy at Hickory Hill to inform him that "I thought we had the man who killed the president . . .

a mean-minded individual . . . in the category of a nut who was an ex-marine who had defected to the Soviet Union."

A few days later, after extensive—and unrecorded—efforts by local authorities to interview Oswald, the roustabout owner of a local strip club, Jack Ruby, stepped forward while Oswald was being transferred to a lockup and stolidly executed him. Ruby would maintain that he had shot Oswald primarily to spare Jacqueline Kennedy the discomfort of returning to Dallas to testify in Oswald's pending trial.

There is a fundamental absurdity to virtually every element of this scenario, a hard Nabokovian drag against the credible. Once investigators moved in and started to sort out the details of the shooting, two lines of inquiry recommended themselves. There were the niceties of the murder— had Oswald acted alone, who put him up to it, were there other shooters? Was law enforcement involved, local or federal, either to help set up the president or to ignore the traditional precautions?

Was there a cover-up? Somehow during the last-minute butchershop surgery at Parkland Hospital and the squabbling between Dallas officials and the feds over custody of John Kennedy's corpse, priceless material began disappearing. From then on, at every key juncture in the evidentiary chain, important physical remains went missing, key documents were embargoed.

One argument that defenders of the Warren Commission Report continue to promulgate is the proposition that if there had been any kind of wide-ranging conspiracy, participants at various levels would have talked by now, won over by book deals or to relieve their consciences or compelled by the glamour of retroactive status. The fact is, individuals *have* come forward, people as close to the plot as Santo Trafficante's lawyer or Johnny Rosselli trying to ingratiate himself with the Church Committee or the belatedly repentant ex-Warren Commission member Gerald Ford, and spelled out with some precision who killed Kennedy, and how.

Lost in a welter of far-fetched and often poorly grounded assassination theorists, many of these genuine directionals have been willfully overlooked. Only with the publication of the Report of the Select Committee on Assassinations in the U.S. House of Representatives on March 29, 1979, did the official door come open a crack: "The committee believes, on the basis of the evidence available to it, that President John F. Kennedy was probably assassinated as a result of a conspiracy," and "that the national syndicate of organized crime, as a group, was not involved in the assassination of President Kennedy, but that the available evidence does not preclude the possibility that individual members may have been involved."

Massive contradictions continued to heave into view. Even during its deliberations in 1964, three of the seven members of the Warren Commission had balked at signing any report maintaining that both victims had been taken down with the same bullet. That archetypal establishmentarian John McCloy conceded that "there is a potential culpability here on the part of the Secret Service and even the FBI. . . ." And as the controversy continued to resurface, even Lyndon Johnson himself acknowledged that "I never believed that Oswald acted alone."

However bloodless Hoover may have sounded to Robert Kennedy, the news of John Kennedy's assassination left the Director an earthquake inside. Elements of the government had failed, catastrophically. If this broke wrong, Hoover could find himself dismissed after forty years of ruthlessly hoarded power. An old man with a pension, as marginalized and quickly forgotten as other eccentric has-beens—like his father, Old Dickerson, all over again.

Within days he flooded the Dallas area with street agents, between sixty and a hundred as the crisis sharpened. Even the mild rebuke implicit in the Warren Commission findings all but unhinged the deeply upset old man. His people would pay: "I do not intend to palliate actions which have resulted in forever destroying the Bureau as the top level investigative organization." Seventeen agents were censured, transferred, or suspended without pay in the immediate aftermath, more than thirty before it was over.

Heavy overlays of headquarters paperwork right after the assassination make clear how desperate the Director was to take complete control immediately and contain this potential bureaucratic train wreck. There is a lot of back-and-forth between Hoover and his senior men as to who *else* will presume to investigate the murders. When, within a day, the *Washington Post* planned to recommend that a presidential commission be formed to examine the details, Hoover called the *Post*'s managing editor himself and killed the idea, at least for one cycle.

It would be better to have Lyndon Johnson release the Bureau's preliminary findings, since, as Hoover quoted the *Post*'s managing editor, "there is so much feeling against the Attorney General it might not be accepted as the complete and true picture notwithstanding the fact that the investigation was made by the FBI." When the editor felt pressured to reopen the possibility of a commission in any case, Hoover accused him of "now going through the action of an adult holding candy before a child and wanting him to beg for it."

Hoover was already well into laying the groundwork for identifying Oswald as a "nut" and Ruby as essentially a "police character," who "brought down sandwiches the second day . . . and was friendly with the police and probably they just let him into the building. . . ." Hoover continues in the tone he reserves for higher authority, more in condescension toward the incompetent locals than in anger: "unfortunately, they had given him a timetable down there on when it was going to take place to the minute."

Inside the embattled Bureau, Hoover is a lot less understanding. On perusing a December 10, 1963 report justifying a reluctance by his Dallas field agents to interview Marina Oswald "because they had developed information that Oswald drinking [sic] to excess and beat up wife on several occasions," Hoover scrawls "certainly an asinine excuse" in the margin, and, a little later, "I just don't understand such solicitude." As to recommendations that "disciplinary actions" be foregone, Hoover leaves no doubt about *his* expectations: "I do not concur," runs one penned-in entry; "such gross incompetency can't be overlooked." Punishment will be meted out, if well below the headquarters level.

The truth was, Hoover and his lieutenants had kept their eyes on Lee Harvey Oswald since 1959, when he defected originally. Most of the extensive FBI file on Oswald was culled ruthlessly at the time of the assassination and would remain unavailable indefinitely. Nevertheless, enough indicators have survived to make it clear that he was much more than just another rootless malcontent so far as the Bureau was concerned. Behind tightly closed doors, Texas officials were initially unwise enough to leak indications to the Warren Commission staff that Oswald had been under FBI control for some time to perform "various tasks pursuant to FBI directives." Unlike Jack Ruby's, Oswald's tax records would never become accessible to any investigative body.

Upon returning from Russia, Oswald had been interviewed as a matter of course by FBI agents on June 26, 1962, in the Fort Worth office. Purportedly alerted by Oswald's subscriptions to Soviet and Trotskyite periodicals from *The Worker* to *Krokodil,* a couple of agents from the FBI stopped by Oswald's apartment in August and found him as evasive and contentious as advertised. When the Oswalds relocated to Dallas in March of 1963, Special Agent James Hosty decided to reopen the case but managed to mislay Oswald, who had moved on temporarily to New Orleans, where he had grown up. While ostensibly hunting for a job, Oswald bedded down with his uncle Charles F. "Dutz" Murret and his Aunt Lillian. Oswald had been close to the Murrets since childhood. Uncle Dutz was an established bookmaker and a seasoned operator of illegal gambling clubs around New Orleans, closely affiliated with Sam Saia, a luminary in Carlos Marcello's empire.

Oswald got a job greasing machinery at the Reily Coffee Company and injected himself immediately into the tumult of local émigré politics. He founded a one-man chapter of the Fair Play for Cuba Committee while endeavoring to ingratiate himself with Carlos Bringuier, a virulently anti-Castro clothier involved with the shadowland émigré effort to mount freelance attacks on the island. Oswald's ostentatious attempt to play both sides against the middle collapsed four days later, on August 9, when he contrived to pass out his Fair Play for Cuba leaflets near Bringuier's store, and Carlos and a pair of equally angry Cuban exiles came after him. All four wound up in jail; the next morning, Oswald told the police lieutenant in charge that he was "desirous of seeing an Agent" of the FBI, and the Bureau's John Quigley stopped by to interrogate this high-strung Marxist drifter. Oswald fed Quigley his usual mélange of half-truths and outright lies. By August 21, Hoover himself was developing an interest and sent New Orleans and Dallas a directive specifying that the man in custody had an FBI identification record number— 327-925-D, according to his fingerprints. What was he up to?

For a recent arrival to town, Oswald found the live ones fast around the Big Easy. Both the address on his leaflets and his post office box indicated that his business address was 544 Camp Street, the moldering Newman building he shared with two of the flashiest walk-ons in the entire assassination road company: W. Guy Banister and David Ferrie. Banister was a back-woods Louisiana naval intelligence veteran who rose in the course of a long grinding career in the FBI to SAC in Chicago: There he was remembered affectionately by Giancana and his friends for his interest in trading, for valuable tips on car thieves and help muscling Commies, a predisposition to look away when the Outfit had something big-league shaking. In 1955 Banister had relocated to New Orleans. The Outfit sent Banister off with a personal introduction to Carlos Marcello, and he quickly snagged a berth as an assistant superintendent in the police department, a job he lost in 1957 for threatening a waiter with a pistol in the Old Absinthe House. With that he regrouped on the second floor of 544 Camp Street as the hulking principal of Guy Banister Associates, a detective agency.

William Turner, a contemporary in the Bureau, remembers Banister as "a shrill racist affiliated with the paramilitary right-wing Minutemen" whose working suite "was an office for the anti-Castro militants and a CIA nerve center for the Bay of Pigs invasion." Banister remained in close touch with the Seat of Government, a dependable resource in a community seething with émigré fanaticism and hard-right activists. Banister's personal secretary, Delphine Roberts, would remember the excitement around the office in 1963 the day the Mob's designated "strategizer," Johnny Rosselli, dropped through to coordinate with Guy. David Ferrie filled in sporadically as a part-time investigator for Banister.

With his kinky red wig and paste-on eyebrows, Ferrie was easy enough to spot as a kind of exotic conjuror among the stumpy bayou gangsters in the entourage of Carlos Marcello. A retired Eastern Airlines pilot known to dabble expertly in a variety of disciplines from research chemistry to hypnosis, Ferrie was a bishop of the apostate Orthodox Old Catholic Church of North America and a voracious, unabashed homosexual. Along with a heavy schedule of drug flights across the Gulf, Marcello trusted him with errands, from mopping up in Guatemala City to helping research and plead cases as a consultant to Marcello's attorney, G. Wray Gill.

Oswald's acquaintanceship with Ferrie is presumed to have originated in the middle fifties, when, according to a number of House Assassination Committee witnesses, Oswald was a cadet in the Louisiana Civil Air Patrol squadron commanded by Captain David Ferrie. Six other witnesses testified to having seen Oswald and Ferrie together in Clinton, Louisiana, in September 1963. Years later, in the course of the elaborate BRILAB sting that the post-Hoover FBI designed to take down Marcello, the normally prudent mobster admitted freely to undercover agent Joseph Hauser that he was well acquainted with Dutz Murret and that the hapless, floundering Oswald had filled in that summer of 1963 as a runner for his uncle's bookmaking enterprises.

Not even a hint of Lee Harvey Oswald's ties to midlevel organized crime around New Orleans shadowed the biographical paragraphs of the Warren Commission Report. Rustled together in three weeks by William Sullivan's Domestic Intelligence Division, the four-volume FBI summary on which the Commission depended never deviated from its lone-assassin thesis. In line with Hoover's phobias, the Commission Report flogged Oswald's Marxism—proof of a diseased mind—and his August radio debate with Carlos Bringuier, a sort of verbal followup to their streetside scuffle.

With regular updates from Guy Banister on the anti-Castro ferment in New Orleans feeding through FBI headquarters supplemented by Oswald's own debriefings, Hoover's insiders that summer and fall of 1963 were more than conscious of their informant's erratic meanderings. Once he had lost his job with Reily Coffee, Oswald started to turn up in counterrevolutionary circles accompanied by a pair of heavyset boys, apparently Cuban, possibly Mexican. Stories surfaced that Oswald and David Ferrie were personally involved; an FBI report later stipulated that Carlos Marcello's attorney G. Wray Gill "had gotten word that Lee Oswald, when he was picked up, was carrying a library card with David Ferrie's name on it."

Rumor mills around the Gulf Coast were starting to grind out increasingly familiar themes. Jose Aleman Jr., a wealthy Cuban in touch with Santo Trafficante, tipped off FBI agents George Davis and Paul Scranton that Trafficante had divulged to him that the president was "going to get it." Meanwhile, Marcello himself confided to the gambling publicist Edward Becker that he was mulling over taking out the president with a "nut," not anybody from his own organization.

Restless, Oswald moved back to Dallas. If the summer was fevered, the autumn was hallucinated. How much displacement occurred might be suggested by the 1964 Warren Commission's treatment of Oswald's purported trip to Mexico City in late September, where he "went almost directly to the Cuban Embassy and applied for a visa to Cuba in transit to Russia." Rebuffed, he "later unsuccessfully attempted to obtain a Soviet visa at the Soviet Embassy. . . ." Arguing with the Cuban consul, "He engaged in an angry argument with the consul," who ultimately charged that "a person like him [Oswald] in place of aiding the Cuban revolution was doing it harm."

Such details were available, the Warren Commission members were given to believe, because of the rich infestation of FBI and CIA microphones and wire taps and informants and surveillance teams concentrated on the Cuban and Soviet embassies in Mexico City. By 1978, after fifteen years throughout which wave after wave of conspiracy investigators chewed over the FBI's original presentation like fire ants feasting on a tethered goat, even the bones had collapsed. Documents were demonstrably bogus, the grainy snapshots recovered from the security cameras were of an unrecognizable, other "Oswald," there had been sightings of the subject in New Orleans when he was supposedly in Mexico City.

Evidence would continue to materialize that ersatz Oswalds were popping up by prearrangement wherever it was useful to establish Lee's presence—practicing on a rifle range, in a gun shop getting his weapon resighted. . . . Several of these Doppelgängers used his name, although he himself was provably elsewhere. Certainly the most elaborately staged of these Oswald manifestations appeared in September 1963 in the Dallas apartment of Silvia Odio, the daughter of an imprisoned Cuban industrialist active in the respectable JURE faction of Cuban émigrés led by Manolo Ray. A gringo look-alike purporting to be Oswald appeared with two Cuban males in a clear effort to link Oswald with legitimate Cuban dissenters.

The seeds of confusion were very expertly sown. By 1978, when the House Assassinations Committee sent its own investigator, Edwin Lopez, to Mexico City, he "returned to Washington convinced beyond all doubt," as John H. Davis relates over the course of his trenchant analysis, "that the real Oswald did not visit either the Russian Embassy or the Cuban Embassy in Mexico City and might not ever have been in Mexico City when he was alleged to have been there by the FBI and the Warren Commission." Overseen by the FBI, the nation had bought a hoax.

Even more astonishing was the collective aphasia the crotchety FBI Director was able to induce among the members of the Commission when it came to Jack Ruby's involvement. While "Ruby was unquestionably familiar, if not friendly, with some Chicago criminals," the Report concludes, "there is no evidence that he ever participated in organized criminal activity." This in the face of testimony by one former staff lawyer for the Kefauver Committee that Ruby was "a syndicate lieutenant who had been sent to Dallas to serve as a liaison for Chicago mobsters" and statements by other witnesses that Ruby was recognized around town as "the payoff man for the Dallas Police Department." In Chicago, Ruby had worked as muscle with the murderous Paul "Red" Dorfman, who came up alongside Sam Giancana in the Capone organization, to wring out Local 20467 of the Scrap Iron and Junk Handler's Union, pronounced "a front for organized crime" by the state of Illinois and "largely a shakedown operation" by the AFL-CIO. Between short-lived sales ventures with novelty items like punchboards, Ruby managed a floating crap game and experimented with strip clubs.

Ruby arrived in Dallas in 1947; even there, the Warren Report maintains, "the evidence does not establish a significant link between Ruby and organized crime." A statement like this would have been preposterous if Ruby had first caught the Bureau's eye *after* he dispatched Oswald, but there is compelling evidence that "Sparky from Chicago," as he was known around the underworld, was functioning as a PCI (Potential Criminal Informant) to the Bureau before he left Illinois. In March 1959, Special Agent Charles W. Flynn started to meet secretly with Ruby to discuss subjects of common interest like "interstate transportation of gambling devices, lottery tickets and obscene matter." Ruby rented a safe deposit box to protect his compensation money.

It was during 1959 that Fidel Castro confirmed his hold on Cuba. Ruby would function as a plenipotentiary for the Mob at every phase of this difficult year for organized crime. At first, like Jimmy Hoffa and others, he attempted to reinsure the Mob's huge vulnerable position on the island by helping run guns in company with Lansky manager Norman "Roughhouse" Rothman to the bearded insurgent. In September, Ruby was evidently tapped by the senior Mafia leadership to look in on and, if possible, ransom out Santo Trafficante himself, under arrest in Cuba inside the minimum-security detention farm at Trescornia. Apparently Ruby's expenses were paid by Meyer Lansky and his brother, and Ruby and Lewis McWillie flew out to Cuba together to pay a visit to the implacable Trafficante.

McWillie was a dapper, seasoned pit boss, close to Joseph Civello and the Campisi brothers, Carlos Marcello's representatives in Dallas. In the hierarchy of crime, McWillie was a good many pay grades up from a grubby, violence-prone strip-club manager like Ruby, and Jack was floored by the honor. Of recent years Ruby had helped McWillie out by shipping him four Cobra handguns after a quick visit to Havana in 1959—Ruby was muling cash out of the Cuban casinos for the Mob—and in May 1963 sent McWillie a .38 in Las Vegas. But the relationship was unmistakably arm's-length. "He sent me tickets to Cuba—think of it, a man like that sending me tickets," Ruby marveled once he was back in Dallas. McWillie had been working the casinos at the Tropicana and the Capri in Havana for the Lanskys and Trafficante until Castro closed them down. In 1961 he took over the gambling floor at the Cal-Neva.

Gamecock that he was, Ruby was so infatuated at the prospect of finding himself in line to perform a service for these legendary syndicate bigshots that the thought of turning them down doesn't seem to have entered his head. In November 1963, they would come up with another chore.

If there was any doubt, Ruby's pattern of associations and telephone records over the weeks immediately preceding the president's assassination suggest strongly that something was brewing. In early October, Ruby and Johnny Rosselli, as always the interface between organized crime and the power elite, are reported to have gotten together twice in small motels in Miami. By then Rosselli was going about his mysterious business under a very heavy FBI surveillance watch. On October 26, Ruby talked on the telephone for twelve minutes with Irwin Weiner, Jimmy Hoffa's investment adviser, who was ultimately tagged by the FBI as "handling all the skimmed money from Las Vegas for Chicago's organized crime community." On October 30, Ruby spoke briefly with Nofio Pecora, Carlos Marcello's third-ranking staff hoodlum and a regular telephone buddy of Ruby's. There was a series of extended calls into November between Ruby and Barney Baker, Jimmy Hoffa's 370-pound senior enforcer.

Throughout November the lines crackled between Ruby and a broad representation at the executive level of organized crime in America. On November 17, Ruby made a quick trip to Las Vegas. Hours before JFK flew into Texas, Ruby was cheered up considerably by a long meeting with syndicate paymaster Paul Rowland Jones, who evidently provided the wherewithal to solve Ruby's gargantuan tax problems. The night before he blew Oswald away, Ruby enjoyed a leisurely dinner in the Egyptian Lounge, a Dallas underworld hangout owned by Ruby's dinner partner, Joseph Campisi. Campisi was a Marcello intimate slated to take over the East Texas territory for Marcello once Joe Civello stepped down.

Well aware of at least the rudiments of the above, the Warren Commissioners nevertheless discovered no "significant link between Ruby and organized crime."

Wriggling inside Hoover's hammerlock, the Warren Commission coughed up the monolithic single-shooter version of events that the Director demanded. Anything less could mean the FBI was guilty of dereliction of duty. Privately, Hoover knew better.

As unstable as J. Edgar Hoover had started to look at times to his counterparts around the government, his memory for detail continued to be phenomenal. "A file concerning Oswald was opened at the time newspapers reported his defection to Russia in 1959," the Director wrote the Warren Commission in 1964, "inasmuch as he was considered a possible security risk in the event he returned to this country." Several CIA divisions were tracking him closely after he got back and alerting the FBI, where field offices in Washington, Miami, Dallas, and New Orleans had been instructed to keep headquarters informed of the activities of this impulsive drifter.

The more sensitive question is whether Oswald was a paid FBI informant. Apart from the claim by former FBI security clerk William Walter that he processed documents to that effect, there was the revelation in chambers by Texas Attorney General Waggoner Carr and Henry Wade, the Dallas district attorney, to Earl Warren and the Commission's senior lawyer J. Lee Rankin that Oswald had been on the FBI payroll for $200 a month since September of 1962 with the informant number S-172. An attempt was immediately made to discredit this shocker by identifying as its source Alonzo Hudkins, a mere newspaper reporter from Houston. But *Hudkins's* source was Allen Sweatt, the chief of the criminal division of the Dallas sheriff's office. Defenders of the Warren Commission results would explain the story away as a stunt by a reporter who "never did like the federals," but the more important point remains that the Warren Commission staff was prevented from even contacting Sweatt or requesting a look at Oswald's FBI file to determine whether he was in fact on retainer all through the year before JFK was murdered. Bureau counterintelligence veterans have since confirmed Oswald's FBI employment.

The way Oswald jumped to demand help from the FBI when he got picked up for disturbing the peace in New Orleans suggested very strongly his presumption that the Bureau was there to look after him. He had a claim. The indefatigable Anthony Summers followed all this up by tracking down another FBI informant in New Orleans that summer of 1963, bar-owner Orest Pena, who maintained—once the heat was off—that Oswald had appeared in his saloon repeatedly with FBI field agent Warren deBrues, who specialized in political groups. Another of Summers's finds, local garage manager Adrian Alba, watched a green FBI Studebaker he serviced slow down outside the Reily Coffee Company and wait until Oswald came out and received a "good-sized . . . white envelope."

Against Oswald's screen, the Director was looking at a pattern of threats to the life of the president that seemed to be getting more ominous and more specific every week. In September 1962 Jose Aleman, the scion of a family of Cuban grandees whose grandfather was Lucky Luciano's lawyer and whose father was in the cabinet in Havana, arranged another audience with Santo Trafficante. Jose was under the thumb of the local FBI, which had him dead to rights for gunrunning. Aleman hoped to persuade Trafficante to intervene and help him secure a $1 million loan from the Teamsters Union. After discussing the brutal treatment Jimmy Hoffa was getting from the Justice Department, Trafficante remarked in his soft, absolute way, "mark my word, this man Kennedy is in trouble and he will get what is coming to him."

Aleman said that Kennedy was going to get reelected.

"You don't understand me," the patient Santo Trafficante said. "Kennedy is not going to make it to the election. He is going to be hit."

Trafficante normally spoke without a lot of passion, but that didn't mean it was a good idea to discount what he said. His reputation rested partly on rumors that he had engineered the extermination of the dreaded Albert Anastasia. Aleman passed Trafficante's threat along to his FBI handlers at the Miami Field Office. Hoover had fair warning.

By November 1963, the *structure* of the attempt on JFK the Mob had in mind was very clearly prefigured. A scheduled November 2 presidential visit to Chicago was abruptly canceled when officials discovered that "there were four men in town who planned an assassination attempt from one of the overpasses from O'Hare into town. They were seized but apparently not arrested." One of the men, a seemingly hapless "Cuban agent referred to as Miguel Casas Saez," had reportedly gravitated to Tampa ahead of the next attempt on Kennedy's life.

On November 9, a "rightwing extremist" named Joseph Milteer told an informant of the Miami police of his group's intention to shoot the president during his scheduled motorcade through downtown Tampa on November 18 "with a high-powered rifle from a tall building." Authorities could be expected to "pick up somebody within hours afterward . . . just to throw the public off." Milteer and his friends had a dupe from the same Fair Play for Cuba Committee with which Oswald went to such extremes to identify: Gilberto Lopez. Milteer told his informant that "this conspiracy originated in New Orleans, and probably some in Miami. . . ." Tapes of Milteer's threats to the Miami police informant arrived in Secret Service and FBI hands on November 12.

Under very heavy police and Secret Service protection, JFK got through his November 18 visit unharmed. Trafficante had evidently been tipped by one of his snitches in local law enforcement that the feds had been alerted to the Tampa plans and called the attempt off. Milteer later told his police informant that "somebody called the FBI and gave the thing away, and of course he was well guarded and everything went 'pluey,' and everybody kept quiet and waited for Dallas."

With *another* presidential motorcade coming up in just four days in Dallas, it might have occurred to the executive braintrust at FBI headquarters that at least a strenuous warning to the White House might be in order. By this point, Bureau experts knew not only whether but pretty much how these people expected to clip JFK.

✳   ✳   ✳

Over the course of his dramatic if ultimately bewildering assault on the Warren Commission results, New Orleans District Attorney Jim Garrison would manage to wing one piece of suggestive evidence. A former Bureau security clerk in the New Orleans office, William S. Walter—the same modest employee who claimed to have processed the paperwork of Oswald in his capacity as Bureau informant—maintained that he had received, on the morning of November 17, 1963, "a TWX message directed to all southern regional offices of the FBI. The message advised that an attempt to assassinate President Kennedy would be made in Dallas on November 22, 1963." A "militant revolutionary group" was behind the planning. Interviewed later by Warren Commission staffers, Walter's FBI colleagues refused to back him up. The Old Man was known to have a big stake in covering up this undying security disaster.

Roughly ten days before Kennedy died, Oswald himself had stormed into FBI headquarters in Dallas and pitched a tantrum over the repeated visits of Special Agent James Hosty, who had been attempting to interrogate his wife, Marina, then living with Mrs. Ruth Paine in Irving, Texas. Oswald had a note prepared for Hosty. If Hosty didn't stop bothering his wife, Hosty's receptionist remembered the note as having said, Oswald would "either blow up the Dallas Police Department or the FBI office."

Hours after the president was taken out, Hosty told a Dallas police lieutenant that "We knew that Lee Harvey Oswald was capable of assassinating the President of the United States, but we didn't dream he would do it." Once Oswald himself was dead, the FBI SAC in Dallas, Gordon Shanklin, presented Hosty with the Oswald note, which he had fished out of Hosty's workbox. "Oswald's dead now; there can be no trial; get rid of it," his supervisor told Hosty, reportedly on orders from Hoover himself. Hosty tore it up and flushed it down the toilet. Too straightforward by half, Hosty suffered through a nightmare of probations and transfers and unpaid suspensions that dead-ended his career.

Too much disclosure just then might well have opened the way to the public revelation that Oswald was one of theirs, which made the Bureau potentially complicitous in the murder of the president. Why hadn't Oswald appeared on the Bureau's "Security Index" for the Dallas area? Within two days, Hoover had canceled his directive to the field to press hard to uncover every lead relating to the Crime of the Century, and in fact suppressed the gathering indications that Marcello, David Ferrie, and Lee Harvey Oswald were all in contact with one another prior to the shooting. Critical files were withheld from the Warren Commission and the House assassination probers fifteen years later; in fact the vital interlude 1962–1964 in Carlos Marcello's long, spotty FBI dossier is unobtainable to this day to anybody pressing a Freedom of Information request.

Having sent a cable to the field rescinding his earlier order to "resolve all allegations pertaining to the assassination," Hoover intervened broadly to cut off speculation. When U.S. Ambassador to Mexico Thomas Mann initiated inquiries as to the chance that there was a Cuban involvement in the shooting, he heard from the Director right away. "The message I received from Hoover . . . was, 'We don't want to hear any more about this case. And tell the Mexican government not to do any more investigating. We just want to hush it up.'" Oswald did it, alone. Case closed.

At every turn, the Bureau moved to step in and freeze the evidence. Beverly Oliver, a singer at Dallas's Colony Club known as the "Babushka Lady" in assassination annals, happened to be standing beside the presidential limousine, filming, when the shooting started. An FBI agent, Regis Kennedy, the New Orleans regular who dismissed Carlos Marcello as a "tomato salesman" in his Bureau updates, reportedly appeared at Beverly's shoulder and grabbed her film, never to appear again. Oliver would subsequently claim to have seen Jack Ruby and Lee Harvey Oswald having a drink together at Ruby's Carousel Club. Immediately after the assassination, Regis Kennedy bobbed up a second time, available to help alibi David Ferrie. It was a busy weekend for all of Carlos Marcello's innumerable flunkies.

When the Zapruder film surfaced, an amateur cameraman's lucky effort to capture the motorcade, which did survive, FBI lab personnel intervened to appropriate the film and somehow reversed the frames during the critical seconds when John Kennedy's brains exploded out of his head, suggesting that the president's skull lurched forward when—once the all-important frames 313–319 were back in place—it would become evident that Kennedy, gripped by his body brace, lurched backward the moment the vital bullet struck him in the temple. The large occipital bone in the back of his skull was plainly blown out by the expanding bullet, permitting the famous "halo" of blood and brain matter to land on Jacqueline and the motorcycle policemen riding to the left rear of the open convertible.

It would become evident that a quickly coordinated if too-often clumsy effort had been made virtually from the moment of the shooting to bamboozle the public. Surviving acoustical evidence—a motorcycle cop in Dealey Plaza had left his radio on, and a tape of his broadcast survived in the local station house—picked up a minimum of six shots during the six to eight seconds during which the attempt occurred. Oswald's elderly mail-order Mannlicher-Carcano was loose and poorly maintained, its sights were off, and he himself was a mediocre marksman badly out of practice. It would take several seconds to chamber each cartridge between shots with his unreliable bolt-action rifle, entirely apart from the time it would take to aim the weapon. Foliage from a large tree in full leaf would have obstructed Oswald's line of fire throughout the critical moments the early shots struck.

The initial shots especially followed on too close for anybody to have fired them from the same rifle; in later years, John Connally was especially strident when it came to ridiculing the "Magic Bullet" theory espoused by Warren Commission staffer Arlen Specter and Representative Gerald Ford, the notion that Oswald's first shot passed through the president's upper torso and then angled around, wounding Connally. "He just wanted a bullet of his own," Nicholas Katzenbach would chuckle to me; at the time, it was no joke. If Kennedy and Connally had been hit by different bullets, perhaps a second apart, then Kennedy had been under attack from a cross-fire, several assailants, a conspiracy. If others were involved, Hoover realized at once, this thing could whipsaw out of control: friends of the Bureau could very well get dragged in.

Another immediate problem was the forensic evidence. As soon as Kennedy's Secret Service contingent unloaded his body at Parkland Hospital, attendants rushed him to Trauma Room One. Charles Crenshaw, one of the emergency-room surgeons who worked on the dying president, would record a small gunshot wound in his throat, another penetration of a couple of inches beside the vertebrae of his upper back, and the results of a "bullet [which] had entered his head through the front, and as it surgically passed through his cranium, the missile obliterated part of the temporal and all the parietal and occipital lobes before it lacerated the cerebellum." The right half of Kennedy's brain had been blown away—Jacqueline herself had appeared in the emergency room clutching much of her husband's brain in one gory hand.

The original autopsy photographs, several of which would disappear, illustrated "a hole in the back of the head, almost two inches above the hairline, about the size of a grapefruit" as well as "a hole in the forehead above the right eye which was a round wound about 3/8 inches thick in diameter which he [the photographer] interpreted as a gunshot wound." Two FBI agents on hand in the emergency room, Francis X. O'Neill and James Sibert, produced diagrams of Kennedy's scalp which backed up the original description of the carnage. There was one more relatively small wound, beneath the heavy hair, on the left side of the president's scalp.

All this would indicate that the president had been shot four times, twice from the front. The overwhelming majority of witnesses that day, 77 of the 107 who gave their statements, reported a very loud explosion, often accompanied by a flash and puff of smoke, from the fenced-in area below and to the right of the presidential limousine, the "grassy knoll" adjacent to the train yard. Unlike the copper-jacketed bullets three casings of which were discovered behind stacked-up boxes at the Book Depository, whatever struck Kennedy on the right forehead and blew away half of his head was in all probability a frangible, soft-core cartridge, directed by a professional.

In 2005 Antoinette Giancana, a daughter of the Chicago Mob boss, assisted by a prominent neurophysiologist and an eminent psychiatrist from the University of Illinois, published *JFK and Sam*, a somewhat sporadic rendition of the unacknowledged history between the Giancanas and the Kennedys. The book peaks with an account of the arrival in Dallas a week before the assassination of James E. Files. Files was an odd-jobs backup for Charles Nicoletti, by then Sam Giancana's best button man. A day later Johnny Rosselli is alleged to have shown up, very much the senior statesman, urbane and fun-loving but businesslike when the moment came, on hand to jolly the soldiers along and clear away whatever logistical problems might emerge.

The delegation from Chicago went about the work with a minimum of wasted energy. There were reportedly meetings with Marcello's resident stooges, including Lee Harvey Oswald and Jack Ruby, to make very sure these bit players would be reliably at their stations when the president came to town. Ruby is alleged to have provided the bogus Secret Service identification badges (which originated with the CIA), with which a few part-time employees of the Mob might be expected to shoo away the curious from the vantage point Files had selected behind the stockade fence on the grassy knoll.

As the presidential motorcade swung into its fateful turn, Nicoletti nailed the president in the back of the head from the adjacent Dal-Tex building; a fraction of a second later Files managed the extremely effective frontal shot with a specially designed "Fireball" XP-100 handgun with a telescopic sight which laid out an exploding bullet with a mercury load. Then Files broke down and chivvied the weapon into his briefcase and turned his reversible plaid jacket gray side out and popped a hat on and bit and discarded the casing—his trademark—and walked away, not in a hurry.

Whatever the limitations of Antoinette Giancana's workup of the Crime of the Century, it made a lot more sense than J. Edgar Hoover's. Before Air Force One, with the new president, and what was left of the old president, and the blood-spattered widow, had permission to lift off and head for Washington, the FBI was moving into Dallas to blanket the community. The Director was determined to establish, fast, that the malefactor here was Oswald, all Oswald, and only Oswald. That meant that facts would need to be altered, suppressed, invented, or enlarged upon to an insane degree to make this one-lung scenario work.

This would be Edgar's bravura performance. What made it much more challenging was Lyndon Johnson's decision, against Hoover's advice— political pressures were building fast—to appoint the Warren Commission. Including Earl Warren himself, there would be seven members on the Commission, and, while several of the more establishment-oriented—Allen Dulles, John McCloy, and Gerald Ford—were already dependably in the Director's pocket, such independent-minded Southerners as Richard Russell, John Sherman Cooper, or Hale Boggs might give Edgar trouble. Fortunately, they were all very busy men.

Hoover's first move was to take over control of the investigation in Dallas—at that time, shooting the president was technically another local homicide, not a federal crime. The Director now pronounced the Kennedy shooting essentially a "civil rights violation." Since Robert Kennedy had recently forced responsibility for civil rights on the unwilling Bureau, Hoover could now proclaim that authority to investigate this murder fell primarily to him. He could also control the investigation of Oswald by shifting responsibility for investigating Oswald to "Crazy Billy" Sullivan, whose Domestic Intelligence Division was already catching the most indefensible of the nutcutting duties, like tapping and bugging Martin Luther King Jr. Better not to permit his Assistant Director for Special Investigations—Organized Crime—Courtney Evans, anywhere near this hotspot. Evans was too close to the Kennedys.

For a day or two the local authorities, starting with the ingenuous Jesse Curry, the Dallas chief of police, threatened to interfere with the public perception of the role of Lee Harvey Oswald, which Hoover intended to pound overnight into the national consciousness. Before the dust started settling, local police sources had been short-sighted enough to leak to the Texas newspapers their discovery that Oswald had been serving for a year as an informant to the FBI. Hoover denied this fervently, meanwhile instructing his Dallas SAC, J. Gordon Shanklin, to "sanitize" Oswald's file, a move the lawyer and assassination historian Mark North would term "wholesale destruction of evidence and nothing less than obstruction of justice."

Within two days of the shooting, under orders from Robert Kennedy's by-the-book Criminal Division Chief Jack Miller, Dallas District Attorney Henry Wade had fallen into line and called a press conference to reinforce the county's slapped-up case against Oswald. Then, after two full days of interrogation of Oswald over the course of which no stenographic record and no tapes of any sort were permitted, Jack Ruby slouched through the knot of reporters and television cameramen waiting in the basement of the police station for Lee Harvey Oswald to be transferred and terminated the unhappy ex-Marine with one perfectly placed slug. After that there was no need for Washington to muffle the loquacious Dallas cops. Apart from his notorious generosity when it came to comping the troopers on the beat in his strip joints, Jack Ruby was widely understood to serve as Carlos Marcello's liaison to the payoff-hungry department.

The Bureau was already at work filling in Oswald's "legend." Unwelcome facts kept getting in the way. For example, Dallas Police Officer J. D. Tippit, whom it was asserted Oswald shot on impulse minutes after dusting the president, was found with three Winchester-Western bullets in his body and one by Remington-Peters, although the spent cartridges on the scene were two and two. Another treatment of the shooting maintains that Tippit was shot with an automatic pistol and Oswald had a standard revolver. The one solid witness to Tippit's murder described a "short and kind of heavy" assailant, still brandishing his pistol, who could not possibly have been Oswald, and was dressed in "khaki and a white shirt." Scuttlebutt suggests that Tippit was waiting on that corner under instructions to kill *Oswald*.

And what about the speed with which the pedestrian Oswald purportedly rushed all over town, fitting in a change of clothes in his rooming house, before turning up in the darkened Texas Theater, evidently expecting to meet a contact? Sixteen police officers, obviously responding to a tip, converged on the dyslexic veteran, already the subject of an all-points and identified to the media as a notorious local Marxist. Less than an hour had passed since John F. Kennedy had died. Oswald showed no sign of powder burns on his cheek, a sure giveaway when somebody has fired a rifle. None of the parts fit.

* * *

More intriguing than mere logistics is the thoroughly calculated seduction of a number of the background figures. The key was building up the impulsive, fundamentally bewildered mental case the authorities had identified almost before the shooting and turning him, in retrospect, into a homicidal mastermind. For this purpose, it was very important to win over the widow, Marina Oswald. As the bride with whom Oswald had returned from Minsk and kept under brutal control, in a kind of slavish destitution, Marina was obviously open to careful, foresighted handling by specialists from the FBI. Unlike the mercurial Oswald, she unequivocally preferred to remain in the United States. Perhaps her best friend throughout those first, awful months in Texas, Ruth Paine, remembers a frightened woman with whom her husband refused to speak English for fear it might help her acclimate herself too quickly and weaken his grip. Ruth, who was mastering Russian, had run into the Oswalds at the same party attended by Lee's CIA handler, the aristocratic White-Russian oil geologist George de Mohrenschildt.

A tall, committed, rather leathery Quaker who knows her own mind, Ruth Paine was privately horrified by the level of squalor and casual abuse to which the obviously vulnerable Marina, a kind of agitated Slavic kewpie doll awakening on another planet, now found herself subjected. No indignity was out of the question. Ruth Paine remembers visiting the pair with their toddler daughter June during the summer of 1963 in New Orleans. Their apartment was primitive; Ruth herself slept on the floor and recalls spraying a big oval around herself with cockroach repellent every night before she slipped beneath her blanket.

For some weeks prior to the assassination Oswald had lived under his alias, Alek Hidell, in a rooming house in Dallas while Marina, again pregnant, boarded with the Paines in nearby Irving. Domestic life with Lee Harvey Oswald upset Marina virtually every time they saw each other, and once he was dead she was utterly susceptible. On finding herself in the course of one shattering day transformed from a gloomy pregnant immigrant into a massive tabloid celebrity, Marina had very little reason not to cooperate with anybody who promised material help, and she evidently did. "Marina Oswald suddenly became rich upon the murder of her husband and the President," Robert Groden notes in his authoritative treatment of the assassination universe. "The Secret Service first hid her away in a motel owned by the Great Southwest Corporation, which was controlled by the Wynne family of Dallas, partners of Clint Murchison. . . . Murchison's lawyers Bedford Wynne and Thomas Webb" had recently been named in a muckraking piece in *Life* as "members of the 'Bobby Baker Set,'" while "'The Texas Murchison family . . . were close to both Lyndon Johnson and above all J. Edgar Hoover. . . .'" Higher authority consumed Marina like a truffle.

With Marina under control, it didn't take a lot of imagination to authenticate serviceable incidents in Lee Harvey Oswald's past. Ruth Paine was a little taken aback one day when "two guys from Secret Service showed up at my door. One of them was their Russian expert. He questioned me in Russian. . . . First he showed me something, a piece of paper. Looked like it wasn't the first page. It said—'If I am in the jailhouse and you want something, here is where you find it. The key to the mail-box is so-and-so. Don't worry, the rent has been paid for the next month.' I didn't recognize the handwriting. I hadn't really seen Oswald's handwriting. It was in Russian. He apparently didn't know the word for key, because he had transliterated the word for key into Russian characters. . . . The Secret Service person said, 'Mrs. Paine, you sent this note to Marina.' We went back and forth for a while, and I was getting pretty upset. Not many people have called me a liar, and I don't take kindly to it."

As things turned out, the note was allegedly found in a book on child-rearing that Ruth had recently shipped off to Marina, although Ruth never noticed the note when she packed it up. "She had hidden the note in the book," Ruth would be told, "as it was very incriminating to Oswald. And he had written it at the time of his attempt on [General Edwin] Walker, left it on his desk when he left to go out to shoot Walker. And Marina found it and was *frantic* with what was going on. And then he came back, according to her testimony ashen and shaken, and saying that he had walked home and that he had tried to shoot this fascist."

Ruth had never actually discussed the Walker shooting with Marina directly. It became an important part of the workup on Oswald based entirely on Marina's well-coached testimony before the Warren Commission, circumstantially supported by the mysterious note. Despite Ruth's many months of offering both Marina and Lee the most honest and unequivocal support they knew, as soon as the FBI moved in, Marina was gone. Ruth Paine's own marriage was coming apart, and she had welcomed Marina's naïve appeal for emotional companionship. "It is hard for you and me to live without a return of our love—interesting, how will it all end?" Marina had written Ruth the previous May. The following December, after Marina was clearly at the mercy of the anonymous authorities, Ruth responded to a letter from Marina: "You closed your face to me. Is it true, have I offended you?"

The note from Oswald which the men from the government claimed to have found in the copy of the *Book of Useful Advice*, a modest text in Russian devoted mostly to subjects like How to Eradicate Pinworms, now offered concrete evidence to help transform the nation's perception of Oswald from that of a badly coordinated would-be quasi-Marxist to somebody with the internal fortitude to blow away a president. Ruth Paine *still* does not recollect that there was in fact any note in the book she sent. Once it reappeared, it served at once as prima facie evidence against Oswald, supplemented by a further confession her FBI handlers extracted from Marina that Lee had contemplated hijacking a plane to Cuba. Marina would now do whatever was expected of her to survive.

Outside investigations of the attempt to shoot General Edwin Walker yielded unconvincing results. The original police report specified that the bullet that narrowly missed the general came from a .30-06 cartridge. Walker himself had looked at the slug which the police dug out of his plaster wall; when the Warren Commission showed him the bullet they now insisted had been fired at him, the standard load from a Mannlicher-Carcano, he insisted that it was certainly not the bullet he looked at earlier, which had been badly mangled. Moreover, a fourteen-year-old neighbor of Walker's had heard the shot and climbed a fence in time to spot two men with two cars. One of the men was putting something into the trunk of a Ford sedan. In his reported confession to Marina, Oswald had supposedly maintained that he had brought off the whole thing, as usual, alone. Traveling exclusively, as always, by bus. Oswald didn't drive.

Unavailable, guarded by the Secret Service, Marina Oswald was interrogated by the FBI forty-six times while the Warren Commission labored over its report. A week after the assassination, Marina was quoted by *Life* magazine as saying "I love Lee. Lee good man. He didn't do anything." But she would quickly find herself expertly coached into providing a great deal of the anecdotal backdrop which impelled the Commissioners to conclude that Oswald was indeed the troubled lunatic who all by himself had managed to destroy John Kennedy.

Just in case, four days after the Warren Commission held its first meeting on December 5, 1963, the FBI turned over to the Commission's lawyers its four-volume summary report of its investigation of the deaths of Oswald and JFK, simultaneously—this infuriated several Commission members— releasing most of its conclusions to the media. To underscore the direction this thing had better take, Deputy Attorney General Nicholas Katzenbach "wrote each member asking them to issue a press release stating that the FBI report said Oswald was the lone assassin."

Hoover was on top of every detail. Through many of the early months, Warren Commission Chief Counsel J. L. Rankin would prove restive, and at one point the Bureau was forced to concede to the Commission members that its acknowledged source "Ruby had been contacted nine times by the FBI in 1959, from March 11 to October 2, 'to furnish information' on criminal matters . . . in view of his position as a night club operator who might have knowledge of the criminal element in Dallas." Hoover demanded that the Commission keep this rather suggestive disclosure away from the public. The Commissioners agreed, and so Jack Ruby went into the Warren Commission's final report as a kind of salty local character fundamentally unaffiliated with organized crime.

By January, her "business adviser" announced that Marina Oswald was now prepared to concede that her husband had killed the president. Testifying before the Commission, Marina met a squad from the Bureau, the Director among them. Shaking hands with Hoover, she would later remark, "I was chilled from top to bottom. It was if you met a dead person; he had a coldness like someone from the grave."

When his turn came before the membership of the Commission, Hoover found it within himself to execute one of those unexpected pirouettes in defiance of the prevailing fanaticism that got him through so many nasty crises throughout his long career. "We found no indication at all that Oswald was a man addicted to violence," the Director blandly assured Hale Boggs, certainly not "a party to the shooting into the house of General Walker." The Walker material had started to look a little thin, and Hoover understood the desirability of covering himself. What the Bureau conjures up, it may at any moment disavow.

Essentially, Earl Warren reminded Hoover, "You have told us that you had no jurisdiction down there in Dallas over this crime."

"That is correct." During the early hours of the crisis, the FBI Director had memoed that he was concerned that the rubes who were bungling the crisis in Texas "really did not have a case against Oswald until we gave them our information," besides which, he now added, "I was so concerned that I asked my agent in charge in Dallas, Mr. Shanklin, to personally go to Chief Curry and tell him that I insisted that he not go on the air any more until this case was resolved." The Bureau was well aware that during his early hours in custody Oswald had tried to retain John Abt, a crack attorney for the American Civil Liberties Union. A lawyer with Abt's skills could bring this entire jerry-rigged hallucination down on all of them.

Once Ruby intervened, Hoover quickly circulated a memo to go on record that he had passed along to the Dallas Police Department rumors the Bureau had picked up emphasizing that Oswald was not safe, that it was important to keep outsiders, the press especially, away from the accused. However relieved the Director might find himself privately that his pop-off informant had now been silenced, it was obviously vital, immediately, to shift the blame. Evidence was apparently altered at every turn. Solid witnesses who insisted that they had encountered Oswald in the second-floor cafeteria while he was presumed to be shooting the president from a sixth-floor window were given, at best, a desultory hearing. Inconsistencies plagued further reports on the death of Officer J. D. Tippit. There was the bullet-hole-in-JFK's-windshield speculation. It was obviously important from the moment the all-Oswald formulation became official to discredit talk about shots originating from the "grassy knoll," and witnesses as highly placed as Kenny O'Donnell, who along with Dave Powers remained convinced that "he had heard two shots that came from behind the fence," were dragooned by the FBI into recanting before the Warren Commission. In 1979, Representative Carl Stokes, the Chairman of the House Select Committee on Assassinations, would admit privately that much more than the disputed "acoustical" evidence pointed to a least two shooters: "We all know that the fatal head shot came from in front." There was, in fact, a conspiracy.

Without question, the weakest link in the single-shooter thesis would remain Jack Ruby. If Oswald had acted alone, what was the point in taking him out? No matter how selectively the Commissioners attempted to sniff their way around his origins, Ruby was no choirboy. At first, protesting that he only wanted to spare the president's widow and Caroline the anguish of Oswald's trial while demonstrating that "a Jew has guts," Ruby seemed to stand up. On trial in 1964, Ruby toyed with his lawyer's defense of mental incompetence, temporary insanity. He remembered how Oswald had appeared in the basement of police headquarters "all of a sudden, with a smirky, defiant, cursing, vicious, Communist expression on his face. I can't convey what impression he gave me. I lost my senses."

But even during the weeks the Commissioners were interviewing him—between bouts of throwing the spittoon in his cell at the light bulb and inserting his finger in the light socket—Ruby pleaded with Earl Warren and others to take him to Washington to debrief him; he would be safe there, he could then tell them things they would find "amazing." It had begun to occur to Ruby that he might very well be facing more than the usual two-to-ten-year

Texas homicide sentence, with time off for good behavior. Ruby might ultimately crack.

By then Hoover's appreciation of the Warren Commission—which he had argued against when Lyndon Johnson brought it up—was small and falling, already anticipating the Report's conclusion that the Bureau had taken "an unduly restrictive view of its role in preventive intelligence work prior to the assassination." Although the Bureau had already subjected one witness to a lie-detector test, "in view of the serious question raised as to Ruby's mental condition, no significance should be placed on the polygraph examination," Hoover informed the Committee and refused twice to permit his technicians to flutter Ruby. They might get answers none of them was prepared to cope with.

Hoover understood right away how flimsy the case was against a will-o'-the-wisp like Oswald. The day after the assassination, the new president was on the telephone pushing the FBI director to lock things up:

JOHNSON: "Have you established any more about the [Oswald] visit to the Soviet Embassy in Mexico in September?"

HOOVER: "No, that's one angle that's very confusing for this reason. We have up here the tape and the photograph of the man who was at the Soviet Embassy, using Oswald's name. That picture and the tape do not correspond to this man's voice, or to his appearance. In other words, it appears that there is a second person who was at the Soviet Embassy."

A week later, in a long memo to his executive staff, Hoover reports having "advised the President that we hope to have the investigation wrapped up today but probably won't have it before the first of the week as an angle in Mexico is giving trouble—the matter of Oswald's getting $6500 from the Cuban Embassy and coming back to this country with it; that we are not able to prove that fact; that we have information he was there on September 18 and we are able to prove he was in New Orleans on that date. . . ." Summing up, the new president "stated that I was more than head of the FBI—I was his brother and personal friend . . . that he has more confidence in me than anybody in town. . . ."

Hoover's gumshoes in Mexico City may have been a little confused, but the Director himself was obviously picking up on the fact that important people out there had prepared for this, that very skillful operatives had laid a false trail. Oswald was to be their sacrifice—their "patsy," in his own word. There was a new president now, and after three years in perdition under the Kennedys, the Director was wising up fast, preparing to pitch in however he could.

* * *

True to form, Hoover made sure he could control the damage by placing a spy of his own on the Warren Commission, somebody to "look after FBI interests." "He was our man, our informant," William Sullivan later wrote of Representative Gerald Ford. Internal FBI paperwork enumerates the documents Ford passed to Deke DeLoach, then chief of Crime Records. Pipelining the Commission's secrets was both improper and illegal. "I should call him any time his assistance was needed," DeLoach reported to The Boss.

A solid American Legion midwesterner, Ford was a great booster of the FBI in Congress and something of a backslapping acquaintance whenever he encountered the Director. But Hoover wasn't one to depend on personal loyalties when it came to Bureau affairs. A source very close to the good times will now divulge that big, lumbering Jerry Ford was very often recognizable among the bipartisan revelers that Ellen Rometsch and her lively cohorts entertained in Fred Black's fun-filled suite at the Sheraton Carlton. It was a time when pills and alcohol laid Betty Ford low. Before long, Hoover had the goods on tape, a turn of events which evidently spurred president-to-be Ford to accommodate DeLoach and the others whenever something sensitive came up behind closed committee-room doors.

Relations within the Commission itself were arm's-length a lot of the time and quite scratchy on occasion; Richard Russell, for example, despised Earl Warren, and all the Commissioners themselves avoided attending more than a handful of the important interviews. Committee Counsel Arlen Specter later wrote that their link to the CIA, Allen Dulles, "may have withheld vital information . . . we were counting on." The four-volume FBI summation on which the Commission based its judgments was, in the opinion of the lawyer who led the subsequent investigation for the House of Representatives, Robert Blakey, "superficial, shoddy and full of holes," and ultimately, as Specter put it, "misled the commission."

Compromised before the Commission met, Ford served the old Director's purposes. He arranged to alter the wording of the Commission's report to indicate that JFK was shot from behind in the neck, not the back, so as to establish the downward angle required by the "magic bullet" thesis to which he and Specter were the primary contributors. Ford would soon utilize his ghosted book *Portrait of an Assassin* to confirm Oswald's guilt, freely including top-secret transcripts from the Commission's proceedings. "Conclusions," Ford would be quoted, "were the work of the Commission."

Burdened with his obligations to Hoover, Ford nevertheless sensed a lot more going on around the assassination than his preoccupied colleagues really wanted to get into, and at one point vexed Earl Warren himself by pressing Ruby about details of his trips to Cuba. Persistent suspicions and perhaps a haunting awareness of unmet responsibilities appear to have stayed with Ford. According to RFK biographer C. David Heymann, "Gerald Ford publicly admitted that in 1975, while President of the United States, he had suppressed certain FBI and CIA surveillance reports that indicated that JFK had been caught in a crossfire in Dallas, and that John Rosselli and Carlos Marcello had orchestrated the assassination plot."

While it is not surprising that Hoover took immediate steps to cover his own broad bureaucratic ass, Robert Kennedy's responses to the presidential murder lifted many an insider eyebrow around Washington. True to form, he attempted to control every upshot. Still numb from Hoover's telephone call, Bobby summoned CIA Director John McCone to Hickory Hill and met him with a single demand: "Did you kill my brother?" Over the next several hours McCone attempted to reassure Kennedy but indicated that he thought two gunmen were involved. McCone was the wrong man to be interrogating—Dick Helms and the others at the operations end of things were careful to tell McCone very little—and by then Bob Kennedy's relations with the clandestine side of the Company were at best iffy.

Drawing on the roughly four million documents which Congress forced the administration to declassify during the nineteen-nineties, Lamar Waldron and Thom Hartmann have their own elaborately developed explanation as to why Jack Kennedy exposed himself to assassination repeatedly during the autumn of 1963. Waldron posits the concern the president and his brother shared that if he varied much from the traditional political warm-up for the 1964 elections, the administration would somehow tip its hand that it was about to spring another clandestine invasion of Cuba in December 1963, what Waldron dubs C-Day. Again, Castro was to be eliminated immediately. Interviews with Dean Rusk and Pierre Salinger appear to support Waldron's thesis.

Hands-on as ever, Robert Kennedy made sure to keep himself in the midst of the planning. Recruited through Bobby's head-knocker Marine General Victor ("Brute") Krulak, Army Captain Bradley Ayers would remember meeting Robert Kennedy in June of 1963 at a "CIA social function" in a house overlooking Biscayne Bay, subsequent to which he was reintroduced to the attorney general "deep in the swampland" after a long ride by airboat when Bobby emerged from a Quonset hut after conferring with Agency officials overseeing preparations for a "planned airborne commando raid" into Cuba, "any time after the first of December." It was from this base that "Colonel" Johnny Rosselli and his big, bad-tempered drinking companion, the New Mexican Indian who ran Miami operations, David Morales, trained recruits in advance of their spoiling forays along the Cuban coast.

The other important staging area for Bobby's incessant "pinprick" reprisals (while JFK secretly explored some back-channel modus vivendi) was of course Louisiana. Robert Kennedy was attempting to keep Hoover and his men on a don't-ask/don't-tell regimen. As with its Miami raid, local FBI officials were flabbergasted when orders came down from Washington to release without charge the McLaney brothers after the Bureau closed in on William McLaney's explosives-laden camp in Lacombe, Louisiana, on Lake Pontchartrain, outside New Orleans. "The Kennedys got us off," McLaney sidekick Steve Reynolds explained. "They were aware of that operation from the start."

Again, Bobby was single-mindedly pursuing family goals through arrangements of his own devising. That conspiracy-minded garage owner, Adrian Alba, told *Frontline* that "RFK's network in New Orleans had considered recruiting Oswald for the Castro assassination plot," and, at the center of RFK's alleged network, Alba put the all-purpose Guy Banister. For all his hard-right credentials, and the constant traffic between his 544 Camp Street detective agency and FBI headquarters, Banister had a long history with the Kennedys' durable gray eminence and fellow FBI old-guardist Carmine Bellino, with whom at one point he had entered into a business partnership. Both Banister and his partner, Hugh Ward, would die abruptly and under extraordinarily murky circumstances just as the Warren Commission was about to publish its report in 1964, two from the first cluster of deaths each investigation incited.

There had evidently been talk of infiltrating Oswald into Cuba ahead of the projected December invasion to serve as a fall guy in the eventuality Castro did get hit. Enough planning had long since leaked, subsequent FBI Director Clarence Kelley wrote, so that "Oswald . . . had information on a CIA plot to assassinate Fidel Castro."

So Robert Kennedy was well briefed when it came to the various New Orleans middleweights. Guy Banister and David Ferrie and even Lee Harvey Oswald were recognizable personalities to the avid attorney general, assorted pieces and pawns he and his trusted intermediaries might expect to move into place with December approaching fast.

Having taken it upon himself to monitor to the nittiest detail the post–Bay of Pigs operations of the CIA, Robert Kennedy was presumably well aware that Oswald had deserted to the Soviet Union, in all probability part of Jim Angleton's longstanding infiltration program. Oswald's primary Agency handler once he was back in Dallas was George de Mohrenschildt, "The Baron," the socialite oil geologist well acquainted with the Bouvier and Bush families. Like David Ferrie, who claimed to have a "letter of marque" from Robert Kennedy personally, Oswald appeared safely co-opted by 1963 as an established Bureau informant. "If the FBI is controlling him," Bobby reportedly conceded before the assassination, "he's no problem."

On November 22, the world turned inside out. David Atlee Phillips, the seasoned CIA operations man who originally mentored the DRE for the Agency before taking over the Alpha 66 infiltration teams constantly processing through the CIA's big amphibious base on Lake Pontchartrain, now found himself startled by the ironic reversals. JFK had gone down, he was to concede privately, according to "the plan we had devised against Castro." Phillips understood reversals. Plagued throughout his later life with charges that he himself was implicated in the assassination, Phillips admitted shortly before he died: "My private opinion is that JFK was done in by a conspiracy, likely including rogue American intelligence people."

The moment he understood fully that his brother had actually died, Robert Kennedy stepped off the edge of his life. The responses he gave to friends who dared to solicit his opinion were misleading, but Kennedy himself clearly perceived, quite quickly, who had brought about this unendurable thing. "I've killed my own brother," he gasped to somebody in the Justice Department. And in a sense, that was true.

To insiders it was apparent immediately that any truly searching examination of the forces behind the JFK assassination would quickly expose the survivors to politically ruinous disclosures. They'd conspired to murder another head of state, engaged in protracted hanky-panky with the Mob, and then of course there were those many awkward assignations involving Judith Campbell Exner and all the others. By November 23, 1963, J. Edgar Hoover's best interests and Robert Kennedy's best interests had conflated perfectly.

The whole thing came around again in 1967, when New Orleans District Attorney Jim Garrison attempted to try in the nation's newspapers his charges against Clay Shaw, a prominent local businessman who Garrison insisted was one of the instruments through whom the CIA had orchestrated the death of John F. Kennedy. The tip-off was the appearance in the Big Easy of Walter Sheridan. Billed as a producer of NBC documentaries, Sheridan claimed to be in town to put together a "White Paper" on the Garrison prosecution effort.

Liaison went through Jack Miller, still running the Criminal Division at the Justice Department, to senior officials at the Agency and the Bureau. In fact, as Sheridan emphasized behind locked doors, "I am here in New Orleans representing Robert Kennedy, and I have been sent down here to stop the probe, no matter what it takes." According to Garrison biographer Joan Mellen, it took the promise to overturn the conviction of Teamster functionary Zachary ("Red") Strate, not the kind of give-back Robert Kennedy went along with readily. In an attempt to coerce a looker from the French Quarter into reversing her earlier testimony in Garrison's support, Sheridan offered her a job on the *Tonight Show*, specifying that if she didn't help out, "He's going down the drain and you're going with him." Bob Kennedy's stocky, angel-faced enforcer still had his own approach to charming a potential witness.

One abiding concern of Bobby's would remain his brother's corpse. An hour and a half after JFK was shot, after the medical group at Parkland Hospital had performed its tracheotomy and felt for bullet holes along the spine and established that most of the back of the president's skull had been blown away—but before the local pathologists were ready to attempt an autopsy— a Secret Service team led by John Kennedy's chief of staff, Kenny O'Donnell, pushed into the operating theater. They demanded the body, no doubt on Robert Kennedy's instructions. The Dallas County Medical Examiner, Dr. Earl Rose, explained that under Texas law no murder victim could be moved until after an autopsy. "It's just another homicide as far as I'm concerned," the judge in attendance declared.

"Go screw yourself," Kenny O'Donnell said. The Secret Service agents "put the doctor and the judge up against the wall at gunpoint," writes Anthony Summers, who interviewed one of the other doctors, "and swept out of the hospital with the President's body."

When the formal autopsy was conducted at the Naval Hospital in Bethesda, Maryland, Robert Kennedy and Jacqueline waited in a nearby office and remained in constant telephone contact with the military aides, Vice Admiral George Burkley and General Godfrey McHugh, while Dr. Pierre Finck was dissecting the cadaver. Finck was specifically ordered not to track the bullet wound in the president's back, presumably an attempt to avoid revealing that JFK's adrenals had been largely reabsorbed, the consequence of his Addison's disease. What we now have of the formal autopsy photographs presents shots of the back of the president's head totally at odds with the depictions by the Parkland surgeons, who would recall something that looked like half of a giant blown egg. Somewhere in the fastness of Bethesda were generated the surviving images of Kennedy's wavy dark locks completely intact, which the official White House photographer, Robert L. Knudsen, admitted to his family must at some point have been very fundamentally altered, with hair that "had been drawn in."

Once the official autopsy was over, the negatives, slides, and the formalin-preserved brain of the dead president were stored in a file cabinet under the control of Admiral Burkley until 1965, when Robert Kennedy arranged for them to pass into the custodianship of JFK's long-time secretary, Evelyn Lincoln, then working on the president's papers at the National Archives.

Angela Novello, Robert Kennedy's secretary over the years, took possession of all this medical evidence until 1966, when Attorney General Ramsey Clark asked for the remains back, as required by a recent law. Bob Kennedy hated the idea, and when the autopsy materials were finally surrendered up from Angela Novello's footlocker, shots of the interior cavity of the president's chest, along with slides of tissue sections and the brain itself, had disappeared.

This meant that later efforts to track the paths of the bullets or determine whether a soft-core round might have left mercury traces as it tore open the president's skull were foreclosed.

In time a story went around Washington alleging that Robert Kennedy had secretly arranged to bury the brain of his dead brother with the rest of him. As for who conspired to murder his brother—the deeply shocked lame-duck attorney general plainly did not want to know. When Lyndon Johnson paid Bobby the courtesy of letting him pick two of the seven dignitaries on the Warren Commission, Kennedy selected John McCloy, an establishment personality to his stubby fingertips, and Allen Dulles, whom his brother had fired, essentially, for incompetence. Implicated as he was in the various Castro-assassination schemes, Dulles could at least be depended on to limit the range of the investigation, Kennedy conceded to William Attwood, "for reasons of national security." To make sure he had one seasoned investigator inside the Warren Commission, Robert Kennedy quietly arranged for Charles Shaffer, one of his Justice Department Get-Hoffa-Squad pit bulls, to serve on the staff and keep an eye out.

Not that it would have mattered much if Kennedy had been hell-bent on tracking down his brother's killers. "The minute that bullet hit Jack Kennedy's head," William Hundley maintains, "it was all over. Right then. The organized crime program just stopped, and Hoover took control back." When the head of the Criminal Division at Justice, Jack Miller, and his assistant, Robert Peloquin, attempted to follow up with the FBI during its investigation of the assassination, they were waved off, on the Director's orders. Reports from the field agents did not go to Kennedy or his deputy, Nicholas Katzenbach.

Nobody seemed to care very much about getting it right. "It's important that all of the facts surrounding President Kennedy's assassination be made public in a way that will satisfy people. . . ," Katzenbach memoed Bill Moyers in the White House three days after the shooting. "The public must be satisfied that Oswald was the assassin; that he did not have confederates who are still at large; and that the evidence was such that he would have been convicted at trial. Speculations about Oswald's motivation ought to be cut off." The cold-blooded liquidation of a U.S. president was now essentially a public-relations challenge.

Over the next few years, Bobby wavered between blaming the murder of his brother on "those Cuban cunts"—the anti-Castro Miami resistance—and "the guy from New Orleans"—Marcello.

One name that kept coming up as an accessory was that of Johnny Rosselli, "Mister Smooth," the soft-spoken Mob facilitator with ties to everybody with underworld connections, from Joseph P. Kennedy to Marilyn Monroe. Rosselli had visited Guy Banister not long before the assassination, then dropped off the FBI surveillance roster for nine days on November 21, during a visit to the Desert Inn in Las Vegas. Like Antoinette Giancana, Bill Bonanno, the son of the New York don, would insist that Rosselli was on the scene, shooting from a storm drain. Another outside witness places Rosselli atop the grassy knoll, handing a rifle to the marksman who presumably potted Jack Kennedy.

Once the historical dust started settling, Rosselli assumed a certain importance as the spin-master for the underworld establishment, a mouthpiece for apologia which backed up the official explanation of the entire disaster. With Jack Kennedy dead and Bobby unwilling to think coherently about organized crime, Rosselli could again begin spending time in his palatial apartment in Los Angeles. He made a devoted effort with Judith Campbell, whose nerves were gone after months of heavy-duty harassment by the FBI. Judy came up pregnant in 1964 and accused first Rosselli, then Frank Sinatra of being the father, evidently hoping to squeeze money for the abortion out of one of them.

Nominated by Frank Sinatra, currently serving as Abbott, Rosselli joined the prestigious Friars Club and began to piece out much of his income around the gin rummy tables. Before long Rosselli discovered that one of the high-stakes players at the club, the rotund Maury Friedman, was fleecing the more gullible members by rigging a peephole system which permitted his shills to spy on the pigeons and tip off their cards. With true Mafioso even-handedness, Rosselli agreed to keep the secret but cut himself in on the proceeds. To compensate, Rosselli arranged Mob financing for Friedman when he started clamoring to erect a new casino, the Frontier, in Las Vegas.

The Warren Commission Report had been released in September 1964, but its raging inconsistencies and the mushrooming of the first crop of conspiracy theorists had excited the maverick district attorney of New Orleans, Jim Garrison, to undertake his dragnet operation. It yielded the potential involvement of David Ferrie, Guy Banister, and a local businessman who doubled as a CIA informant to the Domestic Contact Division, Clay Shaw. Leads pointed at Santo Trafficante. Along with Richard Helms, members of the syndicate were starting to worry. Helms worked very closely with David Atlee Phillips and E. Howard Hunt, both umbilically connected to the Miami Cubans. As Garrison's investigation heated up, on February 22, 1967, his most promising witness, David Ferrie, was discovered dead in his disheveled apartment, false eyelashes still glued becomingly into place. The local coroner quickly proclaimed the death the consequence of a "beery aneurism."

To divert speculation into an alternative direction, early in 1967 Rosselli approached Edward Morgan. Once a senior inspector in the FBI, Morgan had built one of the powerhouse law practices in Washington. Rosselli presented a tale that featured several snipers in the employ of Trafficante, shooters who had been sent out to eliminate Castro, been captured, and ultimately been reprogrammed. The followup here was that they had been turned around —"brainwashed," in some versions—and returned to the United States to dispatch Kennedy. Enraged to find himself a target, the Bearded One was supposedly heard to mutter that "he too could engage in the same tactics."

Hoover himself had been talking up a similar remake of the eternal Leftist Menace, based on a conversation reported to the Bureau by "Solo," the top-level Communist penetrations Jack and Morris Childs, who had stopped by Havana and found the dictator grumbling about all these American-inspired attempts on his life. Yet when KGB Lieutenant Colonel Yuri Nosenko defected shortly after the assassination and insisted that the Soviet services had nothing to do with Oswald in Russia, Hoover and his cosseted informant "Fedora"—Victor Lesiovsky, a double-agent by the CIA's reading—would buy that, too, in hopes of shoring up the Warren Commission conclusions.

So it was more of a shocker even in retrospect when Jack Anderson's column, on March 3, 1967, revealed Rosselli's secret that "Robert Kennedy may have approved an assassination plot which then possibly backfired against his late brother." This left the CIA especially pedaling in air. The questions about CIA complicity in the death of John Kennedy were widely asked for the first time and were never adequately answered.

Always one to develop several themes at once, Rosselli may well have been serving notice that, if the federal government got too close, he had a lot to say. By 1967 the FBI was piecing together the details of the Friars Club scam, and the silver fox was implicated. Ex-CIA Clandestine Services heavyweight William Harvey contributed his legal services, protesting widely that Rosselli was "no more guilty than I am." Early in 1971, Rosselli started serving time in a maximum-security prison on McNeil Island, but not before he made sure Jack Anderson went public with the salient points of the CIA initiatives to tear up Cuba and liquidate Castro.

After he got out, laughing with fellow wiseguys like Jimmy ("The Weasel") Fratianno, Rosselli took to explaining away his 1976 interviews with the Church Committee probers on Senator Richard Schweiker's assassination subcommittee staff as another round of expertly applied smoke up the behind of the G: "Sometimes I'd like to tell them the Mob did it, just to see the expression on their stupid faces. You know, we're supposed to be idiots, right? We hire a punk like Oswald to kill the President and then we get a blabbermouth, two-bit punk like Ruby to shut him up. We wouldn't trust those jerks to hit a fucking dog.

"Anyway, they start questioning me about this bullshit I'd told Morgan years ago. You know, Castro retaliating against Kennedy because of our attempts on his life. I said, 'I have no recollection of receiving or passing on such information.'"

But according to Robert Blakey, the chief counsel directing the 1979 House Committee investigation, Rosselli had already divulged that JFK was shot by "Cubans connected to Santo Trafficante . . . and Oswald had been recruited as a decoy. Oswald may have fired at the President, but the fatal shot was fired from close range. Once Oswald was captured, the mob arranged to have him killed by Ruby. . . ." Ruby was, Rosselli had conceded, "one of our boys," ordered to silence Oswald.

The Church Committee subpoenaed Sam Giancana, Johnny Rosselli, and Santo Trafficante. A week before his scheduled appearance in Washington, somebody with a .22 pistol acquired in a Florida gun shop fired a bullet into the base of Giancana's neck, then one into his mouth and five around his chin. Consequently, Rosselli's appearance before the Committee was moved up. He testified as fully as he had to about the operations against Castro. On April 23, 1976, Rosselli sat down at the Carroll Arms with Senator Schweiker and his staff for questions about the Kennedy assassination. Rosselli was predictably guarded, sliding away from direct references to Trafficante, although alluding to certain Cubans around Santo and promising better during upcoming sessions.

By now a gaunt, aging figure with thin white flossy hair, failing lungs, and an outspoken distaste for the idea of jail or—worse—Sicily, Rosselli presented a danger to his generation's survivors. Personal admirers like Fratianno and Fred Black were starting to hear about a contract that Trafficante had bought on Mister Smooth and attempted to warn their debonair friend. Rosselli didn't seem to care, and on July 16 enjoyed the traditional kiss-off dinner at a waterside restaurant with Trafficante and his wife. Before the end of the month, Johnny disappeared, last seen on a boat owned by a Trafficante associate, and soon afterward his partially decomposed body was discovered, dismembered, in an oil drum floating in Dumfoundling Bay off Miami. He had been smothered, shot, gutted, and packed into the oil drum with his severed legs stuffed in alongside his withered torso.

Another purge was under way to keep the JFK shooting under wraps. Once Blakey's subpoenas got distributed, in addition to Giancana and Rosselli being elaborately taken out in demonstration killings, even the hardworking Charlie Nicoletti went down in this round, three bullets in the back of his head, after which his car was fire-bombed. *Omerta* was still in force.

Every once in a while, across senior Mobland, a confirmatory whisper would find its way into the literature of crime. "We took care of Kennedy . . . together," Sam Giancana would brag to his stepson, and then go on to the details of activating Jack Ruby and enlisting financial backing from the important Texas wildcatters and gunmen from the CIA while J. Edgar Hoover "buried his head in the sand. . . ." Mob lawyer Frank Regano remembered Santo Trafficante joking pointedly with Carlos Marcello: "Carlos, you mark my words, before this thing is over with, they're going to blame you and me for the killing of the president," after which they both broke out laughing. Later, alone with Regano, Trafficante began musing. "God damn Bobby. I think Carlos fucked up in getting rid of Giovanni—maybe it should have been Bobby." In 1980, Joe Hauser looked up from his newspaper to mention that Ted Kennedy was running for the Democratic nomination. "Boy," Hauser remarked, "his brothers sure gave ole Carlos a rough time back when they deported him."

Carlos Marcello's brother Joe had a ready answer. "Don't worry; we took care of 'em, didn't we?"

It was a difficult line to top.

BOOK THREE

THE
AFTERMATH
OF POWER

◆

"Tragedy is a tool for living."

—ROBERT F. KENNEDY, from *Sons and Brothers*,
by RICHARD D. MAHONEY, p. xv

20

The Hamlet Stage

Once its reality sank in, the murder of his brother dealt Robert Kennedy a blow that can only be called existential, utterly life-altering. He hung on as attorney general for a little under ten months, but most of that time, Bob Blakey would recall, "He was a walking zombie. . . . I remember vividly the day I went up to say goodbye to him. Looking at him was like looking right through him to the wall. When we shook hands, his hand was limp."

Kennedy's reaction was primary, tribal: all he was capable of was dragging his dead off the field of battle and hiding and licking his own wounds. This thing he had feared worse than his own death had actually occurred, and Bobby could not hide from himself the fact that, by indulging his own private revulsions along with a yen for well-publicized giant-killing, he had now managed to bring the dynasty down. All of them would have to pay.

For several months he dropped out completely, immobilized. The signature enterprise of his attorney generalship, the campaign against organized crime, ground along on its own inertia, in effect without Bobby. The two-day conference of strike-force coordinators which was winding up the afternoon JFK got shot, a spirited gathering of investigators and prosecutors from around the country that met regularly to update progress against the Mob, never convened again. There wouldn't have been much point. Without the FBI, there simply weren't enough brogans on the pavement to continue the war.

Desultorily, Kennedy made some effort. Before Christmas 1963, Bob mounted a party at the Justice Department to celebrate almost three years of accomplishment, and Hoover—to everybody's surprise—came. Kennedy was handing out engraved gold cufflinks as a souvenir, and it was not in Hoover's nature to ignore something for nothing. Ethel, always there with the needle, accosted "Jedgar," as she called him, by asking whether he didn't think Chief Parker of the Los Angeles Police Force, a celebrity cop Hoover was known to detest, might not be, "if you ever retired . . . the man to replace you?" Hoover reddened noticably and replied in a low voice: "Yes, Ethel."

The fact that Hoover put in an appearance suggested how completely he had regained control. In May 1962, as one more expression of the Oriental punctilio through which the two warlords attempted to manage each other, Robert Kennedy had announced a cake-cutting ceremony to celebrate Hoover's thirty-eighth year as director. Hoover bridled at the thought and let it be known that he was uninterested in any such frivolity and would be spending the day at his desk.

In December 1963 Hoover sent the attorney general a thank-you note for the cufflinks as "a constant reminder of a friendship I shall always treasure." There would be a regular exchange of courtesies until Kennedy left. When the attorney general brought John-John through, Hoover himself showed the dead president's son around his office and promised to send the boy a replica of the missile model in one of the showcases. Kennedy sent the Director a note of thanks in March when Jimmy Hoffa was convicted of jury tampering. When Ethel lost some jewelry in Paris, the Bureau helped get it back. Upon resigning from the cabinet, Kennedy thanked the special agents who backed him up in "the organized crime field," and Hoover responded with "an FBI Agent's gold badge which has been mounted."

All this was foam above an increasingly savage undertow. "Starting at 1:10 on November 22," one Justice Department staffer observed, the FBI "began pissing on the attorney general." Within one day, "we stopped getting information from the FBI on the Bobby Baker investigation. Within a month the FBI men in the field wouldn't tell us anything. We started running out of gas." "Another stiletto from Bobby K," Hoover would write emphatically in a margin when allegations that the Bureau was letting up on crime passed across his desk. It was important to maintain the interval between the public's notion of what they were up to and the actual state of affairs. As for faint praise from this most demanding of the Kennedys: "We don't need any defense from A.G.K. It does us more harm than good."

"These people," Robert Kennedy decided aloud after two weeks, "don't work for us any more." For all Hoover's vagaries, Kennedy had to admit that the Bureau was "the best organized operation within the federal government," and Kennedy's great problem from November on would be to keep Hoover's meticulousness and efficiency from being zeroed in on him. "I knew that, within a few days, he was over at the White House giving dossiers on everybody that President Kennedy had appointed," Bob told Anthony Lewis shortly after resigning. He believed Hoover was tapping Secretary of Defense Robert McNamara's phone "because he thinks there's a conspiracy by McNamara and me to get rid of Hoover." Even before he stepped down, Bob's friend Gerald Tremblay saw how "the bitterness between him and J. Edgar Hoover took away a lot of the pleasure he got out of the Department of Justice."

Among the first victims of this Hoover-directed purge would be two seasoned Robert Kennedy operatives: Carmine Bellino, Joe Kennedy's seasoned bookkeeper still maintaining an eye on the numbers around the White House, and Paul Corbin, an abrasive, self-made, take-no-prisoners knockabout on the Democratic National Committee who was to advance men what Brumus was to dogs. Several of Jack Kennedy's advisers stayed on with the Johnson administration for quite a while, but Bob Kennedy's people were out.

Around the attorney general's office, fresh bruises were apparent wherever anybody looked. After almost three years of being precluded from contacting directly either the president or the White House staff, Hoover now bypassed the attorney general's office entirely and communicated ad nauseam with Johnson. Deke DeLoach, a good personal friend of Johnson's all-purpose aide-de-camp Walter Jenkins, instantly replaced Courtney Evans as the FBI's liaison with the White House. The Bureau now ignored the Department itself whenever clearing judicial nominees, and released its rushed assassination findings to the press without telling anybody, which irked Earl Warren.

It was a campaign of a thousand cuts. Whenever the attorney general flew around the country now there was no sedan from the Bureau to meet his plane. It didn't take many hours after JFK was declared deceased before the direct line from the attorney general's office rang. Hoover let it ring itself out, then barked: "Put that damn thing back on Miss Gandy's desk, where it belongs." Courtney Evans, needless to say, would soon be out of a job.

There had been rumors circulating to the effect that, come the second Kennedy administration, Evans might very well replace Hoover. Even the trim, sandy-haired Evans couldn't carry water on both shoulders while winds like that were blowing up, and he'd done very well to last as long as he had.

One of the stumbling blocks of the Oswald/Ruby investigation was the inconvenient fact that it was more evident day by day that there just might be some Mafia involvement here, but the Mafia experts were all in the Special Investigative Division specifically created to justify the promotion of Courtney Evans to assistant director. Hoover's original motive, to give the Kennedys a polished Irishman they could work with during the Rackets Committee days, had outlived its usefulness by November 22.

Hoover saw his job as largely to foreclose the assassination inquiry, not really to explain anything. He had turned the investigation over to Bill Sullivan's Domestic Intelligence Division. When Evans observed in a memo that, even granted that Oswald had fired the fateful weapon, "The problem is to show motive. A matter of this magnitude cannot be investigated in a week's time," Hoover scrawled across the bottom, in that argument-ending prose of his: "Just how long do you estimate it will take? It seems to me we have the basic facts now." No Mafia experts need apply. Close the investigation down.

Even in his great old age, Evans has about himself something of the deeply saddened, deeply amused quality associated with Jonathan Winters, especially in his Granny Frickert manifestation. He smiles his ancient, rather plangent smile at the very mention of those days. Before long the Director refused to speak to him. Abruptly shorn of responsibilities, an aimless figure drifting around the headquarters, Evans was in a quandary. No fool, Evans asked Al Belmont as to his probable future. "You have no future, Court," the plainspoken Belmont replied. By the middle of December 1964, Courtney Evans had been pushed out to go to work for Nick Katzenbach directly.

By May of 1964, increasingly cut off, Kennedy wrote the Director on the occasion of his fortieth anniversary in the job, lamenting that "In the past few months I have not had the pleasure of associating with you as closely as formerly. I regret this but would not want this occasion to pass without congratulating you on this milestone and wishing you well in the future."

Hoover sent an amiable reply noting how "Time flies by very fast indeed when a person is engaged in the type of work he enjoys doing," which bucked the depressed Kennedy up, momentarily. It was the emptiest of gestures. "I didn't speak to Bobby Kennedy that last six months he was in office," the Director announced to friends, patently pleased with himself.

Kennedy kept up appearances, but he was processing his vision of Hoover. Bob admitted all along that "I knew he didn't like me much," yet it "was not difficult. I mean, it wasn't an impossible relationship." But by the end of 1964, Kennedy would agree that Hoover was dangerous, although "it was a danger that we could control, that we were on top of, that we could deal with at the appropriate time." Later, reflecting aloud to John Bartlow Martin, he would concede that the aging Director was "rather a psycho. . . . I think it [the FBI] is a dangerous organization. He's senile and frightening."

Cut out by Hoover and operating vis-à-vis Johnson in an atmosphere of undisguised mutual distaste, Kennedy accomplished a surprising amount his last nine months in the executive branch. A lot of it was momentum. Under JFK, Lyndon Johnson had agreed to take over the Committee on Equal Employment Opportunities. As the prime sponsor of two related bills during the Eisenhower years, Johnson knew something about the subject, although insiders concluded that both had passed—and John Kennedy had voted for them—largely because Lyndon had watered them down to such an extent that even devout segregationists like Richard Russell found little to interrupt their sleep.

Still, times were changing. Bobby Baker would remember how agitated Johnson got when his black cook and her husband were repeatedly denied access to the comfort stations of Dixie while driving the Majority Leader's car from D.C. to Texas. Once the Kennedy administration settled in, Robert Kennedy later noted, his brother "always felt that Johnson, on civil rights, wanted to get too far involved in it—personally—[more] than was necessary." By 1964 the national polls reflected a populace aroused against Jim Crow; the issue was identified with the martyred JFK, and the public expected action. After a few months of grabbing shoulders and whispering nose-to-nose about huge public-works projects in some wavering Congressman's district and threatening and cajoling on the grand scale, Lyndon Johnson rammed through the extremely effective Civil Rights Act in 1964, followed by the even more effective Voting Rights Act in 1965.

As detailed earlier, Hoover got swept along. With his brother's reelection no longer a factor, Bobby was freed up politically to apply what pressure the Department still had. The mere appearance of Walter Sheridan and his Get-Hoffa-Squad headbreakers in the South was enough to rile Hoover's hairtrigger territorial instincts and pushed him to mandate the Bureau's COINTELPRO subversion of the Ku Klux Klan. Without the Klan, tooth-and-claw white supremacy was effectively defanged.

Another shift was occurring with organized crime. Kingpins around the country sighed with pleasure as the pressure came off after JFK went down; Sam Giancana could again take a leak without tightening up because of some burly fed at the next urinal. But Mortimer Caplin's Internal Revenue investigators were still on the prowl and heavily concentrated on organized crime personalities. By now a whole generation of FBI agents had been blooded when it came to going after the Mob, not merely as figures to shadow and overhear but more and more as hoodlums to clap into prison. Jimmy Hoffa got sent up. Before long, biting new legislation like the RICO Act would revolutionize law enforcement.

Hoover wasn't in any hurry. When Bob Kennedy gave a speech in Georgia in May 1964 during which he stated that Cosa Nostra convictions were up 700 percent over 1960, the Director studied a report on Kennedy's address from his SAC, Atlanta and underlined the statistic. "Is this correct?" he wrote below.

In an answering memo, the agile Courtney Evans attempted to put the boss's troubled old heart at rest. Convictions were up, but the Organized Crime and Racketeering Section "lumped into the figure . . . Labor Management Relations cases, any conviction of a member of the Teamsters, as well as any conviction in gambling matters." Small fry, not the influential dons.

Wave after wave of Great Society legislation included the sort of soft sociological initiatives Hoover detested. The 1964 Criminal Justice Act produced an office subject to the deputy attorney general to deal with social problems—narcotics, juvenile delinquency, even the right of privacy. Kennedy himself pushed the Community Relations Service into the Civil Rights Act, a mediation function directed by the outspoken meliorist Roger Wilkins to confront local disorders with compromise rather than force—a method antithetical to the working style of both Martin Luther King Jr. and J. Edgar Hoover. Every day involved slogging against his internal tide, but Robert Kennedy continued, intermittently, to make himself felt.

Much of his year was taken up with special projects. He led a party that flew to Indonesia in January and mediated a raging dispute between President Sukarno and Malaysia. In June, his brother Edward was very nearly killed in a plane crash in the Connecticut valley. A month later, Bob and Ethel dedicated a memorial in Berlin to the dead president before swinging through Poland, where Kennedy clambered up onto the top of a car in Warsaw and challenged an adoring mob.

It hadn't taken long before Bob styled himself the guardian of his brother's widow. After so many years as the overworked stable boy for a generation over which his brother Jack had long assumed the role of prince, Robert Kennedy now took upon himself the ancient biblical responsibilities. The two investigated Manhattan, where Jackie bought the fifteen-room co-op apartment at 1040 Fifth Avenue. Sans Ethel, they visited Bunny Mellon's vacation house in Antigua, where his sister-in-law introduced the stunned, questing Bobby to Edith Hamilton's *The Greek Way*. It opened him up to classical literature from Aeschylus to Herodotus. "He who learns must suffer," ran the screed from Agamemnon, "and even in our sleep pain that cannot forget, falls drop by drop upon the heart, and in our own despair, against our will, comes wisdom to us by the awful grace of God."

Not to have consummated this tragic intimacy would have bordered on the unnatural. "Well," Fred Dutton would subsequently concede, "he and Jackie consoled each other." A visitor to a house overlooking the Palm Beach compound reported watching Jackie sunbathing on the grass with her halter off as Bobby traipsed over to kneel beside her as they kissed, one hand above and the other below. To assist his sister-in-law with her relocation—the children's trust funds barely met running expenses—Bob donated fifty thousand dollars a year. The free-spending Ethel—forever badgered by the bookkeepers at Joseph P. Kennedy, Inc. to rein in costs, forced to keep the thermostats at Hickory Hill turned way down even in the dead of winter—started to bellyache openly about the "situation" involving her husband and Jackie.

Day to day, Lyndon Johnson was careful to calculate every move when dealing with Kennedy *or* Hoover. His decades of back-fence exchanges with Hoover—the two had been neighbors on Thirtieth Place since 1945—left very little mystique. Hoover would occasionally trip by on a Sunday morning for breakfast with the majority leader and Lady Bird and the two girls, or bestir himself to join the hunt when Edgar, the beagle he himself had given the family, got lost somewhere among the labyrinth of backyard hedges.

This did not mean that Hoover ever intended to give a pass to this towering, shrewd, very often quite uncouth and more often than not monumentally insecure Texan whom one well-aimed bullet had catapulted into the presidency. Confidential FBI files brimmed with documents detailing the doctored poll results that opened the way in 1948 for "Landslide Lyndon" to enter the Senate. Johnson's long, hard-worked association with Billie Sol Estes had gotten a lot of Bureau attention, as well as a vote-buying ruse brought off in Laredo County in 1956.

There were, of course, many women, pre and post the massive 1955 coronary. Johnson had a son by a very talkative constituent. "Have you ever seen anything as big as this?" he would sometimes challenge a colleague before the Capitol urinals, swinging around the beloved member he liked to refer to as "Jumbo" and, according to Marshall Frady, "shaking it in almost a brandishing manner as he began discoursing about some pending legislation." Along with Helen Gahagan Douglas and Clare Boothe Luce—whom Lyndon labeled *mechanical*—the Leader had availed himself of legions of available females; the visionary Lady Bird had long since concluded that "it would be unnatural for him to withhold love from half the people."

Here was a president who routinely invited staffers of both sexes to barge in and exchange ideas while he was defecating. Under any circumstances, there really wasn't much of a basis for authentic rapport between him and Robert Kennedy, who disliked being touched. Midway through a Redskins game, while LBJ sat watching with owner Edward Bennett Williams, Bob Kennedy turned up and started knocking on the door of the box. "Let him pound," the president commanded. Williams attempted to square things with Kennedy the next day. Nevertheless, politics were politics, and both leaders attempted to restrain themselves as 1964 took shape. The outstanding question remained for some months: would Johnson need Kennedy to get himself reelected in November 1964?

Once Barry Goldwater won the Republican nomination on July 15, Johnson concluded that Kennedy wouldn't be necessary, explaining to the divided attorney general that the party would be vulnerable in the border states and the Midwest. "His Adam's apple going up and down like a Yo-yo," in Johnson's retelling, Kennedy had mumbled "I think I could have been of help to you."

Johnson let it be known that he was going to omit from consideration as a running mate any cabinet member or anybody who met regularly with the cabinet. Rather hollowly, Kennedy cracked that he was sorry to have taken so many good men over the side with himself.

Yet Johnson remained apprehensive that, with Bobby still aboard, something could go wrong. "This fella looks at me like he's gonna look a hole through me, like I'm a spy or something," LBJ told John Connally before the 1964 Democratic convention in Atlantic City. After huffing that he would resign at once if Jack Kennedy ever attempted to exploit the Bureau for political purposes, Hoover found himself authorizing Bureau agents to serve as bodyguards on Air Force One or attend on street corners when the presidential motorcade passed. Deke DeLoach and thirty wiremen and undercover agents from the FBI descended on Atlantic City with orders to infiltrate the King and RFK delegations. "There's some thought that Attorney General Kennedy might try to stampede the convention," DeLoach remarked to an agent at the time, and he would shortly inform Hoover that "we were able to keep the White House fully apprised of all major developments during the Convention's course."

Days before the August convention, Robert Kennedy had announced his candidacy for the Senate in New York. The campaign against the moderate Republican Kenneth Keating was harder than anybody expected. Lyndon Johnson, headed for a landslide against Goldwater, appeared in the state to perform on platforms with Kennedy. As executive director of Johnson's campaign, Kenny O'Donnell did what he had to to keep the LBJ loyalists from sabotaging Bobby. In public, Johnson hugged Kennedy and called him "ma boy." Kennedy won by a little over 700,000 votes, although Johnson carried New York by 2.7 million. Johnson's participation had probably secured his Senate seat for Kennedy, but Kennedy refrained from mentioning the president in his victory statement.

As a young lawyer, Ronald Goldfarb had approached his boss in the Justice Department tentatively—"I thought Robert Kennedy was a little fascist from the days he worked for McCarthy"—but Kennedy's intensity about racket-busting had won him over, and Goldfarb pitched in with the New York campaign. Profound changes were obviously occurring. "Such a haunting and dominant personality while he was going through his Hamlet stage," Goldfarb sighs.

Bob wasn't a particularly happy senator. Two hotspur lawyers from the Justice Department, Peter Edelman and Adam Walinsky, moved in to staff his office. Frank Mankiewicz handled press. "Bob didn't do an awful lot," Fred Dutton observes. "He was a quite intense human being. As often as not he would come grumpy to the office, and he wouldn't work it off." Bobby had taken to carrying Jack's old, oversized, discarded tweed coat around, forever leaving it in a car or a hotel room so that he had to send an aide back to retrieve it.

"I found him to be humorless, basically," remarks one of the heavy hitters Ted brought in to advise him. "He could be flippant and fresh, but his humor, to the extent it was humor, was biting, it was sort of attack humor. Narrow." Around the Senate, Bob's attendance was spotty and the reception anybody might get impossible to predict. In hearing rooms or on the floor of the Senate, noticed Ted Kennedy's savvy administrative assistant, David Burke, "you always had the feeling that Robert was ready to explode." The entire deliberative process of the Senate obviously made him nervous, too slow, few if any results.

The ageless Melody Miller was just breaking into politics as a volunteer in Robert Kennedy's Senate office in 1965 and remembers Brumus especially. The hulking, lethargic Newfoundland was regularly sprawled across the entrance to Bobby's inner quarters, delivering a low growl as if to challenge the visitor to justify the seriousness of his business before he was to be permitted to step over the recumbent beast and confront the lurking occupant.

Robert Kennedy himself was sworn in just as his brother Edward was hobbling back to work, propped up inside a steel brace, a line of vertebrae cracked from the airplane crash. In two years, Ted had laid the keel of what would turn into perhaps the most broadly effective career in the Senate during the twentieth century. His patience and intense day-and-night application and talent for collegiality had already made him a kind of apprentice member of "the club," that small knot of Senate insiders who effectively ran the place.

To find himself subordinated to the baby of the Kennedy family, this larky kid who carried the bags for and clowned around with his abstemious elder brothers and predictably got drunk and cranked out rendition after rendition of "Hooray for Hollywood" to their amusement—this seemed the terminal absurdity. I was researching my first book on Edward Kennedy during those years, and inevitably I interviewed Bob. Ted had just made a significant speech on the floor of the Senate, and I put in a good word about Ted's remarks.

Robert Kennedy looked at me a moment, those opaque rather baleful eyes narrowing beneath their slanting folds. "Well," he said finally, "I wonder who wrote it for him."

Bobby was soon well aware that more than two years' seniority separated the brothers. Teddy, whose skills as a gentle tweaker of the pretentious are unrivaled, did what he could to help. Ted's legislative assistant of the era, Dun Gifford, remembers watching Bob take it upon himself to explain the import of some pending amendment to the colleagues "even if he wasn't sure himself exactly what it meant. When he got going on one of these rambles, Ted would whisper or write, 'Well, you just lost Lister—stop talking and let's vote, or you'll lose all the others too,' or, 'Don't you wish you were in the club so you wouldn't have to do all this?' or, 'Do you want me to bail you out?'"

At times, Bobby radiated both the wariness and the low-grade fear of a caged animal. I remember watching him from the Senate press gallery. He moved almost furtively on the floor, darting quick looks over his shoulder.

By the middle sixties Bob had started to let his hair grow; critics on the Right were calling him the Fifth Beatle. His identification with the young, the non-white, the dispossessed was further estranging him from many of his lobby-driven, business-as-usual fellow senators.

Never one to miss an opportunity, Lyndon Johnson made sure to keep Bob from getting too comfortable in the Senate by granting unwelcome favors like honoring Joe Kennedy's demand and nominating Francis X. Morrissey, a municipal judge in Boston and a beloved coatholder to the Ambassador, as a district judge. Both Ted and Bob struggled to prop up the cheerful, spectacularly unqualified dispenser of traffic tickets, but Frank Morrissey couldn't get enough support. The FBI supplied chapter and verse on Morrissey's lackluster performance on the bench to Everett Dirksen, who dismantled him with surgical eloquence throughout the hearings. As one who plugged credentials hard while he was attorney general, the incident hurt Robert Kennedy, which Lyndon no doubt anticipated.

More and more, Bob Kennedy was living his life away from Washington, pumping up the public's recognition of him as a celebrity on the edge. In Chile he confronted a gymnasium packed with angry Marxist students, well fortified with eggs and garbage to throw. On the Amazon, he swam out of a dugout canoe in piranha-infested waters. As they paddled around, Kennedy intoned to the petrified Richard Goodwin that, while "It was impossible to pinpoint the exact time and place when he decided to run for president . . . the idea seemed to take hold as he was swimming in the Amazonian river of Nhamunda." The fact remained that "Piranhas have never been known to bite a U.S. Senator."

When Bobby insisted on struggling up Mount Kennedy in the Yukon with Everest veteran Jim Whittaker, his paralyzed father in Hyannis Port all but attacked the television set, crowing "'Naaaaa, naaaa, naaaa' at the top of his voice," Joe Kennedy's nurse would subsequently write. "He would shake his fist at the set and scream, or if he found a picture in the paper of Bobby in his mountain gear, he would angrily grind it into a ball and throw it across the room."

Reduced to an inarticulate onlooker, the stricken financier had been sidelined bit by bit, even by his devoted family. There had been a time, earlier in his endless efforts at rehabilitation, when there had been some hope of recovering perhaps a measure of speech and movement in a New York clinic. That had quickly foundered—the patient remained demanding and impatient, and his primary caregiver, Ann Gargan, never seemed that interested. There were repeated efforts to get him out into the world—visits to the offices at Park Avenue, Inc., where nervous and confused staffers attempted to show the frustrated and often seemingly incoherent old man important papers which were coming through. Before Jack was shot, a White House lunch had been arranged for Jack, Bobby, Joe, and his old comrade J. Edgar Hoover. It would be hard to conjure up a more bewildering social event.

People did what they could to keep Joe's spirits up. Throughout her Onassis period, Jacqueline made it a point to stop in often, sitting through what mealtimes were possible and patiently and lovingly wiping food and drool from the convalescent's trembling mouth as he attempted to eat. When the Red Sox won the pennant in 1967, Bobby and Teddy joined their wizened father to watch the key game. A member of the household staff remembers an early autumn afternoon when a stiff figure in his wheelchair, wrapped heavily against the weather, was rushed out on the dock at Hyannis Port to watch his children swimming. Through some seeming mishap, the wheelchair tumbled off the edge of the dock and into the frigid water; the boys scrambled over to rescue their father, only to find out that it was a well-shrouded dummy. Watching from the house, the founding father evinced signs of amusement.

The schedule of outside visitors thinned out, year by year. Toward the very end, according to Kennedy chauffeur Frank Saunders, most regular in attendance were Morton Downey, Carroll Rosenbloom, and Joe E. Lewis, the Mobbed-up comedian who so regularly amused the financier over the many decades at syndicate hangouts. The struggling financier needed cheering up. People closest to the old man perceived how alarmed he got at what he clearly regarded as Bobby's self-destructive foolhardiness.

Barrett Prettyman Jr. remembers a sailing trip with Bobby under threatening conditions in "an old boat he had borrowed from some guy. A storm hit, and the next thing you know, when we're all clinging to each other and everything we can hold on to, on the foghorn we heard this voice, saying, 'Senator, your daughter Kathleen has fallen off a horse and is in a hospital.' And Bobby was about to jump overboard, and Ethel *screamed* at him, and told him he had to put a life vest on. And he didn't want to. But he put it on, and jumped overboard and disappeared. Finally came up. And the other boat, which couldn't get close to us, because we were all bangin' back and forth so much, finally got him aboard. Took him back—turned out she was okay. Everybody on our boat was sick. A boom came around and hit young Joe in the back. I thought he'd broken his back. Oh, God—

what a trip! We limped in. I wrote Ethel a note thanking her for a delightful day on the sea. . . ."

Thomas Corcoran, the nephew of Tommy the Cork and himself one of the great downhill ski racers of the period, was also on that chaotic sailing expedition and offers a few more lively details. "Once the sea built up and this smoky sou'wester came in from behind," Corcoran recalls, "we started to learn that a lot of the equipment of the boat really didn't work. . . . Meanwhile, we're running before the wind, and the only people who knew anything about sailing were Ethel and [his former wife] Birdie and myself. The captain went down below and locked himself in his cabin. True story. We were towing a big Boston Whaler on a long line behind and the seas were getting so big that it just snapped the line. The engine didn't work. The radios were broken. . . . As it turned out, we finally pulled in to Tarpaulin Cove and dropped the sails and put the hook down and spent the night. And it wasn't until the next morning, as I recall, that the Coast Guard came back and took everybody off this boat.

"Finally, the next morning, the captain came out of his cabin. Ethel put her hands around his throat. I think that if she had not been pulled off she would have killed the guy. . . ."

These flirtations with death occurred again and again that year. Corcoran remembers a jaunt down the Colorado River with the Kennedys. "The whole family were risk-takers. *Huge* risk-takers. I know that Ethel was very, very proud of all her kids taking risks. The Kennedys invited us to go down the Colorado River with them, on rafts. On that trip was Buchwald, Willi Schaeffler, the ski coach—his usual menagerie of unlikely people. George Plimpton. Jim Whittaker.

"In any event, we were goin' down the Colorado River, and you could hear the rapids ahead of you as you went down. And Kennedy heard them and jumped over the side of the raft without a life preserver on. And so all of them jumped overboard after him. The boatmen were *horrified*. And it sort of put a lot of pressure on anybody else that was along on this thing to follow. And stupidly, I did.

"So they went through the rapids and pulled up on a beach below the rapids. The only guy that was missing was me. I had got caught in a whirlpool over on one side. It kept thrown' me up to get air, and then it sucked me down again. It took probably five minutes to figure out how to get out of this thing, to find a side I could swim out on. Anyhow, I showed up down below. Everybody was relieved. But it was incredibly stupid. There could have been a lot of kids' lives lost."

It was as if violence might be expected to syncopate now all through Bob Kennedy's remaining few years. In September of 1966 Pamela Markham and her sister were at boarding school in Connecticut when they got word that their father, Bob Kennedy's Harvard roommate Dean Markham, and Ethel's brother George Skakel had been killed in a plane crash while out West "hunting or rounding up wild horses, I don't remember which," Pamela remarks.

She was seventeen. Within hours Robert Kennedy showed up in the *Caroline* to conduct the girls home to D.C. Halfway through the flight Kennedy pressed a cup of hot tomato soup on the upset Pamela, which she promptly upchucked. She can still recall the solicitude with which Bob "cleaned her up, almost like a nurse." On landing, Bobby personally drove the girls home and turned them over to her mother. From then on he was careful to remain very close to this shattered family.

Very little of anybody's private life is conducive to legislation, but whatever got out fed an ever-widening perception of Robert Kennedy as something more than human, a Byronic personality too big for Lyndon Johnson's Washington. Hoover—superlative con man that he was, and himself one of the great riggers of publicity—could see where this was going. Once was enough.

Like a regional commander calling down air strikes, Hoover began to target the New York senator. The first salvo landed while Kennedy was still attorney general, courtesy of Roy Cohn, busy dodging the gathering charges of Robert Morgenthau's stubborn prosecutors. A strapping, outspoken lawyer and U.S. Congressman from Bayonne, New Jersey, Cornelius ("Neil") Gallagher, had dealt with a minor pornography charge brought against Roy Cohn arising out of his association with the Union News Company. Over time, the two attorneys fell into an easygoing drinks-after-work relationship; Gallagher several times brought his wife on a visit to the Cohn uptown mansion for dinner with Muddy and plenty of inside political gossip. Bluff and self-assured, the holder of many decorations including three purple hearts and an outstanding combat record, Gallagher had been identified by Lyndon Johnson as the perfect Roman Catholic for his short list of running mates in 1964 until Hoover himself spiked the whole idea.

Roy never scrupled to lean on Gallagher to throw the latest encomium to the Director, some Girl Scout award or a testimonial from an American Legion post, into the *Congressional Record* as a sop to the glory-loving chief of the FBI. The Cohn Gallagher knew had evolved as much in a decade as had Robert Kennedy. Unscrupulous in his business dealings, Cohn now came over as a swart, refulgently smiling, easily forgiving fixer of problems of every dimension. With clients who ultimately ranged from the great universities of New York City and the Catholic diocese to John Gotti and Joe Marcello, Carlos's brother, Cohn was by every definition an executive-level rainmaker in Gotham. Pounded by the IRS, Cohn made money and spent money in vast, untraceable amounts. He pled a lot of cases pro bono.

When Bob Kennedy abruptly put down his base in Manhattan, he found himself forced to pitch hard for support from the likes of Richard Berlin, who managed the Hearst empire, very close to Cohn since they were schoolmates. When Abe Beame ran for mayor, Kennedy had no choice except to campaign for Beame, well aware that Cohn was deeply involved as Beame's major fund-raiser and strategist and routinely represented the Mob's Tammany interests.

Neil Gallagher had remained a "true believer" when it came to Hoover. But he had never cared much for Joe McCarthy or his methods, and once he got onto the House Committee on Government Operations his concern at the range of government-mandated invasiveness led him to chair the Privacy Subcommittee.

One day Roy Cohn called and told Neil that "a friend of ours would like to come down to see you on Monday or Tuesday. . . ." When the friend turned up, it was Sid Zagri, the head lobbyist for the Teamsters, loaded down with documents intended to discredit Robert Kennedy and the strike force and IRS knuckledusters currently roiling the underworld. "We would like you," Zagri said to Gallagher, "to use this as the basis of hearings."

Gallagher threw Zagri out of his office. Roy showed up the next day. "I'm too young and virginal to get mixed up in this pissing contest," Gallagher protested to Cohn.

"The FBI did that full investigation," Cohn explained. The documents "all come from Mr. Hoover and Mr. Deke DeLoach." If Gallagher mounted hearings, "Mr. Hoover will be forever grateful," as would "Jimmy." "They'll support you in your next election, whatever you want, and they'll even hire your law firm for $100,000 a year."

It was still no. "You're going to be sorry," Cohn said.

Gallagher grabbed him by the necktie. "Say, listen, you little son of a bitch, are you threatening me?"

Not exactly, Cohn said, "but I know how they work."

"Who works?"

"The Bureau. If you're not their friend, you're their enemy." If Gallagher wouldn't help, Cohn said, there was always Everett Dirksen or Edward Long over on the Senate side.

Hoover saw his next opportunity when the Senate's Subcommittee on Administrative Practices and Procedure, chaired by the rotund Edward Long of Missouri, started to hold hearings in 1965 into the "armory of electronic snooping devices" the government agencies had started to exploit against helpless citizens. The subcommittee would begin with mail covers, then open up wireline abuses. Long was an outspoken champion of Jimmy Hoffa and a close collaborator with the Teamsters' mobbed-up lawyer, Morris Shenker, from whom he had already pocketed $48,000 over the previous two years. The syndicate was continuously agitated now about electronic surveillance. Furthermore, Long was "out to get Bobby," Bill Moyers tipped Dick Goodwin. "Johnson is egging him on." Deke DeLoach volunteered the resources of the Bureau.

The trick for Hoover here was to immunize the FBI from any unwanted poking around in its own, at best, quasilegal scrounging up of millions of details about the personal lives of numberless citizens while directing the subcommittee toward capers like the alleged bugging and tapping of jury rooms by Walter Sheridan's technicians throughout the Hoffa proceedings. Hoover contrived to offload the defense of FBI practices onto the guileless Nicholas Katzenbach, who had become acting attorney general in September 1964, simultaneously alerting Justice Committee Chairman James Eastland to look out for the Bureau behind the scenes.

It helped that the Bureau's wonderfully productive microphones in Fred Black's copious courtesy suite at the Sheraton Carlton kept turning up evidence that Shenker, by that stage, had run up Long's take well over $100,000. Deke DeLoach, the sonorous Dutch uncle you never forgot could doom your future, explained to Long that compelling an FBI official to testify would "open a Pandora's box, insofar as our enemies in [the] press are concerned." Hoover himself prepared a statement which asserted that "official records . . . make it indelibly clear that the FBI used microphones, as well as wiretaps, during Robert Kennedy's administration of the Justice Department with Mr. Kennedy's knowledge and approval." When Kennedy attempted to get Katzenbach to come back with a statement that as attorney general he, Kennedy, was unaware of the Black microphones or bugging in general, Katzenbach hedged. Kennedy was miffed.

* * *

At a certain level, Long's investigation amounted to a flanking action designed not only for Hoover's purposes but more immediately to provide diversionary cover to Roy Cohn. In full throat, Robert Morgenthau's prosecutors were tearing into Cohn's affairs. By 1966, Cohn and his worried associates had slipped into control of four rather shaky Chicago banks, several with fluctuating assets sloshing back and forth so as to permit such providential commitments as a $65,000 loan to the influential conservative columnist William F. Buckley to purchase a sloop, or $100,000 (unsecured) to Senator Edward Long to finance a chain of high-interest lenders in Missouri. Long's inexperienced son-in-law drew a large salary at one of the banks as chairman. Along with guaranteeing Cohn a legally defensible mechanism for providing important officials with payoffs, Cohn's unexpected emergence as a banker permitted Hoover—through Cohn—to assure himself that Long's dangerous privacy hearings would cut a proper channel. Not that Hoover didn't have plenty of transcripts linking Long to organized crime, if he needed them.

The personal relationship between Cohn and Hoover, while maintained for the record in their constant exchange of polite, mutually laudatory notes, provided opportunities for Hoover to keep Cohn in line with the occasional quick, threatening pinch the Director could deliver like nobody else. In 1963 Cohn's house was burglarized and an assortment of films produced by a company in which Cohn had an interest was taken. Cohn would characterize the art product as "kinky—even to me." In time, Cohn discovered that Hoover had the films. "It was a warning to me never to get too far out of line," Cohn understood. "I thought I was making a joke when I told him to enjoy them. He didn't crack a smile when he told me that he already was." Cohn could tolerate anything; he remained the principal conduit between the Director and the New York columnists, a tremendous plus for Hoover's prestige-enhancing publicity machine.

Like Hoover as a young man, Cohn was at a point in the embellishment of his legend when it was useful to project himself as, at the very minimum, bisexual. He swanked around town with Barbara Walters and the designer Carol Horn. Cohn would ultimately assert that "Hoover was too scared of his own desires to even *have* relationships—male or female." During a late interview, Cohn called Hoover "the most frightened man I ever met," terrified that something he did "would impact that all-important image of his. He would never do anything that would compromise his position as head of the FBI—*ever*."

Subsequently, assessing Hoover's fundamental nature, Cohn would prove willing to take it deeper. Well beyond dispensing disinformation at this point, in the deathbed autobiography he composed with Sidney Zion, Cohn nailed Hoover by way of allusion. "Are you familiar with the term 'killer fruit?'" he quoted Truman Capote. "It's a certain kind of queer who has Freon refrigerating his bloodstream. Diaghilev, for example. J. Edgar Hoover, Hadrian."

What Hoover expected from Cohn in return for those Cuban panatelas at Christmas was access to Roy Cohn's serviceable Mob connections. Even at the second remove, Hoover could easily control Edward Long and his ambitious privacy investigations with a nod to Roy, who just might call in the bank loans that underwrote Long's loan-sharking empire. By influencing his underworld clients to pressure Morris Shenker and the Teamsters, Cohn was in a position either to choke off Long's political survival or keep him going. It would be the publicity that surfaced detailing the $100,000 payoff Long got from Shenker that knocked Long out of the 1968 Democratic primary in Missouri and compelled him to end his career in the penitentiary.

What was expected of Long in 1966 was a flamboyant effort to unearth evidence against the Kennedy Justice Department, exculpating material to spring Jimmy Hoffa. Long contacted DeLoach in search of "any information reflecting that [Walter] Sheridan tapped wires for Bobby Kennedy" or scuttlebutt about Ed Jones, the Kennedy family surveillance specialist still ensconced at Immigration and Naturalization.

At that point Robert Kennedy was settling uneasily into the Senate. Outraged that responsibility for all this distasteful snooping was starting to devolve on *him,* Kennedy agreed to make an appearance before Long and his exacting subcommittee counsel Bernard Fensterwald if other attorneys general were called and if Hoover himself would appear with all his files on the subject. When an article by the disaffected Teamster leader Sam Baron entitled "I Was Near the Top of Jimmy's Drop-Dead List" appeared fortuitously in *Life,* its timing and thrust, to retroactively trash Hoffa, were attributed in a release by Roy Cohn to Kennedy's vindictive media machine. The hectored-looking freshman senator did show up before his committee colleagues to protest heatedly that he had merely referred a reporter to sources. Long quoted Kennedy as pledging: "I'll get Long in the end."

With all this chaff in the air, Hoover sensed his opportunity. In 1964 Fred Black had finally been charged and convicted for tax evasion, and as the extent of the government's surveillance of his Sheraton Carlton hospitality suite became public, Black's lawyer Edward Bennett Williams got the Supreme Court to throw out his conviction on grounds that evidence from such relentless invasion of privacy was inadmissible in a court. The question now animated the nation's editorial columns: Who *authorized* the FBI's bugging of Black? Hoover made it simple: Bobby did it. In a public exchange of letters with his acolyte, Congressman H. R. Gross of Iowa, Hoover stressed that not only was Kennedy "briefed frequently regarding such matters," including the installations in Black's suite, and "exhibited great interest in pursuing" them but also "while in different areas, not only listened to the results of microphone surveillances, but raised questions relative to the obtaining of better equipment."

As proof, Hoover made available such documents as a request Kennedy had signed in 1961 to New York City to lease specified telephone lines in "connection with microphone surveillances." There was a 1961 paper in the files from Kennedy requesting a bug at the Sheridan Carlton on a Mob lawyer, evidently James Haggerty. Affidavits from FBI agents in Chicago and New York emphasized that Robert Kennedy was spellbound listening to the tapes produced by microphones insinuated into the lounges and behind the loading platforms of senior mobsters.

Kennedy's office responded that "Apparently Mr. Hoover had been misinformed" and referred reporters to a letter Kennedy solicited from Courtney Evans, by then in private practice. Evans stated that "Since prior Attorneys General had informed the FBI that the use of microphones, as contrasted to telephone taps, need not be specifically approved by the Attorney General, I did not discuss the uses of any of these devices with you in national security or other cases, nor did I know of any written material that was sent to you at any time. . . ." This statement dovetailed poorly with earlier Evans memos in which he defined his "liaison responsibilities as an FBI official to keep Bobby K. from 'going wild' in connection with investigative matters."

Caught in the middle, Attorney General Nicholas Katzenbach struggled to avoid a situation in which, as he put his dilemma to DeLoach, "former Attorney General Kennedy would make one claim and the FBI would make another type of claim." DeLoach emphasized that the Bureau "did not want the over-all impression to get out that the FBI had operated in an uncontrollable manner in these activities." They were not "a bunch of private eyes."

Nothing was foreclosed, Hoover scrawled into the margin between paragraphs, if "Kennedy continues to feed out untrue information." He surmised that "There must be a penetration of our files to bring up memos to support our position." The Director was obviously shaken that Kennedy would impugn the honor of the Bureau in so public a way. A piece by Dave Kraslow, who worked under Ed Guthman at the *Los Angeles Times,* urging Long to direct his probe at the FBI, prompted Katzenbach to maintain that Kennedy wouldn't pull such a trick. "Just how gullible can he be!" the steamed-up Director scratched between the paragraphs.

Kennedy supporters would claim that anything Kennedy happened to listen to had been taped off microphones presumably planted by local police. That sounded pretty thin. The disenchanted Ed Silberling, who ran the Justice Department's Organized Crime and Racketeering Section with steadily diminishing authority from February 1, 1961 to February 1, 1963, may well have reflected his disappointment at having been elbowed out of his job because certain of his investigations involved Kennedy political assets. He responded to reporters' questions by summoning up the neophyte attorney general of 1961 who pushed the FBI hard to use more "technical equipment" against organized crime. "Everybody . . . knew" that Kennedy "was talking about electronic surveillance—parabolic microphones, spike microphones, bugs—that is, microtransmitters—the whole thing."

All this open furor about electronic surveillance was forcing the administration's hand. Dependent as he was on ambivalent authorization dating back to the Roosevelt era, Hoover was forever writing admonitions like "Let's keep this to a minimum" on requests to surveil. Most of the black bag jobs and bugging installations involved breaking and entering—"trespass"—for which there was uncertain legal cover. As with Black, snooping tainted the evidence. On June 30, 1965, Lyndon Johnson's office distributed a memo which sharply abridged permissible electronic penetrations. The ACLU and the organized criminal community were overjoyed.

However witting Kennedy may have been, Hoover's sense of grievance was deepening. He had been lured into a public forum and labeled a liar. He was not finished with Robert Kennedy yet.

As the sixties deepened, other developments conspired to mousetrap Bobby. Concerned that Jim Bishop, a producer of popularized, sensational treatments of historical incidents, was working on a book about the day of the assassination, the Kennedys arranged to have an author of their own write up the event. Jackie would use the word "hired," and in fact the contract between William Manchester and Harpers pretty largely gave editorial control of the manuscript to the Kennedy faction, invariably a truly bad idea.

Manchester himself was a Kennedy-worshipping, extraordinarily high-strung young historian who over the decades would produce a series of biographies of very large distinction. He had been wounded critically in the head as a Marine officer fighting in the South Pacific. Robert Kennedy had already generated murmurs of bad publicity with his heavy-handed treatment of Red Fay, Jack's PT-boat buddy, whose charming and fundamentally appreciative memoir of his friend got thoroughly gone over by Bobby for what Kennedy regarded as overly familiar references to family members.

When Manchester's first draft of *The Death of a President* began making the rounds, reservations started to collect. With the Kennedys opening a number of normally bolted doors for the author, unexpected details were finding their way into the manuscript. Hoover had somehow made time for Manchester and, along with the usual boilerplate, informed Manchester that the FBI had passed along to the Dallas police a tip that Oswald was going to be murdered once he was removed from the Dallas City Jail. But the Dallas authorities insisted on accommodating the "communications media."

As to John Kennedy's efforts at détente, "The Director told Manchester that he had always felt it better to kick individuals like Khrushchev in the shins once in a while rather than to boot-lick them. The Director explained that Khrushchev was basically an Oriental and that individuals opposing Orientals usually lost face in the Oriental's opinion when fear or trepidation was shown."

Part of the problem with Manchester's unedited material was emphasis. There was an opening scene in which Johnson takes his queasy running mate Jack Kennedy out deer hunting on the LBJ ranch. Johnson came through instantly as a kill-hungry primitive, boorish and overbearing. The whole rendition couldn't help but bring to mind Bobby's own overnight stopover on the Johnson ranch during the autumn of 1959. Coerced into tracking after the Majority Leader in search of quarry, Bobby spotted a deer and let fly with a borrowed shotgun. The recoil knocked him flat and the butt of the weapon cut his brow. Johnson reached way down to assist the candidate's kid brother to his feet. "Son," Johnson had suggested, "you've got to learn to handle a gun like a man."

Anecdotes degrading to a sitting president are rarely well received by commercial publishers, and before long the editors at Harpers were visiting the author in his cottage at Essex, Connecticut. They found Manchester overwrought—he had been writing with a pencil, and his fingers were bleeding. The publisher was already hemmed in—all profits after the first forty thousand copies were slated to go to a Kennedy Memorial Fund—and what the editors had reviewed so far promised big trouble—lawsuits. "I was disturbed by the fact that Lyndon Johnson was seen as a villain," Evan Thomas Sr. would testify in an oral history. "It as almost as though Manchester was saying that Lyndon Johnson was somehow implicated in the assassination."

Manchester responded that Kennedy intermediaries John Seigenthaler and Ed Guthman had cleared the material, and for some months the pileup of serious objections was on the publishers' side. Nobody wanted to put Jacqueline Kennedy through the ordeal of recapitulating, page after page, the worst day of her life.

What seemed to stir Jackie Kennedy out of her lethargy was word that William Manchester's agent had sold the first serial rights to his book to *Look* magazine for a great deal of money—money on which the Kennedy group had no claim. It came to Jackie how frankly she had confessed even the most intimate details of her final hours with her husband to Manchester, secrets concerning her children. She filed suit to enjoin publication of both the book and the excerpts. Manchester had been edited to an extent by then, he told his agent, "where, if the integrity of my manuscript is violated, I have no wish to go on living. . . ."

Well before matters got quite that heavy, Robert Kennedy had anticipated that the publicity this mess was generating would hurt. "Why don't you go ahead and publish the damn book? Get it over with! Get it over with!" he had repeatedly urged Thomas. "My crazy sister-in-law," he exclaimed to Frank Mankiewicz. Jacqueline was being quoted as having assured Manchester coldly that "Anybody who is against me will look like a rat unless I run off with Eddie Fisher," an allusion to Elizabeth Taylor's latest escapade. The remark generated an outstanding cover for *Esquire*.

It got settled, but the nationwide perception of the Kennedy survivors as self-interested Café Society brats, prepared at any moment to chop up anybody not completely subservient to Camelot, arrived as an overlay to the bugging revelations thrown off by the fight with Hoover. By March 1967, Robert Kennedy's Harris poll numbers as opposed to Lyndon Johnson's were shockingly off: he trailed the president 39-61 percent. During the previous autumn, he had led Johnson by a full six points.

Even moves Kennedy made in line of duty, as a committed senator, smacked to many of grandstanding. While Lyndon Johnson was stampeding through the Congress the epic reforms known collectively as the War on Poverty, Kennedy seemed to be making it his business to seek out and publicize life in those intractable pockets of squalor and photogenic misery even the best-intentioned public programs were unlikely to relieve. "His judgments were very quick, the attractiveness of it was that it was all black and white," David Burke will comment now. "You were either good or bad. And therefore if you were poor and deprived it was unconscionable, what was happening to these people. So someone has to pay. . . ."

Wherever Bobby went, observers came away with the sense that this wasn't so much a Senate initiative, or even a United States initiative—it was a Kennedy initiative. To reclaim the Brooklyn slum in Bedford-Stuyvesant, Kennedy made a few telephone calls to acquaintances from Andre Meyer to Tom Watson of IBM and inaugurated a development corporation to resuscitate the neighborhoods. Like Walter Sheridan and the Get-Hoffa Squad, the whole effort proceeded alongside various governmental programs, but entirely under Robert Kennedy's direction.

He arranged for hearings of the Senate Subcommittee on Migratory Labor in support of César Chávez's *huelga* to boycott Schenley Industries, whose vast vineyards were properties of Lewis Rosenstiel, a sponsor to both Roy Cohn and J. Edgar Hoover. He mastered the tragic statistics concerning life on Indian reservations. In Mississippi with the Senate Labor Committee's Subcommittee on Poverty, Robert Kennedy sat deeply moved in a sharecropper's dank, stinking shack in the Delta rubbing a starving black child's swollen rat-bitten belly while tears trickled down his own cheeks. Magazine journalists and photographers swarmed in his wake. Invited by a student union to speak in South Africa, Kennedy bounced by helicopter around the tortured and petrified misery of apartheid, decrying "those who cling to a present which is already dying, who prefer the illusion of security to the excitement and danger which comes from even the most peaceful progress."

Radicalized by sorrow, Kennedy was emerging into a place fewer and fewer could follow him. Junketing through South America during the Lyndon Johnson ascendancy, Robert Kennedy paused to confront the State Department careerist who had been explaining Washington's new policy to him. "Well, Mr. Vaughn," Kennedy responded, "let me see if I understand what you're saying. You're saying that what the Alliance for Progress has come down to is that if you outlaw political parties and close down the Congress and put people in jail, you can get all the aid you want. But if you mess around with an American oil company, then you don't get anything. Is that about right?"

"Yeah," said the foreign service officer, "that's about right."

It was too much sometimes. "What do you think of Che Guevara?" Kennedy demanded one day of Roger Baldwin, founder of the American Civil Liberties Union and a good contact over the decades for J. Edgar Hoover.

"Guevara? I think he is a bandit," Baldwin said.

"I think he is a revolutionary hero," Kennedy said.

It had been several years by then since Kennedy had devoted a good part of his waking day to getting Guevara killed.

And So He Gave Them That

It was not totally unexpected, therefore, when Robert Kennedy began to emerge as a critic of the war in Vietnam. What puzzled many collaborators, from the antiwar movement's Johnny Appleseed Allard Lowenstein to livewires in his office like Jeff Greenfield and Adam Walinsky, was why he took so long.

"There is enough blame to go around," Kennedy admitted in an early statement in opposition to the Johnson administration's policies. In October 1951, he had accompanied his brother the Congressman on a third-world junket. In Saigon, a city besieged by guerrillas, the young Kennedys had met Bao Dai, the corrupt, French-installed head of state, and the commanding French general de Lattre de Tassigny, a Gaullist resistance hero. Both brothers were less than impressed, and Bob had written his father: "Our mistake has been not to insist on definite political reforms by the French toward the natives as prerequisites to any aid. As it stands now, we are becoming more and more involved in the war to a point where we can't back out."

This was a period during which Joseph P. Kennedy and other prominent Catholic laymen and global thinkers like Francis Cardinal Spellman were conspiring with the mystical nationalist Ngo Dinh Diem, lying low at Maryknoll preparatory to the establishment of a Catholic-dominated republic in South Vietnam. There had been meetings of the group at Hyannis Port. After the fall of Dienbienphu in 1954 and the division of the country along the Seventeenth Parallel, Bao Dai was deposed and Diem became the chief of state.

In his seminal treatise on the backdrop of the Vietnamese war, Col. L. Fletcher Prouty, who served as head of special operations for the Joint Chiefs of Staff during the Kennedy years, limned in the largely unnoticed policy decisions that would produce decades of havoc. Half of the mountain of armaments on the docks at Haiphong Harbor in 1945 would wind up with Ho Chi Minh, the stockpile with which he would repel the French. By 1955 at least a million "half-terrorized Tonkinese natives," Roman Catholics, arrived in the South, the majority transported by the U.S. Navy. Beneath the bayonets of the freshly installed Diem regime, these newcomers "began to take over villages, jobs, the police organization, the army, and many of the top jobs. . . ."

To assist Diem, the United States had sent along an advisory team from Michigan State, already a CIA resource, under Diem's political mentor, Wesley Fishel. On Fishel's advice, Diem pushed out the Chinese, for millennia the brokers and middlemen for economic transactions throughout the villages, and expelled the French, whose constabulary system traditionally maintained order throughout the provinces. Northern Catholics were quickly moved into positions of authority. Marginalized, the largely Buddhist farmers and elders of the villages began to revolt, the initial cadre of the Viet Cong.

In 1961, embarrassed by the miscues that produced the Bay of Pigs and fluffed off by Khrushchev in Vienna, Jack Kennedy decided to deal with the outcreep of Communists around the world by energetically backing the regime in Saigon. This was a mistake, and advisers like Undersecretary of State George Ball and Averell Harriman—along with the flagging Dwight Eisenhower and Charles DeGaulle and Douglas MacArthur—had started to tell him that. The mushy standoff the administration managed in Laos was the best anybody could expect short of a ruinous land war in Asia.

Politically, Kennedy needed a victory. Truman had taken a bad beating for "losing China." Characteristically, the calculating young president attempted to control any losses by insisting that the entire undertaking remain a secondary operation overseen by the CIA, directing a regular-army Military Assistance Advisory Group (MAAG) composed of sixteen thousand support personnel, in place mostly to service H-19 Sikorsky helicopters built by Bell.

Helicopters were an unwieldy and ineffective instrument to use in the heavy canopies and rice paddies of Vietnam; a great many got all tangled up and crashed on their own, while others had to fly so low that they were vulnerable to enemy fire, not only from guns but even from bows and arrows. They arrived in the theater, Prouty notes, on instruction from CIA Deputy Director Gen. C. P. Cabell, "shortly after the First National Bank of Boston had arranged for the Textron Corporation to acquire the Bell Helicopter Company." These were the years when the First National Bank of Boston was the creature of its vice chairman, Serge Semenenko, and was floating well-concealed loans to the mobster end of the entertainment industry as well as Meyer Lansky's huge casino promotion in the Bahamas.

There were an undisclosed number of civilian contractors around Saigon as backup for the arriving gunships. These squadrons, totaling five thousand Hueys, were positioned to augment the newly formed Self-Defense Forces of the Saigon government. As our involvement deepened, business-men of every stripe had started to do well by doing good.

Action-oriented as he was during those early months, Robert Kennedy had been swept along. Excited by Maxwell Taylor's theories of flexible response strategy and thoroughly taken in at first by the brainstorms of the quasimilitary huckster Edward Lansdale, Bobby had acquired the nickname "Mr. Counterinsurgency" and instructed reporters during a Saigon stopover in 1962 that this war would be "fought not by massive divisions but secretly by terror, assassination, ambush and infiltration." Before long he had Special Forces bravos scrambling all over the roofs of Hickory Hill for the amuse-ment of his offspring. He kept a green beret on his desk. He took his tactical leads from Marine general Victor "Brute" Krulak, a resolute proponent of saturation bombing against the north.

Bob was as implicated as anybody in the government in the irresponsi-ble dithering that produced the CIA-enabled coup which exterminated the plump, rigid Diem and his manipulative addict of a brother. Between the Saigon government's gruesome "Buddhist barbecues" and intelligence that Diem's brother Ngo Dinh Nhu was in touch with Hanoi with schemes to neutralize the region, it was obviously time to write the Ngo Dinh family off. Cardinal Spellman's fantasy of a Roman Catholic Southeast Asia was caput.

Inside the embattled bureaucracy, by 1964 resentment had started collecting at the extent to which, as a New York senator, Robert Kennedy was attempting to disavow policies and individuals he had strenuously supported while he functioned as a roving troubleshooter for his brother. The CIA smoldered still, and there were murmurs of betrayal throughout the Department of Defense. When Kennedy himself alerted Maxwell Taylor that there was talk around Washington of making him "the scape-goat for American failure," Taylor agreed with his chief sponsor that he was in a bad place, especially for a general, "but here I am—looking more and more like General Custer." The aborigines were gathering, but Bobby had moved on.

Robert Kennedy hated Lyndon anyway, but he became embittered when he heard that the president, in his wettest, windiest pulpit style, had started to regale the faithful around the White House with his judgment that, in view of the government-sponsored murder of Trujillo and Diem, "what happened to Kennedy may have been divine retribution." He compared his predecessor with a cross-eyed boy he'd known growing up, whose "eyes were crossed and so was his character. . . . That was God's retribution for people who were bad and so you should be careful of cross-eyed people because God put his mark on them. . . ."

Emotionally susceptible anyhow, brooding over the classic Greek texts from his sister-in-law with their traumatizing emphasis on the correlation of character and destiny, Johnson's slur hit Robert Kennedy hard. During his final months, in response to a Taylor-McNamara recommendation that the United States start withdrawing troops to exert "selective pressures" on Diem to jettison his brother and broaden his government, JFK had in fact signed National Security Action Memorandum #263, bringing back the first thousand troops by the end of 1963. The rest were expected to clear the region by 1965.

Whether this was essentially a feint or whether Kennedy was genuinely prepared to abandon Southeast Asia to Ho Chi Minh remains a question for historians. What Johnson did, we all know. Having loudly compared the paranoid mandarin Ngo Dinh Diem with Winston Churchill, Johnson demonstrated his manhood to the extent of over 530,000 American fighting men in the war zone, 60,000 dead, and a popular backlash which at times produced something approaching open warfare in the streets of America.

For Robert Kennedy, the buildup of stresses that forced him to break with both the preponderance of his party and the White House was registered month by month. He hated the personalities involved. "I keep myself on a leash, like you would an animal," Lyndon Johnson once said, and the fastidious Kennedy would have agreed with the terminology. "I can't stand the bastard," Robert Kennedy told Richard Goodwin after the pretender had called him in for a meeting, "but he's the most formidable human being I've ever met."

Kennedy attempted to heal the breach. He wrote Johnson in January 1966 that he had been "impressed with the most recent efforts to find a peaceful solution in Viet Nam." The president, obviously hoping to cauterize this potential sore spot, assured Bobby that "You know better than most the gloom that crowds in on a President, for you have lived close to your brother."

But the divide kept opening. By 1967 Robert Kennedy had pretty largely reversed himself. Allied inside the Senate with skeptics like William Fulbright and George McGovern, the ever more shaggy, precociously wrinkled ex-boy wonder was sounding off on programs like *Face the Nation* and asserting that, whatever the people of South Vietnam wanted or didn't want, "we want it, so we're going in there and we're killing South Vietnamese, we're killing children, we're killing women, we're killing innocent people," purportedly because the Communists "are 12,000 miles away and they might get to be 11,000 miles away."

Barricaded in behind the White House fences, the agonized Johnson countered that, should he actually listen to this hypocritical peacenik and give way to the protesters, Kennedy would be the first to pipe up that Johnson had betrayed his brother, "that I had let a democracy fall into the hands of the Communists. That I was a coward. An unmanly man. A man without a spine. Oh, I could see it coming, all right."

From the Senate floor, Bob continued to appeal for bombing pauses, for negotiations, for consideration of a coalition government in Saigon. His brother Ted—who liked the entire embroilment as little as Bobby—characteristically focused on specific situations, practical measures, something to slow this hayride down. He studied the compounding refugee problem. He eased into law a reform of the draft deferment system so middle-class Americans—and their parents—would become aware of what this could mean for *them* if the engagement continued to sharpen. Peaceful demonstrations were turning into the Weathermen.

It was a transforming time, a typhoon of incipient radicalism abroad in the streets. The peace movement required a champion, and, as the 1968 primaries approached, Robert Kennedy, month after month, seemed to be torn among advisers—the old JFK people cautious, Dick Goodwin and Adam Walinsky and Lowenstein already starting to move away, lose patience completely.

To the New Left, the enveloping conflict looked like business by another name—in Vietnam itself, Brown and Root (a very important contributor to Lyndon Johnson's political rise, a predecessor subsidiary of Halliburton) was flush from building the likes of Cam Ranh Bay. Santo Trafficante Jr., very interested in lining up an adequate supply of morphine base from the first-rate Hong Kong laboratories, visited Saigon and one of his young Mafiosi lieutenants, Frank Carmen Furci. Furci ran Trafficante's branch office, to supply dope to the enlisted men's clubs and R-and-R facilities throughout this military empire. With the Kennedys gone, opportunities were surfacing everywhere.

As 1968 opened, Kennedy's poll ratings were coming back. On January 31, as if in response to General William Westmoreland's statements a month earlier that the war was winding down, the Viet Cong and elements of the North Vietnamese Army struck and controlled for a time thirty provincial capitals, including the imperial city Hue, and stormed into the U.S. embassy in Saigon. This, the Tet offensive, was eventually repulsed, but even the man on the street could fathom that military prospects were not good.

The previous November 30, Senator Eugene McCarthy of Minnesota had announced his candidacy as a challenger to Johnson, and in February 1968 won 42.2 percent of the vote and twenty of the twenty-four delegates in the New Hampshire primary. Robert Kennedy had previously charged his brother Ted with the chore of telling McCarthy that he, Bob, intended to get into the race, so Ted—full of foreboding—visited McCarthy but could not quite bring himself to convey the message. Days after McCarthy's triumph, after putting the press and his advisers through a welter of statements about "reassessing the possibility" and "actively reconsidering," and loose talk about what if some sort of presidential commission on Vietnam made his involvement unnecessary—Bobby announced. On March 31, Lyndon Johnson withdrew.

Few events in American history have been more heavily blanketed by journalism than Robert Kennedy's final eighty-five days. It was an up-and-down business, with three generations of family advisers jockeying ceaselessly for position, while Dick Goodwin squirted in and out between the Kennedy factions and the McCarthy camp. Goodwin had enlisted as a McCarthy speechwriter while Bobby flip-flopped. "Bobby's therapy is going to cost the family $4 million," Ted observed, one of those family jokes that takes no prisoners.

Eugene McCarthy himself was already a problem. What began as a gesture took on astonishing gravity after Tet. The sort of energized supporters Kennedy took rather ruefully to referring to as the "A kids" were very quickly out there canvassing for Clean Gene. Throughout white-bread America, Robert Kennedy was harvesting distrust. Eisenhower noted in a letter that it was "difficult for me to see a single qualification that the man has for the Presidency. I think he is shallow, vain and untrustworthy—on top of which he is indecisive." All three of the dignitaries after whom Kennedy had named boys—Maxwell Taylor, Averell Harriman, and Douglas Dillon—preferred other candidates. The urban bosses were already lining up behind Johnson's anointed, Hubert Humphrey. When Kennedy groveled to the extent of asking for an audience with the lame-duck president to establish how active he expected to be in the upcoming campaign, Johnson proclaimed that "I won't bother answering that grandstanding little runt." Subsequently, he informed Kennedy that he expected to stay out.

McCarthy's presence was especially unsettling, presenting as it did the certainty of splitting the protest vote. In the Indiana primary, having listened to the JFK wing and picked up the George Wallace theme of law and order, Kennedy won by 42 to 31 percent against Governor Branigan and 27 percent against McCarthy. The white precincts in Gary, an ethnic center, went decisively against Kennedy. When Martin Luther King was killed on April 4, the deeply upset Kennedy bravely addressed a ghetto mob in Indianapolis and then murmured to an aide, "Well, after all, it's not the greatest tragedy that ever happened in the history of the Republic." Acutely aware of demographics, Kennedy was edging right, hoping to present himself now as mainstream.

Fred Dutton had been a key White House staffer under JFK, and over the course of the 1968 primary season he emerged as Robert Kennedy's closest traveling companion and a principal troubleshooter. A few weeks before he died in 2005 he attempted to sum things up for me: "The last four or five months of his life he was souring on the Vietnam war pretty bad. Johnson was president, and Bobby had to take a back seat to that. The practicalities were that there was a political gain to be harvested from tryin' to disengage or separate yourself from the pro-Vietnam people."

So that was just a practical political decision? I asked.

"Yeah, primarily."

McCarthy skewed the equation. When Jack Newfield asked Bob why he was picking up the white bigots, Kennedy speculated that "Part of it is that Gene comes across as Lace Curtain Irish to those people. They can tell I'm pure Shanty Irish." This reflected theologian Michael Novak's insight that the race pitted "lower-class-Catholicism-become-wealthy against middle-class Midwestern Catholicism, which is rather comfortable and easygoing."

At times the sociology was suffocating. It happened that, not long after the 1968 election, I interviewed McCarthy in the darkened, backlit crypt of his inner office. He was very straightforward. The Kennedys were not fit for office so high, they were spoiled, they weren't civilized enough, they were indifferent Catholics. They played touch football, whereas McCarthy had played semipro baseball. In turn, Bob regarded Gene as on the take to Lyndon Johnson's oil backers as well as "pompous, petty, and venal," and mean to go with it, traceable to the German roots of his family.

Kennedy won in Nebraska. But again, not by enough. Throughout the industrial centers, Humphrey was massing delegates almost by default.

Hoover had been watching carefully, selecting the most effective moment to plant the sword. He had been waiting for months, and his suspicions had never abated. A mid-1965 AIRTEL from his SAC in Newark to the Director conveyed word of "some papers found in a taxi" which "tied in BOBBY KENNEDY with the COMMUNIST PARTY." Guests at a dinner party at which the senator was present reported that "Among the items discussed was how to work out an accommodation with FIDEL CASTRO." The familiar, entrancing smell of sedition was in the wind. Time was past due to bring this recovering young Kennedy down a peg or two.

Not long after that, Neil Gallagher had stopped by his own office on the Hill to sign the mail and discovered "this one letter to Nick Katzenbach, who is now the Attorney General. A letter prepared for me, for my signature. 'Dear Mr. Katzenbach: As chairman of the Special Committee on the Protection of Privacy or whatever we were called in those days, I herewith demand that you come before our committee and bring with you'—this is the Attorney General of the United States, now:—'the authorizations for the illegal bugging of Martin Luther King.'"

Gallagher was dumbfounded. "Where did this letter come from?" Gallagher asked his secretary.

"'Mr. Cohn. Mr. Cohn dictated the letter.'

"'To who?'

"'To me.'"

Gallagher got Roy Cohn on the telephone and pitched a tantrum. As before, Cohn hurried to Washington to explain the situation. "Mr. Hoover dictated this letter," Cohn told Gallagher. "He's sick and tired of Bobby Kennedy proclaiming himself the great liberal when he himself signed the authorizations of this bugging." Cohn showed Gallagher copies.

"Roy, I am everybody's friend, but I'm nobody's whore and I am not that crazy bastard Hoover's whore any more than yours or anybody else's." With that, Gallagher proposed to toss Cohn "through the goddamn window, and if DeLoach is hanging on to you, or Hoover, they're goin' too."

This would not be the last contretemps between the FBI and Gallagher. Hoover understood that it was the authorization to invade the privacy of Martin Luther King that would provide the hot-button issue in 1968. He had already attempted to push some of the responsibility on Nicholas

Katzenbach by producing related documents bearing Katzenbach's alleged signature, which Katzenbach politely repudiated. Katzenbach had irked the Director by in effect reversing Herbert Brownell's 1954 edict that, as concerned the use of "microphone surveillance," where "considerations of internal security and the national safety are paramount," circumstances "may compel the unrestricted use of this technique. . . ." Hoover interpreted this broadly, and it had remained his call. Now Katzenbach mandated that "bugs" would require the same procedures as wiretaps—the attorney general would have to sign off.

The implications of all this had made the massive penetration of the days and nights of Martin Luther King by the Bureau even more of a political hand grenade. The art here was making sure that it landed and detonated in public at exactly the right moment. With Robert Kennedy and his "Ruthless Cannonball" racketing around the country, continuing to pick up momentum, any newsbreak that jeopardized Kennedy's status with blacks and whatever idealists McCarthy couldn't hang on to and civil libertarians and unsophisticated white ethnics was certain to hurt. Bobby's apparent connivance in the wholesale abuse of King's privacy rights could churn his prospects in a hurry.

It happened that the gadfly columnist Drew Pearson had been something of a mouthpiece for Lyndon Johnson for a number of years. He got to throw the grenade. The feature column that he wrote with Jack Anderson, "Washington Merry-Go-Round," had been plinking at Robert Kennedy all spring. One column quoted Papa Joe as characterizing Bobby as a "hater," while another maintained that Bob had arranged to pay off a Hoffa witness. On May 24, obviously calculated to blow up the Oregon primary, Pearson published a column which ran in four top Oregon newspapers and declared that, as attorney general, Robert Kennedy had ordered a wiretap placed on Dr. Martin Luther King. The tap had produced evidence that "a Communist . . . was helping to write King's speeches" while referencing an FBI report which quoted "a confidential informer as claiming that Dr. King 'has been having an illicit affair with the wife of a prominent Negro dentist in Los Angeles since 1962.'"

Identified increasingly with black demands, Robert Kennedy overnight found himself reexamined by the civil-rights leadership, whose martyr he had evidently sold out. Fourth-Amendment devotees had second thoughts. Religious zealots faulted Kennedy because King had strayed. Even converts like Kennedy's black organizer, John Lewis, on loan from the King organization, confessed to Frank Mankiewicz that it was "like someone telling you that your wife is sleeping with someone else. You love her so much you don't want to hear about it." McCarthy strategists were picking up on ruthlessness fast and ran radio ads during which a black voice intoned "I used to be for Robert Kennedy, but then I learned about how he bugged my brother Martin Luther King's phone."

FBI documents dealing with the incident are interesting, in part, as an exhibition of the Bureau's skills at covering its own tracks. Jack Anderson later disclosed to Evan Thomas Jr. that Drew Pearson got the original nod from Lyndon Johnson, obviously on a tip from Hoover. Pearson sent Anderson to DeLoach, who had the knock on Bobby at hand. The Bureau would take the high road, DeLoach said, asserting that Pearson "was doing us a great disservice inasmuch as the article would certainly dry up Negro sources of information. . . ." At Anderson's statement that "Kennedy should receive a death blow prior to the Oregon primary," De Loach sermonized that "The FBI would not become involved in bitter political struggles. . . ."

As to King's sex life and Communist affiliations: Anderson confessed that he had read the extensive FBI report on the subject; DeLoach charged him with having accessed "an old wire tap on King" provided by Ed Weisl Jr. Weisl, another of those lifelong loyalists Roy Cohn picked up at Horace Mann, was the nimble son of the legendary financier Ed Weisl Sr., a Lehman Brothers partner who was close to Johnson.

When, upon being briefed about the King wiretaps a few days before, Weisl offered to suppress the information, DeLoach "told him we held no brief for Kennedy, in view of the shoddy way in which he had treated the FBI; however, we did not want to be involved in any political maneuvers. . . . Weisl stated he would try to keep this from appearing." In other words—go: Just don't implicate us.

What Anderson had been doing, of course, was confirming point by point the material from Weisl that Pearson expected to use in his column. If he had anything wrong, DeLoach would have made that clear. Disclaimer by disclaimer, DeLoach had been protecting the Bureau while unloading on the hated ex-attorney general.

A few years later, engaged in a Pier-Six brawl with the enraged Neil Gallagher—on whom Hoover had let loose his demons of the press—the Director harrumphed in one of his celebrated scrawled-in footnotes that "There would have been no reason to solicit Gallagher's assistance to bring out the facts on Kennedy's participation in the wiretaps on King, for I personally released copies of Kennedy's authorization."

Winning Oregon was important to the campaign as a way of demonstrating that Bobby could carry the Democratic bastions on both coasts. The news break about the King surveillance hurt Kennedy vis-à-vis McCarthy. By then Kennedy had pretty much won over his accompanying press corps, and suddenly there were fresh doubts.

Richard Harwood of the *Washington Post* had previously broken the story that the FBI had been miking and taping King, so assertions that Bobby was behind the whole thing didn't sound totally far-fetched. Harwood, an ex-Marine who traveled with the campaign, had been slow to knuckle under to what the disillusioned Arthur Krock termed the "bristling sensitiveness" with which the Kennedys managed the news, "more cynically and boldly than any previous Administration." When Harwood latched onto an impossible pass during a touch-football break after Bobby jammed the heel of his hand into Harwood's face, the infuriated newsman broke out: "You're a dirty player, and a lousy one, too." The King story could bring down the whole compounding Camelot romance.

Advisers close to Kennedy were disquieted. Pierre Salinger put out the word that Kennedy had never authorized electronic "eavesdropping." As for wiretaps? Only in national security cases. As John Seigenthaler would recall years later, concerns about what exactly Kennedy had agreed to let Hoover do to King hovered over the Kennedy group's California strategy sessions, and damaged morale.

Kennedy lost Oregon to Gene McCarthy, 44.7 to 38.8 percent. This was a telling loss, given that Bob had been running head-to-head against a candidate who seemed to have a lot of trouble getting interested in the issues. Bob held himself accountable, but as John Bartlow Martin noted in his journal, "Robert over-reacted to the Oregon loss and said things that night and next day at the airport in California that he spent the rest of the week trying to climb out of. It really flattened him to lose." This was the first Kennedy loss, the first time the Ambassador wasn't actively involved.

Bob was an unlikely apparition to be running for chief executive by this point. Slight, slouched, half bleary with overfatigue a great part of the time, he kept his gaze down before glancing up from under his hair to release that sheepish grin and attempt some quirky, ambivalent aside. Ethel doled out handfuls of pills at meals, supplemented by B-12 shots. During speeches his hands trembled, and his knees knocked uncontrollably.

The campaigning had taken on an Orphic character, the return of the survivor from the Land of the Dead. Moving through the country's parade grounds and ghettos in an open convertible as a sort of homage-cum-expiation to his slain brother, Kennedy pled his case with mobs so aroused by his very presence that they attacked his person, pulled off his cufflinks and jackets and shoes and struggled to jack Bobby out of the car while his ex-FBI sidekick Bill Barry clutched him around the middle. "My juggler's gift," Barry would later remark about having kept Kennedy intact as long as he did.

By now, winning California was all-important. It was particularly painful for Bob to discover that allies like Walter Reuther from the McClellan days—along with Senator McClellan himself—had cooled on him enough to refuse to support him. Along with pitching heavily for the Chicano vote and touring the Mexican encampments with a debilitated César Chávez barely coming off a hunger strike, it had become necessary for the campaign to alarm Kennedy financial overseer Steve Smith and break loose trust-fund dollars to help their chances. McCarthy had outspent Kennedy in Oregon. It got to the point where genteel advisers like Fred Dutton and John Seigenthaler were following California Assembly power Willy Brown around, bribing one black preacher after the next to load up their sermons and get the devout to the polls for Bobby. This was a variety of dog-meat politics to which the Kennedys hadn't had to stoop since West Virginia.

Worried, Kennedy had agreed to a television debate with McCarthy. It was an unexciting exchange, Kennedy sucking up to the Jewish vote and McCarthy responding in the limpid, supercilious style that was too chilly by then even for the tube. When McCarthy asserted that, if elected president, he would fire J. Edgar Hoover, Kennedy refused to match his promise. Who knew what munitions the vindictive old cocker might yet be hoarding?

Kennedy won in California, 46 to 42 percent. It was a start, but Humphrey could count on a majority of delegates at that stage, a number of whom Kennedy would have to take away on the road by "chasing Hubert's ass all over the country." It looked like an uphill summer. "In those days there were very few primaries," David Burke reflects. Burke was still Ted Kennedy's administrative assistant and alter ego at that point. "And Teddy and I went to many, many convention states. And the delegates to the state conventions, who were all very political people, who dedicated a good portion of their lives to politics—they didn't care for Bobby at all. He wasn't the one they liked, Hubert Humphrey was. Bobby just couldn't shake Humphrey's strength."

Bobby announced the triumph in California to the celebrants in the Royal Suite at the Ambassador Hotel in Los Angeles while parading around with his victory cigar. The atmosphere was charged with several generations' worth of nostalgia. The Ambassador had been the flagship of Meyer Schine's hospitality empire, frequented by politicians and gangsters throughout the postwar decades.

A few minutes before midnight, Kennedy went downstairs to address the crowd in the Embassy Ballroom and then was drawn off by an assistant maitre d' into a side corridor which carried him into a dark pantry passageway where he unexpectedly confronted the kitchen staff. Bob had begun to shake hands when an unstable Palestinian who worked as a groom at Santa Anita stole toward the candidate and emptied his eight-shot .22-caliber pistol at Kennedy's head.

In his journal, John Bartlow Martin compares Robert Kennedy with the peerless bullfighter Manolete. His fans "kept demanding more and more of Manolete," Martin relates, "and he kept giving it, until there was nothing left to give but his life, and so he gave them that. So did Kennedy."

Back at the Seat of Government, the news was received without a great deal of observable shock. "I hope somebody shoots and kills the son of a bitch," the normally taciturn Clyde Tolson had remarked of Bobby during an executive conference earlier that season. Emotional cross-currents ran as powerful as ever. "We hope and pray for your husband's speedy recovery," Hoover wired Ethel at the Good Samaritan Hospital when the news broke. "If my associates or I can be of help in this trying time, please let us know." As soon as Bobby's death was confirmed, Hoover wired: "We all are profoundly saddened over the tragic death of your husband and offer our deepest sympathy to you and your children. His passing leaves a deep void in the hearts of the entire nation, and we pray that God's comforting hand will sustain you in your bereavement." Shortly—as he had done after the murders of John Kennedy and Martin Luther King—Hoover herded Tolson toward the armored limousine to get them out to Pimlico. The Director did hate to miss the opening race.

The investigation into Robert Kennedy's murder was botched even worse than that of the president. While Sirhan had approached Kennedy from the front no closer than 1¹/₂ feet and sprayed bullets into the throng around him, wounding five other people, the autopsy report from the very able Thomas Noguchi of the Los Angeles Coroner's Office stated that the three shots that actually hit Kennedy came from below and behind. All had been fired at point-blank range, less than two inches away, evidenced by the powder burns. Two punctured his shoulder and neck, and the bullet that killed him shattered his mastoid bone and tore into his brain. Kennedy's heart did not stop beating for hours.

Follow-up studies by the Los Angeles field office of the FBI concluded that as many as twelve bullets had been fired, four more than Sirhan could have discharged. Slugs dug out of the woodwork at that time indicated by their scoring that at least two .22 revolvers were in play during the murder. This was an execution by a professional.

Like Oswald, Sirhan Bishara Sirhan was a kind of hapless reject afloat in the shallows of a Mob-dominated culture. A compulsive gambler, Sirhan consorted with minor racketeers like Henry Ramistella in a world under the control of Mickey Cohen. Sirhan's chief defense counsel, Grant Cooper, was tied up with the Rosselli–Friars Club case when he represented Sirhan, and, like Sirhan's other lawyer, Russell Parsons, ignored the coroner's finding that Sirhan was in the wrong position to have killed Kennedy. Parsons was Mickey Cohen's regular lawyer and had himself been investigated by Kennedy during the fifties.

By 1968, Cohen was the king of the Los Angeles branch of the syndicate. He had been grilled excruciatingly by Robert Kennedy during the McClellan hearings and was at the top of the Justice Department's hit list when JFK went down. At one point, Cohen shared the affections of a stripper, Candy Barr, with his pal Jack Ruby. Cohen's prospects were not good under a Robert Kennedy presidency.

Notebooks that turned up in Sirhan's bedroom contained statements—in a hand that experts would not confirm was his—that "Robert F. Kennedy must be assassinated before 5 June 68 . . . sacrificed for the cause of the poor exploited people." But his fellow exercise boys insisted that Sirhan was apolitical, contemptuous of Arabs. At trial, Sirhan maintained that he had blanked out, couldn't remember, wasn't sure where the extra money he was carrying had come from. Everything happened so fast. . . .

Underground, the trolls were chuckling. Years later, hanging out in Antony Marcello's hunting lodge in Louisiana, one secondary California wiseguy got to reminiscing about Bobby: "the bastard," he commented, "thought he was gonna put us all outa business."

His cousin from New Orleans came right back: "Yeah, so we put *him* outa business." Everyone reportedly laughed.

Hoover reviewed the evidence and determined—who could be surprised?—that it was all Sirhan. Another nutty gunman, taking down another Kennedy. He had ignored reported threats to Kennedy from Jimmy Hoffa and a California Minuteman rancher. The day of Robert Kennedy's funeral, the

FBI knocked national coverage of the service off the front pages with an announcement that the presumptive killer of Martin Luther King Jr., James Earl Ray, had been captured in London. The Director would soon be referring to Robert Kennedy as "the Messiah of the generation gap."

Still, violence was clearly abroad in the land, and Hoover ordered another layer of armoring for his limousines. The monsters had now gotten so heavy that they couldn't really go very fast. They required a complete change of tires and new brake linings every few hundred miles. But the Director felt safer, and recommended such precautions to the apprehensive Lyndon Johnson.

Discouragingly, even without "that sneaky little son of a bitch," as Hoover called Kennedy to Dick Nixon while Bob was attorney general, so much that Kennedy started had taken on a momentum of its own. Hoover tended to deride Nicholas Katzenbach as a namby-pamby liberal "hippie," no doubt the only figure in government to perceive the sober-sided legal scholar as a flower child. The Director was especially peeved in 1965 when Katzenbach decreed that *all* forms of electronic surveillance would require the attorney general's signature. Unlike Bobby Kennedy, Katzenbach had no compelling political reason to subject himself to the Director's fiat: his brother wasn't the president, nor was the moderate bureaucrat subject to personal blackmail.

Hoover's infuriating way of Indian-wrestling over issues—seeming to plant his feet solidly, then abruptly giving way and throwing everybody else off balance—wore Katzenbach out. The Director let it be known that he had now decided to discontinue "all techniques—technical coverage, trash covers, mail covers, etc. While it might handicap us I doubt they are as valuable as some believe and none warrant the FBI being used to justify them." Katzenbach was worldly enough to anticipate that, without at least a limited capacity for surveillance, the government would be flying blind and did not want to wind up blamed for some debacle. Having become, as he later testified, "dramatically aware of the lengths to which the Bureau would go in trying to justify its authority," while "My correspondence with Mr. Hoover at that time unavoidably became a bitter one," Katzenbach resigned as attorney general and accepted an appointment a couple of rungs down the bureaucratic ladder as deputy undersecretary of state.

Katzenbach was replaced late in 1966 by *his* deputy, Ramsey Clark. Clark's promotion was tied in some Machiavellian way to the decision of his father, Tom Clark, to resign his seat on the Supreme Court. Hoover had a lot of evidence that one-time Attorney General Tom Clark had done a number of well-remunerated favors earlier in his career, and had taken bribes from Jack Halfen, Carlos Marcello's bagman in Texas. The Director apparently made relevant paperwork available to Lyndon Johnson once LBJ decided that he wanted to find a place on the Court for his crony of many years, Abe Fortas. Tom Clark resigned, and part of the arrangement seems to have been the promotion of Ramsey Clark to the attorney generalship.

Hoover treated Clark like "a small child," DeLoach noticed. The Director decided early that this latest liberal to whom he was theoretically responsible was a publicity-hungry "jellyfish," impossible to pin down. Robert Kennedy, at least, would take a stand. Hoover dubbed Clark the "Bull Butterfly," a reference to the lean Texan's occasional outbursts of willfulness and his tendency to flit from topic to topic. Clark closed down the FBI's surveillance empire and revved up the strike forces. Arrests fell off.

As with so many other enemies he had his eye on, Hoover's reading of Ramsey Clark turned inside out the motivation behind what was going on. There was no file of indiscretions to be had on Ramsey, which put the Director at a serious disadvantage. Clark struggled to get the Director to give him five minutes of productive exchange rather than diatribe after diatribe about Martin Luther King or the outrages of the young. Hoover had visited Clark's house once "and his wife was barefoot!," Hoover disclosed to one newsman. "What kind of person is that?" Ramsey sometimes came to meetings in shirtsleeves.

Annoyingly, Clark refused to permit the Director—who had quickly softened his position—to reinstate the wiretaps on Martin Luther King. He warned the Bureau that any FBI agents caught breaking the law would be energetically prosecuted by the Department's lawyers—Clark obviously had "illegal trespass" in mind, the Bureau's most fervently cultivated nocturnal self-indulgence. He maintained that poverty—not, as Hoover insisted, bad character—was the root of crime. Ultimately, he suggested in interviews that it was long past time to put the Director out to pasture.

The carryover momentum from Kennedy's well-publicized war on organized crime induced Congress to start codifying the murky surveillance and trial requirements. The brightest light on most of the legislation that followed belonged to G. Robert Blakey, a Notre Dame law professor who had watched the bloodletting firsthand as one of Bob Kennedy's prosecutors in the Justice Department. As chief counsel of the responsible subcommittee within the Senate's Judiciary Committee, Blakey brought an expert's know-how to mapping out the pressure points when it came to Organized Crime's America. As Blakey's recommendations got processed into law, the days of pleading the Fifth all afternoon or escaping blame by taking a vacation while a shipment of heroin hit the docks were over for the country's senior hoodlums.

Title III of the Omnibus Crime Control and Safe Streets Act of 1968 established a procedure for obtaining a warrant from a federal court to wiretap for probable cause, simultaneously mandating that each intercept be limited in length and that the subject be informed afterward. Evidence so gathered might now be employed to prosecute cases.

As things worked out, Professor Blakey remembers, Hoover threw his own weight behind the new wiretapping provisions, which authorized pretty much the same procedures that Robert Kennedy had urged on Congress. At that time, Hoover had used his influence with James Eastland to quash such unwarranted interference behind subcommittee doors. But the brouhaha with Kennedy about who authorized what, along with the skittishness around the Johnson administration when it came to unlimited Bureau eavesdropping, now left the politically attuned Director reconciled to a controlled penetration program rather than none at all.

He leaked the hoard of anecdotal detail and statistics about the Mafia piled up by William Sullivan and his ferrets to Sandy Smith for one of those big, splashy exposes in *Life* calculated to inflame public opinion. FBI experts worked closely with Blakey's consultants to draft the legislation. Then Hoover was observed to lean on Jim Eastland and Gerald Ford and the members of the moderate Republican Wednesday Club to prod the draft into law. "Hoover's people were more than willing to enforce it," Blakey says now. "We got perfect cooperation from the FBI."

Paradoxically, one senator who voted against the bill was Robert Kennedy. Privacy has long constituted a nonnegotiable consideration throughout the Boroughs of Greater New York. On the advice of Jack Miller—by now a founding partner of Miller and Cassidy—Kennedy instructed that his vote be paired against the measure. That is not to maintain that Bobby betrayed a great deal of regret when the new law did pass.

Follow-up legislation helped tighten the noose. The Organized Crime Control Act of 1970 made it a lot simpler to compel individuals to testify under a grant of immunity while leaving these same individuals open to prosecution if another witness named them as complicitous. Title IX, the Racketeer Influenced and Corrupt Organizations Statue, RICO, permitted federal prosecutors to obtain convictions when "a pattern of racketeering activity" was provable within a crime group or family.

This meant the bosses could wind up in Lewisburg for the felonies of the soldiers. The FBI had loaded on it jurisdiction over "major gambling operations and hoodlum infiltration of legitimate business." Conviction now carried the risk of federal seizure of Mob assets, even legitimate enterprises acquired with syndicate money. The Federal Witness Protection Program came into existence. Collectively, far more than any foundation or sports stadium, these laws provided Robert Kennedy his lasting memorial. "Had he and Martin Luther King not been killed," in Bob Blakey's opinion, "we couldn't have gotten any of the legislation through the Senate."

For the first few years after Jack Kennedy died and Robert Kennedy abandoned gang-busting, the Justice Department's success rate against organized crime dwindled across the government. But the public was awakened, as were the Bureau's finest. For all the terrifying sorties by mounted apes from the Inspection Division so brilliantly satirized by Joe Schott, there had always been a heavy percentage of FBI street agents who caught the bug from Kennedy, who intended to bring to heel and ultimately destroy the gangsters who controlled their cities. Testicular palookas like Bill Roemer and Neil Welch took their directives from the Seat of Government only so far before listening to their guts. They worked the bricks, increasingly oblivious to the private agenda of J. Edgar Hoover and his selective list of sanitized ex-bootleggers and hoodlum-involved wildcatters.

There had been some disconnect all along between the headquarters and the field. Once Robert Blakey's provisos got turned into law, even Hoover could not offload the national gambling syndicates or Mafia extortion of legitimate businessmen onto Harry Anslinger and the IRS. Local mobsters could continue to corrupt cops and politicians in a given community, but—especially after Hoover died—FBI personnel were in a position to trump anybody else.

One Bureau field supervisor would remember going after gambling paraphernalia or drugs when agents did not trust the local police with advance information. Accordingly, "we would take the police by the hand, not even tell them where we were going, but when we got there let them conduct the raid." Where cases were to be tried in local courts, the FBI field office would type up the warrants and "shop around for an honest judge and a police unit that we could trust."

Hoover was forever proclaiming that he did not want the Bureau transformed into a "national police force," but the process was under way whether he liked it nor not. By 1971, almost a quarter of the active Cosa Nostra membership around Chicago had been convicted "as the result of

Bureau efforts." By 1974, FBI headquarters itself announced that Bureau investigations during the previous year led to "more than 1250 convictions of hoodlums, gambling and vice figures," up in one year from 1026. During his last years, even the Director appreciated that these were indeed impressive statistics to take to Congressman Rooney at appropriations time, and it was cheaper than paying all those ringers to attend Communist Party rallies.

As early as the middle sixties, the dons were falling. In 1965, a federal grand jury deposed Sam Giancana. Wriggling beneath his grant of immunity, Sam had worked a deal through Edward Bennett Williams with William Hundley of the Organized Crime and Racketeering Section which would limit the grilling to relatively harmless questions about petty infractions. Hundley was well aware that Robert Kennedy did not want Giancana turned inside out; by then Hoover was starting to refer to Hundley as organized crime's stooge in the Justice Department. Mindful of *omerta,* Giancana stonewalled and drew a year in the Cook County lockup. After that, he moved to Cuernavaca in Mexico and began to decline rapidly.

That same year, Murray Llewellyn "Curly" Humphreys got rousted by the FBI and died of a coronary blood clot in the aftermath. Always civilized company, Murray the Camel was somebody with whom Joe Kennedy had regularly taken pains to exchange knowledgeable confidences. In time, Allen Dorfman was convicted (although hit before sentencing), and a two-phase FBI sting called OPERATION STRAWMAN took down twenty-nine mobsters at the managerial level, including an aging "Joey Doves" Aiuppa, by then the generalissimo of the Outfit.

For some years, Carlos Marcello was able to fend off close FBI attention, and reporting on the squat, bull-necked Cajun-Siciliano would remain spotty, if amusing at times. In July 1967, the SAC in New Orleans who replaced Regis Kennedy, Patrick Collins, reported that Carlos's wife, Jackie, had become incensed over the don's longstanding affair with "LUCILLE, the beautician." Jackie imposed an 8 P.M. curfew on the powerful gangster; the first time Carlos came in late, she barred the door. Carlos had just availed himself of a sledgehammer when "JACKIE MARCELLO took a shotgun and pointed it out a second story window and ordered CARLOS off the property." From then on, Carlos stuck to the curfew.

SAC Collins carried headquarters instructions to penetrate the Marcello operation to unexpected lengths. He allegedly took up with Marcello's sister-in-law, Bootsie. Meeting Marcello's flight one day, Collins forced his way through a knot of well-wishers to greet the Mafia boss with: "Hey Carlos, guess what? I've been fucking your brother Joe's wife." Carlos flattened him with one punch and wound up serving six months for assaulting an FBI agent. Marcello was believed to have taken the sentence willingly in 1968 rather than risk having his family's dishonor publicized in court proceedings.

By 1979, with Hoover dead and Republican beneficiaries of Marcello's largess like Dick Nixon discredited, the FBI leadership dreamed up a wide-ranging big-store sting to bust Marcello once and for all. Developed by New-Orleans-based Special Agent Harold Hughes and known as BRILAB (bribery and labor), the plan involved breaking into and miking-up Marcello's supposedly impregnable Town and Country office compound before insinuating a string of informants carrying tape recorders in briefcases with false bottoms. The star turn went to Joseph Hauser, a slippery olive-skinned Pole who had escaped from Mauthausen and quickly demonstrated an aptitude for gaming the free-enterprise system. Hauser's gifts at insurance fraud permitted him to make—and lose—several fortunes before finding himself indicted, alongside that flexible lobbyist so valuable to Hoover and Nixon, Irving Davidson, for bribing the trustees of the ever-alluring Teamster Welfare Fund to glom onto insurance contracts.

To escape an excess of prison time, Hauser agreed to collaborate with the FBI. One of the most-thumbed cards in Davidson's Rolodex was that of his client Carlos Marcello. Under Davidson's auspices, Hauser found his way through the Spanish moss and promoted the benefits of his fictitious insurance brokerage, Fidelity Financial Consultants, to the cagey mobster. The reels of tape the FBI collected would reflect the delectable "coonass politics" of Louisiana. Subsequent testimony seemed to implicate top state officials like the commissioner of administration, Charles E. Roemer II, in extravagant kickback schemes.

One of Bob Kennedy's prosecutors at the Justice Department, Mike Fawer, was practicing law in New Orleans by this time. As Charlie Roemer's defense attorney, Fawer would remember how much of the government's case depended on Hauser, "a tool of the FBI. . . . They just had to wind him up and he'd talk." Fawer recalls one tape Hauser recorded "in a men's room, while taking a piss." The adjacent urinal was unoccupied, and Hauser was "making up a conspiracy between two people, one of whom didn't exist."

In August 1981, at seventy-two, Marcello was convicted, on charges largely based on RICO provisions, of conspiracy along with racketeering and mail and wire fraud. This produced a seven-year sentence, to which a Los

Angeles jury added ten for bribing a judge. By then, the fallout of the House Assassination Committee hearings, conducted by the untiring G. Robert Blakey, had started to convince historians that Marcello was the organizing personality behind the murder of John Kennedy. Carlos never talked.

The Kibosh on Those Jaspers

If **Hoover ever dreamed that**, once the Kennedys were gone, he could reassert control, the way the sixties played out was a wrenching disappointment. The Director had bet heavily on Cartha "Deke" DeLoach. DeLoach came from a small Georgia town, Claxton, a tall boy made fatherless at eight and forced to work as hard picking pecans and cotton as any white boy around. His mother ran a boardinghouse. DeLoach was matriculating at a minor law school in Florida when the news that the FBI had captured a band of saboteurs off a Nazi sub inspired him to apply to the Bureau in 1942. Except for a stint in the Navy, there went the next twenty-eight years.

DeLoach has been characterized as rather a pious sort, deep-voiced, with the habit of "speaking softly, moving gently, and oozing humility." As touchy and paranoid as Hoover was becoming year by year, a personality like DeLoach's offered something of a balm. A report he wrote after a stint as liaison with the CIA and the Office of Naval Intelligence caught the Director's eye, and in 1951 Hoover brought him into the headquarters directorate. Throughout the Bureau, assignment to the headquarters was regarded as the quickest route to a colitis condition or a nervous breakdown, but Deke, still in his early thirties, glimpsed nothing but opportunity. For years DeLoach toured the field offices and threw the fear of Hoover into street agents nationwide. Not long after Lou Nichols quit to work for Schenley in 1957, DeLoach took over Crime Records, the vital public relations division which also catered to Congress.

A committed Roman Catholic with seven children, DeLoach remembers Hoover as "a strict authoritarian, a man of very heavy discipline. A godlike figure. He was a man whose bidding you could follow and do great work." Now in the inner circle, DeLoach could appraise for himself the prevailing atmosphere of heavy workaday geniality. During the weekly executive conferences in Tolson's office, the assistant directors were prodded by the Boss to speak their minds, after which Hoover would snap out a decision. Tolson—whose "slavish" obedience to the Director's whims even DeLoach found off-putting—remained for Hoover "an almost indispensable figure at bureau headquarters, but not quite a friend." The occasional flareup of locker-room humor between the two convinced DeLoach that their relationship was "normal." Sometimes DeLoach would travel with Hoover and Tolson; typically they would book a double suite, with Deke allotted the single bedroom. DeLoach could never remember an affectionate gesture between the two cantankerous, aging men. The Director's emotional allegiance remained centered on his mother, and by then "all that was left of Annie Hoover was her Bible."

Sitting in on the same meetings, Courtney Evans reached conclusions of his own. "It was pretty obvious," he acknowledges now, picking his words carefully. "I always surmised that he was active. The pretty boy had finally come along. By the sixties Hoover had probably given it up. Other than Tolson I knew of no close association I might suspect." Like others around Hoover, Evans sensed deep frustration and gathering loneliness. "Hoover had to be the relentless guy, he punished more agents more severely than they needed to be punished," Evans says.

Hoover liked to imagine himself and the select handful of FBI administrators at the top as a kind of omniscient collectivity, a hard beneficent pooled consciousness in place to study and, when necessary, redirect the events of the day. "We'll have to keep an eye on this situation" would be a typical note scribbled into the margins of the thousands of memos flowing across the Director's desk. Badinage was sometimes permitted, if always from the top down. On one of his trips to Miami, Hoover sent DeLoach a postcard with a shot of women in bikinis on the glossy side and the inscription in that too-familiar hand: "I missed you on your last trip, come down again soon."

"My wife wondered what was going on," DeLoach says now. "Despite his rather closeted personality and the monastic life he led to a great extent, Mr. Hoover was a great practical joker."

As LBJ acquired something of a feel for the presidency, his impulse to turn to Hoover whenever something sensitive came up gave way to his politician's apprehension about letting the FBI Director in too close. When Johnson was vice president, according to his loquacious mistress Madeleine Brown, the Director had confronted him with proof that Johnson was the father of Madeleine's son, Stephen. Hoover expected Johnson "to try to influence Kennedy to keep him on as FBI Director," Johnson told Brown. Hoover knew about Stephen, and "he's calling in his marker."

By 1964, Hoover was feeling that hot presidential breath—redolent often of Cutty Sark—demanding that he place his seven thousand or so vulnerable agents at the service of enthusiasms Hoover didn't necessarily agree with. The FBI moved into the South. The Bureau would now be lumbered with the primary responsibility for organized crime. Worst, Hoover had a nagging hunch that he was being circumvented even inside the Bureau.

Compared with Tolson, Hoover appeared frisky enough, but the few who interacted closely with the old tyrant could see that he wasn't what he had been. Apart from prostate surgery, DeLoach says, "I think he had had several small strokes. He was slurring words, not the usual staccato delivery." There had been rumors of a mild heart attack. The leadership was thinning—in 1965, the overworked Al Belmont was pushed out, "about a year short of his thirty-year retirement date. His offense was that he had told the Director the truth more than once too often."

With a sigh, DeLoach moved up, Assistant to the Director, number three after Hoover and Tolson and ultimately responsible for the General and Special Investigative Divisions along with Domestic Intelligence (including the counterintelligence function) as well as his customary role as the master of Crime Records. DeLoach's counterpart over on the administrative side was John Mohr, Mister Inside, who presided over budgets and assignments. A bluff, cunning Dutchman, Mohr lacked the exposure to the world outside which made for success in Washington. Between his political ties and his oversight of so many ongoing investigations, DeLoach was generally regarded as the likeliest successor to the Old Man in the event he stumbled, or retired, or whatever. Hoover obviously favored him: he had now accumulated more immediate power than anybody in the Bureau except Hoover himself had ever wielded.

Slick, hyperalert, a master of the studied compliment, DeLoach seemed to exert a powerful influence wherever Hoover put him, from the American Legion to the White House. Johnson liked him so much it became a problem. The nervous president telephoned DeLoach at the office, from Air Force One, at home on a private line Johnson ordered to be installed when

DeLoach's teenage children tied up the regular number. While LBJ and the Director got along—"They had to, they were like two old dogs chasin' each other in a circle," DeLoach says—Johnson did his business with the FBI increasingly through Deke.

"The president on one occasion called me when I was in Mr. Hoover's office," DeLoach remembers, "and Mr. Hoover handed the phone to me, saying that the president wants to talk to you. And the president said at the time, 'Does it embarrass you for me to be calling you rather than Hoover?' And I said, yessir, it does. And he said, 'Well, Hoover talks so damn fast and so long that I can't understand him sometimes.' And he said, 'Call me when you get back to your office.' I went back to my office and he said, 'I'll promise to call Hoover every once in a while, but again, I can't understand him.'"

DeLoach was rarely hesitant about laying it on. "Thank you for allowing Barbara and me to have a 'moment of greatness' with the world's number one family yesterday afternoon," went one bread-and-butter note. "The informality, yet quiet dignity you possess, never ceases to inspire me. . . ." Johnson must have kept his pants on on that occasion.

DeLoach attempted to deal with the fireworks which resulted when Walter Jenkins, Johnson's top personal aide, got caught making homosexual overtures to a vagrant in the YMCA men's room. While the FBI was investigating the incident, DeLoach persuaded Hoover to send flowers to Jenkins—by then a friend of Deke and his family—in his hospital room. Johnson pushed the FBI to determine either that the Republicans were behind the incident or that Jenkins had been seized by a rare malady of the brain. None of this was credible. In the end, Hoover had to satisfy himself with Johnson's assurance that by sending the flowers he had accomplished "a great humanitarian deed."

Years later Richard Goodwin would write of Johnson as the pressures built as "a textbook case of paranoid disintegration, the eruption of long-suppressed irrationalities." Much the same diagnosis would have summed up Hoover by then. DeLoach was operating between two guttering, unpredictable fires.

Precisely what it took to gratify Hoover is apparent from the final act of the melodrama that played out between the grudge-harboring Director and Congressman Neil Gallagher. As the sixties deepened, Gallagher's rambling invasion-of-privacy hearings had started to sound to the uneasy Director like a drumbeat getting closer. On August 9, 1968, an article titled "The Congressman and the Hoodlum" appeared in *Life* magazine.

Gang-written, it told "the story of the corruption of a U.S. congressman by the Mob." The heart of the expose was the alleged favor-trading between Congressman Gallagher and the Bayonne thug Joe Zicarelli, a capo in the Joe Bonanno family of the Cosa Nostra. Department of Justice wiretaps in 1960 had alerted "authorities" to a series of telephone calls from Zicarelli to Gallagher complaining that, due to "the treachery of a top police official," the Bayonne police "had staked out the key stations of his gambling network." Gallagher was reported to have told Zicarelli that "I got hold of those people [Bayonne police] and there will be no further problem." But it was soon apparent that Gallagher hadn't intervened very effectively, because Zicarelli kept after him by phone and finally attempted to pull him off the floor of the House. Interviewed by the *Life* reporters, Gallagher explained that he was just schmoozing along a potentially troublesome constituent. He himself "never had any influence with the police in Bayonne."

Much of the rest of the article dealt with a pattern of arm's-length relationships between Gallagher and several local business figures with whom Zicarelli was marginally acquainted. One shared commercial interest featured Laetrile, a purported cancer cure fabricated from apricot pits. The eyebrow-raiser had been saved for the end of the article. In February 1967, an enforcer for Zicarelli named Harold ("Kayo") Konigsberg, characterized by "police and federal agents" as "the most dangerous uncaged killer on the east coast," an "animal on a leash for Zicarelli," led FBI agents to the mash pit of a still on a chicken farm that served as a Mafia burial ground. They dug up a pair of orthopedic shoes traced to a missing penny-ante loan shark and bookie, Barney O'Brien. Barney was a neighborhood character best known as the proprietor of a Dairy Treat ice cream stand.

His insanity plea already rejected by the courts, prepared now to accommodate *anybody* in the hope of leniency, Kayo Konigsberg divulged that one night in October 1962 Gallagher had unexpectedly summoned him to remove O'Brien's corpse from his basement and dispose of it. Alerted to Konigsberg's confession, Gallagher called it "the most bizarre story I have ever heard in my life."

Publicity like this wasn't helping as Gallagher revved up for the final three months of his reelection campaign. He contemplated suing *Life*. It was suspected by many that "DeLoach," as ex-FBI agent William W. Turner would write, "who had a reputation as a ruthless operator, leaked data gleaned from wiretaps. . . ." One of the authors of the *Life* piece was Sandy Smith of the *Chicago Sun-Times*, a specialist in Mob affairs whom DeLoach regarded as "not in the Kennedy camp."

"That's a pretty dirty trick the Bureau did to Neil Gallagher," Roy Cohn had commented when an earlier story linking the Congressman and Zicarelli made it into print. "That's just like you, Roy," DeLoach admonished the nimble little attorney, "always standing up for guys who don't stand up for us." When the August 1968 *Life* broadside against Gallagher hit the stands, DeLoach tipped Cohn: "If you still know that guy, you better get word to him to resign from Congress."

Once it became probable that Gallagher would retain his seat, he got a call from his lawyer, Larry Weisman, urgently summoning the harried Congressman to an emergency meeting at the Newark Airport. Immediately following an exchange with Roy Cohn, Weisman had been empowered to tip Gallagher off that "Mr. Hoover is demanding that you resign from Congress in ten days and give up the campaign." Otherwise, "the next story that is going into *Life* magazine," as Gallagher would rephrase it, "is that a guy died in bed with my wife," after which "I . . . panicked, came down from Washington, kept this guy in my basement, and that's when I had to get the local Mafia guys to remove the body."

Furious that these slanders now involved his wife, "a very, very decent woman," Gallagher resolved to fight back. Cohn had authorized Weisman to spell out to his client that he was fresh from "this meeting with Deke DeLoach and this is what they're going to do. They want you out of the goddamn Congress. You're too dangerous for them. You're not their friend, so you're finished."

Cohn left no doubt how serious the threat was—"It comes right from Mr. Hoover." This time it was Gallagher who made the trip to Manhattan. He presented Cohn with what Cohn assumed at first was Gallagher's statement of resignation. It was a speech the Congressman proposed to deliver in the House. It took its energy from the disclosure that "it has been called to my attention that the Director of the FBI and the Deputy Director of the FBI [Clyde Tolson] have been living as man and wife for some twenty-eight years at the public's expense; as a member of Congress we have an oversight duty and that oversight is to make sure that the funds which go to the FBI are properly spent." Gallagher proceeded to specifics: the armored cars, the racetracks, the hotels and dinners and breakfasts. . . . "Jesus," he would exclaim afterward, "I laid it on."

Cohn started to read, and then dropped it out of shock. "Roy, how's the spelling on this?" Gallagher asked. "Is the punctuation okay?"

"My God! He'll go crazy. You can't say anything like this. . . . Where did you get this stuff?"

Some came from jokes floating around Washington for years, Gallagher admitted, "But the other stuff I'll make up, just like they're making up all that shit on my wife." Gallagher pledged to deliver some form of his presentation every day Congress was in session that autumn. "I may go down, but I'm taking that old fag with me."

The next day Cohn called Gallagher: "Mr. Hoover doesn't know why you're mad at him. . . . What do you want him to do?"

Outgunned, the FBI repudiated the transcripts of the wiretaps involving Zicarelli. Mrs. Gallagher was never smeared.

In 1972, convicted by the Nixon administration for tax evasion and perjury and about to undergo a stretch in Allenwood, Neil Gallagher issued a news release detailing the ways ex-Assistant to the Director DeLoach had attempted to blackmail him in *Life*. While insisting that "At this point, I have very little personal sensitivity about being used as a whipping-boy, even by friends," Cohn responded to Neil that "your diatribe against the Bureau was very unfair. . . ." Neither "Mr. Hoover" nor "Mr. DeLoach . . . ever asked me to convey any threat to you." Reviewing the relevant material—to which "Bureau files contain no reference"—Hoover himself scribbled below that "Gallagher is like an octopus spewing forth its black fluid to hide his true character."

Three months before he died in 1986, a very sick and embittered manipulator attempting to square accounts, Roy Cohn cosigned a letter to Gallagher in which he acknowledged "the events that Deke De Louche [*sic*] called Roy and told Roy that the Bureau had information that Barney O'Brien had died in your house and his body was put in the basement and later removed and disposed of, and if Neil did not stop his hearings on evasion [*sic*] of privacy he would make the information public." Unlike the Director, Roy Cohn was ethically incapable of effacing everything.

As front man for the Bureau in the White House as well as Congress and the media, even DeLoach was stretched. A popular television series called *The FBI* premiered in 1965 with the Goldwater enthusiast Efrem Zimbalist Jr. as the brisk Inspector Erskine. Hoover's oversight of this long-running dramatization of Bureau mythology was incessant; DeLoach himself was known to carp at the Boss's compounding list of forbidden sponsors, which ran from alcohol and lingerie to footwear and bathroom products.

But there were now stirrings of resentment audible in the Congress as well as tell-all books about Hoover's foibles. The problematic Ramsey Clark not only vetoed wiretap requests but also unapologetically pulled rank at times and dipped into Justice Department funds to subsidize the International Association of Chiefs of Police, the creature of Quinn Tamm, an ex-assistant director at the Bureau who openly challenged Hoover for supremacy in law enforcement.

No doubt in part to ward off his terrifying sense of the world slipping away, Hoover had started to invest emotionally in the extralegal no-man's-land presided over by William Sullivan. While DeLoach was tall, personable, and not a little bit waxy when confronted with facts he didn't like, Sullivan was a sawed-off, fine-boned intellectual ruffian, the absentminded-professor type who might very well forget that he left a bomb ticking in your desk.

In 1961, the iconoclastic Sullivan had been handed the Domestic Intelligence Division. Brilliant at times and very widely acquainted in Washington—not afraid to consort with individuals on Hoover's No Contact List like the past leader of the American Communist Party, Jay Lovestone—Sullivan had demonstrated his ingenuity by formulating the COINTELPRO—White Hate Groups strategy that trashed the Ku Klux Klan. As widespread protest over the war in Vietnam turned into rioting in the streets, Sullivan saw his opening.

Egged on by Hoover, Sullivan cranked up his COINTELPRO—Black Extremist RM to "expose, disrupt, misdirect, discredit and otherwise neutralize" such radical black elements as threatened public order. The irresistible target just then was the Black Panthers. Along with thoroughly bugging, tapping, and burglarizing this crowd of publicity-crazed would-be revolutionaries, Sullivan's specialists planted informants and churned up rivalries and domestic chaos. Anonymous letters went out to anxious wives of the principal spokesmen about sisters in the movement "shucking and jiving with our Black Men in ACTION, you dig?" A telephone call to the mother of Black Power advocate Stokely Carmichael warning of a Panthers plot to assassinate her son sent Stokely into exile in Africa for years. Bureau surveillance provided the logistics for the police raid in Chicago during which the Panther leadership got badly shot up and Fred Hampton died. Transcripts from the ELSUR placements were scrupulously edited, with all the *motherfuckers* replaced by asterisks to spare the prim old Director and Helen Gandy.

All this was red meat, of course, to the flagging Boss. Something about the wiry Sullivan's combination of impetuousness, brains, and the up-country aplomb to assert that "I was brought up in overalls" if anybody ventured to needle Sullivan about his slovenly, preoccupied presentation—the whole package somehow appealed more every day to Hoover. Through-out the Johnson years, Deke DeLoach was widely regarded as the heir apparent, and Hoover would address him simply by his last name, recognition that he had crossed a well-fortified barrier with the standoffish Director. As the sixties ended, this unique honor also went to Bill Sullivan.

Deke DeLoach could always fall back on his inbred Southerner's aptitude for buttering up their volatile demigod, but now Sullivan—sniffing the director's job—was outrageous. He compared Hoover repeatedly with de Gaulle and Adenauer. He warned Hoover, in underhanded comments along with anonymous letters, that DeLoach had shifted his loyalty to the do-gooders in the Johnson White House, who wanted Hoover out. By 1970, DeLoach was approaching fifty, he had concluded that the Director had no intention of ever leaving office, his many children were approaching college age, and his government salary of $37,000 wouldn't stretch.

Worse yet, situations like the taffy-pull involving Gallagher threatened to crash into headlines. On Lyndon Johnson's orders, late in 1968 DeLoach arranged for the FBI to wiretap Madame Chennault, who was close to Nixon; this turned into a rhubarb for the Bureau once Nixon won a few months later. Jack Nelson of the *Los Angeles Times* was breaking stories which demonstrated that the Bureau had been functioning as an agent provocateur in some of the worst of the segregationist atrocities and that Hoover himself was exploiting Bureau personnel to remodel his house and profiteering from publications ghostwritten by FBI employees. Jack Anderson pulled off a "trash cover" raid on Hoover's own garbage and cataloged every grinds-encrusted grapefruit husk and discarded Gelucil container. Stories floated around Washington that DeLoach was double-billing for certain of his trips, and the *Los Angeles Times* was on the point of printing a scoop linking DeLoach to Victor Frenkil, the contractor who built the new FBI Academy at Quantico.

"DeLoach and I were bitter enemies," Sullivan said afterward. "DeLoach left under a big cloud. He had opposed Hoover, quietly behind the scenes . . . and he wanted to get rid of him." Deeply aggrieved with Sullivan, Deke DeLoach left the Bureau in 1970 to accept a vice-presidency at Pepsico under Donald Kendall, a pal of Richard Nixon. Typically, Hoover sulked and subjected DeLoach to the silent treatment the last few months before he left. DeLoach's finesse and underlying realism were rare at the top of the unraveling Bureau, and during his coherent moments the Director was no doubt aware of that. "I thought you'd never leave me," he admitted to Deke at the end, something of a plaintive note coming from the hard-nosed Director.

✳ ✳ ✳

Richard Nixon and J. Edgar Hoover had been servicing each other's careers at least since the later forties, when Bureau sources supplied files to the rabid, dweebish Congressman on Alger Hiss and Helen Gahagan Douglas. In 1960 the Director had done whatever he could for the Nixon campaign; he hailed Nixon's victory in 1968 and was especially pleased by the appointment of John Mitchell, a phlegmatic municipal bond expert from Nixon's New York firm. After Bobby Kennedy and his two "hippie" successors, the pipe-smoking and seemingly nonchalant new attorney general looked perfect for a collegial relationship, by which Hoover meant: utter permissiveness.

As early as May 1969, Hoover was starting to anticipate problems. The palace guard of business types Nixon had imported from California to micromanage his administration would have to be subjected to control. "There is a ring of homosexualists at the highest levels of the White House," Hoover informed Sullivan. "I want a complete report." The three his inform-ant Drew Pearson had fingered were H. R. Haldeman, John Ehrlichman, and Dwight Chapin. Reluctant to charge this pillbox by himself, Sullivan let the whole thing go. Hoover sent in his rising star, Mark Felt, to depose Haldeman and Ehrlichman as to the extent of their involvement in "homo-sexual parties at a local Washington hotel." The rumor was groundless. Ehrlichman wound up wondering whether "Hoover may have had a part in contriving the accusations."

Hoover's file on Nixon himself was thinner than he liked. Sexually, it appeared that this perennial Republican golden boy restrained himself to an inconvenient extent. Items came in from the legat in Hong Kong and linked the ex-vice president with a Hong Kong hostess, the beautiful Marianna Liu. As was his practice, Hoover himself carried the information to Nixon, unc-tuously assuring the politician that he would "never speak of it to anyone."

What began to dismay the heavy-duty managers around Nixon was the realization that, just as Hoover had no intention of serving as Bobby Kennedy's desk sergeant, he was very often unwilling to accommodate this latest proliferation of buttoned-down hotshots. Not without a payback, at the very least.

The first inklings of how everything worked came during May of 1969 when William Beecher of the *New York Times* released a bombshell on the American raids into Cambodia. Henry Kissinger got upset, along with his aide Colonel Alexander M. Haig Jr. They approached Hoover with demands to wiretap several civil servants as well as a number of reporters known to feed off their offices. Sullivan caught the duty. Before it was over there would be seventeen wiretaps, which produced, as Nixon later lamented, "Just gobs and gobs of material: gossip and bullshitting—the tapping was a very, very unproductive thing."

It was also a very questionable way to conduct government business, producing "political intelligence" from around the government having little or nothing to do with national security. "This is not an FBI operation. This is a White House operation," the Director stressed to Sullivan, and personally made sure all the consumers of this broad-based invasion of privacy signed off on whatever logs and transcripts and summaries they got to peruse. After that the documents wound up in Sullivan's safe, invaluable for blackmailing purposes. The lineaments of Watergate were beginning to rise behind the young Nixon administration.

There was a feeling around the White House office suites that the Old Man had decided to pull in his horns. He refused to help with three bag jobs for the NSA; when Director Richard Helms of the CIA requested assistance with the tapping of a couple of embassies, Hoover said no. He became annoyed with Helms for refusing to reveal the identity of a source in Denver and broke off regular liaison with the Agency, which brought on constipation all across the intelligence community. A request by Ehrlichman to tap columnist Joseph Kraft's home phone met with a no from the Director. Ehrlichman tried the private detective John Caulfield without much success, and ultimately Sullivan went behind the Boss's back and located somebody from the French Secret Service to bug Kraft's room at the George V during the Vietnam peace negotiations. Sullivan remained privately in touch with Jim Angleton, the CIA counterintelligence impresario.

Everything had started to flow around Hoover. In June of 1971 the *New York Times* began to publish the Pentagon Papers, a collection of highly classified documents bearing on information and insider thinking that produced the war in Vietnam. It soon became apparent that the primary leaker was Daniel Ellsberg, a researcher at the Department of Defense and the Rand Corporation. This was the kind of politically freighted situation Hoover never liked anyhow. He consented to an FBI investigation, but when Ellsberg's father-in-law, Louis Marx, appeared on a list of the implicated to be interviewed Hoover had scratched in a NO, which the agent running the investigation took as an H, Hoover's usual mark. He went ahead and grilled Marx.

Louis Marx was a wealthy, conservative toy manufacturer who corresponded from time to time with the Director and filled his outer office each Christmas with presents for children, which senior people at the headquarters might then pick over and take home. This constituted a bonanza for family men like Deke DeLoach, always budgeted to the last penny, and reflected well on the beneficent Director. Anybody who was that generous to the Bureau deserved careful handling. Hoover demoted the presumptuous agent.

Nixon was furious. "If the FBI was not going to pursue the case," he wrote afterward, "then we would have to do it ourselves." On July 17 John Ehrlichman instructed Egil "Bud" Krogh to form a unit to look into situations where Hoover was negligent. Krogh was shortly assisted by ex-Kissinger assistant David Young, CIA veteran E. Howard Hunt, and the ex-FBI gunslinger G. Gordon Liddy. The Plumbers were taking shape. Like the Kennedys, the Nixon White House had decided to pull together its own squad of operatives to circumvent the stodgy, aging Director.

Among the cold-eyed suits who managed the Executive Branch at that point, whatever romance or veneration Washington insiders once accorded Hoover was irrelevant. Spawn of the opposite coast, they did not respect this deteriorating legend particularly. They judged the Bureau's reports as "of poor quality"—conjecture, gossip, hearsay. Unlike the Kennedys, they did not fear the Director. John Ehrlichman was startled to find this living institution "florid and fat-faced . . . apparently without benefit of neck . . . eyes protruding. He looked unwell to me."

When Hoover attempted that initial shot across their bow by alleging their involvement in a "ring of homosexuals" they barely gave Mark Felt the time of day and brushed the whole matter off. Haldeman and Ehrlichman both included notes on the whole absurdity in their published recollections. There would be no memo lurking in Hoover's Personal and Confidential file to take down some official who was starting to get out of hand.

Early in his administration Richard Nixon had attempted to give Hoover the personal access he so unmistakably craved. "Hoover full of hair-raising reports," Haldeman would note after an overnight at Camp David. "He is a real lobbyist, and never quits. And never hesitates to chop everyone else in the process." These memoirs are studded with discussions about how to ease Hoover out, at times including Hoover, who regularly cons the embarrassed president by claiming that, as totally as he remains prepared to go, losing him at that point, before the '72 election, might hurt the party. A story made the rounds to the effect that, when Nixon brought up the issue of age, Hoover assured the president that he, Nixon, was much too young to worry about that.

John Ehrlichman would memorialize one of Richard Nixon's rare attempts to socialize outside the White House. Nixon, Ehrlichman, and Attorney General Mitchell were received by the FBI Director at his Thirtieth

Place residence on October 1, 1969. Accustomed to California palatial, Ehrlichman found Hoover's tight little house "dingy, almost seedy," cluttered as it was with almost-first-rate antiques and hung with photographs of faded film actresses and Hoover himself posing beside forgotten cowboy stars like Tom Mix. A bizarre system of Plexiglas tubes sent dough of various primary colors bobbing up and down the dining-room wall. The faithful giant Crawford had put aside his chauffeur's cap and appeared in a white waiter's jacket to hand around drinks. Steaks and Chasen's chili had been flown in, courtesy of Clint Murchison. Nixon, not to be outdone, bragged about the cottage cheese *he* arranged to fly in from Knudsen's California dairy every week.

With dinner behind them, the Director led the presidential entourage down "the narrowest of basement stairs" to the "recreation room," plastered up with "girlie pinups of the old *Esquire* vintage," including the little lampshade on the bar. It was "his naughty gallery," the astute Ehrlichman observes, "as if it were something he wanted us to know about J. Edgar Hoover."

Clyde Tolson was again recuperating beneath the eye of Hoover's housekeeper, Annie Fields. He made his appearance, looking "pale and pasty," then found his way back upstairs. In 1966, Tolson had suffered a massive ischemic stroke, the first of several which impaired his walking, writing, and speech. For decades, Hoover had depended on Tolson to keep things percolating around the office. His remarkable ability to scan a document at a glance and pick out the single incriminating phrase and buck it back for revision had saved the Director many times. Tolson caught the uglier administrative chores. He never minded firing anybody. A sour, silent presence for most of the final years, Tolson had a gift for playing the rising assistant directors off against each other, preventing any one of them from accumulating too much power.

With Clyde Tolson reduced to shambling invalidism, proportions around the headquarters were changing, fast. People who imagined they understood Hoover sometimes maintained that he was a softie inside, which forced him to present himself as brusquely as he could to the encroaching demands. Without Tolson, enemies he had fended off seemed to be gathering strength. First DeLoach, then William Sullivan had taken on too much importance; perhaps he was making it too easy for those self-serving vipers around the president to displace him with one of his own.

That cool October night in 1969, Ehrlichman would recall, Hoover had rattled on about the cookie-pushers around the State Department, career sticklers who were preventing his people from wiring up the new Soviet embassy. When the party broke up, to Ehrlichman's surprise, the front yard was jammed with reporters and cameramen, obviously alerted by the house-holder. The president himself was forced to offer a statement to the press attesting to how "alert physically and mentally" the Director remained. The Director wasn't passing up any cheap insurance.

It would be hard to exaggerate how thin the Old Man's skin was getting. On discovering in 1970 that the corn-fed young actress Jean Seberg was talking up the Panthers after running into Bobby Seale, Hoover authorized the leak-age of rumors to gossip columnist Joyce Haber and others that Seberg was pregnant by a radical of color.

"Jean Seberg has been a financial supporter of the BPP and should be neutralized," Hoover responded to his Los Angeles field office. The Boss's ferocity when it came to radicals was infecting the troops. "I wonder how she'd like to gobble my dick while I shove my .38 up that black bastard's ass," one of the Los Angeles agents was heard to mutter.

Delicate anyhow, the tormented ingénue miscarried following a *Newsweek* wrap-up of stories about her condition and attempted to kill her-self seven times, "usually on the anniversary of her little girl's birth," observed her heartbroken ex-husband, Romain Gary. She brought it off in 1979.

In 1967, back in private practice, Barrett Prettyman Jr. had made him-self available pro bono to plead cases for clients who would otherwise go undefended. Appointed by the Superior Court to represent a woman who had been flagging down cars at three in the morning and now found herself hauled before the bar and charged with "leading a profligate life," Prettyman mounted an inspired defense. Was this woman any guiltier than, say, J. Edgar Hoover, well known to attend the races and even place a bet from time to time? Certain observers might call that "profligate."

A reporter covering the proceedings picked the comment up, and it was quoted somewhere in the *Washington Post*.

It did not escape the Director's eye. Within a day, a pair of very grim FBI agents showed up at Prettyman's office to present him with a letter from the Director. "I note," Hoover opened, "that you gratuitously injected my name in a case you are representing in the D.C. Court of Appeals referring to my 'numerous' visits to the race track."

After labeling Prettyman's remarks "an unwarranted use of my name to obtain some cheap publicity," and pointing out that he only attended the races, "an entirely legal pastime," on Saturdays "and then infrequently," in company with twenty thousand other people, "including federal and state officials," Hoover drew his own conclusions: "Why you should single me out of this large number can only be that you are vindictively inclined or are hard pressed to make a point completely irrelevant to the true merits of your case.

"In any event, I do not appreciate such despicable use of my name."

It would take digging to come up with a more perfect example of text-book paranoia. The Lefties were converging; whether it be Edward Long or Daniel Berrigan or Cornelius Gallagher or Allard Lowenstein, they were not going to get their satisfaction. He and the Bureau would lie low, avoid the political storms, let the crisis pass.

With so much simmering, Hoover found himself being squeezed to adopt a counterattack being bruited about the White House called the Huston Plan. By the end of 1969 the Peace Movement was turning activistic. In November protesters staged a rally outside the Justice Department building and threw some paint and peed on the lawn, a demonstration of raw power that looked to Attorney General John Mitchell "like a Russian Revolution going on." A lot of middle-class kids were involved, some from influential families, and the Director was disappointingly reluctant, as Sullivan saw things, "to allow his agents to break into embassies, tap telephones, or open other people's mail, even though these were the very investigative techniques to which he owed his publicized successes!"

Nixon, crumbling, was convinced that the Cubans and the Algerians and the Eastern Europeans were behind the antiwar unrest and picked a young and extremely gung-ho White House aide, a lawyer who had recently headed the Young Americans for Freedom, to put some kind of interagency surveil-lance in place. Tom Charles Huston approached the leaders of the four senior intelligence agencies—the CIA, NSA, FBI, and DIA—and with the presi-dent's backing created a committee to design what would amount to a national secret police. Hoover himself—"the last reigning monarch in the Western world," in Huston's view—was to serve as chairman, while a sub-committee run by Bill Sullivan would devise the program.

Hoover didn't like Huston, whose name he could never quite get straight. When the Director spoke for a "historical view" of objective intelli-gence, Huston cut him off by remarking that "We're not talking about the dead past—we're talking about the living present." Huston's forty-three-page program recommended all the usual abuses plus a sweeping array of new opportunities to harass Americans, including a network of campus informers and regular monitoring of American citizens who were discovered to make telephone calls abroad. . . .

Hoover saw the draft, Huston later testified, and "went right through the roof." The Director bore down on Sullivan to rewrite many provisions. Somehow the attorney general had been left out of all this involuted scheming. The Director laid low in his office until the signing ceremony on June 15, 1970, then stood up and read the document aloud, remarking after every section that the FBI expected to continue as before, but "would not oppose other agencies seeking authority of the Attorney General for coverage required by them and therefore instituting such coverage themselves." Many of these initiatives were "clearly illegal." Then Hoover reportedly "landed in Mitchell's office with such a force that the Attorney General was compelled to persuade the White House to back off." Hoover demanded that the president himself sign off each time in writing before he would involve the Bureau. The Huston Plan was dead.

For the feisty Sullivan, Hoover's deftness at sandbagging the Huston Plan amounted to a personal setback. "We've got enough damned coordination in government, too much in fact," Hoover raged to Sullivan. No committee ombudsman would be permitted to look over *his* shoulder. At that point number three in the Bureau, "Crazy Billy" had contributed most of the line-by-line draftsmanship that made the plan so invasive and full of promise to the control freaks around Nixon. In his memoirs, Sullivan would protest that he had never bucked for the promotion, that he was personally a liberal Democrat, that his sick wife Marion had relocated to their New Hampshire farm to protest her husband's frantic involvement with Bureau politics. But Sullivan had now been tagged as somebody with loyalties outside the Bureau.

Addressing a meeting of UPI editors in Williamsburg, Virginia, Sullivan was impolitic enough to respond to a question that it was not the Communist Party that was stirring up the race riots and convulsing the campuses. Back at the headquarters the Director was beside himself, repeating: "How do you expect me to get my appropriations if you keep downgrading the Party?" Testifying before the Senate Subcommittee on Supplemental Appropriations, Hoover attempted to compensate by revealing the existence of a coven of priests and nuns led by Fathers Phillip and Daniel Berrigan who intended to dynamite the power and gas lines serving the capital. The Boss had blurted out the details of one of Sullivan's ongoing investigations. As 1971 opened, legislators across the political spectrum—Congressmen William Anderson and Hale Boggs, Senators George McGovern and Edward Kennedy—were calling for the Director to put an end to his illustrious career. The eternally scavenging press smelled the old warhorse weakening.

At this most perilous of turns, the night of March 8, 1971, a handful of accomplished peaceniks burglarized the FBI files in its resident agency in Media, Pennsylvania, and sent out Xeroxes of reports on many of the Bureau's most sensitive domestic-security penetrations and disruptive COINTELPRO—New Left strategies. The self-designated Citizen's Commission to Investigate the FBI was distributing to members of Congress and sympathetic newspapermen evidence that the Bureau was haunting the college-age children of dovish legislators "to enhance the paranoia endemic in these circles," while advising agents that, when interviewing for local help, they should "be alert for long hairs, beards, pear-shaped heads," etc. All long-standing Hoover anathemas, pear-shaped heads especially.

This was a vast humiliation for the Director and turned him in many quarters from a totem into a laughingstock. A national manhunt ensued, but the Bureau was never able to nail down a conviction. Always sensitive to a shift in the political winds, Hoover discontinued the seven extent COINTELPROs. No need to go through the Palmer-raid backlash all over again. He launched a kind of one-man charm offensive, dressing up in black tie and trading quips with Martha Mitchell at the American Newspaper Women's gala. He was, after all, the country's foremost champion of personal liberty, Roger Baldwin's oldest and most esteemed friend.

He dealt with William Sullivan. On July 1, Hoover summoned Chief Inspector W. Mark Felt and promoted him to a position Hoover had just invented: deputy associate director. This positioned Felt immediately after the dying Tolson and above Sullivan in the precarious Bureau pecking order. Sullivan quickly proved that he understood where everything was heading by packing up the sheaf of receipted logs and transcriptions and summaries from the seventeen illegal wiretaps which Kissinger had demanded—the Pentagon Papers documentation Sullivan knew the Boss would have to have if Nixon ever fully turned against him—and jammed the precious paper-work into an "old, beat-up satchel" with the initials W.C.S. to identify it, olive-drab. He sent it over to Assistant Director for Internal Security Robert Mardian, a reactionary Nixon stooge whose greatest achievement so far had been to weaken desegregation guidelines in the South. Sullivan had already divulged to Mardian that he himself was now "out of channel," and "might in fact be fired," and was prepared to turn over to Mardian documents so potent that with them the Director "could blackmail Mr. Nixon. . . ."

Always alive to danger, Hoover had sensed a threat in Mardian and cautioned Sullivan to avoid "that goddamned Armenian Jew." But it was too late. The satchel with the documents made its way from Mardian to Haldeman to Nixon himself, who called Hoover in to fire him but couldn't get a word in edgewise, swamped as he was by Hoover's outpouring of material about Dillinger and Ma Barker and the shortcomings of Martin Luther King Jr. Nixon lost his nerve. Hoover returned to his office, and a few days after that he signed a new will.

Meanwhile, Sullivan stewed. On August 28, 1971, in prose contorted by the anger and frustration behind it, the mastermind who functioned as the Director's trapdoor to the wised-up Left and ghostwrote his books and fabricated the Oswald mythology and brought into being the entire system of secret guerrilla resistance to Hoover's many enemies sent the Boss a letter to tell him that virtually everything the Director had done recently was ill-considered and self-defeating. Hoover only wanted yes-men, he knew as well as anybody that the American Communist Party was defunct, what was the point of opening still more foreign liaison offices? Our responsibility was in the United States, "and here is where we need to spend the taxpayer's dollar combating crime. And, as our own statistics show we are not doing too well at it here."

"What I am trying to get across to you in my blunt, tactless way is that a number of your decisions this year have not been good ones." The Director was destroying his own reputation. If, upon reading this, Hoover fired Sullivan, "So be it." Everything in the letter was "said for your own good and for the FBI as a whole of which I am very fond."

For Hoover the resentment came through, if not the sorrow. There were a couple of long, noisy exchanges of opinion. "That son of a bitch Sullivan pulled the wool over my eyes," Hoover told one aide immediately afterward. "I treated him like a son and he betrayed me." To Sullivan, Hoover insisted that he had "been giving this controversy between us a great deal of prayer." He had no intention of resigning. "I never thought that you'd betray me," the stricken Director told Sullivan finally, his voice breaking. "That you'd be a Judas too."

"I'm not a Judas, Mr. Hoover," Sullivan said. "And you certainly aren't Jesus Christ."

When Sullivan came to work on October 1, his name was off his office door and the locks had been changed.

* * *

However rough the Nixon years were becoming for J. Edgar Hoover, among the surviving Kennedys the luck ran worse. The Director had kept an eye on Ted Kennedy all along and had a hand in releasing documentation about the cheating scandal at Harvard when Kennedy first ran for a Senate seat in 1962. Under DeLoach's guidance, agents tracked the Kennedy family professionals who scoped out the convention in Chicago in 1968, fearful of a boomlet for the last living brother. Nixon would remain suspicious.

The accident off Chappaquiddick Island in July 1969 reassured the worried Right. Edward Kennedy had risen to become the Whip among the Senate Democrats and demonstrated a level of legislative acumen and energy never discernible in either of his brothers. His personal life bordered on chaotic, which offered some reassurance to the opposition. He drank a great deal.

After Mary Jo Kopechne died, few in the Nixon White House could mistake the opportunity. Along with the entire world's working press, a heavy representation of Bureau investigators descended on the Cape. Reporters on assignment were wiretapped. Not trusting Hoover completely, Nixon authorized his own private detectives, including the resilient John Caulfield and Antony Ulasewicz of Watergate notoriety, to jump in and grub up whatever there was. Close briefly to Robert Kennedy, Mary Jo had worked as an assistant in George Smathers's office and roomed with Bobby Baker's girlfriend. An informant in Colorado had tipped the Bureau that the purse of another of the "Boiler Room Girls" who worked on Bobby's presidential campaign (six young women who had worked on Bobby Kennedy's presidential campaign), Cricket Keough, was found in Kennedy's Oldsmobile. With that, the story was promptly leaked to the tabloids that Cricket and Kennedy had both easily escaped the overturned car while neither was aware that Kopechne was asleep in the back. This reading of events was utterly fallacious; accurate or not, as William Sullivan had commented at the time, it was a better story than the Kennedys came up with.

For Ted, the worst moments arrived while he was attempting to explain this terrible mishap to the fading old patriarch. He approached his father's bed and laid a hand on the withered shoulder. "Dad," he faltered, "I'm in some trouble." His father took his son's hand and held it against his chest. Unsteady because of the huge hematoma still pressing against his brain, the youngest of the children attempted to explain to the source of all their power what happened. When Ted was finished the founding father nodded, patted his son's hand, and closed his eyes.

After that "Mr. Kennedy lost his appetite," his nurse saw, "and I knew he had given up." He died the following November.

By then I was well into my biography of the senator, *The Education of Edward Kennedy,* and I was part of the pack besieging Hyannis Port, and Edgartown, and the locals around Chappaquiddick. I was able to talk with Kennedy at breakfast in his house on Charles River Square not long after his neck brace came off.

A few weeks after his father passed away, I interviewed him again in the Whip's chambers at the Capitol. We covered a lot of topics, including the accident itself, and Kennedy remained calm and realistic in tone. As I was gathering myself up to leave, I offered my condolences on the death of this father.

It was no doubt the wrong thing to mention. I saw Ted sway for a moment, and then his big, round, flushed face trembled and tears started down his cheeks. He hadn't been ready for that, quite yet.

For J. Edgar Hoover, 1972 opened with yet another round of those ritual obeisances the honors-hungry Director expected. Nixon flew him back from Florida on Air Force One and provided a cake for his seventy-seventh birthday along with the companionship of William Rogers. Then secretary of state, Rogers had been one of Hoover's favorite attorneys general. Hoover engineered a formal rapprochement with Lou Nichols and Deke DeLoach; of Sullivan, the Director wrote Nichols "I only wish I had been able to spot his instability long before I did."

Out there in war-weary America, where much of the media was indulging its romance with the firebrands of the New Left, Hoover incarnated more convincingly every day a homegrown Beria. That flat face sagging with bureaucratic gristle, no ears to speak of and a thin trap of a mouth and dark eyes that shone like bearings, alternately beseeching and dismissive—it wasn't a face so much by now as a generic brand, like Coca Cola or the Statue of Liberty. Too many generations at this point had twitched beneath that gaze.

Throughout the winter, Jack Anderson had kept after Hoover in his column, castigating the FBI for loading up its files with "titillating tidbits" about liberal movie actors and black leaders and antagonists to the government like I. F. Stone and Albert Einstein and Paul Robeson. Anderson was literally "lower than dog shit," Hoover assured anybody who would listen: he collected Hoover's garbage and picked over the waste. Then Anderson broke the Dita Beard scandal. The senior Washington lobbyist for International Telephone and Telegraph, Dita Beard had allegedly written a memorandum, of which Anderson had a copy, in which the company pledged to contribute $400,000 to the Republicans if Mitchell would drop three antitrust suits against the company.

Presidential lawyer John Dean hurried over to Hoover to request that FBI laboratories examine the original and declare it a forgery. Hoover was most genial, "delighted to be of service." When the report came back, in time to muddy Richard Kleindienst's confirmation hearings in the Senate as attorney general, the FBI's chief expert concluded that the memo was in all probability authentic. Nixon was furious. "I don't understand Edgar sometimes," he broke out.

Now more than ever, it was vital to bypass this stubborn, difficult old man, who put his Bureau before the administration's priorities. The Committee to Reelect the President was taking shape. The Plumbers were out there.

Hoover himself was in no way befuddled about what was actually happening. That spring the Director and Andrew Tully, a writer who had done a favorable book about the Bureau, settled in for lunch in Hoover's private dining room. After making Tully promise to sit on anything he was about to say until he himself was dead, Hoover proceeded to dissect the palace guard. Asked whether he was under pressure to retire, Hoover responded "Not any more.... I put the kibosh on those jaspers who wanted to get rid of me.... The President asked me what thoughts I had about retirement and I said none, then I told him why. I told him he needed me around to protect him from those people around him. Some of those guys don't know a goddamned thing about due process of law. They think they can get away with murder. I told the president I hoped I'd live long enough to keep those people from getting him into bad trouble.... Some day that bunch will serve him up a fine mess."

But before the spring was over, Hoover couldn't protect anybody. The morning of May 2, a Tuesday, James Crawford parked in front of Hoover's two-story brick Colonial around 8:15 and started up the driveway. He had several rosebushes to plant under the Boss's directive eye. Inside, the two Cairns, Cindy and G-Boy, were yelping—sharp, imploringly, not their usual bark.

Not very long after that Hoover's colored housekeeper, Annie Fields, came out to tell Crawford that she was concerned because she should have heard the shower running upstairs by then. Crawford put his shovel down and trekked into the house and up the stairs to the master bedroom.

The door was open; this was unusual, because the Boss usually locked himself in for the night. Inside, sprawled in his pajama bottoms on the Oriental beside his bed, lay the Director. Hoover normally slept in the nude. He was already cold.

Anthony Summers has plotted the coordinates. By March 1972, he points out, E. Howard Hunt and, especially, G. Gordon Liddy were scratching up ideas for a program they code-named "Gemstone." Along with teams of muggers to break up demonstrators and a chase plane to intercept communications at the Democratic convention, their discussions revolved around ways to murder Jack Anderson. A well-planned auto accident was a possibility, or "Aspirin Roulette," lethal pills in his medicine cabinet.

That spring, there was a rash of break-ins around Washington. Affidavits reached the Watergate Committee attesting to two clandestine entries of Hoover's house, believed to have been "directed by Gordon Liddy." Hoover's doctor, Robert Choisser, was "rather surprised by his sudden death, because he was in good health." But everybody could agree that the Director had suffered from some form of hypertensive cardiovascular disease, so there was no autopsy.

Rumors made the rounds. Richard Nixon had called the night before Hoover died to attempt again to fire him. His toothpaste was poisoned. Hoover did himself in. Perhaps the most reassuring comment of all came from the attorney general–designate, Richard Kleindienst: "It's almost a blessing that he died in his sleep," Kleindienst remarked. That was "a very thoughtful, considerate way for him to cease being the head of the FBI." The Boss had proved himself a dedicated civil servant to the very end.

In 1967 Jules Feiffer produced a wonderful cartoon about "The Bobby Twins," "Good Bobby" and "Bad Bobby." "Good Bobby" was a "courageous reformer" while "Bad Bobby" "makes deals." "Good Bobby" was a "fervent civil libertarian" while "Bad Bobby" was a "fervent wire tapper." And so forth. "If you want ONE Bobby to be your president you will have to take both," Pfeiffer counsels, "for Bobbies are widely noted for their family unity."

Time and honest research have left very few in doubt that there was a "Good Edgar" and a "Bad Edgar." As, little by little, the iniquities of the FBI during J. Edgar Hoover's forty-eight-year reign leak into the accounts of the period, there is a movement afoot—even among conservatives—to disavow the starchy, self-righteous progenitor of the Bureau and scatter his documentary remains among the clinkers of history. Not many today would argue that Hoover lacked shortcomings. He was a bigot, a hypocrite, as unembarrassed a glory-hog as ever rose in public office, a blackmailer of truly fiendish reach, a soft touch for anybody with something for him, and a pretentious dresser who smelled much of the time of perfume. His handshake might fracture your knuckles. He had no compunctions ever about playing God.

But before we agree to chisel his name out of the architrave of the FBI Building in Washington, it might be just as well to think about what the twentieth century in America might have been if Hoover had never appeared. The Old Man's final dance of death with the hard guys of the Nixon administration suggests his legacy. He had a single lifelong bugbear, Communism, and whatever he hated he assumed to have been permeated with its debilitating stench. To combat this abomination Hoover had created his Bureau, a corps of hardened, self-denying professional men—law and accounting preferred—to watch over civilization, by which he meant the bourgeois order of his youth. Their job was to investigate—keep track of whatever was going on around the country—and intervene whenever anything went wrong. Sometimes this involved the courts, although frequently it did not. Politicians remained a necessary evil.

To accomplish his purposes, Hoover fought for an essentially independent FBI. His darlings were not bodyguards, they were not shock troops, and they were not available to pursue the obsession of whichever political appointee happened to be attorney general at the moment. The calculating Director restricted the targets of his Bureau with great care—along with the Lefties, he went after car thieves and kidnappers and the more flamboyant bank robbers and relinquished the more formidable challenges to the Narcotics Bureau, or the Treasury Department's Alcohol, Tobacco and Firearms Division, or the Internal Revenue Service. Hoover was well aware that drugs and gambling and big-league loan-sharking were all tangled up with organized crime, but organized crime was so intermingled with commerce and politics at the top that to let his precious agents get anywhere near something like that was to guarantee their corruption. He needed them clean to combat the Antichrist.

It may be that Hoover's finest performances came during the thirties and early forties, when much of American society was close to dissolution and powerful totalitarian movements of both the Left and the Right threatened seriously to upend our shaky constitutional arrangements. With a wink from FDR, Hoover managed to penetrate extremist groups, from the Communist Party USA to the putsch-minded plutocrats of the Liberty

Lobby to Fritz Kuhn and his German-American Bund, piecing together their strategies and orders of battle and rendering them harmless to the vulnerable New Deal. His instinct to look out for the president and preserve the power relationships throughout the government stayed with Hoover even into his last—unbalanced—decade.

Before and during the First World War, the Germans had mounted effective espionage and sabotage operations against the United States. During World War II, Hoover and his people preempted just about everything the Nazis tried. When bureaucrats in Washington floated the idea of interning the Japanese-Americans on the West Coast, Hoover opposed the proposal, partly on civil-libertarian grounds and mostly because he was convinced that his bird dogs had already identified anybody likely to give the country trouble. Had an FBI been in place in Weimar Germany, the Nazis would in all probability have remained a noisy, ineffectual splinter group.

To a certain extent, Hoover's uncanny success at generating a perception of the Bureau as hard-hitting, superefficient, and impossible for hoodlums at the top to reach made the struggle between Robert Kennedy and Hoover unavoidable. Having discovered his calling on the Rackets Committee, roughing up a succession of corpulent gangsters drenched in toilet water and glittering with pinkie rings, Bob Kennedy had the same visceral abhorrence of the Mob that Hoover displayed toward the Left. Kennedy convinced himself that organized crime was month by month strangulating America. Now it was up to him to save society. Hoover and his immaculate legion were going to have to help.

The way it all came down is the burden of this book. Robert Kennedy died young, but the intensity of his life continued to be directed against organized crime and produced several rounds of very precise lawmaking. Carefully delimited surveillance procedures compelled the Bureau to bring its resources to bear on the fragmenting syndicate. Gambling, that cornucopia into which several generations of hopeful bootleggers had poured their dreams, passed over to corporate America.

The responsibility for civil rights in America had to a great extent been thrust on Robert Kennedy. He took it up; for this, too, he drafted the curmudgeonly Hoover, an especially unhappy accomplice to any disruption of the postbellum status quo around the slumbering South. Bad-mouthing his attorney general as he proceeded, Hoover succumbed in the end to the demands of Lyndon Johnson. Squads of invading FBI were able to demoralize and ultimately collapse the Ku Klux Klan, the terrorist hobgoblin on which the Old Order depended.

At heart a reactionary, Hoover would finally discover when confronted by demands from the Nixon entourage to transform the nation into a police state that he was unprepared to go along. It was too late for that. He and Robert Kennedy had already remade America.

Source Notes

Note systems vary widely, although most serious writers tend to conform in general to the familiar academic norms. We have attempted that here, while providing a few innovations. Anecdotal material about the Kennedys has been floating through this constantly compounding literature for more than half a century. I have tended to attribute a story to the author in whose work I most recently rediscovered it rather than trace it backward through book after book. The fact that there are a number of writers in the field with important contributions has inclined me to reenter the name of the cited writer and his or her book from time to time to avoid confusion, while employing the traditional op. cit. or ibid. where the reference seemed both recent and unmistakable. The Selected Bibliography should provide enough of a lead. Nevertheless, whenever I came to feel that it had been too many pages since I had referenced an important book, I was often inclined to reenter both author and title. The aim, of course, is to speed up and simplify the verification process.

CHAPTER 1

3   Enough bad weather: Kessler, *Sins of the Father*, p. 389; Dallas, *The Kennedy Case*, p. 160.

3   The mansion: Whalen, *The Founding Father*, p. 454; Salinger, *With Kennedy*, p. 36.

4   "She was a woman. . . .": Saunders, *Torn Lace Curtain*, p. 88.

5   "The problem with going along with that": Dutton Interview, 6/2/05.

5   "Jack and Bob will run the show . . . .": Reeves, *A Question of Character*, p. 327.

6   [S]lumped in a chair: Leamer, *The Kennedy Men*, p. 433.

6   They were good together: Heymann, *RFK*, p. 162.

6   "That young man never says please. . . ." Heymann, op. cit., p.163.

6 The party's grand duchess: Wofford, *Of Kennedys and Kings*, p. 31; Reeves, op. cit., p. 85.

7 "If you think it's more important. . . .": Collier and Horowitz, *The Kennedys*, p. 241.

7 "I don't want generalities. . . .": Schlesinger, *Robert Kennedy and His Times*, pp. 205, 206.

7 In 1959, sounding out the prospects: Shesol, *Mutual Contempt*, pp. 10, 32–39, 59; Martin, *Seeds of Destruction*, p. 203.

8 J. Edgar Hoover and Joseph Kennedy: Gentry, *J. Edgar Hoover*, p. 365.

8 At one point: Kessler, op. cit., p. 249.

9 The rumors about Joe Kennedy's: Shesol, op. cit., p. 35; Bradlee, *A Good Life*, p. 206.

9 "Why didn't you tell me. . . .": Collier and Horowitz, op. cit., p. 240.

10 "He began to lecture me. . . .": Seigenthaler Interview, 1/29/05.

12 "He will absolutely take this fellow apart.": Schlesinger, op. cit., p. 205.

12 "You've got your nerve. . . .": Baker, *Wheeling and Dealing*, p. 118.

13 At 6:30 the following morning: Bobby Baker Interview, 5/30/05; Baker, op. cit., pp. 126, 127.

14 Graham, the publisher of: Collier and Horowitz, op. cit., pp. 242, 243; Schlesinger, op. cit., p. 208; Phillip Potter, *The Reporter*, 6/18/64.

14 "According to Michael Janeway": Janeway, *The Fall of the House of Roosevelt*, pp. 178, 179.

14 "Around noon. . . .": Baker Interview, 5/30/05; Schlesinger, *A Thousand Days*, p. 83; Schlesinger, *Robert Kennedy and His Times*, pp. 208–211.

14 "worst hurt Bobby ever suffered": "I think Bobby, he was for Scoop," Edward Kennedy would remember. "Phil Graham was very strongly for Lyndon Johnson. (Interview, 4/8/06) I think my father, to the extent he—he respected Lyndon Johnson, I think he thought about Texas. Also, my father had always been enormously impressed by Mrs. Johnson, who was extraordinarily gracious to my mother."

15 To his brother's consternation: Martin, op. cit., pp. 138, 345; Shesol, op. cit., p. 48.

15 "It was the information J. Edgar Hoover. . . .": Summers, *Official and Confidential*, p. 273.

15 By 1960 Hoover's files: DeLoach, *Hoover's FBI*, p. 37; Spada, *Peter Lawford*, pp. 164, 165; Gentry, op. cit., p. 470.

15–16 That Thursday in July. . . .: Martin, *Seeds of Destruction*, p. 255. Martin quotes Deke DeLoach: "They all knew about Kennedy's desire for sex. . . ." Jack's Senate pal George Smathers would be frank enough during interviews contributory to the ABC documentary "*Dangerous World, The Kennedy Years*": "Jack, Joe and Bobby were all scared to death of Hoover. They knew he knew about Joe and his shady past life. Joe was bad, he had all those businesses. . . ."

16 During Bob's last visit: Shesol, op. cit., pp. 54, 55.

16 Prowling the convention floor: Reeves, op. cit, p. 178; B. Hersh, *The Education of Edward Kennedy*, p. 136; Duncliffe, *The Life and Times of Joseph P. Kennedy*, p. 150.

16 Johnson sympathizers would claim: J. Alsop, *I've Seen the Best of It*, p. 428; Baker, op. cit., pp. 129, 130.

16 "[T]he turmoil in Johnson's private headquarters. . . .": Schlesinger, *A Thousand Days*, p. 56; J. Alsop, op. cit.; Baker, op. cit. p. 129, 130; Baker Interview, 5/30/05.

16–17 Watching over the younger generation: Schlesinger, *Robert Kennedy and His Time*, p. 211.

17 "You have not lost a son. . . .": Reeves, op. cit., p. 121.

CHAPTER 2

18–19 He parlayed *its* profits: Madsen, *Gloria and Joe*, p. 46.

19 Another Board of Strategy regular: Higham, *Rose*, p. 75.

19 P. J. married up: Leamer, *The Kennedy* Men, p. 9; Kessler, op. cit., p. 8; Whalen, *The Founding Father*, pp. 19, 20; Madsen, op. cit., p. 49.

19 At the exacting Boston Latin: Whalen, op. cit., p. 23; Madsen, op. cit. p. 125.

19–20 Joe's hauteur: Koskoff, *Joseph P. Kennedy*, p. 16.

20 A similar quirky performance: Reeves, op. cit., p. 22; Madsen, op. cit. p. 22.

20 When finally Joe did graduate: Whalen, op. cit., p. 24.

20 A classmate would remember: Anderson, *Jack and Jackie*, p. 20.

20 Most unnerving: Whalen, op. cit., p. 24; Duncliffe, op. cit., p. 40.

20 "Joe was the kind of guy. . . ." Whalen, op. cit., p. 27.

20–21 Long-jawed and compact: Duncliffe, op. cit., p. 46.

21 Capitalizing on "a contagious laugh. . . .": Whalen, op. cit., pp. 44, 55; Martin, op. cit., XX–XXI; Madsen, op. cit., p.52.

21 "When I left his office. . . .": Whalen, op. cit., p. 49; Anderson, op. cit., p. 21.

21–22 "Joe was just accommodated . . . .": Kessler, op. cit., p. 130.

22 Another biographer maintains: Gibson, *Rose Kennedy and Her Family*, p. 50; Higham, op. cit., pp. 68–84.

22 As part of her dowry: Duncliffe, op. cit., p. 51.

22 "If you have enough inside information. . . .": Duncliffe, op. cit., p. 71; Hansen, op. cit., p. 59.

22 "When you deal with a businessman. . . .": Martin, op. cit., p. 373.

22 By then Joe's ulcers were kicking up: Madsen, op. cit., p. 106.

23 "Joe was our chief bootlegger": Whalen, op. cit., p. 58; Kessler, op. cit., p. 33; S. Hersh, *The Dark Side of Camelot*, p. 48.

23 Days before he died: Leonard Katz, Costello's primary biographer, observes that Joe came to Costello "for help in smuggling liquor. A deal was worked out in which Kennedy had the liquor dumped at Rum Row and then Costello took over." "[Y]ou had the sense that they were close during prohibition," Katz quotes Costello intimate, columnist John Miller, and then "the way Frank talked you had the feeling that in later years he had tried to reach Joe Kennedy for something and that he was completely ignored . . . . nothing made him angrier. . . ." Katz, *Uncle Frank*, pp. 68, 69.

23 James Seymour signed on: Blair and Blair, *In Search of JFK*, p. 77.

23 Innocence they would deal with: Swanson, *Swanson on Swanson*, pp. 342–344; Fox, *Blood and Power*, p. 55.

23 A 1926 Canadian government: Russo, *The Outfit*, pp. 360, 361; Katz, *Costello*, pp. 68, 69; Messick, *The Mob in Show Business*, p. 32; S. Hersh, op. cit., p. 52; Summers, *Sinatra*, p. 250.

24 Reminiscing to his biographers: Eisenberg, *Meyer Lansky*, pp. 108, 109.

24 Throughout the twenties: At this point, FBI sources indicate, Kennedy inaugurated his bumpy and at times dangerous association with Moe Dalitz, the brains of Detroit's Purple Gang and later Cleveland's Mayfield Road wing of organized crime. Dalitz turned up immediately in Las Vegas to look after the Mob's interests once Bugsy Siegel was out of the way and controlled the swank Desert Inn after 1950 (See Mahoney, p. 383). Joe Kennedy was reportedly an early investor in the resort (see Russo, *Supermob*, p. 221).

24   Kennedy serviced the Caribbean: Leamer, *The Kennedy Men*, p. 40; Russo, *The Outfit*, p. 361; Summers, op. cit., p. 250.

24   The advisability of dealing: Russo, op. cit., p. 397.

24–25 Also known as Curly: Morgan, *Prince of Crime*, p. 136.

25   Stories made the rounds: Giancana, *Double Cross*, pp. 16, 17, 75, 87, 132.

25   "Joe Kennedy was a good friend of W. R.'s. . . ." Davies, *The Times We Had*, (paper) p. 300.

25   "DEAREST JOE . . . ." JFK Library, JPK Collection, apparently 5/9/22.

25–26 While still at Hayden Stone: Whalen, op. cit., p. 55.

26   "Look at that bunch of pants-pressers . . . .": Ibid., p. 75.

26   While he would later claim: Frank Mankiewicz Interview, 6/1/04.

26   One source has it: Giancana, *Double Cross*, pp. 72, 73.

26   The ambitious banker: Whalen, op. cit., p. 76.

27   It was like a convention: Whalen, op. cit., p. 82; Madsen, op. cit., p. 134.

27   The first time: Swanson, op. cit., pp. 305, 306.

27   At their initial lunch: Ibid., pp. 326, 330.

27   Her current and future assets: Higham, op. cit., p. 112.

27   Not long after that: Swanson, op. cit., p. 356.

28   Swanson found herself: Swanson, op. cit., p. 394.

28   Directed by the Central European: Kenneth Anger, *Hollywood Babylon II*, p. 45.

28   In truth, most of the Capitol: Higham, op. cit., pp. 114, 115; Madsen, op. cit., p. 154.

28   Kennedy had been wary all along: Kessler, op. cit., pp. 70, 71.

28   As the misery settled: Whalen, op. cit., p. 95.

28   The International Alliance of Theatrical: Russo, op. cit., pp. 126, 127.

29   Paperwork on Rosselli: Rappleye and Becker, pp. 55, 252; Messick, op. cit., pp. 113, 114; also see FBI main file Johnny Rosselli, (F8-2000-15), 9/16/47; Fox, op. cit., p. 213.

29   When Harry Cohn: Russo, op. cit., p. 154.

29   Sources close to: Russo, *Supermob*, p. 52. Russo has tracked down the engrossing detail that Johnny Rosselli also served as Joe Kennedy's bookie during their California years.

29   Overnight there were several sound systems out there: Whalen, op. cit., pp. 82–86.

29   "Didn't you know, Ed . . .?": Duncliffe, op. cit., p. 67.

29   Kennedy started by denying the chain: *Los Angeles Times*, 10/5/29; Kessler, *Sins of the Father*, p. 53.

29–30 "On her deathbed. . . .": Kenneth Anger, op. cit., p. 35.

30   His longtime backer: Kessler, op. cit., p. 51; Madsen, op. cit., p. 155.

31   Three intense years: Whalen, op. cit., p. 99; Madsen, op. cit., p. 251.

31   Typical was his intervention: Higham, op. cit., pp. 94–95; Whalen, op. cit., pp. 67–68.

31   He formed a backroom alliance: Whalen, op. cit., pp. 107, 109.

32   Franklin Roosevelt's intimate secretary: Janeway, op. cit., p. 103.

32   A Hollywood Kennedy contact: Ted Morgan, *FDR*, p. 365; Kessler, op. cit., p. 96; Blakey, *The Plot to Kill the President*, p. 216.

32   Most useful just then: Swanberg, *Citizen Hearst*, p. 436; Whalen, op. cit., p. 124; Madsen, op. cit., p. 293.

32   By October, Hearst had sent: JFK Library, JPK Collection, Hearst, 10/13/32.

33   During much of the fall: Duncliffe, op. cit., p. 82.

33 A general agent in Boston: Kessler, op. cit., p. 98; *Saturday Evening Post*, 7/2/38, article by Alma Johnson.

33 Flush with cash: Whalen, op. cit., p. 136; Alma Johnson article, p. 60.

33 When Jimmy Roosevelt hinted: Trohan, *Political Animals*, p. 324.

34 Like *his* father: Gid Powers, *Secrecy and Power*, p. 36; Summers, *Official and Confidential*, p. 17.

35 "This is a big city. . . .": JEH Foundation Archives, 4/29/04.

35 Another letter refers: Ibid., 9/8/12.

35 "It is cold here. . . .:" Ibid., undated note.

36 Asked whether Hoover dated: Gentry, op. cit., p. 66; Hack, *Puppetmaster*, p. 30.

36 "My dear old man. . . .:" JEH Foundation Archives, 9/12/12.

36 Annie became its "unofficial housemother": Gid Powers, op. cit., p. 64.

36 Looked after at home: Hack, op. cit., pp. 66, 67.

37 Hoover remained Over Here: Gid Powers, op. cit., p. 104.

37 On June 2, 1919: Gentry, op. cit., p. 74.

37 Within months: Turner, *Hoover's F.B.I.*, p. 179; Gentry, op. cit., pp. 94, 212.

38 Congressional testimony Hoover: Gid Powers, op. cit., p. 73.

38 Hoover put a face: Ibid., p. 81.

38 But rationality: Ibid., pp. 118, 119.

38 Years afterward: Turner, *Hoover's F.B.I.*, p. 181.

38 Within the disorganized government: Gid Powers, op. cit. p. 141.

39 By 1919, for example: Ibid., p. 128.

39 With one colored servant: Demaris, *The Director*, p. 6.

40 To pump his image up: Turner, op. cit., p. 69.

40 Still touchy about the Palmer raids: Gid Powers, op. cit., p. 147; Gentry, op. cit., p. 138.

40 One disillusioned special agent: Schott, *No Left Turns*, p. 10.

41 Each raid: Summers, op. cit., p. 48.

41 Tolson was a go-getter: Theoharis and Cox, *The Boss*, pp. 107, 144.

42 In 1930, the Bureau: Gid Powers, op. cit., p. 157.

42 In one of those gestures of selective aphasia: Gentry, op. cit., p. 328.

42 To improve the efficiency: Gid Powers, op. cit., pp. 382, 383; Nash, *Citizen Hoover*, p. 169.

43 Apparently unflappable: Demaris, op. cit., p. 80; Felt, *The FBI Pyramid*, p. 199; Gentry, op. cit., p. 192.

43 Overloaded with responsibility: Hack, op. cit., p. 188; Turner, op. cit., p. 80.

43 Hottel was a wisecracking: Theoharis and Cox, op. cit., pp. 110, 134, 146.

43 "After settling in. . . .": Turner, op. cit., p. 31.

44 In time, when Hottel's: Theoharis and Cox, op. cit., pp. 110, 201; Hack, op. cit., p. 367.

44 Their flutter with Hottel: Hack, op. cit., p. 233.

CHAPTER 3

45 How deliberately: Gentry, op. cit., pp. 149–151, 162, 163

46 As it happened, Hoover: Theoharis and Cox, op. cit., pp. 111–113.

46 Further obligations would include: Gentry, op. cit., p. 169.

46 In time he would eliminate: Gentry, op. cit., p. 168; Theoharis and Cox, op. cit., p. 129.

47   Purvis reportedly tore: One unfriendly Hoover biography, *Citizen Hoover*, by J. Robert Nash, asserts that "all the evidence in the case clearly points to the fact that Dillinger was never killed outside the Biograph Theater in July, 1934, and that an innocent man was executed in his place": p. 38; see FBI files, Purvis; Mercer Lakeland Association Letter, 4/24/34; Hoover to Purvis, 7/23/34.

47   Hoover's ghostwritten first book: Gentry, op. cit., p. 176.

47   With Dillinger effectively disposed of: Gentry, op. cit., p.179.

47   This outburst hints strongly: J. Robert Nash remarks on the fact that during his emergence in the thirties "Hoover was addicted to gleaming white or pearly gray spats covering mirror-like black shoes" and quoted the contemporary take on the Director as "chubby" and characterized by "a piercing glance, which those who have left his service say is the result of practice before a mirror." Furthermore, "'Hoover walks with a rather mincing step, almost feminine.'": Nash, *Citizen Hoover*, pp. 34, 35.

47   He liked best the converted speakeasies: Turner, op. cit., p. 69; Gentry, op. cit., p. 216.

48   Hoover's appearance: Gabler, *Winchell*, pp. 197, 202.

48   To protect his inflated reputation: Ibid., p. 275.

48   Hank Messick, no doubt: Messick, *Lansky*, p. 100.

48   "I am fed up with you and your friends. . . .": Gabler, op. cit., p. 277.

49   The country's most barefaced killer: Russo, op. cit., p. 221.

49   An acquaintanceship developed: Turner, op. cit., p. 74; Demaris, op. cit., p. 25.

50   Schine put up Hoover: Summers, op. cit., pp. 239, 251; Davis, *Mafia Kingfish*, p. 267.

50   Hoover would let himself be photographed: Fox, op. cit., p. 296.

50   On days in Florida: Messick, op. cit., p. 242.

50   "Mister Attorney General. . . .": Gentry, op. cit., p. 221.

50   Despite denials: Summers, op. cit., p. 250.

50   Designated—self designated: Messick, op. cit., pp. 69, 100, 187; Summers, op. cit., pp. 248, 249.

50   One recent Hoover: Hack, op. cit., p. 272.

51   The extent of the reforms: Gentry, op. cit., pp. 201–211.

51   Himself much more concerned about Harry Bridges: Gentry, op. cit., pp. 206, 211.

51   "One hears in Washington. . . .": *The New Yorker*, 10/5/37, p. 22; Theoharis and Cox, op. cit., p. 155.

51   Both emerging powers: Beschloss, *Kennedy and Roosevelt*, pp. 115, 253.

52   Coughlin favored: Kessler, op. cit., p. 122.

52   As a heavily promoted: Beschloss, op. cit., pp. 127, 257.

52   With an assist: Whalen, op. cit., pp. 132, 145.

52   "He was terribly generous. . . .": Clay Blair interview of Krock, archives, University of Wyoming American Heritage Center, p. 14.

52   The Jews Kennedy dealt with: Whalen, op. cit., pp. 180, 182.

53   It happened: Ronald Brownstein, *Power and Glitter*, p. 148; Janeway, op. cit., pp. 141, 179.

53   Whatever you ask Joe to do: Koskoff, op. cit., p. 86; Kessler, op. cit., p. 143.

53   When *Fortune*: Ralph Martin, *Henry and Clare*, p. 194.

53   "He'd call everybody a son of a bitch. . . .": Martin, *Seeds of Destruction*, p. xx.

53   When it came to Joe's vast acquaintanceship: Ibid., p. 17.

54   An analysis by: Koskoff, op. cit., pp. 192, 193.

54   When Franklin Roosevelt: Kessler, op. cit., p. 127; Koskoff, op. cit., p. 101.

54   "Joe you've been working. . . .": Dineen, *The Kennedy Family*, p. 69.

54   Joseph Kennedy's tenure: Madsen, op. cit., p. 309.

54–55 A State Department summary: Martin, op. cit., p. 153.

55   British antipathy: Koskoff, op. cit., p. 122.

55   Soon after he arrived: *The New York Times*, 11/15/38; Higham, op. cit., pp. 187, 199; Mooney Files, Google on Wohltat.

55   But, enraged: Amanda Smith, *Hostage to Fortune*, pp. 530, 531.

55   A report from J. Edgar Hoover: FBI records, memo 6/9/48, file on J. P. Kennedy, p. 4.

55   Observers on the scene: Koskoff, op. cit., pp. 123, 217; Kessler, op. cit., p. 220; S. Hersh, op. cit., p. 66.

55   "For a man with a weak stomach. . . .": Dallek, *An Unfinished Life*, p. 80; Higham, op. cit., p. 208.

56   "Harry Hopkins had come back. . . .": Clay Blair interview of Krock, University of Wyoming.

56   Openly on the take: Kessler, op. cit., p. 134; Ted Morgan, *FDR*, p. 463.

56   In letters between: Amanda Smith, op. cit., p. 108.

56   Not long after: Schwartz, *Joe Kennedy*, p. 224; Morgan, *FDR*, p. 262; Kessler, op. cit., p. 138.

57   "She said President was worried. . . .": Amanda Smith, op. cit., p. 404.

57   "I never want to see. . . ." Leamer, *The Kennedy Women*, p. 313.

57   For once, Kennedy's stubbornly: Leamer, op. cit., p. 312; Mahoney, op. cit., p. 15.

57   "In April, 1942. . . .": FBI memo, Joseph P. Kennedy file, 6/9/48.

57   The same year, Hoover sent over a letter: Kessler, op. cit., pp. 248, 249; Leamer, op. cit., p. 180, S. Hersh, op. cit., pp. 81, 82; Beschloss, op. cit., p. 242.

58   It would appear: Sullivan, *The Bureau*, p. 48 (paper).

58   A lot of Hoover's dredgings: Morgan, op. cit., pp. 462–466; Fox, op. cit., p. 308.

58   Typically, Hoover made a point: Gentry, op. cit., pp. 228–231

58   After such a noble stand: Ibid., p. 214.

59   In January 1940: Ibid., p. 214.

59   "As I recall. . . .": Ibid., pp. 270, 272; Gid Powers, op. cit., p. 245.

59   What mattered was: Gentry, op. cit., pp. 287–292.

60   "Mr. Hoover, aren't you really ashamed of yourself?": Turner, op. cit., p. 111.

60   He had a reputation: Martin, *Seeds of Destruction*, p. 68.

60–61 Joe Kennedy got a wake-up call: Kessler, op. cit., p. 244.

61   Kick talked Jack up: Ibid., p. 239.

61   It was Inga's assumption: Hamilton, *JFK, Reckless Youth*, p. 429.

61   The Bureau's informant: Leamer, op. cit., p. 296.

62   She attended Goering's wedding: Hamilton, op. cit., pp. 430–432.

62   A column by Inga: Gentry, op. cit., p. 718.

62   Inga's FBI interviewer: Arvad FBI file, 12/12/41.

62   Interestingly, the Washington field office: Hamilton, op. cit., p. 435.

63   "One of Ex-ambassador Kennedy's eligible. . . .": Ibid., p. 438.

63   On January 24: Coordinator of Information, 1/24/42, Arvid FBI files (Kennedy Library); Kessler, op. cit., pp. 246–247.

63   The Savannah special agent in charge: Arvad FBI files, 2/5/42.

63   "That's no reflection on your clothes. . . .": FBI Summary, Arvad files, 1/31/42; 2/3/42.

64   The editor of the *Times-Herald*: Hamilton, op. cit., p. 440.

64   "He is so big and strong": Ibid., p. 442.

64   She would recall old Joe: Kessler, op. cit., p. 246.

64   "She thought the Kennedy family was weird. . . .": Blair and Blair, op. cit., p. 142.

64   It was as if the financier's: The question of Jack Kennedy's ultimate sexuality has fed speculation since his days at Choate. "If it meant getting off, Jack Kennedy

would have inserted his dick in a cement mixer," the unsparing Truman Capote summed it up, and I remember a similar verdict over drinks in the sixties from Larry Laughlin, a Massachusetts politico who served on the PT boats with the deceased president: "Jack Kennedy would fuck a snake if he could get handles on it." (Capote quote: Heymann, *RFK*, p. 14.) Unable spontaneously to empathize, lovemaking was a mechanical process for Kennedy, and his technique was to be described as "awkward and groping and unsure" and "so disastrous that for years later I was convinced I was frigid" by conquests of the period. (Martin, op. cit., pp. 54–55, 101.) Psychologists have speculated that Jack's undisguised resentment of his mother might well have resulted in a buried animosity toward women, the need to avoid being touched except hurriedly for arousal and relief. His libido faltering, the young president increasingly needed extraordinary stimulation—the "strange piece of ass," threesomes, specialty hookers—to perform at all. Admitting finally to his affair with Jacqueline Kennedy during the Kennedy presidency, Undersecretary of Defense Roswell Gilpatrick remembered that "She had certain needs, and I am afraid Jack was capable of giving only so much": Anderson, *Jack and Jackie*, p. 352.

65 "But you know, goddammit, Henry. . . .": Hamilton, op. cit., p. 489.
65 Nothing ever hinted of espionage: Arvad FBI files, February 9, 19, 23, 1942.
65 Meanwhile, Joe Kennedy kept after his son: Hamilton, op. cit., pp. 274, 275.
65 Jack himself was reassigned to a combat unit: "They shagged my ass out of town to break us up," Kennedy later informed Robert Donovan. Wofford, op. cit., p. 215.
65 "He wasn't at all interested. . . .": Blair and Blair, op. cit., p. 151.
65 "Only, you know, his back.": Hamilton, op. cit., p. 494.

CHAPTER 4

66 "Things don't just happen. . . .": Rose Kennedy, *Times to Remember*, p. 269.
67 Anxiety gnawed constantly: Higham, op. cit., p. 34.
67 Where business was concerned: see Billings, *The Fruitful Bow*, private publication, p. 103; JFK Library, JPK Collection, Reisman to Kennedy, 8/15/40.
68 He and his family: Gibson, *Rose Kennedy*, p. 212; Kessler, op. cit., p. 351.
68 Red Chandor: Heymann Collection, SUNY, Box 1, Folder 33.
69 After all those months in California: Swanson, op. cit., pp. 353, 373, 374; Koskoff, op. cit., p. 40.; Martin, op. cit., p. 237; Madsen, op. cit., p. 230.
69 Emerging from the early recession: Bly, *The Kennedy Men*, pp. 19, 20.
69 Another panic set in: Leamer, op. cit., pp. 295, 298, 305.
70 One commentator has written: Martin, op. cit., p. 6; Schwartz, op. cit., p. 106.
70 Clare was as businesslike: Leamer, *The Kennedy Men*, p. 151.
70 Daye brought out a side of Joe: Heymann Collection, SUNY, Box 1, Folder 13, Doris Lilly interview, 6/16/9.
71 "Be sure to lock the bedroom door. . . .": Bly, op. cit., p. 61.
71 Even a glimpse: Leamer, *The Kennedy Women*, p. 230; Martin, op. cit., p. 24; Chandor History, Heymann files, SUNY, op. cit.; also Interview Marianne Strong, 12/13/05.
71 Sex would become a rivalry: Anderson, op. cit., pp. 26, 81; Martin, op. cit., pp. 12, 18, 19; Lester and Irene David, *Bobby Kennedy*, p. 28.
72 "Even if my dad had even. . . .": Rita Dallas, *The Kennedy Case*, p. 145.
72 "My father would be for me. . . .": Wofford, *Of Kennedys and Kings*, p. 39.

72   "You have to understand. . . .": Anderson, op. cit., pp. 80, 81.

72   When Jack finally made it: Martin, op. cit., p. 4.

72   In 1933, touring: Leamer, op. cit., pp. 82, 83.

72   At home on leave: Bly, op. cit., pp. 53, 54; Blair and Blair, op. cit., p. 287.

73   "I'm about to go into my act. . . .": Collier and Horowitz, op. cit., p. 137.

73   After the priests left: Joe Kennedy's devotion to classical music was sustaining and constant. Having majored in music as an undergraduate at Harvard, he collected sheet music for much of the symphonic and operatic repertories. Much of this is available at the Joseph P. Kennedy archive in the Kennedy Library.

73   He inveighed: Heymann Collection, SUNY, Box 4, File 3, Klemmer Interview; McCollough, *Truman*, p. 328.

73   He convinced himself of: Mahoney, op. cit., p. 45.

73   Arthur Krock picked up: Clay Blair interview Krock, p. 13, University of Wyoming, American Heritage Center.

73   Watching closely: Blair and Blair, op. cit., p. 152; Kessler, op. cit., p. 265.

73   A slow pudgy: Higham, op. cit., p. 238.

73   Kathleen Kennedy, "Kick": Leamer, *The Kennedy Women*, pp. 400–411.

74   Lem Billings would paraphrase: Ibid., p. 410.

74   "I'll send my girls to Catholic schools. . . ." Martin, op. cit., pp. 18, 19.

74   "He was referring to Jack and Joe. . . .": Evan Thomas, *Robert Kennedy*, p. 44.

75   "I just got out of about 3 hours. . . .": JFK Library, JPK Collection, Box 5.

75   These were lonely years, desperate at times: Bob was forever attempting to boost the morale of the youngest Kennedy, Teddy, "Whom they'd kind of abandoned," Dick Goodwin has observed. (Goodwin Interview, 6/6/06.) Ted Kennedy himself, reminiscing about relations with his namesake, Joe's sidekick Eddie Moore, remembers his isolated years at Riverdale: "Ed and Mary Moore used to come and pick me up Sundays. We'd go to the Biltmore, have lunch there. Whenever they could, they were always attentive to me. My father was moving around. . . ." (Edward Kennedy Interview, 4/8/06).

76   "Please get on your toes. . . .": Thomas, op. cit., pp. 34-35.

76   One biographer maintains: Heymann, *RFK*, p. 17.

76   Rose, friends, and the younger children: Fox, op. cit., p. 317.

76   "Conversation with the Kennedys. . . .": Heymann Collection, SUNY, Box 1b, Folder 35, Fred Dutton Interview.

76   "We never discussed money in the house. . . .": Kessler, op. cit., p. 44.

76   When one confederate: Laskey, *JFK: The Man and the Myth*, p. 44; Fox, op. cit., p. 316.

77   "Mr. Kennedy shook my hand. . . .": Billings, *The Fruitful Bow*, p. 255.

77   "I wish, Dad. . . .," Bobby wrote: Schlesinger, op. cit., p. 59.

77   "He was the least loved of all the Kennedy children. . . .": Doris Kearns Goodwin, *The Kennedys and The Fitzgeralds*, p. 364; Oppenheimer, *The Other Mrs. Kennedy*, p. 105.

78   Several of the neighbors: Heymann Collection, SUNY, Box 1, Folder 1 (Newman, Korkuch).

78   But attempting to remain a Kennedy: Kup's column, *Chicago Sun Times*, 10/16/57.

78   His life as a boy, Jack Kennedy later admitted: He himself, Jack was frank to concede, had no aspirations to a large family, which he dismissed as "institutional living, children in a cellblock. . . ." Collier and Horowitz, p. 61; David Dalleck, *An Unfinished Life*, p. 69.

78   For Bobby's generation: Madsen, op. cit, p. 182.

78   Watching his middle son in action: Heymann Collection, SUNY, Box 1, Folder 10, William Orrick memo.

79   Bob once got badly cut: James Noonan from *That Shining Hour*, edited by Jean Smith.

79   Rose remembered: Thomas, op. cit., p. 35.

79   "I think he basically was an underdog. . . .": JFK Library, RFK Collection, David Hackett oral history.

79   Sensing Bobby's instinct: Dallas, op. cit., p. 141.

80   Shortly before Jack Kennedy: Blair and Blair, op. cit., p. 346; quote from RFK letter, Heymann Collection, SUNY, Box 1b, Folder 25.

80–81 Dealing with the FBI: Clark Clifford, *Counsel to the President*, p. 178.

81   Under Franklin Roosevelt: As attorney general, Nicholas Katzenbach discovered that, along with FBI limousines, Hoover had been supplying FBI accountants to House of Representatives Appropriations Chairman John Rooney to manage the bookkeeping for his Committee, which in turn set the FBI's budget. Katzenbach Interview, 10/25/05; Gid Powers, op. cit., p. 218.

81   Celler himself groused: Gentry, op. cit., p. 407.

81   "He was a master con man. . . .": Summers, op. cit., p. 25.

82   "I have been looking over the supervisors. . . ." Schott, op. cit., p. 12.

82   William Turner, for many years: Turner, op. cit., p. 70.

82   A burly outspoken: Gid Powers, op. cit., pp. 221, 222.

82   DeLoach remembers: De Loach Interview, 5/30/03.

82–83 After one extremely bumpy plane ride: Schott, op. cit., p. 184.

83   By the time Harry Truman: In *Racial Matters*, Kenneth O'Reilly notes that "Bureau agents had curried favor with prominent Americans since the 1930s and they had chauffeured Kennedy's father around on several occasions during his travels outside the Boston area." (p. 93); Bobby Baker, *Wheeling and Dealing*, p. 18; Hack, op. cit., p. 295.

83   When Hoover's dedicated black manservant: Gentry, op. cit., p. 20; Hack, op. cit., p. 15; Kessler, *The FBI*, pp. 3, 4.

83   His earlier effort: Gentry, op. cit., pp. 176, 448.

83   Visitors approached the icon: Gentry, op. cit., pp. 617, 618; Turner, op. cit., p. 66; DeLoach, op. cit., p. 12; Summers, op. cit., pp. 42, 47.

84   Anything slimy: Gentry, op. cit., pp. 381, 462, 720; Messick, *John Edgar Hoover*, p. 248.

84   The black agent: Gentry, op. cit., p. 462; Messick, op. cit., p. 248.

85   Joseph Schott: Schott, op. cit., p. 193.

85   There is some suggestion: Hoover relic desk in show rooms of the J. Edgar Hoover Foundation, basement of the Scottish Rite Temple, Washington, D.C.

86   Few discovered outside: Gentry, op. cit., pp. 514, 515; Summers, op. cit., p. 118.

86   One prominent psychoanalyst: Summers, op. cit., p. 94; also author interviews with Anthony Summers, Bethesda, MD, 11/18–21/05.

86   In 1946, the Director had consulted: Ibid., p. 95.

86   In *Official and Confidential*: Ibid., p. 241.

87   Hoover showed up regularly: Ibid., p. 254.

87   Susan Rosenstiel's account: Maas, "Setting the Record Straight," *Esquire*, May 1993; Summers, op. cit., p. 447; also Von Hoffman, op. cit., p. 455 (paper).

87   Summers notes: Ibid.; afterward in paperback, p. 515.

87   Professor Athan: Theoharis, *J. Edgar Hoover: Sex and Crime*, pp. 49–51.

87   A summary of KGB files: Andrew and Mitrokhin, *The Sword and The Shield*, p. 235.

88   One corroboratory sidelight: proposal for book from John Klotz, pp. 16, 17; telephone interview with Klotz, 12/12/05.

88   There was an elaborate punctilio: Gentry, op. cit., pp. 50, 232, 284; Theoharis and Cox, *The Boss*, pp. 5, 9, 329.

89   Norman Ollestad: Ollestad, *Inside the FBI*, pp. 163–165.

89   They included, according to Curt Gentry's account: Gentry, op. cit., pp. 51, 302, 434.

89   "The president says the old bitch is going through the change of life. . . .": Ibid., pp. 301, 385.

90   This sort of hypermasculine good time: Gid Powers, op. cit., p. 405.

90   Deke DeLoach cites: DeLoach, *Hoover's FBI*, p. 73.

90   Deep in the printing section: Hack, op. cit., p. 329; Kessler, *FBI*, p. 364; Gentry, op. cit., p. 76.

90   Ray Wannall: Wannall Interview, 10/21/03; Wannall, *The Real J. Edgar Hoover*, p. 59.

90   Another time, Hoover—always the ostentatious gallant: DeLoach Interview, 5/30/04.

91   Apart from putting everybody's adoration to the test: For more Lulley sendups, see Nash, *Citizen Hoover*, pp. 100–102.

91   FBI veterans like Robert Maheu: Maheu Interview, 7/13/04.

91   This left Tolson sitting: Schott, op. cit., pp. 149, 150.

92   Most of the headlines: Morgan, *Reds*, p. 201.

92   "Now that the hunt is on. . . .": Ibid., p. 216.

92   Hoover spread the word: B. Hersh, *The Old Boys*, p. 166.

92   A story made the rounds: Theoharis, *J. Edgar Hoover: Sex and Crime*, pp. 46, 47.

93   In any investigative organization: Schott, op. cit., p. 31.

93   The disillusioned: Morgan, op. cit., p. 249.

93   "By spreading its poison. . . .": Ollestad, op. cit., p. 75.

CHAPTER 5

94   You would, observed Alice Roosevelt Longworth: Stein, *American Journey*, p. 51.

95   His coach would remember: Reeves, *The Life and Times of Joe McCarthy*, pp. 12, 13.

95   But politics is contagious: Ibid., p. 35.

96   According to recently opened records: Morgan, *Reds*, p. 329.

96   But the obstreperous judge: Reeves, op cit., pp. 46–50.

96   After McCarthy went out: Morgan, op. cit., p. 340; Anderson and May, op. cit., p. 60.

97   After thirty steamy months: Morgan, op. cit., pp. 340, 342.

97   "Communists have the same right to vote. . . .": Anderson and May, op. cit., p. 104.

97   In the ensuing general campaign: Ibid., p. 85.

98   Supported by the real estate lobby: Morgan, op. cit., p 354; Oshinsky, *A Conspiracy So Immense*, p. 71.

98   By 1949 most death sentences: Morgan, op. cit., pp. 367, 368

98   A leader among the seventy: Ibid., p. 364.

99   It was to become: McKean, *Peddling Influence*, pp. 196, 197.

100   But Cassara was unexpectedly shot to death: Mahoney, *Sons and Brothers*, p. 437.

100   The Kefauver hearings: Davis, *Mafia Kingfish*, p. 202; Fox, op. cit., p. 315.

100   Not without mixed feelings: Schwartz, *Joseph P. Kennedy*, p. 325; Davis, op. cit., p. 60.

100   But business was business: In *Supermob* Gus Russo points up the extent to which gangsters tended to take up residence in the flagship hotels of the 1946 Conrad Hilton/Arnold Kirkeby merger. Kirkeby, along with Meyer Lansky and Longie Zwillman and Frank Costello, participated in the development of the Nacional Hotel of Cuba, proprietor of the world's largest gambling casino for many years. "Police files in LA and Chicago point to many of the Kirkeby holdings in these cities as meeting spots for the underworld elite: Frank Costello maintained a suite on the thirty-seventh floor of the Waldorf in New York (where he was often seen with Joseph Kennedy). . . .": Russo, *Supermob*, pp. 94–97. Russo also points up the close long-standing association between the Kennedys and Sidney Korshak, the suave Mob lawyer who looked after the Outfit's interests both in Chicago and on the West Coast. When Sidney's brother Marshall received an award as Israel's Bond Man of the Year, the immaculate Sargent Shriver, then running the Merchandise Mart, presented the keynote speech: (Ibid., p. 183).

100   The heirs of Al: Mahoney, op. cit., p. 43.

101   Joe Kennedy had a knack for involving himself: Tip O'Neill, *The Man of the House*, pp. 81, 82, et al.; How serious Joe was about buying himself an important position in national politics is reflected in O'Neill's offhand remark: "Every time a Democrat ran for governor, he would go down to see Joe, who would always send him home with a briefcase full of cash. The word was that if Joe Kennedy liked you, he'd give you fifty thousand dollars. If he *really* liked you he'd give you a hundred thousand." And this in 1950s dollars! O'Neill, op. cit., p. 81.

101   Later, McCarthy would claim: Oshinsky, op. cit., p. 33; Cohn, *McCarthy*, p. 16.

101   "He was very alert, very smart. . . .": LBJ Library, Pearson oral history.

101   In speeches and articles: Collier and Horowitz, op. cit., p.163.

102   Spellman—already a. . . .: Higham, op. cit., pp. 285, 286, 314.

102   "In January 1949. . . .": Reeves, op. cit., 443; McKean, op. cit., pp. 211-213.

102   Jack Kennedy was sounding off: "We never told them how we would have saved Cuba," a rueful President Kennedy observed of the Republicans to Richard Goodwin, "but then they never told us how they would have saved China." (Goodwin Interview, 6/9/06.)

103   He'd been a foot soldier: Collier and Horowitz, op. cit., p. 162.

103   He opposed the Taft-Hartley: Leamer, *The Kennedy Men*, pp. 157–160, 246, 247.

103   Kennedy had set himself up: Priscilla McMillan, the Russian-speaking journalist who researched speeches for John Kennedy and laughed off his advances during his years in the Senate, recalls that insiders were well aware of his struggle with Addison's disease by the middle Fifties. An article appeared in the New York County Medical Society Review in March of 1956 detailing the rigors of Kennedy's back operation; while unnamed, local medical professionals were well aware of the patient's identity. "At that time, you weren't supposed to be able to survive a car crash, a child birth, or surgery if you had Addison's," Pricilla remembers. Waving off his father's pleas to leave well enough alone, JFK insisted on the operation, which very nearly killed him. "I'd rather die than go around in these crutches the rest of my life,'" Kennedy told McMillan. McMillan Interview, 6/9/06.

103   Another dinner guest: Reeves, op. cit., p. 203.

104   Flush sometimes with money: Morgan, op. cit., p. 355; Oshinsky, op. cit., p. 155; Reeves, op. cit., p. 113.

104   What exactly the Kennedys: Van Dusen, *The Power Brokers*, pp. 284, 285.

104   Appearances were everything: Lynne McTaggart, *Kathleen Kennedy*, pp. 12, 14.

105   "They gave him the boat treatment. . . .": Amanda Smith, op. cit., pp. 643, 644.

105   Another weekend: Van Dusen, op. cit., p. 285; Kessler, *Sins of the Father*, p. 318.

105   Eunice was a little too delicate: McTaggart, op. cit., pp. 14, 15.

105   When they were married: Reeves, op. cit., p. 203; Thomas, op. cit., p. 65.

105   "Remind me to check. . . ." Oppenheimer, *The Other Mrs. Kennedy*, p. 157.

105   Tail Gunner Joe could come up: Oshinsky, op. cit., p. 56; Reeves, op. cit., p. 156; Summers, op. cit., p. 179.

106   Whereas Hoover. . . .: Davis, *Mafia Kingfish*, p. 95; Giancana, *Double Cross*, pp. 255, 256; Summers, op. cit., p. 239.

106   Soon after the end: Morgan, op. cit., p. 407.

106   Another friend of Joe's: Messick, *J. Edgar Hoover*, pp. 145, 232; Hack, op. cit., p. 272.

106   Joe McCarthy, posing on the left: Hack, op. cit., p. 284.

106   At that point Del Charro: Phoenix developer Del Webb got his start slapping together the temporary housing in which the American Japanese were interned and quickly moved on as both a builder and a stakeholder in several Mob-dominated hotels, starting with Bugsy Siegel's Flamingo. (See *Interference*, Dan Moldea, p. 67.) Meanwhile, a number of investors with Mob ties and contacts in the office of the Alien Property Custodian and throughout the Warren administration in California picked up the seized Nisei properties cheap and founded venerated private fortunes (see *Supermob*, the penetrating analysis by Gus Russo, pp. 104–115). For Hoover contacts see Mahoney, op. cit., p. 74: "During Hoover and Tolson's twice-yearly betting sojourns at the Santa Anita and Del Mar tracks, underworld figures like Costello and Rosselli fixed races and, for good measure, introduced Hoover and Tolson to lesser mob lights." Also see William Torbitt, op. cit., p.38; Messick, op. cit., pp. 145, 146. That assiduous researcher Peter Dale Scott picked up on another fascinating Del Charro connection. Lee Harvey Oswald's murderer, Jack Ruby, "knew at least one member," E. E. Fogelson, and probably others, notably Billy Byers, "of the influential Murchison-Wynne set of Texas gambling millionaires, the so-called Del Charro set, who among other activities bankrolled the Gettysburg farm of President Eisenhower and paid for the annual Del Mar racetrack holidays of their good friend J. Edgar Hoover." Wynne owned the motel complex into which the FBI and the Secret Service resettled Marina Oswald within hours of the shooting of President Kennedy. See Scott, *Crime and Cover-up*, pp. 44, 45.

107   All this in addition: Theoharis and Cox, op. cit., p. 296, 297; Nash, *Citizen Hoover*, p. 112.

107   "I knew Hoover. . . .": Summers, op. cit., pp. 232, 233.

107   Carlos Marcello settled in: Messick, op. cit., p. 89; Messick, *Lansky*, p. 187; Davis, *Mafia Kingfish*, pp. 312, 425, 426; King, *Lyndon Larouche and the New American Fascism*, p. 352; Moldea, *The Hoffa Wars*, p. 263.

108   As Murchison's spokesman: Davis, op. cit., p. 312; Messick, op. cit., p. 106; *Life*, 5/2/69; DeLoach, *Hoover's FBI*, p. 75.

108   Whenever Edgar came barreling: Gentry, op. cit., p. 159.

108   At certain of the unbuttoned: Theoharis and Cox, op. cit., p. 297; Turner, op. cit., p. 76.

108   Attempting to enlist: Gentry, op. cit., p. 269.

109   When McCarthy returned for his second visit: Theoharis and Cox, op. cit., p. 298.

109   After McCarthy married: Summers, op. cit., p. 189; Demaris, op. cit., p. 162.

109   But soon after the McCarthys: DeLoach Interview, 5/30/03.

CHAPTER 6

110   Within a day: Oshinsky, op. cit., pp. 108, 111.

111   Interestingly enough: Morgan, *Reds*, pp. 489, 490.

111   While he was serving: Ibid., pp. 260, 261.

111   This J. Edgar Hoover: Cohn, *McCarthy*, pp. 8–11.

112   Soon afterward: Reeves, op. cit., pp. 198, 202.

112   Here was a ragtag: Morgan, op. cit., pp. 380–407.

113   In 1950, fueled by $10,000: Reeves, op. cit., p. 447; Oshinsky, op. cit., pp. 175, 216.

113   "Lucas provided the whitewash. . . .": Morgan, op. cit., p. 407.

113   Surine had been flushed out: Anderson and May, op. cit., p. 148.

113   Hoover retained a certain affection for McCarthy: Reeves, op. cit., pp. 493, 494.

113   The blame for the Rosenberg fiasco: Morgan, op. cit., p. 411; Anderson and May, op. cit., pp. 274, 275; Guthman, *We Band of Brothers*, p. 24.

114   As Pearson collapsed: Oshinsky, op. cit, p. 80.

114   He was practically an unpaid member: Morgan, op. cit., p. 487.

114   Sokolsky, who had been a participant: Anderson and May, op. cit., p. 346.

115   A few years earlier: *Newsweek*, June 9, 1947.

115   "We want no Gestapo or Secret Police. . . ." McCollough, *Truman*, p. 367.

115   Somebody would open a bathroom door: Reeves, op. cit, p. 507; Oshinsky, op. cit., p. 162.

116   "[A] man steeped in falsehood. . . .": Morgan, op. cit., p. 413.

116   As soon as the election was behind him: Von Hoffmann, *Citizen Cohn*, p. 416.

117   Walter Winchell's biographer: Gabler, op. cit., p. 455.

117   Roy Cohn began his political education: Cohn, *McCarthy*, p. 22.

117   Having passed the bar: Von Hoffman, op. cit., p. 75.

117   Cohn cut his prosecutorial teeth: Ibid., p. 81.

117   "The way I see it. . . .": Cohn/Zion, *A Fool for a Client*, p. 77; Von Hoffmann, op. cit., p. 94.

117   By 1952 Cohn: Cohn, *McCarthy*, p.91.

118   Cohn maintained: Von Hoffmann, op. cit., pp. 90, 91.

118   When another suspect showed up: Ibid., p. 95.

118   Before that job got serious: Cohn, op. cit., p. 46.

118   Amidst a swarm of overdressed people: Cohn/Zion, op. cit., p. 83.

118   "Here was a man. . . .": Ibid., p. 148.

118   Not long after that: Cohn, *McCarthy*, p. 48; Cohn/Zion, op. cit., p. 88; Collier and Horowitz, op. cit., p. 202.

119   In January of 1953: Roy Cohn had been on Hoover's watch list for years by then. An FBI background report on Cohn of 1/30/48 (NY File No. 77-8747) describes Cohn as "of good morals, trustworthy and loyal," with no foreign sympathies. The issue of loyalty comes up repeatedly during the background report; New York Jews were suspected of Marxist sympathies throughout the period. Also see Collier and Horowitz, op. cit., p. 202.

119   Arthur Krock sat watching: JFK Library, Krock oral history.

119   He liked to vie with his sons: Blair and Blair, op. cit., p. 52.

120   Given Peter's languid: Saunders, op. cit., p. 127; Salinger, op. cit., p. 96; Higham, op. cit., p. 304; Spada, op. cit., p. 84.

120   Attempting to cope: Dallek, op. cit., p. 70.

120   He brought her her first pieces of "serious jewelry": Klein, *All Too Human*, pp. 126, 146.

120   They shared a great deal: Koskoff, op. cit., p. 381.

120   Joe Gargan Jr.: JFK Library, Gargan interview.

121   When Franklin Roosevelt's: Trohan, op. cit., p. 138.

121   Meanwhile the financier: Duncliffe, op. cit., pp. 133, 144.

121   "A lifelong witness. . . .": Billings, op. cit., p. 31.

121   Another courtier who turned up regularly: Ibid., p. 160.

121   This sort of heavy-duty raillery: JFK Library, JPK Collection.

121   Whenever Cavanaugh: Kessler, op. cit., p. 309.

121   "As close as anybody": Edward Kennedy comment, *The Fruitful Bough*, p. 105.

122   "I take it for granted. . . .": JFK Library, JPK Collection, Rosenbloom letters, 1953–1958.

122   After cornering the market: Moldea, op. cit., pp. 77–79.

122   Rosenbloom picked up 53 percent: Moldea, *Interference*, p. 77.

122   A second-generation buccaneer: Higham, op. cit., p. 102; Gibson, *Rose Kennedy*, p. 187.

123   A longstanding acquaintanceship: Moldea, op. cit., pp. 92–96. The Schweiker-Hart hearings of 1971 yielded details about the banking operations of Batista-era Mob fixture Sam Benton, who saw to the repatriation of Cuban gambling profits along with "Mike McLaney, a former casino operator in Havana and a personal friend of J. Edgar Hoover. . . ." Scott, op. cit., p. 17.

123   In 1956, Rosenbloom: Moldea, op. cit., p. 74.

123–124 One social friend: Blair and Blair, op. cit., p. 316.

124   The ultraconservative Ambassador Smith: S. Hersh, *Camelot*, p. 157.

124   "Hope this finds the lovely Miss Janet. . . .": Kessler, op. cit., pp. 292–305.

124   "He was marvelous, you know. . . ." Leamer, *The Kennedy Men*, p. 337.

124   Janet left Kennedy's employ: Kessler, op. cit., pp. 343, 350.

124   "Your note indicates. . . .": JFK Library, JPK Collection, Janet Des Rosiers, 4/10/58, 7/12/62, 12/21/62.

125   Among his many investments: Fox, op. cit., p. 282; Kessler, op. cit., p. 255; Schwartz, *Joe Kennedy*, pp. 323, 325; Van Meter, *The Last Good Time*, p. 116.

125   Over time, the Kennedy boys: Morgan, *Prince of Crime*, p. 136.

125   One contact Kennedy liked to bum around with over the years: Messick, *The Mob in Show Business*, (paper), pp. 41–53.

126   "Bobby was," Joey Gargan saw: JFK Library, Joey Gargan interview.

126   "You couldn't live with him. . . .": Oppenheimer, op. cit., p. 106.

127   In Charlottesville: Ibid., p. 133.

127   "My fiancée. . . .": Thomas, op. cit., p. 57.

127   "Bobby's such a chicken-shit little bastard. . . .": Oppenheimer, op. cit., pp. 137, 151.

127   An untrained English bulldog: Ibid., pp. 132, 134.

127   In college, Robert Kennedy had complained: Leamer, *The Kennedy Men*, p. 241; Thomas, op. cit., p. 251; Schlesinger, op. cit., p. 68.

128   Justice William O. Douglas: Heymann Collection, SUNY, Box 3a, Folder 7, 11/19/50.

128   Joseph P. Kennedy demanded: *The Virginia Law Weekly*, 12/14/50, 3/1/51.

128   In a letter to university president: Heymann Collection, SUNY, Box 3a, Folder 13.

128   Another controversial speaker: *The Virginia Law Weekly*, 5/10/51.

128   One guest was E. Barrett Prettyman Jr.: Prettyman Interview, 5/31/04.

129   As the evening deepened: Thomas, op. cit., p. 65.

129   Still subservient: Schlesinger, op. cit., pp. 82, 83.

129   Bobby liked the work: David and David, op. cit., p. 66; Leamer, op. cit., p. 407.

129   "I have finally solved. . . .": Schlesinger, op. cit., pp. 90–92.

130   "Why don't you tell him off. . . .": Thomas, op. cit., p. 54.

130   As the campaign developed: Robert Kennedy was coming into much sharper focus all around the family. "When Jack was in one of his inaccessible moods, Bobby could always reach him and make him listen to reason," Kennedy niece Mary Jo Clasby would maintain. Kenny O'Donnell saw that "It was Bobby with whom Joseph Kennedy would discuss family matters." (Martin, *Seeds of Destruction*, p. 171.) He'd become not merely the stand-in for the father but the equivalent of the father to his generation, the sibling with the autonomy to go his own way and make decisions on his own, whatever the old Ambassador thought. "Bob was always decisive," Ted Kennedy remembers. "He could make decisions, he didn't mind making them." Jack tended to hesitate, to let himself be conflicted by events. "And Bobby had superb judgment. Jack was lucky to have him, and he had complete confidence in him." As for intergenerational disagreements? "I don't remember a time when Bobby made a call and my father got all worked up about it." (Interview with Edward Kennedy, 4/8/06.) But Ted maintains that he wasn't around during many of the critical junctures, including the row during the 1956 Christmas break when Bobby announced that he was forming the Rackets Committee to go after mobsters in the labor unions. (Reeves, *A Question of Character*, p. 99.)

130   "He just broke his butt. . . .": Collier and Horowitz, op. cit., p. 184.

130   Joe Kennedy quickly set to work: Reeves, op. cit., p. 154.

130   "Oh, bullshit. . . .": Ibid., p. 186.

130   Not that the Ambassador stayed out: Hearst columnist Westbrook Pegler, an occasional luncheon partner of the Ambassador, would report that McCarthy got $50,000 from Joe Kennedy to stay away from Massachusetts. (*The New York Journal-American*, 12/9/60.)

130   "How dare you couple the name. . . .": Collier and Horowitz, op. cit., p. 187.

CHAPTER 7

132   "My father built. . . .": Collier and Horowitz, op. cit., p. 50.

132   "You haven't been elected. . . .": Schlesinger, op. cit., p. 99.

132   "You're right, Gareth. . . .": Heymann, op. cit., p. 68.

133   Cohn, for once: Cohn/Zion, op. cit., pp. 88–89.

133   Cohn would later reminisce: Demaris, op. cit., p. 155.

133   The Truman administration: Von Hoffmann, op. cit., pp. 121–124.

134   "I was rambling, garrulous. . . .": Cohn, *McCarthy*, p. 181.

134   Robert Kennedy's press aide: Guthman, op. cit., p. 18.

134   Murray Marder: Von Hoffmann, op. cit., pp. 180–181.

134   Ralph de Toledano: de Toledano, *RFK*, p. 57.

134   "By asking the Kennedy kid. . . .": Von Hoffmann, op. cit., pp. 181, 182.

134   "Oh, hell. . . .": Schlesinger, op. cit., p. 100.

134–135   Cohn clutched his baton: Kennedy, *The Enemy Within*, p. 291.

135   Much of the truncheon work: Morgan, *Reds,* pp. 430–434.

135   "He always wanted to be somebody . . . .": George Rush, "The Red Baiter and the Billionaire," *Spy Magazine*, March 1991; Von Hoffman, op. cit., p. 150.

135   As the Kefauver: Summers, *Official and Confidential*, p. 190.

135   In and out of a hodgepodge: J. Anthony Lucas, *Harvard Crimson*, May 9, 1954,

136   In 1952, Roy Cohn: Cohn/Zion, *The Autobiography of Roy Cohn*, p. 91.

136   Their partnership: Morgan, *Reds*, p. 443.

136   Challenged to explain: Von Hoffmann, op. cit., pp. 145–154.

137   A bug the High Commissioner's office: Morgan, op. cit., pp. 443, 444.

137   If there was "one thing. . . .": Cohn/Zion, op. cit., pp. 90, 91.

137   It really wasn't much of a surprise: Morgan, op. cit., p. 441.

137   Braced by reporters: Ralph Martin, *A Hero for Our Time*, p. 63; Roberts, *RFK, Biography of a Compulsive Politician*, p. 30.

137   It developed: *The Boston Post,* John Kelso, May 5, 1953; Cohn/Zion, op. cit., p. 89.

137–138   As the hearings rolled on: *The Boston Post*, May 5, 1953.

138   Even Roy Cohn: Cohn/Zion, op. cit., p. 89.

138   A one-time Methodist clergyman: *Rave Magazine*, June 1954; Hilty, *Robert Kennedy*, pp. 78–82; Morgan, op. cit, p. 449.

138   Then Matthews was let go: Hilty, op. cit., pp. 79–82.

139   One FBI memorandum: FBI files, V. P. Keay to Belmont, March 8, 1954.

139   Ex-FBI agent William Turner: Turner, op. cit., pp. 182–183.

139   Lou Nichols, the assistant director: Oshinsky, op. cit., p. 257; Demaris, op. cit., p. 160; Gentry, op. cit., p. 379.

139   "We fed McCarthy all the material. . . .": Summers, op. cit., p. 179; Sullivan, *The Bureau,* (paper), p. 45; Hack, op. cit., p. 288.

139   When McCarthy summoned: Morgan, op. cit., p. 454; Oshinsky, op. cit., p. 321.

140   "Now Chief, let me handle this. . . .": McNeill interview, Herbert Hoover Institute (see Heymann Collection, SUNY, Box 3a, Folder 4).

140   "Working under the old man. . . .": Schlesinger, op. cit., pp. 108; Collier & Horowitz, op. cit., p. 202.

140   Sensing Bobby's admiration: Heymann, op. cit., p. 79.

140   "That must have been a rough game. . . .": Schlesinger, op. cit., pp. 108, 109.

141   Bob immediately called his father: Oppenheimer, op. cit., p. 169; Courtney Evans Interview, 1/19/2005; Bobby Baker Interview, 5/30/05.

141   In 1952, a letter had been forwarded: Theoharis and Cox, op. cit., p. 239.

141   Under pressure: JFK Library, RFK Collection, FBI memo, 3/18/53.

141   The snoop they both feared: Oshinsky, op. cit., pp. 206, 223, 485; *Rave Magazine*, June, 1954; Theoharis and Cox, op. cit., pp. 289–291; Morgan, op. cit., pp. 456, 457.

141   They reportedly argued: Reeves, op. cit., p. 512.

142   The pair would set up: Oshinsky, op. cit., p. 339.

142   Hoover, who socialized very little: Demaris, op. cit., pp. 161, 162.

142   McCarthy could be amusing: Morgan, op. cit., p. 533; Oppenheimer, op. cit., p. 140.

142   The newlyweds were close: Cohn, *McCarthy*, p. 92.

142   At one point: Reeves, op. cit., p. 512.

142   FBI records: FBI records, RFK files, Mooney to Nichols, 3/10/54.

143   "I advised_____. . . .": FBI memo, 1/18/54.

143   " . . . since so far as I know. . . .": FBI memo, 1/21/54.

144   A month later, Nichols: FBI memo, 2/25/54.

144   Still impatient with his career: Heymann Collection, SUNY, Interview of Morton Downey Jr., Box 2b (no folder).

145   Called back to lawyer for the Democrats: Von Hoffmann, op. cit., pp. 203, 204; Thimmesch and Johnson, *Robert Kennedy at Forty*, p. 59; Kennedy, *In His Own Words*, p. 120.

145   But Cohn had telephoned ahead: Hilty, op. cit., p. 86; Gid Powers, op. cit., p. 358.

145   "Robert Kennedy has got to be watched. . . .": Heymann, op. cit., p. 83.

145   It was already apparent: Von Hoffmann, op. cit., p. 204; Nash, op. cit., p. 106; Theoharis and Cox, op. cit., p. 286.

146   "The 'conspiracy group' is sending to McCarthy. . . .": Theoharis and Cox, op. cit., p. 299.

146   When Walter Winchell: Wannall, op. cit., p. 149.

146   "Bobby wanted to get Cohn. . . .": Von Hoffmann, op. cit., pp. 181–183.

146   Robert Kennedy's motives were easier to follow: Robert Kennedy was already maneuvering with great effectiveness to disgrace Schine and so undermine Cohn. Once Committee members started to take a look at Schine's pamphlet *Definition of Communism*, Kennedy "saw it as a way to get at me," Cohn wrote later, "by ridiculing Schine's report. He kept feeding gibe-questions to Senator Henry 'Scoop' Jackson. . . .": (Cohn/Zion, *A Fool For a Client*, p. 156.) A long, handwritten memo from Robert Kennedy to committee-member Senator Stuart Symington survives (Heymann archives, SUNY, Box 4a, Folder 10) in which Kennedy plots to surface—and sabotage—Cohn's efforts to work a back-stage deal with Allen Dulles at the CIA to snag Schine a momentary appointment to the Agency so he can avoid the imminent threat of being drafted, which Bobby, by leaking Schine's draft records to newsman Phil Potter, had now brought down on the lackadaisical object of Cohn's affections. After word of Cohn's intentions got back to McCarthy, Cohn backpedaled and informed his boss that he "agreed to it initially but later turned it down because the Subcommittee was then conducting a preliminary investigation of the CIA."

147   Weekends: Von Hoffmann, op. cit., pp. 213, 214.

147   A high-level Department of Defense: Morgan, op. cit., p. 468.

147   "Schine seems to have the dominant influence. . . .": Oshinsky, op. cit., p. 256

147   "For God's sake," McCarthy: Cohn, *McCarthy*, p. 163.

147   Cohn proclaimed himself incensed: Morgan, op. cit., pp. 470–475.

148   "What once seemed forceful. . . .": Anderson and May, *McCarthy*, pp. 358, 359.

148   McCarthy's main assault: Morgan, op. cit., p. 491.

148   The Army had hired: Cohn, *McCarthy*, p. 209.

149   Hoover himself was irate: Gabler, op. cit., p. 493.

149   "He came into American homes. . . .": Cohn, op cit., pp. 207, 208.

149   "Little did I dream. . . .": Morgan, op. cit., p. 484.

149   Schine proposed a "Deminform": Ibid., p. 498.

149   "Tell Jackson we're going to get him. . . .": Shesol, *Mutual Contempt*, p. 19.

150   "Aw, we got a cute kid here. . . .": Von Hoffmann, op. cit., pp. 243- 244.

150   Informed in time: Hilty, op. cit., p. 88.

150   An FBI memo: June 14, Belmont to Boardman.

150   McCarthy continued to socialize: Koskoff, op. cit., p. 264; Cohn, *McCarthy*, p. 72.

150   Bureaucratically, McCarthy was eviscerated: Oshinsky, op. cit., p. 473.

151   Ideologically, Jack was already walking: Heymann Collection, SUNY, Jean Mannix interview, Box 4a, Folder 1.

151   Aides of the period: Oshinsky, op. cit., p. 33; Dallek, op. cit., p. 189; Thimmisch and Johnson, op. cit., p. 163.

151   Roy Cohn, who looked in often: Morgan, op. cit., p. 506–509; Oshinsky, op. cit., p. 514.

151   This death, Bobby admitted: Hilty, op. cit., p. 89.

151   "I liked him. . . .": Fred Cook, *The Nightmare Decade*, p. 287.

CHAPTER 8

153   Kennedy was more attracted to: Hilty, op. cit., p. 90; Heymann, op. cit., p. 93; Schlesinger, op. cit., p. 118.

153–154 "Just a quick note. . . .": Heymann Collection, SUNY, Box 4b, Folder 9.

154   Douglas minced no words: Hilty, op. cit., p. 91; Schlesinger, op. cit., pp. 122–126.

154   KGB records: Heymann, op. cit., pp. 41, 67, 95.

154–155 Even that most unremitting: Summers, *Goddess*, p. 213.

155   The Investigations Subcommittee: Schlesinger, op. cit., pp. 129–133.

155   In 1956, he attended the Democratic Presidential Convention: Joe Kennedy was vigorously opposed to Jack's candidacy, but that did not mean he remained hands-off. He was reportedly "on the phone repeatedly to John McClellan and Lyndon Johnson, saying 'How's my boy doing, what else should he be doing?'" In retrospect, still unable to stop competing with his sons, he told listeners: "I would have won that nomination for Jack." (Martin, *Seeds of Destruction*, pp. 206, 208).

155   At an early juncture: Mahoney, op. cit., p. 19.

155–156 Two years before: Heymann Collection, SUNY, Box 4a, Folder 2.

156   Eugenie Anderson: Ibid., Box 5b, File 29; Schlesinger, op. cit., p. 135.

156   Around Joseph P. Kennedy: Hilty, op. cit., pp. 95–99.

156–157 "The old man saw this. . . .": Rappleye and Becker, op. cit., p. 202.

157   Douglas didn't get anywhere: Schlesinger, op. cit., p. 142.

157   Once the so-called Rackets Committee: Guthman, op. cit., p. 10; Maheu, *Next to Hughes*, p. 40; Schlesinger, op. cit., p. 141.

158   "Bob is the only man. . . .": Guthman, op. cit., pp. 30–31.

158   McClellan was a low-keyed: Bobby Baker Interview, 5/30/05.

158   "He was a bible-belt Jew hater. . . .": Cohn/Zion, op. cit., pp. 24, 25.

158   To JFK's annoyance: Hilty, op. cit., pp. 102, 103; Mollenhoff, *Tentacles of Power*, p. 5. The stripling Robert Kennedy's knack for befriending and utilizing the press to his own advantage was already impressing Lyndon Johnson and J. Edgar Hoover. (See Interview Deke DeLoach, 5/30/04, Bobby Baker, 5/30/05.)

159   A vaulting, sprawling: Schlesinger, op. cit., pp. 150, 151; Lester and Irene David, *Bobby Kennedy*, pp. 137, 319.

159   Ethel instructed: Dallas, op. cit., p. 228; Oppenheimer, op. cit., p. 150.

159–160 As defensive of the Bureau's: Hilty, op. cit, p. 103.

160   In 1954 Joseph McCarthy: Heymann Collection, SUNY, Box 4b, Folder 9.

160   Sam Giancana shredded: Russo, *The Outfit*, p. 329.

160   When Deputy FBI Director William Sullivan: Davis, *Mafia Kingfish*, p. 87.

160   After such a sighting, even Hoover: For his part, Robert Kennedy had started to refer to his counterparts "in the FBI over there, shuffling papers." (Nash, *Citizen Hoover*, p. 93).

160–161 Apart from his determination: Robert Blakey Interview, 9/22/05; Bobby Baker Interview, 5/30/05.

161   If that didn't work: Lowenthal, *The Federal Bureau of Investigation*, p. 342.

161   Hoover lambasted: Ibid., p. 398.

161   By 1953, for example: Gentry, op. cit., p. 349.

161–162 When key Soviet defector: Summers, *Official and Confidential*, p. 166.

162   Both Deputy Director Sullivan: Sullivan, op. cit., p. 38; Turner, op. cit., p. 16.

162   White himself had expired: Robert Lamphere, *The KGB-FBI War*, pp. 82–89.

162   While Truman was President: Demaris, op. cit., p. 106; Clifford, op. cit., p. 190.

163   As Hoover's reluctance to deal with organized crime: de Toledano, *J. Edgar Hoover*, pp. 262, 263.

163   The Director never mentioned: Nash, op. cit., p. 144.

163   Reacting to all the publicity: Theoharis and Cox, op. cit., pp. 322–323.

163   The Top Hoodlum program: Ibid., p. 257.

164   As "SAC of a field office. . . .": Felt, op. cit., p. 47.

164   Sam Giancana: Brashler, *The Don*, p. 170.

164   Richard Ogilvie: Theoharis and Cox, op. cit., p. 323.

165   The Rackets Committee hearings: Jack Kennedy's above-the-fray approach, especially to politics in Massachusetts, made his father uneasy. Joe advised against the way Jack elbowed aside party regular "Onions" Burke in 1956 and ignored the petition circulated by House Majority Leader John McCormack to spring from the penitentiary James Curley, Honey Fitz's lifelong nemesis, who had after all succumbed to the Ambassador's entreaties—and bribes—to permit his sallow, unmotivated son to grab the Eleventh District seat in 1946. Long on the Ambassador's payroll, John McCormack would play an important—if well-disguised—role as Joe Kennedy's backup vote-counter on the convention floor in 1960. (See Blair and Blair, *The Search for JFK*, pp. 550, 551, as well as my McCormack interview for *The Education of Edward Kennedy*.)

165   The Teamster president: Hilty, op. cit., p. 106.

165   Beck's mind worked slowly: Guthman, op. cit., p. 52.

165   "As a committee counsel. . . .": Russell Baker, Heymann, op. cit., p. 124.

165–166 When Kennedy asked for background: Hilty, op. cit., p. 124.

166   The director of the Bureau of Narcotics: Heymann, op. cit., pp. 98, 99.

166   A call girl Jack Kennedy frequented: Ibid., p. 230.

167   "I knew about it," Kennedy's FBI liaison: Ibid., p. 99.

167   "He was a great civil libertarian. . . .": DeLoach Interview, 5/30/04.

167   Stephen Fox compared: Fox, op. cit., p. 323.

167   "Bobby doesn't care how he wins. . . .": de Toledano, *RFK*, p. 244.

167   Another time Joe told Oleg Cassini: Cassini, *I'd Do It All Over Again*, p. 218.

167   With adverse witnesses: Heymann Collection, SUNY, Box 4b, Folder 10; *Saturday Night*, 10/25/58.

168   A widely noted piece: Hilty, op. cit., p. 116.

168   Kennedy did himself no good: Schlesinger, op. cit., pp. 188, 189.

168   "No one," Hundley said, was "breaking their back. . . .": Hilty, op. cit., pp. 117–119.

CHAPTER 9

171   He made a unique impression: Regano, *Mob Lawyer*, p. 92.

171   His mood was normally: Schlesinger, op. cit., p. 40.

172   Cheyfitz hoped: Ibid., p. 153.

172   Before long "Bobby kept peppering. . . .": Heymann, op. cit., pp. 124, 125.

172   "Twenty years ago. . . .": Schlesinger, op. cit., p. 166; Mahoney, op. cit., p. 28.

172   As it happened: Messick, *J. Edgar Hoover*, p. 182; Kennedy, *The Enemy Within*, p. 46.

173   Hoffa's detectives: Collier and Horowitz, op. cit., p. 222; Schlesinger, op. cit., p. 151.

173   "He kept looking at me. . . .": Heymann, op. cit., p. 126; Thomas, op. cit., p. 79.

173   If Hoffa were to be acquitted: Hilty, op. cit., p. 110.

173   Eight of the twelve jurors were black: Evan Thomas, *Edward Bennett Williams*, pp. 112, 113; Thomas, *Robert Kennedy*, p. 80; Hilty, op. cit., pp. 110, 111; Collier and Horowitz, op. cit., p. 223.

174   "You can tell Bobby Kennedy for me. . . .": Schlesinger, op. cit., p. 156.

174–175 The Teamsters Central States, Southeast: Reid and Demaris, *The Green Felt Jungle*, p. 83.

175   Over the years: Russo, op. cit., p. 349; Davis, op. cit., p. 111.

175   Besides McClellan, Patrick McNamara: Schlesinger, op. cit., pp. 143, 144.

175   When McCarthy passed on: Hilty, op. cit., p. 118.

175   The Republicans were increasingly concerned: Thimmesch and Johnson, op. cit., p. 177; Thomas, *Edward Bennett Williams*, p. 128; Salinger, op. cit., pp. 187, 188.

176   "When the going would get rough. . . .": Hilty, op. cit., p. 116.

176   Another attorney who matched wits: de Toledano, *RFK*, p. 176.

176   At times Bobby's charges: Davis, op. cit., p. 86.

176   Red meat to Bob: Russo, op. cit., p. 316.

176   The son of Curly Humphreys: Sheridan, *The Fall and Rise of Jimmy Hoffa*, pp. 15, 16.

176   This peeved Bobby: Kennedy, *The Enemy Within*, p. 90; Thimmesch and Johnson, op. cit., p. 71; Schlesinger, op. cit., p. 165; Hilty, op. cit., p. 113.

177   "His face seemed completely transformed. . . .": Kennedy, op. cit., pp. 34, 35.

177–178 An acquaintance of the period: Stein, op. cit., p. 156.

178   Typical of the flotsam: Schlesinger, op. cit., p. 164; David and David, op. cit., p. 116.

178   One very big fish: see Davis, *Mafia Kingfish*, early chapters.

178–179 At Meyer Lansky's direction: Regano, *Mob Lawyer*, p. 129.

179   In 1938 an undercover FBI agent: see extensive Marcello FBI files.

179   Impressed, in 1944 the New York Mob: Blakey, op. cit., p. 241.

180   "I used to stuff de cash in a suitcase. . . .": Davis, op. cit., p. 36.

180   A Louisiana native, Joe Civello: Regano, op. cit., p. 135.

180   One tipoff to Marcello's eminence: Davis, op. cit., pp. 72, 78, 237, 238.

180   When Robert Kennedy: Blakey, op. cit., p. 257; Goldfarb, *Perfect Villains, Imperfect Heroes*, p. 76.

181   What about the United Automobile Workers: Schlesinger, op. cit., p. 170.

181   A union member who demanded: de Toledano, *RFK*, pp. 121–125.

182   Even Goldwater was at a loss for words: Schlesinger, op. cit., p. 180.

182   Insiders labeled Bobby "a one-man firing squad for Jack": de Toledano, *RFK*, p. 134.

182   Russell Baker, returning to the hearing room: Heymann, op. cit., p. 92.

182   Right-wing commentator Ralph de Toledano: de Toledano, op. cit., p. 72; FBI internal memo, 9/19/59, Jones to DeLoach.

182–183 Joseph Rauh, sitting in: Schlesinger, op. cit., p. 179.

183   On discovering that Hoffa had a wiretap expert: Hilty, op. cit., pp. 127, 128; Sheridan, op. cit., p. 172.

183   Having decided: Kennedy, op. cit., p. 265.

183   It developed that Kennedy had instigated: Victor Navasky subsequently remarked of Kennedy that he "had little difficulty accommodating the notion that there were two kinds of justice, one for society's enemies, another for its victims." (Navasky, *Kennedy Justice*, p. 460.)

183   Thus, Bob could later write: Kennedy, op. cit., p. 292.

184   A year later, The *Washington Post*: Hilty, op. cit., p. 131.

184   FBI Assistant Director Alex Rosen: FBI memo, Rosen to Hoover, 3/7/59.

184   As the months passed: Hilty, op. cit., p. 116.

184   As the ubiquitous Lem Billings commented: Collier and Horowitz, op. cit., p. 225.

184   "All you're doing. . . .": Heymann, op. cit., p. 121.

185   "The committee's chief clerk. . . .": Fox, op. cit., p. 329.

185   La Verne Duffy: Shesol, op. cit., p. 20.

185   Guthman appreciated the way: Guthman, op. cit., p. 56.

185   With outsiders, he maintained a reputation: Wofford, op. cit., p. 32.

186   The Eisenhower administration remained disinterested: Kennedy, op. cit., pp. 78, 117, 140, 141.

186   Pressure was exerted on Bobby: Arthur Krock, *Memoirs*, p. 243.

186–187 Committee investigators, Kennedy wrote: Kennedy, op. cit., p. 80.

187   One committee senator who disliked Bobby all along: Mahoney, op. cit., XIV–XV, pp. 26, 27.

187   At one point, Al Capone's attorney: Ibid., p 38.

187   In pursuit of Paul Dorfman: Kennedy, op. cit., p. 87.

188   A piece of harsh, Republican-inspired legislation: Hilty, op. cit., p 122.

188   Their father had been right about one thing: Bly, *The Kennedy Men*, p. 61.

CHAPTER 10

189   Everybody is familiar: Theodore White, *The Making of the President, 1960*, pp. 260, 288, 289.

189   This required the critical involvement: Russo, op. cit., pp. 366, 375; a series of lists survives in Joseph P. Kennedy's personal files on 1960, within which he parcels out the work of telephoning major politicos around the country among key Kennedy managers. Hy Raskin catches the responsibility for Mayor George Chacharis of Gary, Indiana, while Ted Sorenson is tasked to contact Paul Ziffren a powerful Los Angeles attorney with top Mob connections. Joseph P. Kennedy papers, JFK Library; see Russo, *Supermob*.

190   They all knew from the beginning: White, op. cit., p. 57.

190   Mayor Richard J. Daley in Chicago: Kessler, op. cit., p. 347; Fox, op. cit., p. 332; White, op. cit., p. 125.

190–191 At Joe's bidding: Russo, op. cit., pp. 358, 359.

191   United Artists boss: Ibid., p. 166, et. al.

191   Widely regarded as a toady: Ibid., pp. 220–222.

191   Through George Smathers: See *Rolling Stone*, 5/20//76, pp. 43, 44 (Howard Kohn).

192   Sinatra's mother, Dolly: Schwartz, *Joseph P. Kennedy*, p. 389; Kitty Kelley, *His Way*, pp. 1, 14; FBI records, Sinatra file; Summers, *Sinatra*, pp. 257, 274, 275.

192–193 I was Frank's pimp: Van Meter, *The Last Good Time*, p. 170.

193 "Forever on the move. . . .": Summers, *Sinatra*, p. 257.

193 Toward the end of the year: S. Hersh, op. cit., p. 182; Russo, op. cit., pp. 232, 233.

193 Gangsters like Willie Moretti: Van Meter, op. cit., pp. 232, 233.

194 Once the large challenges: Martin, *Seeds of Destruction*, pp. 224, 247, 248; Bobby Baker Interview, 5/30/05.

195 Once the Chicago Outfit: Russo, op. cit., p. 375; Rappleye & Becker, op. cit., p. 205; Van Meter, op. cit., p. 172.

195 D'Amato: Summers, *Sinatra*, p. 258.

195 When Vincent ("Jimmy Blue Eyes"): Russo, op. cit., p. 370.

195 A deal was struck: S. Hersh, op. cit., pp. 144, 145; Russo, op. cit., pp. 278, 280.

195 Sinatra had long since arranged: Kennedy, op. cit., p. 94; Russo, op. cit., p. 363; Fox, op. cit., p. 333.

196 By then, Hoffa had secretly committed: Moldea, *The Hoffa Wars*, p. 108.

196 Ted Kennedy was reportedly: S. Hersh, op. cit., p. 96.

196 Nobody must draw attention: Ibid., p. 100.

196 The forthright Cardinal Cushing: Mahoney, op. cit., p. 53.

196 Once details drifted back: *IMAGE*, 3/29/92, David Talbot.

196 Bobby was more autonomous every day: Heymann Collection, SUNY, Dutton Interview, Box 2b, Folder 31.

196 Confronting the demands of a reformer: Mark Lane, *Plausible Denial*, p. 10.

197 "You know, Franklin. . . .": Schlesinger, op. cit., p. 199.

197 Charles Buckley: Whalen, op. cit., p. 452.

197 In West Virginia, historically: Schlesinger, op. cit., pp. 200–220.

198 "It was with great regret that I learned. . . .": FBI internal files, JFK Assassination Series, 11/9/54.

198 The next day Deke presented: S. Hersh, op. cit., p. 149; DeLoach, op. cit., p. 37.

198 In fact, agent reports: FBI internal files, DeLoach to Mohr, 4/19/60.

198 DeLoach would remember well: DeLoach Interview, 5/30/04.

198 "Mr. Hoover was familiar. . . .": Ibid., see Davis, *The Kennedys*, p. 278.

199 In March of 1960: FBI files, Carlos Marcello, SAC New Orleans to Director, 3/23/60 (94-37374-23); also John F. Kennedy files, SAC Los Angeles to Director, 4/1/60.

199 Two weeks after that, Hoover's: FBI files, John F. Kennedy, SAC Los Angeles to Director, 4/1/60—much of this series reappears in the JFK Assassination Collection in the National Archives.

199 FBI teletypes: FBI internal files, John F. Kennedy Files, 3/29/60; Kelley, op. cit., pp. 272, 274.

200 "Dear Bob. . . .": Robert Kennedy Files, FBI, 4/22/58.

200 Robert Kennedy came back: Ibid., 5/13/58.

200 "Dear Mr. Hoover," he wrote the Director: Ibid., 9/11/56.

200 A backgrounder as early as July 1955: Ibid., 7/20/55.

200 FBI informants inside Kennedy's subcommittee: FBI records, Jones to DeLoach, 7/20/55 (77-51387).

201 The Director is quoted as remarking: FBI, Robert Kennedy files, Jones to DeLoach, 11/4/55.

201 There was the 1956 meeting in Hoover's office: Ibid., Jones to DeLoach, 9/19/59.

201 The Director advised Kennedy that before any such move: Ibid.

201 [W]hen FBI officials were about to scoop up: Ibid.

201   Intimidated by the Bureau: Ibid.

201   The Bureau's in-house review: RFK FBI files, McGrath to Rosen, 3/4/60.

202   Kennedy understood what it meant when the Director: RFK FBI files, Jones to DeLoach, 9/19/59.

202   Weeks after John Kennedy was elected president, an internal FBI: RFK FBI files, Jones to DeLoach, 11/7/60.

202   Two weeks later: RFK FBI files, 12/22/60.

202   It wouldn't be long before: Schlesinger, op. cit., p. 260.

203   Carroll Rosenbloom: Moldea, *Interference*, p. 110.

203   The Democratic National Committeeman: Kelley, op. cit., p. 281.

203   On election day, Hoover dispatched: FBI records, 11/8/60; Summers, op. cit., pp. 274, 275.

204   Soon after Kennedy took his oath: S. Hersh, op. cit., p. 153.

204   The ten other assistant directors: Gentry, op. cit., p. 476.

204   The standards kept changing: Schlesinger, op. cit., p. 248.

204   Agents in the field labeled: Turner, op. cit., p. 4.

204   Clyde was slowing down: Hundley Interview, 10/13/04.

205   Jack had been toying: Schlesinger, op. cit., p. 229.

205   "Do you realize that high-pitched. . . ." de Toledano, op. cit., p. 12.

205   The old man: Cassini, op. cit., p. 217.

205   "I sometimes wish that Bobby. . . .": de Toledano, op. cit., p. 9.

205   "In the first place, I thought nepotism. . . .": Schlesinger, op. cit., p. 229.

205   "To Bobby—who made the impossible. . . .": Ibid., p. 232.

205   Drew Pearson wrote: Ibid, p. 229.

205–206 "Thank you very much, Clark. . . ." Clifford, op. cit., p. 337.

206   When Jack's worldly stablemate: Kessler, op. cit., p. 361.

206   The president-elect obeyed: S. Hersh, op. cit., p. 154.

206   Robert Kennedy was telling his brother: Robert Healy Interview, 4/12/03.

206   The Director was well aware: DeLoach Interview, 5/30/03.

206   Making the rounds that day with Bobby: John Seigenthaler Interview, 9/21/05.

207   "I didn't like to tell him that. . . .": Summers, op. cit., p. 277; DeLoach Interview, 5/30/03.

CHAPTER 11

208   "On January 13, 1961. . . .": RFK FBI file, 5/23/61.

208   "All the Kennedys were afraid of Hoover. . . ." Summers, *Official and Confidential*, p. 274.

208   "Whatever else he did, John Kennedy admonished. . . .": Gentry article, *Mirabella*, August 1981.

209   "Well, I think I'll open the door of the Georgetown house. . . .": Schlesinger, op. cit., p. 233.

209   The Justice Department was huge: Thimmesch and Johnson, op. cit., p. 90; Navasky, *Kennedy Justice*, p. 25.

210   "We are not going to inject ourselves into. . . .": FBI internal memo, 2/20/60.

210   "They all have the same problem. . . .": Navasky, op. cit., p. 7.

210   As deputy attorney general: Schlesinger, op. cit., p. 237.

211   The young Kennedy remembered White from an embassy: Hamilton, *JFK, Reckless Youth*, p. 269.

211   Four years later: Ibid., p. 542.

211   Joe Kennedy threw business: Bobby Baker Interview, 5/20/05.

211   The incoming president expected White: Nicholas Katzenbach, watching developments as the number three appointee in the Department, confirms all this in no uncertain terms: "Byron could have had a bigger job in the administration than deputy attorney general. But they wanted Byron there as an anchor. That was important. Bobby was impulsive. . . ." Katzenbach Interview, 10/26/05.

211   "I can't see that it's wrong to give him. . . ." Schlesinger, op. cit., pp. 236-237.

211   Miller was another lawyer: Bobby Baker Interview, 5/20/05.

212   "Kennedy knew he was obviously not qualified. . . .": Katzenbach Interview, 10/26/05.

212   Virtually Kennedy's first move: JFK Library, RFK Collection, Ronald Goldfarb oral history.

213   Kennedy was far-sighted enough: Schlesinger, op. cit., p. 268.

213   For Hundley all this amounted: Hundley Interview, 10/13/04.

213   Robert Kennedy invited Ed into: JFK Library, RFK Collection, Silberling oral history, p. 3.

214   In short order, the head count: Ronald Goldfarb, *Perfect Villains, Imperfect Heroes*, pp. 50, 57; Moldea, *The Hoffa Wars*, p. 169.

214   One of the activists Silberling hired: Jay Goldberg interview, 1/8/05.

215   As Silberling saw it, "Bob Kennedy's primary concern. . . .": JFK Library, RFK Collection, Silberling oral history.

216   The summer of 1961: Jack Miller Interview, 10/12/04.

216   They passed so quickly: JFK Library, RFK Collection, William Geogheghan oral history; Fox, op. cit., p. 336; Russo, op. cit., p. 410.

217   By now Clyde Tolson: DeLoach Interview, 5/31/04.

217   "Let the dumb asshole. . . .": Summers, op. cit., p. 367.

217   "My God, Deke. . . .": DeLoach Interview, 5/31/04.

217   "Mister Hoover had had prostrate surgery": Ibid.

218   It filled up quickly with furniture: Schlesinger, op. cit., p. 239; Summers, op. cit., p. 277.

218   "And Christ, what an office it was. . . .": Robert Healy Interview, 4/12/03.

218   "You would go and see him in his office. . . .": Stein, op. cit., p. 316.

219   Bob sent word over: Theoharis and Cox, op. cit., p. 326; Taylor Branch, *Parting the Waters*, p. 408.

219   One early decision: JFK Library, RFK Collection, Hundley oral history, 12/9/70; Hundley Interview, 10/13/04.

219   Once—humiliation!—: Gentry, op. cit., p. 477.

219   Another time Kennedy invited: Heymann, op. cit., p. 205.

219   The safe was open, Robert Kennedy Jr. recollects: Exchange with Robert Kennedy Jr., 10/29/04.

220   In February 1961 Hoover called: Robert Kennedy FBI file, 2/13/61.

220   A month later: Ibid., 3/15/61.

220   Resolutely, according to an in-house memorandum: Ibid., Jones to DeLoach, 3/20/61.

221   A few days later another memo lands: Ibid., 3/24/61.

221   But Bobby had already signed, Joe was told: Bly, *The Kennedy Men*, p. 111.

221   Wald died abruptly: Schlesinger, op. cit., p. 263.

221   He tended to travel in a small party: JFK Library, RFK Collection, Courtney Evans oral history.

222   The versatile Evans: Gid Powers, op. cit., p. 363.

222   Kennedy's lapses of judgment: Heymann, op. cit., p. 99.

222   Kennedy's insistence on moving around: Stein, op. cit., p. 292.

222   "Both sides believed in me": Goldfarb, op. cit., p. 56; Felt, op. cit., p. 63.

222   "They were too much alike. . . .": Hilty, op. cit., p. 224.

223   "Once, when Bobby had come in with a pack. . . .": Welch, *Inside Hoover's FBI*, p. 4.

CHAPTER 12

224   A failure to file tax returns: JFK Library, RFK Collection, William Hundley oral history, pp. 18–23.

224   One of JFK's priorities: Schlesinger, op. cit., pp. 286–287.

226   But Hoover was following: William Hundley Interview, 10/13/04.

227   Along with Charles A. Buckley: Navasky, op. cit., pp. 411–413.

227   Months before, when word reached the president: Schlesinger, op. cit., p. 283.

227–228 The item in the *Wall Street Journal*: Navasky, op. cit., p. 413.

228   Information about ongoing Bureau investigations: JFK Library, RFK Collection, Silberling oral history, p. 55.

228   The trail quickly led to a sometime: Navasky, op. cit., p. 417.

228   My own impression was that if: Silberling, op. cit., pp. 57–58.

229   "O'Donnell was in favor. . . .": Navasky, op. cit., p. 418.

229   "What this administration needs. . . .": Goldfarb, op. cit., p. 161.

229   "If Vincent Keogh were actually indicted. . . .": Navasky, op. cit., p. 417.

229   "I knew I had to try this sucker. . . .": Goldfarb, op. cit., p. 173.

229   "The Bureau has refused to do it. . . .": JFK Library, RFK Collection, Hundley oral history.

229   "Sherlock Holmeses must have their fun. . . .": Ibid.; FBI records, RFK files.

229   "Go back and tell your client. . . .": Goldfarb, op. cit., p. 175; Navasky, op. cit., p. 418.

229–230 "Every time Eugene Keogh's name was mentioned. . . .": Navasky, op. cit., pp. 418–419.

230   The distracted attorney general himself: Silberling oral history, op. cit., pp. 47–48.

230   "I said I wanted a legal opinion. . . .": Navasky, op. cit., p. 317.

231   Tangentially, the financier: Higham, op. cit., p. 318; Whelan, op. cit., p. 53.

231   More immediately: Joe Kennedy and Morton Downey: Hinckle and Turner, *Deadly Secrets*, p. 105.

231   Joe Kennedy himself accompanied Somoza: Higham, op. cit., pp. 346, 348, 371. Characteristically, despite having personally helped negotiate the CIA-directed arrangements that made the Bay of Pigs landing possible, Joe Kennedy repudiated the entire failed effort to Kennedy biographer William Manchester: "I know that outfit and I wouldn't pay them a hundred bucks a week. It's a lucky thing they were found out early." (William Manchester, *Portrait of a President*, p. 35.)

231   Shortly before JFK's inauguration: Higham, op. cit., pp. 348, 371.

231   Shortly after the inaugural: Speriglio, *The Marilyn Conspiracy*, (paper), p. 47.

231   One important resource: Thomas McCann, *An American Company*, pp. 93–94.

231–232 Richard Goodwin, throughout those inaugural months: Hinckle and Turner, op. cit., p. 113.

232   Robert Kennedy as well lingered on the telephone: Richard Goodwin, who frequently found himself trapped between the brothers, remembers the president as a "very smart guy, but he was a coldly calculating guy. You'd look into those killer eyes of his. . . ." With Bobby, for all his widely advertised arrogance and immaturity, insiders often found empathy. "Bobby was passionate, impetuous," Goodwin maintains, echoing other Kennedy insiders. "I loved the guy." (Goodwin Interview, 6/9/06.)

        When dealing with people he respected, Robert Kennedy could be depended on to display a level of personal kindness, even forgiveness, rare in a politician. I myself remember skiing with the senator, taking a tumble after which a ski came loose, then watching with astonishment while Kennedy sideslipped down to recover my lost ski and then clambered painfully up the icy mountainside to assist me with freezing fingers into my binding. The loyalty Robert Kennedy commanded among his troops came immediately out of this instinctive generosity toward people he cared about.

232   "The old man wanted to go in on air strikes. . . .": Martin, *Seeds of Destruction*, p. 326.

232   Many years afterward, with the detachment: Goodwin, *Remembering America*, p. 143.

232   After the debacle: Schlesinger, op. cit., pp. 416, 442.

232   Joe complained to Rose: Higham, op. cit., p. 352; Rose Kennedy, *Times to Remember*, p. 342.

232   But after hearing Jack blame: Reeves, *A Question of Character*, p. 272.

232   Once emotions leveled off: Hinckle and Turner, op. cit., p. 105.

232   After bickering with Khrushchev: Reeves, op. cit., p. 299.

232–233 Bobby alone among the children: Schlesinger, op. cit., p. 94.

233   They traded calculated digs: Martin, op. cit., p. 309.

233   Bob was "absolutely incorruptible": Ben Bradlee, *A Good Life*, p. 243; Stein, op. cit., p. 68.

234   Behind this ever-increasing shift: Dallek, op. cit., p. 195; S. Hersh, op. cit., pp. 234–237; Klein, *All Too Human*, pp. 93, 94; Anderson, *Jack and Jackie*, pp. 49, 155. In his posthumously issued autobiography, *American Spy*, E. Howard Hunt quotes James Angleton on "how Mary [Meyers] and [John F.] Kennedy would drop LSD before making love": Hunt, p. 134.

234   Bobby took his place, often justifying: JFK Library, RFK archive, Silberling oral history, p. 48.

234–235 In June of 1962: Robert Kennedy FBI files, Evans to Belmont, 6/4/62.

235   "I don't care if there's panther piss in there. . . ." Anderson, op. cit., p. 303.

235   "Management in Jack's mind. . . .": Schlesinger, op. cit., p. 598.

235   Maxwell Taylor would observe: Martin, *Seeds of Destruction*, p. 333; Reeves, *A Question of Character*, p. 273.

235   Just before the dinner: Leamer, *The Kennedy Women*, p. 435.

235   "I guess Dad decided. . . .": Reeves, op. cit., pp. 88, 288.

235   "My father would be for me. . . .": Wofford, op. cit., p. 39.

235   "Jack, if you don't want the job. . . .": Matthews, op. cit., p. 187.

236   Ex-Harvard Dean James Landis: Higham, op. cit., p. 374.

236   Anthony Gallucio: Martin, op. cit., p. 228.

236   JFK's personal secretary: Martin, op. cit., pp. 312, 359.

236   He told his old friend Charles Spalding: Ibid., p. 473.

236   Later on, Harris Wofford: Ibid., p. 25.

236–237 The Robert Kennedys attracted headlines: Oppenheimer, op. cit., p. 247.

237   At a St. Patrick's Day dinner: de Toledano, *RFK*, p. 17.

237   Robert Junior's menagerie: Warren Rogers, *When I Think of Bobby*, p. 138.

237   Except for Evan Bernard: Oppenheimer, op. cit., p. 183; Rogers, op. cit., p. 109.

237   A sign on the front lawn: Hilty, op. cit., pp. 259, 260.

237   If a visitor seemed: Sidorenko, *Robert F. Kennedy*, p. 149; David and David, op. cit., p. 137.

237   Her one reliable meal: Oppenheimer, op. cit., p. 250.

237   He encouraged rough-housing: Hilty, op. cit., pp. 96, 97, 496.

238   She converted the reprobate: Oppenheimer, op. cit., p. 245.

238   "After the party got rolling. . . .": Ibid., p. 246.

238   When *Life* characterized Bobby: Schlesinger, op. cit., p. 598.

238   One constant in Bob Kennedy's life: Warren Rogers, op. cit., pp. 93–98.

238   "Once was enough for me. . . .": de Toledano, *RFK*, p. 20.

239   "Brumus was always a big problem. . . .": Stein, op. cit., p. 160.

239   Brumus, who would normally lay sprawled: Melody Miller Interview, 6/1/05.

239   It was quickly brought to the Director's attention: Thomas, op. cit., pp. 117, 186; Heymann, op. cit., p. 215; Gentry, op. cit., p. 476.

239–240 Soon after Robert Kennedy was installed: David and David, op. cit., p. 126; Thimmesch and Johnson, op. cit., pp. 90, 91.

240   Tolson was profoundly disgusted: Schott, op. cit., p. 192; Gid Powers, op. cit., p. 355; Gentry, op. cit., p. 653.

240   The neophyte attorney general: Navasky, op. cit., p. 11.

240   Bobby pushed his brother to commute: Schlesinger, op. cit., pp. 42, 345; JFK Library, RFK Collection, Anthony Lewis oral history.

241   Robert Kennedy's lurking egalitarianism: Schlesinger, op. cit., p. 290; JFK Library, RFK correspondence.

241   Kennedy played this very cute: Stein, op. cit., p. 83 (Peter Maas).

241   Take the Chacharis investigation: Kennedy, op. cit., pp. 200, 201.

241   Wyn Hayes' ramifying: Jay Goldberg Interview, 1/8/05.

242   Cole supplied the exhilarated prosecutor: Navasky, op. cit., p. 423.

243   Chacharis took preemptive action: Ibid., p. 421.

243   With Chacharis's grand-jury appearance: Ibid., pp. 422, 423.

243   The evidence against the mayor: Goldberg Interview, 1/8/05.

243–244 In tears, Chacharis now protested: Ibid.

244   Goldberg reappeared in Washington: Navasky, op. cit., p. 422; Goldfarb, op. cit., pp. 166–168.

244   John Seigenthaler was in the room: Seigenthaler Interview, 4/4/05.

244   Within minutes, Bob had Secretary of Labor Arthur Goldberg: Robert Blakey interview, 9/22/05.

244   His bosses let Jay present his indictments: Navasky, op. cit., p. 423; JFK Library, RFK Collection, Silberling oral history, p. 18.

245   In *The Enemy Within*: Kennedy, op. cit., p. 283.

245   Kennedy—who had repeatedly assaulted witnesses: Alexander Bickel, *The New Republic*, 1/9/61; Kennedy, op. cit., p. 299.

245   Throughout John Kennedy's presidential run, Richard Gosser: Goldfarb, op. cit., pp. 132, 133, 180.

246   "Great. But can't you guys come up with a steel company president once in a while?": Ibid., p. 132.

246   Immediately across the Ohio River from god-fearing Cincinnati: Ibid., p. 92.

246   April was naked, too: JFK Library, RFK Collection, Silberling oral history, p. 52.

246–247 "All this was new to Rutterman. . . .": Goldfarb, *Perfect Villains, Imperfect Heroes*, pp. 94, 104, 105, 106, 121; Navasky, op. cit., p. 61.

247   The foot soldiers, as usual: Goldfarb, op. cit., pp. 21, 22, 235, 237.

247   His attempt to exploit the FBI: Navasky, op. cit, pp. 62–64, 415, 416.

248   Soon after investigators for the Park and Wildlife Service: Davis, *The Kennedys*, p. 313.

248   Until the Nixon administration pushed him out: Messick, *Lansky*, pp. 268, 269; Fox, op. cit., p. 312; Moldea, *Interference*, pp. 286, 471.

249   A pending indictment of officials: Goldfarb, op. cit., p. 159.

249   Before long Congressman William Green: Navasky, op. cit., p. 412.

249   "What shall I tell Dad?": Navasky, op. cit., p. 409.

249–250 "I had little or no regard for Jack Miller's. . . ." JFK Library, RFK Collection, Silberling oral history, p. 16.

250   For his part, Miller could not miss: JFK Library, RFK Collection, Herbert (Jack) Miller oral history.

250   One aspiring prosecutor: Fawer Interview, 10/6/04.

250   What success Silberling had required keeping: JFK Library, RFK Collection, Silberling oral history, p. 19.

250   "[I]f there was a conference taking place. . . .": Ibid., p. 21.

250   The key to getting something underway, plainly: Ibid., p. 15.

250–251 "I guess I was as much a part. . . .": Courtney Evans Interview, 1/19/05.

251   "Silberling was a terrible problem," Katzenbach is frank: Katzenbach Interview, 10/26/05.

251   The faithful Jay Goldberg: Goldberg Interview, 1/8/05.

CHAPTER 13

252   That needs a second look, too: It appears that there *were* individuals from whom the Kennedys refused to take money. When hard-right wildcatter H. L. ("Daddy") Hunt sent in a contribution, Bobby put his aide Ralph Dungen on a plane to hand the check straight back to the Texas billionaire. It was Jack's intention to cut back the oil depletion allowance, and Bobby intended to investigate this entire crowd of the newly rich Texas oilmen, many of whom were intimates of J. Edgar Hoover and several of whom were partners with Kennedy's father. "This man will have to be prosecuted if we're elected," Bob told John Seigenthaler. (Mahoney, op. cit., p. 85) Hunt was to prove an implacable enemy; of the Kennedy administration he was to express himself shortly before November 22, 1963: there was "no way to get these traitors out of government except by shooting them out." (Ibid., p. 256).

252   Marcello himself tipped off: Russo, op. cit., p. 367.

252   Politely, Marcello told Bobby no: Davis, op. cit., p. 139; Fox, op. cit., p. 340; Halfen's buried role in Southwestern politics surfaces in Peter Dale Scott's brilliant monograph on the Kennedy assassination, *Crime and Cover-up*. "Jack Harold Halfen," he alleges, "channeled money from the Dallas-Chicago mob's slot machines in Houston to Texas politicians as high (he claimed) as Lyndon Johnson. But Halfen also 'smuggled guns and surplus American bombers to Fidel Castro,' in a deal that apparently involved Carlos Prio Socarras and his Texas associate, Ruby's Cuban business contact, Robert R. McKeown," op. cit.,

p. 44. All this casts forward, of course, to Ruby's many gangland services prior to shooting Lee Harvey Oswald (See Chapter 19).

252–253 Meanwhile the bantam don: Davis, *Mafia Kingfish*, pp. 356, 520; Rappleye and Becker, op. cit., p. 204; Moldea, *The Hoffa Wars*, p. 108.

253 An FBI surveillance tape: Blakey, op. cit., p. 242; Marcello FBI file, 3/16/61; Kelley, op. cit., p. 295.

253 After advising Kennedy: Davis, op. cit., pp. 104, 151, 255.

253 There was some indication of Hoover's: Marcello FBI file, 3/3/61.

253 But none of the subsequent: Ibid., 7/27/67; Blakey, op. cit., p. 257.

253 Regis Kennedy would continue: Davis, op. cit., pp. 115, 116, 255; Blakey Interview, 9/11/05.

253 Ed Silberling's lawyer: Chandler, *Brothers in Blood*, p. 85.

253 One of Marcello's flunkies: Marcello FBI file, SAC New Orleans to Director, 2/22/61; Davis, op. cit., p. 288.

254 Conducted to San Jose Pinula: Goldfarb, op. cit., p. 74.

254 Pining for an early release: Marcello FBI file, L'Allier to Belmont, 4/28/60.

254 Since "The FBI had refused. . . .": Goldfarb, op. cit., p. 74.

254 Able at last to demonstrate: Rappleye and Becker, op. cit., p. 230.

254 The opera-bouffe sequence: Goldfarb, op. cit., p. 147.

255 "It is possible," reads the FBI memo: Marcello FBI file, Belmont to Parsons, 3/2/61.

255 Memoing back: Ibid., Evans to Parsons, 3/3/61.

255 Furthermore, everyone involved was well aware: Davis, op. cit., p. 102.

255 No contact was permitted: Ibid., p. 91; Hilty, op. cit., p. 205.

255 "I didn't have no pajamas. . . .": Davis, op. cit., p. 95.

255–256 Meanwhile Attorney General Robert Kennedy: Ibid., p. 92; Rappleye and Becker, op. cit., p. 149.

256 But the important paper in town: Davis, op. cit., p. 96.

256 Marcello's family returned to Louisiana: Blakey, op. cit., p. 293.

256 "If I don't make it, Mike. . . .": Davis, op. cit., pp. 98, 99; Chandler, op. cit., p. 192.

256 There is compelling evidence: Marcello FBI file, 8/27/67; Blakey, op. cit., p. 243.

256 Alongside his perennial colleague: Moldea, op. cit., p. 87.

257 Davidson lived around the corner: Summers, *Official and Confidential*, p. 233. Throughout his long career in public relations, Davidson would give a new meaning to the term *fixer*. By sharing an office with Jack Anderson, the antic little manipulator stayed ahead of breaking scandals, which often involved his clients. The Kennedy brothers had barely initiated an investigation, left largely to Senator Fulbright, into Davidson's many sleights of hand (especially where they concerned the Teamsters and the powerful Murchison family) when the president was assassinated. Scott, op. cit., pp. 11, 27.

257 While he would deny: Moldea, op. cit., p. 107.

257 As soon as word got around that Marcello: Marcello FBI file, Belmont to Parsons, 4/23/61.

257 Furthermore, a June 16, 1961 FBI report: Davis, op. cit., p. 100.

257–258 In his definitive biography of Marcello: Ibid., p. 100.

258 "My first love is Jimmy Hoffa. . . .": *The Saturday Evening Post*, 4/4/59 (John Bartlow Martin).

258 Kennedy intended to incarcerate Hoffa: Bernard Spindel, *The Ominous Ear*, p. 118.

258 The story went around: Shesol, op. cit., p. 20.

258   "His almost angelic appearance. . . .": Kennedy, *The Enemy Within* (paper), p. 168.

258–259 Sheridan did not scruple: Mollenhoff, op. cit., p. 338; James Neal Interview, 2/18/05.

259   "It burned my ass": Ed Silberling: Navasky, op. cit., p. 456.

259   Most of Sheridan's cadre: Ibid., p. 463.

259   Five years of spadework: Moldea, op. cit., p. 76; Spindel, op. cit., p. 44.

259   Two trials of Hoffa: Navasky, op. cit., p. 252.

259   A month after the November elections: Sheridan, *The Fall and Rise of Jimmy Hoffa*, p. 159.

259   To secure a $395,000 loan: Moldea, op. cit., pp. 38, 58, 102.

260   That William Rogers, during the terminal weeks: Sheridan, op. cit., pp. 155, 156, 166.

260   Shortly after the change of administration: Navasky, op. cit., p. 462.

260   By early July 1961: Sheridan, op. cit., p. 177; Moldea, op. cit., pp. 111, 113, 122.

260   William ("Big Bill") Presser: Navasky, op. cit., p. 462; Mollenhoff, op. cit., p. 195.

260–261 Johnny Dio: Sheridan, op. cit., p. 204; Moldea, op. cit., pp. 110, 118.

261   Puerto Rican muscleman: Navasky, op. cit., p. 462.

261   With an initial payment of $4,000: *The Saturday Evening Post*, 7/11/59 (Martin); Moldea, op. cit., pp. 43, 80.

261   Edward Bennett Williams, watching: Thomas, *Edward Bennett Williams*, p. 117.

261   Walter Sheridan himself: Sheridan, op. cit., pp. 210–255.

262   Nevertheless, a few years later Robert Kennedy himself: Navasky, op. cit., p. 465.

262   FBI sources later specified: Fred J. Cook, *The Nation*, 2/20/67, "Anything To Get Hoffa."

263   Furthermore, as Get-Hoffa lawyer, Charles Shaffer put it: Navasky, op. cit., p. 466.

263   This did not mean that Hoover intended: Fred J. Cook article, op. cit.; Trohan, op. cit., pp. 339–340.

263   So events in Nashville: James Neal Interview, 2/14/05.

263   So Hoover looked away: Sheridan, op. cit., pp. 238, 250.

264   "I have signed orders," he announced: Ibid., p. 254.

264   "During my first year as an organizer. . . .": Hoffa, *The Real Story*, p. 86.

264   Showily unpretentious: Moldea, op. cit., pp. 62, 63.

264   He normally used cash: Mollenhoff, op. cit., pp. 319–344.

265   One of Hoffa's lawyers: Regano, *Mob Lawyer*, pp. 142, 143.

265   Hoffa was obviously cracking: Sheridan, op. cit., pp. 205, 206.

265–266 Hoffa's morale didn't improve: Franco, *Hoffa's Man*, pp. 226–234.

266   "Everyone in my family forgives. . . .": Brill, *The Teamsters*, p. 38.

266   Shortly before the Chattanooga trial: Fred Cook, *The Nation*, 4/27/64.

267   The two had evidently collaborated: Moldea, op. cit., pp. 122, 149.

267   Furious with Bobby Kennedy: Goldfarb, op. cit., p. 194; Moldea, op. cit., p. 148.

268   Days later, one A. Frank Grimsley: Fred Cook, *The Nation*, 4/27/64; de Toledano, *RFK*, p. 238.

268   Even the lead prosecutor didn't know: James Neal Interview, 2/14/05.

268   Hoffa flew in Bernard Spindel: Fred Cook, *The Nation*, 4/27/64; Sheridan, op. cit., p. 272.

269   One of the jurors told Jim Neal: James Neal Interview, 2/18/05.

269   Outcries from the Hoffa bench: Fred Cook, *The Nation*, 4/27/64.

269   Two defendants got off: Perhaps the most revealing study of how Mob financing worked was to appear in *Forbes*, 9/29/80 (James Cook). By then the

Teamster Fund under Allen Dorfman was running over two billion dollars in assets, providing a bonanza of kickback money to its managers from most of the Vegas casinos as well as faltering construction plungers like Webb and Knapp.

269   One was Nicholas Tweel: Moldea, op. cit., p. 50; Russo, *The Outfit*, p. 315.

270   Many of these cross-connections: Ralph and Estelle James, *Hoffa and The Teamsters*, p. 20.

270   A previously undisclosed trust agreement: Sheridan, op. cit., p. 372.

270   Many of the manipulations: Moldea, op. cit., p. 174; Sheridan, op. cit., p. 374.

270   By 1964, employers were shoveling: James and James, op. cit., pp. 216, 247, 248, 273, 277.

271   Hoffa had been on kitchen-table terms: Moldea, op. cit., p. 49.

271   The diminutive lobbyist: Davis, op. cit., p. 425.

271   Already in legal peril: Navasky, op. cit., p. 479; Sheridan, op. cit, p. 376.

271   In March 1965, Hoffa himself: Sheridan, op. cit., p. 407.

271   By then the syndicate: Moldea, op. cit., pp. 260, 279, 441.

272   At that point Audie Murphy: Moldea, op. cit., p. 279; Davis, op. cit., p. 309; Peter Dale Scott referenced Sheridan to the effect that "The Mafia had placed a million dollars in the hands of Garrison's friend Carlos Marcello. The Garrison inquiry, according to Sheridan, became a means of applying pressure to have the government's chief anti-Hoffa witness, E. G. Partin, recant his testimony." Scott, op. cit., pp. 27, 28. Scott had also pieced together the connection between Jack Ruby contact Nofio Pecora, D'Alton Smith's brother-in-law, and the Smith 1970 indictment for alleged securities fraud along with Marcello, Charles Tourine, Mike McLaney and Sam Benton. . . . Ibid., p. 46.

272   Partin understood that he would probably stay alive: Moldea, op. cit., p. 279; Davis, op. cit., p. 309.

272   After Lyndon Johnson became president: Bobby Baker Interview, 5/30/05.

272   "The federal government seemed to get after Edward Grady Partin. . . ." James Neal Interview, 2/14/05.

272–273 A minimum of $50,000 a year: Davis, op. cit., p. 130.

273   The Get-Hoffa Squad got Hoffa: Navasky, op. cit., pp. 447, 478, 493.

273   Apart from the fact that senior water carriers: James and James, op. cit., p. 66.

274   "The Bureau didn't want anything to do with Partin. . . .": Navasky, op. cit., pp. 274, 275.

274   In Nashville, under Sheridan's guidance: Ibid., p. 489.

274   Sheridan himself later remarked: Ibid., p. 40.

275   In 1968, Ted Kennedy passed along: Adam Clymer, *Edward M. Kennedy*, p. 111.

275   In one of the great unavoidable set-pieces: Davis, op. cit., p. 109; Rappleye and Becker, op. cit., pp. 237, 238.

CHAPTER 14

276   Justice Department publicists: Navasky, op. cit. p. 49.

276   On June 5, 1961: Davis, *Mafia Kingfish*, pp. 101, 102.

276   It was already too late: Ibid., pp. 102, 139.

276   As late as January 1963: Ibid., pp. 137, 139, 237, 238.

277   What made this collar especially awkward for Bobby: Russo, *Live by the Sword*, p. 67.

277–278　The Palm Beach Country Club was Jewish: Kessler, op. cit., p. 84; Marianne Strong Interview, December 2005; Another golfing buddy of McLaney's was Florida Senator George Smathers: George Smathers would subsequently reveal to several interviewers that, walking with the president on the South Lawn of the White House, JFK conceded before the Bay of Pigs landing that "There is a plot to murder Castro. Castro is to be dead by the time the thousand Cuban exiles trained by the CIA hit the beaches." "Someone was supposed to have knocked him off" Smathers told Ralph Martin, "and there was supposed to be absolute pandemonium." (Martin, *Seeds of Destruction*, p. 327.)

278　By then, Bobby had been designated: Russo, op. cit., p. 38.

278　Under the policy direction: Ibid., p. 44.

278　"Everyone at CIA was surprised. . . .": Ibid., p. 37.

279　Throughout the remaining 2 1/2 years: Survivors of the Kennedy administration have been particularly vehement about disowning Cuba. "Richard Bissell was the author, frankly, of the whole thing," Richard Goodwin recalls. As for Operation Mongoose, "the sabotage and all that bullshit, none of which had the slightest impact on Cuba." (Interview, 6/9/06.) Richard Helms, attempting a late autobiography, cites, "Richard Goodwin's plan for MONGOOSE" as the basis of the entire frantic misadventure. (Helms, *A Look Over My Shoulder*, p. 198.)

279　Ex-ambassador to Cuba William Pawley: Hinckle and Turner, op. cit., pp. 147, 148; Scott references William Pawley as a contact of Trujillo and the Somozas, "whose own business connections overlapped those of the Teamster-Murchison Miami-Cuban network." Scott, op. cit., p. 12.

279　Well connected in aviation circles: Ibid., p. 181.

279　The FBI had tipped Bobby: Russo, op. cit., p. 69.

280　The raid netted "a ton of dynamite. . . .": Hinckle and Turner, op. cit., p. 224.

280　Bobby sent him up and down the east coast: Russo, op. cit., p. 69; Waldron, *Ultimate Sacrifice*, p. 564.

280　Simultaneously, intriguing with his friend: Waldron, op. cit., p. 41; Waldron's projection is reinforced by what Tad Szulc of *The New York Times* characterized in print as "the Artime-Nicaraguan plan, Operation Second Naval Guerrilla, which was counting on the assassination of Castro by Rolando Cubela alias AMLASH." Scott, op. cit., p. 10.

281　The emissary himself, Reynolds indicates: Russo, op. cit., p. 70.

281　Rosselli's availability: Fonzi, *The Last Investigation*, pp. 372, 376.

281　As Chicago's man on the Coast: Rappleye and Becker, op. cit., pp. 82–145.

282　In 1955, the Outfit's: Russo, op. cit., pp. 306, 307.

282　By 1957 Johnny Rosselli: Rappleye and Becker, op. cit., p. 163; Kessler, op. cit., p. 43; Russo, *The Outfit*, p. 314.

282　He helped distribute cash: Martin, *Seeds of Destruction*, p. 339.

283　Rosselli's most versatile contact man: Hinckle and Turner, op. cit., p. 23; Dade County (FL) police records: Russo, op. cit., pl 362.

283　In fact, well before Robert Kennedy resigned: FBI Rosselli file, cable, 11/9/62, 92-3267-371

283　"How much can I count on from the boys in Las Vegas?": Summers, *Sinatra*, p. 258; Russo, op. cit., p. 376; Davis, *The Kennedys*, p. 239.

283　"If Jack had known about some of the telephone calls. . . .": O'Donnell and Powers, op. cit., p. 83.

283　As the Las Vegas FBI reported: Mahoney, op. cit., p. 38.

283–284　There is some evidence that the cunning Lansky: Russo, *The Outfit*, pp. 367, 368.

284　It hadn't come easily; since 1927: Eisenberg, *Lansky*, pp. 109, 110.

284　"He's taking care of his end, Blondie. . . .": Russo, op. cit., p. 375.

284　So he was more than an interested party: Rappleye and Becker, op. cit., p. 163.

284　While owned on paper: It is not impossible that Morton Downey was telling the whole story when he mentioned in the memorial volume Ted Kennedy pulled together in his father's memory that "He once loaned me $500,000 to close a very important deal," and that this was the money that provided the stake Downey took in the Tropicana. (See the privately printed book, *The Fruitful Bough*, p. 35) But Joe Kennedy's pattern of investing makes it more probable that Downey was, as usual, a straw. That indefatigable researcher Gus Russo observes in a footnote: "Other evidence suggests that Kennedy also had some involvement in the Flamingo and Dalitz's Desert Inn, according to Desert Inn former employee Annie Patterson. In two letters to Moe Dalitz, Patterson informed him that Joe Kennedy had told her of his close friendship with Meyer Lansky and how Lansky informed Kennedy that 'he was not receiving his full share of the take skim.' According to Patterson, this was the original reason for the wiretapping of the Desert Inn under Bobby Kennedy." (Russo, *Supermob*, p. 221).

284　Downey was the real surprise: Reid and Demaris, *The Green Felt Jungle*, p. 71; Russo, *The Outfit*, p. 315.

285　It has been said: Russo, op. cit., pp. 375, 376.

285　"He may be old," Walter Winchell: Fox, op. cit., p. 315.

285　The ambassador had been a denizen: Van Meter, op. cit., p. 176; Russo, op. cit., pp. 376, 377.

286　"He had considerable experience in the bygone era. . . .": S. Hersh, op. cit., p. 47.

286　In time, the Bureau ran up 343: Fox, op. cit., p. 282, 315; Gentry, op. cit., p. 470.

286　The financier would normally arrive: Fox, op. cit., p. 374; Schwartz, *Joseph P. Kennedy*, p. 323.

286　Throughout reactionary Palm Beach: S. Hersh, op. cit., p. 27; Kessler, op. cit., p. 365; Clymer, op. cit., p. 23.

286　Excruciating pain: Higham, op. cit., p. 320; Kessler, op. cit., p. 336.

286　Janet Des Rosiers: Leamer, *The Kennedy Men*, p. 338.

286–287　The confidence and vibrancy: "I think if you check old Joe's will," Charles Roberts of *Newsweek* told Ralph Martin, "you'll find that he left this young woman some oil leases in Louisiana." (Martin, *Seeds of Destruction*, p. 239).

287　A follow-up FBI memo: Russo, *The Outfit*, p. 377.

287　What appears to have happened: Rappleye and Becker, op. cit., p. 208; Hellerman, *Wall Street Swindler*, pp. 105, 108.

287　The investment was troubled, almost immediately: Hellerman, op. cit., p. 108; Summers, *Sinatra*, p. 292; Kelley, *His Way*, pp. 320–323; Van Meter, op. cit., pp. 198, 199.

287　While it lasted, the Cal-Neva's ownership: Russo, op. cit., pp. 376, 389; Mahoney, op. cit., pp. 78, 122; O'Donnell and Powers, *Johnny We Hardly Knew Ye*, p. 142.

288　Allen Dulles, something of a hanger-on: S. Hersh, op. cit., pp. 150, 151; Clifford, op. cit., pp. 350, 351, Higham, op. cit., pp. 312–317.

288　By 1960, the financier's: Kessler, op. cit., pp. 327, 328; Gibson, *Rose*, pp. 171, 267.

289　Financial analysts: Bly, op. cit., p. 324; Koskoff, op. cit., p. 322; Schwartz, op. cit., p. 423.

289　When Rose Kennedy upbraided: Duncliffe, op. cit., p. 154.

289   For years, specialists: Bly, op. cit., p. 325.

289   On December 10, 1961: Higham, op. cit., p. 360.

289   He wasn't the same: Ibid.; Saunders, op. cit., p. 94.

290   Most of the threats and all the raw: A. Giancana, *Mafia Princess*, pp. 248, 249.

290   Sinatra had in fact already approached: Rappleye and Becker, op. cit., pp. 233, 234.

290   When Sinatra brought the problem up: Bly, op. cit., p. 117.

290   The volatile patriarch: Summers, *Sinatra*, pp. 282, 283.

290   What no doubt alarmed: Davis, *The Kennedys*, p. 403; Schwartz, op. cit., p. 415; Blakey, op. cit., pp. 61, 79.

290   An FBI wiretap: Reeves, *A Question of Character*, p. 214; "JFK and the Mobster's Moll," *Time*, 12/29/75.

291   "I get awfully blue sometimes. . . ." Reeves, op. cit., p. 473; Leamer, *The Kennedy Men*, p. 589.

291   When Bobby telephoned: Kessler, op. cit., p. 369.

291   Throughout recent months, Rose: Saunders, op. cit., pp. 94, 121.

291   "My son, my poor poor son. . . .": Dallas, op. cit., p. 147.

291   "Why, oh why. . . ." Summers, *Sinatra*, p. 287.

292   As first lady: Madsen, op. cit., p. 19; Martin, op. cit., p. 188.

292   Presidential aides remember: Anderson, op. cit., p. 327; Mahoney, op. cit., p. 140.

292   Judith Campbell: *The New York Times*, April 12, 1976; Judith Exner, *My Story* (paper), p. 116.

293   In August 1960: S. Hersh, op. cit., p. 163; Interview Robert Maheu, 7/13/04; All the details of the Howard Hughes/Maheu/Las Vegas scenario may never be known. Maheu has told me that Hughes bought up the casinos largely as a way of deferring the tremendous capital gains bill consequent to selling TWA. Other sources—Peter Dale Scott, for example—maintain that once Bobby and the Rackets Committee moved in on Hoffa the syndicate needed a replacement banker and arranged for Hughes to buy the Mob out while the same functionaries continued to run the gambling floors and evacuate the skim. (See Scott, op. cit., p. 29.) Maheu maintains that the flow of cash was watched carefully by state and federal authorities and the various governments got an honest count.

      There has been a recurrent rumor that the purpose of the Watergate burglars in breaking into Larry O'Brien's office was to lift documents that linked the Nixon administration to Howard Hughes; at that time, Hughes was the top CIA contractor. Scott traces the Nixon administration's "first ill-starred contacts with Robert Bennett of the CIA-front Mullen Agency," which led to "Nixon's inability to keep the Hughes-Intertel representative in Washington, Robert Bennett . . . from leaking stories to Robert Woodward which would ultimately force Nixon from office." Scott, Ibid, pp. 26, 30. Many throats were deep by the early Seventies.

293   Rosselli's was a familiar name: Rappleye and Becker, op. cit., p. 154; S. Hersh, op. cit., pp. 163–167; Fonzi, op. cit., p. 373; Scott identifies "Standard Fruit and Steamship," which made payments to Central American governments and later, along with Frank Sturgis and Howard Hunt, was accused of plotting the assassination of Panamanian President Omar Torrijos. Standard Fruit and Steamship has also been named for its role on ensuring Mafia control of corrupt Longshoremen's union locals in the United States (one ILA local owned the building at 544 Camp Street)." Scott, op. cit., pp. 15, 16. The building at 544 Camp Street would provide a base in New Orleans to both Lee Harvey Oswald

and Guy Banister, the FBI retiree at the center of Kennedy assassination speculation. (See Chapter 19.)

293   This would be Sam Giancana: A. Giancana, *Mafia Princess*, pp. 211–212;
Rappleye and Becker, op. cit., p. 177; Wofford, op. cit., p. 400.

294   The third stooge in this hapless cabal: Ragano, op. cit., pp. 12, 17, 46.

294   A second-generation fixture: Deitche, *Cigar City Mafia*, p. 90.

294   He was a prime collaborator: Messick, *Lansky*, pp. 209, 210.

294   During the months Fidel Castro: Kantor, *Who Was Jack Ruby?* p. 134.

294   After Havana fell: Deitche, op. cit., pp. 101, 102.

294   Looking back, Johnny Rosselli: Ibid., p. 108.

295   CIA files document: Kantor, op. cit., pp. 26, 27.

295   Castro exacted: Ibid., p. 135.

295   Personally the fastidious Trafficante: Ragano, op. cit., p. 39.

295   With Trafficante functioning: Russo, *The Outfit*, pp. 242, 246; Goldfarb, op. cit.,
pp. 268, 269

295   Meyer Lansky's widow: Summers, *Sinatra*, pp. 259, 260.

295   Peter Lawford described: Spada, op. cit., p. 208; Exner, op. cit., p. 117; Roemer,
Man Against the Mob, p. 280; Giancana, *Double Cross*, p. 301; Davis, *The
Kennedys*, p. 317.

296   This was by no means boudoir talk: Brashler, op. cit., p. 136; Giancana, *Double
Cross*, p. 302.

296   A private investigator named Arthur: S. Hersh, op. cit., p. 289.

296   A March 8, 1961 FBI report: Giancana, *Mafia Princess*, p. 218.

296   On the early suggestion: S. Hersh, op. cit., p. 289.

297   At midday on March 22: Mahoney, op. cit., pp. 156–158.

297   "If you have seen Mr. Kennedy's eyes get steely. . . .": Wofford, op. cit., p. 400.

298   On May 9 Bob Kennedy: Ibid., pp. 400, 401.

298   A day later, expertly spinning his web: FBI memo, Hoover to Tolson, 5/10/61.

298–299 In Chicago: Roemer, *Man Against the Mob*, pp. 213, 214.

299   *Life*'s mob expert: Sandy Smith, *The Fix*, 9/1/67, pp. 22, 23.

299   All across Cook County: Russo, *The Outfit*, pp. 301, 339.

299   At Giancana's elbow: Waldron, op. cit., pp. 229, 551–555; Mahoney, op. cit.,
pp. 75, 76.

299   *Time* magazine later reported: Hinckle and Turner, op. cit., p. 82.

299   An experienced wireman: Rappleye and Becker, op. cit., p. 178.

299   After painful reflection: Sandy Smith, op. cit.

299   The trio of special agents: Russo, *The Outfit*, pp. 340, 349.

300   "If he went to dinner. . . .": Roemer, op. cit., p. 260.

300   "He put his head right up under my chin. . . .": Ibid., pp. 148, 149.

300   Accordingly, in time the Bureau put: Ibid., p. 185.

300   In *The Dark Side of Camelot*: S. Hersh, op. cit., pp. 311, 312.

301   According to Justice Department insiders: Courtney Evans Interview, 1/19/05.

301   "J. Edna. . . .": Mahoney, op. cit., p. 78.

301   When Tolson went into the hospital: Gentry, op. cit., p. 479.

301   As his frustrations deepened: Heymann, *RFK*, p. 215.

302   "We tried to prove. . . .": Hundley Interview, 10/13/05.

302   By 1962, the Bureau: Courtney Evans Interview, 1/19/05.

302   Roemer describes: Roemer, op. cit., pp. 214–217.

303   The seasoned William Hundley: Hundley Interview, 10/13/05.

303   It was already too late: Roemer, op. cit., p. 217.

303   By then, Jack Kennedy had stayed away: Rappleye and Becker, op. cit., p. 234.

303–304 Robert Kennedy, as usual: O'Donnell and Powers, op. cit., p. 380.

304   Receiving word of the presidential: Van Meter, op. cit., p. 186.

304   Any Mob effort to dust Castro: Russo, *Live by the Sword*, p. 523.

304   By answering at all: Davis, *The Kennedys*, p. 339

304   Chicago Special Agent in Charge Marlin Johnson: Russo, *The Outfit*, pp. 446, 447.

304   "He knows too much. . . .": Ibid.

305   One writer remarks, "FBI. . . .": Davis, *Mafia Kingfish*, p. 92.

305   FBI records detail: FBI Rosselli files, teletype 11/9/62 (92-3267-371); Schwartz, op. cit., pp. 412, 413.

305   Early in 1963, openly demoted: Navasky, op. cit., p. 62.

305   Years later, reflecting on the Giancana embroilment: Heymann, op. cit., p. 416.

CHAPTER 15

306   Dr. Jacobson's "miracle tissue regenerator. . . .": Bly, op. cit., p. 86; Gibson, op. cit., p. 177.

306   His doctors prescribed Tuinal: Schwartz, op. cit., p. 379.

306   Much as he appreciated the backup: It appears that Robert Kennedy brought in his own wiretappers to listen in on White House reporters during a stopover by JFK in Newport, Rhode Island, while the president himself tapped the calls of both his wife and his brother, Robert. (Michael Beschloss, *Kennedy and Khrushchev*, p. 347.)

307   "This will destroy us politically. . . ." Schlesinger, op. cit., p. 387.

307   "I'm the president. . . .": Baker, op. cit., pp. 97, 98.

307   It got down often enough: Ibid., p. 99.

307   "He was not a systematic organizer. . . .": Katzenbach Interview, 11/26/05; Navasky, op. cit., p. 199.

307   Bobby reportedly stuck: S. Hersh, op. cit., p. 35.

308   As the months passed: Thimmesch and Johnson, op. cit., p. 122.

308   "Bobby was like a wounded animal. . . .": S. Hersh, op. cit., p. 216.

308   "I'm afraid, Mr. President. . . .": Goodwin, *Remembering America*, p. 445.

308   What his restive subordinates: Schlesinger, op. cit., p. 808.

308   Impressed at that point: Rappleye and Becker, op. cit., pp. 195, 196.

308–309 Thomas Parrott: Sidorenko, op. cit., p. 49.

309   "Oh, shit, the second most important man. . . .": S. Hersh, op. cit., p. 279.

309   Taylor himself: Leamer, *The Kennedy Men*, p. 612.

309   By 1961 William Harvey: B. Hersh, *The Old Boys*, p. 398 (paper).

310   Quickly dubbed "the colonel": Rappleye and Becker, op. cit., pp. 146, 147, 223, 224; Hinckle and Turner, op. cit., p. 77.

310   Bob Kennedy would subsequently characterize: RFK, *In His Own Words*, p. 378.

310   The Kennedy brothers "were just absolutely obsessed. . . .": S. Hersh, op. cit., p. 268.

310   After decades of holding his tongue: Russo, *Live by the Sword*, p. 431.

310   He directed the Agency to provide him: Leamer, *The Kennedy Men*, p. 610.

310–311 "Bobby was absolutely convinced. . . .": S. Hersh, op. cit., p. 286.

311   McLaney is said to have offered: Russo, op. cit., pp. 69, 70.

311   He and three other Get-Hoffa Squad: Ibid., p. 407.

311   Along with Bobby's friend John Reilly: deToledano, *RFK*, pp. 206–208 (paper).

311   Determined to begin to efface: Schlesinger, op. cit., p. 468.

311–312 When enough private-sector cash: Prettyman Interview, 5/3/04.

312   No forms, no wait, no haggling: As word got back to the professional military of Robert Kennedy's independent deal-making with the Soviets, communal rage was starting to reach a level that evidently threatened a takeover of the nation by the Pentagon. Bobby's good friend John Reilly, who ran security at the State Department, lends credence to the statement in Khrushchev's memoirs that Soviet Ambassador Anatoly Dobrynin "in a visit with Bob Kennedy, was informed by Bob Kennedy that one of the reasons that President Kennedy had to settle the Cuban missile matter was because he was fearful of an overthrow by the military in the United States." (JFK Library, Reilly oral history interview, 12/6/70).

      Researching his forthcoming book on Robert Kennedy and the CIA, David Talbot found evidence of senior brass attacking the Kennedy administration as a "culture of treason," with Curtis LeMay referring to the Kennedy brothers as "cockroaches," while Admiral Arleigh Burke dismissed them as "appeasers, decadent like Joe Kennedy." The Kennedys in turn were contemptuous of the general they found in place as chairman of the Joint Chiefs of Staff, Lyman Lemnitzer and regarded the combat-intoxicated head of the Strategic Air Command, LeMay, as "a madman." (Talbot address before conference of the Assassination and Research Archives, 11/19/05).

      Justification for the Kennedy attitude is to be found in James Bamford's important new book, *Body of Secrets*, which reprints a JCS proposal of the period urging the U.S. Government to mount a wide-scale provocation intended to justify the eagerly awaited invasion of Cuba, OPERATION NORTHWOODS. American methods were to include a bogus "Communist Cuban terror campaign in the Miami area, in other Florida cities and even in Washington," to include "sinking a boatload of Cuban refugees (real or simulated)" along with a fake Cuban air force attack on a civilian jetliner and a "Remember the Maine" incident involving the detonation of a U.S. ship in Cuban waters, to be attributed to Cuban sabotage.

      The whole venture smacks of OPERATION CANNED GOODS, which Hitler's Sicherheitsdienst impresario Reinhard Heydrich staged with Polish corpses in 1939 as a pretext to invade Poland. As it happens, a number of Heydrich's senior staffers had been smuggled into the United States after World War II to advise our intelligence services. In 1962, fortunately, Robert McNamara stepped on OPERATION NORTHWOODS. (See fifteen-page U.S. Government TOP SECRET document, "Chairman, Joint Chiefs of Staff, Justification for US Military Intervention in Cuba, 3/13/62.)

312   From the early days of the administration: Schlesinger, op. cit., pp. 499–501.

312–313 Hoover had been introduced around the offices: Hack, *Puppetmaster*, p. 316.

313   Simply thinking about preemptive air strikes: Schlesinger, op. cit., pp. 507, 525.

313   Not that Robert Kennedy was squeamish: Spindel, op. cit., pp. 85–88.

313   With the Alliance for Progress: See Church Committee Assassination Hearings—Trujillo.

314   In March 1961: Rappleye and Becker, op. cit., p. 226.

314   One of Joe Kennedy's regular golfing partners: Cassini, *I'd Do It All Over Again*, pp 217–228; Higham, op. cit., p. 430.

314   Documents that soon leaked: S. Hersh, op. cit., pp. 197, 198.

314   After George Smathers failed: Rappleye and Becker, op. cit., p. 225.

315   Once Oleg began to supply Jacqueline Kennedy: Anderson, op. cit., p. 244.

315   The Ambassador had once tried: Kessler, op. cit., pp. 260, 261, 284; Reeves, op. cit., pp. 138, 230; Klein, op. cit., p. 209; Anderson, op. cit., pp. 154, 244.

315   One Narcotics Bureau contact: See Heymann Collection, SUNY, Box 2b (both Downey and Diller Interviews).

315   Rose Kennedy was fond of Igor's: Higham, op. cit., p. 371.

315   Igor's wife, the thirty-eight-year-old: Cassini, op. cit., p. 228.

316   From Hoover's vantage point: Ibid., pp. 218, 225.

316   Another supporter who wound up overboard: Van Meter, op. cit., p. 174.

317   By then, Sinatra had retained: Schwartz, op. cit., pp. 411, 412.

317   Closer to home, Bobby found himself caught: Moldea, *Interference*, pp. 90, 91; Russo, *Live by the Sword*, pp. 89, 526.

318   Everybody took a step back: Moldea, op. cit., pp. 176, 459.

318   No doubt the most painful: Navasky, op. cit., pp. 427–442.

319   In 1964, fighting for his seat: Guthman, *This Band of Brothers*, p. 300.

319   Ultimately, closeted in the attorney general's: Navasky, op. cit., pp. 395–397.

320   One of the more puzzling revelations: S. Hersh, op. cit., pp. 315–317; also FBI Assassination Series, National Archives, Evans to Belmont, 8/17/62, Rosselli investigation.

320   Courtney Evans comes closest: Evans Interview, 1/19/05.

320   Joe Kennedy was concerned: Evan Thomas, *Edward Bennett Williams*, p. 163.

321   Their first meeting on February 1: Heymann, op. cit., pp. 304, 305.

321   Like the sisters' giggled warning: Cassini, op. cit., p. 224.

321   "For all her romanticism and masochism. . . .": Heymann, op. cit., p. 305; also see Speriglio, *The Marilyn Conspiracy*, p. 41.

321   James Spada's biography: Spada, op. cit., p. 307.

321   Arthur Schlesinger remembers: Schlesinger, op. cit., p. 590.

322   By the spring of 1962: Summers, *Official and Confidential*, pp. 297, 298.

322   Hoover himself sent over word: Ibid., p. 297.

322   On the telephone to George Terrien: Oppenheimer, op. cit., p. 235.

322   "Oddly enough. . . .": Cassini, op. cit., pp. 217, 218.

322   Marilyn's "sleeping pills buddy": Spada, op. cit., p. 308.

323   On stolen time: Summers, *Goddess*, pp. 226, 227.

323   Marilyn told Jeanne Carmen: Bly, *The Kennedy Men*, p. 127; also *The Los Angeles Times*, 8/5/05 (Los Angeles County Prosecutor, John Miner).

323   One regular visitor to the Lawford house: Summers, *Goddess*, p. 251.

323   When Bob caught Marilyn: Speriglio, op. cit., p. 215.

323   Slatzer had been in and out: Summers, *Goddess*, pp. 24, 25.

323   As they lounged on the beach: Speriglio, op. cit., pp. 46–48.

324   Bobby had maintained "that he was powerful enough. . . .": Speriglio, op. cit., p. 87; Slatzer, *The Curious Death of Marilyn Monroe*, p. 4.

324   When Fred Otash: Heymann, op. cit., pp. 315, 316; Summers, *Goddess*, p. 265; Davis, *Mafia Kingfish*, p. 239.

324   Meanwhile, Hoffa's highly regarded wireman: Summers, op. cit., pp. 296, 297.

324   Spindel, who anticipated: Spada, op. cit., pp. 310, 311.

324   To demonstrate his matchless technical: Summers, *Goddess*, p. 263.

324   Hoover kept other files: Summers, *Official and Confidential*, p. 296.

324–325 One, which is evidently intended: FBI Airtel, SAC Newark to Director #61465.

325   An outside technician: A confidential source.

325   For months, remarked one FBI onlooker: Summers, *Goddess*, p. 240.

325   Tipped off that Marilyn was bugging: Spada, op. cit., p. 318.

325   Incredulous at reports that Bobby: Gibson, *Rose Kennedy*, p. 183.

325   Furthermore, it began to dawn on Bob: Summers, *Official and Confidential*, p. 297; *Goddess*, p. 245. Frederick Vanderbilt Field: Anthony Summers, *The Reader's Digest*, October 2006.

325   Several biographers refer: Summers, *Goddess*, p. 285.

325–326 George Smathers: S. Hersh, op. cit., p. 104.

326   On June 26, Robert Kennedy reappeared: Summers, op. cit., p. 284; Speriglio, op. cit., pp. 103, 104.

326   Peter Lawford flew up with her: Russo, *The Outfit*, p. 432; Giancana, *Double Cross*, p. 436.

326   "Mooney thought she was a pig. . . .": Confidential source.

326   Soon afterward, the FBI microphone: Russo, op. cit., p. 432.

326   While never insensitive to the fact: Heymann, op. cit., p. 385; Speriglio, op. cit., p. 94.

326   Marilyn's ex-husband, Joe DiMaggio: Van Meter, op. cit., pp. 190, 191.

327   She evidently did not get a lot of satisfaction: Spada, op. cit., p. 315; Heymann, op. cit., p. 320.

327   Floundering now for self-respect: Summers, *Goddess*, p. 296.

327   The bar association had reserved a large suite: Slatzer, op. cit., pp. 18, 250, 251; Speriglio, op. cit., pp. 166, 169, 170, 183, 214; Martin, *Seeds of Destruction*, p. 383.

327   Marilyn had been up most of the night before: Summers, op. cit., pp. 305, 350.

327   "Marilyn presently lost it. . . .": Heymann, op. cit., p. 322.

327   Around seven, Lawford called Marilyn: Summers, op. cit., pp. 333, 341.

328   This compounding Hollywood tragedy: The reliability of *Double Cross* is challenged regularly by writers in the field, up to and including Robert Maheu (Interview, 6/13/04). This book is patched together largely out of hearsay, often second- and thirdhand. Nevertheless, where the details are as precise as they are here, and accord with other, more immediate sources, they constitute a contribution to the literature of organized crime.

328   When the Chicago don discovered: Giancana, *Double Cross*, pp. 437, 438.

328   Spindel's wireman later insisted: Speriglio, op. cit., pp. 200, 201.

328   It was Giancana's intention to implicate Bobby: Summers, op. cit., pp. 322–347.

329   As recently as August 2005: *The Los Angeles Times*, 8/4/5/05; Speriglio, op. cit., pp. 110–114.

329   Like the coroner Dr. Thomas Noguchi: Slatzer, op. cit., p. 229. Noguchi would subsequently remark that tissue samples had unaccountably been destroyed before the head toxicologist could test them. Anthony Summers, *Reader's Digest*, October 2006.

329   This was a familiar routine for the volatile actress: Summers, *Goddess*, p. 347.

329   But the call stayed with him: Speriglio, op. cit., p. 13.

329   "We'd hauled her before because of the barbiturates. . . .": Summers, op. cit., pp. 345, 346; Slatzer, op. cit., p. 245.

330   At 4:35 A.M., Sergeant Jack Clemmons: Speriglio, op. cit., pp. 13–18, 104, 205, 206. Milton Rudin, the attorney for both Marilyn and Mob contact Frank Sinatra, was there and seemingly in charge. Summers, *Reader's Digest*, October 2006.

330   Within hours, Peter Lawford had joined his wife: Heymann, op. cit., p. 324.

330   "It was really taken rather lightly . . . .": Summers, op. cit., p. 316.

331   Hamilton was reportedly able to prevent the transfer: Summers, op. cit., p. 337.

331   To make very sure that none of this leaked: Ibid., p. 335; *Official and Confidential*, pp. 296, 300, 301.

331   Los Angeles Police Chief William Parker: Slatzer, op. cit., pp. 26, 229; Speriglio, op. cit., p. 194.

331   Years later, Deke DeLoach: Summers, *Official and Confidential*, pp. 296, 301; Interview, May 30, 2006.

331   Years later, a remnant in the otherwise shredded FBI file: Spada, op. cit., p. 319.

332   Reporting back to Al Belmont: FBI memo, Evans to Belmont, 8/20/62, (FOIA FN 77-51337); Director FBI to the Attorney General, 7/8/64.

CHAPTER 16

333   By 1963, Arthur Schlesinger observed: Hilty, op. cit., p. 285.

333   "Jack Kennedy had been privately scornful. . . .": Davis, *The Kennedys*, p. 340.

334   Jack Kennedy went along with both of them: Schwartz, op. cit., p. 340.

334   "I did not lie awake at night worrying. . . .": O'Reilly, *Racial Matters*, p. 50.

334   Harris Wofford, the administration's civil rights advisor: Davis, *The Kennedys*, p. 342.

334   For J. Edgar Hoover, the dilemmas that arose: O'Reilly, op. cit., p. 66.

334   "Hoover didn't want to be involved in anything. . . .": Courtney Evans Interview, 1/19/05.

334   While Hoover had not lost his sensitivity: Gentry, op. cit., p. 602.

335   As riots broke out: O'Reilly, op. cit., pp. 12, 13.

335   When Jamaican-born Marcus Garvey: Ibid., pp. 14–16.

335   When civil libertarian Joe Rauh: Ibid., p. 27.

335   Eisenhower's first attorney general: Ibid., pp. 46–52.

335   At a cabinet-level presentation: Gentry, op. cit., p. 441.

336   Emmett Till: O'Reilly, op. cit., p. 41.

336   He commented to one Justice Department aide: David and David, op. cit., p. 188.

336   Paradoxically, Hoover appears to have shared: Gid Powers, op. cit., pp. 323, 324.

336   Hunted down by the renegade FBI author: Ollestad, op. cit., pp. 163–165.

336   "He wanted me to lower our qualifications. . . .": Schlesinger, op. cit., p. 292.

337   "Mister Hoover assigned me to go. . . .": DeLoach Interview, 5/30/03.

337   "We thought Hoover was shipping the same black agent. . . .": JFK Library, RFK Collection, Reilly oral history; Taylor Branch, *Parting the Waters*, p. 389.

337   In his seminal study *Kennedy Justice*: Navasky, op. cit., p. 122.

337–338 "The General had yielded to the Director. . . .": Ibid., p. 113.

338   Doar roamed the South: O'Reilly, op. cit, pp. 52–54; Branch, op. cit., pp. 386, 387.

338   Doar would stay on into the Kennedy administration: Wofford, op. cit., pp. 67, 154.

338   Hoover sent along a report "insinuating that Wofford. . . .": Hilty, op. cit., pp. 296, 297.

339   The most immediate problem for the Kennedy administration: O'Reilly, op. cit., pp. 70–73.

339   Kennedy had them boxed up and deposited: Wofford, op. cit., p. 124.

339   Clarence Mitchell, the NAACP's man: Ibid., p. 140.

339–340 To assure Thurgood Marshall a seat: Navasky, op. cit., p. 277.

340   "Tell your brother": Eastland: Ibid., p. 285.

340   "Who is telling these people they can get in line?": Ibid., p. 275.

340   In company with Cox: Ibid., pp. 277, 291, 305, 306.

340   As late as June 1963: Newfield, op. cit., p. 23.

340   "Each case," Victor Navasky wrote: Navasky, op. cit., p. 112.

341   As Burke Marshall would note in retrospect: Ibid., p. 101.

342   The Kennedys promptly leafleted the nation's black churches: Marshall Frady, *Martin Luther King, Jr.*, pp. 75–79.

342   A representative of the Freedom Riders had called on Robert Kennedy: Arsenault, *Freedom Riders*, p. 111.

342   On May 14, a mob turned over a bus full of demonstrators: Wofford, op. cit., p. 151; Boates, *Let the Trumpet Sound*, p. 174.

342   Tipped off to Connor's arrangement: Wofford, op. cit., pp. 152, 206.

342   By then Bob Kennedy's administrative assistant: Seigenthaler interview, 4/4/05; Arsenault, op. cit., p. 163.

343   When King shrugged off Kennedy's request: Frady, op. cit., p. 80.

343   The word in the station house: Navasky, op. cit., p. 139; Schlesinger, op. cit., p. 297.

343   Advised well in advance of the Klan's intentions: Wofford, op. cit., p. 152; Arsenault, op. cit., p. 136.

343   Placate "that old man," Jack Kennedy had told his brother: Branch, op. cit., p. 402.

343   Hoover was already turning Martin Luther King: Gentry, op. cit., p. 602.

343   Periodically, it occurred to Bobby that the FBI could help: Navasky, op. cit., p. 14.

344   Once the tumultuous summer was over: Boates, op. cit., pp. 176–178.

344   "There's nobody in the whole country that's got the spine. . . .": Ibid., pp. 74, 75.

344   "Look, Governor, why don't you just let this. . . .": Seigenthaler Interview, 4/4/05.

344   "There goes the South," Robert Kennedy expired: Ibid.

344   Levison was of a type: Garrow, *The FBI and Martin Luther King, Jr.* (paper), p. 232; Frady, op. cit., p. 43.

345   Levison's presence in the King entourage must have been flagged for Kennedy early: Branch, *Parting the Waters*, p. 406.

345   A Bureau informant, "Solo. . . .": Garrow, op. cit., pp. 40, 41.

345   Rustin had arranged for Levison to meet King: Branch, op. cit., p. 168.

345–346 The FBI had been surveilling and even bugging: Harris Wofford Interview, 4/7/05.

346   Early in 1960, a couple of agents: Garrow, op. cit., p. 42.

346   "[Levison's] skills," David Garrow would observe: Ibid., p. 26.

346   His capacities, he explained, were acquired: Ibid., p. 28.

346   Rauschenbusch condemned America: Oates, op. cit., pp. 25, 26.

346   But day to day, Levison provided: Garrow, op. cit., pp. 28, 29.

346   "Stanley was this seemingly loyal, mousy, ever-willing-to-do-work. . . .": Wofford Interview, 4/7/05.

347   Finishing up his doctoral dissertation: McKnight, *The Last Crusade*, p. 6.

347   Harris Wofford saw Bureau cables indicating: Wofford, op. cit., p. 214; Wofford Interview, 4/7/05; Branch, op. cit., p. 227.

347   A memo suggested that Levison's contribution: Branch, op. cit., pp. 255–256.

348   "Some of these problems you have created yourself. . . .": Ibid. pp. 610–611.

348   On January 8, 1962, Hoover sent a letter: Garrow, op. cit., p. 26.

348   When Charles E. Whittaker: Branch, op. cit., p. 584.

348   Meanwhile, Chief Justice Earl Warren: Schlesinger, op. cit., p. 377.

348   After a mid-January meeting with civil rights leaders: Seigenthaler Interview, 4/4/05.

349   Working another favorite channel: Garrow, op. cit., p. 48.

350   At that point, the FBI's own Atlanta field office: Ibid., p. 48.

350   William Sullivan, the peppery: Garrow, op. cit., p. 48; Schlesinger, op. cit., p. 356.

350   When Byron White got his back up after the initial warning: Branch, op. cit., pp. 516, 564, 565.

350   Hoover continued to stonewall his superiors: Gentry, op. cit., pp. 503, 508.

350   FBI "suicide squads" had been breaking into: O'Reilly, op. cit., p. 134.

350   One bemused underling suggested: Morgan, *Reds*, p. 566.

350   U.S. District Judge J. Robert Elliot: Oates, op. cit., p. 195; Hilty, op. cit., p. 337.

351   To Roy Wilkins and most of the other: Frady, op. cit., p. 54.

351   "One of the greatest problems we face with the FBI. . . .": *The New York Times*, 11/18/62; Oates, op. cit., p. 200.

351   Forever willing to commit to the extra mile on paper: Gentry, op. cit., p. 506.

351   "It would appear obvious that Reverend King. . . .": FBI memo, DeLoach to Mohr, 1/15/63.

351   Hoover would ultimately divulge: Gentry, op. cit., p. 417.

351   Before that was set the U.S. marshals: Hilty, op. cit., p. 344

352   JFK, Bobby remarked, was "torn. . . .": Ibid., p. 345.

352   When John Kennedy tried to explicate his motives during a follow-up: Ibid., p. 346.

352   Bobby's efforts that May to enlist Jimmy Baldwin: Schlesinger, op. cit., pp. 330–335.

352   Another bloodbath threatened: Hilty, op. cit., p. 366; Oates, op. cit., p. 244.

352   This tense long week of bumpercars: Frady, op. cit., p. 113.

352   "Who better to prick the conscience of the country. . . ?": Seigenthaler Interview, 4/4/05; Oates, op. cit., pp. 232, 233.

352   "The administration's poll numbers were collapsing. . . .": Oates, op. cit., pp. 244-247.

353   "An injured, maimed, or dead child. . . .": Frady, op. cit., p. 111.

353   By then the relationship between Bob Kennedy and King: Seigenthaler Interview, 4/4/05.

353   King "held no public office. . . .": Branch, op. cit., p. 836.

353   The previous autumn, a few weeks before King chastised: Ibid., p. 675.

353   By 1963, King was long aware that O'Dell: Ibid., p. 675.

353   Confronted by King, O'Dell: Ibid., p. 646.

353   John Seigenthaler was again dispatched: Seigenthaler Interview, 4/4/05.

354   Still fuming over King's November challenge: Branch, op. cit., p. 678.

354   The Childs brothers, whom even the head of the American Party: Andrews and Mitrokhin, op. cit., p. 290.

354   Reinforcement came from Victor Lesiovsky: Schlesinger, op. cit., pp. 356–357.

355   Kennedy remembered King as "always sort of dismissing. . . .": Branch, op. cit., p. 836.

355   When King rejoined that Hoover regarded: Thomas, *Robert Kennedy*, p. 253; Branch, op. cit., p. 837.

355   It is easy to imagine King's almond-shaped eyes: Ibid., p. 837.

355   Kennedy turned the conversation to the Profumo scandal: Schlesinger, op. cit., p. 358.

355   "I guess Hoover's buggin' him, too. . . .": Oates, op. cit., p. 248.

355   As for the charges against O'Dell and Levison: Branch, op. cit., p. 844.

356   Marshall met Young in New Orleans: Branch, op. cit., p. 852; Oates, op. cit., p. 250.

356   Along with the fact that, on Robert Kennedy's orders: Davis, *Mafia Kingfish*, p. 242.

356   When Harris Wofford reached him: Oates, op. cit., pp. 248–250.

356   On June 30, a story obviously pieced together: Gentry, op. cit., p. 508; Branch, op. cit., p. 850.

357   Already under pressure from Hoover: Branch, op. cit., p. 853.

357   "We were against putting a wiretap on King," DeLoach insisted: DeLoach
        Interview, 5/31/04.
357   Courtney Evans emphasized: Branch, op. cit., p. 855.
357   Courtney Evans helped debunk: Ibid., pp. 254–256.
357   When SCC chairman John Lewis: O'Neill, op. cit., p. 126; Branch, op. cit., p. 876.
358   The March proceeded peacefully: Branch, op. cit., p. 883.
358   "Onetime Communist Organizer Heads Rev. King's office. . . .": Ibid., p. 857.
358   King's mood swings were becoming more pronounced: Ibid., p. 859.
359   With Jones and his friends the talk switched around: Davis, op. cit., p. 338.
359   These exchanges went straightaway to Robert Kennedy: Garrow, op. cit., p. 67.
359   "I'm away from home twenty-five to twenty-seven. . . .": Summers, *Official and
        Confidential*, p. 353.
359   Beyond that, he was the glamour preacher: Frady, op. cit., p. 67.

CHAPTER 17

360   Around the Justice Department: Branch, op. cit., p. 402.
360–361   Traditional restraints on the media were loosening: S. Hersh, op. cit., p.
        391.
361   Until that summer, the cerebral: Staking out the range of Jack Kennedy's com-
        plicated sexuality has stymied biographers all along. Several have not hesitated
        to speculate about the universally magnetic if easily bored politician's true ori-
        entation, dwelling on his relations with his roommate at Choate, Lem Billings.
        A hulking, clumsy, weak-eyed, rather self-effacing doctor's son from Pittsburg,
        Billings and his battered suitcase showed up in Hyannis Port during JFK's
        midadolescence in the midst of a holiday break, over the course of which
        Billings managed to scald himself badly. He devoted the rest of his visit to recu-
        perating in the local hospital. From then on, the genteel and impressionable
        Lem remained a mainstay among the Kennedys.
            Jack and Lem bonded; Kennedy's many hilarious letters to Lem about
        his own miserable health and his increasingly predatory love life provide the
        best insight available as to the true emotions of the guarded scion. As late as
        1942 Kennedy twitted his adoring friend, labeling him a "glutton for punish-
        ment. . . . After you hear someone call you a fairy and discuss it for two solid
        hours and argue whether you did or did not go down on Worthington Johnson.
        . . ." (See Nigel Hamilton, *JFK, Restless Youth*, p. 470). The truth was, Lem was
        ultimately homosexual, although Truman Capote's offhand characterization of
        Billings—"I didn't care for him. I used to see him at Studio 54. He would often
        be high on one drug or another, bragging how he used to give JFK blow jobs in
        the Lincoln Bedroom." (Heymann, *RFK*, p. 514)—was probably unfair and fal-
        lacious. But even Jackie Kennedy was heard to carp of Lem that he had been "a
        houseguest of mine every weekend since I've been married"(Blair and Blair, p.
        31), and one of the Hyannis Port retainers remarked of Billings to the new
        chauffeur: "He's always here. I think he sleeps with Jack more than Jacqueline
        does." (Saunders, op. cit., p. 46.)
            As it happens, I knew Lem Billings in passing toward the end of his
        bereft middle age. His attachment to John Kennedy, and subsequently to Bobby
        and later on to Bob's older boys, came through in every exchange. A fundamen-
        tally gentle soul and obviously a born pushover, Lem provided Jack a comforting
        foil in the midst of JFK's illness-wracked and increasingly hectic career. One of

Kennedy's psychic priorities was plainly to present himself as a sexual swordsman non pareil, but as his forties set in, still upset about his mother, no recreational drug or cortisone implant was enough to guarantee much more than an embarrassingly brief performance. Accordingly, extraordinary stimulation seemed to be in order—the threesomes, the dress-up games, the startling insouciance when it came to political fallout. "He was very fatalistic," George Smathers would observe. "When I first knew him, sometimes it seemed that women and death were all he talked about." (Anderson, op. cit, p. 83.)

361   Like those daily injections of steroid-laced: Morgan, *Reds*, p. 561.

361   FBI files indicate: JFK Assassination files, National Archives (94-34-44-H); (*The Washington Post*, 12/16/77); Hoover to RFK, 6/6/63 (official and confidential); Hilty, op. cit., p. 253.

361   Jack Kennedy and the tiny but strong-minded: S. Hersh, op. cit., pp. 330–331.

361   The president resented 'the gall of the man': Ibid., p. 314.

361   In 1959, an incensed Georgetown housewife: Ibid., p. 107.

362   In early June 1963: FBI, RFK files, Hoover to RFK, 6/6/63 (official and confidential); FBI, JFK Assassination Files, 6/30/61, (94-37374).

362   By July 23, 1963, the attorney general: FBI, JFK Assassination Files, National Archives, 7/23/63, Branagan to Sullivan; 7/24/63, Evans to Belmont.

362–363 A month earlier, the Bureau's Domestic Intelligence Division: FBI, JFK Assassination Files, 6/29/63, (94-37374-154).

363   Two of the hookers in the Keeler ensemble: Hilty, op. cit., p. 252; S. Hersh, op. cit., pp. 391–398.

363   Hoover "already knew of the accusations": Hilty, op. cit., pp. 252, 558.

363   The Kennedys endeavored to kill the story: FBI, JFK Assassination Files, Evans to Director, 7/2/63 and 7/3/63 (several memos).

363–364 Joe Kennedy had cultivated intimate ties: S. Hersh, op. cit., p. 394.

364   For Hoover, by then, it was a question of survival: undated FBI memo, July 1963, Callahan to Director (FM-77-51337).

364   The wife of a German army sergeant: Baker, op. cit., p. 80.

364   On July 3, 1963: Typically, on the usual pretext of providing the White House with advanced warning, Hoover quickly inserted himself into the prospective crisis and "added to the attorney general's fears when he told him that, according to an FBI informant's report in July, 'Rometsch said that she was sent to this country to get information.'" (S. Hersh, *Camelot*, p. 403).

364   She would be linked in future FBI investigations: FBI, Ellen Rometsch files, (2/27/65).

364–365 According to several historians: Baker, op. cit., pp. 78, 80.

365   On August 21, 1963: S. Hersh, op. cit., pp. 400, 401.

365   By the early sixties, Baker was out: Baker, op. cit., pp. 170, 171.

365–366 In October, once Baker was attracting headlines: Theoharis and Cox, op. cit., p. 348.

366   The attorney general had recently gotten into: Seigenthaler Interview, 9/20/05; Anderson, op. cit., p. 306.

366   One of Jack's bird dogs: David and David, op. cit., p. 182; Anderson, op. cit., p. 159.

366   One evening Thompson was having drinks: Baker Interview, 5/30/05.

366   Years earlier, Mollenhoff: "US Expels Girls Linked to Officials," *The Des Moines Register*, 10/26/63.

367   The attorney general dispatched La Verne: Branch, op. cit., pp. 312, 313.

367   Hoover toyed with his tortured: FBI, Ellen Rometsch files, memo 11/7/63, Hoover to Assistant Directors.

368   Hoover's October 28 memo: FBI Ellen Rometsch files, memo 10/28/63; Branch, op. cit., p. 913

368   Hoover followed up immediately with a memo: FBI, JEH memos to assistant directors, 10/29/63.

369   Now that Bobby Kennedy was his new best friend: FBI, Belmont to Tolson, 10/29/63.

369   On hearing that "the President was personally interested": FBI, DeLoach to Mohr, 10/28/63.

370   Joe Valachi, a soldier in the Genovese family: Turner, op. cit., pp. 171–173.

370   Sullivan was widely regarded as the odd bird: Unger, FBI, pp. 295, 296; O'Reilly, op. cit., p. 128; DeLoach, op. cit., p. 280.

370   "The Party views the struggle for equal rights. . . ." O'Reilly, op. cit., p. 127.

371   "A few months went by before he would speak to me," Sullivan later wrote: Sullivan, The Bureau (paper), p. 248.

371   On August 30, he groveled his way through an apology: O'Reilly, op. cit., p. 130.

371   On October 4, William Sullivan, avidly seeking redemption: FBI, J. F. Bland to Sullivan, 10/4/63; Branch, op. cit., pp. 906, 907. According to Hoover's subsequent memo on the subject: Hack, op. cit., p. 326; FBI memo, Director to Attorney General, 6/10/69.

372   What Hoover does not mention in his memo of record was the fact: FBI memo, 10/25/63, Evans to Belmont.

372   "Bobby thought it was absolute blackmail. . . .": JFK Library, RFK Collection, Katzenbach oral history, pp. 62, 63.

372   It could be that enough of the Bureau's unobtrusive little green: O'Reilly, op. cit., p. 137.

373   Once, off guard, he confided that he had had: Gentry, op. cit., p. 529.

373   A rich man's son: Schlesinger, op. cit., p. 277.

373   A July 6, 1961 memo survives: FBI Internal files, Evans to Belmont, 7/6/61.

373   But there is a lot of reason to believe that Kennedy: Hilty, op. cit., p. 121; Thomas, Robert Kennedy, p. 118.

373   Ed Silberling, still nursing his bruises: The Manchester Union Leader (NH), 2/2/67.

373   In some situations there were probably facts: JFK Library, RFK Collection, Courtney Evans oral history, 11/6/70.

374   Having held back key files for five years: Turner, op. cit., pp. 100, 101.

374   John Seigenthaler was in the room: Seigenthaler Interview, 4/4/05.

374   A Division-Five conference: Branch, Pillar of Fire, pp. 195, 196.

374   To supplement its electronic snooping: McKnight, op. cit., p. 23.

374   At one stage the Bureau specialists: O'Reilly, op. cit., p. 137.

375   It would become a joke with Abernathy: Navasky, op. cit., p. 150.

375   After eleven reels of nondescript, informal: Branch, op. cit., p. 207.

375   "This will destroy the burrhead!": Summers, Official and Confidential, p. 354.

375   They already had enough, as Sullivan noted: Branch, op. cit., p. 207.

375   "The fact that King and twelve acquaintances. . . .": DeLoach Interview, 5/30/04.

375–376 In his posthumously published expose of the Hoover FBI: Sullivan, op. cit., p. 140.

376   The letter urged King to "look into your heart. . . .": Oates, op. cit., p. 331.

376   "The purpose of the tape," Sullivan wrote: Sullivan, op. cit., p. 142.

376   "Sullivan prepared a letter in the Martin Luther King case. . . .": Wannall, *The Real J. Edgar Hoover*, p. 105.

376–377 "Since World War II the FBI recruited. . . .": O'Reilly, op. cit., p. 148.

377   Berl Bernhard had persevered: Bernhard Interview, 4/15/05.

377   Hoover fumed—"They had to dig deep. . . .": Davis, *Mafia Kingfish*, p. 338.

377   The Director turned to his long-time ally: Branch, op. cit., p. 483.

377   King should have gotten the "top alleycat" prize: Gid Powers, op. cit., p. 418.

378   On November 18, 1964 Hoover summoned: Branch, op. cit., p. 156.

378   When the startled DeLoach passed Hoover: DeLoach Interview, 5/30/04.

378   Vacationing in Bimini: Branch, op. cit., p. 157.

378   Alarmed bystanders: Branch, op. cit., p. 361; Navasky, op. cit., p. 39, et al.; Wofford, op. cit., p. 209.

378   While DeLoach continues to deny having taken any part: Theoharis and Cox, op. cit., p. 357; O'Reilly, op. cit., p. 148.

379   Bureau attempts to float rumors: Branch, op. cit., p. 533; Wofford, op. cit., p. 212.

379   When his headquarters braintrust advised the Director: Branch, op. cit., p. 528.

379   By July 2, 1964, after a winter: Branch, op. cit., p. 387.

380   Furthermore, he harbored a lifelong distaste for the Ku Klux Klan: O'Reilly, op. cit., p. 162.

380   This was the twentieth unsolved explosion in "Bombingham": Branch, op. cit., pp. 137, 138.

380   Important power centers in America: Navasky, op. cit., p. 236.

380   Despite the decades of walking their dogs together: DeLoach Interview, 5/30/04.

380   As Hoover approached the mandatory federal retirement age: Theoharis and Cox, op. cit., pp. 356, 357.

380   "Hoover walks in with an armload of files, smiling. . . .": Gus Russo, private citation, quoting Martin Underwood.

381   With his brother gone: Navasky, op. cit., p. 19.

381   Hoover soon wrote Ramsey Clark off: Turner, op. cit., p. 101.

381   As "Freedom Summer" broke across the South: O'Reilly, op. cit., pp. 161, 162.

381   Hoover at once memoed Burke Marshall: Navasky, op. cit., p. 118.

381–382 At this point Kennedy and Marshall recommended to Johnson: Navasky, op. cit., p. 162; Gid Powers, op. cit., pp. 412, 413.

382   The South was difficult for his men, Hoover once remarked: de Toledano, *J. Edgar Hoover*, p. 334.

382   "I really don't think the black community knows or appreciates the work the FBI did. . . .": Kessler, *The FBI* (paper), p. 403.

382   On July 10, 1964, Johnson flew the Director: Wannall, op. cit., p. 80; Turner, op. cit., p. 319.

382   Received by local politicians as a hero: Branch, op. cit., p. 397.

383   Referred to behind his back around the management suite as "Crazy Billy": Branch, *Parting the Waters*, p. 903; O'Reilly, op. cit., p. 299.

383   Across the South, within a year, 2,000 Klansmen: Gid Powers, op. cit., pp. 413, 414; Navasky, op. cit., pp. 101, 114.

383   Incoming Attorney General Katzenbach: Navasky, op. cit., p. 414.

384   By now Hoover was permitting: Roemer, *Man Against the Mob*, p. 234; Blakey, op. cit., pp. 238, 239.

384   "The Klan did push us to the limit," Deke DeLoach admits: DeLoach Interview, 5/30/04.

384   According to ex-SAC Neil Welch: Welch, *Inside Hoover's FBI*, pp. 105, 106; Gentry, op. cit., p. 692.

385   Rumors, possibly authenticated: Branch, *Pillar of Fire*, p. 529.

385   A $25,000 payoff produced: Navasky, op. cit., p. 437; Boates, op. cit., p. 308.

385   On March 25, 1965, four Klansmen: O'Reilly, op. cit., pp. 196, 197.

385   When the shocked LBJ: Gid Powers, op. cit., p. 410.

385   The trick was to guide the process: Turner, op. cit., p. 136.

386   Worse, when they got back: Navasky, op. cit., pp. 22, 23.

386   As late as 1964, irked by word that Marshall: O'Reilly, op. cit., pp. 75, 78, 81.

386   "If the country knew what we know about King's goings on. . . .": Hilty, op. cit., pp. 26, 27.

386   Frank Mankiewicz remembers that by the later sixties: JFK Library, RFK Collection, Mankiewicz oral history.

386   As the televised rerun of the funeral reached the moment when Jacqueline Kennedy: Branch, op. cit., p. 250.

CHAPTER 18

388   The FBI had obviously weathered: W. Mark Felt, *The FBI Pyramid*, pp. 62, 197.

388   "Sokolsky would call me twice a week. . . .: DeLoach Interview, 5/31/04.

388–389 Bob looked into Sokolsky's apartment: Guthman, op. cit., pp. 17, 18.

389   When Roy returned from the glory years: DeLoach Interview, 5/31/04.

389   Roy was to assert: Cohn/Zion, *The Autobiography of Roy Cohn*, p. 14.

389   Along with half the hoods: Davis, *Mafia Kingfish*, p. 471; Cohn/Zion, op. cit., p. 268; Bly, op. cit., p. 202.

390   He matured quickly: Cohn, *A Fool for a Client*, p. 160; *Life*, 9/5/69 (William Lambert).

390   Let's put it this way, Juliana warned him: Cohn/Zion, op. cit., p. 159.

390   Antennae bristling, Cohn faked: Von Hoffmann, *Citizen Cohn* (paper), pp. 260–263.

390   Before long Cohn heard: Ibid., p. 260; Cohn/Zion, op. cit., p. 178.

391   What baffled even Bob Kennedy's Justice Department: Von Hoffmann, op. cit., pp. 266, 267.

391   Roy was broadly connected: Cohn, *McCarthy*, p. 72.

391   The president was apprehensive, Williams told Fugazy: Thomas, *Edward Bennett Williams*, p. 163.

391–392 Much of his business: *Life*, 9/5/69 (William Lambert); Von Hoffmann, op. cit., p. 322.

392   Before long the fighters and the hotels: Von Hoffmann, op. cit., p. 274.

392   "It's almost worth all the headaches. . . .": *The Wall Street Journal*, 2/28/63 (Ed Cony).

392   "Being anti-Communist does not automatically excuse. . . .": Von Hoffmann, op. cit., p. 267.

393   Lansky's most trusted lieutenant: Robert Maheu Interview, 7/13/04; Von Hoffmann, op. cit., p. 272.

393   "If you hit me, nigger. . . .": *The Mafia Encyclopedia*, p. 96.

393   A well-informed source places Cohn: John Klotz, book proposal, p. 4; Klotz Interview 12/15/05; Russo, *The Outfit*, pp. 349, 351.

393   Dalitz cut *his* friends in: In the financial shadows of this comprehensive deal, along with Roy Cohn, it is not hard to detect Joe Kennedy, who, according to

Gus Russo's sources (see Russo, *Supermob*, p. 221), was one of Dalitz's backers in the Desert Inn. Hoover, obviously well aware of the Ambassador's interest, had taken advantage of Robert Kennedy's comparative innocence where it came to his father's business connections during the first months of his attorney-generalship in 1961 and had gotten Bobby to sign off on two years of wide-ranging "electronic surveillance of the homes and hotel offices of some twenty-five Mafiosi in the Las Vegas area. . . ." On May 16, 1963, by which date Robert Kennedy was more skittish every day about initiating prosecutions that might well implicate his family, Hoover began to circulate the results of his investigation, two volumes entitled "The Skimming Report," which "detailed the inner mechanics of the Mafia's massive and untaxed diversion of gambling profits in Las Vegas." Hoover would subsequently protest that within three days of its issuance the information in "The Skimming Report" was getting bandied about among senior criminals. Hoover blamed William Hundley, the streetwise chief of Bobby's Organized Crime and Racketeering Section, for leaking to the Mob, presumably on Bobby's orders. Hundley would blame the FBI. The Director's noose was continuing to tighten. (Mahoney, p. 232.)

A Top-Secret internal summary (5/27/66) prepared on Hoover's instructions and widely disseminated specified that Courtney Evans "did acknowledge that Kennedy must have known that our information came from microphones in view of the fact that Hundley kept Kennedy advised of FBI coverage" and "Hundley, due to his background and experience, obviously knew that the type information included in our reports on Las Vegas activities came from microphones." (Heymann Collection, SUNY, Box 15a, Folder 6.) The basic document recommending the authorization for microphone penetration of Fred Black's offices as well as Suite 438-40 of the Sheraton-Carlton Hotel was Evans to Belmont, December 28, 1962 (Fred Black file). The memo specifies that "Robert G. Baker . . . is affiliated with Black and other individuals who have a joint interest in the Serv-U-Corporations." Like so many others throughout this narrative, Black was very close to the ubiquitous Johnny Rosselli.

393 Once shares of the resulting partnership: *Wall Street Journal*, 2/28/63.

394 Another Mob carryover was Allard Roen: *New York Times*, 4/10/63 (Homer Bigart).

394 Garfield and Irving Pasternak: *Wall Street Journal*, 9/5/63 (Ed Cony).

394 Cohn apparently told the gamblers: Messick, *J. Edgar Hoover*, p. 177.

394 Irving Younger, at that point an assistant United States attorney: *Commentary*, October 1976.

395 Once a grand jury was in place, Cohn: de Toledano, *RFK*, p. 222.

395 "When Internal Revenue came. . . .: Ibid., p. 222; *New York Times*, 9/6/63 (Edward Ranzal); Station WMCA, Barry Gray interview, 9/9/63.

395 Cohn was already worried enough to send a wire to Walter Winchell: Cohn FBI file, SA to SAC New York, 6/12/62 (58-1232-18S); *New York Daily Mirror*, 5/12/62.

395 One acquaintance of Roy's attempted: Von Hoffmann, op. cit., p. 266; *New York Times*, 4/10/64 (Homer Bigart); Fulton Lewis Jr. broadcast, 9/5/63 (Lewis collection, Syracuse University.)

396 "I think that history speaks for itself. . . .": *New York Times*, 9/6/63.

396 Robert Kennedy was following all this closely: *New York Post*, 9/5/63 (Normand Poirier); *New York Times*, 4/10/64.

396   Cohn accused the U.S. Attorney of "inspiring managed news leaks. . . .": Barry Gray interview, 9/9/63.

396   Robert Kennedy had backed Morgenthau by feeding a reporter: *Life*, 10/4/63 (William Lambert).

396   Another ally in the press: *New York Times*, 11/18–22/63.

397   At one point, Morgenthau's lead attorney: Von Hoffmann, op. cit., p. 275.

397   Ultimately, the verdict depended: Ibid, p. 293.

397   Roy was a celebrity: Cohn/Zion, op. cit., pp. 276, 277.

397   Until the Nixon administration: *Life*, 9/5/69 (Lambert); *Wall Street Journal*, 2/28/63.

397   When Cohn's attorney suffered a heart attack: Von Hoffmann, op. cit., p. 346.

398   "Roy and Hoover were very close. . . .": Ibid., p. 282.

398   FBI files of the period highlight the Director: Ibid., p. 282.

398   When Byron White insisted that the Bureau bug: FBI internal memo, McGrath to Rosen, 3/1/62.

398   The special agent in charge": FBI files, SAC NY to Director, 2/23/62.

398   Meanwhile, attempts by the FBI to establish Morton Robson's: FBI files, memo ASAC AM Bryant, Division II to SAC, 8/3/62, (58-1232), part of Airtel SAC Las Vegas to Director, 8/2/62, (58-1232289).

398   A July 13, 1962 FBI memo: FBI files, Evans to Belmont, 7/13/62 (58-5100).

399   By July 1962, with the United Dye investigation: FBI files, AS Larson to McGrath, 7/28/62 (58-5100-93).

399   DeLoach, back from a short leave by August: DeLoach to Mohr, 8/1/62 (58-5100-96).

399   As long as Robert Kennedy was attorney general, the Director: *New York Magazine*, (Peter Maas), 6/23/69; *New York Times*, 9/2/69; *Life*, 9/5/69 (Lambert).

399   As if to test Cohn beyond all reason: Guthman, op. cit., p. 17.

399   "[J]ust as Cohn is extraordinarily gentle. . . .": *The New York Journal American*, 3/25/62.

399   Standing on the steps of the Central Synagogue: FBI files, Roy Cohn, DeLoach to Mohr, 12/17/62 (62-97564).

400   One of the legions of pages over whom he in turn bestowed: *The Columbia Journalism Review*, November-December 1997, (Lance Morrow).

400   Doing well for others: *Life*, 11/22/63.

401   "When you been in the business of raising campaign funds. . . .": Bobby Baker Interview, 5/30/05.

401   As founder and majordomo: FBI file Ellen Rometsch, memo Rosen to Belmont, 11/8/63.

401   A gargantuan, rough-spoken: Schlesinger, op. cit., p. 374.

401   It weighed on Kerr especially: Baker Interview, 5/30/05.

402   Kerr put together a $400,000: Baker, op. cit., pp. 170, 171; *Life*, 11/22/63.

402   "Bobby Baker a partner with Meyer Lansky?": Baker Interview, 5/30/05.

403   Her tolerance and inventiveness comes through: *Life Magazine*, 11/22/63.

403   Around the end of 1962: FBI memo, Gale to DeLoach, 5/27/66.

404   The entente between Fred Black and Levinson: FBI memo, Evans to Belmont, 12/28/62 (92-6171-42).

404   Bobby glimpsed an opportunity to undermine: *Life*, 11/22/63 (Lambert).

404   Reynolds was still upset because Johnson: S. Hersh, op. cit., p. 83.

405   The aggrieved Reynolds: National Archives, Learning Curve, Internet, Fred Black.

405   "He's mean, bitter, vicious. . . .": Robert Kennedy, *In His Own Words*, p. 417.

405   While JFK was president: Shesol, op. cit., pp. 107, 108.

405   Responding to an interviewer's question: Kennedy Library, RFK Collection, Frank Mankiewicz oral history.

405   "A few days later," Brennan recalls: National Archives, *Learning Curve* (Bobby Baker), p. 19.

405   Well-substantiated rumors flew around the Capitol: Russo, *Live By The Sword*, pp. 283, 290; Davis, *Mafia Kingfish*, p. 283; Scheim, *Contract on America*, p. 222.

406   Earlier, when Justice Department prosecutor William Bittman: Baker, op. cit., p. 199.

406   Characteristically, although stonewalling the Department: Baker himself found out that Liakakis was exploiting her job to pillage Bobby Baker's private files when Clyde Tolson, of all people, recuperating in the hospital from yet another stroke, told a nurse who was close to the Baker family that Georgia was "a paid government informant and had been for years." Liakakis, like Rometsch, had been involved with Bobby's Rackets Committee investigator La Verne Duffy and could be squeezed with the threat of prosecution for insufficient payment of taxes. Baker himself insists she was helping out a later boyfriend, an FBI agent. Liakakis had arranged to store several boxes of the records of Sy Pollock, a fast-moving attorney who had become a confidant of Carlos Marcello and was already headed for the penitentiary. A trove like that in Baker's basement predictably tempted the ever-vigilant Hoover, and he hadn't resisted. (Baker, pp. 256–257; Baker Interview, 5/30/05.)

406   Once indictments started to come down: Baker, p. 183.

406   After November 1963 reportedly threatening Hoover directly: National Archives, Learning Curve, Fred Black; FBI files, DeLoach to Tolson, 7/12/66.

406   Then McInerney got killed: Baker Interview, 5/30/05.

407   "You know, J. Edgar Hoover came to me. . . .": Baker, op. cit., pp. 267, 268.

CHAPTER 19

408   A few minutes later, Hoover called back to report: Schlesinger, op. cit., pp. 607, 608; Russo, *Live By The Sword*, pp. 302–303. Also see Katzenbach Interview, 10/26/05.

409   Then came the gunshots: Mahoney, op. cit., p. 292.

409   Within the hour Hoover: Ibid., p. 295.

410   Only with the publication of the Report: Warren Commission Report, 9/24/64, p. 1.

411   Even during its deliberations in 1964: Thompson, *Six Seconds in Dallas*, p. 210; Livingstone and Groden, *High Treason*, pp. 156, 227, 365.

411   Within days he flooded the Dallas area: Posner, op. cit., p. 82; Gid Powers, op. cit., p. 389.

411   Seventeen agents were censured: Gentry, op. cit., p. 549; Turner, op. cit., p. 237.

411   There is a lot of back-and-forth: Hoover to executive conference, 11/19/63.

411   Hoover was already well into laying the groundwork: Weisberg, *Whitewash II*, p. 225.

412   On perusing a December 10, 1963 report: FBI memo, J. H. Gale to Tolson, 12/10/63.

412   The truth was, Hoover and his lieutenants: Newman, *Oswald and the CIA*, pp. 19, 153.

412   Behind tightly closed doors, Texas officials: confidential FBI sources; Lane, *Plausible Denial*, pp. 55, 367; Gentry, op. cit., p. 554; Posner, op. cit., p. 348. Several FBI officials of the period have assured me that Oswald was indeed an FBI informant during the year before JFK was shot; FBI counterintelligence expert William Tafoya, who has seen the Bureau's classified documentary coverage of the assassination, adds that Oswald was cut off several months before the assassination as "too crazy" for the Bureau to deal with: "You didn't need to be a psychiatrist to know that there was something wrong with him. That's what happened after the second meeting." (Tafoya Interview, 1/15/07). Ex-SAC Warren Tabruiez would admit to having been Oswald's handler. (Rex Bradford, Mary Farrell Foundation, Address to Assassination and Research Archives Conference [11/18/05]. Whenever the subject of Oswald came up before the Commission, agents were instructed to avoid the questioning, having dropped the investigation under orders. Hoover was plainly petrified at the prospect that the Oswald provenance might surface.

412   Upon returning from Russia: Newman, op. cit., p. 264; Posner, op. cit., pp. 79–81, 268.

412   Oswald had been close to the Murrets: Scheim, *Contract on America*, p. 43; Davis, *Mafia Kingfish*, p. 122.

413   All four wound up in jail: Newman, op. cit., pp. 335–338.

413   Both the address on his leaflets: Summers, *Conspiracy*, pp. 322–323.

413   Banister was a backwoods Louisiana: Newman, op. cit., p. 209; Giancana, *Double Cross*, pp. 111, 255, 256.

413   William Turner, a contemporary: Turner, op. cit., p. 305.

413–414 Banister's personal secretary: Summers, op. cit., pp. 379–380.

414   A retired Eastern Airlines pilot: Davis, *Mafia Kingfish*, p. 130; Russo, op. cit., p. 329.

414   Oswald's acquaintanceship with Ferrie: Blakey, op. cit., pp. 177, 346; Scheim, op. cit., p. 44; Davis, op. cit., pp. 128–129, 187; Livingstone and Groden, op. cit., pp. 248, 251; Report of U.S. House of Representatives, Select Committee on Assassinations, March 29, 1979, pp. 144–145. Rustled together in three weeks by William Sullivan's: Russo, *Live By The Sword*, pp. 334, 355; Warren Commission Report, p. 383. Scott observes that "Hoover's rush to name his assassin publicly was motivated, according to his former assistant William C. Sullivan, by a desire to cut off, or at least circumscribe, an independent inquiry by the Warren Commission." Like Hoover's Assistant Director for Inspection James Gale, Hoover knew that "The FBI had much to hide, and he was looking for ways to hide it." Scott, op. cit., p. 4. Gale would note, suggestively, that "with Oswald's background we should have had a stop [look-out card] on his passport, particularly since we did not know definitively whether or not he had any intelligence assignments at the time." Ibid, p. 6. *At the time.* This is the language bureaucrats take to established operatives.

414   With regular updates from Guy Banister: Livingstone and Groden, op. cit., p. 161; Blakey, op. cit., p. 177; Davis, op. cit., p. 195.

414   Stories surfaced that Oswald and David Ferrie: Waldron, *Ultimate Sacrifice*, p. 745.

415   Meanwhile, Marcello himself confided: Gentry, op. cit., p. 465.

415   How much displacement occurred: Warren Commission Report, p. 388.

415   Evidence would continue to materialize: Livingstone and Groden, op. cit., pp. 282, 304, 305; Waldron, op. cit., pp. 536–537; Weisberg, *Whitewash I*, p. 226.

415–416 By 1978, when the House Assassinations Committee: Davis, op. cit., pp. 149, 150; Hoover was also dubious; See Newman, op. cit., 54.

416   While "Ruby was unquestionably familiar. . . .": Warren Commission Report, p. 697.

416   This in the face of testimony: Moldea, *The Hoffa Wars*, p. 267.

416   In Chicago, Ruby had worked as muscle: Scheim, op. cit., p. 75.

416   Ruby arrived in Dallas in 1947: Warren Report, p. 707.

416   A statement like this: Scheim, op. cit., p. 204; Russo, op. cit., p. 494; Kantor, *Who Was Jack Ruby?* p. 88; Summers, *Conspiracy*, pp. 128, 466. Also *New Times*, "The Secret Life of Jack Ruby," William Scott Malone, 1/23/78; House of Representatives Report on Assassinations, p. 151.

        Peter Dale Scott records that "the Warren Commission received reports linking Ruby to a nationwide network of which [Dave] Yarras was a part . . . linked to the anti-Castro operations and securities operations of Mike McLaney and Sam Benton. . . . ," Scott, op. cit., p. 43.

416–417 At first, like Jimmy Hoffa: Scheim, op. cit., pp. 197, 198; Kantor, op. cit., p. 13.

417   Of recent years Ruby had helped McWillie: Rappleye and Becker, op. cit., pp. 245, 246; Gentry, op. cit., p. 551.

417   "He sent me tickets to Cuba. . . .": Kantor, op. cit., p. 131.

417   McWillie had been working the casinos: Blakey, op. cit., p. 299.

417   In early October, Ruby and Johnny Rosselli: Rappleye and Becker, op, cit., pp. 245, 246; Scheim, op. cit., pp. 215, 237–239.

417   On October 26 Ruby talked: Davis, op. cit., p. 144; Scheim, op. cit., p. 240. Scott suggests that the Warren Commission shied away from authorizing an investigation into Ruby's telephone records because Ruby's testimony was starting to establish his link to Alfred McLane, a key Murchison attorney, who "was killed in a taxi in New York."

417–418 There was a series of extended calls: Kantor, op. cit., pp. 22–24.

418   Throughout November the lines crackled. . . .: "One reason Bobby was reluctant to get into the JFK assassination was because—you know, Jack Ruby. Somebody looked up his long-distance phone records the month before it happened and they almost matched, name for name, the people Bobby had called before the Rackets Committee." (Interview Frank Mankiewicz, 6/1/04). Kennedy insiders like Mankiewicz agree that Walter Sheridan remained close to Bobby, his "avenging Angel," as David Talbot puts it; Talbot claims that RFK sent Sheridan to New Orleans primarily to determine "What Marina really knew." (Talbot, 11/19; Talbot Interview, 5/16/06).

418   Hours before JFK flew into Texas: Ibid., p. 215.

418   "A file concerning Oswald was opened. . . .": Scheim, op. cit., pp. 19, 290, 291.

418   The more sensitive question. . . .: Interestingly enough, Gerald Ford early slips the charge that the Commission members were startled at the claim that Oswald was an FBI informant into his ghost-written 1965 treatment of Oswald, *Portrait of the Assassin* (p. 14). Unfortunately, throughout the rest of the narration he ignores it.

418   Apart from the claim: North, *Act of Treason*, p. 511.

418   An attempt was immediately made to discredit: Epstein, *The Assassination Chronicles*, pp. 59, 60.

419   Defender of the Warren Commission results: Posner, op. cit., p. 348.

419   The indefatigable Anthony Summers: Summers, op. cit., pp. 310–312.

419   Trafficante normally spoke without a lot of passion: Waldron, *Ultimate Sacrifice*, p. 414.

420   A scheduled November 2 presidential visit to Chicago: Ibid., p. 226.

420   Milteer told his informant: Ibid., pp. 660–661. Milteer was a wealthy racist with ties to Guy Banister and a leadership role in the Pedro de Valles group, which had concluded that assassination was the last, best hope for changing the administration. (Peter Dale Scott Interview, November 20, 2005.)

420   Under very heavy police and Secret Service protection: Ibid., pp. 691–692.

420–421   A former Bureau security clerk: Turner, op. cit., p. 118; Posner, op. cit., p. 155; Crenshaw, *Trauma Room One*, pp. 39, 40.

421   If Hosty didn't stop bothering: Gentry, op. cit., pp. 544–546, 549, 550.

421   Why hadn't Oswald appeared on the Bureau's "Security Index": Schlesinger, op. cit., p. 65; Posner, op. cit., pp. 82, 461.

421–422   Critical files were withheld from the Warren Commission: Davis, op. cit., p. 535.

422   Having sent a cable to the field: Davis, *The Kennedys*, p. 454.

422   When U.S. Ambassador to Mexico Thomas Mann: Russo, op. cit., p. 343.

422   Beverly Oliver, a singer: Livingstone and Groden, op. cit., pp. 363, 398.

422   Immediately after the assassination, Regis Kennedy: Summers, *Conspiracy*, p. 506.

422   When the Zapruder film surfaced: Livingstone and Groden, op. cit., pp. 197, 198; Lane, *Plausible Denial*, p. 355.

422   The large occipital bone in the back: The most revealing exchange on the details of JFK's primary wound is to be found in *Neurosurgery*, Volume 54, Number 6, June 2004; and particularly in the response by Gary Aguilar, Cyril Wecht, and Rex Bradford in the September 2005 (Volume 57, Number 3) issue of *Neurosurgery*. Most telling was the lead examining pathologist Dr. Clark Kemp's statement—Clark was Parkland's chairman of neurosurgery—that "there was a large, gaping wound in the right posterior part with the cerebellar tissue being damaged or exposed." The chief of anesthesia reported that Jackie Kennedy handed him "a large chunk of her husband's brain . . . it was less than half a brain there."

422   Surviving acoustical evidence: Livingstone and Groden, op. cit., pp. 211, 224; Weisberg, *Whitewash II*, p. 95; Thompson, op. cit., p. 295. For details of this continuing debate on this point see *Science and Justice*, 2001: 41 (1): 21–32; *Los Angeles Times*, January 27, 1979.

     I remain indebted to Professor Gary Aguilar at the University of California and Stanford. The acoustical evidence is updated in Jefferson Morley's piece in the March 2005 *Reader's Digest*.

423   It would take several seconds to chamber: Livingstone and Groden, op. cit., pp. 152, 189.

423   The initial shots especially: Ibid., pp. 20, 322, 405.

423   "He just wanted a bullet of his own. . . .": Katzenbach Interview, October 26, 2005.

423   If Kennedy and Connally had been hit. . . .: Again, for technical detail with regard to this and other forensic matters I owe a debt to Dr. Aguilar. Recent work at the Forensic Science Center at the Laurence Livermore Laboratory has repudiated the early claim of FBI metallurgists that Kennedy and Connally were struck by the same "magic bullet." Several gunmen are indicated. See *The Mercury News*, August 20, 2006.

423   Charles Crenshaw, one of the emergency-room surgeons: Crenshaw: op. cit., pp. 62, 67, 238. Also see Martin, *Seeds of Destruction*, p. 454.

423   The original autopsy photographs: Livingstone and Groden, op. cit., pp. 3, 419.

423–424 Two FBI agents on hand: Crenshaw, op. cit., p. 229.

424   All this would indicate that the president: Robert Blakey, the committee counsel for the U.S. House of Representatives investigation into the JFK assassination, told me that he had concluded that Oswald had been "roped into the plot to kill the president" and that the shooter on the grassy knoll was tasked with eliminating Oswald before he could figure out—as he quickly did—that it was not the Communists who were after Kennedy; realizing this, once he felt safe in custody Oswald attempted to hire John Apt, the lawyer for the American Civil Liberties Union. Ruth Paine's husband Michael had been urging the headstrong re-defector to look to the ACLU rather than the American Communist Party to effect meaningful reform. (Blakey Interview, September 22, 2005; Ruth Paine Interview, March 23, 2006.)

424   The overwhelming majority of witnesses that day: Ibid., p. 54.

424   In 2005 Antoinette Giancana: A. Giancana, *JFK and Sam*, pp. 189–203.

424   There were reportedly meetings with Marcello's resident stooges: Livingstone and Groden, p. 29.

424   As the presidential motorcade swung: Thompson, op. cit., pp. 137, 179–280; A. Giancana, op. cit., pp. 191, 192, 204; Livingstone and Groden, op. cit., p. 184.

425   The Director now pronounced the Kennedy shooting: North, op. cit., p. 392.

425–426 For a day or two the local authorities: Ibid., p. 393.

426   Within two days of the shooting: Ibid., p. 393.

426   Apart from his notorious generosity when it came to comping: Ibid., p. 394.

426   Unwelcome facts kept getting in the way: Weisberg, *Whitewash*, pp. 57, 58; *Whitewash II*, p. 225; Crenshaw, op. cit., p. 78; Summers, op. cit., p. 119; A. Giancana, op. cit., p. 120. Also see A. Giancana, op. cit., p. 112.

427   Perhaps her best friend throughout those first: Ruth Paine Interview, March 23, 2006.

427   Ruth, who was mastering Russian: Gaeton Fonzi, an investigator for Robert Blakey's House Investigation of the JFK assassination has identified from CIA files de Mohrenschildt, "The Baron," as "The Agency's debriefer of Oswald when the Marine Defector returned from Russia. . . ." (Fonzi, *The Last Investigation*, p. 312.) The CIA was simultaneously bankrolling the anti-Castro hotheads of the Cuban DRE (the "Revolutionary Student Directorate"), who were assuring listeners of their "bitter animosity" toward the president and their intention to buy weapons "as soon as we take care of Kennedy." When CIA inspector John Whitten began to uncover the extent of Agency involvement in the DRE and the FBI's clandestine efforts to pump up Oswald's Fair Play for Cuba Committee, Whitten was hurriedly reassigned by CIA Operations chief Richard Helms, himself pressured by Angleton. See the *Miami New Times*, April 12, 2001 (Jefferson Morley); Morley Interview, November 19, 2003. Also see "The Good Spy," Jefferson Morley, *The Washington Monthly*.

427   "Marina Oswald suddenly became rich. . . ." Livingstone and Groden, op. cit., pp. 242, 243; Hosty, *Assignment Oswald*, p. 88. Hosty identifies the motel as "The Inn of the Six Flags," Adjacent to the Six Flags over Texas amusement park. *Life*, November 22, 1963. Scott carries all this further by citing the "continuing influence often associated with Bedford Wynne." The Secret Service

not only selected Marina's motel but "arranged for her to be interviewed in the presence of an organizer of de Mohrenschildt's CIA-subsidized church parish. The Secret Service helped arrange for the motel's manager to resign and become Marina's manager." Scott, op. cit., pp. 35, 37.

428   Ruth Paine was a little taken aback: Paine Interview, op. cit.

428   "It is hard for you and me to live without a return of our love. . . .": North, op. cit., pp. 273, 292.

429   Once it reappeared it served at once: Ibid., p. 456. Most of the details concerning Marina in North's book are reiterated in Gerald Ford's memoir of the Oswald investigation, *Portrait of an Assassin*.

429   Walker himself had looked at the slug. Livingstone and Groden, op. cit., p. 181; Epstein, *Legend*, p. 491.

429   Unavailable, guarded by the Secret Service: North, op. cit., pp. 449, 500; Hosty, op. cit., pp. 92–93. A couple of years after the Kennedy shooting, Priscilla (Johnson) McMillan spent five months in residence with Marina Oswald in the Dallas area while preparing to write her landmark biography *Lee and Marina*. The woman Priscilla remembers was still in her twenties, self-centered and self-absorbed, a careless mother to her two daughters, and very difficult to pin down.

While Special Agent James Hosty, an FBI internal subversion specialist, repeatedly suggests that Marina was probably a Soviet "sleeper," who hung onto Oswald to worm her way into the United States and lie low (see *Assignment Oswald*, p. 75, etc.), McMillan found her much too slovenly for anything as demanding as espionage. Trained in Russia as a pharmacist, even with Lee gone Marina made at best a desultory effort to learn English. She remembered her months of exchanges with the FBI with revulsion and equated the Bureau with "the Soviet Secret Police." As a subject, McMillan remembers, "I made her go over and over each incident because I was trying to figure out, of her different versions, which one had actually happened." (McMillan Interview, June 9, 2006). On this mercurial witness, the Warren Commission hung its case. Peter Dale Scott cites the memo of a Warren Commission counsel: "Marina had repeatedly lied . . . on matters which are of vital concern." Scott, op. cit., p. 36.

Never overburdened with subtlety, Marina responded to Chief Counsel Rankin by recalling that "Sometimes the FBI agents asked me questions which had no bearing or relationship, and if I didn't want to answer they told me that if I wanted to live in this country, I would have to help in this matter, even thought they were often irrelevant. That is the FBI. I think they should not count on my practically becoming their agent if I desire to stay and live in the United States." (Weisberg, *Whitewash*, p. 134). As late as September of 1964, under Senatorial questioning, Marina maintained that "if he [Oswald] did any shooting that he was not shooting at President Kennedy." (Weisberg, *Whitewash II*, p. 18.)

429   To underscore the direction this thing had better take: North, op. cit., p. 475.

430   Through many of the early months, Warren Commission Chief Counsel: Ibid., pp. 498, 519.

430   Shaking hands with Hoover, she would later remark: Ibid., p. 516.

430   When his turn came: "Hoover lied his eyes out to the Commission," House Majority Leader Hale Boggs commented afterward. "On Oswald, on Ruby, on their friends, the bullets, the gun, you name it. . . .": Summers, *Official and Confidential*, p. 314.

430   "We found no indication at all that Oswald. . . .": Ibid., p. 531.

430   "That is correct. . . .": Stoked up, by now, Marina was telling her handlers that her husband had been out gunning for Richard Nixon and she had restrained him bodily and that he had contemplated hijacking a plane for Cuba. All this sounded overdone to the Commission interrogators, and so these assertions tended to be discounted officially as of "no probative value"—the pot-shot at Walker was all they were after to establish Lee's homicidal proclivities. See Sylvia Meagher, *Accessories After the Fact*, pp. 240, 241.

430   During the early hours of the crisis, the FBI Director had memoed: North, op. cit., pp. 426, 433, 434.

431   Solid witnesses who insisted that they had encountered Oswald: Lane, *Plausible Denial*, p. 364.

431   Inconsistencies plagued further reports on the death: Deitche, *Cigar City Mafia*, p. 129.

431   It was obviously important from the moment the all-Oswald formulation: U.S. House of Representatives Assassination Report, p. 74; Livingstone and Groden, op. cit., pp. 211, 321, 336; Scheim, op. cit., p. 209.

431   He remembered how Oswald had appeared in the basement: Russo, op. cit., p. 497.

431   But even during the weeks the Commissioners were interviewing him: Blakey, op. cit., p. 334; Russo, op. cit., p. 498.

432   By then Hoover's appreciation of the Warren Commission: Turner, op. cit., p. xxii.

432   Although the Bureau had already subjected one witness: Scheim, op. cit., p. 161; Demaris and Wills, *Jack Ruby*, p. 200.

432   Hoover understood right away how flimsy: Newman, op. cit., p. 354; Posner, op. cit., p. 82.

432   The day after the assassination: The new president's need to involve *himself* in staging the aftermath of the JFK shooting is revealing. Charles Crenshaw, one of the surgeons who had struggled to resuscitate JFK, would write of "the call I received from Lyndon Johnson while we were operating on Lee Harvey Oswald. President Johnson told me that a man in the operating room would get a death-bed confession from Oswald." Crenshaw, *Trauma Room One*, p. 14.

432   A week later, in a long memo to his executive staff: FBI internal records, Hoover to Staff, 11/29/63 (Assassination Series).

433   "He was our man, our informant. . . .": Sullivan, *The Bureau*, p. 53; Summers, op. cit., p. 318; Lane, op. cit., p. 43.

433   Relations within the Commission itself were: A. Giancana, op. cit., pp. 50, 51; Livingstone and Groden, op. cit., p. 216; Thompson, *Six Seconds in Dallas*, p. 209.

433–434   Burdened with his obligations to Hoover: Kantor, op. cit., p. 6.

434   According to RFK biographer G. David Heymann: Heymann, op. cit., p. 361.

434   Still numb from Hoover's telephone call: Davis, *The Kennedys*, p. 461; Livingstone and Groden, op. cit., p. 308; Gentry, op. cit., p. 557.

434   Again, Castro was to be eliminated immediately: Livingstone and Groden, op. cit., p. 355.

434   Hands-on as ever, Robert Kennedy: Waldron, op. cit., p, 562.

435   As with its Miami raid, local FBI: Russo, op. cit., p. 184.

435   It was from this base: Morales would become a legend at the action end of the Clandestine Services, a meat-saw available to more polished operatives like David Attlee Phillips. A recent expose by the BBC places Morales in the Ambassador Hotel ballroom the night Bobby Kennedy died and quoted Morales—who liked to brag when he drank, which was a lot of the time—as exclaiming to friends: "I was in Dallas when we got the son of a bitch and I was

in Los Angeles when we got the little bastard." BBC Newsnight, November 21, 2006.

435 Again, Bobby was single-mindedly pursuing: Waldron, op. cit., p. 243; Livingstone and Groden, op. cit., pp. 124, 125, 133.

435 Enough planning had long since leaked, subsequent FBI Director: Waldron, op. cit., p. 252.

435 Having taken it upon himself: Livingstone and Groden, op. cit., pp. 113, 161; Fonzi, *The Last Investigation*, p. 312. The way this worked is spelled out in a suppressed intra-office memo put together by Jefferson Morley, a reporter and editor at *Washington Post*. When Morley confronted Jane Roman, a key CIA officer in Angleton's counterintelligence shop, with initialed routing slips tracking Oswald's movements from 1959 to 1963, she admitted that after January 1963 the Oswald file along with FBI reports had been moved over to "the Agency's Cuba hands," specifically the "Special Affairs Staff" created by the Kennedy brothers after MONGOOSE collapsed to "take over the job of coordinating the secret campaign to bring down Castro's government. . . ." Morley memo, pp. 8, 13, 14. Thanks to James Lesar, president of the Washington-based Assassination and Research Archives Center, for providing a transcript of this internal memo along with related government files on Johnny Rosselli and other corroboratory material.

436 Oswald's primary Agency handler: The role of George de Mohrenschildt was probably the most demanding of that of any of the walk-on players around the Kennedy assassination. Scott points out that "the Oswald family's exotic 'babysitter' in Dallas, White Russian Baron George de Mohrenschildt," had once worked overseas for a Murchison oil company (Three States Oil and Gas) as well as "an oil trust uniting a Trujillo associate . . . with a representative . . . of the Batista Falla family behind the Lake Pontchartrain training camp." He remained "a personal friend of the CIA representative in Dallas, J. Walter Moore." Scott, op. cit., pp. 34, 35. Responsible people close to the details, from Robert Groden to James Lesar, seem inclined to believe that the CIA was the organizing entity behind the Kennedy assassination. (Exchange with Robert Groden, December 2, 2006.) Richard Helms's name comes up, and even that of the director in 1963, the straight-laced John McCone. As somebody who has spent considerable time with Helms and many others at the top of the Sixties Agency, such a scenario strikes me as unlikely.

436 "If the FBI is controlling him," Bobby reportedly conceded: Mellen, *A Farewell to Justice*, p. 380.

436 JFK had gone down, he was to concede privately: Waldron, op. cit., p. 241.

436 Plagued throughout his later life with charges: *IMAGE* Magazine, Sunday, 3/29/92 (David Talbot).

436 The moment he understood fully. . . .: Richard Goodwin, a constant throughout Robert Kennedy's later career, tends to support that: "And of course that was why he felt guilty too. Maybe it was his pursuit of organized crime that brought this down." (Goodwin Interview, 6/9/06.)

436 "I've killed my own brother. . . .": Waldron, op. cit., p. 243.

437 In fact, as Sheridan emphasized: Mellen, op. cit., pp. 189, 192. Also see *New York Review of Books*, Richard Popkin, 9/14/67.

437 An hour and a half after JFK: "Had I been asked to testify," one pathologist later wrote, "I would have told them that there is no doubt in my mind that the bullet that killed President Kennedy was shot from the front." Crenshaw, op. cit., p. 14.

437   "Go screw yourself," Kenny O'Donnell said: Summers, *Conspiracy,* p. 42; Crenshaw, op. cit., p. 19.

437   When the formal autopsy was conducted at the Naval Hospital: Davis, *Mafia Kingfish,* pp. 291–296; Livingstone and Groden, op. cit., pp. 8, 289, 496; Posner, op. cit., pp. 303–308.

437   When Lyndon Johnson paid Bobby the courtesy: Russo, op. cit., p. 363.

438   To make sure he had one seasoned investigator: Davis, *The Kennedys,* pp. 460, 461.

438–439   "The minute that bullet hit Jack Kennedy's head. . . .": Summers, op. cit., p. 332.

439   When the head of the Criminal Division at Justice: Davis, *Mafia Kingfish,* pp. 242, 243.

439   "It's important that all of the facts. . . .": Posner, op. cit., pp. 404, 405; Gentry, op. cit., p. 547.

439   Over the next few years: William Hundley told Richard Mahoney, author of *Sons and Brothers,* that one of his partners associated with the law firm of Edward Bennett Williams, Tom Wadden, a "longtime friend and attorney of Rosselli's, subsequently confirmed Rosselli's role in plotting to kill the president." (p. 229). Another of Wadden's partners, Leslie Scherr, also close to Rosselli, claims never to have heard a word about this, although he admits freely that for all his warmth and generosity and savoir faire and those "piercing gray eyes," Johnny was allegedly "Al Capone's major hit man, and I suspect this is true, or real." (Scherr Interview, 6/7/06.) Wadden's widow Mary would remember going to dinner with the affable gangster. Midway through the meal the waiter made a mistake. Rosselli darkened. The resulting scene left the Waddens deeply frightened. (Mary Wadden Interview, 5/26/06.) Certain response patterns never change.

439   One name that kept coming up as an accessory: Thomas, op. cit., p. 337; Summers, op. cit., p. 326; Rappleye and Becker, op. cit., pp. 247, 248; Deitche, op. cit., p. 179. Day by day details can be gleaned from Rosselli's FBI file (HQ 92 – 3267, plus LA 92-113).

439–440   He made a devoted effort with Judith Campbell: Rappleye and Becker, op. cit., p. 252; FBI Sinatra file (92-143-2834).

440   As Garrison's investigation heated up, on February: Mellen, op. cit., p. 106.

440   Enraged to find himself a target: Rappleye and Becker, op. cit., p. 268.

440–441   Hoover himself had been talking up a similar remake: Blakey, op. cit., p. 145; Newman, op. cit., p. 428.

441   Yet, when KGB Lieutenant Colonel Yuri Nosenko: Summers, *Conspiracy,* p. 201.

441   "Sometimes I'd like to tell them the Mob did it. . . .": Demaris, *The Last Mafioso,* p. 389.

441   But according to Robert Blakey, the chief counsel: Blakey, op. cit., p. 386; Summers, op. cit., p. 495, 503; Livingstone and Groden, op. cit., p. 328; Davis, op. cit., p. 329.

442   Ruby was, Rosselli had conceded, "one of our boys": Scheim, op. cit., p. 124.

442   A week before his scheduled appearance in Washington: Summers, op. cit., p. 502.

442   On April 23, 1976, Rosselli sat down at the Carroll Arms: Davis, op. cit., p. 373.

442   Rosselli didn't seem to care: Rappleye and Becker, op. cit., p. 319; Summers, op. cit., p. 503.

442   He had been smothered, shot, gutted: Russo, op. cit., p. 346.

442–443   "We took care of Kennedy. . . together. . . .": S. Giancana, *Double Cross,* pp. 457, 467.

443   Mob lawyer Frank Regano: Regano, op. cit., pp. 151, 348.

443   In 1980, Joe Hauser looked up from his newspaper: Davis, op. cit., p. 424.

CHAPTER 20

447   He hung on as attorney general: Goldfarb, op. cit., p. 312.

448   Ethel, always there with the needle: Guthman, op. cit., p. 266.

448   In May 1962: Hilty, op. cit., p. 231; de Toledano, *J. Edgar Hoover*, p. 294.

448   In December 1964: Gid Powers, op. cit., pp. 291, 292; FBI, RFK Files, Morrell to DeLoach, February 24, 1964, (77-51387); RFK Files, Robert Kennedy to Hoover, 3/30/64.

448   When Ethel lost some jewelry in Paris: FBI cable, RFK Files, 6/11/64.

448   Upon resigning from the cabinet, Kennedy thanked the special agents: FBI, Robert Kennedy File, Hoover to Robert Kennedy, 9/1/64.

448   "Starting at 1:10 on November 22. . . .": Davis, *Mafia Kingfish*, p. 297.

448   Within one day "we stopped getting information from the FBI. . . .": Turner, op. cit., p. 174.

448   "Another stiletto from Bobby K. . . .": FBI Internal Memo, Belmont to Tolson, 9/22/65.

448   "These people," Robert Kennedy decided aloud: Summers, *Official and Confidential*, p. 332.

448–449 For all Hoover's vagaries, Kennedy had to admit: Robert K. Kennedy, *In His Own Words*, pp. 127, 131, 291.

449   Even before he stepped down, Bob's friend: JFK Library, RFK Collection, Tremblay oral history.

449   Among the first victims of this Hoover-directed purge: Shesol, op. cit., pp. 189, 192.

449   After almost three years of being precluded from communicating: Navasky, op. cit., p. 65.

449   Hoover let it ring itself out: Schott, op. cit., pp. 204, 205; Davis, op. cit., p. 297.

450   When Evans observed in a memo: Gentry, op. cit., p. 548.

450   No fool, Evans asked Al Belmont: Gentry, op. cit., pp. 55, 152, 583.

450   By May 1964, increasingly cut off: Gid Powers, op. cit., pp. 391, 392.

450–451 Bob admitted all along that I knew he didn't like me much": Hilty, op. cit., p. 224.

451   But by the end of 1964 Kennedy would agree: Robert F. Kennedy, *In His Own Words*, p. 184.

451   Later, reflecting aloud to John Bartlow Martin: Davis, *The Kennedys*, p. 348.

451   Bobby Baker would remember how agitated: Baker, *Wheelin' and Dealin'*, p. 71.

451   Once the Kennedy administration settled in, Robert Kennedy: Robert F. Kennedy, *In His Own Words*, p. 77.

452   When Bob Kennedy gave a speech in Georgia: FBI Records, Robert Kennedy File, SAC Atlanta to Director, 5/26/64.

452   In an answering memo: FBI Records, Robert F. Kennedy File, Evans to Belmont, 6/2/64.

452   Kennedy himself pushed the Community Relations Service: Gid Powers, op. cit., pp. 399, 400.

453   "He who learns must suffer. . . .": Schlesinger, op. cit., p. 618.

453   Not to have consummated this tragic intimacy. . . .: Assorted visitors and friends couldn't help but notice that the only framed portrait in Jacqueline Kennedy's Manhattan living room was of Robert Kennedy. (Mutual acquaintance; see Martin, op. cit., p. 53.)

453   "Well," Fred Dutton would subsequently concede: Dutton Interview, 6/2/05.

453   A visitor to a house overlooking the Palm Beach compound: Heymann, op. cit., pp. 286, 287.

453   Hoover would occasionally trip by: Gentry, op. cit., pp. 557, 558.

453   Confidential FBI files: Gentry, op. cit., p. 559.

454   "Have you ever seen anything as big as this?": *New York Review of Books*, Marshall Frady, "The Big Guy," 11/14/02.

454   Here was a president who routinely invited staffers: Goodwin, *Remembering America*, p. 256.

454   Midway through a Redskins game: Thomas, *Edward Bennett Williams*, p. 182.

454   "His Adam's apple going up and down like a Yo-yo. . . .": Schlesinger, op. cit., p. 662.

454   "This fellow looks at me like he's gonna look a hole. . . .": Branch, *Pillar of Fire*, p. 422.

454   After huffing that he would resign at once: Hilty, op. cit., p. 246; Theoharis and Cox, op. cit., p. 337; Gentry, op. cit., p. 561.

455   "There's some thought that Attorney General Kennedy. . . .": Schlesinger, op. cit., p. 663; Shesol, op. cit., pp. 216, 217.

455   As executive director of Johnson's campaign, Kenny O'Donnell: O'Donnell and Powers, *Johnny We Hardly Knew Ye*, p. 401.

455   As a young lawyer, Ronald Goldfarb: JFK Library, RFK Collection, Goldfarb oral history.

455   "Bob didn't do an awful lot. . . .": Dutton Interview, 6/2/05; Newfield, op. cit., p. 31.

455   In hearing rooms or on the floor of the Senate: David Burke Interview, 9/16/05.

456   The ageless Melody Miller: Melody Miller Interview, 5/31/05.

456   Ted's legislative assistant of the era, Dun Gifford: Stein, op. cit., p. 183.

457   More and more, Bob Kennedy was living his life. . . .: The omnipresent Billings would explain to Collier and Horowitz: "Bobby didn't know that his father was trying to stop this thing that had gotten started—this Kennedy daring of the gods. The two of them never understood each other on this." (Collier and Horowitz, op. cit., p. 340).

457   In Chile he confronted a gymnasium packed: Schlesinger, op. cit., pp. 696, 698.

457   As they paddled around: R. Goodwin, op. cit., p. 442.

457   When Bobby insisted on struggling up Mount Kennedy: Dallas, op. cit., p. 276.

457   Reduced to an inarticulate onlooker: Dallas, op. cit., p. 275.

458   Toward the very end, according to Kennedy chauffeur: Saunders, *Torn Lace Curtain*, p. 193.

458   Barrett Prettyman Jr.: Prettyman Interview, 5/31/04.

459   Thomas Corcoran, a nephew of Tommy the Cork: Corcoran Interview, 11/15/05.

460   A strapping, outspoken lawyer and U.S. Congressman: Von Hoffman, op. cit., p. 259.

460   Bluff and self-assured, the holder: Gentry, op. cit., p. 589.

461   When Bob Kennedy abruptly put down his base: Newfield, op. cit., pp. 149, 150.

461   One day Roy Cohn called and told Neil: Von Hoffman, op. cit., pp. 285, 286.

462   Hoover saw his next opportunity: Gentry, op. cit., p. 586.

462   Furthermore, Long was "out to get Bobby": Shesol, op. cit., pp. 349, 350.

462   Hoover contrived to offload the defense of FBI: FBI memo, DeLoach to Tolson, 1/9/67; Theoharis and Cox, op. cit., p. 363.

462   It helped that the Bureau's wonderfully productive: Turner, op. cit., p. 90.

462   Deke DeLoach, the sonorous Dutch uncle: Gentry, op. cit., pp. 587, 588.
462   Hoover himself prepared a statement: Theoharis and Cox, op. cit., p. 365.
462   When Kennedy attempted to get Katzenbach: Shesol, op. cit., p. 351; Katzenbach Interview, 10/26/05.
463   In full throat, Robert Morgenthau's prosecutors: *Life,* 9/9/69 (William Lampert); Von Hoffmann, op. cit., p. 301 (paper).
463   Not that Hoover didn't have plenty of: Gentry, op. cit., p. 586.
463   In 1963 Cohn's house was burglarized: Hack, *Puppetmaster,* p. 330.
463   Cohn would ultimately assert: Ibid., p. 272.
464   Well beyond dispensing disinformation: Cohn/Zion: *The Autobiography of Roy Cohn,* p. 235.
464   It would be the publicity that surfaced: Theoharis and Cox, op. cit., p. 365.
464   Long contacted DeLoach in search of: FBI Memo, DeLoach to Tolson, 1/9/67 (94-923).
464   Outraged that responsibility for all this distasteful snooping: Sheridan, *The Fall and Rise of Jimmy Hoffa,* pp. 399–400; FBI Memo, DeLoach to Mohr, 3/3/65 (77-513871772).
464   Long quoted Kennedy as pledging: Navasky, op. cit., p. 481.
464–465 In 1964 Fred Black had finally been charged: FBI Records, Robert Kennedy Files, DeLoach to Tolson, 1/9/67; *Time,* 12/3/66.
465   Hoover made it simple: FBI Files, Hoover to Gross, 12/28/66; DeLoach to Tolson, 12/24/65; DeLoach to Tolson, 7/11/66; Hoover to Tolson, 6/12/68.
465   Kennedy's office responded that: State University of New York, David Heymann Collection, Box 15a, Folders 6, 7, 10, letters 2/17, 5/27, 1966.
465   This statement dovetailed poorly with: FBI Files, DeLoach to Tolson, 3/23/66.
465   Caught in the middle, Attorney General Nicholas Katzenbach: FBI Records, Robert Kennedy Files, DeLoach to Tolson, 12/20/65 (77-511587); Gale to DeLoach, 12/30/65; DeLoach to Tolson, 1/28/66.
466   He responded to reporters' questions: *The World Journal Tribune* (Special), 12/31/66 (Leslie Whitten). Also see JFK Library, RFK Collection, Silberling oral history, 3/22/71. Also: FBI Memo, DeLoach to Tolson, 12/23/66.
466   Jackie would use the word "hired": Thomas, op. cit., p. 330.
466   Robert Kennedy had already generated murmurs: Schlesinger, op. cit., pp. 760–761.
467   As to John Kennedy's efforts at détente: FBI Records, Robert Kennedy File, DeLoach to Mohr, 6/4/64 (77-5387).
467   Johnson came through instantly: Thomas, op. cit., p. 331.
467   "Son," Johnson had suggested: Shesol, op. cit., p. 10.
467   They found Manchester overwrought: Columbia University Library, Evan Thomas Sr. oral history (1964), pp. 128–130.
468   Manchester had been edited to an extent: Schlesinger, op. cit., p. 762.
468   "Why don't you go ahead and publish the damn book?": Columbia University Library, Evan Thomas Sr. oral history, p. 133.
468   Jacqueline was being quoted: Thomas, op. cit., p. 331.
469   "His judgments were very quick. . . .": David Burke Interview, 9/16/05.
469   Wherever Bobby went, observers: Schlesinger, op. cit., pp. 786, 787.
469   He arranged for hearings of the Senate Subcommittee: Mahoney, op. cit., p. 311.
469   In Mississippi with the Senate Labor Committee's: Schlesinger, op. cit., p. 795.
469   Invited by a student union: Ibid., p. 745.

469   Junketing through South America: Stein, op. cit., p. 152.

470   It was too much sometimes: Mahoney, op. cit., p. 317.

CHAPTER 21

471   Both brothers were less than impressed: Schlesinger, op. cit., p. 92.

472   In his seminal treatise on the backdrop: Prouty, *JFK*, pp. 105–109.

472   This was a mistake, and advisors like Undersecretary of State: Schlesinger, op. cit., p. 703.

472–473 Helicopters were an unwieldly: Prouty, op. cit., pp. 109–114.

473   These were the years when the First National Bank: Messick, *The Mob in ShowBusiness* (paper), pp. 222–231.

473   Excited by Maxwell Taylor's theories: Hilty, op. cit., pp. 461–472; Sheehan, *A Bright Shining Lie*, pp. 178, 179.

473   Bob was as implicated as anybody in the government: George Smathers told Ralph Martin: "I think Jack thought Bobby screwed up on Diem's assassination . . . that he knew something before Jack knew anything about it. . . ." (Martin, p. 447.) Family honor was involved. Robert Kennedy subsequently insisted that he personally had been against the coup, but Bobby had a way of rounding the corners of history when pushed for the truth. "Hell, I was the one who saved his life," Bob told Richard Goodwin when Goodwin cautiously inquired as to whether Bob had been involved in the plots to eliminate Castro. (Goodwin Interview, 6/9, 6/26/06.)

473   When Kennedy himself alerted Maxwell Taylor: Branch, *Pillar of Fire*, p. 572.

474   Robert Kennedy hated Lyndon anyway: Wofford, op. cit., p. 417.

474   During his final months, in response: Hilty, op. cit., p. 469; O'Donnell and Powers, op. cit., pp. 13, 17; Prouty, op. cit., p. 116.

474   "I keep myself on a leash. . . .": Marshall Frady, *New York Review of Books*, 11/14/04.

474   "I can't stand the bastard. . . .": R. Goodwin, op. cit., p. 415.

474   He wrote Johnson in January 1966: Kennedy Library, RFK Collection, RFK to LBJ, 1/26/66; LBJ to RFK, 1/27/66.

475   Allied inside the Senate with skeptics: Schlesinger, op. cit., p. 824.

475   Barricaded in behind the White House fences: Shesol, op. cit., p. 261.

475   Santo Trafficante Jr., very interested in lining up an adequate supply: McCoy, *The Politics of Heroin*, p. 253.

476   The previous November 30: Schlesinger, op. cit., p. 832.

476   Days after McCarthy's triumph. . . .: Ibid., p. 850; Thomas, op. cit., pp. 360, 365. It happened that I was a part of a small skiing party that included the Robert Kennedys several weeks before the New Hampshire primary of 1968. Bobby hadn't yet announced. We were all eating tasteless sandwiches from the Kennedy hamper when somebody asked Bobby whether he still had his sights set on Jimmy Hoffa. "Why should I bother about Hoffa when I've got Lyndon?" Kennedy cracked. Standing behind the senator, I pulled out a notebook to take down the exchange; Bobby caught me writing and reprimanded me; I came back in kind. He was plainly quite nerved up where the question of his candidacy was involved and probably had already decided to announce.

476   "Bobby's therapy is going to cost. . . .": Newfield, op. cit., p. 220.

476   Eisenhower noted in a letter: Schlesinger, op. cit., p. 859.

477   When Kennedy groveled: Oppenheimer, op. cit., p. 310.

477 In the Indiana primary, having listened: Newfield, op. cit., p. 225.

477 When Martin Luther King was killed: JFK Library, RFK Collection, oral history, Adam Walinsky, 11/22/76.

477 A few weeks before he died in 2005 he attempted: Fred Dutton Interview, 6/2/2005.

477 When Jack Newfield asked: Newfield, op. cit., p. 58.

477 This reflected theologian Michael Novak's: Stein, op. cit., p. 236.

477 It happened that, not long after the 1968 election: Eugene McCarthy Interview for my book, *The Education of Edward Kennedy;* see notes in that 1972 volume.

477–478 In turn, Bob regarded Gene as on the take: Thomas, op. cit., pp. 360, 367.

478 A mid-1965 AIRTEL: FBI Files, SAC Newark to Director, 6/14/65 (77-51381-1790).

478 Not long after that, Neil Gallagher: Von Hoffman, op. cit., pp. 329, 330.

479 He had already attempted to push some of the responsibility on Nicholas Katzenbach: Gentry, op. cit., pp. 406, 583.

479 It happened that the gadfly columnist: Thomas, op. cit., p. 378.

479 The tap had produced evidence that "a Communist. . . .": Witcover, *85 Days,* p. 212, (paper).

479–480 Even converts like Kennedy's black organizer, John Lewis: Thomas, op. cit., p. 380.

480 The Bureau would take the high road, DeLoach said: FBI Files, DeLoach to Tolson, 5/21/68 (100-106670).

480 As to King's sex life: FBI Files, DeLoach to Tolson, 5/17/68; Von Hoffman, op. cit., p. 71.

480 When, upon being briefed about the King wiretaps: FBI Files, DeLoach to Tolson, 5/17/68 (77-51387).

480–481 A few years later, engaged in a Pier-Six brawl: FBI Records, Neil Gallagher Files, T. S. Emory to Cleveland, 4/20/72 (FM 62 975 64).

481 Richard Harwood of the *Washington Post: Washington Post,* 5/16/68.

481 Harwood, an ex-Marine: Johnson, reportedly quite worked up at the prospect of a Robert Kennedy candidacy, was leaking information to the press intended to finish Bobby off. The president was allegedly telling reactionaries that Robert Kennedy had Martin Luther King on his payroll. Concerned that the half-crazed LBJ might now try anything, Bobby "worried that the President might well blacken the Kennedy name by publicly releasing everything that Hoover knew about Marilyn Monroe." (Martin, pp. 525, 555) Newfield, op. cit., p. 262. Also *Fortune Magazine,* Arthur Krock, March 1963.

481 Pierre Salinger put out the word: Thomas, op. cit., p. 379.

481 As John Seigenthaler would recall: Seigenthaler Interview, 4/4/05.

481 Bob held himself accountable: John Bartlow Martin Journal, p. 55 (unpublished); SUNY, David Heymann Collection, Box 30-A, Folder 4.

481 Ethel doled out handfuls of pills: Ibid., p. 29; Thomas, op. cit., p. 383.

482 "My juggler's gift": Heymann, op. cit., p. 466.

482 It was particularly painful for Bob: Martin, Journal, p. 30.

482 It got to the point where genteel advisors: Ibid., p. 59; *RFK, In His Own Words,* p. 371.

482 Kennedy won in California. . . .: Thomas, op. cit., p. 388. Robert Kennedy understood his predicament. "Bob said he had to get McCarthy to withdraw, because McCarthy might have beat him in the New York primary," Richard Goodwin will concede. "The bosses might have gone with him [Kennedy] because they thought he might be the winner. If McCarthy's support and

money fell away it would have been hard for him. That's what we were work-ing on. It was a long shot. . . .": Goodwin Interview, 7/9/06.

482   "In those days there were very few primaries. . . .": David Burke Interview, 9/16/05.

483   Bob had begun to shake hands when an unstable Palestinian: Moldea, *The Killing of Robert F. Kennedy,* p. 191; Davis, *Mafia Kingfish,* p. 349.

483   In his journal, John Bartlow Martin: Martin Journal, p. 35.

483   "I hope somebody shoots and kills the son of a bitch. . . .": Gentry, op. cit., p. 606.

483   "We hope and pray. . . .": FBI Records, RFK Files (77-51337), 6/5/68.

    Shortly—as he had done after the murders: Hack, op. cit., p. 370.

483   The investigation into Robert Kennedy's murder. . . .: Ralph Martin has discov-ered that "There was also the fact that the Los Angeles police had destroyed three rolls of film confiscated from an eyewitness who took pictures at the very moment shots were being fired. Of 3470 police interviews on tape only 301 were kept." (Martin, p. 566.) Also Moldea, op. cit., p. 221.

483   Sirhan had approached Kennedy from the front: Moldea, op. cit., p. 88; Davis, op. cit., p. 350.

484   Follow-up studies by the Los Angeles field office of the FBI: Moldea, op. cit., pp. 261–266.

484   A compulsive gambler, Sirhan consorted: Ibid., p. 105; Davis, op. cit., p. 351.

    Sirhan's chief defense counsel, Grant Cooper: Davis, op. cit., pp. 353–355; Moldea, op. cit., p. 116.

484   Underground, the trolls were chuckling: John Davis observes that a prison informant at Lewisburg "told the FBI that he had heard Jimmy Hoffa and New York Mafia boss Carmine Gallante, an ally of Carlos Marcello's, discussing a 'mob contract to kill Bob Kennedy,'" while another FBI informant tipped the Bureau off about a "wealthy southern California rancher" with Minuteman ties, who hated Kennedy because of his support for Caesar Chavez, who "pledged $2000 toward a $500,000 to $750,000 Mafia contract to kill the sena-tor in the event he could receive the Democratic nomination for President." (Davis, *Mafia Kingfish,* p. 345.) There is no indication that the Bureau ever passed the threats along to the Kennedy campaign. The pattern is alarmingly similar to the layers of involvement and support behind the JFK assassina-tion—in the former case, the major oil wildcatters were reputedly the financial backers, according to Johnny Rosselli; see Chapter 19. Davis, op. cit., p. 347.

485   The day of Robert Kennedy's funeral, the FBI knocked national coverage: Demaris, *The Director,* p. 224; Heymann, op. cit., p. 215.

485   The monsters had now gotten so heavy: William Hundley Interview, 10/13/04.

485   Discouragingly, even without "that sneaky little son of a bitch. . . .": "In my view, Hoover was senile," Katzenbach says now. "I always tried to meet with him in his office, because I couldn't get him out of mine. He would agree to almost any-thing, and then he would talk endlessly about anything—Perle Mesta's jewels, details about her house, stupid stiff like that. People asked whether I could have fired him. I could have, but he was so powerful that the next day I'd have been fired and he'd have been reinstated." (Katzenbach Interview, 10/26/05). Also, Summers, *Official and Confidential,* p. 279.

485   The Director let it be known that he had now decided: Theoharis and Cox, op. cit., p. 393.

486   Clark's promotion was tied in some Machiavellian way: Russo, *The Outfit,* pp. 380, 464.

486   Hoover treated Clark like "a small child": DeLoach, op. cit., pp. 222, 252.

486   Clark struggled to get the Director to give him: Gentry, op. cit., pp. 578, 599.

486–487 The brightest light on most of the legislation: Moldea, *Interference,* p. 179.

487   Title III of the Omnibus Crime Control: Unger, *FBI,* p. 400; Fox, op. cit., p. 397; Russo, *The Outfit,* p. 466.

487   As things worked out, Professor Blakey remembers: Blakey Interview, 9/23/05.

488   One Bureau field supervisor: Ungar, op. cit., p. 401.

489   Hundley was well aware that Robert Kennedy: Russo, *The Outfit,* p. 453.

489   That same year Murray Llewellyn: Ibid., p. 458.

489   In July 1967 the SAC in New Orleans: FBI Records, Marcello File, AIRTEL, SAC New Orleans to Director, 7/27/67 (92-2713-452).

490   He allegedly took up with Marcello's sister-in-law: Davis, *Mafia Kingfish,* pp. 322, 323; FBI Internal Memo, 5/2/68.

490   By 1979, with Hoover dead: Davis, op. cit., p. 321.

490   The star turn went to Joseph Hauser: Ibid., pp. 418–436.

490   One of Bob Kennedy's prosecutors at the Justice Department: Mike Fawer Interview, 10/6/04.

        In August 1981, at seventy-two: Davis, op. cit., pp. 493, 501.

CHAPTER 22

492   DeLoach came from a small Georgia town: Ungar, op. cit., pp. 279–281.

493   A committed Roman Catholic: DeLoach Interview, 5/30/03.

493   Tolson—whose "slavish" obedience: DeLoach, op cit., p. 65.

493   DeLoach could never remember an affectionate gesture: DeLoach Interview, 5/31/ 04.

493   Sitting in on the same meeting, Courtney Evans: Evans Interview, 1/19/05.

493–494 "My wife wondered what was going on," DeLoach says now: DeLoach Interview, 5/31/04.

494   When Johnson was vice president, according to his loquacious mistress: Summers, *Official and Confidential,* p. 336.

494   Apart from prostate surgery, DeLoach says: DeLoach Interview, 5/30/03.

494   The leadership was thinning—in 1965, the overworked Al Belmont: Gentry, op. cit., p. 583.

495   Johnson liked him so much: Ungar, op. cit., p. 287; DeLoach Interview, 5/31/04.

495   "The president on one occasion called me. . . .": DeLoach Interview, 5/30/03.

495   DeLoach was rarely hesitant about laying it on: Summers, op. cit., pp. 338, 339.

495   DeLoach attempted to deal with the fireworks: Sullivan, *The Bureau,* pp. 68, 69 (paper).

495   Years later Richard Goodwin would write: R. Goodwin, op. cit., p. 398.

496   On August 9, 1968: *Life* article by Russell Sackett, Sandy Smith, and William Lambert.

496–497 It was suspected by many that "DeLoach": Turner, op. cit., p. xx.

497   One of the authors of the *Life* piece was Sandy Smith: DeLoach, op. cit., p. 317.

497   "That's a pretty dirty trick the Bureau did. . . .": Gentry, op. cit., p. 590.

497   Once it became probable that Gallagher would retain his seat: Von Hoffman, op. cit., pp. 332, 339.

497   It took its energy from the disclosure: Gentry, op. cit., pp. 589, 590.

498   While insisting that "At this point I have very little personal sensitivity. . . .": FBI

Records, Cohn File, Cohn to Gallagher, 4/28/72; T. J. Emery to Cleveland, 4/20/72 (FM62-97564).

498   Three months before he died: Von Hoffman, op. cit., p. 446, appendix (paper).
498   A popular television series called *The FBI*: Turner, op. cit., pp. 115, 116.
498   Hoover's oversight of this long-running: Branch, *Pillar of Fire*, p. 544.
499   The problematic Ramsey Clark: Turner, op. cit., pp. 222, 223.
499   Egged on by Hoover: Gentry, op. cit., pp. 602, 618–623.
499–500 Something about the wiry Sullivan's combination: Ungar, op. cit., p. 297.
500   He compared Hoover repeatedly with de Gaulle and Adenauer: Wannall, *The Real J. Edgar Hoover*, p. 147; DeLoach Interview, 9/11/05.
500   On Lyndon Johnson's orders, late in 1968: Gentry, op. cit., p. 608.
500   Jack Nelson of the the *Los Angeles Times:* Ibid., pp. 651, 652.
500   Jack Anderson pulled off a "trash cover" raid: Ibid., p. 669.
500   Stories floated around Washington that DeLoach was double-billing: Ungar, op. cit., p. 295.
500   "DeLoach and I were bitter enemies. . . .": Demaris, *The Director,* p. 217.
500   Deeply aggrieved with Sullivan: DeLoach Interview, 9/11/05.
501   "There is a ring of homosexualists. . . .": Gentry, op. cit., p. 624.
501   Hoover sent in his rising star, Mark Felt: Haldeman, *The Ends of Power,* p. 66; Erlichman, *Witness to Power,* p. 160.
501   Sexually, it appeared that this perennial Republican golden boy: Sullivan, op. cit., pp. 197, 198.
501–502 The first inklings of how everything worked: Gentry, op. cit., pp. 632, 637.
502   Before it was over there would be seventeen wiretaps: Ambrose, *Nixon,* p. 273.
502   "This is not an FBI operation. This is a White House operation. . . .": Gentry, op. cit., p. 637.
502   He refused to help with three bag jobs for the NSA: Ibid., pp. 639, 645.
502   It soon became apparent that the primary leaker was Daniel Ellsberg: Ibid., p. 684.
503   Louis Marx was a wealthy: Hoover's loyalty to people who had been helpful to him endeared him to his friends. Nick Katzenbach recalls the *frisson* that erupted in the Justice Department when Hoover paid a friendly call on Frank Costello after the aging Mafia boss was finally sent up the river on a tax charge. (Katzenbach Interview, 10/26/05.)
503   "If the FBI was not going to pursue the case. . . .": Nixon, *The Memoirs of Richard Nixon,* p. 513.
503   On July 17, John Erlichman instructed Egil: Gentry, op. cit., p. 686.
503   They judged the Bureau's reports as "of poor quality": Erlichman, op. cit., pp. 156, 158.
503   "Hoover full of hair-raising reports. . . .": Haldeman, op. cit., p. 53.
503   These memoirs are studded: Ibid., p. 270.
503   Accustomed to California palatial: Erlichman, op. cit., pp. 160, 162.
504   In 1966, Tolson had suffered: Hack, op. cit., pp. 354, 364.
504   The president himself was forced to offer a statement to the press: Gentry, op. cit., pp. 640, 641.
504   On discovering in 1970 that the corn-fed: Gid Powers, op. cit., pp. 458–460; Gentry, op. cit., pp. 640, 641.
505   In 1967, back in private practice, Barrett Prettyman Jr.: Private letter, J. Edgar Hoover to E. Barrett Prettyman Jr., 2/6/67; Interview Prettyman, 5/31/04.

506   In November protesters staged a rally: Sullivan, op. cit., p. 286.

506   A lot of middle-class kids were involved: Ibid., p. 205.

506   Tom Charles Huston approached: Ibid., pp. 284–288.

507   Hoover saw the draft, Huston later testified: Demaris, *The Director*, p. 290.

507   The Director laid low in his office until the signing ceremony: Gentry, op. cit., p. 656.

507   Then Hoover reportedly "landed in Mitchell's office. . . .": Demaris, op. cit., p. 290; DeLoach Interview, 9/11/05.

507   "We've got enough damned coordination. . . .": Sullivan, op. cit., p. 212.

507   In his memoirs. Sullivan would protest: Sullivan, op. cit., p. 202.

507–508   Back at the headquarters the Director was beside himself: Gentry, op. cit., p. 660.

508   Testifying before the Senate Subcommittee on Supplemental Appropriations: Ibid., p. 665.

508   At this most perilous of turns: Ibid., pp. 674, 675.

508   The self-designated Citizens' Commission to Investigate the FBI: Ungar, op. cit., pp. 140, 141, 492.

508   Always sensitive to a shift in the political winds: Gentry, op. cit., pp. 682, 683.

508–509   Sullivan quickly proved that he understood where everything was heading: Demaris, *The Director*, pp. 250–252.

509   Always alive to danger, Hoover: Gentry, op. cit., pp. 689–691.

509   On August 28, 1971: Sullivan, op. cit., pp. 242–245.

509   "That son of a bitch Sullivan pulled the wool. . . .": Wannall, op. cit., p. 147.

509   To Sullivan Hoover insisted: Gentry, op. cit., p. 695.

510   The Director had kept an eye on Ted Kennedy: Sullivan, op. cit., p. 57.

510   Along with the entire world's working press: Gentry, op. cit., p. 638; Ambrose, op. cit., p. 284.

510   With that, the story was promptly leaked to the tabloids: Gentry, op. cit., p. 642.

510–511   For Ted, the worst moments arrived: Dallas, op. cit., pp. 338–343.

511   Hoover engineered a formal rapprochement: Gentry, op. cit., p. 711.

512   Throughout the winter, Jack Anderson had kept after Hoover: Ibid., pp. 718, 719.

512   Presidential lawyer John Dean: Ibid., pp. 715, 716.

512   That spring the Director and Andrew Tully: Summers, *Official and Confidential*, p. 408.

513   Not very long after that Hoover's colored housekeeper: Gentry, op. cit., pp. 19–21.

513   Anthony Summers: Summer, op.cit., pp. 412–421; Livingstone and Groden, op. cit., p. 362.

513   Perhaps the most reassuring comment of all: Demaris, *The Director*, p. 237.

513   In 1967 Jules Feiffer produced: reproduced in Schlesinger, op. cit., p. 807.

515   With a wink from FDR, Hoover managed to penetrate: Gentry, op. cit., p. 205, passim.

515   When bureaucrats in Washington floated the idea: Wannall, op. cit., p. 69.

Selected Bibliography

The books listed here are indeed part of a much larger body of scholarship. Most of these titles reappear in the source notes and are intended to key the reader to the published work under discussion. For a wider bibliography, please consult the bibliographies of my two earlier works about the Kennedy family, *The Education of Edward Kennedy* and *The Shadow President*. Magazine, interview, and documentary excerpts are dealt with throughout the source notes.

Adler, Bill (Editor). *Robert Kennedy Statements: The Kennedy Wit*. New York: Bantam, 1964 (paper).
———. *A New Day*. New York: New American Library, 1968 (paper).
———. *The Robert F. Kennedy Wit*. New York: Berkley Medallion, 1968 (paper).
Alsop, Joseph. *I've Seen the Best of It*. New York: Norton, 1992.
Ambrose, Stephen. *Nixon*. New York: Simon & Schuster, 1989.
Anderson, Christopher. *Jack and Jackie: Portrait of an American Marriage*. New York: Avon Books, 1977 (paper).
Anderson, Jack, and Ronald W. May. *McCarthy: The Man, the Senator, the "Ism."* Boston: Beacon, 1952.
Andrew, Christopher, and Vassily Mitrokhin. *The Sword and The Shield: The Secret History of the KGB*. New York: Basic Books, 1999.
Anger, Kenneth. *Hollywood Babylon II*. New York: Simon & Schuster, 1975.
Anslinger, Harry J. *The Protectors*. New York: Farrar, Straus, 1964.
Arsenault, Ray. *Freedom Riders*. New York: Oxford University Press, 2006.
Baker, Bobby, with Larry L. King. *Wheeling and Dealing: Confessions of a Capitol Hill Operator*. New York: Norton, 1978.
Beschloss, Michael. *Kennedy and Roosevelt: The Uneasy Alliance*. New York: Norton, 1980.
Blair, Joan, and Clay Blair Jr. *The Search for JFK*. New York: Berkley/Putnam's, 1976.
Blakey, G. Robert, and Richard N. Billings. *The Plot to Kill the President*. New York: Times Books, 1981.

Bly, Nellie. *The Kennedy Men: Three Generations of Sex, Scandal and Secrets*. New York: Kensington Books, 1996.

Bowles, Chester. *Promises to Keep*. New York: Harper & Row, 1971.

Bradlee, Ben. *A Good Life: Newspapering and Other Adventures*. New York: Simon and Schuster, 1995.

Branch, Taylor. *Parting the Waters: America in the King Years: 1954–63*. New York: Simon and Schuster, 1988.

———. *Pillar of Fire: America in the King Years: 1963–65*. New York: Simon and Schuster, 1998.

Brashler, William. *The Don: The Life and Death of Sam Giancana*. New York: Harper and Row, 1977.

Brill, Stephen. *The Teamsters*. New York: Simon and Schuster, 1978.

Brownstein, Ronald. *Power and Glitter*. New York: Pantheon, 1990.

Buckley, William F. Jr., and L. Brent Bozel. *McCarthy and His Enemies: The Record and Its Meaning*. Chicago: Regnery, 1954.

Cassini, Igor, with Jeanne Molli. *I'd Do It All Over Again*. New York: Putnam's, 1977.

Chandler, David. *Brothers in Blood*. New York: Dutton, 1775.

Clifford, Clark. *Counsel to the President*. New York: Random House, 1991.

Clymer, Adam. *Edward M. Kennedy: A Biography*. New York: Morrow, 1999.

Cohn, Roy. *McCarthy*. New York: New American Library, 1968.

———. *A Fool for a Client: My Struggle Against the Power*. New York: Hawthorn Books, 1971.

Collier, Peter, and David Horowitz. *The Kennedys: An American Drama*. New York: Summit, 1984.

Cook, Fred J. *The FBI Nobody Knows*. New York: MacMillan, 1964.

———. *The Nightmare Decade: The Life and Times of Senator McCarthy*. New York: Random House, 1971.

Crenshaw, Charles A., M.D., *Trauma Room One: The JFK Medical Coverup Exposed*. New York: Paraview Press, 2001.

Dallas, Rita, with Jeanira Rattliffe. *The Kennedy Case*. New York: Putnam's, 1973.

Dallek, Robert. *An Unfinished Life: John F. Kennedy 1917–1963*. New York: Little Brown, 2003.

David, Lester, and Irene David. *Bobby Kennedy: The Making of a Folk Hero*. New York: Dodd, Mead, 1986.

Davies, Marion. *The Times We Had*. New York: Ballantine, 1985 (paper).

Davis, John H. *The Kennedys: Dynasty and Disaster 1848–1993*. New York: McGraw-Hill, 1984.

———. *Mafia Dynasty: The Rise and Fall of the Gambino Crime Family*. New York: HarperCollins, 1993.

———. *Mafia Kingfish: Carlos Marcello and the Assassination of John F. Kennedy*. New York: McGraw Hill, 1989.

Davison, Jean. *Oswald's Game*. New York: Norton, 1983.

Deitche, Scott M. *Cigar City Mafia: A Complete History of the Tampa Underworld*. New York: Barricade Books, 2004.

DeLoach, Cartha. *Hoover's FBI: The Inside Story by Hoover's Trusted Lieutenant*. Washington, D.C.: Regnery, 1995.

Demaris, Ovid. *The Director: An Oral Biography of J. Edgar Hoover*. New York: Harper's, 1975.

———. *The Last Mafioso: Jimmy "The Weasel" Fratianno*. New York: Bantam, 1981 (paper).

de Toledano, Ralph. *J. Edgar Hoover: The Man in His Time.* New Rochelle, NY: Arlington House, 1973.

———. *RFK, The Man Who Would Be President.* New York: Putnam's, 1967.

Dinneen, Joseph F. *The Kennedy Family.* New York: Little Brown, 1959.

Duncliffe, William J. *The Life and Times of Joseph P. Kennedy.* New York: Macfadden (paperback original), 1965.

Ehrlichman, John. *Witness to Power: The Nixon Years.* New York: Simon & Schuster, 1986.

Eisenberg, Dennis, and Uri Dan and Eli Landau. *Meyer Lansky: Mogul of the Mob.* New York: Paddington, 1979.

Epstein, Edward Jay. *The Assassination Chronicles.* New York: Carroll and Graf, 1992 (paper).

Ewald, William Bragg Jr. *Who Killed Joe McCarthy?* New York: Simon and Schuster, 1984.

Exner, Judith. *My Story.* New York: Grove Press, 1977 (paper).

Fay, Paul B. Jr. *The Pleasure of His Company.* New York: Dell, 1966 (paper).

Felt, Mark. *The FBI Pyramid: From the Inside.* New York: Putnam's, 1979.

Fonzi, Gaeton. *The Last Investigation.* New York: Thunder's Mouth Press, 1993.

Ford, Gerald R., and John R. Stiles. *Portrait of the Assassin.* New York: Simon and Schuster, 1965.

Fox, Stephen. *Blood and Power: Organized Crime in Twentieth-Century America.* New York: Morrow, 1989.

Frady, Marshall. *Martin Luther King Jr.* New York: Viking, Penguin Group, 2002.

———. *Wallace.* New York: Random House, 1996 (paper).

Gabler, Neal. *Winchell: Gossip, Power and the Culture of Celebrity.* New York: Knopf, 1994.

Garrow, David J. *The FBI and Martin Luther King Jr.* New York: Penguin, 1981 (paper).

Gentry, Curt. *J. Edgar Hoover: The Man and the Secrets.* New York: Norton, 1991.

Gershenson, Alvin. *Kennedy and Big Business.* Beverly Hills: Book Company of America, 1964 (paper).

Giancana, Antoinette, and John R. Hughes, Thomas H. Jobe. *JFK and Sam: The Connection Between the Giancana and Kennedy Assassinations.* Nashville: Cumberland House, 2005.

Giancana, Antoinette, and Thomas C. Renner. *Mafia Princess: Growing Up in Sam Giancana's Family.* New York: Morrow, 1984.

Giancana, Sam, and Chuck Giancana. *Double Cross.* New York: Warner Books, 1992 (paper).

Gibson, Barbara, and Ted Schwarz. *Rose Kennedy and Her Family.* New York: Birch Lane Press, 1995.

———. *The Kennedys: The Third Generation.* New York: Thunder's Mouth Press, 1993.

Goldfarb, Ronald. *Perfect Villains, Imperfect Heroes.* New York: Random House, 1995.

Goodwin, Doris Kearns. *The Fitzgeralds and the Kennedys.* New York: Simon & Schuster, 1987.

Goodwin, Richard. *Remembering America: A Voice from the Sixties.* Boston: Little Brown, 1988.

Guthman, Edwin. *We Band of Brothers: A Memoir of Robert F. Kennedy.* New York: Harper & Row, 1971.

Hack, Richard. *Puppetmaster: The Secret Life of J. Edgar Hoover.* Beverly Hills: New Millennium Press, 2004.

Haldeman, H. R. *The Haldeman Diaries.* New York: Putnam's, 1994.

Haldeman, H. R., with Joseph DeMona. *The Ends of Power.* New York: Times Books, 1978.

Hamilton, Nigel. *JFK: Reckless Youth.* New York: Random House, 1992.

Hellerman, Michael, with Thomas C. Renner. *Wall Street Swindler*. Garden City: Doubleday, 1977.

Helms, Richard. *A Look Over My Shoulder: A Life in the Central Intelligence Agency*. New York: Random House, 2002.

Hersh, Seymour. *The Dark Side of Camelot*. Boston: Little Brown, 1997.

Heymann, C. David. *A Woman Named Jackie*. New York: Lyle Stuart, 1989.

————. *RFK: A Candid Biography of Robert F. Kennedy*. New York: Penguin Putnam, 1998.

Higham, Charles. *Rose: The Life and Times of Rose Fitzgerald Kennedy*. New York: Pocket Books, 1995.

Hilty, James W. *Robert Kennedy: Brother Protector*. Philadelphia: Temple University Press, 1997.

Hinckle, Warren, and William Turner. *Deadly Secrets: The CIA-Mafia War Against Castro and the Assassination of JFK*. New York: Thunder's Mouth Press, 1992.

————. *The Fish Is Red: The Story of the Secret War Against Castro*. New York: Harper and Row, 1981.

Hoffa, James, as told to Oscar Fraley. *The Real Story*. New York: Stein and Day, 1975.

Hoover, J. Edgar. *Masters of Deceit: The Story of Communism in America and How to Fight It*. New York: Holt, Rinehart and Winston, 1958.

————. *Persons In Hiding*. Boston: Little, Brown, 1938.

Hosty, James P. Jr. *Assignment: Oswald*. New York: Arcade, 1996.

Hunt, E. Howard. *My Secret History in the CIA, Watergate and Beyond*. Hoboken, NJ: John Wiley and Sons, Inc., 2007.

James, Ralph C., and Estelle Dinerstein James. *Hoffa and the Teamsters: A Study of Union Power*. Princeton: Van Norstrand, 1965.

Janeway, Michael. *The Fall of the House of Roosevelt*. New York: Columbia University Press, 2004.

Kantor, Seth. *Who Was Jack Ruby?* New York: Everest House, 1978.

Katz, Leonard. *Uncle Frank: The Biography of Frank Costello*. New York: Drake, 1973.

Kelley, Kitty. *His Way*. New York: Bantam, 1986.

Kennedy, Edward M. *The Fruitful Bough*. Privately printed, 1965.

Kennedy, Robert F. *Robert Kennedy in His Own Words*. New York: Bantam, 1988.

————. *The Enemy Within*. New York: Popular Library, 1960 (paper).

————. *To Seek a Newer World* (speeches). New York: Bantam, 1967 (paper).

Kennedy, Rose Fitzgerald. *Times to Remember*. New York: Doubleday, 1974.

Kessler, Ronald. *The FBI*. New York: Simon & Schuster/Pocket Books, 1993 (paper).

————. *The Sins of the Father*. New York: Warner Books (paper), 1996.

King, Dennis. *Lyndon LaRouche and the New American Fascism*. New York: Doubleday, 1989.

Klein, Edward. *All Too Human: The Love Story of Jack and Jackie Kennedy*. New York: Simon & Schuster/Pocket Books, 1996 (paper).

Koskoff, David E. *Joseph P. Kennedy: A Life and Times*. Englewood Cliffs, NJ: Prentice-Hall, 1974.

Krock, Arthur. *Memoirs*. New York: Funk & Wagnalls, 1968.

Lacey, Robert. *Little Man: Meyer Lansky and the Gangster Life*. Boston: Little Brown, 1991.

Lamphere, Robert, and Tom Schachtman. *The FBI-KGB War*. New York: Random House, 1986.

Lane, Mark. *Plausible Denial: Was the CIA Involved in the Assassination of JFK?* New York: Thunder's Mouth Press, 1991.

———. *Rush to Judgment.* New York: Holt, Rinehart and Winston, 1966.

Lasky, Victor. *Robert F. Kennedy: The Man and the Myth.* New York: Trident, 1968.

Lawford, Patricia Seaton, with Ted Schwarz. *The Peter Lawford Story.* New York: Carroll & Graf, 1988.

Leamer, Laurence. *The Kennedy Men.* New York: Morrow, 2001.

———. *The Kennedy Women.* New York: Ballantine, 1994 (paper).

———. *Sons of Camelot.* New York: Morrow, 2004.

Lincoln, Evelyn. *Kennedy and Johnson.* New York: Holt, Rinehart & Winston, 1968.

———. *My Twelve Years with John F. Kennedy.* New York: Bantam, 1966 (paper).

Livingstone, Harrison Edward, and Robert J. Groden. *High Treason: The Assassination of JFK and the Case for Conspiracy.* New York: Carroll & Graf, 1980 (paper).

———. *Killing Kennedy and the Hoax of the Century.* New York: Carroll & Graf, 1995.

Lowenthal, Max. *FBI.* New York: Westport, CT: Greenwood Press, 1950.

Madsen, Axel. *Gloria and Joe.* New York: William Morrow/Arbor House, 1988.

McCann, Thomas. *An American Company.* New York: Crown, 1976.

McCarthy, Joe. *The Remarkable Kennedys.* New York: Dial, 1960.

McClellan, Barr. *Blood, Money and Power.* New York: Hanover House, 2003.

McCoy, Alfred. *The Politics of Heroin.* Brooklyn, NY: Laurence Hill Books, 1991 (paper).

McKean, David. *Peddling Influence.* Hanover, NH: Steerforth, 2004.

McKnight, Gerald D. *The Last Crusade.* New York: Westview Press, 1998.

McMillan, Priscilla Johnson. *Marina and Lee.* New York: Harper & Row, 1997.

McWhorter, Diane. *Carry Me Home.* New York: Simon & Schuster, 2001.

Maheu, Robert, and Richard Hack. *Next to Hughes.* New York: HarperCollins, 1992.

Mahoney, Richard D. *Sons & Brothers: The Days of Jack and Bobby Kennedy.* New York: Arcade, 1999.

Mailer, Norman. *Oswald's Tale.* New York: Random House, 1995.

Manchester, William. *The Death of a President.* New York: HarperCollins, 1967.

———. *Portrait of a President.* Boston: Houghton Mifflin, 1962.

Markmann, Charles, and Mark Sherwin. *Kennedy: A Sense of Purpose.* New York: St. Martin's, 1961.

Marrs, Jim. *Crossfire: The Plot That Killed Kennedy.* New York: Carroll & Graf, 1989.

Martin, Ralph. *Henry and Clare.* New York: Putnam's, 1991.

———. *Seeds of Destruction: Joe Kennedy and His Sons.* New York: Putnam's, 1995.

Martino, John, in collaboration with Nathaniel Weyl. *I Was Castro's Prisoner: An American Tells His Story.* New York: Devin-Adair, 1963.

Matthews, Christopher. *Kennedy & Nixon: The Rivalry That Shaped Postwar America.* New York: Simon & Schuster, 1996.

Meagher, Sylvia. *Accessories After the Fact.* New York: Bobbs-Merrill, 1967.

Mellen, Joan. *A Farewell to Justice.* Dulles, VA: Potomac Books, 1991.

Messick, Hank. *Lansky.* New York: Putnam's, 1971.

———. *The Mob in Show Business.* New York: Pyramid, 1973 (paper).

———. *John Edgar Hoover.* New York: David McKay, 1972.

Messick, Hank, and Burt Goldblatt. *The Mobs and the Mafia.* New York: Thomas Crowell, 1972.

Miller, Merle. *Plain Speaking.* New York: Berkley, 1973.

Moldea, Dan E. *The Hoffa Wars: Teamsters, Rebels, Politicians and the Mob.* New York & London: Paddington Press, 1978.

———. *Interference: How Organized Crime Affects Professional Football.* New York: Morrow, 1989.

————. *The Killing of Robert F. Kennedy: An Investigation of Motive, Means, and Opportunity.* New York: Norton, 1995.

Mollenhoff, Clark R. *The Tentacles of Power: The Story of Jimmy Hoffa.* Cleveland and New York: World, 1965.

Morgan, John. *Prince of Crime.* New York: Stein & Day, 1985.

Morgan, Ted. *Reds.* New York: Random House, 2003.

Nash, Jay Robert. *Citizen Hoover: A Critical Study of the Life and Times of J. Edgar Hoover and his FBI.* Chicago: Nelson-Hall, 1972.

Navasky, Victor S. *Kennedy Justice.* New York: Atheneum, 1971.

Newfield, Jack. *Robert Kennedy: A Memoir.* New York: Dutton, 1969.

Newman, John. *Oswald and the CIA.* New York: Carroll & Graf, 1995.

Nixon, Richard. *The Memoirs of Richard Nixon.* New York: Grossset & Dunlap, 1978.

North, Mark. *Act of Treason.* New York: Carroll & Graf, 1991.

Oates, Stephen B. *Let the Trumpet Sound: The Life of Martin Luther King Jr.* New York: Harper & Row, 1982.

O'Donnell, Kenneth, and David F. Powers with Joe McCarthy. *"Johnny We Hardly Knew Ye": Memories of John Fitzgerald Kennedy.* Boston: Little, Brown, 1972.

Ollestad, Norman. *Inside the F.B.I.* New York: Lyle Stuart, 1967.

O'Neill, Thomas. *The Man of the House.* New York: Random House, 1987.

Oppenheimer, Jerry. *The Other Mrs. Kennedy: Ethel Skakel Kennedy.* New York: St. Martin's, 1994.

O'Reilly, Kenneth. *Racial Matters.* New York: Free Press/Macmillan, 1989.

Oshinsky, David M. *A Conspiracy So Immense: The World of Joe McCarthy.* New York: Free Press, 1963.

Otash, Fred. *Investigation Hollywood.* Chicago: Regnery, 1976.

O'Toole, George. *The Assassination Tapes.* New York: Penthouse Press, 1975.

Posner, Gerald. *Case Closed: Lee Harvey Oswald and the Assassination of JFK.* New York: Random House, 1983.

Powers, Richard Gid. *Secrecy and Power: The Life of J. Edgar Hoover.* New York: Free Press, 1987.

Prouty, L. Fletcher. *JFK: the CIA, Vietnam and the Plot to Assassinate John F. Kennedy.* New York: Birch Lane, 1992.

Quirk, Lawrence J. *Robert Francis Kennedy.* Los Angeles: Holloway House, 1968 (paper).

Ragano, Frank. *Mob Lawyer.* New York: Scribners, 1994.

Rappleye, Charles, and Ed Becker: *All-American Mafioso: The Johnny Rosselli Story.* New York: Doubleday, 1991.

Reeves, Richard. *President Kennedy: Profile of Power.* New York: Simon & Schuster, 1993.

Reeves, Thomas C. *The Life and Times of Joe McCarthy: A Biography.* New York, Stein and Day, 1982.

————. *A Question Of Character: The Life of John F. Kennedy.* New York: Free Press/Macmillan, 1991.

Reid, Ed, and Ovid Demaris. *The Green Felt Jungle.* Cutchogue, NY: Buccaneer Books, 1963.

Roberts, Allen. *Robert Francis Kennedy: Biography of a Compulsive Politician.* Brookline Village, MA: Brandon Press, 1984.

Roemer, William F. Jr. *Accardo.* New York: Ivy Books, 1996 (paper).

————. *Man Against the Mob.* New York: Donald I. Fine, 1989.

Rogers, Warren. *When I Think of Bobby: A Personal Memoir of the Kennedy Years.* New York: Harper Collins, 1993.

Ross, Douglas (editor). *Robert F. Kennedy: Apostle of Change.* New York: Pocket Books, 1968 (paper).

Rowe, Robert. *The Bobby Baker Story.* New York: Parallax, 1974.

Russell, Dick. *The Man Who Knew Too Much.* New York: Carroll & Graf, 1992.

Russo, Gus. *Live by the Sword.* New York: Bancroft, 1998.

————. *The Outfit: The Role of Chicago's Underworld in the Shaping of Modern America.* New York and London: Bloomsbury, 2001.

————. *Supermob.* New York and London: Bloomsbury, 2006.

Salinger, Pierre. *With Kennedy.* Garden City: Doubleday, 1966.

Saunders, Frank, with James Southwood. *Torn Lace Curtain: Life with the Kennedys, Recalled by Their Personal Chauffeur.* New York: Holt, Rinehart & Winston, 1982.

Schaap, Dick. *RFK.* New York: Signet Books, 1968 (paper).

Scheim, David E. *Contract on America: The Mafia Murder of President John F. Kennedy.* New York: Shapolsky, 1988.

Schlesinger, Arthur M. Jr., *Robert Kennedy and His Times.* Houghton Mifflin, 1978.

————. *A Thousand Days.* Boston: Houghton Mifflin, 1965.

Schott, Joseph L. *No Left Turns.* New York: Praeger, 1975.

Schwarz, Ted. *Joseph P. Kennedy: The Mogul. The Mob. The Statesman. And The Making of an American Myth.* Hoboken: John Wiley & Sons, 2003.

Scott, Peter Dale. *Crime and Cover-up.* Santa Barbara, CA: Open Archive Press, 1993 (paper).

Shannon, William V. *The Heir Apparent: Robert Kennedy and the Struggle for Power.* New York: MacMillan, 1967.

Sheehan, Neil. *A Bright Shining Lie.* New York: Random House, 1988.

Sheridan, Walter. *The Fall and Rise of Jimmy Hoffa.* New York: Saturday Review Press, 1972.

Shesol, Jeff. *Mutual Contempt.* New York: Norton, 1997.

Sidorenko, Konstantin. *Robert F. Kennedy: A Spiritual Biography.* New York: Crossroad Publishing Company, 2000.

Sifakis, Carl. *The Mafia Encyclopedia.* New York: Facts on File, 1987.

Slatzer, Robert F. *The Life and Curious Death of Marilyn Monroe.* New York: Pinnacle House, 1974.

Smith, Amanda. *Hostage to Fortune: The Letters of Joseph P. Kennedy.* New York: Penguin, 2001.

Smith, Jean. *That Shining Hour.* Private remembrances of Robert Kennedy.

Spada, James. *Peter Lawford: The Man Who Kept the Secrets.* New York: Bantam, 1991.

Speriglio, Milo. *The Marilyn Conspiracy.* New York: Pocket Books, 1986 (paper).

Spindel, Bernard B. *The Ominous Ear.* New York: Award House, 1968.

Stein, Jean. *American Journey: The Times of Robert F. Kennedy.* New York: Harcourt Brace Jovanovich, 1970.

Sullivan, William. *The Bureau: My Thirty Years in Hoover's FBI.* New York: Pinnacle Books, 1979 (paper).

Summers, Anthony. *Conspiracy.* New York: McGraw-Hill, 1980.

————. *Goddess: The Secret Lives of Marilyn Monroe.* New York: MacMillan, 1985.

————. *Official and Confidential: The Secret Life of J. Edgar Hoover.* New York: Putnam's, 1993.

Summers, Anthony, and Robbyn Swann. *Sinatra: The Life.* New York: Knopf, 2005.

Swanson, Gloria. *Swanson on Swanson.* New York: Random House, 1980.

Theoharis, Athan G., and John Cox. *J. Edgar Hoover, Sex and Crime: An Historical Antidote.* New York: Ivan R. Dee, 1993.

——. *From the Secret Files of J. Edgar Hoover.* Chicago: Ivan R. Dee, 1991.

——. *The Boss: J. Edgar Hoover and the Great American Inquisition.* Philadelphia: Temple University Press, 1988.

Thimmesch, Nick, and William Johnson. *Robert Kennedy at 40.* New York: Norton, 1965.

Thomas, Evan. *The Man to See: Edward Bennett Williams.* New York: Simon & Schuster, 1991.

——. *Robert Kennedy: His Life.* New York: Simon & Schuster, 2000.

Thompson, Josiah. *Six Seconds in Dallas: A Micro-Study of the Kennedy Assassination.* New York: Bernard Geis Associates (Random House), 1967.

Thompson, Robert E., and Hortense Meyers. *Robert F. Kennedy: The Brother Within.* New York: Dell, 1962 (paper).

Torbitt, William. *Nomenclature of an Assassination Cabal.* Mae Brussell Archive, 1970.

Trohan, Walter. *Political Animals.* New York: Doubleday, 1975.

Tully, Andrew. *Inside the FBI.* New York: McGraw-Hill, 1980.

Turner, William W. *Hoover's F.B.I.* New York: Thunder's Mouth Press, 1993.

Ungar, Sanford J. *FBI.* Boston: Atlantic Monthly Press, 1975.

Vanden Heuvel, William, and Milton Gwirtzman. *On His Own: RFK 1964–68.* New York: Doubleday, 1970.

Van Dusen, Thomas. *The Power Brokers.* Toronto: Collins, 1976.

Van Meter, Jonathan. *The Last Good Time.* New York: Crown, 2003.

Von Hoffman, Nicholas. *Citizen Cohn: The Life and Times of Roy Cohn.* New York: Bantam Books, 1988 (paper).

Waldron, Lamar. *Ultimate Sacrifice.* New York: Carroll & Graf, 2005.

Wannall, Ray. *The Real J. Edgar Hoover: For the Record.* New York: Turner Publishing Co., 2000.

Warren Commission. *Report of the Warren Commission on the Assassination of President Kennedy.* New York: McGraw-Hill, 1964 (paper).

Weisberg, Harold. *Whitewash: The Report on the Warren Report.* Hyattstown: Harold Weisberg, 1965.

——. *Whitewash II: The FBI-Secret Service Cover-up.* Hyattstown: Harold Weisberg, 1966.

Welch, Neil J., and David W. Marston. *Inside Hoover's FBI: The Top Field Chief Reports.* New York: Doubleday, 1984.

Whalen, Richard J. *The Founding Father.* Washington, D.C.: Regnery, Gateway, 1993.

White, Theodore. *The Making of the President, 1960.* New York: Atheneum, 1961.

Wills, Garry. *The Kennedy Imprisonment: A Meditation on Power.* Boston: Little Brown, 1981.

Wills, Garry, and Ovid Demaris. *Jack Ruby.* New York: New American Library, 1967.

Witcover, Jules. *85 Days: The Last Campaign of Robert Kennedy.* New York: Putnam's, 1969.

Wofford, Harris. *Of Kennedys and Kings: Making Sense of the Sixties.* New York: Farrar Straus and Giroux, 1980.

Wolf, George, with Joseph DiMona. *Frank Costello: Prime Minister of the Underworld.* New York: Morrow, 1974.

Zion, Sidney. *The Autobiography of Roy Cohn.* Secaucus, NJ: Lyle Stuart, 1988.

Acknowledgments

This book attempts to cast a very wide net, and over the years questions arose which very few could answer. I sought those few individuals out. Most agreed to confide in me, although certain sources did not want their names involved, and I have accordingly left them out. The rest I have cited, checking carefully in most cases to make sure my notes accorded precisely with my tapes of the interviews.

Three tracks of history are interwoven here: the history of the Kennedy family, the history of the FBI and its progenitor J. Edgar Hoover, and the history of organized crime in America. One track continually illuminates the others, and out of this effort has come, I hope, an interpretation of the third quarter of the twentieth century in America quite different from anything published so far, both incident by incident and overall.

Treatments of the Kennedys abound, especially the recent contributions from academia, and one follows the next with comparatively little variation, excepting from time to time a newly declassified document or two. An exception in this case was Arthur Schlesinger Jr.'s *Robert Kennedy and His Times,* 1978. Massive yet sprightly, Professor Schlesinger utilized a broad array of personal documents, many unavailable to most scholars at the time, as well as his own longstanding relationship of deep trust with his subject to produce a work that will probably stand as the definitive biography, however protective of Bobby it would appear to many. The appearance in 2000 of the much less reverent *Robert Kennedy* by Evan Thomas—which Schlesinger could not get himself to read—knocked some of the spots off the Robert-Kennedy-as-pugnacious-archangel projection. A third book worth citing is Jack Newfield's dead-on memoir, also *Robert Kennedy.* Victor Navasky's *Kennedy Justice* identified early Bobby's galaxy of blind spots as attorney general, and studies by James Hilty and Richard Mahoney proved insightful at times.

Once I began to understand the importance of Joe Kennedy in framing this narrative I went back to a number of people and sources to help me rethink the fundamental psychodynamics of the Kennedys. Richard Whalen's pioneering *The Founding Father* opened the way. Another very revealing book, all but unobtainable these days, was *The Search for JFK*, by Joan and Clay Blair Jr., in which the key interviews suggested strongly the emotional dishevelment at the heart of the Kennedy family relationships. This theme would be carried out in Lawrence Leamer's encompassing trilogy on the several generations, Nigel Hamilton's biting *JFK, Reckless Youth*, and Ralph Martin's thoughtful analysis throughout *Seed of Destruction.* This list goes on and should be evident from the notes. The very open access I could depend on at every stage of preparation to the archives of the JFK Library, including the Robert F. Kennedy Collection and the private papers of Joseph P. Kennedy, much enriched many passages.

The scholarship on J. Edgar Hoover describes a narrower orbit. The three principal biographies are *The Boss*, by Theoharis and Cox, Curt Gentry's *J. Edgar Hoover,* and *Secrecy and Power* by Richard Gid Powers. Several waves of subsequent books fill in the chinks, most famously *Official and Confidential* by Anthony Summers, with its celebrated presentation of the FBI chief at a party in a frock. Beyond that I am beholden to Cartha ("Deke") DeLoach for a great deal of help and hospitality and Dr. Ray Batvinis of the J. Edgar Hoover Foundation for a wide array of private documents and personal items, not least Hoover family letters to the troubled J. Edgar as a very young child. Wide-ranging employment of the FBI's own priceless files, months of immersion, provided the locomotive for this book.

Mob chronicles tend to disclosures as shadowy and difficult to pin down as the underworld itself. Books by the Giancana family, Sam Giancana's stepson and daughter, have come under attack as to details and veracity, but many of the particulars line up with revelations from more highly regarded sources; the trick is to know which to take seriously and how much. Hearsay by its nature does not lend itself to a verifiable close chronology. Fortunately, a new and trustworthy generation of Mob historians has come into the canon, starting with Hank Messick and Ovid Demaris. Along with Robert Maheu, I am particularly beholden to both the fine books and the solid advice from Dan Moldea and—especially—Gus Russo, both of whom have raised the study of organized crime to the level of serious scholarship. Two books that bristled with suggestive insights were *Mafia Kingfish* by Bouvier cousin and Kennedy historian John H. Davis and *All-American Mafioso* by Charles Rappleye and Ed Becker.

Many survivors of Bob Kennedy's universe along with a horde of writers in the field have been good enough to speak with me at length, a number several times. They include:

INTERVIEWS

Mark Allen
Gary Aguilar
Bobby Baker
James Bamford
Berl Bernhardt
Robert Blakey
David Burke
Thomas Corcoran
Cartha (Deke) DeLoach
Robert Denz
John Douglas
Joe Dolan
Fred Dutton
Courtney Evans
Mike Fawer
Mike Feldman
Richard Goodwin
Jay Goldberg
Ron Goldfarb
Ed Guthman
Milton Gwirtzman
Robert Healy
David Heymann
William Hundley
Nicholas Katzenbach
Senator Edward Kennedy
John Klotz

Jerry McKnight
Priscilla McMillan
Serio Maccioni
Robert Maheu
Scott Malone
Frank Mankiewicz
Melody Miller
Dan Moldea
Jefferson Morley
James Neal
Ruth Paine
Barrett Prettyman Jr.
Gus Russo
John Seigenthaler
Leslie Scherr
Arthur Schlesinger Jr.
Peter Dale Scott
Lawrence Silberman
Amanda Smith
Marianne Strong
Anthony Summers
William Tafoya
David Talbot
Mrs. Thomas Wadden
Ray Wannall
Richard Whalen
Harris Wofford

I've also looked for assistance to a number of institutions around the country. Much gratitude goes out to the indispensable professionals at:

The Assassination and Research Archives: (James Lesar)
The Associated Press: (Kim Waldman)
The Association of Former Intelligence Officers: (Special Thanks to Gene Poteat, Elizabeth Bancroft)
Boston University (Mugar Memorial Library): (the late Howard Gotlieb, Vita Paladino)
Brown Memorial Library, Bradford, New Hampshire: (Meg Fearnley)
Columbia University Library
The J. Edgar Hoover Foundation: (Dr. Ray Batvinis)
FBI Headquarters (The Freedom of Information and Privacy Section): (Steve Tilley, Martha Murphy, Sally Ann Cummings, Alan Walker)
The JFK Library: (Steve Plotkin, Jennifer Quand, Megan Desnoyers, Maryrose Grossman)
The Library of Congress: (Jeff Bridger, Barabara Moore)
The Massachusetts Historical Society
The National Archives
St. Petersburg, Florida, Public Library: (Special thanks to Jodee Roberson)
The State University of New York at Stony Brook, New York, Special Collections: (Kristen Nyitra)
The University of Wyoming: (Carol Bowers)

I was particularly grateful to come upon David Heymann's archive at the State University of New York at Stony Brook. While preparing his own controversial biography of Robert Kennedy, Heymann undertook an amazing dredging operation across the entire Kennedy literature and came across many documents and literary detritus of every category perhaps of more use to me than to him. For this and other favors, I thank him.

This book has provided a bumpy ride. For encouragement, practical help, and valuable professional advice I am grateful to a number of fellow writers. Foremost among these were Peter Golenbock, Larry Leamer, Tom Powers, Gus Russo, Richard Whalen, Arthur Schlesinger Jr., and Anthony Summers. Many others did what they could when the occasion arose.

A work on this scale soon calls for major technical support. I have depended every summer on Luci Koban, and for a time on Annamaria Colburn, and throughout the long winter season on Linda Angel and Julie

Saffan. As always, occasionally with a sigh, my wife of so many years, the tire-less Ellen, has stood by and pitched in.

Without the enthusiasm and persistence of my agent, Larry Kirshbaum, this book might never have seen publication. My thanks to him and Will Balliett, Herman Graf, Jamie McNeely, Shaun Dillon, and Karen Auerbach of Carroll & Graf, and to copyeditor Phillip J. Gaskill. It has been a long campaign.

Index